Public Administration

PUBLIC ADMINISTRATION AND PUBLIC POLICY

A Comprehensive Publication Program

Executive Editor

JACK RABIN
Professor of Public Administration and Public Policy
School of Public Affairs
The Capital College
The Pennsylvania State University—Harrisburg
Middletown, Pennsylvania

Additional Volumes in Preparation

Online at www.netLibrary.com

Principles and Practices of Public Administration, edited by Jack Rabin, Robert F. Munzenrider, and Sherrie M. Bartell

Annals of Public Administration

Public Administration

A Comparative Perspective

Sixth Edition

Ferrel Heady

Professor Emeritus
The University of New Mexico
Albuquerque, New Mexico

MARCEL DEKKER, INC.   NEW YORK · BASEL

ISBN: 0-8247-0480-0

This book is printed on acid-free paper.

Headquarters
Marcel Dekker, Inc.
270 Madison Avenue, New York, NY 10016
tel: 212-696-9000; fax: 212-685-4540

Eastern Hemisphere Distribution
Marcel Dekker AG
Hutgasse 4, Postfach 812, CH-4001 Basel, Switzerland
tel: 41-61-261-8482; fax: 41-61-261-8896

World Wide Web
http://www.dekker.com

The publisher offers discounts on this book when ordered in bulk quantities. For more information, write to Special Sales/Professional Marketing at the headquarters address above.

Current printing (last digit):
10 9 8 7 6 5 4 3 2 1

PRINTED IN THE UNITED STATES OF AMERICA

To the memory of my parents.

Preface

This is the sixth edition of a book first published in a shorter version 35 years ago. At that time, I commented that some readers might consider it overdue and that others might regard it as premature. Recognition that in a sense each view was correct led me to assert both a claim and a disclaimer. The claim was that I was making the first comprehensive effort to assess the state of the comparative study of public administration and to characterize the administrative systems in a wide range of present-day nation-states. The disclaimer was that the book did not attempt to provide a definitive treatment for a field probably not yet ready for the task to be performed. My objective was to respond to an existing need felt by many students, teachers, and researchers who had chosen to explore the fascinating problems of comparison among national systems of public administration.

This objective has not altered substantially, nor have the difficulties of trying to meet it. Over the intervening years, no similar comprehensive treatment has appeared, although the volume of literature on comparative public administration has expanded enormously and much of it has been made more accessible. Diversities of approach have continued to characterize the field, leading to numerous assessments expressing disappointment in actual accomplishments when contrasted to earlier promise. The field has also continued to go through periods of expansion and contraction, with many current indications of a new upswing in interest.

In this and earlier revisions, I have had several aims in view. The most obvious is updating to take into account recent developments in various national systems of public administration. The last few years have brought unprecedented major politico-administrative changes—most notably in what had been the Soviet Union and in Eastern Europe, but also in several more developed democracies and in some regions of the developing world. The global superpower system that emerged after World War II, and the Cold War it generated, are now history, but the shape of what lies ahead has become even more difficult to predict. Some countries, such as Russia and China, have seen dramatic changes in their present situations and future prospects.

In addition, current conditions in comparative public administration and closely related fields of study such as development administration and comparative public policy are discussed. Options are also examined for progress in the future. Recent contributions to the literature on societal change have been taken into account in the discussion of concepts of system transformation. The classification system for dealing with political regime types in developing countries has been updated, and in some instances different countries have been used as case examples. Significant recent shifts in the distribution of countries among these regime types are described and analyzed.

The basic approach chosen for this study continues "to bring within the range of consideration administrative systems that have wide variations among them, and to make the task manageable by focusing on public bureaucracies as common governmental institutions and by placing special emphasis on relationships between bureaucracies and political regime types."

Although wanting to acknowledge contributions from several sources for whatever merits the book may possess in either its original or revised forms, I do not intend to expose any of the contributors to blame for its defects. I am grateful to the Horace H. Rackham School of Graduate Studies at the University of Michigan and to the East-West Center at the University of Hawaii for providing funds, facilities, and time which allowed me to plan and complete the original manuscript, and to the School of Public Administration at the University of New Mexico for facilitating the work of expansion and revision. Many professional colleagues—particularly those with whom it has been my good fortune to associate at Michigan, New Mexico, and the East-West Center, and in the Comparative Administration Group and the Section on International and Comparative Administration of the American Society for Public Administration—have given me the benefit of their help. I am especially indebted to Wallace S. Sayre and William J. Siffin, both now deceased, and to Edward W. Weidner for detailed comments and suggestions, which were often followed. Fred W. Riggs has over the years made many perceptive and useful comments on revisions as they appeared. Dwight Waldo, who was generous in providing a foreword for several previous editions, was unable to do so again because of deteriorating health which led to his death in October, 2000. I wish to acknowledge with gratitude his friendship over the years and his notable lifetime contributions to the literature of public administration. To students in courses I have taught in comparative public administration, including in recent years those in the Spanish-language version of the MPA program at New Mexico and at El Colegio de Mexico in Mexico City, I owe much for their willingness to offer constructive criticisms of working drafts of the manuscript.

Sybil L. Stokes, then a member of the Michigan Institute of Public Administration staff, provided expert editorial assistance and advice when the first edition was being prepared. Bruce H. Kirschner, then a graduate assistant at New Mexico, was equally helpful in working on the second edition, particularly in analyzing bureaucratic elite regimes and presenting case examples of them. For the third edition, Virginia T. Rood was invaluable in manuscript preparation, and I had competent and willing help in library searches and other essential tasks from graduate assistants Karen H. Ricci, Victoria Marquez, Scott V. Nystrom, and Karen L. Ruffing. Similar substantial contributions were made in preparation of the fourth edition by administrative secretary Frances M. Romero and graduate assistants Franklin G. Lim, Irene Gomez, Mary Frances A. Lim, and Annette S. Paez, and in preparation of the fifth edition by graduate assistants Linda Callaghan, Jacqueline Lee Cox, Jennifer S. Mayfield, and Michael C. Ashinin. Finally, I want to acknowledge with special thanks the multiple valuable contributions of graduate assistant Ellen Greene in the completion of this sixth edition.

My wife, Charlotte, has provided support and encouragement in what became a long-term task requiring commitments from both of us. For this I am appreciative and grateful.

Ferrel Heady

Contents

1

Comparison in the Study of Public Administration

PUBLIC ADMINISTRATION AS A FIELD OF STUDY

Public administration as an aspect of governmental activity has existed as long as political systems have been functioning and trying to achieve program objectives set by the political decision-makers. Public administration as a field of systematic study is much more recent. Advisers to rulers and commentators on the workings of government have recorded their observations from time to time in sources as varied as Kautilya's *Arthasastra* in ancient India,[1] the *Bible*, Aristotle's *Politics*, and Machiavelli's *The Prince*, but it was not until the eighteenth century that cameralism, concerned with the systematic management of governmental affairs, became a specialty of German scholars in Western Europe. In the United States, such a development did not take place until the latter part of the nineteenth century, with the publication in 1887 of Woodrow Wilson's famous essay, "The Study of Administration," generally considered the starting point. Since that time, public administration has become a well-recognized area of specialized interest, either as a subfield of political science or as an academic discipline in its own right.

Despite several decades of development, consensus about the scope of public administration is still lacking, and the field has been described as featuring heterodoxy rather than orthodoxy. A current text reviews the intellectual development of the field under the heading of public administration's "century in a quandary,"[2] and a recent survey describes trends in the study of public administration as moving "from order to chaos."[3] Such features may be strengths rather than weaknesses, but they do rule out a short, precise, and generally acceptable definition of the field. The identification of tendencies and of shared subjects of concern is more feasible, and is all that is necessary for our purposes.

Public administration is presumably an aspect of a more generic concept—administration, the essence of which has been described as "determined action taken in pursuit of conscious purpose."[4] Most efforts to define administration in general add the element of cooperation among two or more individuals and view it as cooperative human effort toward reaching some goal or goals accepted by those engaged in the endeavor. Administration is concerned with means for the achievement of prescribed ends. Administrative activity can take place in a variety of settings, provided the crucial elements are present: the cooperation of human beings to perform tasks that have been mutually accepted as worthy of the joint effort. The institutional framework in which administration occurs may be as diverse as a business firm, labor union, church, educational institution, or governmental unit.

Public administration is that sector of administration found in a political setting. Concerned primarily with the carrying out of public policy decisions made by the authoritative decision-makers in the political system, public administration can be roughly distinguished from private, or nonpublic, administration. Of course, the range of governmental concern may vary widely from one political jurisdiction to another, so that the dividing line is wavy rather than clear-cut.

In the United States, actual usage in the past somewhat narrowed the range of administrative action dealt with in most writings on public administration, with the result that the term came to signify primarily "the organization, personnel, practices, and procedures essential to effective performance of the civilian functions assigned to the executive branch of government."[5] This was acceptable for purposes of emphasis but was unduly restrictive as a definition of the scope of public administration. Consequently, in recent years the tendency has been to move away from such a restricted range of concerns, even though no consensus has emerged as to the exact boundaries of the field. One indication is the gradual abandonment of the sharp dichotomy between politics and administration made by earlier writers such as Frank J. Goodnow and Leonard D. White. Paul H. Appleby, whose career combined varied experiences both as a practitioner and an academic, was one of the first to stress the interrelationships rather than the differences between the policy-making and policy-execution aspects of governing, in his influential book *Policy and Administration*, published in 1949.[6] Since then, the dominant view has come to be that students of administration cannot confine themselves to the implementation phase of public policy. Indeed, one of the basic textbooks states that "the core of public administration is politics and public policy," and that "public administration can be defined as the formulation, implementation, evaluation, and modification of public policy."[7] One way of stressing this linkage has been the widespread use of case studies in the teaching of public administration. These case studies are narratives of the events constituting or leading to decisions by public administrators, taking into account "the personal, legal, institutional, political, economic, and other factors that surrounded the process of decision," and trying to give the reader "a feeling of actual participation in the action."[8]

Earlier assumptions about public administration as a field of study continue to be questioned. Only a few of the most prominent of these suggestions for evaluation made during recent decades will be described briefly.

Interest in the comparative study of administration across national boundaries, which gained momentum in the middle of the century, soon made apparent the inadequacies of a narrow culture-bound definition of public administration. As we shall see, the comparative administration movement inevitably had to turn to a more comprehensive view concerning the scope of public administration than had been generally accepted in the United States before World War II.

Another line of questioning of earlier assumptions appeared as a by-product of the unrest centering on university campuses during the late 1960s and early 1970s, and found expression in the teaching, writing, and professional activities of younger public administrators both in academia and in government. Generally labeled the "new" public administration, this movement not only reaffirmed the breakdown of the politics-administration dichotomy, it also challenged the traditional emphasis on techniques of administration and stressed the obligations of public administrators to be concerned with values, ethics, and morals, and to pursue a strategy of activism in coping with the problems of society.[9]

In the closing decades of the century, two significant proposals for reassessment have become prominent. They differ in essential respects and tend to point in different directions. These proposals are most commonly labeled "postmodernism" and "new public management."

Postmodernism is a designation with a variety of meanings. Indeed, it has been described as "one of those words whose linguistic career resembles that of a kitchen sponge. . . . It has become worthless for most purposes; a pattern of random and expanding usage has rendered it so."[10] The semantic problem begins with the fact that the term itself seems to challenge the common dictionary meanings of "modern" and "modernism," defined respectively as "of, pertaining to, or characteristic of the present or most recent past; contemporary," and "a practice, idiom, thought or behavior pattern, art form, etc., characteristic of modern times." As Wasserstrom points out, "we are living in a post-*something* era, the exact nature of which remains unclear."[11] In one form or another, postmodernism has been utilized to describe trends in such varied fields as architecture, sociology, literary criticism, feminism, and history, without consensus as to what designation would be most appropriate to indicate what is happening. In public administration, the most noteworthy contributions to date are *Postmodern Public Administration: Toward Discourse*, by Charles F. Fox and Hugh T. Miller,[12] and *The Language of Public Administration: Bureaucracy, Modernity and Postmodernity*, by David John Farmer.[13] These books are reviewed and evaluated perceptively in "Postmodernism and Public Administration's Identity Crisis," by O. C. McSwite,[14] where they are described as "the cornerstones of what . . . will be a quickly burgeoning literature of post-modern public administration." The claim made for them is that they will help heal the splits that beset the field of public administration, "divisions between those who hold feelings of certainty and those who hold feelings of doubt," by a way of talking that covers over these splits "with common ground, that resolves certainty and doubt into productive dialogue."[15] The thrust of this approach is clearly away from primary reliance on rationality as a producer of answers that can be depended upon, implying that the quest for certainty, in the words of Camilla Stivers, is "not only quixotic but oppressive."[16]

New public management, on the other hand, is described by Stivers as the most recent manifestation of the repeated urge among students of public administration to develop a science of administration with principles of universal validity. It is closely related to the "reinventing government" movement in the United States and other countries,[17] which in turn is linked to preferences for limiting the scope of governmental action, decentralizing authority, contracting out, privatization of public services, and evaluation of performance based on assessment of outcomes. Although the words are essentially synonyms, "management" is preferred over "administration" as a better indicator of such objectives. A succinct statement of the basic concepts of this framework is provided by Lawrence R. Jones and Fred Thompson.[18] One of its most convinced and ardent advocates is Owen E. Hughes of Australia, who argues that

> the traditional model of administration is obsolete and has been effectively replaced by a new model of public management. This change represents a paradigm shift from a bureaucratic model of administration to a market model of management closely related to that of the private sector. Managerial reforms mean a transformation, not only of public management, but of the relationships between market and government, government and the bureaucracy, government and the citizenry, and bureaucracy and the citizenry.[19]

The potential directions proposed for American public administration by postmodernism and new public management currently provide a focus for discussion among leaders in the field. Examples are a recent symposium on "Leadership, Democracy, and the New Public Management"[20] presenting a range of views on the merits of this approach, and a collection of papers under the heading "From Market Entrepreneurialism to Postmodern Intellectualism: Where Should a Divided Field Be Headed?"[21] proposing several middle ground alternatives which attempt to combine or reconcile these competing themes, but without any clear consensus as to what should be done.

On one point crucial to our concerns, postmodernism and new public management are in agreement. Both stress the importance of the comparative dimension in advancing administrative studies. Farmer's book, in particular, "is challenging the public administration community to broaden itself beyond the American parochialism that has traditionally afflicted it."[22] The new public management movement has been multinational from the beginning. The International Public Management Network includes individuals from many countries, and now publishes the *International Public Management Journal* "to provide a forum for sharing ideas, concepts and results of research and thinking about alternative approaches to problem solving and decision making in the public sector."[23]

These summary statements about the fuzzy focus of public administration hide a host of knotty problems—conceptual, definitive, semantic—that do not have to be explored here. Sharp differences of opinion do indeed exist among students of public administration on important issues of approach and emphasis, but should not obscure basic agreement on the central concerns in administrative studies. These concerns include (1) the characteristics and behavior of public administrators—the motivations and conduct of the participants in the administrative process, particularly those who are career officials in the public service; (2) the institutional arrangements for the conduct of large-scale administration in government—organizing for administrative action; and (3) the environment or ecology of administration—the relationship of the administrative subsystem to the political system of which it is a part and to society in general. This combination of concerns, proceeding from the more circumscribed to the more comprehensive, provides a basic framework both for the analysis of particular national systems of public administration and for comparisons among them.

SIGNIFICANCE OF COMPARISON

The purpose of this study is to offer an introduction to the comparative analysis of systems of public administration in the nation-states of today.[24] This is not entirely a new venture, of course. European scholars have been comparativists for at least two hundred years, as shown by the work of Prussian cameralists during the eighteenth century and by French students of public administration during the nineteenth. These studies tended to emphasize issues related to the continental system of administrative law, but the French literature particularly anticipated many of the concepts dealt with later by American public administration theorists.[25] In the United States, there has been a recurring interest by American statesmen and scholars in experience elsewhere. Among the founders of the American constitutional system and government leaders during its first century, this was mainly for purposes of adapting foreign experience to American needs. Pioneers in the study of public administration such as Woodrow Wilson, Frank Goodnow, and Ernst Freund drew upon European experience in their efforts to understand and improve American administration, but most subsequent writers concentrated on the local scene, with only incidental references to other systems of administration. Comparison and historical perspective were certainly not the main thrusts in most of the literature on public administration produced in the United States before the decade of the 1940s.[26] The limitations and hazards of such parochialism have now been recognized, and we have entered a new era in administrative studies that stresses comparative analysis.

Persuasive reasons lie behind this reorientation. Those attempting to construct a science of administration have recognized that this depends, among other things, on success in establishing propositions about administrative behavior which transcend national boundaries. This requirement was pointed out by Robert Dahl, in an influential 1947 essay, when he said:

> the comparative aspects of public administration have largely been ignored; and as long as the study of public administration is not comparative, claims for "a science of public administration" sound rather hollow. Conceivably there might be a science of American public administration and a science of British public administration and a science of French public administration; but can there be a "science of public administration" in the sense of a body of generalized principles independent of their peculiar national setting?[27]

Formulating general principles concerning public administration in the United States, Great Britain, and France may be difficult enough, but this would be quite inadequate in a world having the great number and diversity of national administrative systems that must now be included in our field of interest. Administration in current and former Communist countries and in the multitude of recently independent nations scattered around the globe must also be taken into account. Even cursory observation brings home the complexities involved in describing and analyzing the administrative variations and innovations that have developed in these settings.

Aside from the demands of scientific inquiry, there are other advantages to be gained from a better understanding of public administration across national boundaries. The increasing interdependence of nations and regions of the world makes comprehension of the conduct of administration of much more importance than in the past. The degree of success shown by Zaire, Bolivia, and Indonesia in organizing for administrative action is no longer just a matter of intellectual curiosity; it is of immense practical significance in Washington, Moscow, and London, not to mention Manila, Cairo, and Beijing.

Various administrative devices developed abroad may also prove worthy of consideration for adoption or adaptation at home. The influence of Western patterns of administration in the newly independent countries is well known and easily understandable. Less obvious is the growing interest in larger countries concerning administrative machinery originated in smaller nations. An example is the Scandinavian office of Ombudsman, designed for protection of the public against administrative abuse or inadequacy, which has been widely studied and, in numerous instances, transplanted in Western Europe, the United States, countries of the British Commonwealth, Japan, and some of the new states.[28] Another example is the establishment in the Indonesian president's cabinet of several "junior ministers," with boundary-spanning functions designed to achieve better coordination on a government-wide basis in the implementation of crucial development programs (such as food crops, transmigration, and community housing) involving two or more national departments as well as provincial government agencies.[29] On a broader front, some of the most extensive and crucial use of government corporations has been occurring in the developing nations, and they have joined more developed countries in worldwide experiments with privatization.[30] The laboratories for administrative experimentation provided by the emergence of many new nations should, in the future, continue to offer numerous instances of innovations in administration worthy of the attention of more established countries.

PROBLEMS OF COMPARISON

Recognizing the need for comparison is much easier than coping with some of the problems posed by efforts to compare on a systematic basis.

The basic dilemma is that any attempt to compare national administrative systems must acknowledge the fact that administration is only one aspect of the operation of the political system. This means inevitably that comparative public administration is linked closely to the study of comparative politics, and must start from the base provided by recent and current developments in the comparative study of whole political systems.[31]

During the last half century, comparative politics has been through transitions that deserve to be called revolutionary.[32] This has resulted from a combination of dramatic expansion of the range of coverage of the subject and a decisive rejection of approaches to comparison common before World War II. A field that was largely confined to consideration of the political institutions of a handful of countries in Western Europe and North America, plus only a scattering of other countries, such as selected members of the British Commonwealth and Japan, suddenly confronted the urgent need to account in its comparisons for a welter of additional nations which had emerged on the world scene, with the resulting problem of numbers and diversity. The United Nations now has over 180 member states, and there are others waiting to get in, excluded from membership, or not wanting to be included. Moreover, their diversity is more of a complication than their number, since they range so widely in area, population, stability, ideological orientation, economic development, historical background, governmental institutions, future prospects, and a host of other relevant factors. Students of comparative politics must somehow undertake to provide a framework for comparison that can cope with such complexity.

The insistence on inclusion of the nations of Asia, Latin America, and Africa signifies recognition of the fact that these countries occupy approximately 63 percent of the land area of the earth and contain over 75 percent of the world's population. These statistics are particularly significant in view of the waning age of imperialism and colonialism, the "revolution of rising expectations" among the peoples of these countries, and the battleground they furnish for rivalry among competing world powers and political ideologies. As expressed by Ward and Macridis, it became essential that "the discipline of comparative politics keep abreast of such developments and expand its frames of reference and concern so as to include the political systems of these emergent non-Western areas. This is easy to say, but hard in practice to do."[33]

Nevertheless, the response to these needs has been impressive, with substantial, although not complete, agreement on means of fulfilling them. The common objectives have been that the purview of comparative studies must be capable of including all existing nation-states; that comparison, in order to be significant, must be based on the collection and evaluation of political data in terms of definite hypotheses or theories; and that some alternative to a simple institutional basis for comparison must be found.[34]

Heroic efforts have been made to define key concepts and formulate hypotheses for systematic testing. Attempts to define "political system" had first priority, with the result that a political system is now generally described as that system of interactions in a society which produces authoritative decisions (or allocates values) that are binding on the society as a whole and are enforced by legitimate physical compulsion if necessary. The political system, in the words of Gabriel Almond, is "the legitimate, order-maintaining or transforming system in the society."[35] According to Ward and Macridis, government is the official machinery by which these decisions are "legally identified, posed, made, and administered."[36] In a recent contribution, Herbert Kitschelt prefers the more inclusive term "political regime," defined as "the rules and basic political resource allocations according to which actors exercise authority by imposing and enforcing collective decisions on a bounded constituency."[37] Such formulations are intended to include a variety of states—developed and developing, totalitarian and democratic, Western and non-Western. They also embrace types of primitive political organizations that do not qualify as states in the sense used by Max

Weber, that they monopolize the legitimate use of physical force within a given territory. Other key concepts that have received much attention but are the subject of more disagreement are political modernization, development, and change. Further consideration of the issues involved in these concepts is given in Chapter 3.

The basic analytical framework that has been most generally accepted is a form of systems theory known as *structural functionalism*, originated and elaborated by sociologists such as Talcott Parsons, Marion Levy, and Robert Merton for the study of whole societies, and later adapted by political scientists for the analysis of political systems. In the terminology of structural-functional analysis, structures are roughly synonymous with institutions and functions with activities. Structures or institutions perform functions or activities. The linkage between structures and functions cannot be broken, but priority can be given in analysis either to the structural or functional aspects of the total system. Whether the preferred approach is through structure or function, the central question, as Martin Landau has pointed out,[38] is always some form of "[w]hat functions are performed by a given institution, and how?"

A simplified summary of the literature of comparative politics during recent decades is that a functional emphasis gained the upper hand and became accepted in what is often termed "mainline" comparative politics, but that currently there is a growing tendency toward reversing this preference and focusing primarily on political structures. This sequence will be explored under the labels of "functionalism" and "neo-institutionalism."

Functionalism

The most influential of the comprehensive efforts to substitute a functional approach for the earlier more traditional institutional approach to comparative politics was led by Gabriel A. Almond.[39] As to the advantage of this approach, his basic claim was that it attempted "to construct a theoretical framework that makes possible, for the first time, a comparative method of analysis for political systems of all kinds."[40] The indictment against comparisons on the basis of specialized political structures such as legislatures, political parties, chief executives, and interest groups was that such comparisons are of only limited utility because similar structural features may not be found in different political systems, or they may be performing significantly different functions. Almond conceded that all political systems have specialized political structures, and that the systems may be compared with one another structurally. He saw little to be gained from this, however, and a serious danger of being misled. Instead, he argued that the correct functional questions should be asked, asserting that "the same functions are performed in all political systems, even though these functions may be performed with different frequencies, and by different kinds of structures."[41]

What are these functional categories? Let us begin by saying they are derived from consideration of the political activities that take place in the most complex Western political systems. Thus, the activities of associational interest groups led to derivation of the function of interest articulation, and the activities of political parties to the function of interest aggregation. In its revised form, this scheme of analysis suggests a sixfold functional breakdown for the internal conversion processes through which political systems transform inputs into outputs. These functions are (1) interest articulation (formulation of demands); (2) interest aggregation (combination of demands in the form of alternative courses of action); (3) rule-making (formulation of authoritative rules); (4) rule application (application and enforcement of these rules); (5) rule adjudication (adjudication in individual cases of applications of these rules); and (6) communication (both within the political system and between the political system and its environment). The innovation in this list is clearly in the functions that have been traditionally related to policy-making rather than policy execution, which detracts considerably from the usefulness of this analytical framework to those principally interested in the administrative aspects of comparative study.

Despite the generally favorable reception given to the Almond functional approach, it did not escape sharp criticism. Leonard Binder acknowledged that it was an advance over institutional description, but dismissed it with the curt observation that it "may be praised as interesting or perceptive, without compelling further attention." He conceded that the categories, being broad and ambiguous, could be universally applied. The scheme claimed to facilitate the analysis of whole political systems, but Binder felt that it would be accepted "only if it lends itself to the analysis of specific systems as well as to problems of comparison, and only if the implicit assumptions of the scheme accord with the theoretical assumptions of individual researchers." The root defect that Binder saw was that these functions, having been located by "the device of generalizing what appeared to the theorist to be the broad classes of political activity found in Western political systems," were "derived neither logically nor empirically." He asked why these functions should be selected and not others, and he challenged the supposition that "a limited number of functions . . . comprise the political system." Further, he argued that the weakness of the scheme was evidenced by the fact that the authors who attempted to apply the Almond scheme in the volume it introduced "judiciously avoided remaining within its limiting framework or, in the case of the 'governmental functions,' made it clear how insignificant has been the effort to apply the traditional categories of Western political science."[42]

Another critic of Almond's input-output model was Fred W. Riggs, who admitted that it was useful for the study of developed political systems, but found it inadequate for the analysis of transitional systems, such as that of India, which was, of course, precisely the kind of system to which Almond thought it would be most applicable. Riggs felt that a different model was needed for such a polity, which has "inputs which do not lead to rule-making, and rules which are often not implemented." The requirement was for "a two-tiered model, a system which distinguishes between 'formal' and 'effective' structures, between what is pre-scribed ideally and what actually happens."[43] Riggs suggested as more appropri-ate for such political systems his own "prismatic model," which we will explore in more detail in Chapter 2.

An additional attack on the functional approach came from critics who associated this school of thought with a basic philosophical bias favoring the political systems which had evolved in liberal Western capitalist societies, and who argued that analytical schemes such as Almond's operate in practice to justify and perpetuate the status quo in developing countries to the benefit of the advanced industrialized societies and to the detriment of the countries subjected to study by social scientists using this methodology. This judgment has been made particularly by the dependency development theorists whose views are examined in Chapter 3.

Finally, and more recently, functionalism has been questioned by a variety of "neo-institutionalists" who differ in important respects but are in agreement that the primacy of emphasis on functions should be replaced by increasing attention to structures.

Neo-institutionalism

The phrase "return to the state" conveys the thrust of this proposed reorientation toward a new emphasis in comparative politics on institutional comparisons. In addition to a burgeoning literature,[44] this trend is evidenced by organizational developments such as creation of the International Institute of Comparative Government, based in Switzerland, "to coordinate studies of government struc-tures, activities, and policies on a genuinely cross-national basis,"[45] and the establishment by the International Political Science Association of a Research Committee on the Structure and Organization of Government, which in 1988 initiated publication of a new quarterly journal, *Governance: An International Journal of Policy and Administration.*

Revival of the concept of the "state" in some form is a common theme, with variations in detail as to definition but concurrence that "state" needs to be distinguished from both "society" and "government." The state and the society are viewed as distinct, despite being inevitably linked together. Likewise, the state is more inclusive than the government of the day and the institutional apparatus through which it operates. Basically, the emphasis is placed on the state and its institutions, composed, as Fesler says, "of a multitude of large and small parts," but sharing five interrelated characteristics: taking actions, holding distinctive values, having a history, sharing organization cultures, and maintaining power structures.[46] As both its advocates and its critics agree, this concept of the state differs from those of "mainstream" political scientists (based on behavioralism, pluralism, and/or structural functionalism) and of neo-Marxists. Even Almond, who generally is unimpressed by the statist movement, agrees that it "has drawn attention to institutional and particularly administrative history," and that this is "all to the good."[47]

Another aspect of neo-institutionalism is that it has generated a revival of concern with normative issues associated with such traditional concepts as "the public interest" and "civil science." Fesler, for example, welcomes reexamination of what has often been referred to in a derogatory way as the myth of the public interest. "The simple fact," he says, "is that the public interest is an ideal. It is for administrators what objectivity is for scholars—something to be strived for, even if imperfectly achieved, something not to be spurned because performance falls short of the goal."[48] Robert H. Jackson has argued for the benefits of a renewed interest in civil science, defined as "the study of rules which constitute and govern political life within and between sovereign states."[49] He maintains that there is a need "to resurrect and renew civil science in the comparative analysis of all countries today including those of Africa, Asia, Oceania, the Middle East, and—not least—Eastern Europe."[50] He distinguishes between "civil science" and "social science," which in his terminology is essentially what I call "mainstream" political science. He is not advocating replacement of the approach of "social science" with that of "civil science," but rather views them as equally important and related to one another in a complementary rather than a competitive way.

One facet of the neo-institutional literature of particular interest to us is the notion of "stateness" for use in making cross-societal comparisons. As early as 1968, J. P. Nettl argued that "more or less stateness is a useful variable for comparing Western societies," and that "the absence or presence of a well-developed concept of state relates to and identifies important empirical differences in these societies."[51] More recently, this idea of degree of stateness (referring to the relative scope and extent of governmental power and authority) has been applied more globally by Metin Heper, who has undertaken to distinguish four types of polity based on their degrees of stateness and to identify corresponding types of bureaucracy.[52] We will examine this application of neo-institutionalism more fully in Chapter 2.

The neo-institutionalist thrust has now been around long enough to generate a critical reaction, mostly centered on the clarity and utility of the "state" as a focus. For instance, Pye deplores trying to bring back into vogue "the hoary, 18th–19th century concept of the 'state' as a unitary phenomenon," and suggests that culture is the concept "which makes it possible to merge many differences in attitudes and behavior into categories while still preserving an appreciation for the diversity that characterizes most of human life."[53] Mitchell advocates an approach that can account "for both the salience of the state and its elusiveness."[54] Jackman argues that it would be most fruitful to concentrate on the study of "political capacity" among contemporary nation-states.[55]

Although this summary has touched on only selected aspects of neo-institutionalism in comparative politics, it should be enough to demonstrate the impact already made and still being made on the more dominant functionalist school of thought.

Keeping in mind the centrality of the linkage between comparative politics and comparative public administration, it ought now to be evident that the problems of comparing national systems of administration are formidable. The primary requirement is that some way must be found for singling out the administrative segment of the political system as a basis for specialized comparison. This cannot be done without involvement in issues related to the comparison of whole political systems, where there is ferment and progress but no consensus. The dominant tendency has been to substitute a functional approach to comparison for one emphasizing political structures and institutions. Insofar as the functional approach receives exclusive or even preferred recognition as the proper basis for comparisons of less than whole political systems, a problem is created for the comparative study of administration. The reason is that the full range of concerns of public administration as a field of academic inquiry is less easily identified with one or more functions in a framework such as Almond's than with particular familiar institutions in Western political systems. The movement toward a new institutionalism has made a structural emphasis less difficult to justify, but does not make the choice either easy or obvious. This problem will be readdressed and dealt with in Chapter 2.

POSTWAR EVOLUTION OF COMPARATIVE STUDIES

A sustained effort to undertake comparative analysis in public administration has occurred since mid-20th century.[56] Beginning soon after the end of World War II, a comparative administration "movement" gained momentum, with enthusiastic and industrious devotees whose efforts have evoked enthusiastic praise from some quarters for impressive accomplishments and criticism from others for what are regarded as pretentious claims.

The timing and vigor of this movement resulted from a combination of factors: the rather obvious need for this extension of range in public administration as a discipline; the exposure of large numbers of scholars and practitioners of administration to experience with administration abroad during wartime, postwar occupation, and subsequent technical assistance assignments; the stimulation of the largely contemporary revisionist movement in comparative politics which has already been summarized; and the rather remarkable expansion of opportunities during the 1950s and 1960s for those interested in devoting themselves to research at home or field experience abroad on problems of comparative public administration.

Manifestations of these developments were numerous during the first two decades after the end of World War II. A growing number of colleges and universities offered courses in comparative public administration, and some of them made it a field of specialization for graduate study. Professional associations extended recognition, first through the appointment in 1953 of an ad hoc committee on comparative administration by the American Political Science Association, and later by the establishment in 1960 of the Comparative Administration Group affiliated with the American Society for Public Administration. The latter group, usually abbreviated as CAG, grew vigorously with the help of generous support from the Ford Foundation. The CAG, under Fred W. Riggs as chairman and leading spokesman, mapped out and entered into a comprehensive program of research seminars, experimental teaching projects, discussions at professional meetings, special conferences, and exploration of other ways of strengthening available resources, such as through the expansion of facilities for field research.

The most tangible product of these early endeavors was an output of published writings on comparative public administration which soon reached voluminous proportions and led, despite the short span of time, to several attempts to review and analyze the literature produced by the early 1960s.[57] Classification of this literature is best done by subject matter or focus of emphasis rather than chronological order, since it appeared in a variety of forms more or less simultaneously. I have suggested as a useful scheme of classification one which divides this literature as follows: (1) modified traditional, (2) development-oriented, (3) general system model-building, and (4) middle-range theory formulation.

The modified traditional category showed the greatest continuity with earlier more parochially oriented literature. The subject matter was not markedly different as the focus shifted from individual administrative systems to comparisons among them, although there was often a serious effort to utilize more advanced research tools and to incorporate findings from a variety of social science disciplines. This literature may be further subdivided into studies made from a comparative perspective of standard administrative subtopics, and those which undertook comparisons of entire systems of administration. Topics in the first subcategory included administrative organization, personnel management, fiscal administration, headquarters-field relations, administration of public enterprises, regulatory administration, administrative responsibility and control, and program fields such as health, education, welfare, and agriculture.

The second subcategory included a number of studies that were basically descriptive institutional comparisons of administration in Western developed countries, with special emphasis on administrative organization and civil service systems.[58] Also worthy of mention is an outline for comparative field research formulated by Wallace S. Sayre and Herbert Kaufman in 1952, and later revised by a working group of the American Political Science Association subcommittee on comparative public administration. This research design suggested a three-point model for comparison, focusing on the organization of the administrative system, the control of the administrative system, and the securing of consent and compliance by the administrative hierarchy.[59]

Advocates of a focus on "development administration" sought to concentrate attention on the administrative requisites for achieving public policy goals, particularly in countries in which these goals involved dramatic political, economic, and social transformations.[60] "Development," according to Weidner, "is a state of mind, a tendency, a direction. Rather than a fixed goal, it is a rate of change in a particular direction. . . . The study of development administration can help to identify the conditions under which a maximum rate of development is sought and the conditions under which it has been obtained."[61] He contended that existing models for comparison were of limited use because "they make inadequate provision for social change; characterize modern bureaucracy in very inaccurate ways; are unduly comprehensive, all-inclusive and abstract; and fail to take account of the differences in administration that may be related to the goals that are being sought." Hence, he urged the adoption of development administration as a separate focus for research, with the end object being "to relate different administrative roles, practices, organizational arrangements, and procedures to the maximizing of development objectives. . . . In research terms, the ultimate dependent variable would be the development goals themselves."[62] Although work with a development administration emphasis need not be normative, in the sense of a choice among development goals by the researcher, much of it has had a prescriptive coloration.

Dwight Waldo, among others, was intrigued by this approach and argued that a concentration on the theme of development might "help to bring into useful association various clusters of ideas and types of activity that are now more or less separate and help clarify some methodological problems," even though he admitted that he found it impossible to define development, as used in this connection, with precision.[63] Although the term did raise serious questions about what it meant and what was included and excluded, development administration continued as a focus of attention because it had the virtue of consciously relating administrative means to administrative ends, and of deliberately spotlighting the problems of administrative adjustment faced by emerging countries seeking to achieve developmental goals. As Swerdlow remarked, "poor countries have special characteristics that tend to create a different role for government. These characteristics and this expanded or emphasized role of government, particularly as it affects economic growth, tend to make the operations of the public administrator significantly different. Where such differences exist, public administration can be usefully called development administration."[64]

The remaining two groups were more typical of the dominant mood among students of comparative public administration during this period, and indeed of comparative politics as well. In contrast to the first two categories, the emphasis here was much more self-consciously on the construction of typologies or models for comparative purposes, and there was a strong concern to keep these value-free or value-neutral. The word "model" was used here, as by Waldo, to mean "simply the conscious attempt to develop and define concepts, or clusters of related concepts, useful in classifying data, describing reality and (or) hypothesizing about it."[65] Interdisciplinary borrowing was extensive, primarily from sociology, but to a considerable extent also from economics, psychology, and other fields. This emphasis on theory and methodology was repeatedly noted, often praised as indicative of sound preparation for future progress, as well as frequently disparaged as a preoccupation diverting energies that might better have been devoted to the conduct of actual field studies of administrative systems in operation. Any attempt to classify this plethora of models must be somewhat arbitrary, but the most useful distinction was made by Presthus, who distinguished between theorists attempting broad, cross-cultural, all encompassing formulations and those advancing more modest and restricted "middle-range" theories.[66] Diamant likewise discerned "general system" models and "political culture" models among contributions in comparative politics.[67]

Among those who preferred the general system approach to comparative public administration, Fred W. Riggs was clearly the dominant figure. As I have said elsewhere, "mere acquaintance with all of his writings on comparative theory is in itself not an insignificant accomplishment."[68] Drawing essentially upon concepts of structural-functional analysis developed by sociologists such as Talcott Parsons, Marion Levy, and F. X. Sutton, Riggs, in a series of published and unpublished writings, over a period of years formulated and reformulated a cluster of models or "ideal types" for societies, designed to contribute to a better understanding of actual societies, particularly those undergoing rapid social, economic, political, and administrative change. This work culminated in his book, *Administration in Developing Countries: The Theory of Prismatic Society*,[69] which continues to be probably the most notable single contribution in comparative public administration.

Another prominent source of comprehensive model-building was equilibrium theory, postulating a system of inputs and outputs as a basis of analysis. John T. Dorsey outlined an approach to theory of this type in his "information-energy model," which he believed might be useful in the analysis of social and political systems in general as well as for a better understanding of administrative systems.[70] Dorsey later used this scheme in an analysis of political development in Vietnam.[71] The model was later tested by William M. Berenson, who used aggregate data from a universe of fifty-six nations to examine the validity of propositions drawn from the information-energy model linking three ecological variables (energy, information, and energy conversion) to bureaucratic development in the Third World. His conclusion was that the model failed to offer an adequate explanation for bureaucratic changes in the countries studied.[72] Interest in this model has since waned.

As Waldo observed, the central problem of model construction in the study of comparative public administration is "to select a model that is 'large' enough to embrace all the phenomena that should be embraced without being, by virtue of its large dimensions, too coarse-textured and clumsy to grasp and manipulate administration."[73] The alleged gap between such "large" models and the empirical data to be examined led Presthus and others to stress the need for middle-range theory rather than theory of "cosmic dimension," to use his phrase. He advised social scientists working on comparative administration to "bite off smaller chunks of reality and . . . research these intensively."[74] Similar expressions of preference for middle-range theories were made at about the same time in the field of comparative politics.[75]

By the early 1960s, the most prominent and promising middle-range model available for comparative studies in administration had already been established as the "bureaucratic" one, based on the ideal-type model of bureaucracy formulated by Max Weber but with substantial subsequent modification, alteration, and revision. Waldo found the bureaucratic model useful, stimulating, and provocative, its advantage and appeal being that this model "is set in a large framework that spans history and cultures and relates bureaucracy to important social variables, yet it focuses attention upon the chief structural and functional characteristics of bureaucracy."[76] He correctly pointed out that not much empirical research had actually been done using the bureaucratic model. However, this deficiency applied to other models as well, and there was at least a base of such studies upon which to build, with others on the way. The most notable such research, despite substantial flaws in execution, was Morroe Berger's *Bureaucracy and Society in Modern Egypt*,[77] but there were a number of other partial treatments of bureaucracy in particular countries, either in separate essays or as parts of analyses of individual political systems. The entire subject of the role of bureaucracy in political development had been explored in depth in papers prepared for a conference sponsored in 1962 by the Committee on Comparative Politics of the Social Science Research Council and published the following year in a volume edited by Joseph LaPalombara.[78] The bureaucratic perspective for comparison was thus already well rooted during the formative period of the comparative public administration movement.

This review of the literature during the emergence of comparative studies in public administration provides a base for describing the flowering of the movement during the decade beginning in the early 1960s. Trends which continued into this period of expansion had already been identified and encouraged by Fred Riggs in an essay published in 1962.[79] He discerned three trends which have been generally accepted as important and relevant. The first was a shift from normative toward more empirical approaches—a movement away from efforts to prescribe ideal or better patterns of administration toward a growing interest in descriptive and analytic information. This consideration has already been mentioned, but it should be noted that the popular development administration theme often had a strong prescriptive motivation. The second trend was a movement from what Riggs called idiographic toward nomothetic approaches. Essentially this distinguished between studies concentrating on unique cases and those seeking generalizations. Model-building, particularly of the general system type, showed this nomothetic inclination. The third trend was a shift from a predominantly nonecological to an ecological basis for comparative study. Riggs described the first trend as being fairly clear by the time he wrote, but considered the other two as just emerging. Obviously, he approved of these trends and was trying to encourage them. Indeed, he stated that his personal preference would be "to consider as 'truly' comparative only those studies that are empirical, nomothetic, and ecological."[80]

THE HEYDAY OF THE COMPARATIVE ADMINISTRATION MOVEMENT

"The time of greatest vitality, vigor, influence, etc." is the dictionary definition of heyday, describing accurately the comparative administration movement during the period of about a decade beginning in 1962, the year in which the Comparative Administration Group received initial funding from the Ford Foundation through a grant to the American Society for Public Administration, CAG's parent organization. During these years, students of comparative public administration demonstrated an amazing productivity, and their field of interest grew rapidly in glamor and reputation.[81]

CAG Programs

At the core of all this activity was the Comparative Administration Group, with a membership composed of academics and practitioners, including a considerable number of "corresponding members" from countries other than the United States, reaching a total in 1968 of over 500. The principal source of financial support was the Ford Foundation, which made grants to CAG of about half a million dollars in all, beginning in 1962 with a three-year grant which was extended for a year and then renewed in 1966 for five additional years. In 1971 this support was not renewed again, and after that CAG resources were much reduced, with a corresponding curtailment of programs. The primary focus of interest of the Ford Foundation was on the administrative problems of developing countries, and the CAG was expected to analyze these problems in the context of societal environmental factors found in these countries. The foundation had a strong development administration orientation and was eager to see a transfer of knowledge from CAG programs to practical applications through technical assistance projects and domestic developmental undertakings within the target countries.

The CAG spun an elaborate network for carrying out its obligation to stimulate interest in comparative administration, with special reference to development administration problems. The primary device chosen initially was a series of summer seminars, held two per year over a three-year period at different universities, involving in each instance about a half dozen senior scholars who prepared papers on a common theme, plus graduate assistants and visiting consultants. Later, special conferences and seminars were scheduled on various topics both in the United States and abroad. In addition, a number of small subgrants were made for experimental teaching programs.

A committee structure evolved under CAG auspices as areas of interest became identified. Several had a geographical orientation, relating to Asia, Europe, Latin America, and Africa. Others had a subject matter focus, including committees on comparative urban studies, national economic planning, comparative educational administration, comparative legislative studies, international administration, organization theory, and systems theory. These committees were not equally active or productive.

The work of CAG was reflected principally in publications which it spawned, either directly or indirectly. A newsletter was issued regularly as a means of internal communication. More than 100 occasional papers were distributed in mimeographed form. After editing and revision, many of these were later published under various auspices. The primary outlet was provided by the Duke University Press, which published seven volumes in cooperation with CAG from 1969 through 1973, including general collections on political and administrative development and "frontiers" of development administration, volumes on development administration in Asia and in Latin America, studies of temporal dimensions and spatial dimensions of development administration, and a comparative analysis of legislatures. For a five-year period, from 1969 to 1974, the quarterly *Journal of Comparative Administration* was issued by Sage Publications in cooperation with CAG. There were also, of course, numerous articles published in other scholarly journals in the United States and abroad which were written by CAG members.

Paralleling these research efforts, a corresponding growth was taking place in the teaching of courses in comparative and development administration in the United States, as evidenced by a 1970 report of a CAG survey which enumerated a proliferation of offerings beginning in 1945 at one institution and growing to over thirty by the time of the survey, but it also revealed very little uniformity as to approach, emphasis, or level of presentation. This interest in comparative aspects of administration was also reflected in the curricula and publications of numerous schools and institutes of public administration scattered around the world, usually as products of technical assistance projects, although the record was uneven as to the quantity and quality of these efforts.

Characteristic Features

The record of this "golden era" in comparative public administration is basically a continuation and expansion of what had already begun during the postwar period. The sheer bulk and great diversity of the output makes generalizations hazardous. Nevertheless, it is possible to identify some characteristic features which not only show what was accomplished but also foreshadow some of the predicaments faced later by the comparative administration movement.

One obvious enduring influence can be traced to the large-scale postwar effort to export administrative know-how through unilateral and multilateral technical assistance programs. The CAG inherited the then favorable reputation and shared many of the attitudes associated with the public administration technical assistance efforts of the 1950s. Experts in public administration, not only from the United States but from numerous European countries as well, were scattered around the world, engaged in similar projects to export administrative technology, largely drawn from American experience, to a multitude of developing countries. Looking back, one of these experts describes the scene as follows:

> The 1950s was a wonderful period. The "American Dream" was the "World Dream"—and the best and quickest way to bring that dream into reality was through the mechanism of public administration. . . . The net result of all this enthusiastic action was that in the 1950s public administration was a magic term and public administration experts were magicians, of a sort. They were eagerly recruited by the United States' aid-giving agencies and readily accepted by most of the new nations, along with a lot of other experts as well.[82]

Another well-informed participant observer takes 1955 as the baseline year, and describes it as "a vintage year in a time of faith—faith in the developmental power of administrative tools devised in the West. It was a sanguine year in a time of hope—hope that public administration could lead countries toward modernization. It was a busy year in a brief age of charity—the not-unmixed charity of foreign assistance."[83]

Members of the CAG, many of whom had been or still were active participants in such programs, shared as a group most of the assumptions of the public administration experts, at least initially. Siffin has provided an accurate and perceptive analysis of the orientations which marked this era, noting several major features. The first was a tool or technology orientation. The best developed and most widely exported of these processes were in the fields of personnel administration and budgeting and financial administration, but the list included administrative planning, records management, work simplification, tax and revenue administration, and at least the beginnings of computer technology. Part of the tool orientation was a belief that use of the tools could be essentially divorced from the substance of the governmental policies which they would be serving. Second, there was a structural orientation which placed great emphasis on the importance of appropriate organizational arrangements, and assumed that organizational decisions could and should be based on rational considerations. For the most part, organizational forms then popular in the West were thought of as the most fitting, and organizations recommended for the developing countries usually emulated some model familiar to the expert at home.

Underlying these administrative manifestations were certain value and contextual orientations which helped explain the specifics of technical assistance recommendations. The instrumental nature of administration was the core value, with related supportive concepts of efficiency, rationality, responsibility, effectiveness, and professionalism. Education and training projects, including the sending of thousands of individuals to developed countries and the establishment of about seventy institutes in developing countries, were designed to inculcate these values as well as transmit technical know-how in specific subjects. Probably most important of all, these normative elements, particularly the commitment to responsibility as a basic value, were in Siffin's words "predicated upon a certain kind of socio-political context—the kind of context which is distinguished in its absence from nearly every developing country in the world." This context included economic, social, political, and intellectual aspects drawn mainly from U.S experience and to some extent from other Western democratic systems. Politically, for example, these systems operated "within reasonably stable political frameworks, with limited competition for resources and mandates. In this milieu, administrative technologies provided *order* more than *integration*. The political context of administration was generally predictable, supportive, and incrementally expansive." In this and other respects, Siffin concluded that "the radical differences between the U.S. administrative context and various overseas situations were substantially ignored."[84]

It would be unfair to infer that misconceptions prevalent in the technical assistance efforts of the 1950s were accepted without question by students of comparative public administration during the 1960s. As a matter of fact, many of them voiced doubt and skepticism about approaches being used and opposed particular reform measures in countries with which they were familiar. Nevertheless, the comparative administration movement at its height can accurately be described as imbued with a pervasive overall mood of optimism about the practicality of utilizing administrative means to bring about desirable change. Commentators who disagreed on many other matters agreed in making this assessment. In a review of several of the major books produced by the CAG, Garth N. Jones remarked that they "make a case for positive intervention into the affairs of men. Men can take destiny in their hands, control, and mold it." Noting that many of the papers under review systematically eviscerated "past approaches and efforts in planned development in public administration," Jones pointed out that even so "scarcely a word is mentioned that questions the approach of positive intervention. The main task is to find a better way by which to do this."[85]

Peter Savage, who served as editor of the *Journal of Comparative Administration*, observed that the study of administration from a comparative perspective "possesses a peculiar quality; a concern for the management of action in the real world, for creating organizational and procedural arrangements that handle specified and identifiable problems in the public realm." Indigenous to the comparative administration movement, in his opinion, had been "a belief in the possibility of managing change by purposive intervention by administrative institutions."[86]

Even more than before, during the 1960s development administration became a term often used in the titles of books and articles with a comparative thrust. No doubt this reflected in part the faith in positive results just discussed and behind that the desire to assist developing countries in meeting their overwhelming problems. It was also responsive to the core interest of the Ford Foundation as chief financial benefactor in directing CAG programs toward developmental topics. Furthermore, it proved attractive to leaders in the developing countries themselves by highlighting an intent to assist in reaching domestic goals. From a more strictly scholarly point of view, strong arguments were made as to the benefits to comparative studies of a developmental focus. Whatever the motivations, development administration largely displaced comparative administration in the labeling of CAG output. This was shown most significantly in the Duke University Press series of books, each of which had in its title either the word "development" or "developmental," and none of which had "comparative."

Despite the trend toward greater usage, little progress appeared in defining more precisely what development administration meant. Riggs, in his introduction to *Frontiers of Development Administration*,[87] said that no clear answer could be given as to how the study of development administration differed from the study of comparative administration or the study of public administration generally. He did identify two foci of attention—the administration of development and the development of administration. In the first sense, development administration referred "to the administration of development programs, to the methods used by large-scale organizations, notably governments, to implement policies and plans designed to meet their developmental objectives."[88] The second meaning involved the strengthening of administrative capabilities, both as a means to enhance the prospects for success in carrying out current development programs, and as a by-product of prior programs such as in education.[89] Writings under the heading of development administration did indeed explore both of these facets, but were not by any means confined to one or the other of these subjects of inquiry. As a matter of actual practice, development administration came in the 1960s to be synonymous with, or at least not clearly distinguishable from, comparative public administration. The two terms became virtually interchangeable. This usage was in part an affirmation of the faith in positive intervention for societal reform held by most of those identified with the comparative administration movement.

Among the middle-range models for comparative studies, bureaucracy continued to be widely preferred. Ramesh K. Arora identified the construct of bureaucracy drawn from the work of Max Weber as "the single most dominant conceptual framework in the study of comparative administration."[90] A large proportion of the literature dealt in one way or another with bureaucracies— refining what was meant by the term bureaucracy, describing particular national or subnational bureaucratic systems, classifying bureaucracies as to type on the basis of dominant characteristics, debating the problem of relationships between bureaucracies and other groups in the political system, and so forth. Lacking, however, was any outpouring of field studies on the current operations of developing bureaucracies, in part because of the scarcity of financial support for the substantial costs involved.

The most conspicuous trait of the comparative administration literature during this period, nevertheless, was an extension of the search for comprehensive theory, with contributions from a wide range of social scientists, not just from students of public administration and political science. Savage noted the production of much "grand theory," and commented that if one envisioned a high and a low road to science, then certainly comparative administration "tended to travel loftily,"[91] and undervalued the approach of systematic inquiry directed toward reducing indeterminacy. James Heaphey found "academic analysis" to be the foremost among a few "dominant visions" in his analysis of characteristics of comparative literature.[92] Jamil E. Jreisat also concluded that the research orientation leading in influence had been macro-analysis of national administrative systems, with emphasis tending to be at "the level of grand theory in the sociological tradition."[93] All those who surveyed the output of the comparative administration movement during its peak agreed on this pervasive, but not dominant, characteristic.

When all of these partially overlapping and partially competing forces had been taken into account, the overwhelming impression was that diversity had been the hallmark of the movement, recognized as such by both its enthusiasts and its detractors. Fred Riggs, acknowledging that "dissensus prevails," with no agreement on "approach, methodology, concept, theory, or doctrine," considered this a "virtue, a cause for excitement," normal in a preparadigmatic field.[94] As Peter Savage put it, comparative administration "started with no paradigm of its own and developed none." No orthodoxy was established or even attempted. "The net result has been paradigmatic confusion, as much a part of Comparative Administration as it is held to be of its parent field, Public Administration."[95] This failure to draw the boundaries and set the rules of comparative administration as a field of study became, as we shall see, a main complaint of those disenchanted with accomplishments made by the CAG.

RETRENCHMENT, REAPPRAISALS, AND RECOMMENDATIONS

The years from about 1970 through the early 1980s became for comparative public administration a period of lessened support and lowered expectations. The exuberance of CAG's heyday was replaced by a mood of introspection. Individuals long identified with CAG joined earlier detractors and younger scholars in reappraising the past record and making recommendations for the future of comparative administration as a focus of study and action.

Retrenchment

Foreshadowing these trends in the comparative administration movement itself came a downshift in the attention devoted to public administration as a category for technical assistance efforts. Emphasis on these programs continued into the mid-1960s, but declined rapidly and sharply beginning about 1967. By the early 1970s the annual rate of support from the United States for public administration aid was less than half what it had been during the decade from the mid-1950s to the mid-1960s. International as well as U.S. technical assistance agencies shifted their attention from administrative reform efforts to complex programs with an economic orientation designed to foster indigenous economic growth through policies jointly worked out by domestic and international agencies. As Jones dramatically put it, the public administration technicians, the POSDCORB types of the 1950s, were exterminated by a new animal "as fearsome and aggressive as the ancient Norsemen—the new development economists."[96] Projects high on the priority list of the experts in development economics largely displaced the administrative know-how export projects favored earlier. This transition not only reduced the number of practitioners in technical assistance agencies affiliated with the CAG, it also sharply curtailed even the theoretical possibilities of bringing the work of CAG to bear directly on technical assistance programs.

The 1970s also brought several direct alterations and reductions in the scope of activities of the comparative administration movement itself. The end of Ford Foundation support has already been mentioned. No substitute financial sponsor materialized with help approaching the level provided during the 1960s. Even during those years, the CAG was turned down in its search for funds to support field research in developing countries on any substantial, systematic, and planned basis. The *Journal of Comparative Administration*, after only five years of existence as the primary vehicle for scholarly research in the field, ceased publication in 1974. Although this move involved a merger into a new journal, *Administration and Society*, rather than outright extinction, it clearly meant a more diffused focus with no assurance that the broader scope would assure success either. Publications in the Duke University Press series continued to appear as late as 1973, but these were products of work done several years earlier. Reports from university campuses indicated a falling off of student interest in comparative administration courses, and there was evidence that fewer doctoral dissertations were being written in the field.

Perhaps most symbolically if not substantively important, the Comparative Administration Group itself went out of existence in 1973, when it merged with the International Committee of the American Society for Public Administration to form a new Section on International and Comparative Administration (SICA). SICA continued with much the same membership, and engaged in many of the same activities as CAG, such as participation in professional meetings, issuance of a newsletter, and distribution of occasional papers, but all at a somewhat reduced level.

Reappraisals

These indications of decline were accompanied, and probably stimulated, by a series of critiques of the comparative administration movement, usually in the form of papers presented at professional meetings, several of which were subsequently published. These deserve our attention, not only for what they had to say about shortcomings and disappointments, but also about prescriptions and predictions.

The usual takeoff point was that the comparative administration movement, after over a quarter of a century in which to prove itself, including a decade of rather lavish support, needed now to be scrutinized for results.

Peter Savage took as his point of reference the propositions that any "fresh ideas, theories, and perspectives in Political Science have about a decade to 'make it' before they are dropped and replaced by even fresher ones," and that the first few years are the easiest. During this time, the "honey-pot syndrome" emerges, with money and professional rewards accorded the progenitors of the new movement. After that, "orthodoxy begins and the crucial test is then upon the innovation, namely to produce some results. If this does not happen, the pot is assumed not to contain honey, or not the right kind of honey, and it is quietly and sometimes abruptly abandoned in favor of an even newer one."[97] He thought comparative administration was no exception, and that the time for testing the honey in the pot had come.

Whatever the worth of this notion, comparative public administration certainly was well enough established to become one target of the general tendency to question older orthodoxies which surfaced dramatically at the turn of the decade of the 1970s. No doubt linked to campus unrest, in turn stemming from reaction to the unpopular war in Vietnam, this revolt against the establishment appeared in one form or another in all the social sciences and in some of the natural sciences. In the form of what was usually called the "new" public administration movement, this combination of attack and reform proposals reached its peak about 1970, just as comparative public administration was facing straitened circumstances and completing its period of scholarly probation. Comparative administration turned out to be attractive to some of the leaders of the "new" public administration because of its own relative newness, and also the subject of their skeptical questioning.

However stimulated, the tone of the appraisers was essentially negative, and they expressed generally unfavorable judgments. A few sample quotations will suffice to illustrate: "The auguries for Comparative Administration are not good."[98] Described as a declining and troubled field which had made only minimal progress, it was charged with lagging "far behind the fields to which it is most closely related in its application of systematic research technologies."[99] Comparative public administration was "floundering at a time when other social scientists have finally come to appreciate the central role bureaucracy and bureaucrats play in the political process."[100] Development administration as an academic enterprise appeared ill-prepared to meet the challenge it faced at a critical juncture. "Need and opportunity beckon: performance falls short."[101]

Like the writers in comparative public administration whose work they were analyzing, the evaluators did not by any means fully agree with one another as to what was wrong and what ought to be done about it, but there were some readily identifiable common themes.

The most frequent complaint was that comparative public administration had by then had time enough but had failed to establish itself as a field of study with a generally accepted range of topics to be addressed, and that despite the inclination to theorize no consensus had been achieved permitting primary attention to be given to empirical studies designed to test existing theories about cross-national public administration.

Keith Henderson, writing in 1969 about the "identity crisis" in the field, asked what was *not* within the scope of comparative public administration. Calling attention to the diversity of titles in CAG publications, he observed that although "there are certain dominant themes (the developing countries, the political system, etc.) it is hard to know what the central thrust might be and equally hard to find anything distinctly 'administrative' in that thrust. Seemingly, the full range of political science, economic, sociological, historical, and other concerns is relevant."[102]

Lee Sigelman made a content analysis of the entire output of the *Journal of Comparative Administration* as the primary vehicle for scholarly publication in the field, and found that in comparative public administration "no single topic or set of questions came close to dominating." Among substantive categories, he placed the highest percentage of articles (14.6 percent) under the heading "policy administration," followed by categories such as concepts (of bureaucracy, institution-building, etc.), structural descriptions of organizations in various national settings, and studies of bureaucratic values and behavior. His residual category of "other" had the most entries (22 percent), "embracing an astounding array of topics, e.g., communication models for social science, time, the ombudsman, law, problems of causal analysis, the nature of the political process, party coalitions, and anti-bureaucratic utopias." To Sigelman, this suggested that "students of administration have not narrowed their interest to a manageable set of questions and topics. A substantial amount of their effort continues to be spent in activity that can best be characterized as 'getting ready to get ready'—exploring epistemological matters, debating the boundaries of the field, and surveying the manner in which concepts have been used."[103] Jones remarked even more acidly that the CAG movement "never got much beyond the researching of the definition stage of the subject. Some would say it did not even reach that stage."[104]

Similar concerns were reiterated elsewhere, often by commentators who observed that the prospects for integration had seemed promising only a few years earlier but had not materialized. For example, Jreisat believed that "the absence of integrative concepts and central foci in comparative research and analysis" was a critical problem, manifested in recent CAG literature indicating a "wide range of seemingly independent concerns." He explored the reasons for the "kaleidoscopic development" of comparative research, such as the movement from culture-bound to cross-cultural studies, the diverse backgrounds and interests of social scientists from a variety of disciplines, the absence of cumulativeness in acquiring administrative knowledge, and particularly the lack of an identifiable core that would enable scholars "to distinguish an administrative phenomenon when they see one and to sift out its critical aspects from the uncritical ones." Recognizing that there were reasons initially for sacrificing conceptual rigor for substantive breadth and methodological experimentation, Jreisat asserted that such justification "is less convincing after more than two decades of research in the comparative field and because prospective evolution toward consolidation and synthesis is not emerging."[105]

The indictment basically was that students of comparative administration had simultaneously shown an unseemly addiction to theorizing and a lack of ability to offer theories which could win acceptance and be tested empirically. Savage said that the literature displayed "a melange of idiosyncratic theoretical formulations and organizing perspectives, many of which have more to do with academic or personal fancy than with any generally acceptable cumulative purpose." Using an illustration from Riggs, he suspected that the proposals "were often not so much theories, in any scientific sense of the word, as they were fantasies."[106] J. Fred Springer claimed that development administration was "starved for theories which will guide the pooling of empirical knowledge, orient new research, and recommend administrative policy."[107] Sigelman likened the plight of comparative public administration to that of the Third World nations being studied, in the sense that like them the field was caught in a vicious circle. Reliable data must be brought to bear on theoretically significant propositions for research to be meaningful, but Sigelman believed that comparative administration had been sorely lacking in both reliable data and testable propositions, resulting in theoretical and empirical underdevelopment, and presenting the strategic problem to students in the field of how to break out of the circle of stagnation.[108]

Explanations for this plight were not obvious, but one suggestion offered was that students of comparative administration had not kept pace with progress in closely related fields, and that this helped account for the lag in accomplishment. Sigelman made an unfavorable contrast of the analytic techniques employed in the comparative administration literature against those used in research in comparative politics. According to his content analysis of the *Journal of Comparative Administration*, less than one-fifth of the articles published were at all quantitative in their techniques, and only half of these used what he defined as "more powerful" measurement techniques. Most of the works published consisted of essay-type theoretical or conceptual pieces, or were empirical but nonquantitative, such as case studies. On the other hand, three out of every four articles published in *Comparative Political Studies*, representing comparative politics research, had been empirical in character, with the preponderance of these falling into the "more powerful" quantitative category. Linked to this fault, Sigelman also found that cross-national studies were the exception rather than the norm, with 70 percent of the studies which focused on national or subnational units examining administration in only one national setting, 15 percent comparing a pair of national settings, and only 15 percent undertaking comparisons on a larger scale.

Taking a different tack, Jong S. Jun faulted comparative public administration for not keeping pace with its own parent field of public administration, and suggested that revival in comparative studies must incorporate recent developments in the broader discipline, particularly with regard to organization theory.[109]

Turning to another theme, the term development administration became a frequent target, but from different angles of attack. Garth Jones bluntly scolded the CAG for appropriating and obfuscating this concept. He viewed development administration as "a polite way to talk about administrative reform, and this in all cases means political reform." After commending the CAG writers for recognizing that political reform must precede administrative reform and that the two cannot be separated, he found little else to say by way of approval of how the

CAG had dealt with development administration. To start with, he accounted for the shift in CAG usage from comparative public administration to development administration in a very simple fashion, calling it a device to secure money for research. By changing the name of the "game" to development administration, the CAG seized upon a term more marketable to the Ford Foundation. Besides being more exciting, the term was also more difficult to define, but not as difficult as the CAG tried to make it. Moreover, he thought that the work of CAG scholars fell more properly in the area of development politics than development administration, and that they had very little to offer of practical utility to those who wanted to know how to "reform an archaic accounting system, integrate new national planning methodology within a dynamic administrative program, organize and administer a new national family-planning effort, or design management operations for a new irrigation system." In sum, he accused the CAG of adopting the term development administration for its own advantage, without actually contributing much to the solution of development administration problems. The CAG stayed in its ivory tower and away from the field of action.[110]

A quite different complaint came from Brian Loveman, who raised questions about assumptions in the development administration literature concerning the ability of governments to strengthen administrative capabilities and carry out plans for meeting developmental objectives.[111] He grouped CAG members with others labeled liberal democratic theorists who were alleged to share these assumptions, similar to ideas about development and development administration held by Marxist-Leninist theorists as well. His summary conclusion was that both the liberal democratic and socialist models of development cost more than they were worth to developing societies. These models, in his judgment, called for an "administered society" antagonistic to the important value of expanded human choice as an alternative to the extension of intervention by government administrators. In short, development cannot, or at least should not, be administered.

Loveman's criticism thus contrasted with the one made by Jones. He accused the CAG of overidentification with the aims of development administrators, and overinvolvement in development administration programs. He quoted Milton Esman, a CAG spokesman, as writing that much of the change desired must be induced, and therefore managed. He identified the CAG as sharing the assumption that development can be administered and that it requires administration by a politico-administrative elite. The quest for such an elite had led often to the military as a stabilizing or modernizing force. According to Loveman,

> By the 1970s, administrative development and development administration had become euphemisms for autocratic, frequently military, rule that, admittedly, sometimes induced industrialization, modernization, and even economic growth. But this occurred at a great cost in the

welfare of the rural and urban poor and a substantial erosion if not deletion of the political freedoms associated with liberal democracy.[112]

He mentioned Brazil, Iran (before the fall of the shah), and South Korea as "showcases." The CAG role, in his interpretation, had been both to elaborate an academic ideology of development and to encourage participation by its members in programs to induce development.

Ambivalence also showed up in related evaluations of the "relevance" of the comparative administration movement. CAG documents had frequently expressed the desire to have the work of CAG prove useful to technical assistance experts and to officials in developing countries, and this was one of the explicit expectations from the Ford Foundation grants. However, except for agreement on somewhat peripheral matters such as the establishment of links among scholars from various countries, the usual judgment was negative as to the success of CAG in achieving relevancy.

Disappointment on this score was conceded by Fred Riggs in a 1970 newsletter when he noted that CAG had an ivory tower image and had failed to form a bridge between academic life and practice. Others agreed, and some tried to explain why. Jones found little in CAG writings "that will contribute to social technologies related to the burning issues of the day such as population control, environmental protection, and food production. These authors undoubtedly have something to say here, but it is best that they start all over again."[113] Savage concurred that CAG did not produce much in the way of socially useful knowledge. It was not a matter of producing "bad medicine," but "no medicine." These judgments may have been overly severe in what was expected of CAG, but whatever the worth of CAG efforts, there was another problem of getting attention and acceptance. Jones, speaking as a former practitioner, had this comment which he no doubt intended not to be restricted to one individual: "As much as I admire Fred Riggs, and I do, his thinking had little relevance for my kind of problems. Certainly the AID [U.S. Agency for International Development] bureaucracy was not willing to accept it."[114] B. B. Schaffer wrote that CAG members "had their conferences and wrote their papers, but the practitioners did not seem to take much notice and changes in developing countries did not seem to be directly affected."[115]

These were typical common assessments, focused on the question of relevance to developing countries. Jreisat added an unusual fillip by pointing out that comparative studies had so concentrated on emerging countries and their problems that little was offered of theoretical or practical utility in Western, particularly American, contexts.

Some critics, on the other hand, seemed to view the comparative administration movement as all too relevant. In opposing the outcomes of technical assistance and development administration programs in recipient countries, they directly or implicitly chastised the CAG for participation by some of its members, and for its desire to be supportive to practitioners. Loveman, as part of his argument that development cannot be administered, repeatedly spoke of "United States-AID-CAG" models, doctrines, or programs of development administration. He credited the CAG with providing "an intellectual grounding for American foreign policy in the 1960s." According to his version, the failure of liberal democratic regimes to "develop" gradually made it clear that "United States policy and the CAG would have to make ever more explicit the relationship between growth, liberal democracy, anti-Marxism, and a strategy giving first priority to political stability." For this to occur, the problem of administrative development had to be resolved. "Administrative development had to precede effective development administration; any concern for constraints on bureaucratic authority had to be subordinated to the need to create effective administrative instruments." Hence the CAG and United States policy-makers turned to programs intended to build up administrative elites, often military elites. Recommendations of CAG spokesmen such as Esman "to be less concerned with control of the development administrators and more concerned with the capabilities of these elites to carry out developmental objectives" were heeded by officials making U.S. government policy, with the unfortunate consequences, as seen by Loveman, already mentioned. The point in connection with the relevancy issue is that Loveman, far from viewing the CAG as detached from and ignored by governmental technical assistance policy-makers, evidently pictured CAG members as closely allied with these officials and highly influential in crucial policy decision-making.[116]

The relevancy issue, then, received plenty of attention, with quite a spread of opinion on it. Few regarded the CAG as achieving the degree of relevancy desired by its members or its sponsors, but the explanations for the deficiency varied. As Jreisat put it, "although the cry of non-relevance is common, it comes to us from different sources for different reasons and, consequently, the remedial suggestions are not always consistent."[117] With measures of relevancy uncertain, and with such inconsistency in assessing the situation and what ought to be done about it, probably the only certain conclusion is that not all the commentators could have been right, but those who reported a close working collaboration between the CAG as a group entity and official policy-makers produced little evidence to support this interpretation.

Balancing somewhat the negative thrust of this review of the retrenchment evidence and the critical reappraisals, it should be noted that even the more severe critics of the CAG and its record (such as Jones, Jreisat, and Jun) acknowledged the impressive productivity of the 1960s and the vast accumulation of knowledge in comparative public administration which resulted. Others who had been more closely identified personally with the CAG (such as Savage and Siffin) were even more apt to temper their criticism with reference to specific accomplishments.

Savage emphasized that the intentions were commendable, despite flaws in priorities and methods, and that overall the legacy of the CAG could be viewed with considerable satisfaction. He mentioned, for example, that comparative studies had "shed a bright light on the existence and importance, in many settings, of the public bureaucracy," and had called attention insistently to the importance of the administrative factor in political analysis. At the same time, he believed that the comparative administration movement had made a dent in "the myth of managerial omnipotence" by its increasing recognition and exploration of the cultural shaping of administrative techniques, and by identifying factors that must be taken into account when making prescriptions for administrative reform. More generally, he credited the movement with building bridges with comparative politics and other subfields in the discipline of political science, and providing a kind of "demonstration effect" of the attractions of venturing into unfamiliar territory. He thought a lot of brush had been cleared out by the pursuit of false leads which other scholars need no longer pursue. He also made the point, often overlooked, that the failure of the movement to achieve some of the early promises had "more to do with the complexities and intractabilities in its chosen domain than with faulty purpose."[118] Siffin, more directly concerned with efforts to export administrative technology, gave credit to students of comparative administration for inquiring into the reasons for technology transfer failures, and commended their attention to environmental factors as inhibitors in attaining development administration objectives.

Recommendations

Simultaneously and as a part of the reassessment efforts came analyses as to causes of past problems and recommendations for the future.

The most often recurring complaint, as already indicated, had been that comparative public administration had never been able to reach paradigmatic consensus. As might be anticipated from this, the most common recommendation was that this deficiency had to be remedied if this field of study was to achieve intellectual standing and academic maturity. Repeatedly, the point was stressed that an adequate paradigm must be sought to bring coherence, purpose, and progress.

Given the urgency of the need expressed, one naturally looks hopefully for suggestions as to what the basis for consensus should be. On this score, most critics were embarrassingly silent or vague. Some immediately qualified the call for an accepted paradigm by disavowal of any intention to establish a paradigmatic orthodoxy in comparative public administration. "The search for common ground," according to Jreisat, was "not necessarily a call for the establishment of precise and rigid boundaries."[119] The main disappointment, however, was that when it came to specifics, the suggestions made were strongly reminiscent of those voiced much earlier, near the beginning of the movement's heyday. We find repeated the caution expressed in 1959 by Robert Presthus against "cosmic" theory and the advice to seek instead "middle-range" theory. Jreisat asserted, for instance, that "a higher degree of synthesis and relevance of comparative analysis may be attained through conceptualization of critical administrative problems at the 'middle range' level and involving institutions rather than entire national administrative systems."[120] Lee Sigelman described his views as representing "a meaningful middle ground between the present state of affairs and unrealistically optimistic schemes for improving it." Also in line with a preference already established by the early 1960s, Sigelman stated as his conviction that the future of comparative public administration lay in studies of bureaucracies, in "examinations of the backgrounds, attitudes, and behaviors of bureaucrats and those with whom they interact."[121]

Even though these commentators presented no drastically new directions to improve comparative studies, they did provide a number of thoughtful, useful, and helpful suggestions, some of which have since been acted upon. Most of these had to do with methodologies to be used, data to be gathered, or subjects to be studied—all rather persistent concerns of comparative administration students.

An exception was the contention by Jong S. Jun that methodological considerations had received too much attention, and that the problem was essentially one of epistemology rather than methodology. Jun raised questions as to the limits and validity of human knowledge as it is brought to bear on the comparative study of systems of administration. He presented what was essentially an epistemological critique of the structural-functional and bureaucratic models, which he regarded as the dominant ones, arguing that both models failed "to explore the subjective meaning of social action, to provide a mechanism for organizational change, and to consider the renewal effects of conflict-induced disequilibrium." He detected a common tendency for the researcher to superimpose "his perspective and method onto a culture not his own." Tending to imitate natural science methodologies, social scientists have had in his view inadequate tools to cope with the incredible variety of data from the world's political and administrative systems and have been unable to generate a suitable comparative perspective. His suggestion for a different conceptual framework, which he did not elaborate, was that scholars should adopt a phenomenological approach to comparative study to provide a new perspective for analyzing other cultures. He maintained that with this approach "the need becomes apparent to bracket one's own feelings and separate them from one's perceptions," and that this perspective would be "a useful way of standing aside from our presuppositions and cultural biases, and looking at someone else a good deal more in their own terms," but he did not give illustrations as to how this perspective would be applied. Richard Ryan has also stressed the importance of a contextual approach to reduce perceptual biases of development administrators, and he has provided several specific examples.[122]

On the themes of scope and method rather than psychological approach, several related points were made. Sigelman deplored the loss of focus on *administration* in comparative public administration, and believed that the advice that students of administration should study unrelated or loosely related substantive fields was equivalent to institutionalizing that loss of focus. Continuing "the seemingly never-ending quest for an all-inclusive analytic framework" seemed to him "positively perverse." He quoted as applicable to comparative public administration Jorgen Rasmussen's supplication "O Lord, deliver us from further conceptualization and lead us not into new approaches." In his view, scholars in the past had "spent so much time and energy debating issues of comparison, putting forth general analytic frameworks, and sketching out the environment of administration that we have been diverted from the study of administration itself."[123]

Both Peter Savage and J. Fred Springer called attention to choices in comparative studies among different levels of analysis. Although their terminology differed somewhat, they both were referring to a range of options running from whole social systems through descending levels of inclusiveness to units such as institutions, organizations, and even individuals. Springer argued that reliance on one level of analysis decreased the prospects for understanding complex systems. He stressed the use of concepts, such as those from role theory, which might have utility "in relating phenomena at different levels of analysis, and in sensitizing the analyst to contextually specific patterns of interaction and behavior." He cited a number of studies which had penetrated "into the structure of national bureaucracies to identify important contextual effects within the organization," including role analyses of public officials in Indonesia and Thailand, and a cross-national multilevel study of the administration of rice production projects in Indonesia, the Philippines, and Thailand.[124]

The problem of data for research was another serious matter addressed. The growth of availability of data from a multitude of countries was evident, but this did not equate with comparability and reliability of data. Sigelman stressed the importance of new strategies of data collection and maintenance, examining the matter at both the system or macrolevel of research, and at the microlevel. In both instances, he concentrated on comparative studies involving bureaucracies, which he considered should be the core of future research endeavors. He was quite pessimistic about the availability of data for systematic testing of hypotheses in system level studies, leaving the testing of macrolevel theory to be done primarily with judgmental data derived from experts considered to be knowledgeable, using methods such as the Delphi technique, which Sigelman recommended as promising. With regard to microlevel research, Sigelman believed that many potentially significant studies on bureaucracy had already been undertaken, but that many had never been published or had appeared in journals devoted to specific geographical areas that were not noticed by comparative administration students. Besides the problem of inaccessibility, he identified two other acute deficiencies. Only occasionally had the research been cross-national in scope, and the literature was scattered and diffuse. "Different scholars with different research perspectives use different instruments to interview different types of bureaucrats in examinations of different problems in different nations." In short, microlevel research was noncumulative. Sigelman proposed an institutionalized mechanism for data maintenance through establishment of an archive of comparative administration research, arguing that this "could go far toward bringing some order to the chaos of micro-level administrative studies."[125]

As to the subject matter focus for research, certainly there was no consensus beyond the dominant view that the choice of substantive topic should be designed to test middle-range theory. Indeed, if anything, the range of suggestions broadened rather than narrowed. Bureaucracy as a common institution in political systems continued to be most frequently recommended as the target with the greatest promise for research efforts, although as we will discover in the following chapter, different people had different ideas even as to the meaning of bureaucracy, not to mention how it ought to be studied on a comparative basis.

A persistent strain in the recommendations of the commentators was that new advances in the area of organization theory could be brought to bear fruitfully in the analysis of organizational units of interest to comparative administration researchers, whether these might be whole national bureaucracies or bureaucratic subunits. Springer called for supplementing earlier work aimed at individual or systemic levels with increasing attention to conceptual and empirical work at the organization level. Jun advocated the introduction of concepts from modern organization theory which would focus attention on organizational change and development in a cross-cultural context. He referred particularly to experiments in industrial democracy or self-management attempted in several countries, and commented that comparisons among such experiments would "provide a new avenue for learning about the effectiveness of different organizations in different cultural settings."[126]

Jreisat concurred that cross-cultural comparisons at the organizational level had rarely been attempted, even though studies of formal organizations within one cultural setting such as the United States, with stable environmental influences, were advanced and sophisticated. He regarded the few ventures which had been made toward comparative organizational theory as not representing genuine cross-cultural comparisons and as "not seriously concerned with the various possible patterns of human interaction which may be prevalent outside the limits of customary Western styles of behavior."[127] Jorge I. Tapia-Videla also asserted that research and writing in comparative public administration had not been much influenced by theoretical progress in the area of organization theory.[128] With a few exceptions, such as *Bureaucratic Politics and Administration in Chile* by Peter Cleaves,[129] Tapia-Videla found that the potential benefits of blending organization theory into the comparative study of administration had not been realized. He himself then examined the characteristics of public bureaucracies in Latin America, and the relationships between these bureaucracies and the "corporate-technocratic" state which had emerged in several Latin American countries as well as elsewhere in the Third World.[130]

Public policy-making was another subject receiving much attention during the 1970s. Attempts were being made on one hand to analyze the process of policy-making in a descriptive way, and on the other to analyze outputs and effects of policy in a fashion which was more prescriptive and aimed to improve both the process and the content of public policy.[131] With few exceptions, however, policy-making studies had not been comparative across countries, leading Jun in 1976 to urge comparative policy analysis as an additional field for pioneering work which might serve both scientific and practical purposes.[132]

This survey of recommendations made in connection with the reassessment efforts of the decade of the 1970s paves the way for consideration of what has been happening during recent years in comparative public administration, an appraisal of the current state of the field, and prognostication about future developments.

PROSPECTS AND OPTIONS

By 1980 the prospects for the comparative public administration movement were obviously not as bright as they had once seemed to be. The period of massive technical assistance in public administration which had helped launch the movement was over. The CAG, which had been the organizing force during the years of greatest activity, had lost its separate identity, and the programs it initiated had been ended or cut back. As a source of action-oriented plans for dealing with problems of development administration, the movement had generally been judged disappointing. At any rate, whatever the impact, it had lessened. Moreover, earlier optimistic expectations about the possibilities of transferring or inducing change in developing societies had come into question as many of these nations were suffering from increasing rather than decreasing problems of economic growth and political stability. As an academic or intellectual enterprise, comparative administration had moved from a position of innovation and vitality to a more defensive posture, reacting to charges that the promises of its youth had not been fulfilled and to advice from various quarters as to remedial measures.

During the decades of the 1980s and 1990s, however, there has been a reassuring revival of activity in comparative public administration. The exuberance of the movement's youth has not been regained, but the field may have attained maturity—a stage of development bringing fewer drastic changes but presenting a new set of challenges and problems.

One obvious trend has been toward a proliferation of comparative studies concerned with public administration broadly conceived, and a branching off into subspecialties by many comparativists. Our interest focuses on what I will call "core" comparative public administration, but supplemental attention needs to be given to at least two of these branching but closely related subjects—development administration or management, and comparative public policy. Some treatment has already been given to each of these foci of interest, particularly the former. They share the characteristic that they concentrate on something less than the comprehensive study of national administrative systems as the entities or subjects being compared. They also have in each instance demonstrated a tendency to assert and to seek recognition of their separateness.

For these reasons, we will review in sequence rather than together the prospects and options first of development administration/management, then comparative public policy, and finally "core" comparative public administration.

Development Administration/Management

Since the early days of the comparative administration movement, development administration has been continuously studied. A great deal of effort has gone into setting boundaries as to what is and what is not included, improving strategies for implementation of development projects, and evaluating the results of what has continued to be a massive network of activity. Unfortunately, the results in each instance have been either disappointing or inconclusive.[133] As a result, development administration has been a subject of perennial controversy, and has presented issues that seem to be intractable to resolution. At best, as Siffin observes, it is "the indicative but imprecise label for a set, or at least a potential batch, of problems."[134]

Although widely used for more than four decades, why has this term "development administration" never been given an agreed-upon definition, despite extended discussion and arguments on the matter? As we have seen, the original intent in coining and popularizing the phrase is not in doubt. It was to concentrate attention on the administrative requisites for achieving public policy goals, particularly in the less developed countries. This purpose was linked to an assumption that the more developed countries could assist in this effort through a process of diffusion or transfer of administrative capabilities already possessed. As a phenomenon, development administration appeared to be confined to certain countries under certain circumstances, existing in some nation-states but not in others. This was the most common understanding during the heyday of the comparative administration movement, when the CAG was concentrating its attention on comparative studies with a developmental focus, leading to the terms development administration and comparative administration being regarded almost as synonyms.

As time passed, critics properly pointed out that even the so-called developed countries have difficulties in reaching their public policy goals, and hence should be viewed as sharing problems of development administration. The implication was that since all systems of public administration have goals and objectives to be achieved, development administration could best be used simply as a designator having to do with the degree of success achieved in movement toward the chosen purposes. Under such a definition, however, the Hitler regime in Nazi Germany could be considered as a model example of development administration, because of its proven ability to eliminate six million Jews in its campaign of extermination. Surely no user of the term had this application in mind, so some meaning needed to be sought which would specify more satisfactorily what public policy goals are appropriate as development administration targets.

My preferred choice for doing this is to accept the suggestion of George Gant in his book *Development Administration: Concepts, Goals, Methods*, published in 1979.[135] Gant himself is generally credited with having coined the term "development administration" in the mid-1950s when he was on the staff of the Ford Foundation, so his book represented a quarter century of thinking and writing on the subject.

Gant's approach is to avoid definitions which limit the general applicability of concepts such as "development" and "development administration." As he sees it, development is not an absolute but is a relative condition, with no country ever qualifying as fully developed.[136] Development administration is defined in a similar way. Originally it referred to the focusing of administration "on the support and management of development as distinguished from the administration of law and order." According to Gant, the term came to denote "the complex of agencies, management systems, and processes a government establishes to achieve its development goals. . . . Development administration is the administration of policies, programs, and projects to serve development purposes." It is characterized by its purposes, which are "to stimulate and facilitate defined programs of social and economic progress," by its loyalties, which are to the public rather than to vested interests, and by its attitudes, which are "positive rather than negative, persuasive rather than restrictive."[137]

Such concepts and definitions mean that every country is concerned with and has its own problems of development administration, centered in what Gant calls "nation-building departments or ministries," in fields such as agriculture, industry, education, and health. These agencies, in comparison to more traditional ones, have special requirements with regard to structure, planning capabilities, staff analysis services, and a variety of professionally trained personnel. The original emphasis is also retained on the newly independent nations, which can be expected to have particularly acute problems in these areas, and the expectation is continued that at least to some extent less developed countries can benefit from the accumulated experience of those more developed.

Most later commentators during the decade after Gant's book was published indicated essential agreement with him. Nasir Islam and Georges M. Henault suggested that the label development administration could best be applied "to designing, implementing and evaluating policies and programmes leading to socio-economic change."[138] Asmeron and Jain said that development administration "refers to an aspect of public administration in which the focus of attention is on organizing and managing public agencies and government departments at both the national and sub-national levels in such a way as to stimulate and facilitate well-defined programmes of social, economic and political progress."[139] Huque concurred that the term development administration indicates that "the administrative activities in developing countries are not concerned merely with the maintenance of law and order and the execution of public policies, but also with modernization, economic development and the extension of social services," and that these functions are of "overwhelming importance" in developing countries,[140] but he was skeptical as to the existence of a "science of development administration" that could be of much assistance.[141]

It is crucial to recognize that development administration, viewed this way, is not synonymous with either public administration or comparative public administration. As Gant explains, development administration is "distinguished from, although not independent of, other aspects and concerns of public administration. Certainly the maintenance of law and order is a prime function of government and is basic to development, although it precedes and is not usually encompassed within the definition of development administration." Similarly, the provision of essential communications and educational facilities, and the maintenance of judicial and diplomatic systems, would have an impact on but not be an integral part of development administration.[142]

Without insisting on any particular definitive meaning for development administration, it seems to me that at least we should abandon earlier tendencies to use it interchangeably with comparative public administration, and that we should reject any implication that the domain of comparative public administration is confined to issues of development administration, however defined.

This divergence does not mean, however, that significant shifts involving development administration are no longer relevant for comparative public administration. Strategies of management for technical assistance programs aimed at developmental objectives are of central concern to specialists in development administration, and continue to be of interest to those focusing on the overall comparison of national systems of administration.[143]

Recent years have in fact produced a major reassessment and reorientation of technical assistance goals and strategies, resulting from mounting evidence that efforts to transfer administrative technologies had turned out often to have little discernible impact or else had produced unanticipated negative consequences, and this in turn has led to current efforts to redirect the thrust of work in development administration/management. In simplest terms, what occurred first was a shift from one to another mode of thinking about development and development administration. Islam and Henault labeled them model I and model II. The first model was associated with the technical assistance programs of the first two decades after World War II. The second was identified with the restructuring which has taken place since the late 1960s in the aid-giving projects of the World Bank and other multilateral development agencies, as well as of the U.S. Agency for International Development and other bilateral agencies. Both models can be thought of as appropriate under certain circumstances, rather than as competing alternatives or substitutes, one of which must always be chosen as preferred over the other, but the presumption is that the second is currently more suited to the requirements of developing countries.

The earlier Western model of development administration emphasized administrative reform in organizational structural arrangements, personnel management, budgeting, and other technical fields, and assumed that transference of administrative technology from one culture to another was feasible, without any necessary concurrent reformation in political, social, or economic conditions. It implied the separability of policy-making and policy execution, but its critics have argued that in fact it had an underlying ethnocentric bias based on Western values such as stress on economic growth as measured by gross national product (GNP), organizational and professional specialization, and an achievement orientation for determining social status—all of which were misrepresented as neutral indicators of development. The tendency was to concentrate on advances in administrative technology and isolate these from the activities really important for development, leading Islam and Henault to comment that "the hallmark of the Model I era was planning without implementation."[144]

The second model made a more direct connection between public policy and administrative technology, beginning with policy choices and necessary institutional infrastructure and then moving to appropriate administrative technology. An early recognition of this tendency was shown in the work of Milton Esman and his associates, who focused on the process of "institution-building" through an interuniversity research program intended to systematize the cross-cultural analysis of institutions as appropriate units for comparison. During the 1960s empirical data were collected and analyzed for a number of countries, including Yugoslavia, Venezuela, Nigeria, Jordan, and Ecuador.[145] Jreisat described this model and suggested modifications of it intended to focus less exclusively on developing societies, to place more emphasis on cross-cultural comparison, and to draw more heavily on research in organization theory.[146] Siffin concurred as to the need for more knowledge to be marshaled about organizational design and the effects of alternative organizational arrangements, with special attention to environmental factors not intrinsic to the organizations themselves. He noted that traditional administrative technology efforts aimed more at *maintenance* needs than *developmental* needs, whereas the essence of development is not to maintain, but to effectively create. Typically "the need for ability to design and implement arrangements involving technologies is greater than the need for the technologies," calling for a "developmental design strategy" focusing on the process of institution-building.[147]

Increasing attention also has been directed to the fundamental impact of cultural factors on development administration.[148] For example, as part of a symposium on cultural differences and development, Bjur and Zomorrodian presented what they described as "a conceptual framework for developing context-based, indigenous theories of administration." They assumed that "any administrative theory which pretends to describe existing reality, to guide administrative practice and clarify legitimate administrative objectives must necessarily spring from the cultural values which govern social interactions and dominate intra- and inter-organizational relationships," implying that different cultures have different value mixes, and that usually these differ from the mix in secular Western societies that have produced the most commonly accepted theories of administration. Hence when it comes to borrowing administrative techniques from outside a culture, they advised that unqualified adoption is never appropriate, but that the right approach is "self-conscious adaptation or, if the value mismatch is too marked, the invention of suitable tools and techniques consonant with the regnant value system."[149] Staudt, Huque, and I have all called attention to cultural factors at various levels of analysis (societal, bureaucratic, organizational, work group, etc.), and Staudt has pointed out both the importance of and the current limited knowledge about cultural influences at all levels.[150]

With this reorientation in approach came a shift in emphasis for technical assistance projects to the concept of "basic needs," which is how Islam and Henault labeled their model II pattern of development. The policy objective is to make a direct attack on "absolute poverty," in World Bank terminology. The *content* of GNP becomes more important than its rate of growth, and the rural sector of the economy becomes the major focus for development. The aim is to bring about agricultural transformation through a decentralized system of small locally controlled organizations rather than through large-scale governmental organizations, requiring strengthening of local governments, increased local participation, creation of new intermediary organizations, and other major changes in socio-political conditions. The inference is that appropriate administrative technology will be much different under a model II approach. This requirement is stressed by Islam and Henault, who insist that a "new management strategy" must be formulated as developing countries focus on planned agricultural rural development as their primary policy goal.

Resultant issues considered were whether such a new management strategy has been or can be devised, and to what extent and in what manner more developed countries should continue their efforts to transfer administrative technologies to those less developed. On the latter point, disillusionment with the record of experience was evident. Numerous technical assistance projects had admittedly failed, even when judged by the least demanding criteria as to their success. Skeptics pointed out that supposedly policy-neutral assistance programs had often in fact bolstered and preserved, or protected beyond their time, repressive political regimes,[151] leading to the implication that administrative technology assistance activities are inevitably part and parcel of undesirable overall intervention in the affairs of other nations.

Others, such as Esman, who is a knowledgeable and respected longtime student and practitioner of development assistance in public administration, reacted in more of an upbeat mood.[152] He saw the disillusionment among developmentalists in all fields as being replaced by a recognition of opportunities available within a more limited and realistic assessment of what is possible. Along with acknowledgment of the absence of general consensus on development strategies had come realization that modernization is not unilinear or inevitable, that technical assistance is a high risk enterprise, "beset with daunting problems,"[153] and that public administration, in his words, "is a profoundly plural, not a universal phenomenon."[154] Consequently, he foresaw demand for technical cooperation in public administration as likely to follow two parallel tracks. The first was responding to requests for help in building fundamental governmental functions, which can be done basically in what he referred to as the well-established "Point IV mode," corresponding to model I of Islam and Henault. The second track, along the lines of their model II, was the area of creative growth but also of problems, because it is characterized by high levels of uncertainty, severe resource limitations, and a need for creative administrative responses. Esman foresaw a fresh orientation, with emphasis on innovation and experimentation rather than the transfer of known technologies.

In the resulting development administration literature, much attention was devoted to devising management strategies for model II-type projects,[155] with a pronounced tendency to formulate and lay out a suggested sequence of activities designed to avoid pitfalls and enhance prospects for success. One such effort, by Marc Lindenburg and Benjamin Crosby, focused on the political dimension in managing development, and offered a model for political analysis designed to be useful for development administrators, supplemented by a number of case studies for use as teaching devices in applying the model.[156] Another, by Gregory D. Foster, presented an "administrative development intervention methodology," calling first for a demanding list of activities to clarify environmental and policy matters, followed by a strategy for implementation comprising two major stages—a *preparatory* stage and an *operational* stage—each with specified steps to be taken.[157] Dennis A. Rondinelli and Marcus D. Ingle, although they were concerned with and tried to identify recurrent pervasive obstacles created by broad environmental or cultural factors, focused more directly on effective implementation of development plans and programs. They formulated a strategic approach to implementation consisting of six elements or steps to be taken: broad reconnaissance; strategic analysis and intervention; identification of the sequence for incremental interventions; engaged planning to protect and promote new programs; reliance on uncomplicated management procedures and use of indigenous institutions; and a facilitative style of management with less dependence on hierarchical controls and more reliance on local initiative and discretion.[158] Kathleen Staudt pointed to the persistent dearth of participation by women in development activities, citing numerous specific case examples.[159] David C. Korten stressed what he called a "learning process approach" to replace the more usual "blueprint approach," and attached great importance to voluntary action and the role of nongovernmental organizations (NGOs).[160] His emphasis was on leadership and teamwork at the local level, with reliance on help from knowledgeable outsiders. He perceived this process as ordinarily proceeding through time over three stages: learning to be *effective*, learning to be *efficient*, and learning to *expand*. Successful programs and their sustaining organizations were not "designed and implemented," but "evolved and grew." Instead of careful preplanning of projects as the basic unit of development action, he advocated a switch to "action based capacity building" as an alternative to recurring failures in rural development activities crucial to progress in development administration.[161] In updating and elaborating on his people-centered approach after reviewing events through the 1980s, Korten later reached the pessimistic conclusion that the "development industry" has become a "big business, preoccupied more with its own growth and imperatives than with the people it was originally created to serve. Dominated by professional financiers and technocrats, the development industry seeks to maintain an apolitical and value-free stance in dealing with what are, more than anything else, problems of power and values." The only hope he sees for dealing with the development crisis "rests with people who are driven by a strong social commitment rather than by the budgetary imperatives of huge global bureaucracies."[162] Hence, he stresses the potential role of voluntary nongovernmental organizations (NGOs), particularly those operating in the southern part of the globe, and presents an agenda for action during the 1990s.[163]

This sampling indicates common concerns but differences in response. This diversity is matched by the range of opinion as to how much progress has been made or can be expected in identifying appropriate strategies for managing development activities. Marcus Ingle is one of the most optimistic believers in the existence of a science of management from which such management technology can be derived. He has advocated "a more generic and less contextual approach to development administration," claiming that its appropriateness "stems primarily from the fact that it is consistent with first principles, and only secondarily with the fact that it is situationally adapted. In fact, by definition the substantive core of appropriate management technology does not need to be adapted, it is universally applicable in any context."[164] He thinks that a preliminary technology based on such an approach has already evolved, and that prospects for future advances are excellent. Korten represents a much more cautious point of view. He faults the "blueprint approach" of models stressing definite goals, a definite time frame, and carefully specified resource requirements, because it is usually not well suited to the unpredictabilities of rural development activities. The implementing organizations in his preferred "learning process approach" are not valued for their ability to adhere to detailed prepared plans, but for having "a well developed capacity for responsive and anticipatory adaptation."[165] He shows little confidence in the workability of universal or widely applicable management technology strategies. Esman also favors a pluralistic strategy of development that encourages the exploration of alternative channels for providing services through the use of "multiorganizational service networks,"[166] including contracting out to private enterprise and reliance on nongovernmental organizations (NGOs).

It is still much too early to pass judgment on the success or failure of the various proposed systematic approaches to the implementation of model II or second track development administration programs, but past experience would suggest that the better part of wisdom is to be modest rather than overconfident in predicting success.

The most recent contributions to the literature on development administration or "development management" (which is becoming the more commonly used term) tend to focus on strategies for implementing policy change.[167] As Brinkerhoff puts it, the common concern is to deal with "the translation of policy reforms and program intentions into results that ultimately produce benefits and better lives for citizens" in countries of the developing world.[168] Emphasis is placed on the analysis of case studies considered to be relatively successful. Global trends (economic and financial, technological, environmental, and sociopolitical) impact on public managers and must be taken into account. As a result, development management is now viewed as an applied discipline reflecting four facets of concern: an explicitly interventionist orientation; a source of analytical tools adapted from various social science disciplines; a value dimension emphasizing self-determination, empowerment, and equity in the distribution of development benefits; and process intervention in pursuit of objectives addressing these values.

Development administration/management thus is a topic exhibiting continual ferment and debate, with increasing tendencies to move toward greater autonomy as these issues are pursued. Nevertheless, the interests and concerns of development administration and core comparative public administration will continue to be intermingled.

Comparative Public Policy

Beginning in the mid-1970s, interest in comparative public policy has expanded enormously, paralleling in many ways the earlier history of the comparative public administration movement, both in achievements and uncertainties. The proliferation of studies in comparative public policy has resulted in numerous books, a large volume of journal articles (many in journals devoted exclusively to policy matters), graduate and undergraduate course offerings, and specialized panels and conferences sponsored by professional associations and other organizations.[169]

As had occurred previously in comparative public administration, this rapid growth has resulted in a diversity of approaches, leading to suggestions as to how the burgeoning output should be classified, intellectual debate as to whether consensus on a paradigm should be sought and if so what it should be, and proposals as to future research priorities. We can only highlight some of these issues, without treating them in detail.

The central focus is not in dispute. Comparative public policy, according to pioneers in the field, "is the cross-national study of how, why, and to what effect government policies are developed."[170] Although the research undertaken can—and has—varied in emphasis, clearly the subject is more restricted than the coverage of either comparative politics viewed as the study of whole political systems, or comparative public administration viewed as concerned with their administrative subsystems.

Four substantive fields are emphasized in a major contribution to comparative policy research,[171] indicating major thrusts in the literature. These are environmental policy, education policy, economic policy, and social policy. In addition to examining the "state of the art" in each of these areas, the authors address issues of strategy, methodology, and application, and they comment on past results and future directions.

Although it has rapidly established its own divergent identity, comparative public policy is of great significance for us.[172] In the first place, it is the most impressive success story to date in applying on a comparative basis a major reorientation which has taken place in the United States, thus responding to the criticism that comparative studies have not kept pace with recent domestic trends. Second, comparative public policy research is also trying to cope with the dilemmas of dealing with cross-cultural factors, although in this case the sequence has been to move from more familiar American and European settings to the developing world, rather than the reverse order which was taken by the comparative administration movement.[173] Third, this subfield also confronts the familiar criticism that "the very existence of sharply different conceptualizations and research foci has severely inhibited cumulative scholarship,"[174] and that more unity of approach would be desirable.[175] Fourth, researchers are charged with producing studies that lack relevance for policy-makers and are chided for being overly fond of theorizing and speculating.[176] Finally, there is a similar ambiguity as to whether comparative public policy refers to comparisons among nation-states or more generally to use of a comparative methodology in public policy analysis.[177]

Efforts to tie together comparative studies in public policy and in public administration have been rare. Guy Peters has addressed the need he sees for more adequate conceptualization of the policy-making role of organizations in his contribution to the Ashford volume,[178] pointing out that a powerful policy-making role for the bureaucracy is probably a prerequisite for effective government in contemporary society, despite political pressure to minimize it, and that the crucial question is how to blend professional competence with mandates for policy change coming from elected politicians. Randall Baker has edited a volume intended to spearhead a major effort to introduce more comparative materials, including public policy components, into the curricula of public administration programs in the United States.[179] He deliberately uses the word "management" in the title instead of "administration" to stress the "applied and practical nature" of the undertaking, and because it connotes dynamism and change, but he explicitly says that this does not imply that government is a business.[180] The modules in this collection combine in about equal proportions what would usually be considered administrative (bureaucratic reform, public finance and budgeting, planning, intergovernmental relations) and policy (international trade, criminal justice, environmental protection, industrial competitiveness) matters. This may become a vehicle both for curricular reform to enhance comparative content and for bringing about closer ties between comparative public policy and other foci for comparison.

Core Comparative Public Administration

At the center of comparative studies in public administration during the past two and a half decades have been several developments which characterize the present situation and set the stage for the future as we come to the beginning of the 21st century.

One tendency has been to reappraise objectives for comparative administrative studies by scaling down somewhat claims for the attainment of scientific status and predictability of results from research efforts. Jonathan Bendor touched on these issues perceptively in a discussion of developmental versus evolutionary theories, in which he admits that evolutionary theory does have lower predictive power, but notes that this is not the only criterion of theoretical merit. Predictions from inadequate hypotheses may be precise but inaccurate. Explanatory power and predictive power are not the same; adequate explanation is not dependent on the capacity to predict correctly. He mentions that biologists consider evolutionary theory adequate for the explanation of evolutionary processes, despite the fact that the theory generates only weak predictions, and suggests that social scientists might also settle for understanding rather than foresight.[181]

Related to this is recognition that comparative public administration not only has been and is in a preparadigmatic state, but is likely to remain so for some time to come. No consensus has appeared bringing the coherence, purpose, and progress sought earlier by some. Diversity continues to be more descriptive of comparative studies in administration than does uniformity or orthodoxy. Those whose aim is the scientific testing of precisely stated hypotheses as a basis for prediction remain frustrated and unhappy about the rate of progress. I have argued earlier that escape from the kind of paradigmatic uncertainties long characteristic of the parent discipline of public administration is not required for comparative study and research, and that coercive superimposition of a feigned consensus would be futile and stifling.[182] There now seems to be more acceptance of the view that a real consensus will emerge if and when work done in the field leads to it in a cumulative fashion, but that premature urging of it as the top priority would be counterproductive.

During these same years, there is no question in my mind that there has been an increasing recognition of the bureaucratic model within middle-range theory as the dominant conceptual framework for comparative public administration. This emphasis on comparative studies of bureaucratic systems does not meet Kuhn's requirements for a scientific paradigm, but it does provide a focus that has proved its utility. No substitute has been suggested or advocated recently, to my knowledge. Meanwhile, most of the current output is based on this foundation in theory.

The growing volume of work in comparative public administration, much of it already published and some of it still in progress, is a notable feature of the current situation which contrasts with the lull of activity that was a cause of concern during the reappraisals made in the mid-1970s. Included in this output is periodical literature, which has continued to appear in a wide variety of professional journals.[183] In addition, numerous basic texts and several recent publications covering public administration generally include chapters or passages dealing with comparative administration.[184]

Some examples of this activity, more comprehensive in scope, are summarized at this point. Others, dealing with specific topics, regions,[185] or countries, are referred to in subsequent chapters.

The most significant of these contributions in terms of its intent to assess the present state of affairs and prescribe for the future has been offered by B. Guy Peters.[186] It should be pointed out immediately that Peters in his 1988 book differed markedly from the rather rosy statement that I have just made concerning prospects in comparative public administration. Indeed, he said then that his presentation was "about the apparent decline in the study of comparative public administration," which he described as a field of inquiry in political science that "once displayed great promise and for some time made great strides," but "is now the concern of relatively few scholars . . . and has become mired in endless descriptive studies of rather minute aspects of administrative structure or behavior in single countries, with little theoretical and conceptual development."[187] The validity of these judgments will be examined as we proceed.

At this point, I want to concentrate on what I regard as the more positive aspects of his analysis. First, he accepted, as his title indicates, that the comparison of public bureaucracies should be the principal objective, and he attempted "middle-range or institutional theories" while disclaiming any intent to "articulate an overarching paradigm for public administration." Second, he identified "perhaps the first and most fundamental problem facing the comparative study of public administration" as being "the absence of any agreement as to what we are studying—as to what, in the language of the social sciences, constitutes the dependent variable." He pointed out that other institutions in government have readily available dependent variables, such as voting in legislatures and decisions in courts, but that such dependent variables have not been identified for public bureaucracies so as to permit use of "modern" social science techniques. Third, he selected four dependent variables which he thought would be useful in the process of cross-national comparison. These were (1) people who are public employees, (2) public sector organizations, (3) behavior within public organizations, and (4) the power of the civil service in making public policy. A chapter was devoted to each variable, and the purpose of the book was described by the author as "only to illustrate the ways in which each of them can be used."[188]

Other recent impressive additions to the literature have included wide-ranging comparative surveys of public administration from a variety of perspectives. Donald C. Rowat and V. Subramaniam have edited similar volumes—one focusing on developed democracies and the other on developing countries.[189] Each contains contributions on specific countries by informed experts, plus chapters providing overviews of regions or related national systems and analyses of problems and emerging trends. Another valuable study is *Public Administration in World Perspective*, containing an essay on the state of the art in comparative administration by the editors, O. P. Dwivedi and Keith Henderson, a series of country or regional studies including both developed and developing areas, and an appraisal of future prospects by Gerald and Naomi Caiden which is basically optimistic that a revitalization of comparative administration is occurring and which includes a list of suggestions as to areas "ripe for comparative treatment."[190]

Ali Farazmand is the editor of two even more ambitious projects. One is a *Handbook of Comparative and Development Public Administration*,[191] with chapters on historical administrative systems, public administration in developed capitalist and socialist nations and in developing nations (on a regional basis), and analyses of administrative performance and political responsibility in a variety of social settings. The second, a *Handbook of Bureaucracy*,[192] is a compendium that includes historical and conceptual perspectives on bureaucracy and bureaucratic politics, chapters on the diversity of bureaucratic-societal relationships, and sections dealing with bureaucracy and bureaucratic politics organized by region.

Three final examples are Baker's *Comparative Public Management*, already mentioned; *Public Administration in the Global Village*, edited by Jean-Claude Garcia-Zamor and Renu Khator,[193] which combines several theoretical and conceptual chapters with case studies concerning development administration in different settings; and *Bureaucracy and the Alternatives in World Perspective*,[194] edited by Keith M. Henderson and O. P. Dwivedi, which is a collection of studies concerning choices as to national systems of public administration that are indigenous rather than imposed or copied.

This wave of contributions is not without its share of criticisms, but the focus has shifted primarily to the issue of methodological sophistication from the broader array of shortcomings noted in earlier critiques.

Peters has offered the most comprehensive brief as to this deficiency, its causes, its consequences, and its cure. The alleged deficiency, in short, is that comparative public administration has lagged far behind other areas in political science in progress toward meeting tests of scientific rigor as measured by the canons of normal social science. Some causes for this are examined, such as the absence of a useful theoretical language, the shortage of indicators, and the importance of "minute and subtle differences" in comparative administration.[195] The consequences are that comparative public administration does not conform "to the usual standards of scholarship in the contemporary social sciences,"[196] and must strive to "be made more a component of 'mainstream' political science."[197] Peters repeatedly contrasts progress in comparative public policy with this retardation in comparative public administration, accounting for it in part by "the presumed greater ease of measurement and hence the appearance of greater 'scientific rigor' in the comparative study of public policy."[198] The remedy proposed is to identify dependent variables such as those already mentioned, and to study them in ways that are both empirical and comparative, using quantitative information or systematic reasoning in conformity with modern social science requirements. In the conclusion to his 1988 book, Peters expressed the hope that the contents had "advanced us at least a few yards down that long and difficult road."[199]

Without presenting a detailed analysis, I can summarize my reaction by saying that although Peters contended that the low status of comparative public administration was traceable to its failure to be sufficiently *both* empirical and comparative, and he sought to remedy this, he seldom succeeded in accomplishing what he recommended. Being empirical was not the problem, but being comparative was. The comparisons that were made (this was acknowledged by the author and attributed to data constraints and his own knowledge) were almost completely limited to the United States and a few European countries—all Western industrialized democracies. Some models that he used (such as those dealing with interactions between politicians and bureaucrats) seemed to be applicable only to parliamentary or presidential democracies, and not to the much larger number of contemporary political entities which had regimes dominated by single parties or by professional bureaucrats. I had no doubt that he was to be commended and encouraged for what he had already done and proposed to do. However, his criteria for progress—that research must be empirical and quantitative, and hence limited to situations in which the database available for analysis is fully adequate—were not the same as mine, and they should not, in my judgment, be accepted as necessary requirements for legitimate efforts in comparative public administration. In my view, the best available approaches for the comparative study of public administration over the whole range of existing national political systems should be pursued, even though empirical and quantitative measurements are not always possible. If this means some loss of status or prestige in relation to comparative public policy or other fields of inquiry where such measurements are more readily available, so be it.

My reading of the most recent discussion of these issues by Peters is that he has considerably softened his earlier barrage of criticisms about the methodological deficiencies in comparative public administration relative to comparative public policy and comparative politics. He acknowledges that "there is now substantially more skepticism about the progress of comparative policy studies," and concedes that "rather than being peculiar to comparative public administration, the malaise of comparative studies may be a very widespread phenomenon." As to methodology, he says that in the complex world of administration, "identifying independent and dependent variables may require as much faith as science, so that somewhat less precise methods and language may be useful." He suggests some such alternative approaches that might be tried and even acknowledges that efforts to be more sophisticated might turn out to be counterproductive. I am in full agreement with his concluding statement that "most of the issues that confound students of comparative public administration in 1994 are the same issues that have plagued us for decades and that have plagued students of comparative politics in general for the same length of time," and that "there is no quick technological fix for most of our research questions, nor any methodological medicine that will cure all our ills."[200]

These comments reflect the persistence of differences of opinion as to past accomplishments and future priorities in comparative studies of public administration. Nevertheless, my perception is that these differences are not as great as they once were, because of general acceptance (including by Peters and myself) of a primary focus on comparing public bureaucracies. In doing this, some may prefer comparisons that are more limited but more sophisticated methodologically, others comparisons that are more comprehensive even though less sophisticated. Both approaches may lead to worthwhile contributions.[201]

The shifts in approach and emphasis that have taken place since the early days of the comparative administration movement have naturally led to efforts to put labels on basic characteristics distinguishing between time periods. Two recent such efforts, although using different terms to describe earlier and later dominant trends, agree that the principal turning point was in the early 1980s.

Eric Welch and Wilson Wong identify what they see as two "methodological trajectories" that have emerged from the comparative administration literature, referring to them as "traditionalist" and "revisionist" perspectives.[202] The first is ascribed to founders of the field (including Fred Riggs and myself), focusing on public bureaucracies as subsystems within the political, economic, and social contexts of nation-states, and the second to Guy Peters and others, who criticize the lack of cumulative knowledge that has been produced due to what they view as inadequate use of scientific methodology. Welch and Wong consider that both approaches are necessary, but advocate a synthesis that will bridge what they judge to be the resulting gaps of theory and practice with regard to Western and non-Western nations in the emerging framework of global pressures on public bureaucracies.

The second analysis is by George M. Guess, who contrasts what he calls "classical" and "new" comparative public administration.[203] He describes the main difference in emphasis between these periods as being a concentration on transformation of whole systems earlier, and more recently a focus on the application of theory to comparative policy and management problems more narrowly defined. He obviously approves of the current trends, which he thinks are converting comparative public administration into "an eclectic mix of disciplines contributing diverse hypotheses and findings to a larger body of applied knowledge,"[204] drawing upon such diverse perspectives as public choice and institutional economics, functionalism and systems analysis, political culture, and "government reinvention."

Meanwhile, another topic which continues to be discussed is the relationship between comparative public administration and the larger fields of public administration and political science. As long ago as 1976, Savage, Jun, and Riggs all questioned the virtue and feasibility of trying in the future to emphasize the separate identity of comparative public administration as a field of study. Savage, drawing a parallel with the effect of the behavioral movement on political science, argued that the impact of the comparative movement had been significant and lasting enough that a "movement" was no longer needed, because its concerns and perspectives had become a part of the broader disciplines. As he put it: "The movement's ten years are up and it passes. I judge that while it did not produce in sufficient ways to forestall its decline as a movement, its legacies are being absorbed into the larger Political Science and Public Administration. . . . The problems which spawned the movement have not gone away. If anything, they have become exacerbated."[205] Jun expressed the view that comparative administration as an isolated field had served its purpose and should become an integral part of the larger field of public administration, which could be enriched by placing it in a world context.[206] Riggs also has foreseen convergence, but in the sense that comparative administration would become the master field within which American public administration would be only a subfield.[207] Peters agrees that the direction pointed out by Riggs "would certainly be the one offering the opportunity for the greatest theoretical development," and emphasizes how crucial it is "to foster more and better comparative studies."[208]

However expressed, I concur with the cardinal point that it is neither necessary nor feasible to strive for restoration of the degree of autonomy and separatism once characteristic of the burgeoning comparative public administration movement. The time has come to blend the comparative perspective with the traditionally parochial national emphasis of study and research in public administration. This promises to remedy some of the deficiencies in depth of analysis attributed to comparative efforts, but it also will enrich general public administration by widening the horizon of interest in such a way that understanding of one's own national system of administration will be enhanced by placing it in a cross-cultural setting.

Meanwhile, an overview of public administration from a comparative perspective cannot be undertaken without deciding upon a framework for presentation. It should be clear from this historical review of the evolution of comparative studies that systems of public administration in existing nation-states can only be treated comparatively after a choice of focus has been made among numerous and partially conflicting alternatives. The task of selecting a focus for comparison is faced in Chapter 2.

NOTES

1. For a brief biographical note on this author, see S. R. Maheshwari, *Administrative Thinkers* (New Delhi: Macmillan India Limited, 1998), Chap. 1, "Kautilya," pp. 1–9.

2. Nicholas Henry, *Public Administration and Public Affairs*, 7th ed. (Upper Saddle River, NJ: Prentice-Hall, 1999), Chap. 2, pp. 26–51.

3. Lennart Lundquist, "From Order to Chaos: Recent Trends in the Study of Public Administration," in Jan-Erik Lane, ed., *State and Market: The Politics of the Public and the Private* (London: Sage Publications, 1985), Chap. 9, pp. 201–230. An excellent recent short summary is Donald F. Kettl, "Public Administration: The State of the Field," in Ada W. Finifter, ed., *Political Science: The State of the Discipline*

II (Washington, DC: American Political Science Association, 1993), Chap. 16, pp. 407–428.

4. Fritz Morstein Marx, ed., *Elements of Public Administration*, 2nd ed. (Englewood Cliffs, NJ: Prentice-Hall, 1963), p. 4.

5. *Ibid.*, p. 6.

6. Paul H. Appleby, *Policy and Administration* (University, AL: University of Alabama Press, 1949).

7. James W. Davis, Jr., *An Introduction to Public Administration: Politics, Policy, and Bureaucracy* (New York: Free Press, 1974), p. 4.

8. Harold Stein, ed., *Public Administration and Policy Development* (New York: Harcourt, Brace, and Company, 1952), p. xxvii. This case book, supplemented by other cases published by the Inter-University Case Program, has been the primary source of public administration cases used in the United States.

9. The main source book, containing papers presented at a conference in 1968, is Frank Marini, ed., *Toward a New Public Administration: The Minnowbrook Perspective* (Scranton, PA: Chandler Publishing Company, 1971). For a later presentation by a leading spokesman for this point of view, refer to H. George Frederickson, *New Public Administration* (University, AL: University of Alabama Press, 1980). A twentieth anniversary Minnowbrook conference was held in 1988, surveying trends during the intervening years. "Minnowbrook II: Changing Epochs of Public Administration," a symposium edited by Frederickson and Richard T. Mayer, based on papers presented at this conference, is in *Public Administration Review* 49, No. 2 (March/April 1989): 95–227.

10. Jeffrey N. Wasserstrom, "Are You Now or Have You Ever Been . . . Postmodern?," *The Chronicle of Higher Education*, September 11, 1998, pp. B4–B5, at p. B4.

11. *Ibid.*, p. B5.

12. (Beverly Hills, CA: Sage Publications, 1994). See also Gary M. Woller, ed., "Public Administration and Postmodernism," *American Behavioral Scientist* 41, No. 1 (September 1997); and Mario A. Rivera and Gary M. Woller, eds., *Public Administration in a New Era: Postmodern and Critical Perspectives* (Burke, VA: Chatelaine Press, 2000).

13. (University, AL: University of Alabama Press, 1995).

14. *Public Administration Review* 55, No. 2 (March/April 1997): 174–181. O. C. McSwite is the pseudonym for Orion F. White and Cynthia J. McSwain.

15. *Ibid.*, pp. 179, 180.

16. Stivers, "Between Public Management and Post-Modernism: The Future of Public Administration," prepared for the 1999 National Conference of the American Society for Public Administration, mimeographed, 4 pp.

17. See David Osborne and Ted Gaebler, *Reinventing Government: How the Entrepreneurial Spirit is Transforming the Public Sector* (Reading, MA: Addison-Wesley, 1992).

18. "The Five Rs of the New Public Management," in Lawrence R. Jones, Kuno Schedler, and Stephen W. Wade, eds., *Advances in International Comparative Management*, Supplement 3, *International Perspectives on the New Public Management* (Greenwich, CT: JAI Press Inc., 1997), pp. 15–45. The five Rs are: restructuring, reengineering, reinventing, realigning, and rethinking. See also Sandford

Borins, "What the New Public Management is Achieving: A Survey of Common-wealth Experience," *Ibid.*, pp. 49–70; and Nancy C. Roberts and Raymond Trevor Bradley, "Research Methodology for New Public Management," paper presented at the International Public Management Network workshop in Siena, Italy, July 28–30, 1999, 33 pp. mimeo. Table 1 (on pp. 24 and 25) presents a comparison between "Public Administration" and "New Public Management." For a more complete articulation of new public management concepts, see Lawrence R. Jones and Fred Thompson, *Public Management: Institutional Renewal for the 21st Century* (Stamford, CT, Ablex-JAI Press, 1999), Vol. 10 in the series Research in Public Policy Analysis and Management, JAI Press.

19. *Public Management and Administration: An Introduction*, 2nd ed. (New York: St. Martin's Press, Inc., 1998), p. 242.

20. *Public Administration Review* 58, No. 3 (May/June 1998): 189–237.

21. Prepared by Charles Goodsell, H. George Frederickson, Richard J. Stillman II, Camilla Stivers, and Robert Kramer for the 60th National Conference of the American Society for Public Administration, 1999, mimeographed, 17 pp.

22. McSwite, "Postmodernism and Public Administration's Identity Crisis," p. 177,

23. (New York, NY: Elsevier Science, Inc.). See the "IPMN Mission Statement" on the inside back cover of each issue, authored by L. R. Jones, co-editor.

24. Charles T. Goodsell, in his convenor's introduction to a panel on "The New Comparative Administration Applied to Service Delivery" at the 1980 Annual Conference of the American Society for Public Administration, and in "The New Comparative Administration: A Proposal," *International Journal of Public Administration* 3, No. 2 (1981): 143–155, has suggested that the scope of the term comparative administration should be enlarged to include comparisons at supranational and subnational levels of analysis, embracing "all studies of administrative phenomena where the comparative method—in some guise—is explicitly employed." This proposed extension of scope in defining comparative administration seems to me more confusing than helpful; therefore, I have retained the more accepted usage which focuses on cross-national comparisons. International administration, concerned with the administrative operations of agencies created by sovereign nation-states as instrumentalities for international or regional cooperation, is also outside the scope of this study, although comparative and international administration share many attributes and face numerous similar issues. For a discussion of connections between these two fields, see Ferrel Heady, "Issues in Comparative and International Administration," in Jack Rabin, W. Bartley Hildreth, and Gerald J. Miller, eds., *Handbook of Public Administration*, 2nd ed. (New York: Marcel Dekker, 1998), Chap. 16, pp. 571–594.

25. Daniel W. Martin, "Deja Vu: French Antecedents of American Public Administration," *Public Administration Review* 47, No. 4 (1987): 297–303.

26. For a fuller historical survey, see Ferrel Heady, "Comparative Public Administration in the United States," in Ralph C. Chandler, ed., *A Centennial History of the American Administrative State* (New York: Free Press, 1987), Chap. 15, pp. 477–508. Refer also to Fred W. Riggs, "The American Tradition in Comparative Administration," prepared for the 1976 National Conference of the American Society for Public Administration, mimeographed, 28 pp. For a recent critique of

the "culture of modernity," see Guy B. Adams, "Enthralled with Modernity: The Historical Context of Knowledge and Theory Development in Public Administration," *Public Administration Review* 52, No. 4 (July/August 1992): 363–373.

27. Robert A. Dahl, "The Science of Public Administration: Three Problems," *Public Administration Review* 7, No. 1 (1947): 1–11, at p. 8.

28. Donald C. Rowat, ed., *The Ombudsman Plan: The Worldwide Spread of an Idea*, 2nd rev. ed. (Lanham, MD: University Press of America, 1985).

29. For descriptions and evaluations of this innovation, see Garth N. Jones, "Bureaucratic Structure and National Development Programs: The Indonesian Office of Junior Minister," in Krishna K. Tummala, ed., *Administrative Systems Abroad*, rev. ed. (Lanham, MD: University Press of America, 1982), Chap. 13, pp. 335–358; and "Boundary Spanning and Organizational Structure in National Development Programs: Indonesian Office of Junior Minister," *Chinese Journal of Administration* No. 33 (May 1982): 75–116.

30. For an overview, see Ezra N. Suleiman and John Waterbury, eds., *The Political Economy of Public Sector Reform and Privatization* (Boulder, CO: Westview Press, 1990). The pros and cons are analyzed perceptively in Donald F. Kettl, *Sharing Power: Public Governance and Private Markets* (Washington, DC: The Brookings Institution, 1993). A recent comprehensive treatment is Terry L. Anderson and Peter J. Hill, eds., *The Privatization Process: A Worldwide Perspective* (Lanham, MD: Rowman & Littlefield Publishers, Inc., 1996).

31. See Alfred Diamant, "The Relevance of Comparative Politics to the Study of Comparative Administration," *Administrative Science Quarterly* 5, No. 1 (1960): 87–112.

32. For recent overviews of comparative politics as a field of study, refer to Ronald H. Chilcote *Theories of Comparative Politics: The Search for a Paradigm* (Boulder, CO: Westview Press, 1981); Howard J. Wiarda, ed., *New Directions in Comparative Politics* (Boulder, CO: Westview Press, 1985); Louis J. Cantori and Andrew H. Ziegler, Jr., eds., *Comparative Politics in the Post-Behavioral Era* (Boulder, CO: Lynne Rienner Publishers, 1988); Mattei Dogan and Dominique Pelassy, *How to Compare Nations*, 2nd ed. (Chatham, NJ: Chatham House Publishers, 1990); Martin C. Needler, *The Concepts of Comparative Politics* (New York: Praeger, 1991); John D. Nagle, *Introduction to Comparative Politics: Political System Performance in Three Worlds*, 3rd ed. (Chicago, IL: Nelson-Hall Publishers, 1992); Gabriel A. Almond, G. Bingham Powell, Jr., and Robert J. Mundt, *Comparative Politics: A Theoretical Framework* (New York: Harper Collins, 1993); Mattei Dogan and Ali Kazancigil, eds., *Comparing Nations: Concepts, Strategies, Substance* (Oxford: Basil Blackwell, 1994); and Mark Irving Lichbach and Alan S. Zuckerman, eds., *Comparative Politics: Rationality, Culture, and Structure* (Cambridge: Cambridge University Press, 1997).

33. Robert E. Ward and Roy C. Macridis, eds., *Modern Political Systems: Asia* (Englewood Cliffs, NJ: Prentice-Hall, 1963), pp. 3–4.

34. "Comparison is significant only if it seeks to interpret political data in terms of hypotheses or theories. Interpretation must deal with institutions as they really function—which sometimes differs radically from the way in which they are supposed to function. It is also desirable that agreement be reached on the frame

within which research is to be pursued. The comparative method thus requires an insistence on the scientific nature of inquiry, a focus on political behavior, and orientation of research within a broad analytic scheme." Bernard E. Brown, *New Directions in Comparative Politics* (New York: Asia Publishing House, 1962), pp. 3–4.

35. Gabriel A. Almond and James S. Coleman, eds., *The Politics of the Developing Areas* (Princeton, NJ: Princeton University Press, 1960), p. 7.
36. Ward and Macridis, *Modern Political Systems*, p. 8.
37. Herbert Kitschelt, "Political Regime Change: Structure and Process-Driven Explanations?," *American Political Science Review* 86, No. 4 (1992): 1028–1034, at p. 1028.
38. Martin Landau, "On the Use of Functional Analysis in American Political Science," *Social Research* 35, No. 1 (1968): 48–75, at p. 74.
39. Almond and Coleman, "Introduction: A Functional Approach to Comparative Politics," *The Politics of the Developing Areas*, pp. 3–64. For later reformulations and applications of this approach, see Gabriel Almond, "A Developmental Approach to Political Systems," *World Politics* 17, No. 2 (1965): 183–214; Gabriel A. Almond and G. Bingham Powell, Jr., *Comparative Politics: System, Process, and Policy*, 2nd ed. (Glenview, IL: Scott, Foresman and Company, 1978); and Gabriel A. Almond and G. Bingham Powell, Jr., *Comparative Politics Today*, 5th ed. (New York: Harper Collins, 1992).
40. Almond and Coleman, *The Politics of the Developing Areas*, p. v.
41. *Ibid.*, p. 11.
42. Leonard Binder, *Iran: Political Development in a Changing Society* (Berkeley, CA: University of California Press, 1962), pp. 7–10.
43. Fred W. Riggs, *Administration in Developing Countries: The Theory of Prismatic Society* (Boston: Houghton Mifflin, 1964), pp. 456–457.
44. Major sources include: J. P. Nettl, "The State as a Conceptual Variable," *World Politics* 20 (1968): 559–592; Alfred Stepan, *State and Society: Peru in Comparative Perspective* (Princeton, NJ: Princeton University Press, 1978); Eric Nordlinger, *On the Autonomy of the Democratic State* (Cambridge, MA: Harvard University Press, 1981); Stephen Krasner, "Approaches to the State: Alternative Conceptions and Historical Dynamics," *Comparative Politics* 16 (1984): 223–246; James G. March and Johan P. Olsen, "The New Institutionalism: Organizational Factors in Political Life," *American Political Science Review* 78, No. 3 (1984): 734–749; Peter Evans, Dietrich Rueschemeyer, and Theda Skocpol, eds., *Bringing the State Back In* (Cambridge, MA: Harvard University Press, 1985); Metin Heper, ed., *The State and Public Bureaucracies: A Comparative Perspective* (Westport, CT: Greenwood Press, 1987); Rogers M. Smith, "Political Jurisprudence, the 'New Institutionalism,' and the Future of Public Law," *American Political Science Review* 82, No. 1 (1988): 89–108; Gabriel A. Almond, "The Return to the State," *American Political Science Review* 82, No. 3 (1988): 853–874; Eric A. Nordlinger, Theodore J. Lowi, and Sergio Fabbrini, "The Return to the State: Critiques," *American Political Science Review* 82, No. 3 (1988): 875–901; Robert H. Jackson, "Civil Science: Comparative Jurisprudence and Third World Government," *Governance* 1, No. 4 (1988): 380–414; James W. Fesler, "The State and Its Study," *PS: Political Science & Politics*

21, No. 4 (1988): 891–901; James A. Caporaso, ed., *The Elusive State: International and Comparative Perspectives* (Newbury Park, CA: Sage Publications, 1989); James G. March and Johan P. Olsen, *Rediscovering Institutions: The Organizational Basis of Politics* (New York: Free Press, 1989); Szymon Chodak, *The New State: Etatization of Western Societies* (Boulder, CO: Lynne Rienner, 1989); Milton J. Esman, "The State, Government Bureaucracies, and Their Alternatives," in Ali Farazmand, ed. *Handbook of Comparative and Development Public Administration* (New York: Marcel Dekker, 1991), Chap. 33, pp. 457–465; Lucian W. Pye, "The Myth of the State: The Reality of Authority," in Ramesh K. Arora, ed., *Politics and Administration in Changing Societies: Essays in Honour of Professor Fred W. Riggs* (New Delhi: Associated Publishing House, 1991), Chap. 2, pp. 35–49; Timothy Mitchell, "The Limits of the State: Beyond Statist Approaches and Their Critics," *American Political Science Review* 85, No. 1 (1991): 77–96; John Bendix, Bertell Ollman, Bartholomew H. Sparrow, and Timothy P. Mitchell, "Going Beyond the State?," *American Political Science Review* 86, No. 4 (1992): 1007–1021; and Robert W. Jackman, *Power without Force: The Political Capacity of Nation-States* (Ann Arbor, MI: The University of Michigan Press, 1993).

45. *Proposal for an International Institute of Comparative Government* (Lausanne: IICG, 1986).
46. Fesler, "The State and Its Study," p. 894.
47. Almond, "The Return to the State," p. 872.
48. Fesler, "The State and Its Study," p. 897.
49. Jackson, "Civil Science: Comparative Jurisprudence and Third World Governance," p. 380. Refer also to Jackson's earlier paper, "Civil Science: A Rule-Based Paradigm for Comparative Government," prepared for the 1987 Annual Conference of the American Political Science Association, mimeographed, 25 pp. A similar perspective, applauding more attention to the role of normative ideas in law, is taken by Rogers M. Smith in "Political Jurisprudence, the 'New Institutionalism,' and the Future of Public Law."
50. Jackson, "Civil Science: Comparative Jurisprudence and Third World Governance," p. 408.
51. Nettl, "The State as a Conceptual Variable," p. 592.
52. Heper, *The State and Public Bureaucracies.*
53. Pye, "The Myth of the State: The Reality of Authority," pp. 35, 46.
54. Mitchell, "The Limits of the State," p. 77.
55. Jackman, *Power without Force.*
56. The best comprehensive bibliographical sources are Ferrel Heady and Sybil L. Stokes, *Comparative Public Administration: A Selective Annotated Bibliography*, 2nd ed. (Ann Arbor, MI: Institute of Public Administration, The University of Michigan, 1960) for the earlier period; and Mark W. Huddleston, *Comparative Public Administration: An Annotated Bibliography* (New York: Garland Publishing, 1983) for the years 1962 to 1981. More specialized sources on important segments of the comparative administration literature are Allan A. Spitz and Edward W. Weidner, *Development Administration: An Annotated Bibliography* (Honolulu: East-West Center Press, 1963); and Manindra K. Mohapatra and David R. Hager,

Studies of Public Bureaucracy: A Select Cross-National Bibliography (Monticello, IL: Council of Planning Librarians, Exchange Bibliography #1385–1387, 1977).

57. These included Ferrel Heady, "Comparative Public Administration: Concerns and Priorities," in Ferrel Heady and Sybil L. Stokes, eds., *Papers in Comparative Public Administration* (Ann Arbor, MI: Institute of Public Administration, The University of Michigan, 1962); and Dwight Waldo, *Comparative Public Administration: Prologue, Problems, and Promise* (Chicago: Comparative Administration Group, American Society for Public Administration, 1964). Earlier treatments are cited in these essays.

58. Poul Meyer, *Administrative Organization: A Comparative Study of the Organization of Public Administration* (London: Stevens & Sons, 1957); Brian Chapman, *The Profession of Government* (London: George Allen & Unwin, 1959); the parts dealing with administration in Herman Finer, *Theory and Practice of Modern Government*, rev. ed. (New York: Holt, Rinehart & Winston, 1949); Fritz Morstein Marx, *The Administrative State* (Chicago: University of Chicago Press, 1957).

59. This research design is discussed in Fred W. Riggs, "Relearning an Old Lesson: The Political Context of Development Administration," *Public Administration Review* 25, No. 1 (1965): 72–75.

60. Leading early expositions of this view are found in Edward W. Weidner, "Development Administration: A New Focus for Research," in Heady and Stokes, *Papers*, pp. 97–115; Irving Swerdlow, ed., *Development Administration Concepts and Problems* (Syracuse, NY: Syracuse University Press, 1963); and Milton J. Esman, "The Politics of Development Administration, " in John D. Montgomery and William J. Siffin, eds., *Approaches to Development: Politics, Administration and Change* (New York: McGraw-Hill, 1966), pp. 59–112. A later valuable contribution, focusing on the developmental role of the civil service in India, was V. A. Pai Panandiker and S. S. Kshirsagar, *Bureaucracy and Development Administration* (New Delhi: Centre for Policy Research, 1978).

61. In Heady and Stokes, *Papers*, p. 99.

62. *Ibid.* pp. 103, 107.

63. Waldo, *Comparative Public Administration*, p. 27.

64. Swerdlow, *Development Administration*, p. xiv.

65. Waldo, *Comparative Public Administration*, p. 15.

66. Robert V. Presthus, "Behavior and Bureaucracy in Many Cultures," *Public Administration Review* 19, No. 1 (1959): 25–35.

67. Diamant, "The Relevance of Comparative Politics," pp. 87–112.

68. Heady and Stokes, *Papers*, p. 4.

69. See Note 43.

70. Dorsey, "An Information-Energy Model," in Heady and Stokes, *Papers*, pp. 37–57.

71. Dorsey, "The Bureaucracy and Political Development in Vietnam," in Joseph LaPalombara, ed., *Bureaucracy and Political Development* (Princeton, NJ: Princeton University Press, 1964), pp. 318–359.

72. William M. Berenson, "Testing the Information-Energy Model," *Administration and Society* 9, No. 2 (August 1977): 139–158. For a commentary raising questions both as to the model itself and the adequacy of Berenson's test of it, see Charles T.

Goodsell, "The Information-Energy Model and Comparative Administration," *Administration and Society* 9, No. 2 (August 1977): 159–168.

73. Waldo, *Comparative Public Administration*, p. 22.
74. Presthus, "Behavior and Bureaucracy in Many Cultures," p. 26.
75. See, for example, Brown, *New Directions*, pp. 10–11.
76. Waldo, *Comparative Public Administration*, p. 24.
77. Morroe Berger, *Bureaucracy and Society in Modern Egypt* (Princeton, NJ: Princeton University Press, 1957).
78. LaPalombara, *Bureaucracy and Political Development*.
79. Fred W. Riggs, "Trends in the Comparative Study of Public Administration," *International Review of Administrative Sciences* 28, No. 1 (1962): 9–15.
80. *Ibid.*, p. 15.
81. An informative general treatment of the evolution of comparative administration up to 1970 is available in Ramesh K. Arora, *Comparative Public Administration* (New Delhi: Associated Publishing House, 1972), Chap. 1, pp. 5–29.
82. Garth N. Jones, "Frontiersmen in Search for the 'Lost Horizon': The State of Development Administration in the 1960s," *Public Administration Review* 36, No. 1 (1976): 99–110, at pp. 99–100.
83. William J. Siffin, "Two Decades of Public Administration in Developing Countries," *Public Administration Review* 36, No. 1 (1976): 61–71, at p. 61.
84. *Ibid.*, pp. 64–66.
85. Jones, "Frontiersmen in Search," pp. 105–106.
86. Peter Savage, "Optimism and Pessimism in Comparative Administration," *Public Administration Review* 36, No. 4 (1976): 415–423, at pp. 419–420.
87. Fred W. Riggs, *Frontiers of Development Administration* (Durham, NC: Duke University Press, 1971).
88. *Ibid.*, p. 6.
89. *Ibid.*, pp. 3, 6, 7.
90. Arora, *Comparative Public Administration*, p. 37.
91. Savage, "Optimism and Pessimism," p. 419.
92. James Heaphey, "Comparative Public Administration: Comments on Current Characteristics," *Public Administration Review* 29, No. 3 (1968): 242–249, at pp. 242–243.
93. Jamil E. Jreisat, "Synthesis and Relevance in Comparative Public Administration, *Public Administration Review* 35, No. 6 (1975): 663–671, at p. 667.
94. Riggs, *Frontiers of Development Administration*, p. 7. Paradigm is used here in the meaning suggested by Thomas S. Kuhn in *The Structure of Scientific Revolution*, 2nd ed. (Chicago: University of Chicago Press, 1970). He says (pp. 10, 11) that "the study of paradigms prepares the student for membership in the particular scientific community with which he will later practice. . . . Men whose research is based on shared paradigms are committed to the same rules and standards for scientific practice. That commitment and the apparent consensus it produces are prerequisite for normal science" He regards social sciences generally as in a preparadigmatic stage, as compared to the physical sciences.
95. Savage, "Optimism and Pessimism," p. 417.
96. Jones, "Frontiersmen in Search," p. 101. POSDCORB was a word coined by Luther

Gulick as an abbreviation for Planning, Organizing, Directing, Coordinating, Reporting, and Budgeting.

97. Savage, "Optimism and Pessimism," p. 417.
98. *Ibid.*
99. Lee Sigelman, "In Search of Comparative Administration," *Public Administration Review* 36, No. 6 (1976): 621–625, at p. 623.
100. *Ibid.*, p. 625.
101. J. Fred Springer, "Empirical Theory and Development Administration: Prologues and Promise," *Public Administration Review* 36, No. 6 (1976): 636–641, at p. 636.
102. Keith Henderson, "Comparative Public Administration: The Identity Crisis," *Journal of Comparative Administration* 1, No. 1 (May 1969): 65–84, at p. 75.
103. Sigelman, "In Search of Comparative Administration," p. 622.
104. Jones, "Frontiersmen in Search," p. 102.
105. Jreisat, "Synthesis and Relevance," p. 655.
106. Savage, "Optimism and Pessimism," p. 417.
107. Springer, "Empirical Theory and Development Administration," p. 636.
108. Sigelman, "In Search of Comparative Administration," p. 623.
109. Jong S. Jun, "Renewing the Study of Comparative Administration: Some Reflections on the Current Possibilities," *Public Administration Review* 36, No. 6 (1976): 641–647, at p. 645.
110. Jones, "Frontiersmen in Search," p. 103.
111. Brian Loveman, "The Comparative Administration Group, Development Administration, and Antidevelopment," *Public Administration Review* 36, No. 6 (1976): 616–621.
112. *Ibid.*, p. 619.
113. Jones, "Frontiersmen in Search," p. 103.
114. *Ibid.*, p. 102.
115. B. B. Schaffer, "Comparisons, Administration, and Development," *Political Studies* 19, No. 3 (September 1971): 327–337, at p. 330.
116. Loveman, "The Comparative Administration Group," pp. 618–619.
117. Jreisat, "Synthesis and Relevance," pp. 666–667.
118. Savage, "Optimism and Pessimism," pp. 420–422.
119. Jreisat, "Synthesis and Relevance," p. 665.
120. *Ibid.*, p. 663.
121. Sigelman, "In Search of Comparative Administration," p. 624.
122. See Jun, "Renewing the Study of Comparative Administration," pp. 643–644; and Richard Ryan, "Comparative-Development Administration," *Southern Review of Public Administration* 6, No. 2 (1982): 188–203.
123. Sigelman, "In Search of Comparative Administration," p. 623.
124. Springer, "Empirical Theory and Development Administration," pp. 639–640. For a published version of the latter study, see Richard W. Gable and J. Fred Springer, "Administrative Implications of Development Policy: A Comparative Analysis of Agricultural Programs in Asia," *Economic Development and Cultural Change* 27, No. 4 (July 1979): 687–704.
125. Sigelman, "In Search of Comparative Administration," pp. 623–625.
126. Jun, "Renewing the Study of Comparative Administration," pp. 645–646. A later

example was the interest shown in other countries, including the United States, concerning Japanese practices in achieving worker satisfaction, setting up quality circles, conducting research and development activities, and contributing in other ways to Japan's success in competing in the world market. See, for example, William Ouchi, *Theory Z: How American Business Can Meet the Japanese Challenge* (New York: Addison-Wesley, 1981).

127. Jreisat, "Synthesis and Relevance," p. 668.

128. Jorge I. Tapia-Videla, "Understanding Organizations and Environments: A Comparative Perspective," *Public Administration Review* 36, No. 6 (1976): 631–636.

129. Peter Cleaves, *Bureaucratic Politics and Administration in Chile* (Berkeley, CA: University of California Press, 1975).

130. As Joel S. Migdal has observed, this term was later transformed "from one concerned parochially with traditional Iberian and Latin American societies to one dealing with the dynamics of change in a number of regions." See "Studying the Politics of Development and Change: The State of the Art," in Ada W. Finifter, ed., *Political Science: The State of the Discipline* (Washington, DC: The American Political Science Association, 1983), pp. 309–338, at p. 319. Hence it will be useful to us later in the classification of political regime types in developing countries.

131. For important examples of this literature, see Yehezkel Dror, *Public Policymaking Reexamined* (San Francisco: Chandler Publishing Company, 1968); Thomas R. Dye, *Understanding Public Policy*, 3rd ed., (Englewood Cliffs, NJ: Prentice-Hall, 1978); and Aaron Wildavsky, *Speaking Truth to Power: The Art and Craft of Policy Analysis* (Boston: Little, Brown and Company, 1979).

132. Jun, "Renewing the Study of Comparative Administration," p. 646.

133. These matters are discussed in my unpublished paper, "American Public Administration in Cultural Perspective: Lessons for and Lessons from Other Cultures," in more detail than is possible here. Recent published summaries of various views about development administration include: Ahmed Shafiqul Huque, *Paradoxes in Public Administration: Dimensions of Development* (Dhaka, Bangladesh: University Press Limited, 1990), pp. 112–114, 150–151; William J. Siffin, "The Problem of Development Administration," Chap. 1, pp. 5–13, in Ali Farazmand, ed., *Handbook of Comparative and Development Public Administration* (New York: Marcel Dekker, 1991); and H. K. Asmeron and R. B. Jain, "Politics and Administration: Some Conceptual Issues," Chap. 1, pp. 1–15, in Asmeron and Jain, eds., *Politics, Administration and Public Policy in Developing Countries: Examples from Africa, Asia and Latin America* (Amsterdam: VU University Press, 1993).

134. Siffin, "The Problem of Development Administration," p. 9.

135. George Gant, *Development Administration: Concepts, Goals, Methods* (Madison, WI: The University of Wisconsin Press, 1979).

136. "There is not a fixed point at which a people, region, or country passes from a state of underdevelopment to a state of development. The relative condition of development, rather, is comparative and ever changing—it fluctuates according to what is needed, what is possible, and what is desired. Development is relative also in terms of the possible; it fluctuates according to what is feasible at any particular time. A country which utilizes its resources effectively is considered to be more developed than a country which does not." *Ibid.*, p. 7. Presumably a country which utilizes its

resources with 100 percent efficiency could be considered fully developed. Obviously no country qualifies or is likely to qualify. More recent commentators concur. Milton Esman concedes that "the concept of development has been and remains imprecise," but says that "it connotes steady progress toward improvement in the human condition; reduction and eventual elimination of poverty, ignorance, and disease; and expansion of well-being and opportunity for all. It entails rapid change, but change alone is insufficient; it must be directed to specific ends. Development involves societal transformation—political, social, and cultural as well as economic; it implies modernization—secularization, industrialization, and urbanization—but not necessarily Westernization. It is multi-dimensional, with scholars and practitioners disagreeing, however, on relative emphasis, priority, and timing." Quoted from *Management Dimensions of Development: Perspectives and Strategies* (West Hartford, CT: Kumarian Press, 1991), p. 5. H. K. Asmeron and R. B. Jain state that the concept of development "refers to the changes and improvements that have to be made in the socio-economic and political aspirations of society as integral components of the nation-building process. In particular, development is closely associated with nationally and locally initiated concrete socio-economic programmes and projects and with the creation of national and grassroots organizations in which the people can meaningfully participate in the formulation and implementation of policies." Quoted from "Politics and Administration," p. 5.

137. Gant, *Development Administration*, pp. 19–21.
138. Islam and Henault, "From GNP to Basic Needs: A Critical Review of Development Administration," *International Review of Administrative Sciences* 45, No. 3 (1979): 253–267, at p. 258.
139. Asmeron and Jain, "Politics and Administration," p. 5.
140. Huque, *Paradoxes in Public Administration*, pp. 113–114.
141. "Principles of administration developed in the West are seldom relevant to the needs and circumstances prevailing in the developing world. The two types of societies vary, often to a considerable degree, in almost all respects. . . . Principles and procedures aimed at efficiency and economy may turn out to be counterproductive when applied to different circumstances. This represents the principal paradox of administration viewed in terms of development." *Ibid.*, pp. 150–151.
142. Gant, *Development Administration*, p. 21.
143. For a detailed chronological review of the links between comparative public administration and U.S. programs of foreign aid, see George Guess, "Comparative and International Administration," in Rabin, Hildreth, and Miller, *Handbook of Public Administration*, Chap. 14, pp. 477–497.
144. Islam and Henault, "From GNP to Basic Needs," p. 257.
145. W. Blase, *Institution Building: A Source Book* (Beverly Hills, CA: Sage Publications, 1973).
146. Jreisat, "Synthesis and Relevance," pp. 668–670.
147. Siffin, "Two Decades of Public Administration," pp. 68–70.
148. Wesley E. Bjur and Asghar Zomorrodian, "Towards Indigenous Theories of Administration: An International Perspective," *International Review of Administrative Sciences* 52, No. 4 (1986): 397–420; A. S. Huque, *Paradoxes in Public Administration*, "Administrative Behaviour Across Cultures," in Chap. 3, pp. 65–70; Ferrel

Heady, "The Cultural Dimension in Comparative Administration," Chap. 5, pp. 89–100, in Arora, *Politics and Administration in Changing Societies*; Kathleen Staudt, *Managing Development: State, Society, and International Contexts* (Newbury Park, CA: Sage, 1991), Part I, Chap. 3, "The Cultural Context," pp. 35–61.

149. Bjur and Zomorrodian, "Toward Indigenous Theories of Administration," pp. 397, 400, 412.

150. "Attention to culture is fundamental to development work. Many levels of culture are part of that work, from the national level, to ethnic and class levels, to gender, organization, and disciplinary. Each cultural level has its insights and applications, but caveats about each level exist as well." Staudt, *Managing Development*, p. 56.

151. South Korea, Chile, Argentina, and Iran were cited as showcase examples before the political reforms that since have occurred in each case. For an example of soul-searching by Americans concerning Iranian public administration assistance projects during the regime of the shah, see the following articles in *Public Administration Review* 40, No. 5 (1980): John L. Seitz, "The Failure of U.S. Technical Assistance in Public Administration: The Iranian Case," pp. 407–413; Frank P. Sherwood, "Learning from the Iranian Experience," pp. 413–418; William J. Siffin, "The Sultan, the Wise Men, and the Fretful Mastodon: A Persian Fable," pp. 418–421; and John L. Seitz, "Iran and the Future of U.S. Technical Assistance: Some Afterthoughts," pp. 432–433.

152. See Esman's earlier article, "Development Assistance in Public Administration: Requiem or Renewal," *Public Administration Review* 40, No. 5 (1980): 426–431; and his more recent book, *Management Dimensions of Development*.

153. Esman, *Management Dimensions of Development*, p. 160.

154. Esman, "Development Assistance in Public Administration," p. 427.

155. For a brief review, see George Honadle, "Development Administration in the Eighties: New Agendas or Old Perspectives?," *Public Administration Review* 42, No. 2 (1982): 174–179. For fuller treatments, refer to Coralie Bryant and Louise G. White, *Management Development in the Third World* (Boulder, CO: Westview Press, 1982); John E. Kerrigan and Jeff S. Luke, *Management Training Strategies for Developing Countries* (Boulder, CO: Lynne Rienner Publishers, 1987); Dennis A. Rondinelli, *Development Administration and U.S. Aid Policy* (Boulder, CO: Lynne Rienner Publishers, 1987); Louise G. White, *Implementing Policy Reforms in LDCs: A Strategy for Designing and Effecting Change* (Boulder, CO: Lynne Rienner Publishers, 1990); Esman, *Management Dimensions of Development*; and Staudt, *Managing Development*.

156. Lindenburg and Crosby, *Managing Development: The Political Dimension* (West Hartford, CT: Kumarian Press, 1981).

157. Foster, "A Methodological Approach to Administrative Development Intervention," *International Review of Administrative Sciences* 46, No. 3 (1980): 237–243.

158. Rondinelli and Ingle, *Improving the Implementation of Development Programs: Beyond Administrative Reform*, SICA Occasional Papers Series, No. 10 (Washington, DC: American Society for Public Administration, 1981, Mimeographed) 25 pp.

159. See the index heading "Women in administration" in Staudt's book, *Managing Development*.

160. See Korten's influential article, "Community Organization and Rural Development:

A Learning Process Approach," *Public Administration Review* 40, No. 5 (1980): 480–511; and his more recent book, *Getting to the 21st Century: Voluntary Action and the Global Agenda* (West Hartford, CT: Kumarian Press, 1990).

161. Korten, "Community Organization and Rural Development," p. 502.

162. Korten, *Getting to the 21st Century*, p.ix.

163. For another work devoted to the contributions of NGOs, refer to Thomas F. Carroll, *Intermediary NGOs: The Supporting Link in Grassroots Development* (West Hartford, CT: Kumarian Press, 1992).

164. Ingle, "Appropriate Management Technology: A Development Management Perspective," prepared for the 1981 National Conference of the American Society for Public Administration, mimeographed, 23 pp., at p. 17.

165. Korten, "Community Organization and Rural Development," p. 498.

166. Refer to Esman's *Management Dimensions of Development*, especially Chaps. 5 and 6.

167. Pioneering efforts in this direction are Coralie Bryant and Louise G. White, *Managing Development in the Third World* (Boulder, CO: Westview Press, 1982); White, *Creating Opportunities for Change: Approaches to Managing Development* (Boulder, CO: Lynne Riener, 1987); Douglass North, *Institutions, Institutional Change, and Economic Performance* (Cambridge and New York: Cambridge University Press, 1990). Major recent examples are Derick W. Brinkerhoff, ed., "Implementing Policy Change," *World Development* 24, No. 9 (Special Issue, September 1996): 1393–1559; Anirudh Krishna, Norman Uphoff, and Milton J. Esman, eds., *Reasons for Hope: Instructive Experiences in Rural Development* (West Hartford, CT: Kumarian Press, 1997); Norman Uphoff, Milton J. Esman, and Anirudh Krishna, *Reasons for Success: Learning from Instructive Experiences in Rural Development* (West Hartford, CT: Kumarian Press, 1998); John M. Cohen and Stephen B. Peterson, *Administrative Decentralization: Strategies for Developing Countries* (West Hartford, CT: Kumarian Press, 1999); and Derick W. Brinkerhoff and Jennifer M. Coston, "International Development Management in a Globalized World," *Public Administration Review* 59, No. 4 (July/August 1999): 346–361.

168. Brinkerhoff, "Implementing Policy Change," editor's preface, p. 1393.

169. For valuable surveys of these accomplishments and problems during the formative stage, see Keith M. Henderson, "From Comparative Public Administration to Comparative Public Policy," *International Review of Administrative Sciences* 47, No. 4 (1981): 356–364; and M. Donald Hancock, "Comparative Public Policy: An Assessment," pp. 283–308, in Finifter, *Political Science* (includes a select bibliography). For more recent comprehensive surveys of the field, refer to Douglas E. Ashford, ed., *History and Context in Comparative Public Policy* (Pittsburgh, PA: University of Pittsburgh Press, 1992); and Stuart S. Nagel, ed., *Encyclopedia of Policy Studies*, 2nd ed., revised and expanded (New York, NY: Marcel Dekker, 1994).

170. Arnold J. Heidenheimer, Hugh Heclo, and Carolyn Teich Adams, *Comparative Public Policy: The Politics of Social Choice in Europe and America* (New York: St. Martin's Press, 1975), p. i.

171. Meinolf Dierkes, Hans N. Weiler, and Ariane Berthoin Antal, eds., *Comparative Policy Research: Learning from Experience* (New York: St. Martin's Press, 1987).

172. This mutuality of concerns is not always acknowledged by writers in comparative public policy. As Naomi Caiden points out in her review of *Comparative Policy Research* [in *Public Administration Review* 48, No. 5 (1988): 932–933], this book makes no reference to the work of the Comparative Administration Group or its successors, and dismisses public administration as "ethnocentric and parochial" (p. 18).

173. Hancock estimated that approximately 70 percent of policy analysis work had dealt with advanced industrial democracies of Western Europe and North America, as contrasted with about 10 percent in either Latin America or Asia, and almost none in the Middle East and Africa ("Comparative Public Policy: An Assessment," p. 299). Hugh Heclo, in another review of *Comparative Policy Research* [in *American Political Science Review* 82, No. 2 (1988): 652–653], makes this relevant comment: "We should worry more about the parochialism in our choice of countries and the true equivalency of issues in different national settings."

174. Hancock, "Comparative Public Policy," p. 293.

175. "The aspirations for comparative policy research have been set high, and understandably results have fallen short. There are plenty of data, and even some theorizing, but the approach has not been systematic. It has been difficult to control variables in comparative context, and differences come to overwhelm similarities. Theoretical assumptions diverge. Countries for study are chosen accidentally. Studies are often descriptive and lack theoretical interest. American methods and concepts are uncritically transferred to other contexts. Complexity and uncertainty defeat reliable prediction. Values and preferences pervade and influence analysis. Lack of a general theoretical framework hinders cumulation of research results." This is Naomi Caiden's summary of the situation in her review of *Comparative Policy Research* in *Public Administration Review*, previously cited. She goes on to observe: "All of this no doubt sounds familiar. The literature of comparative public administration is permeated with discussions of precisely these problems."

176. Heclo's review of *Comparative Policy Research* in *American Political Science Review*, previously cited, includes this tart observation: "Students of comparative public policy have enough theories, hypotheses, methodological tools, and conferencing opportunities to keep them going into the next century. What they do not have are decent data."

177. This was reflected, for example, in the scope statements of program sections for the 1983 annual meeting of the American Political Science Association, with one on public policy analysis and another on comparative politics: public policy. The issue is also mentioned by Henderson, "From Comparative Public Administration to Comparative Public Policy," p. 364.

178. Peters, "Public Policy and Public Bureaucracy," Part III, Chap. 13, pp. 283–315, in Ashford, *History and Context in Comparative Public Policy*.

179. Randall Baker, ed., *Comparative Public Management: Putting U.S. Public Policy and Implementation in Context* (Westport, CT: Praeger, 1994).

180. *Ibid.*, p. 7.

181. Jonathan Bendor, "A Theoretical Problem in Comparative Administration," *Public Administration Review* 36, No. 6 (1976): 626–630.

182. See my article, "Comparative Administration: A Sojourner's View," *Public Administration Review* 38, No. 4 (1978): 358–365, at p. 364.

183. The most comprehensive survey of this periodical literature is a content analysis of 253 articles published in twenty journals during the years 1982–1986. The investigators concluded that the literature is indeed substantial, and that it demonstrates the continued vitality of comparative public administration but also its lack of a clear identity. Important characteristics noted are "a significant practitioner component, substantial orientation towards policy recommendations, a relative paucity of theory-testing studies, wide and mature coverage of a range of topics, and methodological practices that seem slightly better than in the past but still far from ideal." See Montgomery Van Wart and N. Joseph Cayer, "Comparative Public Administration: Defunct, Dispersed, or Redefined?," *Public Administration Review* 50, No. 2 (March/April 1990): 238–248.

184. Examples include Chandler, *A Centennial History of the American Administrative State*; Rabin, Hildreth, and Miller, *Handbook of Public Administration*; Naomi B. Lynn and Aaron Wildavsky, eds., *Public Administration: The State of the Discipline* (Chatham, NJ: Chatham House Publishers, 1990); and Richard J. Stillman II, *Preface to Public Administration: A Search for Themes and Direction* (New York: St. Martin's Press, 1991).

185. A survey of administrative research in Europe since 1980, by Hans-Ulrich Derlien, concludes that secondary analysis of comparable national studies in subfields such as organizational structure and personnel policies is quite common, but that there has been a scarcity in research that is "*comparative by design* involving data collection in two or more countries." See Derlien, "Observations on the State of Comparative Administration Research in Europe—Rather Comparable than Comparative," *Governance* 5, No. 3 (July 1992): 279–311.

186. Peters' views are presented most fully in *Comparing Public Bureaucracies: Problems of Theory and Method* (Tuscaloosa, AL: The University of Alabama Press, 1988); and more briefly and recently in "Theory and Methodology in the Study of Comparative Public Administration," Chap. 6, pp. 67–91, in Baker, *Comparative Public Management*.

187. Peters, *Comparing Public Bureaucracies*, p. xiii.

188. *Ibid.*, pp. 2, 13, 24.

189. Donald C. Rowat, ed., *Public Administration in Developed Democracies: A Comparative Study* (New York: Marcel Dekker, 1988); and V. Subramaniam, ed., *Public Administration in the Third World: An International Handbook* (Westport, CT: Greenwood Press, 1990).

190. O. P. Dwivedi and Keith Henderson, eds., *Public Administration in World Perspective* (Iowa City: Iowa State University Press, 1990).

191. Ali Farazmand, ed., *Handbook of Comparative and Development Public Administration* (New York: Marcel Dekker, 1991).

192. Ali Farazmand, ed., *Handbook of Bureaucracy* (New York: Marcel Dekker, 1994).

193. (Westport, CT: Praeger, 1994).

194. (New York, NY: St. Martin's Press, 1999).

195. Peters, *Comparing Public Bureaucracies*, pp. 22–24.

196. *Ibid.*, p. xiv.

197. *Ibid.*, p. 13.
198. *Ibid.*, p. 12. Peters did not cite specific examples of successful comparative public policy research, however. As has already been noted, this field has also been the target for a barrage of criticism.
199. *Ibid.*, p. 189.
200. Peters, "Theory and Methodology in the Study of Comparative Public Administration," pp. 71, 82–86.
201. Charles C. Ragin, in *The Comparative Method: Moving Beyond Qualitative and Quantitative Strategies* (Berkeley, CA: University of California Press, 1987), addresses this problem perceptively. "I was trained," he states, "as are most American social scientists today, to use multivariate statistical techniques whenever possible. I often found, however, that these techniques were not well suited for answering some of the questions that interest me. . . . This book represents an effort to step back from traditional statistical techniques, in comparative social science especially, and to explore alternatives. . . . The problem is not to show which methodology is best but to explore alternative ways of establishing a meaningful dialogue between ideas and evidence" (pp. vii, viii).
202. Eric Welch and Wilson Wong, "Public Administration in a Global Context: Bridging the Gaps of Theory and Practice between Western and Non-Western Nations," *Public Administration Review* 58, No. 1 (January/February 1998): 40–49.
203. George M. Guess, "Comparative and International Administration," in Rabin, Hildreth, and Miller, *Handbook of Public Administration*, 2nd ed., Chap. 15, pp. 535–569.
204. *Ibid.*, p. 542.
205. Savage, "Optimism and Pessimism," p. 422.
206. Jun, "Renewing the Study of Comparative Administration," p. 647.
207. Riggs has expressed this view more than once, using different words. See, for example, "The Group and the Movement," p. 652; and "Epilogue: The Politics of Bureaucratic Administration," in Tummala, *Administrative Systems Abroad*, rev. ed., Chap. 15, p. 407.
208. Peters, *Comparing Public Bureaucracies*, p. 3.

2

A Focus for Comparison

BUREAUCRACY AS A FOCUS

Of the many ways to organize a survey of the existing state of knowledge concerning administration in various countries, I have chosen the institution of the public bureaucracy as the means for comparison.

In view of the preference of many leading students of comparative politics for a functional or nonstructural approach, it is certainly legitimate to ask why the structure or institution of bureaucracy should be selected as the subject for comparative administrative analysis rather than a function such as Almond's rule application. The answer does not lie in a general judgment that a functional approach to comparative study of whole political systems is inferior to a structural approach; rather, it is a decision that the bureaucracy as a specialized political structure offers a better basis for treatment than would a choice of one or more functional categories. Our objective is comparison of public administration across polities, not the comparison of whole political systems. Such a narrowing of interest forces us to choose the most promising basis for comparison for the particular purpose (in this case public administration)—a basis that will simultaneously include enough, but not too much, and can promise data for comparison in the polities covered. For the student of public administration, the structure of bureaucracy has some advantages over the function of rule application, or any functional alternative that has been suggested.

The major objections made by Almond and others to comparative studies that have a structural emphasis are that structures may vary substantially from system to system, and like structures in different systems may have significant functional differences that are overlooked. These cautions do not seem to vitiate the utility of a structural approach in the comparative study of public administration. Apparently bureaucracy as a specialized structure is common to all contemporary nation-states, as is explained later. On the second point, to focus on the public bureaucracy is not automatically to ignore the probability that it performs functions other than rule application. Indeed, if all structures are multifunctional, as Almond hypothesizes, it may be just as valuable for comparative studies to focus on a universally existing structure and to investigate the different functions it performs as it is to focus on one function and identify the structures that perform it. Tracing a given function through a multitude of structures would appear to present problems of conceptualization and research at least as great as singling out one structure and analyzing the functions it performs.[1]

Any partial comparative analysis of political systems presents a dilemma, whether the approach is functional or institutional. This may not be serious in Western countries where there is a high degree of correlation across systems between structures and corresponding functions, but either approach runs into serious difficulties in the developing countries. Comparison by function may be more difficult in practice than in theory, since we have had very little of it, and it calls for identification of vaguely formed or strange structures through which the function under study may be carried out. On the other hand, structural comparison has hazards more easily identifiable, including the absence or precarious existence of comparable institutions, and the danger of assuming that similar structures will always have equivalent functions.

A structural basis of comparison is feasible if the institution or institutions being studied actually exist in corresponding form in the political systems under study, and if notice is taken of variations in the functional role of these institutions in different systems.

From another angle, it might be argued that comparison of bureaucratic structure and behavior is deficient because it offers only partial coverage of topics traditionally dealt with in books on public administration in particular countries, such as administrative organization and management, fiscal and personnel administration, relations between levels of government and levels of administration, and administrative law. One response is that a common framework for treatment is less observable now than was the case a few years ago, so that variation in perspective is more acceptable. The more compelling reason, however, is that a sweeping comparison across national boundaries requires some organizing concept to avoid burial under an avalanche of data about a multitude of diverse administrative systems. Bureaucracy provides such an organizing concept, one which certainly is at the core of modern administration even though public administration and public bureaucracy are not synonymous, and which has impinging upon it all the other forces that have in the past interested students of public administration.

Before proceeding, we need to examine with care and in some detail how the term bureaucracy has been used by different people, the confusions of meaning and understanding that have resulted, and the meaning given to bureaucracy as used here.

CONCEPTS OF BUREAUCRACY

The term bureaucracy has often been attacked as contrived, ambiguous, and troublesome. All of these charges are accurate. Nevertheless, bureaucracy is a word that has demonstrated great staying power. Even most of its critics have concluded that there is more to be gained by keeping it (provided it is given the meaning they prefer) than by abandoning it. And that is essentially the position taken here.

The origins of the word are not entirely clear. Morstein Marx gives it a French pedigree, identifies a Latin ancestor of long ago, calls it a hideous example of teaming French with Greek, and counts it as among the notorious words of our age.[2] He points out that it was first used in the French form *bureaucratie* by a French minister of commerce in the eighteenth century to refer to the government in operation, spread to Germany during the nineteenth century as *Burokratie*, and has since found its way into English and many other languages. As a subject for scholarly inquiry, the term is primarily associated with the German social scientist Max Weber (1864–1920), whose writings on bureaucracy have stimulated a flood of commentary and further research.[3]

What is probably the most common usage of bureaucracy may distract us, but it need not detain us. In popular language, bureaucracy is most often employed as a "political cussword," and is cast in the role of villain by opponents of "big government" or "the welfare state." Sometimes this meaning appears in academic writing as well, two often quoted examples being Harold Laski's definition in the 1930 edition of the *Encyclopedia of the Social Sciences*, and the treatment by Von Mises in his book, *Bureaucracy*.[4] Most social scientists define bureaucracy in a way intended to identify a phenomenon associated with large-scale complex organizations, without any connotation of approval or disapproval. A usage that is value-neutral, it identifies bureaucracy as neither hero nor villain, but as a form of social organization with certain characteristics.

The confusion in bureaucratic theory comes from differences in approach in describing these characteristics, and failure to distinguish among these approaches.[5] The ambiguity can be traced to Weber's own formulations, and despite a high degree of agreement and consistency concerning some essential earmarks of bureaucracy, it continues down to the present.

The dominant tendency is to define bureaucracy in terms of an organization's basic structural characteristics. The most compact formulation is that of Victor Thompson, who characterizes the bureaucratic organization as composed of a highly elaborated hierarchy of authority superimposed upon a highly elaborated division of labor.[6] From Weber on, most writers on bureaucracy have enumerated the structural dimensions of bureaucracy, with minor variations in their formulations, both in content and breakdown of items, but with substantial agreement among them. Richard H. Hall has tabulated characteristics of bureaucracy as listed by a number of authors, including Weber, Litwak, Friedrich, Merton, Udy, Heady, Parsons, and Berger.[7] From the longer roster of characteristics, Hall picked six dimensions of bureaucracy for special attention. These were (1) a well-defined hierarchy of authority; (2) a division of labor based on functional specialization; (3) a system of rules covering the rights and duties of positional incumbents; (4) a system of procedures for dealing with work situations; (5) impersonality of interpersonal relationships; and (6) selection for employment and promotion based on technical competence. This list can serve very well as a summary of the most commonly mentioned structural earmarks of bureaucracy.

A second tendency has been to define bureaucracy in terms of behavioral characteristics, or to add these to the structural characteristics, the result being a pattern of behavior presumed to be bureaucratic. Opinion varies considerably on what kind of behavior deserves to be so labeled. One option is to emphasize normal, desirable, functional traits positively associated with attainment of the objectives of bureaucratic organizations. Friedrich, for example, stresses traits such as objectivity, precision and consistency, and discretion. He describes these traits as "clearly and closely related to the measure-taking function of administrative officials."[8] They "embody rules defining desirable habit or behavior patterns of all the members" of such a bureaucratic organization and they were originated by "men of extraordinary inventiveness who were laying the basis of a rationalized society by these inventions."[9] Eisenstadt speaks approvingly of a type of dynamic equilibrium that a bureaucracy may develop in relation to its environment, in which the bureaucracy maintains its autonomy and distinctiveness by behavior retaining its structural differentiation from other social groups but recognizing the claims of those legitimately entitled to exercise supervisory controls over the bureaucracy.[10]

A more common emphasis, which shows up in the work of many other authors, highlights behavioral traits which are basically negative, "dysfunctional," pathological, or self-defeating, tending to frustrate the realization of the goals toward which the bureaucracy is supposed to be working. Robert Merton has made the classic statement of this point of view.[11] He is concerned with the fact that "the very elements which conduce toward efficiency in general produce inefficiency in specific instances" and "also lead to an overconcern with strict adherence to regulations which induces timidity, conservatism, and technicism." Stress on "depersonalization of relationships" leads to conflict in relations with bureaucratic clientele. Specific behavioral orientations often mentioned are "buck passing," red tape, rigidity and inflexibility, excessive impersonality, over-secretiveness, unwillingness to delegate, and reluctance to exercise discretion. Behavior of this sort is typical of the "trained incapacity" of the bureaucrat. The implication is that behavior which is most typically bureaucratic is behavior emerging from overemphasis on the rationality of bureaucratic organization and dysfunctional in its effects, suggesting a model for bureaucratic behavior which would stress these contradictory or self-defeating traits. This continues to be a common orientation. Morstein Marx talks of such traits as "ailment of organization," explained by the fact that "the bureaucratic type of organization gives rise to certain tendencies that pervert its purpose. Some of its strength—and in extreme cases all of it—is drained off constantly by vices that paradoxically spring from virtues."[12] Michel Crozier describes his valuable study, *The Bureaucratic Phenomenon*, as a scientific attempt to understand better this "malady of bureaucracy." He explains that the subject to which he refers in speaking of the bureaucratic phenomenon "is that of the maladaptations, the inadequacies, or to use Merton's expression, the 'dysfunctions,' which necessarily develop within human organizations."[13]

Either of these paths toward defining bureaucracy in terms of behavior leads to distinctions between patterns of behavior that are "more" or "less" bureaucratic, with the meaning of such descriptions being uncertain unless the kind of behavior that has been labeled "bureaucratic" is clearly understood. This approach may also result in identifying the "process of bureaucratization" with a pronounced inclination toward a patterned combination of behavioral traits, usually pathological, such as Eisenstadt's use of the word bureaucratization to mean "the extension of the power of a bureaucratic organization over many areas beyond its initial purpose, the growing internal formalization within the bureaucracy, the regimentation of these areas by the bureaucracy, and in general a strong emphasis by the bureaucracy on the extension of its power."[14]

A third method for dealing with bureaucratic behavior has been suggested by Peter Blau, who defines bureaucracy in terms of achievement of purpose, as an "organization that maximizes efficiency in administration or an institutionalized method of organized social conduct in the interests of administrative efficiency."[15] In modern society, with its necessities for large-scale operation, this probably requires that certain basic organizational characteristics be present, including hierarchical arrangements, specialization, professionalization to some degree, a set of operational rules, and a basic commitment to rational adaptation of means to ends. Although Blau recognizes the tendencies for bureaucracies to develop behavior patterns which detract from the attainment of legitimate objectives, he does not accept the view that all behavior that deviates from the formal expectation or seems irrational is in fact dysfunctional. He suggests a category of behavior of a somewhat different kind, which he terms "irrational but (perhaps) purposeful."[16] Behavior having its source in undercommitment to rationality may be dysfunctional, but this must be judged by results rather than by reference to a preconceived set of behavioral traits which are assumed to accompany the structural components of bureaucracy. The test as to the propriety of behavior would be its contribution to fundamental bureaucratic goals. Behavior which is pathological in one bureaucracy may be healthy in another. This would seem to make both structural and behavioral characteristics of bureaucracy somewhat variable, since the test for whether or not an organization is a bureaucracy is whether it is achieving its purpose, and the elements of structure and behavior that this requires may shift from time to time and place to place.

As indicated by this resume, considerable agreement exists as to the basic organizational characteristics of bureaucracy, but there is much less certainty as to the behavioral traits associated with it. Three alternatives have been presented for designating a pattern of behavior as "bureaucratic." One points toward normal, functional, desirable behavior to be expected and accepted as natural in bureaucratic operations. Another stresses dysfunctional behavior which is likely to develop from the rationalistic orientation of bureaucracy and the structural features designed to maintain it. The third alternative relates the propriety of behavior to the bureaucratic environment and results in a more flexible standard as to what behavior is bureaucratic in the sense of being functional.

Of course, all of these considerations are important, and the selection of any one of these aspects as critical to the definition of bureaucracy is quite justifiable. It is crucial to clarity of understanding, however, to make an explicit choice.[17] I have argued elsewhere[18] that Morroe Berger's pioneering study, *Bureaucracy and Society in Modern Egypt*, is flawed by a failure to do this, and that this affects his conclusion that theories of bureaucracy developed in the West have serious shortcomings for the analysis of bureaucracies both in Western and non-Western settings.[19] His view as to the inadequacy of existing theory is based mainly on the fact that responses to the questionnaire which he used in his study did not conform to his expectations. In his research he made certain assumptions about "Western norms" of bureaucratic behavior, and he discovered upon analysis of the questionnaire data that the Egyptian civil servants most highly exposed to Western influences did not, as he had anticipated, come closest to what he had assumed to be the Western norms. Berger pays relatively little attention to the structural side of bureaucratic theory, but he implicitly assumes that a model of bureaucracy would combine structural and behavioral features. As to behavioral attributes, he quotes Merton and seems to imply that on the behavioral side a model for bureaucracy would stress dysfunctional or pathological tendencies, along the lines of the second alternative discussed earlier. Nevertheless, he combines traits generally considered pathological or dysfunctional with others usually viewed as functional or desirable, in constructing his research tools for measuring "typical" or "Western" bureaucratic behavior. In short, his assumptions as to "the bureaucratic pattern of behavior," which he apparently equates with "the Western bureaucratic pattern of behavior," seem not to conform with his own citation from bureaucratic theory as to the behavioral components of bureaucracy. The hybrid or bifurcated model of bureaucracy which he uses results in confusion which might have been avoided by greater consistency in the approach used for identifying behavioral components, or by defining bureaucracy in a way which avoids attaching the label of "bureaucratic" to any particular pattern of behavioral traits.

My choice of the most useful way to view bureaucracy is as an institution defined in terms of basic structural characteristics.[20] Bureaucracy is a form of organization. Organizations either are bureaucracies or they are not, depending on whether or not they have these characteristics. Regarding bureaucracy as characteristic of the structure of an organization does not mean that all bureaucracies are identical as far as structure is concerned. Some promising efforts have been made to conceptualize elements that can be considered dimensions of organizational structure, the objective being to rate organizations on a continuum for each of the dimensions, with the position of a particular organization on all these dimensions jointly forming a profile of its structure. This structural profile can then be used, it is hoped, to characterize the organization for purposes of comparison.[21]

A principal advantage of selecting a structural focus in defining bureaucracy, rather than incorporating a behavioral component as well, is that it allows us to consider all patterns of behavior that are actually found in bureaucracies equally deserving to be called bureaucratic behavior. One pattern of behavior is not singled out as somehow entitled to be labeled bureaucratic, leaving other behavior patterns, also found in existing bureaucracies, to be described as non-bureaucratic or less bureaucratic. This practice has been the source of much confusion that can be eliminated.

The approach suggested does not ignore or de-emphasize differences in behavioral tendencies in bureaucracies. On the contrary, it facilitates the identification and classification of these patterns, which are extremely significant and should be primary objects for analysis and comparison. Behavioral traits, more than structural elements, are what distinguish one bureaucracy from another. These patterns can be expected to vary from bureaucracy to bureaucracy and from time to time in a given bureaucracy, but other than that we know very little about this highly complicated subject.[22] A theory of bureaucracy and techniques of comparative study which will facilitate exploration of these problems is an objective of the highest priority. "Intuitively . . . people have always assumed that bureaucratic structures and patterns of action differ in the different countries of the Western world and even more markedly between East and West. Men of action know it and never fail to take it into account. But contemporary social scientists . . . have not been concerned with such comparisons."[23] A structural characterization of what constitutes bureaucracy will not in itself accomplish much along this line, but it should at least clear away part of the debris so as to make progress somewhat easier.

THE PREVALENCE OF PUBLIC BUREAUCRACY

What are the generally accepted organizational features common to all bureaucracies? Do bureaucracies with these essential features exist in all or nearly all of the political systems of the world, so that they afford an actual basis for comparison of public administration across national boundaries? If bureaucracies are uniformly found to be in operation in modern polities, what points about their structure and behavior should be selected as most productive for purposes of comparative study? As has already been mentioned, there are almost as many formulations of the essential characteristics of bureaucracy as there are writers on the subject (and they have been plentiful). Nevertheless, the area of agreement on the structural or organizational features that are central is substantial. The variations come mostly in the way the structural aspects are expressed and in the divergence that comes when behavioral traits are added.

The pivotal structural characteristics can be reduced to three: (1) hierarchy, (2) differentiation or specialization, and (3) qualification or competence.[24] Hierarchy is probably the most important because it is so closely associated with the effort to apply rationality to administrative tasks. Max Weber viewed this effort as explaining the origin of the bureaucratic form of organization. He refers to hierarchy as involving principles and levels of graded authority that ensure a firmly ordered system of superordination and subordination in which higher offices supervise lower ones. Such a formal scheme of interlocking superior-subordinate relationships is intended to provide direction, cohesion, and continuity. Specialization in organization is a result of division of labor, which in turn is a requirement for accomplishment in cooperative human endeavor to master the environment and reach complex goals. Specialized allocation of tasks means differentiation within the organization of what sociologists refer to as roles. The structure of organization must provide for a functional relationship of these roles. Qualification "refers to these functions or roles and requires that the person playing a certain role must be qualified for it, typically in highly developed bureaucracies by adequate preparation and education."[25] Such intensive preparation might justify referring to professionalism in connection with this aspect, but competence and qualification are preferable because these terms hint at fitting the official to the role as it is conceived in the particular context. Competence might or might not require what would be considered professionalized training in a highly specialized society.

Other features of a structural sort are also frequently mentioned, but these are somewhat more peripheral, or are closely related to those already mentioned, such as a body of rules governing the behavior of members, a system of records, a system of procedures for dealing with work situations, and size sufficient at least to ensure a network of secondary group relationships.

It should be noted that this treatment of bureaucracy differs substantially from Weber's formulation of an "ideal-type" or a "fully developed" bureaucracy. His "ideal-type" was not intended to represent reality but was an abstraction that highlighted certain features, a "mental construct" which, in his words, "cannot be found empirically in reality."[26] As Arora observes, Weber "seemed to be clear in his mind that the ideal-type does not represent 'reality' *per se*, but is only an abstraction weaving an exaggeration of certain elements of reality into a logically precise conception."[27] Such an "ideal-type" is based on a combination of inductive and deductive analysis, and presumably has heuristic value even though it does not match any existing instance of the phenomenon being studied.

This formulation, on the other hand, is intended to identify actual organizations as bureaucracies if they have the specified characteristics. Moreover, Weber's formulation combined organizational with behavioral aspects, whereas this one confines the definition of bureaucracy to a minimal number of key structural characteristics.

There seems to be little doubt that a viable polity in the world today must have a public service that meets these criteria for a bureaucracy.[28] The necessities of governmental operation require large-scale organization of a bureaucratic type, with a definite internal hierarchical arrangement, well-developed functional specialization, and qualification standards for membership in the bureaucracy.[29] This does not mean that uniformity, even of these structural features, is assumed. Certainly, variations in operating characteristics are anticipated among bureaucracies in different political settings. Bureaucratic adaptation and innovation should be expected, particularly in the newer developing nations and in some socialist societies.[30]

In order to compare the public bureaucracies of the entire range of existing political entities, on what parts of these bureaucracies and on what aspects of bureaucratic activity should we concentrate to make the attempt manageable and to take into account realistically the available stock of reliable information?

To begin, let us use what LaPalombara calls "an accordion-like conceptualization of the bureaucracy."[31] The bureaucrats of major interest to us will generally be "those who occupy managerial roles, who are in some directive capacity either in central agencies or in the field, who are generally described in the language of public administration as 'middle' or 'top' management."[32] This is the higher civil service as the term is used by Morstein Marx to mean "the relatively 'permanent' top group composed of those who share, in different degrees, in the task of directing the various agencies," including *administrative, professional,* and *industrial* categories, *staff* as well as *line* personnel, and *field service* as well as *headquarters* officials.[33] In relation to the total number of people in the public service, this will be a small proportion, probably not more than 1 or 2 percent. This more restricted concept of the bureaucracy is most relevant when the concern is bureaucratic participation in the formation of public policy.[34]

The usual convention in public administration literature has been to concentrate on the civil, rather than the military, bureaucracy. This has been an understandable, and for the most part acceptable, emphasis for the study of administration in Western democratic systems. However, neglect of the military bureaucracy would be a serious omission in making comparisons on a global basis, in view of the numerous instances of nation-states in which the military has not consistently in the past conformed, or does not now conform, to a role of subordination to civilian political leadership. This role for the military has been common in many Latin American countries since independence. A large proportion of the newly independent countries have started with or turned to military or semimilitary regimes, with the frequency increasing until recently. Sporadically, such regimes have appeared elsewhere in long established polities. In such circumstances, where the higher military leadership has collaborated with or dominated the civil bureaucracy in making major public policy decisions, this participation in political rule will be of direct interest to us, although we will not deal with the military bureaucracy as it operates within the sphere of conventional military activity.

This perspective for a comparative survey of public administration, focusing on the institution of bureaucracy as it adapts to environmental conditions (particularly to the degree of social and economic development and to the configuration of the political system), does not claim to be the only one, or even necessarily the best of possible perspectives. It has been picked because it is relatively manageable, because it can rely upon a fairly adequate accumulation of basic data, and because it offers the promise of leading to future comparative research that will be both more exact and more comprehensive. A focus on bureaucracy also has the advantage that it has already been recognized as the most commonly accepted basis for comparative studies.[35]

With this background, recognizing that the subject matter is highly complicated and that available information sources are limited, we will seek to compare the higher civil and, where relevant, military bureaucracies in a variety of existing political systems, taking the following questions as the most pertinent ones for our purposes:

1. What are the dominant internal operating characteristics of the bureaucracy reflecting its composition, hierarchical arrangements, pattern of specialization, and behavioral tendencies?
2. To what extent is the bureaucracy multifunctional, participating in the making of major public policy decisions as well as in their execution?

3. What are the principal means for exerting control over the bureaucracy from sources outside it, and how effective are those external controls?

As these questions indicate, our interest is not confined to a comparison of structural variations, but extends to an exploration of differences in behavior patterns among bureaucracies.

Before trying to answer these questions in particular polities or types of political systems, let us consider two general background factors that can be expected to influence markedly the characteristics of bureaucratic systems. One is a fairly immediate and easily discernible factor—the organizational setting for public administration, including the pattern of departmentalization and the extent of public sector employment. The other, less tangible and more complex, but of much greater significance, is the political, economic, and social environment in which the bureaucracy functions, often referred to as the "ecology of administration." At a minimum, we must identify those environmental features that have the greatest impact in shaping and reshaping the bureaucracy.

ORGANIZATIONAL SETTING

Departmentalization

A necessary consequence of hierarchy and specialization in large scale organization is an orderly arrangement of units into successively larger and more inclusive groupings. This process of departmentalization has occurred in a remarkably uniform way in countries that vary greatly in their political orientations and other aspects of their administrative systems. The basic unit is the department or ministry, with each one representing a major organizational subdivision of administration. Brian Chapman identified five "primordial fields of government"—foreign affairs, justice, finance, defense and war, and internal affairs—represented in Europe's past by primary ministries with origins dating back to the Roman system of administration.[36] With the growth of governmental responsibilities and services, new ministries emerged from what had been the residual category of internal affairs, adding units in such fields as education, agriculture, transport, trade, and more recently, social security and health.[37] Richard Rose has analyzed the growth in the number of central government departments in a variety of Western nations during the period from the middle of the nineteenth century to the early 1980s, and reports that the average has gone from 9.4 to 19.2 per country.[38] Jean Blondel states that the most rapid expansion was from the late 1940s to the mid-1970s, when the average rose from about twelve to almost eighteen.[39]

Despite substantial differences in number at the lower and upper ends of the range, and the emergence of some distinctive patterns of departmentalization,[40] the impression one gets from reviewing current rosters of ministries in many countries is one of uniformity or close similarity rather than of wide variation. Central government ministries normally number from around twelve to about thirty, depending on the degree to which the country concerned prefers specialized or composite units, the range of governmental program areas, the size of the country's population, ideological considerations, geographical location,[41] and other factors. Switzerland, with only seven central government departments, was reported by Chapman as having a record low number, presumably reflecting the country's small size, restricted scope of government intervention, and confederative constitutional arrangements emphasizing autonomy for the member cantons.[42]

Several other countries (mostly small ones) have ten ministries or less. A more usual figure is around twelve, found in countries as different in size, location, political configuration, and level of development as the United States, Panama, Portugal, Thailand, Japan, Colombia, and the Netherlands. Another cluster occurs around twenty, including Indonesia, South Africa, South Korea, Morocco, Canada, Greece, and Burma. Also in this group are several countries, among them Burundi, Iran, Israel, Madagascar, Mexico, Nepal, and the Philippines, which had fewer units earlier, indicating a tendency toward gradual proliferation. Among countries having a higher number and more short-range fluctuation in the total are several with parliamentary governments such as Italy, Great Britain, and former or current members of the British Commonwealth, as well as the USSR, the People's Republic of China, Poland, Cuba, and other Communist countries. For the first group the explanation is probably the ease of making changes by action of the cabinet in some parliamentary systems, and in the second group the extensive sweep of direct state responsibility for economic and industrial enterprises. The USSR probably was a record setter both as to fluctuation and total number of ministries. Fainsod gives the tally at intervals during the thirty-year period from the mid-1920s to the mid-1950s, showing only ten at the start, moving up to fifty-nine in 1947, hovering around fifty for several years, and then dropping sharply to twenty-five in 1953.[43] However, during the next thirty-five years the total moved up again dramatically, reaching seventy-seven by 1976 and a high of about eighty in the late 1970s,[44] and then declining somewhat to fifty-seven in the late 1980s shortly before the USSR dissolved. Successor units in the Commonwealth of Independent States (CIS) tend to have considerably smaller totals (in 1993 the number in the Russian Federation was twenty-three, and in the Ukraine twenty-five).

Comparative analysis of ministerial or departmental operational characteristics has been minimal. One landmark study of ministerial careers was undertaken by Jean Blondel, who analyzed available data on more than 20,000 ministers who had been in office throughout the world between 1945 and the mid-1980s.[45] In the context of six geographical areas (Atlantic, communist, Latin

America, Middle East and North Africa, Africa south of the Sahara, and South and East Asia), he presented preliminary generalizations about the social backgrounds of ministers, their career routes to office, their duration in office, and some of the behavioral patterns they exhibited. Two major problems were identified: the prevalent shortness of tenure, and reconciliation of the competing priorities between specialization and representation. Blondel's pessimistic overall assessment is that the ministerial career, in many countries of the contemporary world, "is one of the least attractive of all careers: it is short; it begins and ends by accident; and it places many in positions that do not necessarily correspond to their training or ability."[46]

Relationships among ministries and the process of decision-making within cabinets have received even less attention, most of it confined to Western parliamentary systems. The most informative study[47] reported that no clear-cut model of cabinet structure emerged, but that "the idea of a hierarchical pyramid of individual ministers topped by cabinet committees, topped by cabinet, topped by the prime minister, with implied delegation downwards and upwards referral of all strategic or important decisions" was inaccurate. Instead, most cabinet systems exhibited "interrelated but fragmented decision arenas," with cabinet committees playing critical roles of coordination and conflict resolution and with few decisions being made by the full cabinet.[48] These generalizations were supported by case examples of cabinet structures in seven countries (United Kingdom, Canada, Australia, New Zealand, Denmark, the Netherlands, and Switzerland).

Organizational features other than the lineup of core ministries or departments are likely also to have a significant impact on the bureaucracy. In most countries, an outcropping of administrative agencies has developed that does not fit within the ministerial system. These include central agencies set up for purposes of coordination and control. Sometimes they are units that have split off from parent ministries and are on their way to becoming full-fledged ministries but have not yet arrived. They may be agencies, such as the independent regulatory commissions in the United States, that have deliberately been given an autonomous status because of the nature of the controls they wield over private interests. The most common form of incremental organization in recent decades is the government corporation, which has been popular in many countries displaying wide differences in the role of government in the economy. The corporate form has had a special appeal in the newer nations struggling toward industrialization under governmental auspices. The autonomy often accorded to these public corporations in staffing and related matters may have profound effects not only on that part of the bureaucracy in the corporations but on the remainder of the public service as well.

Variations in the way in which the core ministries and other units of organization are tied to the organs of political leadership are also of obvious significance. These include such differences as those between: unitary and federal arrangements for territorial distribution of governmental powers; presidential and parliamentary systems for organizing executive-legislative relationships; single-party, two-party, and multiparty patterns in political party systems; and various procedures for providing interest group representation in the conduct of administration. All of these choices concerning the structure of government machinery and the conduct of government business have direct and traceable effects on the bureaucracy.

One manifestation of the "neo-institutionalist" movement discussed earlier is a growing interest in examination of these structural features of governmental systems. The most comprehensive treatment up to now is *Organizing Governance, Governing Organizations*, a volume edited by Colin Campbell and B. Guy Peters, reflecting a regeneration of concern with institutions, "while retaining some better understanding of the behavior of individuals within organizations and institutions."[49] The contributors provide not only general analyses of organizational issues and their cross-national dimensions, but also treatments of experience in specific countries (including Great Britain, the United States, Canada, Australia, Switzerland, and Bangladesh).

The relative capabilities of parliamentary and presidential systems has been receiving increased attention. The most thorough analysis to date is contained in a 1993 publication edited by R. Kent Weaver and Bert A. Rockman,[50] who contribute introductory and summing up essays. Other participants in this project offer cross-national analyses which assess the role of government institutions in influencing outcomes in various policy areas (energy, environment, industrial change, pensions, trade, military security, and others). These comparative case studies are not limited to the impact of presidential, parliamentary, or hybrid institutional arrangements, but examine also other explanatory factors affecting government capabilities. As the editors state, this study "addresses a highly complex set of questions wrapped within a disarmingly simple one—whether parliamentary government is superior to the separation of powers." They do conclude that differences among parliamentary regimes are at least as important as differences between parliamentary and presidential regimes, but observe that "as with most simple questions, we find no simple answers." Their summary comment is that institutions "do not provide panaceas, but they do have predictable risks and opportunities. Serious debate about institutional reform and design must be based on an understanding of the balance between those risks and opportunities."[51]

Other recent undertakings are aimed more directly and explicitly at the issue of relative viability of the parliamentary and presidential options, especially for developing countries. Initiated primarily by Abdo Baaklini of the State University of New York at Albany and Fred W. Riggs of the University of Hawaii, a Committee on Viable Constitutionalism (COVICO) was set up in 1993, with about twenty founding members.[52] Its program includes exchanges of information, seminars, publications, and other activities to identify the essentials for constitutional viability of various options for democratic governance—parliamentary, presidential, or mixed. At the University of California, Irvine, the Research Program on Democratization convened a conference on the design of constitutions, also held in 1993, with similar objectives.[53] These are indications of a growing interest in such institutional issues, which will receive more attention later.

Public Sector Employment

Another factor in the organizational setting is variation in the extent and distribution of public employment from one country to another. Reliable and up-to-date information is difficult to locate, particularly for developing countries. The most recent available data has been compiled by Donald C. Rowat, showing public employees as a percentage of population in twenty-one developed countries and thirty-six developing countries.[54] The range in total public sector employment is from a high of 16.31 percent in Sweden to a low of 0.83 percent in Burundi, with the median between five and six percent.

As these statistics show, the extent of public employment is considerably higher in the developed countries (at around eight percent of the population) than in the developing countries (around four percent). Japan (at 4.44 percent) has by far the lowest proportion among the developed group, with the United Kingdom and Denmark ranking behind Sweden at the top. Most of the developing countries are below Japan (exceptions are Mauritius, Sri Lanka, Argentina, Panama, Bahamas, and Egypt). Ranked next to Burundi in the lowest category (all with under three percent) are Senegal, Benin, Guatemala, Uganda, India, Tanzania, Liberia, and Kenya.

Another important difference between the developed and the developing countries as shown in this compilation is that in the developed group more public employees work for state and local units of government, whereas in the developing group more work for central governments. Employment in public enterprises shows marked variation in both developed and developing countries, with Great Britain and Sri Lanka having high proportions, for example, and the United States and Guatemala having proportions that are quite low.

It is possible to reach some very general conclusions from the available data, such as that the developed countries have larger but more decentralized public sectors and the developing countries have smaller but more centralized ones, but the information is too incomplete and spotty for comprehensive across-the-board analysis.[55] Nevertheless, in dealing with any particular country, it is important to profile its public sector employment as precisely as possible in relation to others based on the data at hand.

Civil Service Systems

Each nation faces the necessity of organizing for the management of its civilian public sector employees. The resulting civil service systems have frequently been described individually, but until recently little comparative analysis has appeared. Beginning in the early 1990s, a major effort was launched with this objective under the auspices of a research consortium initiated by university professors in the United States and the Netherlands and later joined by participants from several other countries. The focus of this research is on civil service systems rather than on more inclusive public service systems with military components added, although attention is given to civil-military relationships as well as to the political and social environment in which the civil service functions.

The first publication of this consortium[56] has background chapters on the need for comparative research, on theory and methodology, and on data requirements and availability. Other contributions deal with the history and structure of civil service systems, with contextual factors, with the special characteristics of civil service in developing countries, and with changes and transformations either in process or anticipated. A concluding chapter by the editors summarizes the analytic framework and synthesizes the contents.

Because of the need for selectivity in discussing this research, and because it is most relevant for our purposes, I will concentrate on my own contribution, which is an attempt to present broad groupings, or configurations, of existing civil service systems.[57] The intent is to identify categories that will account for most, but not necessarily all, contemporary national systems. Five variables are used in the analysis: (1) relation of the civil service system to the political regime; (2) socio-economic context of the system; (3) focus for personnel management functions in the system; (4) qualification requirements for entering and performing as a member of the system; and (5) sense of mission held by members of the system. Several points on a continuum for each of these variables are then utilized to describe particular civil service systems. For example, with regard to relationship to the political regime, the options are ruler responsive, single party responsive, majority party responsive, and military responsive. The options as to the organizational focus for personnel management in the system are assignment of this responsibility directly to or under the chief executive, placing it in an independent agency such as a civil service commission, dividing it by function between two separate units, or decentralizing it on a ministry-by-ministry basis. Four groupings or configurations of civil service systems are derived from the interactions among these five variables: *ruler trustworthy, party controlled, policy receptive,* and *collaborative.* Table 1 summarizes this analysis, and includes examples of civil service systems in each configuration.

My assumption is that most, but not all, existing national civil service systems can be appropriately placed in one of these categories. Exceptions are

TABLE 1 Configurations of Civil Service Systems

Variables	Ruler trustworthy	Party controlled	Policy receptive	Collaborative
Relation to political regime	Ruler responsive	Single party or majority party responsive	Majority party responsive	Military responsive
Socio-economic context	Traditional	Corporatist or planned centrally	Pluralist competitive or mixed	Corporatist or planned centrally
Focus for personnel management	Chief executive or ministry-by-ministry	Chief executive or ministry-by-ministry	Independent agency or divided	Chief executive or ministry-by-ministry
Qualification requirements	Patrimony	Party loyalty or party patronage	Professional performance	Bureaucratic determination
Sense of mission	Compliance or guidance	Compliance or cooperation	Policy or constitutional responsiveness	Cooperation or guidance
Examples	Saudi Arabia Iran Brunei	China Cuba Egypt	France Great Britain United States	South Korea Indonesia Ghana

instances in which political transition is currently too drastic and unpredictable for placement (as in former republics of the USSR, countries of Eastern Europe, and South Africa), countries with a recent history of pendulum-like swings from one form of political regime to another (such as Brazil, Nigeria, and Turkey), and countries with extremely chaotic political situations (such as Haiti or Zaire). Recognition also needs to be given to the possibility of future emergence of new configurations. In any event, one organizational factor affecting the conduct of public administration in any country will be the nature of its civil service system.

THE ECOLOGY OF ADMINISTRATION

An ecological approach to public administration is usually traced to the writings of John M. Gaus,[58] who drew upon the work of sociologists during the 1920s concerned with the interdependence of human life and its surrounding environment, who had in turn borrowed from botanists and zoologists seeking to explain how plant and animal organisms adapt to their environments. Such an approach, in his words, "builds . . . quite literally from the ground up; from the elements of a place—soils, climate, location, for example—to the people who live there—their numbers and ages and knowledge, and the ways of physical and social technology by which from the place and in relationship with one another, they get their living."[59] Gaus was primarily concerned with identifying key ecological factors for an understanding of contemporary American public administration, and he explored a list of factors which he found to be particularly useful: people, place, physical technology, social technology, wishes and ideas, catastrophe, and personality.

If ecological considerations were helpful in studying one's own administrative system, they would obviously be doubly important in comparative studies, and this was recognized early by Riggs and other pioneers in the field.[60] Later, R. K. Arora stressed that cross-cultural administrative analysis "should focus upon the interaction between an administrative system and its external environment, and also study the dynamics of socio-administrative change in the context of such interaction."[61] In Arora's judgment, more success had been achieved in the treatment of the social environmental impact on the administrative system than in the reciprocal treatment of the bureaucracy's influence on the environment, and he called for a more balanced interactional analysis.[62]

We will accept this recommendation that a systematic effort should be made to relate public administration to its environment, in much the same way that the science of ecology is concerned with the mutual relations between organisms and their environment. Of course, social institutions are not living organisms, so the parallel is at most suggestive. The point is that bureaucracies, as well as other political and administrative institutions, can be better understood if the surrounding conditions, influences, and forces that shape and modify them are identified and ranked to the extent possible in the order of relative importance, and if the reciprocal impact of these institutions on their environment is also explored.

The environment of bureaucracy may be visualized as a series of concentric circles, with bureaucracy at the center. The smallest circle generally has the most decisive influence, and the larger circles represent a descending order of importance as far as the bureaucracy is concerned. We may view the largest circle as representing all of society or the general social system. The next circle represents the economic system or the economic aspects of the social system. The inner circle is the political system; it encloses the administrative subsystem and the bureaucracy as one of its elements.

Without undertaking any full exploration of the ecology of public administration, we can try to pick out the environmental factors impinging on bureaucracy that would seem to be most helpful in answering the questions posed earlier regarding bureaucracies. Comparative analysis requires a preliminary classification of the nation-states in which these bureaucracies function, based on the environmental factors that are deemed to be most decisive.

The basic categories employed here are not original; they are already widely known and used. The first classification is "developed" and "developing" societies, referring to clusters of characteristics, primarily of a social and economic nature, that are identified with development as contrasted to underdevelopment or partial development. This is a classification based on the outer environmental circles, with consequences for the bureaucracy that may be considered secondary.

"Development" is admittedly debatable as a criterion for classification, with drawbacks as well as advantages. For these reasons, the following chapter is devoted entirely to a detailed discussion of the concept of development and related concepts such as modernization and change. Pending this review as to various meanings given to development and related terms, and recognizing that such terms in themselves have invidious implications, we can nevertheless capture the essential theme from this statement by Milton Esman: "Development denotes a major societal transformation, a change in system states, along the continuum from peasant and pastoral to industrial organization. The assimilation and institutionalization of modern physical and social technology are critical ingredients. These qualitative changes affect values, behavior, social structure, economic organization and political process."[63]

In terms employed by sociologists such as Talcott Parsons who use a structural-functional approach to study social systems, the more traditional, less developed societies would tend to be predominantly ascriptive, particularistic, and diffuse. In other words, they would confer status based on birth or inherited station rather than personal achievement; they would favor a narrow base rather than more generalized bases for making social decisions; and given social structures would be likely to perform a large number of functions rather than a few. More developed modern societies, on the other hand, would tend to be achievement-oriented, universalistic, and specific.[64]

The words "developing" or "less developed," referring to the countries that are undergoing this process of social transformation, seem preferable to such alternative adjectives as backward, poor, undeveloped, underdeveloped, emerging, transitional, and even expectant. This profusion of terms has led to the facetious comment that the terminology develops faster than do the developing countries. We shall consider developing, less developed, emerging, and transitional as acceptable and more or less interchangeable.

The concept of development does not purport to sort societies into classes of opposites, but only to locate them along a continuum. Our interest is to compare countries that are commonly placed toward the upper end of a scale of development with some of those rated lower on the development scale. Rather than using a simple two-way differentiation between more and less developed countries, it will be helpful and more discriminating to group contemporary nation-states into four tiers as to their developmental levels, with the upper two tiers containing more developed and the lower two tiers less developed countries. The group of countries generally conceded to be in the first tier of most highly or fully developed is quite small compared to the total number of existing nation-states, and these countries are geographically concentrated. They include Great Britain and a few members of the British Commonwealth, such as Canada and Australia, most of the countries of western continental Europe, the United States, and perhaps only Japan among the nations of the so-called non-Western world. The former USSR was generally considered as belonging to this group, whereas it is doubtful that any of its successor states currently should be. Some of them, however, such as the Russian Federation, along with a number of countries in southern and eastern Europe, the so-called "Little Tigers" of Asia (South Korea, Taiwan, Hong Kong, and Singapore), and perhaps the People's Republic of China because of its exceptional potential and remarkable recent advances, qualify as second tier examples. The overwhelming majority of present-day countries fall into the third or fourth tiers, indicating that although they are all less developed, significant differences exist between those in the third tier (such as Mexico and Turkey) and those in the fourth (such as Haiti and Bangladesh).

The second major classification is one of political systems (using types derived from suggestions by students of comparative politics) for both the more developed and the less developed countries. These political system differences are assumed to encompass environmental factors that have the most direct and consequential effects on bureaucracies.

The concept of political culture has become a key tool for attempts to differentiate among political systems. Defined as "the values, attitudes, orientations, myths, and beliefs that people have about politics and government and particularly about the legitimacy of government and their relation to government,"[65] political culture is assumed to have a major impact on the direction of national political development, and numerous formulations have been offered classifying political systems in relation to the political cultures nurturing them. An early and influential example was use by Almond and Verba of "the civic culture" as a label identifying political characteristics shared by Great Britain and the United States.[66] Ronald Inglehart has recently reviewed the linkage between cultural orientations and their major political consequences in more than a score of societies, mostly located in Europe but including Japan and a few developing countries.[67] One important product of "neo-institutionalism," with its emphasis on the importance of "the state," is the identification by Metin Heper and his associates of four ideal types of polities based on their degree of "statenesss," and linkage of these types of polity with corresponding types of bureaucracy.[68] These are examples of classification systems that are intended either to be global in their application, or concentrate primarily on developed countries. Other studies have focused on the classification of polities in less developed countries. A recent illustration is Andrain's *Political Change in the Third World*,[69] which draws upon earlier work by David Apter in suggesting four models for such political systems (folk, bureaucratic-authoritarian, reconciliation, and mobilization), with each having implications for the exercise of political power and the processing of policy issues. This is the latest in a lengthy series of proposals for classifying the polities of developing countries, dating as far back as 1960, which will be discussed in more detail in Chapter 7.

The purpose in mentioning these examples is not to offer a comprehensive survey of all the relevant suggestions for classifying political systems but only to indicate the variety of options available. My assumption is that special emphasis should be placed on political regime characteristics as a variable in the explanation of differences in patterns of behavior among national public bureaucracies. Most of our attention later is devoted to examining the interactions between political regimes of various types and their bureaucracies, within the two broader categories first of developed and then developing countries. For developed countries, these political regime characteristics can be identified on a case-by-case basis, or by considering pairs or small groups of countries with similar or closely related political regimes. For the more numerous developing countries, an essential preliminary step is to group them according to some appropriate political regime classification scheme, prior to dealing with country-by-country variations.

This emphasis on the importance of political regime type in understanding national public bureaucracies is not based on the assumption that regime type is the only variable explaining differences in bureaucratic behavior, or that it is necessarily the most important in every instance. Numerous other factors undoubtedly are also relevant, with the mix of variables differing from country to country. Among those which have previously been studied or suggested (in addition to degree of "stateness," as already mentioned) are historical bureaucratic traditions; colonial legacies; institutional inertia; and external forces exerted by other governments, international agencies, or multinational corporations.[70] The factor receiving the most concentrated attention recently is the issue of the appropriate model for administrative reform to make government work better, which in turn is derived from differing views about governance. B. Guy Peters has provided the most comprehensive and informative analysis of this matter in *The Future of Governing: Four Emerging Models:*[71]

> Few governments have remained untouched by the wave of reform that has swept through the public sector over the past several decades. The magnitude of reform undertaken in most political systems may have been unprecedented, at least during peacetime, but the reforms themselves have also tended to be extremely piecemeal and unsystematic. The absence of clear vision and integrated strategies may partly explain why the results of the reforms have tended to disappoint so many of their advocates.

Therefore, he undertakes to explicate "several more integrated visions of possible futures for the state and its bureaucracy."[72] He offers four such models of government (market, participative, flexible, and deregulated), indicating major features of each, as shown in Table 2.[73]

Cross-national explorations of the relative importance of all such factors should be encouraged, and for an understanding of any single nation-state bureaucracy all of the pertinent factors should be investigated. The reason for devoting special attention to relationships between political regime types and bureaucracies is that the variable of regime type will always be present and is likely to be highly significant.

MODELS OF ADMINISTRATIVE SYSTEMS

Social scientists have suggested using models, corresponding to real world phenomena, to guide investigation and analysis of administrative practices that actually prevail in existing polities. A well-chosen model highlights general characteristics and their interrelationships in a way that facilitates the gathering and interpretation of data about whatever subject matter is being studied. The inevitability of using models of some kind for systematic study of any topic has often been pointed out.[74] The problem lies in choosing a model that matches reality closely enough to aid in comprehending it.

We do have an array of proposed models for the conduct of public administration and the operations of bureaucracy in a variety of countries, with some intended to be applicable on a global basis and others designed to focus more directly on either developed or developing countries. Heper's 1987 formu-

TABLE 2 Major Features of the Four Models

	Market Government	Participative Government	Flexible Government	Deregulated Government
Principal diagnosis	Monopoly	Hierarchy	Permanence	Internal regulation
Structure	Decentralization	Flatter organizations	"Virtual organizations"	No particular recommendation
Management	Pay for performance; other private-sector techniques	TQM; teams	Managing temporary personnel	Greater managerial freedom
Policy-making	Internal markets; market incentives	Consultation; negotiations	Experimentation	Entrepreneurial government
Public interest	Low cost	Involvement; consultation	Low cost; coordination	Creativity; activism

lation falls into the first category. He suggests four basic types of polity based on degree of "stateness" and identifies six types of bureaucracy corresponding to these polity types. Table 3 summarizes this model building effort.[75] It will be useful and will be referred to from time to time, as an aid in characterizing certain systemic political-administrative relationships, but it has the drawback in my view of overemphasizing "stateness" by selecting this factor as the basic one for classifying polities and bureaucracies both historically and currently.

The most utilized model of bureaucracy is the Weberian or "classic" model which has already been discussed. Although not limited to them, this model applies essentially to the countries of Western Europe, which are the prototypes for developed or modernized polities. This classic model of bureaucracy not only incorporates the essential structural characteristics that have been postulated as definitive of bureaucracy as a form of organization—hierarchy, differentiation, and qualification. It also specifies a network of interrelated characteristics, both structural and behavioral, which identify bureaucracy of this type. An underlying assumption is that the pattern of authority, which lends legitimacy to the system, will be legal-rational rather than traditional or charismatic, and that within the bureaucracy rational means will be used to comply with the commands of the legitimate authority. Bureaucracy is above all a form of organization dedicated to the concept of rationality, and to the conduct of administration on the basis of relevant knowledge. This calls for a series of arrangements. Recruitment is based on achievement as demonstrated competitively rather than on ascription, and similar criteria are to determine subsequent movement within the bureaucracy. Service in the bureaucracy is a career for professionals, who are salaried and have tenured status, subject to discipline or removal only on specified grounds following specified procedures. Administrative roles are highly specialized and differentiated; spheres of competence are well defined and hierarchical relationships are thoroughly understood. The bureaucracy is not an autonomous unit in the political system but is responsive to external controls from legitimized political authority, although there are tendencies toward evasion and self-direction.

This simplified model has been widely used to guide descriptions of, and comparisons among, bureaucracies in modern nation-states, even though it does not accurately depict any of them. The closeness of fit varies among political system subtypes in the modernized polities. The greatest conformity is in such bureaucracies as those in Germany and France, which we have designated as "classic" bureaucracies. The model is essentially acceptable when it is applied to numerous other developed countries with a Western political tradition, including not only Great Britain and the United States but also Canada, Australia, New Zealand, and several of the small European countries. As we move away from these core countries toward other polities which have been categorized as developed but which are more removed from the Western European political orbit, this classic model becomes increasingly less applicable. Nevertheless,

TABLE 3 Types of Polity and Corresponding Types of Bureaucracy

Personalist polity	Ideological polity		Liberal polity	Praetorian polity
State = Ruler	State = Bureaucracy	State = Party	Absence of a predominant state	No state
Personal servant bureaucracy "Machine model" bureaucracy	"Bonapartist" or *Rechtsstaat* bureaucracy	Party-controlled bureaucracy with residues of historical bureaucratic ruling tradition	Weberian "legal-rational" bureaucracy	Spoils system bureaucracy is part of a Hegelian civil society

Source: Reprinted by permission of Greenwood Publishing group, Westport, CT, from *The State and Public Bureaucracies* edited by Metin Heper, Figure 1, p. 20. Copyright © 1987 by Metin Heper.

despite substantial divergences, the model was generally considered helpful for purposes of comparison in analysis of the former USSR, and it will be used here in our examination of the case of Japan.

When bureaucracies in the less developed countries become the object of attention, however, the inadequacy of the classic model becomes so apparent that it is nearly always abandoned in favor of models chosen because they are presumed to correspond much more closely to actuality in these societies. The best known and most elaborate model has been formulated by Fred Riggs in his "prismatic-sala" combination for developing countries and their administrative subsystems.[76] No brief summary can do justice to the intricacies of this model or familiarize the uninitiated with the specialized vocabulary used in presenting it, but we can indicate its dimensions and implications.[77]

There is some ambiguity concerning the link Riggs sees between the prismatic model and existing societies. "Fused" and "differentiated" societies are models constructed deductively from contrasting assumptions about the relationship between structures and the number of functions they perform. A structure is "functionally diffuse" when it performs a large number of functions, "functionally specific" when it performs a limited number of functions. The "fused" hypothetical model is of a society in which all component structures are highly diffuse; in the "diffracted" model component structures are highly specific.[78] These models cannot be found in the real world, but they "can serve a heuristic purpose by helping us to describe real world situations." Some real world societies may resemble the fused model, others the diffracted.

The "prismatic" model, as originally presented by Riggs, is of the same hypothetical type as the fused and the diffracted. Designed to represent a situation intermediate between the fused and diffracted ends of a continuum, it combines relatively fused traits with relatively diffracted ones. It refers to a social system that is semidifferentiated, standing midway between an undifferentiated fused society and a highly differentiated diffracted society. Although its characteristics are derived deductively also, there may be societies that have characteristics resembling those of the model. Logically speaking, it would seem quite plain that no actual society would be either completely fused or completely diffracted; all would be to some degree prismatic in the sense of being intermediate. On a scale measuring the degree of functional specificity of structures, presumably the pure prismatic model as originally conceived by Riggs represented a society at midpoint between the fused and diffracted models, although this was not made entirely clear.

In *Prismatic Society Revisited*, Riggs complicates matters further by introducing new connotations for "prismatic." He now refers to his original conceptualization as a mistaken "one-dimensional approach," and offers a new definition of prismatic society, based on a "two-dimensional approach." The original dimension was degree of differentiation, ranging from undifferentiated through semidifferentiated to highly differentiated societies, with the fused, prismatic, and diffracted models corresponding to these three stages along the dimension of differentiation.

The second dimension now introduced has to do with the degree of integration among structures in a society that is differentiated. This dimension is insignificant in the fused society model because it is undifferentiated, and the possibility of malintegration among social structures does not arise. With the process of differentiation comes the possibility of malintegration or lack of coordination among social structures. Riggs illustrates by comparing the problem to that of coordinating sounds from the different specialized instruments in a symphony orchestra. When the conductor's baton provides proper direction for coordination, the cacophony of instruments being tuned up or playing out of synchronization is replaced by the sounds of a symphonic performance. Integration has been achieved in the differentiated sounds of the various instruments. Likewise, differentiated social systems can be ranked on a malintegrated-integrated scale.

The problem is not with recognition of the possibility that differentiated societies may differ as to their degree of integration, or that very highly differentiated societies may turn out to be also extremely malintegrated, with dire consequences. The terminological difficulty is that Riggs has chosen to redefine the prismatic model by expanding it to include any society that is differentiated but malintegrated. A corresponding reinterpretation of the diffracted model makes it refer to any society that is differentiated and integrated. Hence prismatic and diffracted are no longer models next to one another on a one-dimensional scale based on degree of differentiation. Instead the usage now suggested for these terms would have them refer to any society that is not fused, at any point along a scale of differentiation, with the distinction being that prismatic societies are malintegrated and diffracted societies are integrated. This in turn leads to the suggestion that prefixes be attached to both the prismatic and diffracted types to indicate stages in the degree of differentiation. These shifts in terminology are indicated by Figure 1, showing first the one-dimensional and then the two-dimensional approach.[79]

The advantage claimed by Riggs is that the two-dimensional approach recognizes that "prismatic" conditions may occur in societies at any level of differentiation, or to put it in terms of contemporary nation-states, such conditions need not be confined to less developed countries, but may occur in developed countries as well. This enables him to explore recent phenomena in the United States and other developed nations that may manifest increasing malintegration "in the form of urban crises, race riots, student uprisings, popular apathy, the hippy phenomenon, and the profound turbulence wrought by a continuing war in Vietnam."[80]

Our concern, however, is primarily the value of the prismatic model in understanding developing societies, which is what Riggs originally had in mind.

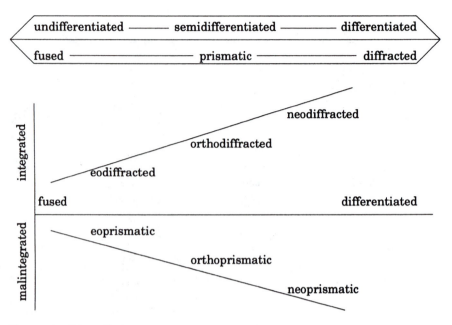

FIGURE 1   Prismatic types.

Although Riggs has stressed the deductive nature of these models, he has also emphasized their relevance for understanding phenomena in real societies, saying that he has been "fascinated by the prismatic model not only as an intellectual game but also as a device that might eventually help us understand more about administrative behavior in transitional societies."[81]

Despite the shift in usage by Riggs, clearly his claim for relevance is still focused on the type of prismatic society that is semidifferentiated and mal-integrated, that is, on what his latest formulation labels orthoprismatic society. For purposes of brevity and clarity, in discussing the prismatic model we will be referring essentially to the societal type which he earlier simply called prismatic and now prefers to call orthoprismatic. This appears to be quite in keeping with his own emphasis, as indicated by this statement: "Since prevalent conditions in third world countries provided the initial impetus and data for creation of the prismatic model, it seems fitting to apply the label 'orthoprismatic' to the characteristic syndrome of the kind of malintegrated differentiated society that we find best illustrated in some, though not necessarily all, the countries of the third world."[82]

The prismatic model in its entirety deals with the full range of social phenomena and behavior, subsuming political and administrative aspects. In other words, it is a model pertaining to the ecology of administration in a type of society. This model is "intrinsically paradoxical."[83] Riggs examines the economic sector (describing it as a "bazaar-canteen" pattern), the elite groupings ("kaleidoscopic stratification"), social structures, symbol systems, and political power patterns. He then turns more specifically to public administration in prismatic society, and evolves the sala model for the administrative subsystem. In line with the general configuration of the prismatic model, administrative functions in such a society "may be performed both by concrete structures oriented primarily toward this function and also by other structures lacking this primary orientation."[84] Such a situation calls for an alternative to conventional ways of thinking about the conduct of public administration, since these are related to experience in Western societies, which are closer to the diffracted model (or neodiffracted in the more recent formulation).

Riggs is interested in bureaucracies and how they differ in his models. He uses what he calls a "simplified structural definition" of bureaucracy, similar to the one adopted for our purposes, which recognizes wide operational variations among bureaucracies which meet the basic structural requirements. Traditional bureaucracies in societies closer to the fused model were functionally quite diffuse: "each official typically performed a wide range of functions, affecting political and economic as well as administrative functions." In well-integrated differentiated societies approximating the neodiffracted model, bureaucracies have become much more functionally specific "as the chief—though by no means the only—agents for performing administrative tasks." Indeed, Riggs strongly suggests that such a "functionally narrowed bureaucracy," effectively controlled by other political institutions, "may well be one of the requisite institutional means for achieving integration in a differentiated society."[85] Bureaucracies in the transitional prismatic societies are intermediate as to the degree of their functional specialization, and they contribute to malintegration by not meshing well with other institutions in the political system.

In discussing the locus of bureaucratic action in each of the three principal models, Riggs suggests a choice of terms for each one, as well as a general term to cover them all. He chooses "bureau" for the more comprehensive purpose, and suggests "chamber" to denote the fused bureau, and "office" the diffracted one. For the prismatic bureau, he employs the word "sala," used in Spanish and other languages (including Arabic and Thai) to refer to various kinds of rooms, among them government offices, thus suggesting the "interlocking mixture of the diffracted office and the fused chamber which we can identify as the prismatic bureau."[86]

The profile of administration and the role of the bureaucracy in the sala as drawn by Riggs rest basically on his treatment of the power structure in prismatic society. He finds that the scope of bureaucratic power, in the sense of the range of the values affected, is only intermediate in the prismatic setting, but that the weight of bureaucratic power (referring to the extent of participation in making decisions) is very heavy as compared to either the fused or diffracted models. This is particularly so in polities that have patterned their bureaucratic systems after more diffracted foreign examples. Rates of political and bureaucratic growth are imbalanced in prismatic society. There the bureaucracy has the advantage in competition with other political institutions, which might be better able to control the bureaucracy in more diffracted societies, whether pluralistic or totalitarian. The weight of bureaucratic power in prismatic society tempts bureaucrats to interfere in the political process.

A second and corollary proposition concerning prismatic administration is that the heavy weight of bureaucratic power lowers administrative efficiency, in the sense of cost relative to accomplishment, with the result that such an administration is less efficient than that in either a fused or a diffracted system. The sala is associated with unequal distribution of services, institutionalized corruption, inefficiency in rule application, nepotism in recruitment, bureaucratic enclaves dominated by motives of self-protection, and, in general, a pronounced gap between formal expectations and actual behavior. Administration in the sala model is "basically wasteful and prodigal." Many factors combine in prismatic society to "heighten administrative profligacy." Riggs concedes that this is a "gloomy view" but maintains it is one which "seems to grow out of the logic of the prismatic model."[87]

Influential though it has been, this prismatic-sala model of Riggs' has also received much adverse criticism, particularly from those who object to the pessimistic tone admitted to by Riggs himself. R. K. Arora discusses at some length the "negative character" of the prismatic model, claiming that it has a Western bias, and that the terms chosen to describe prismatic theory are value-laden, emphasizing only the negative aspects of prismatic behavior.[88] Michael L. Monroe has described prismatic theory as reflecting standards from a Western frame of reference, and faults Riggs for overlooking evidence of prismatic behavior in countries such as the United States.[89] E. H. Valsan[90] and R. S. Milne[91] have argued that "formalism," meaning in Riggsian terms the gap between what is formally prescribed and actually practiced, may have positive as well as negative consequences, depending on the circumstances. These reactions have undoubtedly influenced Riggs in making the modifications contained in *Prismatic Society Revisited*. It should be noted, however, that Riggs never has made any claim about how well the sala model fits any existing transitional society, and indeed has emphasized a need to research the extent to which the sala attributes actually are to be found in particular developing countries. All he has asserted is that his model-building effort "rests on a substratum of empiricism."[92]

Before exploring the utility of these models, we devote the following two chapters to treatment of two exceedingly important background factors: the concepts of modernization, development, and change; and the historical anteced-ents of administration in contemporary nation-states.

NOTES

1. For a fuller explanation, see Ferrel Heady and Sybil L. Stokes, eds., *Papers in Comparative Public Administration* (Ann Arbor, MI: Institute of Public Administration, The University of Michigan, 1962), pp. 10–11. William J. Siffin has explored the issue as to whether the structural bureaucratic perspective deserves continued use and concludes that it does merit further reliance in traveling what he calls the "low road" to science, equivalent to what others have referred to as "middle-range" theory. Even though he concedes the limited capacity of structuralism as a tool, Siffin argues that abandoning it will not help the situation much. See his "Bureaucracy: The Problem of Methodology and the 'Structural' Approach," *Journal of Comparative Administration* 2, No. 4 (1971): 471–503.

2. Fritz Morstein Marx, *The Administrative State* (Chicago: University of Chicago Press, 1957), pp. 16–21.

3. For excellent introductions to this literature, see Robert K. Merton et al., eds., *Reader in Bureaucracy* (New York: Free Press of Glencoe, Inc., 1952); Peter M. Blau, *Bureaucracy in Modern Society* (New York: Random House, 1956); Alfred Diamant, "The Bureaucratic Model: Max Weber Rejected, Rediscovered, Reformed," in Heady and Stokes, *Papers*, pp. 59–96; Henry Jacoby, *The Bureaucratization of the World* (Berkeley, CA: University of California Press, 1973).

4. Both Laski and Von Mises are quoted in Wallace S. Sayre, "Bureaucracies: Some Contrasts in Systems," *Indian Journal of Public Administration* 10, No. 2 (1964): 219.

5. Ferrel Heady, "Bureaucratic Theory and Comparative Administration," *Administrative Science Quarterly* 3, No. 4 (1959): 509–525.

6. Victor A. Thompson, *Modern Organization* (New York: Alfred A. Knopf, Inc., 1961), pp. 3–4.

7. Richard H. Hall, "Intraorganizational Structural Variation: Application of the Bureaucratic Model," *Administrative Science Quarterly* 7, No. 3 (1962): 295–308.

8. Carl Joachim Friedrich, *Man and His Government* (New York: McGraw-Hill Book Company, 1963), p.471. For a fuller presentation of Friedrich's views on bureaucracy, see in particular Chap. 18, "The Political Elite and Bureaucracy," and Chap. 26, "Taking Measures and Carrying On: Bureaucracy."

9. Carl Joachim Friedrich, *Constitutional Government and Democracy*, 4th ed. (Boston: Blaisdell Publishing Company, 1968), pp. 44–45.

10. S. N. Eisenstadt, "Bureaucracy, Bureaucratization, and Debureaucratization," *Administrative Science Quarterly* 4, No. 3 (1959):302–320. He contrasts this preferred type of equilibrium with two other less desirable main possibilities, which he labels bureaucratization and debureaucratization, each of which results from patterns of aberrant bureaucratic behavior which overextend the role of bureaucracy, in the first instance, and weaken or subvert it in the second.

11. Robert Merton, "Bureaucratic Structure and Personality," in *Social Theory and Social Structure* (New York: Free Press of Glencoe, Inc., 1949), Chap. 5; reprinted in *Reader in Bureaucracy*, pp. 361–371.

12. Morstein Marx, *The Administrative State*, pp. 25–28.

13. Michel Crozier, *The Bureaucratic Phenomenon* (Chicago: University of Chicago Press, 1964), pp. 4–5.
14. Eisenstadt, "Bureaucracy, Bureaucratization, and Debureaucratization," p. 303.
15. Blau, *Bureaucracy in Modern Society*, p. 60.
16. *Ibid.*, p. 58: "To administer a social organization according to purely technical criteria of rationality is irrational, because it ignores the nonrational aspects of social conduct."
17. "Most writers have kept these aspects distinct . . . and have not attempted any rigorous analysis or formal definition of bureaucracy. They have been content to take some selection of structural, behavioral, and purposive aspects as characterizing a bureaucratic organization." D. S. Pugh et al., "A Conceptual Scheme for Organizational Analysis," *Administrative Science Quarterly* 8, No. 3 (1963): 297.
18. Ferrel Heady, "Bureaucratic Theory and Comparative Administration," *Administrative Science Quarterly* 3, No. 4(1959): 509–525.
19. Morroe Berger, "Bureaucracy East and West," *Administrative Science Quarterly* 1, No. 4 (1957):518–529.
20. For a fuller discussion, see Ferrel Heady, "Recent Literature on Comparative Public Administration," *Administrative Science Quarterly* 5, No. 1 (1960):134–154.
21. Pugh et al., "A Conceptual Scheme for Organizational Analysis," pp. 298 ff.
22. As Friedrich has pointed out, the problems presented by the behavioral aspects of bureaucracy are considerably more complex than those associated with the structural aspects. He observes that

> although a certain similarity is observable, the behavior of bureaucrats varies widely in time and place without there being any clear-cut pattern of development. Nor is this fact to be wondered at. The behavior of all persons in a particular cultural context is bound to be molded by the values and beliefs prevalent in that culture. Thus the Chinese official, motivated by the doctrine of Confucius and his followers, will be much more concerned with good manners than the Swiss official, while the latter, motivated by the teachings of Christianity and more especially (typically) by a Protestant and Pietist version of Christian beliefs, will be more concerned with honesty and duty.

Friedrich, *Man and His Government*, p. 470.
23. Crozier, *The Bureaucratic Phenomenon*, p. 210.
24. This formulation of the organizational aspects of bureaucracy has long been identified with Carl J. Friedrich. It was first presented (with Taylor Cole) in *Responsible Bureaucracy: A Study of the Swiss Civil Service* (Cambridge: Harvard University Press, 1932), and appeared more recently in *Man and His Government*, pp. 468–470.
25. *Ibid.*, p. 469.
26. Quoted by Diamant in Heady and Stokes, *Papers*, p. 63.
27. Ramesh K. Arora, *Comparative Public Administration* (New Delhi: Associated Publishing House, 1972), p. 51. Arora has a fuller explanation of the nature of ideal-type constructs.
28. Fred Riggs, for example, states that "it is clear that all contemporary states recognized

by the United Nations have bureaucracies." *Frontiers of Development Administration* (Durham, NC: Duke University Press, 1970), p. 388.

29. This statement continues to be accurate, in my opinion, even though recognition needs to be given to the widespread interest in recent years in trends toward "debureaucratization," with relatively "open" systems of management replacing claims of specialized expertise, and other modifications of earlier orthodoxies of bureaucratization. For a discussion of these modifications in the bureaucratic model, see Demetrious Argyriades, "Bureaucracy and Debureaucratization," in Ali Farazmand, ed., *Handbook of Comparative and Development Public Administration* (New York: Marcel Dekker, 1991), Chapter 40, pp. 567–598.

30. See Kalman Kulcsar, "Deviant Bureaucracies: Public Administration in Eastern Europe and in the Developing Countries," in Farazmand, *Handbook of Comparative and Development Public Administration*, Chapter 41, pp. 587–598.

31. Joseph LaPalombara, "An Overview of Bureaucracy and Political Development," in Joseph LaPalombara, ed., *Bureaucracy and Political Development* (Princeton, NJ: Princeton University Press, 1963), p. 7.

32. *Ibid.*

33. Morstein Marx, "The Higher Civil Service as an Action Group in Western Political Development," *ibid.*, p. 63.

34. I am deliberately excluding "political" appointees in the executive branch, such as heads of agencies; under, deputy, and assistant secretaries; and other officials chosen by and serving at the discretion of the incumbent executive branch political leadership. In this usage, I differ from the preference of Fred W. Riggs, who uses bureaucracy to refer to "all appointed officials regardless of their tenure in office, their civil/military status, or their rank." Riggs, "Bureaucratic Links Between Administration and Politics," in Farazmand, *Handbook of Comparative and Development Public Administration*, Chapter 35, pp. 485–509, at p. 486.

35. As early as 1964, Dwight Waldo found the bureaucratic model useful, stimulating, and provocative. *Comparative Public Administration: Prologue, Problems, and Promise* (Chicago: Comparative Administration Group, American Society for Public Administration, 1964), p. 24. Writing several years later, Arora identified the construct of bureaucracy drawing upon the work of Max Weber as "the single most dominant conceptual framework in the study of comparative administration." *Comparative Public Administration*, p. 37. In 1976 Jong Jun and Lee Sigelman both reaffirmed this preference. Jun called for continued study of "the structures, functions, behaviors, and environments of bureaucracy" in his article "Renewing the Study of Comparative Administration: Some Reflections on the Current Possibilities," *Public Administration Review* 36, No. 6 (1976):641–647, at p. 644. Sigelman stated as his conviction that the future of comparative public administration lay in studies of bureaucracies, in "examinations of the backgrounds, attitudes, and behaviors of bureaucrats and those with whom they interact." "In Search of Comparative Administration," *Public Administration Review* 36, No. 6 (1976):621–625, at p. 624. Guy Peters has reinforced this priority in his more recent book, *Comparing Public Bureaucracies: Problems of Theory and Method* (Tuscaloosa, AL: The University of Alabama Press, 1988).

36. Brian Chapman, *The Profession of Government* (London: George Allen & Unwin, 1959), pp. 48–61.
37. For comprehensive treatments as to how patterns of organization developed in various countries, see Poul Meyer, *Administrative Organization: A Comparative Study of the Organization of Public Administration* (London: Stevens & Sons, 1957); and Jean Blondel, *The Organization of Governments: A Comparative Analysis of Governmental Structures* (London: Sage Publications, 1982), especially Chapter 2, "The Development of Modern Government." For discussions of recent reorganization and reform efforts, refer to Gerald E. Caiden, "Administrative Reform," in Farazmand, *Handbook of Comparative and Development Public Administration*, Chapter 27, pp. 367–380; and B. Guy Peters, "Government Reform and Reorganization in an Era of Retrenchment and Conviction Politics," in Farazmand, *Handbook of Comparative and Development Public Administration*, Chapter 28, pp. 381–403.
38. Richard Rose, *Understanding Big Government* (London: Sage Publications, 1984), p. 157.
39. Blondel, *The Organization of Governments*, p. 176.
40. These are discussed in Rose, *Understanding Big Government*, pp. 177–203.
41. Blondel found that among developing countries, those in Latin America tended to have the fewest ministries and those in the Middle East and Africa the most, with South and Southeast Asia countries in between. *The Organization of Governments*, p. 179.
42. Chapman, *The Profession of Government*, p. 49. Switzerland still has only seven ministries, but this is not a modern record low number. Nepal, for example, had only six ministries in the mid-1970s, although the number has grown considerably since then.
43. Merle Fainsod, *How Russia Is Ruled*, rev. ed. (Cambridge: Harvard University Press, 1964), p. 333.
44. Blondel, *The Organization of Governments*, pp. 189–194.
45. Jean Blondel, *Government Ministers in the Contemporary World* (Beverly Hills, CA: Sage Publications, 1985).
46. *Ibid.*, p. 274.
47. Thomas T. Mackie and Brian W. Hogwood, eds., *Unlocking the Cabinet: Cabinet Structures in Contemporary Perspective* (Beverly Hills, CA: Sage Publications, 1985).
48. *Ibid.*, pp. 31–32.
49. Colin Campbell, S. J., and B. Guy Peters, eds., *Organizing Governance, Governing Organizations* (Pittsburgh: University of Pittsburgh Press, 1988), p. 4. See also George M. Thomas, John W. Meyer, Francisco O. Ramirez, and John Boli, *Institutional Structure: Constituting State, Society, and the Individual* (Beverly Hills, CA: Sage Publications, 1987).
50. R. Kent Weaver and Bert A. Rockman, eds., *Do Institutions Matter? Government Capabilities in the United States and Abroad* (Washington, DC: The Brookings Institution, 1993).
51. *Ibid.*, p. 41.
52. See Committee on Viable Constitutionalism, "Summary Report of Preliminary Meeting, 10–11 June 1993, at Tokai University in Honolulu," 11 pp. mimeo.

53. See the conference program and attached "Notes on the Design of Constitutions," by Harry Eckstein, 15 pp. mimeo.

54. Donald C. Rowat, "Comparing Bureaucracies in Developed and Developing Countries: A Statistical Analysis," prepared for the XIVth World Congress of the International Political Science Association, 1988, 39 pp. mimeographed, at pp. 28 and 29. Rowat presents similar information on smaller groups of nineteen developed democracies and nine developing countries in "Comparisons and Trends," Chap. 25 in Rowat, ed., *Public Administration in Developed Democracies: A Comparative Study* (New York: Marcel Dekker, Inc., 1988), at pp. 442–443.

55. These generalized findings are confirmed by Salvatore Schiavo-Campo in "Reforming the Civil Service," *Finance & Development* (September 1996): 10–13. He adds additional information concerning regional differences, indicating that government employment as a percentage of the population is highest in the developed countries of the Organization for Economic Cooperation (OECD), and becomes progressively lower in Eastern Europe and the former Soviet Union, the Middle East and North Africa, Latin America and the Caribbean, Asia, and Sub-Saharan Africa (where there has been a sharp deterioration since the 1970s). A firmer data base has permitted the publication in the mid-1980s of a detailed statistical study of public employment covering six large democracies—Great Britain, France, Italy, Sweden, West Germany, and the United States. See Richard Rose et al., *Public Employment in Western Nations* (Cambridge: Cambridge University Press, 1985).

56. Hans Bekke, James L. Perry, and Theo A. J. Toonen, eds., *Civil Service Systems in Comparative Perspective* (Bloomington, IN: Indiana University Press, 1996).

57. Ferrel Heady, "Configurations of Civil Service Systems," in Bekke, Perry, and Toonen, *Civil Service Systems in Comparative Perspective*, Part 4, Chapter 10, pp. 207–226.

58. John M. Gaus, *Reflections on Public Administration* (University, AL: University of Alabama Press, 1947).

59. *Ibid.*, pp. 8–9.

60. See, for example, Fred W. Riggs, *The Ecology of Public Administration* (Bombay: Asia Publishing House, 1961); and "Trends in the Comparative Study of Public Administration," *International Review of Administrative Sciences* 28, No. 1 (1962): 9–15.

61. R.K. Arora, *Comparative Public Administration* (New Delhi: Associated Publishing House, 1972), p.168. The subtitle of Arora's book is *An Ecological Perspective.*

62. *Ibid.*, p. 175.

63. Milton J. Esman, "The Politics of Development Administration," in John D. Montgomery and William J. Siffin, eds., *Approaches to Development: Politics, Administration & Change* (New York: McGraw-Hill Book Company, 1966), p. 59.

64. For a fuller discussion of this application of the structural-functional approach, see Riggs, *Administration in Developing Countries* (Boston: Houghton Mifflin, 1964), pp. 19–27.

65. Samuel P. Huntington and Jorge I. Dominguez, "Political Development," Chap. 1, pp. 1–114, in Fred I. Greenstein and Nelson W. Polsby, eds., *Handbook of Political Science*, Volume 3, *Macropolitical Theory* (Reading, MA: Addison-Wesley Publishing Company, 1975), at p. 10.

66. Gabriel A. Almond and Sidney Verba, *The Civic Culture* (Princeton, NJ: Princeton University Press, 1963).

67. Ronald Inglehart, "The Renaissance of Political Culture," *American Political Science Review* 82, No. 4 (1988): 1203–1230.

68. Metin Heper, ed., *The State and Public Bureaucracies: A Comparative Perspective* (New York: Greenwood Press, 1987).

69. Charles F. Andrain, *Political Change in the Third World* (Boston: Allen & Unwin, 1988).

70. Debate about variables to explain differences in bureaucratic behavior was stimulated by a 1980 comparative study based on data from Turkey and South Korea, which explored the proposition that the political roles of public bureaucracies vary significantly with political regime types, and suggested that in the two countries studied historical bureaucratic traditions appeared to be more helpful than regime type in explaining variance in bureaucratic roles. See Metin Heper, Chong Lim Kim, and Seong-Tong Pai, "The Role of Bureaucracy and Regime Types: A Comparative Study of Turkish and South Korean Higher Civil Servants," *Administration and Society,* 12, No. 2 (August, 1980):137–157. Fred W. Riggs wrote a rejoinder, "Three Dubious Hypotheses: A Comment on Heper, Kim, and Pai," *Administration and Society,* 12, No. 3 (November, 1980):301–326. He criticized their interpretation of previous writings in comparative public administration (including some of his and some of mine), suggested revised hypotheses from the ones they had used, and reanalyzed their data as supporting the importance of regime type as one of the factors affecting bureaucratic performance. This exchange highlights the need for additional studies, representing a range of regime types and bureaucratic traditions, to identify the relative importance of these two factors, preferably bringing in other variables as well.

71. (Lawrence, KS: University Press of Kansas, 1996).

72. *Ibid.*, p. 16.

73. *Ibid.*, p. 19. For related discussions, see Klaus Konig, "Three Worlds of Public Administration Modernization," *International Journal of Organization Theory and Behaviour* 1, No. 4 (1998): 481–520; and Ali Farazmand, "Professionalism, Bureaucracy, and Modern Governance: A Comparative Analysis," in Farazmand, ed., *Modern Systems of Government: Exploring the Role of Bureaucrats and Politicians* (Thousand Oaks, CA: Sage Publications, 1997), Chapter 2, pp. 48–73.

74. A favorite statement is that of Karl Deutsch: "We are using models, willing or not, whenever we are trying to think systematically about anything at all." In "On Communications Models in the Social Sciences," *Public Opinion Quarterly* 16, No. 3 (1952):356.

75. Heper, *The State and Public Bureaucracies*, p. 20.

76. The most complete and comprehensive formulation is in Riggs' *Administration in Developing Countries*. A more recent updated presentation, including a number of clarifications and modifications, is in *Prismatic Society Revisited* (Morristown, NJ: General Learning Press, 1973).

77. The following sentence gives a hint about the terminological innovation:

> We have seen how the inefficiency of the sala is reinforced by the price indeterminacy of the bazaar-canteen, by pariah entrepreneurship and intrusive access to the elite, by the agglomeration of values, by strategic spending and strategic learning as instruments of elite recruitment, by poly-communalism and poly-normativism, by double-talk, blocked throughputs, bifocalism and equivocacy, by the dependency syndrome, interference complex, and the formalism effect.

Administration in Developing Countries, p. 284.

78. *Ibid.*, pp. 23–24. This relationship between model name and structural characteristics is given incorrectly on p. 23, correctly on p. 24.
79. Riggs, *Prismatic Society Revisited*, pp. 7–8. These illustrations are adapted from those used by Riggs.
80. *Ibid.*, p. 7.
81. Riggs, *Administration in Developing Countries*, p. 401.
82. Riggs, *Prismatic Society Revisited*, p.8.
83. Riggs, *Administration in Developing Countries*, p. 99.
84. *Ibid.*, p. 33.
85. Riggs, *Prismatic Society Revisited*, pp. 24–25.
86. Riggs, *Administration in Developing Countries*, p. 268.
87. *Ibid.*, p. 424. These themes are developed primarily in "Bureaucratic Power and Administrative Prodigality," Chap. 8, pp. 260–285.
88. Arora, *Comparative Public Administration*, pp. 121–123.
89. Michael L. Monroe, "Prismatic Behavior in the United States?" *Journal of Comparative Administration* 2, No. 2 (1970): 229–242.
90. E. H. Valsan, "Positive Formalism: A Desideratum for Development," *Philippine Journal of Public Administration* 12, No. 1 (1968): 3–6.
91. R. S. Milne, "Formalism Reconsidered," *Philippine Journal of Public Administration* 14, No. 1 (1970): 21–30. "Given the existence of a divergence between personal goals and organizational goals, it is possible to create institutional arrangements so that the official's pursuit of self-interest may at the same time promote organizational goals." *Ibid.*, p. 27. Although such "positive formalism" cannot be expected to occur very often in developing countries, Milne suggests that it be practiced as much as is practicable.
92. Riggs, *Administration in Developing Countries*, p. 241. Despite the passage of time since he presented the prismatic-sala model, the contributions of Riggs continue to receive recognition and critiques. See S. R. Maheshwari, *Administrative Thinkers* (New Delhi: Macmillan India Limited, 1998), "Fred W. Riggs," Chapter 19, pp. 215–232. The annual meeting of the International Studies Association held in Washington, DC, during February, 1999, featured an evaluation of his work, including papers on his contributions to comparative public administration by Howard McCurdy, Robert Gamer, Abdo Baaklini, and others. Riggs himself has been writing an "intellectual odyssey," not yet published, which includes an account of how his thinking on comparative public administration has evolved.

3

Concepts of System Transformation

The close linkage between the study of comparative politics and the study of comparative public administration has already been pointed out, as has the fact of disagreement among students of comparative politics concerning key concepts relating to modifications over time in the characteristics of political systems. Because of the extreme importance of these issues to our concerns with the administrative aspects of these systems, this chapter is devoted to an exploration of concepts usually discussed under terms such as "modernization," "development," or "change."

To begin, it must be recorded that the literature on these matters has now grown to be enormous. No attempt at exhaustive treatment of it is made here. Moreover, standardization of terminology has not occurred, so that use of the same words by different commentators may give an appearance of agreement that further analysis shows to be wrong. This lack of standardization also forces upon us a choice as to what terms to use and what meanings to attach to them.

This cluster of concepts does represent, however, a sharing of some basic interests on the part of students of political systems. They are seeking to explain variations on a comparative and chronological basis among nation-states. These concepts have in common the twin goals of comprehensiveness and realism. Comprehensiveness here means global scope with a time dimension, embracing as a minimum political systems which qualify as nation-states, and permitting historical, contemporary, and futuristic treatment of them. Realism means ability to explain what has happened, is happening, or may happen in terms that go beyond a descriptive institutional approach to emphasize the dynamics of political transformation.

Conceptualization along these lines is an integral part of the dramatic revolution in comparative political studies since the end of World War II, and therefore reflects stages in the growth of these studies, with more recent writers building upon or dissenting from what earlier ones have had to say. The focus is on major societal transformations involving a complex of social, economic, and political factors. For our purposes, treatment of these attempts can be grouped, in an order that is chronological to some extent but not completely, under the broad headings of modernization, development, and change.

MODERNIZATION

Modernization is in one sense the most comprehensive of these terms, but it is also, as we shall see, the most culture- and time-bound. Daniel Lerner describes modernization as a systemic process involving complementary changes in the "demographic, economic, political, communication, and cultural 'sectors'" of a society.[1] Modernity may presumably be thought of in terms of the society as an entity, or it may be segmented into phases such as economic or political. As Inkeles and Smith have stated, the term "modern" has "many denotations and carries a heavy weight of connotations."[2] The word, taken literally, refers to "anything which has more or less recently replaced something which in the past was the accepted way of doing things." Scholars, in attempting to give the term more specificity with reference to the nation-state, have included as defining features of modernity such manifestations as "mass education, urbanization, industrialization, bureaucratization, and rapid communication and transportation." Inkeles and Smith go on to point out that "the more or less simultaneous manifestation of these forms of social organization as a set certainly was not observed in any nation before the nineteenth century, and became really widespread only in the twentieth." Therefore, modernity may be conceived of as "a form of civilization characteristic of our current historical epoch, much as feudalism or the classical empires of antiquity were characteristic of earlier historical eras."[3]

Sometimes modernization is described in somewhat more generalized language, but the context makes it clear that the reference point is the same. For example, Monte Palmer states that modernization "refers to the process of moving toward that idealized set of relationships posited as *modern*." However, he also indicates that "the term *modern* will be used to refer to an *idealized* pattern of social, economic, and political arrangements that is yet to be achieved but is approximated by the world's more economically developed states."[4]

In other words, this orientation centers on a relatively recent and still ongoing historical process, whether the word modernization is used or some substitute, such as development, with the same meaning. Whatever may be the hazards of defining modernization generically, there is much less uncertainty about what people who commonly refer to modernization actually do have in mind: the political systems, and the interrelated economic and social systems, that are actually found in a limited number of nation-states. Diamant states that "it should not be necessary to define precisely what is meant by modernization, except to say it is the sort of transformation which we have come to know in Europe and North America and in less complete forms in other parts of the world."[5] As Edward Shils comments, these states of Western Europe, North America, and the English-speaking dominions of the British Commonwealth "need not *aspire* to modernity. They *are* modern. It has become part of their nature to be modern and indeed what they are is definitive of modernity. The image of the Western countries, and the partial incorporation and transformation of that image in the Soviet Union, provide the standards and models in the light of which the elites of the unmodern new states of Asia and Africa seek to reshape their countries."[6] Eisenstadt likewise asserts that political modernization can be equated historically with "those types of political systems which developed in Western Europe from the seventeenth century and which spread to other parts of Europe, to the American continent, and, in the nineteenth and twentieth century, to Asian and African countries."[7]

In this perspective, the evolution of political and administrative institutions in Western Europe becomes of crucial importance not only to the nation-states that have taken shape there, but also to the other countries that have already modernized or developed politically, and to the scores of nations both old and new that strive toward modernization. As Reinhard Bendix says, "today we face a world in which the expansion of European ideas and institutions has placed the task of nation-building on the agenda of most countries, whether or not they are ready to tackle the job."[8] The political system these countries have sought in large measure to emulate is one that had its origins in Western Europe. The principal features connected with modernization in a political system were developed there. Political modernization in this sense (like industrialization) can be initiated only once,[9] hence the experience continues to be significant to both "developed" and "developing" societies, even though every polity evolves along a path of its own.

Despite the obvious relevance of modernization thus viewed to the actualities of historical events in recent decades, Western scholars have been troubled by the ethnocentric nature of this approach, a feeling that has been more than shared by their non-Western colleagues. This led fairly early to attempts at formulation of models of modernization that were less openly tied to the examples of particular countries in Europe and North America. A notable example from the literature of comparative administration is the essay published in 1957 by Fred W. Riggs, entitled "Agraria and Industria—Toward a Typology of Comparative Administration,"[10] in which he proposed to establish "ideal or hypothetical models of public administration in agricultural and industrial societies"[11] to provide a basis for empirical analysis of administrative systems. Useful as this effort was at the time, Industria turned out to be descriptive of the United States in all significant respects, and Agraria matched closely the characteristics of Imperial China, as Riggs himself later acknowledged. Moreover, the implication was that the process of modernization was unilinear, from Agraria to Industria, with some kind of historical imperative moving actual societies from one model toward the other.[12]

All these, and many other formulations that could be mentioned, share the tendency to equate modernization with emulation of a few existing nation-states. They take as given that the elites of modernizing societies strongly desire to bring about societal transformations that will make them as much as possible like the modern prototype, as soon as possible. Modernization is to be measured by the degree of actual achievement of this objective.

With this treatment in mind, Joseph LaPalombara argued as long ago as 1963 that the concept was a "serious pitfall," and suggested that its use be suspended, at least for the time being. His objections took three forms. First, he was disturbed by the confusion caused by the tendency to substitute economic system or social system for political system, particularly when this leads to the implication that a "modern" political system is one that exists in a highly industrialized society, with high per capita output of goods and services. Second, he argued that the concept is "often implicitly and perhaps unintentionally" normative, using an Anglo-American standard for modernity. Third, he thought that such a term suggests "a deterministic, unilinear theory of political evolution," whereas change in political systems should be viewed as "neither evolutionary nor inevitable."[13]

Going beyond the points mentioned by LaPalombara, note that little attention is given in this approach to speculation, prediction, or prescription as to the future of nation-states that are already considered modernized. How they may evolve in coming years is an unfaced question. The impression might even be that these modernized societies have reached a condition of near perfection, which leads to regarding further modification as likely to be harmful and retrogressive. The future lies in limbo or in a state of suspended animation. The only benchmark is the modernized society of today, to be maintained by those societies that have arrived at that point and to be achieved by those which have not.

Linked with the obvious deficiency of seeming to ignore the inevitable future, modernization so conceived labors under a semantic difficulty. The primary dictionary definition of the word "modern" is "of, pertaining to, or characteristic of the present or most recent past; contemporary." If modernization is defined in terms of the characteristics of certain contemporary societies, this seems to be equivalent to redefinition by confining what is modern to what is characteristic of the present. At the very least, if accepted, this imposes an obligation on coming generations of word coiners to devise a new term for what will be contemporary then rather than now.

DEVELOPMENT

A second group of analysts has sought to escape from these dilemmas by avoiding a definition that centers on what is, and instead focuses on a condition or set of conditions that may or may not exist in a particular political system or society at a particular time. Although the term they use is not always the same, I have chosen to discuss this orientation under the label of "development."

Development, like modernization, is widely employed without having acquired an agreed-upon meaning. Uphof and Ilchman refer to it as "probably one of the most depreciated terms in social science literature, having been used vastly more than it has been understood."[14] According to Joseph J. Spengler, development in general takes place "when an index of that which is deemed desirable and relatively preferable increases in magnitude."[15] More than in the case of modernization, development tends not to be discussed in total societal terms, but to be segmented into phases such as economic or political development.

The economists have vigorously pursued the study of development or growth economics. Economic development is understood to entail "the diversion of a nation's scarce resources and productive powers to the augmentation of its stock of productive wealth and to the progressive enlargement of its gross and net national product of goods and services."[16] The objective may be stated in aggregate or in per capita terms, so that an index of accomplishment is readily available, whatever may be the problems associated with securing accurate economic data or with designing strategy for economic development. Among economists, disagreements have not been so much over the concept of economic development as over the means of accomplishing it, with growing divergence of views as to obstacles and strategies for overcoming them. The earlier optimistic belief that there is a common road toward economic growth, expressed for example in *The Stages of Economic Growth* by W. W. Rostow,[17] has given way to much more cautious and tentative explanations and prognostications, with a tendency on the part of contending schools of thought to shift from a more narrowly economic to a broader political economy perspective.[18]

Political Development

Among political scientists, in contrast to the consensus among economists as to what they mean by economic development, the very concept of political development has been assigned various meanings and has been a cause of dispute.[19]

As already indicated, political development has sometimes been used as the equivalent of political modernization, subject as a result to the same objections.

Most formulations, however, have endeavored to avoid the kind of pitfall mentioned by LaPalombara, at least by trying to identify characteristics of political development rather than simply pointing to specific nation-states as being politically developed. This is so for nearly all of the ten major meanings of political development enumerated by Pye in 1966, the exception being the one which considers political development to be the same as political modernization, in the sense of Westernization. However, Pye found most of the other meanings to be partial, insufficient, or overly value-laden. His own inclination was to stress the importance of increasing political capability and the interlinkage of political development with other aspects of social change as a multidimensional process.

In their review of the literature on political development from the early 1960s through 1975, Huntington and Dominguez commented that definitions "proliferated at an alarming rate," partly because the term had positive connotations for political scientists, hence they "tended to apply it to things that they thought important and/or desirable," using it to perform "a legitimating function rather than an analytical function." As they indicated, discussions on political development often focused "more on development *toward* what than on development *of* what." According to these authors, the term was used in four different general ways: geographical, derivative, teleological, and functional. They explained the meaning of each, giving most attention themselves to the derivative approach, conceiving political development "as the political consequences of modernization."[20] For our purposes, it will be worthwhile to describe several of the formulations that have been influential as descriptions of the prerequisites of a developed political system. Certainly one of the most fully elaborated of these is the contribution of Almond and Powell.[21] Political development, in their view, is the consequence of events which may come from the international environment, from the domestic society, or from political elites within the political system itself. Whatever the source, these impulses "involve some significant change in the magnitude and content of the flow inputs into the political system."[22] When the political system as it exists is unable to cope with the problem or challenge confronting it, development occurs if the system has capabilities for successful adaptation to meet the challenge. Otherwise, the result will be retrogression or negative development.

Four types of problems or challenges are identified which put an existing political system under such a strain: state-building, nation-building, participation, and distribution or welfare. Almond and Powell then suggest five factors which affect the process of political development and help explain variations among systems. These are (1) whether the problems come successively or cumulatively, (2) the resources available to the system, (3) whether or not other systems of the society develop in step with the political system, (4) the extent to which the existing system is geared for change and adaptation, and (5) the creativity or stagnation of political elites since this may be a decisive factor in the ability of the system to accommodate.

These authors stress functionalism in their comparative framework for the study of political systems and use a threefold classification of functions as important for political analysis. These different levels of functioning are capabilities, conversion functions, and system maintenance and adaptation functions. Without trying to trace the analysis in detail, the conclusion of Almond and Powell is that political development, in accordance with these variables, is a cumulative process of (1) role differentiation, (2) subsystem autonomy, and (3) secularization.[23]

As part of their discussion of differentiation, these authors predict that "higher capabilities depend upon the emergence of 'rational' bureaucratic organizations . . . a system cannot develop a high level of internal regulation, distribution, or extraction without a 'modern' governmental bureaucracy in one form or another. . . . Likewise, the development of something like a modern interest-group or party system seems to be the prerequisite to a high development of the responsive capability."[24]

Another influential study is a product of the Committee on Comparative Politics of the Social Science Research Council, growing out of a workshop sponsored by the committee. *Crises and Sequences in Political Development*, edited by Leonard Binder, with five other contributors, reduces political development to three key concepts: equality, capacity, and differentiation.[25] Collectively, these are called the development syndrome.[26]

Consisting of these three basic dimensions, the development syndrome is a combination of congruencies and contradictions. The three elements in the syndrome are at the same time congruent and interdependent, and incongruent and potentially conflictive. Because of these contradictions, the process of development and modernization are regarded as interminable. "We cannot logically envisage a state of affairs characterized at once by total equality, irreducible differentiation, and absolute capacity. Moreover, not only is development interminable, but the course it takes in concrete polities is extremely variable and unpredictable."[27]

Patterns of political development in the newly developing countries are of primary concern to this group of scholars, and they direct their main attention to crises of political development faced by these polities with a degree of intensity not imposed on nation-states that emerged earlier. Five of these crisis-type issues are suggested, and then analyzed in the light of the three components of the development syndrome. The five are crises of identity, legitimacy, participation, penetration, and distribution.[28] These categories are efforts to provide a framework for the analysis of potential crises. The bulk of the volume is devoted to separate articles that deal with each of these crises, plus a contribution by Sidney Verba on a sequential model for their occurrence.[29] Verba's essay mainly raises questions which need to be answered before such a model is possible, but he does agree with Almond and Powell that the overlapping or accumulation of problems makes each harder to solve, and that this is the common predicament faced by the newer nations.

The treatment by Binder and his associates is an example of defining political development in terms of the functional requisites of a modern or developed political system. As Binder says, "the idea of political development is that in modern systems identity will be politicized, legitimacy will be based in part on performance, governments will be capable of mobilizing national resources, the majority of the adult population will be participant citizens, political access will be ubiquitous, and material allocations will be rational, principled, and public."[30]

Helio Jaguaribe presents one of the most interesting comprehensive theories of political development.[31] He reviews the earlier literature in a different way from Huntington and Dominguez, making a twofold classification of it. Writers of his first group understand political development as political modernization. This "historically situated" process corresponds closely, of course, to our previous review of writings under the heading of modernization, although Jaguaribe includes in this group some scholars whose work we have referred to in this section on development. Jaguaribe's second group includes those who understand political development as political institutionalization. He regards the referents of political institutionalization as political mobilization, political integration, and political representation, but points out that former writers have tended to use only one of them. He includes Pye and Karl W. Deutsch[32] in this group, but regards Huntington as the most noteworthy advocate of political development as "the institutionalization of political organizations and procedures."[33]

In his own theory, Jaguaribe attempts to build upon the work of these two schools of thought by proposing a formulation of political development as political modernization plus political institutionalization. He considers that Pye[34] and Apter,[35] although using different terms and categories, substantially share the same conceptual frame, and that Myron Weiner[36] and Irving Horowitz[37] do also at least partially.

This theory, abbreviated $PD = M + I$, is elaborated on by Jaguaribe in great detail.[38] When fully laid out, Jaguaribe's model provides a grid for comparative analyses of political systems, linked to these twin basic components of modernization and institutionalization.[39]

Another crucial point made by Jaguaribe is that political modernization and political institutionalization are closely interrelated, and that political development requires an appropriate balance between the two. A pronounced imbalance in the form of a high level of modernization and a low level of institutionalization makes the political system dependent on the successful use of violence. An imbalance of the opposite kind, with a high level of institutionalization and a low level of modernization, adversely affects the operational capability of the political system. Participational variables, although indispensable for political development, cannot be sustained without sufficient political modernization.

A final thesis of Jaguaribe's theory has to do with what he terms the three aspects of political development: (1) development of the capability of the political system; (2) development of the contribution of the political system to the overall development of the concerned society; and (3) development of the responsiveness of the political system. Any one of these taken alone, as he sees it, would be too restrictive a view. Of these three aspects, Jaguaribe considers the development of the system's capability as a necessary precondition of the other two, and hence the "most general," and presumably the most basic, aspect of political development. Maximum general political development is achieved "when the concerned polity, besides maximizing its capability . . . , and besides contributing to the overall development of the society . . . , also achieves maximum political consensus." This stage, however, is one "which no modern political system has ever achieved and which can only be viewed as an ideal type."[40]

Numerous other authors could be cited who have offered their own variations on the theme of the key characteristics found in developed polities. Harry Eckstein has explored dimensions for ascertaining whether the political performance of a system is adequate.[41] He proposes four that satisfy his criteria: durability, civil order, legitimacy, and decisional efficacy. Robert W. Benjamin also argues that any systematic explanation of political development must employ some method of measurement of system characteristics and performance. However, he chooses different key dimensions of political development as a process: political participation, political institutionalization, and national integration. The process, he believes, "may be viewed as a historically identifiable set of political changes associated with the onset of industrialization in any given society."[42] His own study is a comparative analysis involving Japan, India, and Israel.

Monte Palmer asserts that the challenge of political development is "to create a system of political institutions capable of controlling the state's population, of mobilizing the state's human and material resources towards the ends of economic and social modernization, and of coping with the strain of social, economic, and political change without abdicating its control and mobilization roles."[43] The importance of institutions in managing conflict is accorded similar stress by Powelson, who points out that this capacity "requires national consensus on an economic and a political ideology. These ideologies are defined as the ways in which individuals envisage the economic and political systems—how they operate, and how just they are. Ideological consensus in turn is fostered by a popular nationalism, which therefore plays a positive role in growth rather than the negative one usually attributed to it by economists."[44]

Capability as a Primary Requisite   Although overlapping in part and differing in part, all of these commentators on political development present versions that identify some combination of characteristics thought to be requisite for classification of a nation-state as politically developed. Many of them give a prominent or even pivotal role to a requisite variously labeled with terms such as capacity, capability, or sustained growth potential.

Some authorities have chosen to single out and emphasize this characteristic as itself definitive of political development. In doing this, they have been motivated both by conceptual preferences and by a desire to avoid some of the difficulties of too close an association of political development with the contemporary polities of a few highly industrialized Western societies. In some of his earlier writings, Gabriel Almond used "change" and "development" as synonyms, and formulated a thesis in terms of the performance capabilities of political systems, according to which political systems change or develop "when they acquire new capabilities in relation to their social and international environments."[45]

S. N. Eisenstadt and Alfred Diamant are leading proponents of this approach which equates political development with the ability of a political system to grow or adjust to new demands put upon it. Eisenstadt views sustained political growth as "the central problem of modernization" and says that "ability to deal with continuous change is the crucial test of this growth."[46] Diamant objects to any conception of political development that equates it with the process by which traditional political systems change "into certain forms of democracy as developed in what is loosely called the West," because such a conception "excludes as irrelevant the political experience of a large number of polities and might lead us to conclude that there has been no form of political development in most parts of the world outside Europe and a few sections of the American hemisphere." Hence he defines political development in its most general form as "a process by which a political system acquires an increased capacity to sustain successfully and continuously new types of goals and demands and the creation of new types of organizations."[47]

This formulation is intended to do several things. It avoids the suggestion that there are identifiable stages of political development or that development requires the creation of particular kinds of political institutions. It permits the possibility that traditional symbols and institutions may be successfully utilized for modernization. It implies nothing about eventual success or failure, since the process is not irreversible but can stop even after it has persisted for some time.

Commendably, these ways of understanding political development avoid too pronounced an identification with Western democratic political systems such as those of Great Britain or the United States. A different question may be raised about them, however, because they seem to come extremely close to equating political development with political survival. If political development or modernization is "a generic process of successfully sustaining new demands, goals, and organizations in a flexible manner,"[48] any political system that has managed to maintain its identity over a considerable period of time, particularly under conditions of challenge or stress of any magnitude, would seem to qualify as developed or modernized, whatever might be its characteristics as a political system—other than that it still exists. In other words, somewhat different problems may crop up unless we can distinguish between political modernity or development on the one hand, and political survival on the other. If this is not done, there is the hypothetical possibility, at least, of having to regard as developed political systems such as that of Great Britain, which made drastic political adaptations but responded incrementally over a long period of time; Communist China, which attempted within a single generation the remolding of a society and its political life by revolutionary means; Thailand, which has maintained political identity for centuries against a series of internal and external threats with only limited modification of social institutions; and the remnants of a society that might successfully manage to maintain the rudiments of a political system following a nuclear holocaust. These political systems would seem to have in common the attribute of survival, rather than any other more definite characteristics of modernity or development.

Negative Political Development　Thus far, we have reviewed a variety of attempts to define or explain political development. Generally they have shared what might be called a positive orientation, in the sense that they have indicated what polities have achieved political development and why, or they have pointed toward requirements to be met by polities striving to become politically developed. The stress has been on the potentialities for movement from a less desirable to a more desirable general situation in the political system.

Another train of thought has concentrated on the more negative aspects of the subject, either by dealing with the circumstances that lead to movement away from rather than toward development, or by exploring the factors external or internal to political systems that hinder or inhibit development. Some of this attention has been given by scholars who also have discussed political development in general theoretical terms, but much of it has come from skeptics or critics of the bulk of writing on political development.

Samuel Huntington has provided the most penetrating analysis of breakdowns in political development, or political decay.[49] His concern is to probe the conditions under which societies undergoing social and economic change that is rapid and disruptive can realize political stability.

Huntington proposes what he calls the "political gap" hypothesis as an explanation. He groups the aspects of modernization most relevant to politics into two broad categories: social mobilization and economic development. Social mobilization means a change in "the attitudes, values, and expectations of people" from those associated with the traditional world to those associated with the modern world, as a consequence of such factors as "literacy, education, increased communications, mass media exposure, and urbanization." Economic development refers to "the growth in the total economic activity and output of a society," measured by per capita gross national product, level of industrialization, and level of individual welfare gauged by indices such as life expectancy and caloric intake. "Social mobilization involves changes in the aspirations of individuals, groups, and societies; economic development involves changes in their capabilities. Modernization requires both."[50]

On the assumption that social mobilization is much more devastating than economic development, Huntington hypothesizes that the gap between these two forms of change furnishes a measure of the impact of modernization on political stability. Traditional man is exposed to new experiences in the process of social mobilization that promote new levels of wants and aspirations which transitional societies have difficulties in satisfying. Because the ability to respond increases much more slowly than the wants, "a gap develops between aspiration and expectation, want formulation and want satisfaction, or the aspiration function and the level-of-living function. This gap generates social frustration and dissatisfaction. In practice, the extent of the gap provides a reasonable index to political instability."[51]

This gap is manifested in phenomena such as income inequalities, inflation, widespread corruption, and a widening spread between the city and the countryside which in turn leads to unrest from the rising urban middle class based on a belief that the society is still dominated by the rural elite and often leads to a rural mobilization or "Green Uprising" due to resentment of urban upthrust.

Although using somewhat different terminology, Huntington makes the same point as Jaguaribe that political systems can be distinguished by their levels of political institutionalization and their levels of political participation, and that the stability of any given polity is related to a proper relationship between these two levels.

Many new states are institutionally deficient when they are confronted with rapid social mobilization and increasing demands on the political system. The expansion of political participation needs to be accompanied by the development of strong, complex, and autonomous political institutions, but the usual effect is to undermine traditional institutions and obstruct the development of modern political institutions. Huntington feels that this tendency toward political decay has been neglected, and that concepts of modernization or development are, as a result, not as relevant as they should be to many of the countries that are optimistically considered to be modernizing or developing. In seeking clues as to which societies during the modernization process have better prospects of avoiding political decomposition, Huntington looks to the nature of their traditional political institutions. If these are weak or nonexistent, prospects are poor. If the bureaucratic structure is highly developed and autonomous, the nature of the structure will make adaptation to broader political participation hard, as shown by the highly centralized bureaucratic monarchies of China and France. Societies with more pluralistic feudal systems such as existed in England and Japan proved to be more able to absorb new middle class groups into the political system. These historical examples he considers instructive in assessing the prospects of contemporary modernizing states.

However, even if adaptation to middle class political participation is successful, the ultimate test is the expansion of participation to the urban working class and the rural peasantry to achieve "a fully participant, highly institutionalized modern polity." If institutional adjustment takes place, the result is in Huntington's terms a participant society. Otherwise, the outcome is a mass praetorian society. In either case, the societies have high levels of political participation, but they differ in how their political organizations and procedures are institutionalized. In the mass praetorian society, political participation is "unstructured, inconstant, anomic, and variegated. . . . The distinctive form of political participation is the mass movement combining violent and nonviolent, legal and illegal, coercive and persuasive actions." Popular involvement at a high level in the participant polity, on the other hand, "is organized and structured through political institutions," which must be capable of organizing mass participation in politics. The distinctive institution of the modern polity for this purpose is the political party. Other political institutions in modern political systems are adapted or carried over from traditional political systems. Since 1800, political party development has paralleled the development of modern government. Where earlier political institutions continue to be the primary sources of continuity and legitimacy, parties play a secondary and supplemental role. Where the traditional political institutions collapse, or where they are weak or nonexistent, the role of the party is quite different. "In such situations, strong party organization is the only long-run alternative to the instability of a corrupt or praetorian or mass society. The party is not just a supplementary organization; it is instead the source of legitimacy and authority." The prerequisite for stability in these circumstances is "at least one highly institutionalized political party." He cites the examples of the emergence of one strong party in each case from the Chinese, Mexican, Russian, and Turkish revolutions.[52]

From this perspective, modernization is dangerous and traumatic. It is very likely to lead to political breakdown and decay because political institutions are inadequate to respond to the new demands resulting from the expansion of political participation. The political party as an institution is the most promising device for avoiding political decay and gaining political order.

A couple of subpoints in Huntington's presentation are of particular importance to us. One is that he does not equate popular participation in politics with popular control of government. In his definition of participant polities, both constitutional democracies and Communist regimes qualify. At the time he wrote, he considered both the United States and the USSR to be participant polities, although they had arrived there by different routes, had adopted very different forms of government, and had assigned widely variant roles to the political party as an institution. Related to this point, Huntington noted that one reason for the appeal of Communist and Communist-type movements in modernizing countries had been that they could overcome the scarce supply of authority chronic in these societies. This aspect of his analysis, of course, is now subject to reexamination in view of the collapse of the USSR and other Communist regimes. Presumably his response would be that in these instances the dominant party lost its power to insure political order, which was maintained elsewhere, as in the People's Republic of China.

The same basic theme of disenchantment with the prospects of many transitional countries is sounded by Heeger in his book, *The Politics of Under-development*.[53] These countries are seeking political order and political stability, but they are frustrated because they discover that underdevelopment threatens to become permanent rather than a transitory stage. After exploring the sources of this widespread political instability and explanations given for it, Heeger summarizes by noting that the consistent answer to the question as to why under-developed states are unstable politically is that their political institutions lack the capability to deal with the consequences of social and economic change. The usual reaction is to make recommendations as to how the political institutions might improve in their capabilities and eventually provide the means for reaching a stable political equilibrium. Heeger doubts the feasibility of expecting this to happen, and develops the view that in these polities a more likely outcome is that conflict becomes the norm. He then examines in some detail this political instability, giving particular attention to the role of the military when it gains political power, and to relations between the military and the civil bureaucracy. Contrary to other commentators, who have found that military regimes might be useful in a transition to greater political stability, Heeger passes a negative judgment, saying that such regimes only exacerbate the existing fragmentation. Heeger's orientation, therefore, is far removed from those who view development as unilinear and inevitable, or who anticipate that in the future contemporary underdeveloped states will come to resemble closely any variant of current developed polities.

A sobering but somewhat less pessimistic appraisal is found in John Kautsky's *The Political Consequences of Modernization*.[54] This author also casts doubt on the assumption that there is any single path to political development. He perceives politics as group conflict, and is primarily interested in the political change that results from conflict. His analysis draws a sharp distinction histori-cally between the processes of political change involved in modernization from within as contrasted with modernization from without. In either case, the politics of traditional societies is transformed, but modernization from within has native origins, is relatively slow, and involves continued predominance of the aristocracy. This is basically the way currently developed countries became modernized, but they are not likely to be models for countries that are now underdeveloped. These countries are caught up in the process of modernization from without, through such agents as colonialism, a modernizing aristocracy influenced from the outside, and foreign and native capital. The impact of modernization from without results in different effects on various segments of the traditional society, but the modernizing elements bring about revolutionary political change. Usually this is followed by postrevolutionary conflict among the modernizers, which often leads to the use of mass terror, regimentation, and persuasion, to the suppression of opposition, to drives for rapid industrialization, and to frequent changes in the group basis of the modernizing regimes. A condition of balance may or may not emerge eventually. If it does, it may be after a second-wave revolution of modernizers. Another prospect is an aristocratic reaction that may usher in a Fascist regime. If a balance that is persistent becomes established, the prospects of the modernizing country markedly improve. The longer a balance lasts in the polity, the better become its chances for further survival.

Dependency Theories

The overwhelming importance of external environmental factors forms the basic thesis of social scientists who have advocated dependency theories of development. The dominant note is that what is commonly called underdevelopment is the consequence of a state of dependence by one society on another, and a secondary theme is that this dependency condition is repeated within the affected society by an internal colonialism which one segment of the society imposes on another segment. The net effect is a situation which allows little prospect for improvement without a drastic alteration of both the external environment and the internal system.[55]

Originating among economists who were concerned with dependency aspects of economic development, this emphasis on dependency has been extended by sociologists to social development in general and by political scientists to political development in particular. Although they share this common orientation, these dependency social scientists have offered a wide spectrum of philosophic backgrounds, geographical interests, and prescriptive recommendations. Some have written from what is clearly an orthodox Marxist perspective; some have not. Many leaders in the elucidation of dependency points of view have been Latin Americans, but others have been social scientists from developing areas elsewhere in the world and many have been located in countries considered developed, including the United States and other nations viewed as imposing dependency status abroad.

In contrast to diffusion concepts which regard development as a positive process of importation or borrowing by less advanced from more advanced societies, dependency theorists believe that the impact of external factors is essentially negative, in the form of pressure and influence from "metropolitan" developed countries on "peripheral" developing countries.

During the peak period of their influence, before the world altering political events that occurred in the Soviet Union and Eastern Europe beginning in the late 1980s, dependency theorists were divided into two main groups. Those with an orthodox Marxist or neo-Marxist interpretation tended to view the dependency condition as the historically inevitable outcome of "capitalistic imperialism," with the United States as the primary imposer of obstacles to autonomous development, and with Latin America as the prime example of a developing area fitting the dependency model. Linked to this perspective was often a spirited attack on social science research methodology as it had evolved in the United States, particularly through the structural-functional approach, which was accused of serving as a tool of imperialistic capitalism by supporting the diffusion concept, by advocating the "end of ideology" as a means of promoting Western pluralism, by rationalizing the status quo, and by offering a generally distorted interpretation of the situation in the dependent countries.

Other supporters of the basic thesis offered as an explanation the emergence after World War II of a new bipolar international system, replacing the international balance of power system stemming from the Napoleonic era. In this emerging "interimperial" system, the United States and the Soviet Union appeared as the two superpowers, with the United States in a role of general primacy but with the Soviet Union holding a status in the current world order that was basically the same except that its primacy was less pervasive and more regionally focused. A few other nation-states (including Japan, China, and the nations of Western Europe as a group) were viewed as enjoying autonomy in the sense of being able to make crucial domestic decisions and to resist overt aggression, or in other words, to maintain national viability in the interimperial system. The rest of the world was in a condition of dependency, including the older nation-states in Latin America and scattered here and there elsewhere, and the many newer nation-states of Asia and Africa. Some movement between categories was hypothesized before the end of the century, from autonomy to dependency and vice versa, but this was anticipated to be quite limited and not altering the outlook for most dependent countries. Another frequently noted aspect of this analysis was the developmental cleavage in the world between the north, where the superpowers and autonomous nation-states were mostly located, and the south, which had nearly all of the dependent countries. The distinction between capitalism and socialism, on the other hand, was either dropped or muted to secondary status, with both the United States as a capitalist democracy and the USSR as a socialist state considered as being more alike than different because, despite their ideological and regime variations, both superpowers in the new imperial situation created conditions of dependency.

Some theorists divided dependency into subtypes based on substantive and chronological considerations. Jaguaribe, for example, delineated four forms of dependency as appearing historically in roughly chronological order: classic colonialism, neo-colonialism, satellite dependency, and provincial dependency.[56]

Such long-range scenarios for the future of the contemporary nation-states of the developing world were a far cry from optimistic earlier prognostications that these societies were embarked on a road that would lead them after a period of trials and tribulations to a situation in which they would match very closely the characteristics of the limited number of already developed countries. The only ray of hope held out was that some countries not enjoying superpower status might be able to pursue a course of autonomous development, and that others of the currently dependent nation-states might be able to achieve that option later, either singly in a few instances or in combination with other nation-states in the same geographical region.

As indicated above, the dependency theorists emphasized the overwhelming impact of the external environment on developing societies, and devoted their main attention to an examination of the relationships between metropolitan and peripheral countries, but they also explored the resultant domestic societal characteristics within the dependent nations, rejecting as myths several prevailing theses concerning the nature of these societies, such as that they are dual societies with a modernized sector and a backward sector that has not yet caught up, and that progress will be achieved by diffusion of the products of industrialism to backward and traditional zones.

The counterinterpretation proposed consisted of several propositions, the most important being the concepts of internal colonialism, stagnation, marginality, and denationalization. The notion of internal colonialism is basically that the international relationship of dominance by metropolitan over peripheral countries is repeated internally by a comparable dominance by domestic elitist groups linked to foreign governments and multinational corporations over submerged elements in the society unable to resist being kept in a status of internal dependency. Stagnation refers to the static character of the economies of Latin America and other underdeveloped areas, to the lack of achievement of a process of self-sustained growth. The concept of marginality came to mean basically the phenomenon of nonparticipation or very limited participation by large proportions of the people in underdeveloped countries in economic, social, and political activities beyond the most minimal levels. Used originally to refer to the inhabitants of a variety of substandard living quarters on the margins of the principal cities, the term later acquired this more generalized connotation. The combined phenomena of stagnation and marginality were viewed as mutually reinforcing and operating in a process of circular causation to drive the typical dependent country deeper into a corner of underdevelopment. The process of denationalization was in turn seen as an impending consequence of these other factors, resulting in the actual transfer of control over relevant decisions to actors loyal to another nation.

Aside from economic aspects, these hypotheses concerning dependency have not been the subject of much comparative empirical study. An exception is an examination by Sofranko and Bealer of the relationship between patterns of modernization and domestic stability in seventy-four countries.[57] These authors attempted to test the assumption that unevenness of development among the institutional sectors of a developing society is apt to exist, and that the degree of imbalance and the pattern which the imbalances assume have consequences for domestic instability. They gave primary concern to political, economic, and educational institutions. Contrary to expectations, their findings revealed little relationship between magnitudes of imbalance for these political, economic, and educational sectors considered singly and instability. However, when the notion of sectoral imbalance was invoked, relationships between particular patterns of imbalances and instability did emerge. The summary findings by Sofranko and Bealer were that isolated disequilibria in a sector of society did not need to be highly disruptive, but that widespread imbalances appeared to have considerable impact on overall stability. Although this study does not deal with the question of the extent to which imbalances arise from outside sources, it does seem to confirm that patterns of widespread imbalances of the type alleged by dependency theorists to be imposed from without do exist, and that such extensive sectoral imbalances indeed have a negative impact on overall stability in developing societies.

As already mentioned, dependency theorists have differed among themselves in various ways, including their views on what strategies ought to be followed by the leadership in dependent countries to cope with current dependency conditions. Those interpreting dependency as the outcome of the global spread of capitalism played down any imperialistic tendencies on the part of Communist powers such as the USSR or China, and saw the path of revolutionary socialism as the answer. Writers who regarded dependency as the product of a new imperialism, shared by the United States and the USSR, tended to look upon the options available to the dependent countries as quite restricted, and to advise their leaders to seek an accommodation under the best circumstances available subject to the hegemony of one of the superpowers. Their outlook was essentially pessimistic, with the most hopeful prospect being avoidance of a nuclear confrontation between the superpowers and the consolidation of a modern Pax Romana, with its advantages in terms of stability and its price in terms of institutionalized submission on the part of dependent regions of the world.

A third, somewhat less negative, point of view has been that possibilities for autonomous development do exist and that they should be taken advantage of to the fullest possible extent. This option stresses a reformist approach under the leadership of local elites, making maximum use of discretion left by operation of the international system. This alternative is usually described by such terms as "autonomous capitalism" or "state capitalism." The assumption is that it will be a mixed system with strong state involvement in planning and execution of plans, and with public enterprises playing a prominent role. Where national entities are small or weak, particularly in Latin America and Africa, groupings of existing nation-states may be a condition for exploring any realistic prospects for autonomous development. Advocates of autonomy place great emphasis on the importance of local innovation and willingness to experiment. For example, a Malaysian commentator named Inayatullah has argued that the lack of an adequate level of development in Asian countries is due in part to overreliance on borrowing from external sources and insufficient creativity in evolving new development models. He considers modernization to be a process that is historically and culturally specific and doubts the relevance of any foreign model of development evolved in different cultural and historical circumstances. This places, he believes, "the main burden of evolving an appropriate model of development on a society itself, by examining what it can learn and maintain from its own history and culture, by full comprehension of the constraints and opportunities available in its internal and external environments."[58] For instance, he doubts the relevance for Asian societies of the elements of traditional capitalism and liberal democracy from the Western model as compared to the concepts of the nation-state or of an instrumental public bureaucracy. Another common theme is the extreme importance of timing, of taking advantage of opportunities before they disappear. A number of writers urging autonomy for Latin America, with Jaguaribe being prominent among them, have been discouraged that such a strategy is not being actively pursued where it has chances for success. They warn that developmental autonomy may be a short-lived option that will be gone by the end of the century.

In recent years, the dependency approach has been subjected to numerous evaluative critiques aimed at identifying its strong and weak points. Moreover, dependency theorists are still trying to cope with the implications of the dissolution of the Soviet Union and the end of the Cold War which, for example, has largely wiped out the underpinnings of the dual superpower version of dependency theory.

One critique, by Michael J. Francis, while acknowledging the widespread and pervasive acceptance of dependency thinking, especially by leaders in developing countries, presents an analysis of the dependency literature which distinguishes between propositions that are supported by substantial evidence, and others that are more controversial and less verifiable.[59] Tony Smith also points out deficiencies, but stresses that recently the dependency approach has made notable gains in sophistication. He discusses three refinements that are significant responses to changes in the situation in the developing countries.

One is recognition that the dual economy is not as rigid as believed earlier, and that economies in some countries are becoming more advanced. Another is placement of new emphasis on the crucial role of the state, and urging of more assertive action on the part of the state as an agent for change. Third is more recognition of the diversity of these countries and a growing appreciation of the significance of local factors. This is leading to discussion of stages or degrees of dependency, thus going beyond simply saying that a country is or is not dependent. Smith summarized the situation in the mid-1980s by asserting that dependency literature took a major step forward when it admitted evidence about change and then formulated new concepts to deal with the new developments, meanwhile reaffirming its primary doctrinal belief in the dependence of the periphery on the core and in the preeminence of economic affairs. With these advances, his judgment was that the dependency paradigm was in its prime, having since the early 1970s largely displaced the older developmentalist or diffusionist perspective. Nevertheless, dependency theories are still frequently challenged as to their validity, either with respect to Latin America, or with regard to specific East Asian countries demonstrating rapid economic progress during these same two decades.

Rethinking Development

The revisionist trend just reviewed among dependency theorists extends to other students of development as well, and indicates that there is in process a rather fundamental reappraisal of "development" as a rubric for describing major societal transitions.[60]

Although differing in many ways, these commentators share some points of view. One is that they express dissatisfaction with "development" as a term and a concept, without being able to come up with a satisfactory substitute to replace it. As a result, they continue to employ the terminology that they find wanting. Apter, a long time student of these issues,[61] raises this basic question as to whether the term itself ought to be abandoned. Development, he asserts, is "so imprecise and vulgar that no doubt it should be stricken from any proper lexicon of technical terms." He adds that "concepts like modernization and modernism" should be dropped also. "Despite its (and their) shortcomings, however," he predicts, "this will not happen."[62] His explanation is that developmental theory "remains intrinsically important despite its confusions. One reason is that its ideas are so embedded in our thinking that they have a life of their own, a life quite divorced one might add from developmental practice." Besides, he foresees "no single forthcoming theoretical approach" that is likely to be satisfactory.[63] In arguing that underdevelopment is "a state of mind," Harrison parts company with the dominant stress in the development literature on economic factors, particularly by dependency theorists, and at least by implication suggests that a new framework for analysis is needed. Mittelman believes that it is crucial to examine "traditional lore" about the less developed countries and their future prospects, because "attention is centred on the wrong issues and neglects major questions."[64] These are typical comments reflecting dissatisfaction with current conceptual categories.

A second shared tendency is to call for more stress on the linkages among different aspects of the process of development, but without consensus as to where the emphasis should be. Some authors (including Apter, Migdal, Lee, and Jackman) place an institutionalist focus on the state. Believing that this is "a time for tentativeness rather than conclusions," Apter concedes that the ideas he presents "do not pretend to be tightly integrated into a single system," but says that they are "linked together in terms of problems studied in the field as well as interpreted in comparative terms." Underlying themes he explores include the relation between development and democracy, the problem of innovation and marginality, and questions of violence and governability. The bulk of his presentation consists of discussion of problems that tend to work either for or against the state. Migdal finds that strong states in Asia, Africa, and Latin America have been a rarity (examples are Israel, Cuba, China, Japan, Vietnam, Taiwan, North Korea, and South Korea), and that major societal dislocation has been a necessary, but not sufficient, condition for their emergence. Once existing patterns of social control have been broken, other "sufficient" conditions he suggests are favorable timing, the existence of a serious military threat from outside or from communal groups inside, the presence of social groups from which capable state bureaucrats can be drawn, and the availability of skillful top leadership. In his study of state-building in the present-day developing countries, Lee concludes that the primary determinant has been transnational linkages of these states to the modern world-system, rather than intranational variables such as industrialization or political class struggle. "Overall," he states, "implications of the expansion of the state seem to be positive for national economic development in dependent capitalist countries. Increased roles and expanded state capacities to regulate and control economic resources and to formulate and enact development policies make statist development a viable strategy."[65] Jackman, on the other hand, emphasizes that there are wide variations in the political capacity of nation-states, and that many of them continue to be weak and ineffective, making development difficult or impossible.

Taking direct issue with the emphasis placed on economic factors by Lee and by the dependency theorists generally, Harrison argues that it is *culture* ("the values and attitudes a society inculcates in its people through various socializing mechanisms, e.g., the home, the school, the church") that "principally explains, in most cases, why some countries develop more rapidly and equitably than others."[66] Based on twenty years of technical assistance experience in Latin America, he examines and contrasts the records of pairs of countries

(Nicaragua and Costa Rica, the Dominican Republic and Haiti, Barbados and Haiti, Argentina and Australia) that he considers to have started with the same basic resource endowment but to have developed very differently. He also reviews societal cultural patterns in Spain, Spanish America, and the United States that might help explain these differential results. His basic thesis is that some patterns of cultural characteristics impel or facilitate development and others impede or undermine it, and he asks how the first pattern can be reinforced and the second pattern weakened. "In the case of Latin America," he concludes, "we see a cultural pattern, derivative of traditional Hispanic culture, that is anti-democratic, anti-social, anti-progress, anti-entrepreneurial, and, at least among the elite, anti-work."[67] He suggests means to "design and orchestrate a coherent program of cultural change," with emphasis on leadership, religious reform, education and training, the media, development projects, management practices, and child-rearing practices.[68] Harrison thus is a strong advocate of culture as the principal determinant of development, while downplaying but not ignoring noncultural factors. His position contrasts most sharply with that of dependency theorists, particularly since each is based on an interpretation of Latin American experience.

Several books take a political economy stance, stressing the interlocking roles of economic and political factors in development. Contributors to the Bates volume, for example, seek to "teach ways of doing political economy" using a "collective choice" approach, recognizing that markets are imperfect and that institutions other than markets allocate resources.[69] Political interventions are viewed as not necessarily supportive of growth and development. Political elites often behave in ways that are politically rational but economically irrational, resulting in economic costs that retard development.[70] In contrast to such negative consequences of political factors, Seitz focuses more positively on the role politics plays in solving key problems involving social changes caused by or accompanying economic growth, such as "living standards, population growth, food production and consumption, energy use, the environment, and the use of technology."[71]

Mittelman invokes an even broader complex of factors. He argued in 1988 that underdevelopment is best understood "in terms of the interplay of capital accumulation, the state and class forces. The relationship among these factors defines the strategy of development adopted in a given historical context."[72] This basic approach is retained in the 1997 reformulation he has made in collaboration with Mustapha K. Pasha. Figure 1 is a visualization used to indicate the dynamics of this triangular relationship.[73]

The third similarity among these reappraisals is the tendency to foresee a variety of possible alternative futures for less developed countries rather than movement along some common path. Mittelman and Pasha describe three basic strategies which will be detailed later: the conventional route of joining global

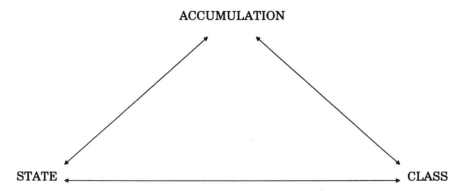

FIGURE 1 The dynamics of development and underdevelopment.

capitalism, the exit option of withdrawing from (and perhaps later re-entering) global capitalism, and the alternative path of "weaving through" global capitalism. Turner and Hulme stress the importance of diversity and creativity, emphasizing that there is no "one best way" for the public sectors in developing countries to improve their performance. They examine the impact of international and organizational environmental factors in making choices as to primary reliance on such alternatives as state-centered programs, market-oriented forces, and contributions of non-governmental organizations. Werlin proposes "political elasticity" theory as a means for better understanding and mastery of what he calls the "mysteries of development." This concept advocates that governmental authorities integrate and alternate "soft" (linking incentives to persuasion) and "hard" (including disincentives and coercion) forms of political power. In this way, their role takes on "rubber band" and "balloon" characteristics, allowing decentralization or delegation of power without losing control, or expansion of influence affecting wider circles of respondents. Doing this requires the selection of appropriate political "hardware" and, more importantly, "software" to balance the struggle for competitive advantage and the struggle for consensus as forms of political power. "Somehow," he asserts, "we need to find room for legality, authority, hierarchy, accountability, control, responsibility, expertise and judicial neutrality to give credibility to decentralization, empowerment, choice, participation, community development, and the other concepts favored by the proponents of . . . 'the hollow state:' the shifting of responsibility for public services away from the central government to local governments, communities, and the private sector."[74]

The range among these possibilities is too great for all of them to be conveniently grouped under one label such as "development," despite the failure of these authors to agree upon another term. We will take a closer look at some of these alternatives in the following section.

CHANGE

Uneasiness about the general applicability of both the terms modernity and development has been voiced frequently, even by those who have continued to use one or the other, or both. For instance, as noted earlier, Joseph LaPalombara as long ago as 1963 pointed out pitfalls resulting from concepts of modern, modernity, and modernization. His concerns seemed to be about equally applicable to concepts such as developing and development, yet his essay and the book containing it, which he edited, carries the title *Bureaucracy and Political Development*. Gabriel Almond and his associates have been primarily concerned with the process of change in political systems but have tended to prefer to talk in terms of political development rather than political change, even though in practice they seem to consider the two phrases to be substitutable one for the other.

John Kautsky, writing in 1972 in *The Political Consequences of Modernization*, confines the concept of modernization in a rather unusual way to the social and economic antecedents and consequences of industrialization, and excludes the political antecedents and consequences. The latter are his main concerns. In dealing with them, he deliberately avoids both the terms political modernization and political development, for the reason that "these concepts suggest development toward a single pattern and in a single direction, often . . . the one generally referred to as Western democracy." He prefers the more neutral concept of political change to either political modernization or political development, in order to "leave the question of which way politics changes under the impact of modernization open for our investigation rather than to foreclose it by the use and the definition of a term."[75] He then proceeds to write about political change under the impact of modernization as defined, with particular attention to modernization of traditional societies from within and from without, and to the politics of modernizing regimes.

In their review of trends in the literature, Huntington and Dominguez point out that in the late 1960s and early 1970s, "political scientists who had been talking about political development began to think in more general terms about theories of political change," and they note that as the tradition-modernity dichotomy becomes less useful for political analysis, which appears to be the case, "it seems likely that the study of political development will become increasingly divorced from the study of modernization and more closely identified with broader study of political change." They expect this to result in more attention to cultural factors than to levels of modernity in comparative studies, and to the identification of "distinctive patterns of political beliefs and behavior for the Latin, Nordic, Hindu, Arab, Chinese, Slav, Japanese, Malay, African, and possibly other major cultural groupings."[76] They also anticipate more of a focus on how changes in particular components of a political system relate to changes in other components.[77]

The extent to which such a shift toward substitution of the concept of change for modernization and development actually takes place in the future remains to be seen, but it does appear to be a desirable trend. It offers the obvious advantage of replacing terms that are subjective and value-laden with a concept that is more neutral and value-free. That in itself should be a sufficient reason for a gradual transition in usage.

Another consideration may become even more persuasive. Aside from its value connotations and identification with particular groupings of nation-states considered to be modernized or more developed on the one hand, or traditional or less developed on the other, the terminology linked to modernization and development as concepts has a very limited capability for dealing with potential future change that may occur among nation-states in each of these groupings. Current terminology encounters great difficulty, as previously mentioned, in coping with change which moves societies now tabbed as developed toward some future condition in which their characteristics might be substantially different. Modernization and development are static concepts as they relate to what may be in the offing.

A different set of problems crops up with regard to the developing societies. Their future, as built into the adjective itself, is presumably to be movement in the direction already taken by developed societies, and the key questions to be answered are how they follow and at what pace. But what if all or some of these countries are either incapable of, or not desirous of, taking such a path? How do we deal with change in these cases if it is in some other direction than that already taken by societies whose course can be traced historically?

Signs are already on the horizon, or even above it, that indicate something about what is coming. Should these changes materialize, they would soon convert these potential conceptual dilemmas into actual ones. Therefore, we need to have a brief further look at recent forecasts and speculations concerning upcoming changes in both the so-called developed and developing countries.

Competing Conceptions of the Future

This task is complicated because of the increasingly wide spectrum of perceptions as to likely future trends. Despite frequent references to a "new world order" following the collapse of the Soviet domain, no consensus has emerged as to the characteristics of what will replace the old dual superpower global configuration, or as to the consequences for both more developed and less developed countries.

Without trying to examine the whole range of projections about change in the post–Cold War world, I will mention two examples that seem to me to represent extremes of optimism and pessimism about future trends.

An upbeat assessment, or at least one that recognizes the possibility of positive progress, is by Harlan Cleveland in his book *Birth of a New World: An Open Moment for International Leadership*, published in 1993.[78] Cleveland presents an action agenda for shaping world history in the near future, based on strategies and structures discussed by a multi-national group of about thirty experts, of which he was one, during the late 1980s. Seeking to seize the opportunity presented by "this open moment of world-scale ferment," Cleveland discusses the implications of such diverse phenomena as the erosion of superpower resulting in a "nobody-in-charge world . . . more volatile and more crisis-prone" than the earlier confrontation of "nuclear-tipped superpowers;" the leakage of power from the modern nation-state and the emergence of new power wielding entities at super-national and subnational levels; the "outbreak of cultural diversity" with the resulting "boiling over of resentments in the name of almost forgotten or newly discovered cultural traditions;" the numerous instances of collaborative success in dealing with such problems as weather forecasting, eradication of infectious diseases, and cooperation in outer space; and the dwindling relevance for development of geography as compared to access to technological data. A key element in Cleveland's strategy for taking advantage of opportunities and reducing dangers is the building of "a global public sector" that will regulate trade and money by a mix of two levels of activity (collective standard setting by international public authorities, and uncentralized market-driven international business activity). For leadership in carrying out this agenda, he relies on "the club of democracies" or "coalition of the willing," with the United States as a pivotal force.[79]

At the opposite end of the scale of projections is Samuel P. Huntington's expectation that global politics in coming years will center on a "clash of civilizations."[80] Although the title of his original presentation was framed as a question, there is no doubt as to what Huntington anticipates. His hypothesis is that the fundamental source of conflict in the foreseeable future will not be primarily ideological or primarily economic, but will be cultural. He asserts that nation-states "will remain the most powerful actors in world affairs, but the principal conflicts of global politics will occur between nations and groups of different civilizations. The clash of civilizations will dominate global politics. The fault lines between civilizations will be the battle lines of the future."[81]

Huntington's prime evidence, of course, is what has been happening since the end of the Cold War in Eastern Europe, especially in what was Yugoslavia, with the confrontation in Kosovo during 1999 as the most recent example. His presentation features a map showing the dividing line from north to south in Europe around 1500 between Western Christianity on the west and Orthodox Christianity and Islam on the east, and traces the current problems to this long existing confrontation between civilizations. Arguing that civilization identity will be increasingly important, he states that the post-1990 world is being shaped into a world of civilizations, the major ones being Western, Latin American, African, Islamic, Sinic, Hindu, Orthodox, Buddhist, and Japanese. Disclaiming any intent to advocate the desirability of conflicts, Huntington nevertheless concludes that "violent conflicts between groups in different civilizations are the most likely and most dangerous source of escalation that could lead to global wars," and that "a central focus of conflict for the immediate future will be between the West and several Islamic-Confucian states."[82] His intent is to offer "an interpretation of the evolution of global politics after the Cold War. It aspires to present a framework, a paradigm, for viewing global politics that would be meaningful to scholars and useful to policymakers."[83] He concludes that in the emerging era with clashes of civilizations as the greatest threats to world peace, the surest safeguard against world war is to create an international order based on the commonalities shared by all peoples in all civilizations.

Of course, there are also many intermediary speculations about the future, falling in between these examples, which cannot be examined one by one. The term being used most frequently to describe the post–Cold War world is "globalization." Thomas L. Friedman has recently written about this era of globalization, using the Japanese luxury automobile Lexus, assembled primarily by robots, to represent "all the burgeoning global markets, financial institutions and computer technologies with which we pursue higher living standards today," and the olive tree symbolizing "millions of people in developing countries," for whom "the quest for material improvement still involves walking to the well, plowing a field barefoot behind an ox or gathering firewood and carrying it on their heads for five miles." He views the Lexus and the olive tree as wrestling with each other, with the challenge of globalization being, both for countries and individuals, "to find a healthy balance between preserving a sense of identity, home and community and doing what it takes to survive within the globalization system." Globalization as a system depends on how well this balance is struck. "A country without a Lexus will never grow or go very far. A country without healthy olive trees will never be rooted or secure enough to open up fully to the world. But keeping them in balance is a constant struggle."[84]

This diversity among competing conceptions indicates that in reality the future will present a variety of illustrations of suggested situations, or mixtures among them, making it advantageous to have available a roster of possible explanatory hypotheses.

A subsidiary issue raised by some of the analyses is whether nation-states should continue to be the primary focus of attention, in view of the appearance on the scene of so many public agencies below and above the national level, as well as of non-governmental entities in the private and voluntary sectors. It should be noted that both Cleveland and Huntington, who differ so greatly in their prognostications, concur in the continued centrality of the nation-state, even after recognizing the increasing importance of these other actors.[85] Similarly, Robert Jackman, while focusing on variations in their political capacity, recognizes that nation-states "are clearly the basic unit of analysis in the contemporary international order," and that preservation of this system "is legitimized by the doctrine of the right to national self-determination and by the principle of noninterference in the 'internal' affairs of other states."[86] The shape of the future may indeed be different, but for now continued concentration on nation-state comparisons appears to be fully justified.

Following these general observations, we are now ready to turn to more specific discussions of change in the two groupings of countries already identified.

In More Developed Countries

Social forecasting about the future of advanced industrial countries has taken shape in the concept of postindustrial society, with the implication that this emerging type of society will be as distinctly different from industrial society as this form was from agrarian society. In the United States, Daniel Bell has been the best known expositor of this formulation of what lies ahead.[87]

The transition discussed by Bell and numerous other social scientists in this country and abroad does not lead clearly to a new type of society with fully laid out characteristics. The very label that has gained general acceptance indicates this. The choice of a term using a prefix meaning "after in time" or "following" is almost an admission that industrial society is much better understood than what is expected to succeed it. Bell acknowledges this, in explaining his preference over alternatives such as the knowledge society, the information society, the professional society, the programmed society, the credential society, the technetronic society, and other possible choices based on salient aspects of what is deemed to be emerging.[88] He does not anticipate that the postindustrial society will achieve the degree of societal unity "which was characteristic of capitalist civilization from the mid-eighteenth to the mid-twentieth century," and so he thinks that the prefix "post" indicates an appropriate sense of "living in interstitial time."[89] He does identify, however, the major source of structural transformation as "the change in the character of knowledge,"[90] and he discusses several dimensions of the consequent social structure modifications that he foresees taking place during the next half-century.

The core of this concept is that technology and theoretical knowledge will have an increasing role in the functioning of society. The professional and technical class will be pre-eminent. Levels of education and affluence will rise. The university will be the primary institution of the postindustrial society. Conflict will be generated between populism and elitism by the meritocracy principle which is central to the allocation of position in such a society.

Ramifications will include a change in the economic sector from a goods-producing to a service economy, with white-collar workers, particularly professionals and scientists, becoming predominant in the labor force. Cultural norms will be profoundly affected, with the primacy of theoretical knowledge promoting confidence in technological assessment and control, expanding the scope of political decision-making, and fostering a pervasive cultural orientation toward the future.

Recent writing along these lines has not further clarified, and may even have blurred further, a delineation of what is anticipated. Whereas earlier various labels were suggested as most descriptive, the preference now seems to be to retreat even from the once popular term "postindustrial" to the more neutral concept of a "process of postmodernization" which will give rise "to a form of society which is radically different from that given within modernity." The adjective "postmodern" is defended as best describing this emerging form of society, mainly because "it is still indeterminate and problematic: we have no firm knowledge of what it is but only that it is not modernity. . . . Therefore we concentrate on the processes of change which produce postmodern social forms, the processes of postmodernization, rather than a vision of the new society."[91]

An aspect of this line of thinking of special import to us is that the forecast of postindustrialism or postmodernization has not been confined to the United States and Western Europe. Bell viewed the same basic social pattern is in prospect also for Japan, a non-Western capitalist society, and for the Soviet Union, a noncapitalist Western or semi-Western society. Neither geographic location nor the distinction between capitalism and socialism were viewed as crucial considerations.[92] Communist theorists have tended in the past with a few exceptions to avoid substituting this kind of analysis for more orthodox Marxist views as to the role of the working class as the agent of change and as to expectations for achieving a classless society. However, European social scientists with a neo-Marxist orientation, such as Alain Touraine, took a different approach to the postindustrial theme. Recognizing the decisive role of science and technology and the emergence of scientific and technical personnel in all industrial societies, they were inclined to reinterpret the usual Marxist view as to the role of the working class, or to enlarge the definition to include the increasingly important technically trained personnel.[93]

Since the Soviet Union disintegrated, attention has turned increasingly to the future of capitalism in the world, despite its apparent victory as the outcome of the Cold War. Some authors stress the likelihood that with modifications the basic institutions of capitalism will persist. For example, in *Contemporary Capitalism: The Embeddedness of Institutions*,[94] the editors argue that although there is no one best set of institutional arrangements for organizing modern societies, the economic institutions of capitalism are not static entities and are capable of responding to changing circumstances. Essay contributors examine various possibilities. The editors conclude that "taming the market has always been more rewarding over the longer term than myopically following it," and they call for the construction of new forms of a mixed economy, pointing out that "one of the major challenges of our time is to create a new theory of democracy for governing institutions nested in a world of unprecedented complexity, one in which subnational regions, nation-states, and continental and global regimes are all intricately linked."[95]

David C. Korten is much more critical of recent trends. He contends that in the 1980s capitalism triumphed over communism, and in the 1990s "it triumphed over democracy and the market economy. For those of us who grew up believing that capitalism is the foundation of democracy and market freedom, it has been a rude awakening to realize that under capitalism, democracy is for sale to the highest bidder and the market is centrally planned by global mega-corporations larger than most states."[96] In an earlier work,[97] he had focused on the dysfunctions of this new global capitalism. In this one, he turns to what he terms "democratic, market-based" alternatives, setting forth an agenda for a "post-corporate-post-capitalist civilization" based on freedom that is responsible, "mindful markets," economic democracy, and restoration of the rights of "living persons" as against those of corporate entities.[98]

What these prognostications as to the postindustrial or postmodern society have in common, despite their variations in detail, is that a transition is already well underway which is taking modernized, developed, industrial societies into a period as traumatic and disruptive as they faced earlier themselves, or as is faced by the present-day modernizing, developing, industrializing societies, and with the outcome equally indeterminate. The contours of the societal future for this group of countries seem to have become more blurred rather than more clearly defined as we have moved through the decade of the 1990s.[99] For such forecasts to have any accuracy at all, they will require as a by-product more adequate social science terminology concerning change in the general social system and in the political subsystem.

In Less Developed Countries

With regard to the less developed countries as a group, predictions about their future are much more diverse. Few expectations are now being expressed that all or most of them will soon, if ever, become replicas of existing developed countries.

As we have seen, instances of negative political development have increased, preventing numerous countries from changing their political systems to conform with requirements for them to be considered developed by most writers on the subject. Dependency theorists generally have had a low level of expectation about prospects for success, although they are giving more recognition to the possibility of exceptions. Authors who have recently been rethinking development and exploring alternative concepts have, as already mentioned, usually anticipated alternate paths rather than a common path for the countries currently seeking to become more developed.

To what extent do we have suggestions as to what these options might be? Harrison, who credits culture or "state of mind" as the primary cause of divergent national developmental histories, clearly considers that the record shows varying degrees of success and failure, but he does not devote much attention to delineating categories or means of measurement. Bates and his colleagues offer a number of case studies dealing with the political economy of development, showing a variety of results, but do not offer a summing up at the end.

Seitz does identify three approaches that have been used in seeking to reach development goals, labeling them the "orthodox," "radical," and "growth-with-equity" approaches. He also examines three alternative futures for these countries, suggesting that all three will be part of what actually happens. These are "doom," "growth," and "steady-state." He apparently favors the "growth-with-equity" approach, and indicates that the "steady-state" future is the one that developing nations generally should strive for, since "we live in a world in which some of the resources needed to support life are finite." He goes on to observe that this "would not mean the absence of growth, but the growth which would be emphasized would be intellectual, moral, and spiritual rather than the growth of material objects."[100]

Mittelman and Pasha present a more fully rounded analysis, using a political economy framework. They outline three strategies of development, based on the premise that the current world system offers only a quite limited range of realistic choices. Each option carries both promises and risks. For each strategy, they present country case studies illustrating the reasons for the choice and the consequences of making it.

The most conventional route is to join global capitalism, with Brazil as the prime example. This strategy, when stripped to its essentials, is "to embrace global capitalism; tighten monetary and fiscal policy while accelerating privatizations and easing state monopolies so as to gain revenue; accumulate capital from above and outside in order to expand the stock of machinery and other productive equipment; exploit natural resources to sell on the world market; and concentrate income in the fists of the upper echelon of society and major foreign investors while promising that wealth will ultimately percolate down to the needy."[101] The record shows "miracle" growth rates until 1974 and "respectable" growth rates in later years. This was accomplished, however, through inflationary means and the amassing of a huge foreign debt. During the 1990s, Brazil has been struggling to get out of this noose of debt with only limited success. The Newly Industrializing Countries (NICs) of Asia (Taiwan, South Korea, Singapore, and Hong Kong) are presented as on a second track toward joining global capitalism. Their relatively remarkable economic performance, at least until recently, has been accompanied by an "underside of growth" which has concentrated power in an authoritarian state in some instances and has contributed to degradation of the environment.

The second alternative is what Mittelman and Pasha call the exit option of withdrawing from and then re-entering global capitalism, illustrated by the People's Republic of China under and after Mao. The legacy of this strategy was the elimination of old power alignments and a metamorphosis in production, with low inflation and a significant reduction in reliance on external market forces. Counterbalancing these features has been a record of introduction and then reversal of economic policies, extensive coercion, and top-heavy governmental and bureaucratic structures. "In the final analysis," in their judgment, "China under Mao was unable to solve the problem of underdevelopment through policies designed to generate internal accumulation and (though not entirely by choice) to constrict external sources of capital accumulation." China's subsequent re-entry into the global political economy receives a mixed evaluation, suggesting "both the opportunities and uncertainties of development in an evolving world order."[102]

"Weaving through global capitalism" is the term for the third alternative, represented by the African country of Mozambique. The principal features of this strategy, which emerged from the colonial legacy of the country, were "creating new party and state organs, hastening a rural transformation, promoting heavy industry and redefining links with the international economy."[103] While acknowledging that Mozambique has encountered "an awesome combination of natural and social disasters," and that the economy has been in a state of "acute distress," Mittelman asserts that "several vital factors which foster development" may be found there, and that "elements of its strategy for escaping underdevelopment cannot be erased from historical memory and could suggest important lessons."[104]

Although these thumbnail summaries of alternative strategies tend to underscore the hazards of each, the basic outlook of Mittelman and Pasha is optimistic, as the title of their book indicates. The task, they assert, is to "identify principles which can be adapted to varied conditions." They point out lessons learned, such as that these countries cannot rely on stimuli generated by the advanced capitalist countries, that limits to exploitation can be set by the underdeveloped countries, that concrete measures can be devised and adopted but improvements do not come easily or steadily, and that it is hard to measure progress. "Although the escape from underdevelopment calls for a monumental feat," they conclude, "we can devise novel ways to abolish the grim conditions in which the majority of humankind has been condemned to live and chart strategies for the course ahead."[105]

A recent contribution by Julie Fisher to the problem of political development emphasizes the increasing importance of non-governmental organizations (NGOs).[106] The emergence of indigenous NGOs over the last three decades is credited with strengthening the institutions of civil society, which in turn promotes increased governmental responsiveness and accountability. She presents evidence that the prospects for achieving sustainable development and democratization are thus enhanced.

A quite different analysis comes from Paul Cammack, who argues that political development theorists since the 1950s have claimed to be aiming toward postulation of a universal theory, but were actually presenting a theory of political change in societies in the process of capitalist modernization, which was designed to promote capitalist rather than socialist development. He reviews this literature in detail, concluding that it is largely ideological in character, and that it should be replaced by a restatement of "a critical Marxist perspective on global politics and political economy for the twenty-first century."[107] He describes his book as a small contribution to that "large enterprise," presumably to be pursued in the future. My interpretation of his position is that although he concedes that "the capitalist system in the 1990s, for the first time in world history," can be described as "genuinely global in scale,"[108] capitalism is historically specific, and should eventually give way to some form of socialism as the preferable future for the currently less developed countries.

Many of these analyses and suggestions were made prior to the events in territories of the former Soviet Union, in Eastern Europe, in Africa, and elsewhere, that have prompted recent predictions by Huntington and others[109] stressing the hazards of cultural and ethnic group conflicts as barriers to development. The long-range accuracy of these warnings has not yet been proven or disproven, and little has been written advising as to strategy for mitigating such problems. At the very least, these recent events raise new issues affecting development programs.

The emphasis in all these discussions of future prospects for the developing countries is on incapacities for development and the explanatory reasons, and on recommended remedial measures, with slight attention being given to the question of whether development in the usually understood sense is a desirable goal.

This fundamental issue has been raised in recent years by some social scientists. Their position is that the contemporary advanced industrial societies are rapidly losing their appeal as models for underdeveloped countries. Instead, these leader societies, as they have previously been regarded, are being reduced to antireference groups in the context of global society. In brief, the argument is that the newer nation-states of the world no longer are aiming toward development of the kind considered attractive in recent decades, but are in actuality searching for and experimenting with alternative models as they shape their futures. They are groping for paths of societal change different from the road taken by present-day industrialized societies. The direction chosen may therefore be one not previously tried by countries ordinarily considered developed. More-over, it may be a direction now foreclosed to these societies because of choices and commitments made in the past. If so, the historical experience of these countries becomes relevant less as a guide than as a warning. The developing countries as a group still share common characteristics and face similar problems, which justify treating them as a major societal category, but standard development theory and practice are unresponsive to their requirements.

Such views have not yet jelled into any stabilized form, but the phrase most used to describe them is social systems delimitation, and the leading spokesman has been Alberto Guerreiro Ramos.[110] This concept is intended as an alternative to conventional approaches to the allocation of resources and personnel in social systems, which are claimed to be predicated upon the requirements of the market and its utilitarian ethos. The individual in society is considered primarily as a jobholder and an insatiable consumer, and the socialization process is geared toward improving individual capacity to succeed in employment and in consumption. Organizational and institutional effectiveness, in turn, is assessed from the standpoint of their contribution to the maximization of societal economic activities, leading to unidimensional types of organizational theory and practice, and undesirable policy science models of public choice.

Social systems delimitation offers a counterapproach. It is undergirded by what Ramos propounds as "the new science of organizations," only the outlines of which can be suggested here. The concern is not only with social systems required to enable individuals to succeed in a market-centered society, but also in all human societies. Ramos charges that standard organization theory, as derived from the time of Adam Smith to the present, has failed to provide an accurate understanding of the complexity of social systems analysis and design, because its psychological underpinnings have been confined by the market-centered society.

Ramos proposes to replace this unidimensional model of social systems analysis and design with what he calls the "para-economic paradigm," which emphasizes the notion of delimitation. The view of society implied by delimitation is that it consists of a variety of enclaves, of which the market is one—but only one and not necessarily the most important. The governance system should be designed with ability to formulate and implement policies required for optimal transactions between these social enclaves. Organization theory needs to be reoriented so that it deals not only with the hierarchical and coercive requirements of organizations engaged in market-centered economizing activities (economies, which include essentially all bureaucracies, both private and public), but also with the attributes of institutional arrangements in which members are peers (isonomies), and those in which an individual or small group provides direction but the personal choice of members is maximized and their subordination to formal controls is minimized (phenonomies). The role of the state would become that of fostering a multicentric society by formulating and enforcing "allocative policies supportive not only of market-oriented pursuits, but of social settings suited for personal actualization, convivial relationships, and community activities of citizens as well." This delimitative model is intended by Ramos to be generally applicable, as he puts it, "both in centric and peripheral nations." It represents his vision of postindustrial society, already partially realized and to be pursued further by what he calls a "do-it-yourself" approach.[111]

Whatever the eventual impact may be, for the near future social systems delimitation will be most relevant to a rethinking of the meaning of development and to a possible reshaping of public policy goals in developing countries. The quality of social life, according to Ramos, should be based on productive activities which enhance the sense of community of citizens. Since these activities are not necessarily to be assessed from the standpoint inherent in the market, strategies of allocation of resources and personnel at the national level should reflect an optimal combination of one-way transfers resulting from public policy decisions as well as two-way market-type transfers. This calls for expertise congenial to social systems delimitation for economic planning and budgeting in an expanded role for public policy-makers. Ramos is optimistic about prospects for doing this, suggesting that "there are many possibilities for the nations of the so-called underdeveloped world to recover immediately from their peripheral condition, if only they would find their own political will and thus free themselves from the syndrome of relative deprivation which they have internalized by taking the advanced market society as the scenario of their future."[112]

Proponents of social systems delimitation are thus convinced not only that this is a preferable theoretical base, but also that it is already in the process of acceptance by public opinion in developing societies, resulting in rejection of the example provided by advanced industrial societies, both capitalist and socialist, which have achieved high levels of material welfare through the development and application of technology. Along with this goes skepticism about extrapolating from the historical experience of European countries and the United States to predict or plan the course of developing countries.

The published writings to date on social systems delimitation are rather vague and unspecific as to actual or potential application of these theories in particular countries. The only cited instances of national efforts along these lines seem to be China during the Maoist period, Yugoslavia before its breakup, and Tanzania, without elaboration as to just how delimitation techniques have been applied. The Mozambique strategy as described by Mittelman and Pasha might be added as a more recent example. Both Ramos and Dunn seem to be in agreement that a model of development based on social systems delimitation would depend on a large measure of national self-reliance and inventiveness within the society. It would not be modernization by imitation of advanced industrial societies, and it would certainly reject any notion of unilinear evolution in the process of change.

Another more current and less cohesive example of reconceptualization is a collection of essays by several social scientists from various disciplines and with different points of view, all of whom addressed the issue of *how* rather than *what* to think about the future of these countries.[113] United by concern about what they regard as the failure of contemporary development theory to be sufficiently relevant to the dynamic histories of the peoples of Latin America, Africa and Asia, they describe their joint effort as offering insight "into the link between democracy and raising productivity; the respective influence of technology and social relations in industrialization; the contribution to and participation in development of peasants, primitives, and other, often ignored, stereotyped peoples; the conflict between individual freedom and authoritarianism; the changing relations of governments and bureaucracies to other governments, institutions and subject populations, and the political alliances formed around development issues." Underscoring what they regard as "the contradiction and crises inherent in contemporary Western models of development," they express general dissatisfaction with much of current social science, including modernization theory, mainstream development economics, behavioralism, dependency theory, world systems analysis, and modes of production analysis.[114] This broadside attack is not matched, however, by an articulated set of counter propositions.

As this review of concepts of modernization, development, and change has shown, "development" continues to be the most commonly used of these terms, but the degree of consensus on what development means and of satisfaction as to its adequacy is markedly less now than it was twenty plus years ago. This is especially evident in the work of the dependency, postindustrial, social systems delimitation, and reconceptualization theorists. It is legitimate to ask, therefore, whether the term "development" and related words should be abandoned altogether, and whether a distinction should continue to be made between a group of nation-states considered developed and another group considered to be underdeveloped or developing. Recognizing the handicaps involved, the position here is that in the contemporary world a distinct difference does exist and will continue to exist for at least the next few decades between these two sets of nation-states, and that the nation-state will continue to be the dominant system for societal organization.[115]

During our time, the so-called Western nations, plus some remnants of the former Soviet Union and countries of Eastern Europe, Japan, a few "Little Tiger" countries of East and Southeast Asia, and perhaps the People's Republic of China, do in fact have characteristics in common that justify grouping them together for purposes of analysis of their systems of public administration. The other present-day nation-states, although more numerous and displaying a dazzling and complex variety, also share characteristics making it worthwhile to consider them as a second major grouping, with identifiable subgroups. Perhaps some substitute set of terms will eventually be proposed and generally accepted, but that has not yet happened.

During recent decades, the phrase "Third World" came into common use with reference to the developing nations, but it is no longer realistically relevant. The first and second worlds in this triad were the United States and other Westernized democracies on the one hand, and the USSR and its satellites in Eastern Europe and elsewhere on the other. From early on this designation was misleading, because although Third World countries were originally supposed to be unaligned with either of the two superpowers, many of them in fact had close associations with one or the other, or even with both. The crucial consideration, however, is that the Second World does not now exist. The land areas and the populations are still there, but what justified calling them "Second World" no longer applies. Although it will not happen overnight, the sooner we abandon the label "Third World" the better.[116]

For our purposes, therefore, this usage never was an improvement, and it certainly isn't now. I do not propose to attempt the introduction of a novel alternative. Hence, we will use these categories of developed and developing nation-states as we proceed, even though for purposes of analytical progress in future comparative studies, I agree that there are advantages in shifting discussions of basic societal transitions from development, as the most prevalent term used, to the more generic and neutral concept of change.

NOTES

1. Daniel Lerner, *The Passing of Traditional Society* (New York: Free Press, 1958), p. 401.
2. Alex Inkeles and David H. Smith, *Becoming Modern* (Cambridge, MA: Harvard University Press, 1974), p. 15.
3. *Ibid.*, pp. 15, 16.
4. Monte Palmer, *The Dilemmas of Political Development* (Itasca, IL: F.E. Peacock Publishers, 1973), pp. 3, 4. Reproduced by permission of the publisher, F. E. Peacock Publishers, Inc., Itasca, IL. *Dilemmas of Political Development* is now available in a fourth edition, © 1989 by F. E. Peacock Publishers, Inc.
5. Alfred Diamant, "Political Development: Approaches to Theory and Strategy," in John D. Montgomery and William J. Siffin, eds., *Approaches to Development: Politics, Administration and Change* (New York: McGraw-Hill, 1966), p. 25.
6. Edward Shils, *Political Development in the New States* (The Hague: Mouton and Company, 1962), p. 10.
7. S. N. Eisenstadt, "Bureaucracy and Political Development," in Joseph LaPalombara, *Bureaucracy and Political Development* (Princeton, NJ: Princeton University Press, 1963), p. 98.

8. Reinhard Bendix, *Nation-Building and Citizenship* (New York: John Wiley & Sons, Inc., 1964), p. 300.

9. "Industrialization can be initiated only once; after that its techniques are borrowed; no other country that has since embarked on the process can start where England started in the eighteenth century. England is the exception rather than the model." *Ibid.*, p. 71.

10. In William J. Siffin, ed., *Toward the Comparative Study of Public Administration* (Bloomington, IN: Department of Government, Indiana University), pp. 23–116.

11. *Ibid.*, p. 28.

12. These considerations led in part to the reformulation by Fred W. Riggs of "fused" and "diffracted" for the polar types, with intermediate systems as "prismatic," as he explains in the preface to *Administration in Developing Countries: The Theory of Prismatic Society* (Boston: Houghton Mifflin, 1964).

13. Joseph LaPalombara, ed., *Bureaucracy and Political Development* (Princeton, NJ: Princeton University Press, 1963), pp. 35–39.

14. Norman T. Uphof and Warren F. Ilchman, eds., *The Political Economy of Development: Theoretical and Empirical Contributions* (Berkeley, CA: University of California Press, 1972), p. ix.

15. Ralph Braibanti and Joseph J. Spengler, eds., *Tradition, Values and Socio-Economic Development* (Durham, NC: Duke University Press, 1961), p. 8.

16. *Ibid.*, p. 9.

17. The most recent version is *The Stages of Economic Growth: A Non-Communist Manifesto*, 3rd ed. (New York: Cambridge University Press, 1990). Rostow's current assessment, taking into account the transformations in the former Soviet Union and Eastern Europe, is contained in the Preface, pp. ix–xxxviii. He predicts the emergence of a "Fourth Graduating Class . . . to full technological maturity," during the first half of the twenty-first century (including Argentina, Turkey, Brazil, Mexico, Iran, India, China, Taiwan, Thailand, and South Korea).

18. For an overview of these trends, refer to Charles K. Wilber, ed., 4th ed. *The Political Economy of Development and Underdevelopment* (New York: Random House, Inc., 1988).

19. Several summarization efforts have been made of the literature on political development. An early influential summary and analysis was by Lucian W. Pye in *Aspects of Political Development* (Boston: Little, Brown and Company, 1966). Later comprehensive reviews are Helio Jaguaribe, "Review of the Literature," *Political Development: A General Theory and a Latin American Case Study* (New York: Harper & Row, 1973), Chap. 8, pp. 195–206; Samuel P. Huntington and Jorge I. Dominguez, "Political Development," in Fred I. Greenstein and Nelson W. Polsby, eds., *Handbook of Political Science*, Volume 3, *Macropolitical Theory* (Reading, MA: Addison-Wesley Publishing Company, 1975), Chap. 1, pp. 1–114; Fred W. Riggs, "The Rise and Fall of 'Political Development'," in Samuel L. Long, ed., *The Handbook of Political Behavior*, Volume 4 (New York: Plenum Press, 1981), Chap. 6, pp. 289–348; Joel S. Migdal, "Studying the Politics of Development and Change: The State of the Art," in Ada W. Finifter, ed., *Political Science: The State of the Discipline* (Washington, DC: The American Political Science Association, 1983), pp. 309–338; and Stephen Chilton, *Defining Political Development* (Boulder, CO:

Lynne Rienner Publishers, 1988) and *Grounding Political Development* (Boulder, CO: Lynne Rienner Publishers, 1990).

20. Huntington and Dominguez, "Political Development," pp. 3–5.
21. Gabriel A. Almond and G. Bingham Powell, Jr., *Comparative Politics: A Developmental Approach* (Boston: Little, Brown and Company, 1966).
22. *Ibid.*, p.34.
23. "In our treatment of political structure we have emphasized role differentiation and subsystem autonomy as criteria of development, and in our treatment of political culture and socialization we have stressed the concept of secularization as a criterion of development. Similarly, in our treatment of the conversion process of politics, the themes of differentiation, structural autonomy, and secularization have served to distinguish the varieties of ways in which these functions are performed. In our treatment of the capabilities of political systems we have argued that particular levels and patterns of system performance are associated with levels of structural differentiation, autonomy and secularization. Finally, our classification of political systems is a developmental one in which the variables of structural differentiation, autonomy, and secularization are related to other aspects of the functioning of particular classes of political systems—their conversion characteristics, capabilities, and system maintenance patterns." *Ibid.*, pp. 299–300.
24. *Ibid.*, pp. 323–334.
25. Leonard Binder et al., eds., *Crises and Sequences in Political Development*, # 7 Series Studies in Political Development (Princeton, NJ: Princeton Paperback, 1974); published for Social Science Research Council. Copyright 1971 by Princeton University Press. Excerpts reprinted by permission of Princeton University Press.
26. For explanations of these concepts, see particularly Chap. 2, "The Development Syndrome: Differentiation-Equality-Capacity," pp. 73–100, by James S. Coleman. Capacity includes the attribute of rationality in governmental decision-making. Historically, this rationalization of government has been marked by "the emergence of a centralized civil bureaucracy staffed by personnel whose recruitment and status mobility are governed by achievement norms, and whose decisions reflect what Weber termed formal rationality (i.e., procedural formalization and the consistency of principle in decision-making). The peculiarly modern feature of this development is not the existence of centralized bureaucracy. Rather it is the predominance, pervasiveness, and institutionalization of the rational-secular orientation in political and administrative processes. This orientation is an absolutely indispensable ingredient in the creative capacity of a developing polity." *Ibid.*, p. 80.
27. *Ibid.*, p. 82.
28. These crises are discussed in detail by Binder in Chap. 1, particularly at pp. 52–67.
29. Sidney Verba, Chap. 8, "Sequences and Development," pp. 283–316.
30. Binder, Chap. 1, "The Crises of Political Development," pp. 64–65.
31. Helio Jaguaribe, *Political Development: A General Theory and a Latin American Case Study* (New York: Harper and Row, 1973). Copyright 1973 by Helio Jaguaribe. Excerpts by permission of Harper Collins Publishers.
32. Karl W. Deutsch, "Social Mobilization and Political Development," *American Political Science Review* 55 (September 1961): 493–514.
33. Samuel P. Huntington, "Political Development and Political Decay," *World Politics*

17, No. 3 (April 1965): 386–430, at p. 393. See also his book, *Political Order in Changing Societies* (New Haven, CT: Yale University Press, 1968).

34. Pye, *Aspects of Political Development*.

35. David E. Apter, *The Politics of Modernization* (Chicago: University of Chicago Press, 1965).

36. Myron Weiner, "Political Integration and Political Development," *Annals* 358 (March 1965): 52–64.

37. Irving Horowitz, with Josue de Castro and John Gerassi, eds., *Latin American Radicalism* (New York: Vintage Books, 1969).

38. Jaguaribe, "A Comprehensive Theory of Political Development," in *Political Development*, Chap. 9, pp. 207–218.

39. *Ibid.*, pp. 210–211.

40. *Ibid.*, pp. 213–217.

41. Harry Eckstein, *The Evaluation of Political Performance: Problems and Dimensions* (Beverly Hills, CA: Sage Publications, 1971). A related work based on a comparative analysis of twelve countries, using Eckstein's conceptual groundwork, is Ted Robert Gross and Muriel McClelland, *Political Performance: A Twelve-Nation Study* (Beverly Hills, CA: Sage Publications, 1971).

42. Roger W. Benjamin, *Patterns of Political Development* (New York: McKay, 1972), p. 11.

43. Palmer, *The Dilemmas of Political Development*, p. 3.

44. John B. Powelson, *Institution of Economic Growth: A Theory of Conflict Management in Developing Countries* (Princeton, NJ: Princeton University Press, 1972), p. ix.

45. Almond's original formulation of the kinds of capabilities required for development is in "Political Systems and Political Change," *American Behavioral Scientist* 6, No. 10 (June 1963): 3–10. A later version is in "A Developmental Approach to Political Systems," *World Politics* 17, No. 2 (January 1965): 183–214.

46. Eisenstadt, "Bureaucracy and Political Development," p. 104.

47. Alfred Diamant, *Bureaucracy in Developmental Movement Regimes: A Bureaucratic Model for Developing Societies* (Bloomington, IN: CAG Occasional Papers, 1964), pp. 4–15. See also his *Political Development: Approaches to Theory and Strategy*, prepared for the Comparative Administration Group, Summer Seminar, Indiana University, 1963, pp. 19–25.

48. Diamant, *Bureaucracy in Developmental Movement Regimes*, p. 14.

49. Samuel P. Huntington, "Political Development and Political Decay," *World Politics* 17 (1965): 386–430; *idem, Political Order in Changing Societies* (New Haven, CT: Yale University Press, 1968).

50. *Ibid.*, pp. 33–34.

51. *Ibid.*, pp. 53–54.

52. *Ibid.*, pp 86–92.

53. Gerald A. Heeger, *The Politics of Underdevelopment* (New York: St. Martin's Press, 1974).

54. John Kautsky, *The Political Consequences of Modernization* (New York: John Wiley & Sons, 1972).

55. Numerous publications in several languages present variations of these views. For

an excellent summary, see Tony Smith, "The Dependency Approach," in Howard J. Wiarda, ed., *New Directions in Comparative Politics* (Boulder, CO: Westview Press, 1985), Chap. 6, pp. 113–126.

56. For elaboration of these distinctions, see Jaguaribe, *Political Development*, pp. 381–385.

57. Andrew J. Sofranko and Robert C. Bealer, *Unbalanced Modernization and Domestic Instability: A Comparative Analysis* (Beverly Hills: CA: Sage Publications, 1972).

58. Inayatullah, *Transfer of Western Development Model to Asia and Its Impact* (Kuala Lumpur, Malaysia: Asian Centre for Development Administration, 1975), pp. 88–105.

59. Michael J. Francis, "Dependency: Ideology, Fad, and Fact," in Michael Novak and Michael P. Jackson, eds., *Latin America: Dependency or Interdependence?* (Washington, DC: American Enterprise Institute for Public Policy Research, 1985), pp. 88–105.

60. Major examples of such studies include David E. Apter, *Rethinking Development: Modernization, Dependency, and Postmodern Politics* (Beverly Hills, CA: Sage Publications, 1987); Joel S. Migdal, *Strong Societies and Weak States: State-Society Relations and State Capabilities in the Third World* (Princeton, NJ: Princeton University Press, 1988); Su-Hoon Lee, *State-Building in the Contemporary Third World* (Boulder, CO: Westview Press, Inc., 1988); Lawrence E. Harrison, *Underdevelopment Is a State of Mind: The Latin American Case* (Lanham, MD: University Press of America; 1985); Robert H. Bates, ed., *Toward a Political Economy of Development: A Rational Choice Perspective* (Berkeley: University of California Press, 1988); John L. Seitz, *The Politics of Development: An Introduction to Global Issues* (New York: Basil Blackwell, Inc., 1988); James H. Mittelman, *Out From Underdevelopment: Prospects for the Third World* (New York: St. Martin's Press, 1988); Stephen Gill and David Law, *The Global Political Economy: Perspectives, Problems, and Policies* (New York: Harvester Wheatsheaf, 1988); Herman E. Daly and John B. Cob, Jr., *For the Common Good: Redirecting the Economy toward Community, the Environment, and a Sustainable Future* (Boston, MA: Beacon Press, 1989); Ezra N. Suleiman and John Waterbury, eds., *The Political Economy of Public Sector Reform and Privatization* (Boulder, CO: Westview Press, 1990); Alvin Y. So, *Social Change and Development: Modernization, Dependency, and World-System Theories* (Newbury Park, CA: Sage Publications, 1990); Samuel P. Huntington, *The Third Wave: Democratization in the Late Twentieth Century* (Norman, OK: University of Oklahoma Press, 1991); Jan K. Black, *Development in Theory and Practice: Bridging the Gap* (Boulder, CO: Westview Press, 1991); Merilee S. Grindle and John W. Thomas, *Public Choices and Policy Change: The Political Economy of Reform in Developing Countries* (Baltimore, MD: Johns Hopkins University Press, 1991); Robert W. Jackman, *Power without Force: The Political Capacity of Nation-States* (Ann Arbor, MI: University of Michigan Press, 1993); James H. Mittelman and Mustapha K. Pasha, *Out from Underdevelopment Revisited: Changing Global Structures and the Remaking of the Third World* (New York: St. Martin's Press, 1997); Mark M. Turner and David Hulme, *Governance, Administration and Development: Making the State Work* (West Hartford, CT: Kamarian Press, 1997); and Herbert H. Werlin, *The Mysteries of Development:*

Studies Using Political Elasticity Theory (Lanham, MD: University Press of America, 1998).

61. The first edition of his *The Politics of Modernization* was published in 1965 (Chicago: University of Chicago Press).
62. Apter, *Rethinking Development*, p. 7.
63. *Ibid.*, pp. 9, 10.
64. Mittelman, *Out From Underdevelopment*, p. xiii.
65. Lee, *State-Building in the Contemporary Third World*, pp. 165–166.
66. Harrison, *Underdevelopment Is a State of Mind*, p. xvi.
67. *Ibid.*, p. 165.
68. *Ibid.*, pp. 169–176. Wooten, in *A Revolution in Arrears*, centers on management practices, and spotlights the role as change agents of innovative entrepreneurs.
69. Bates, *Toward a Political Economy of Development*, pp. 2–3.
70. "A major reason why politically rational choices are not economically optimal is that expenditures that represent economic costs might well be regarded by politicians as political benefits. Thus price distortions may create opportunities for rationing; although it is economically inefficient, rationing allows commodities to be targeted to the politically faithful. And government regulation may transform markets into political organizations, ones in which too few transactions take place at too high a cost but ones that can be used to build organizations supportive of those in power." *Ibid.*, p. 244.
71. Seitz, *The Politics of Development*, pp. xi, xii. Subsequent chapters deal with specific problem areas.
72. Mittelman, *Out From Underdevelopment*, p. xiv.
73. *Ibid.*, p. 80, Figure 4.1. See also Mittelman and Pasha, *Out From Underdevelopment Revisited*, p. 92.
74. *The Mysteries of Development*, pp. 9–10. A number of these books, with Huntington's *The Third Wave* being the best known, have stressed the evidence of a worldwide movement toward increased political competition. Apter, for instance, concurs that the long-run tendency is that "development will generate democracy," but he adds that this will not be done easily, and that "there are snares along the way—snares that result in violence and affect the future of the state itself." *Rethinking Development*, pp. 10, 11. This literature will be examined in more detail in Chap. 7.
75. Kautsky, *The Political Consequences of Modernization*, pp. 21–22.
76. Huntington and Dominguez, "Political Development," p. 96.
77. An effort at computer modeling of complex change involving demographic, economic, and political variables, applied to the political experience of Turkey and the Philippines during the 1950s, is made in Ronald D. Brunner and Garry D. Brewer, *Organized Complexity: Empirical Theories of Political Development* (New York: The Free Press, 1971).
78. (San Francisco, CA: Jossey-Bass Publishers).
79. *Ibid.*, pp. xvii, 25, 31–43, 44–55, 78, 147–148, 150–162, 204–223.
80. See his article, "The Clash of Civilizations?," *Foreign Affairs* 72, No. 3 (Summer 1993): 22–49, and his later book, *The Clash of Civilizations and the Remaking of World Order* (New York: Simon & Schuster, 1996).

81. "The Clash of Civilizations?," p. 22.

82. *Ibid.*, pp. 25, 48.

83. *The Clash of Civilizations and the Remaking of World Order*, p. 13. As might be expected, Huntington's analysis has provoked lively debate, both pro and con. See, for example, several responses in *Foreign Affairs* 72, No. 4 (September/October 1993): 2–26. For a later exposition similar to Huntington's, with stress on the rise of religious nationalism, refer to Mark Juergensmeyer, *The New Cold War?: Religious Nationalism Confronts the Secular State* (Berkeley, CA: University of California Press, 1993).

84. Thomas L. Friedman, *The Lexus and the Olive Tree: Understanding Globalization* (New York: Farrar, Straus and Giroux, 1999), pp. 28, 30, 35, 36. An earlier related study addressing "globalization" as a problem is Roland Robertson, *Globalization: Social Theory and Global Culture* (Newbury Park, CA: Sage Publications, 1992).

85. ". . . for the foreseeable future, world affairs will be dominated by a comparatively few postindustrial states, fewer than a dozen if the European Community is counted as one, a couple of dozen on issues that tempt European states to make their mark separately." Cleveland, *Birth of a New World*, p. 204. "Nation states will remain the most powerful actors in world affairs. . . ." Huntington, "The Clash of Civilizations?," p. 22.

86. *Power without Force*, p. 22.

87. Daniel Bell's thesis is set forth most fully in *The Coming of Post-Industrial Society: A Venture in Social Forecasting* (New York: Basic Books, 1973).

88. Of these alternatives, "information society" probably has been most used. This preference has been reinforced by Walter B. Wriston, in *The Twilight of Sovereignty* (New York: Charles Scribner's Sons, 1992). He argues that as the result of an information revolution as profound as the industrial revolution we have now entered a new era which he prefers to call the "Information Age." Perhaps the most ambiguous label is "technetronic society," coined by Zbigniew Brzezinski in *Between Two Ages: America's Role in the Technetronic Era* (New York: Viking Press, 1970). He describes such a society, at p. 9, as one that is "shaped culturally, psychologically, socially, and economically by the impact of technology and electronics—particularly in the area of computers and communications."

89. Bell, *The Coming of Post-Industrial Society*, p. 37.

90. *Ibid.*, p. 44.

91. Stephen Crook, Jan Pakulski, and Malcolm Waters, *Postmodernization: Change in Advanced Society* (Newbury Park, CA: Sage Publications, 1992), pp. 2, 3. The most specific suggestion as to "a defining outcome of postmodernization" is "an increased level of cultural effectivity," which is a way of saying that "culture as opposed to society or as opposed to material relationships is an expanding source of the causes of change in other arenas." *Ibid.*, p. 2 and Note 3, p. 42. See also John Hassard and Martin Parker, eds., *Postmodernism and Organizations* (Newbury Park, CA: Sage Publications, 1993), which concentrates more narrowly on "a conceptual framework for postmodern organizational analysis."

92. Writing in 1973, Bell said that "both systems, Western capitalist and Soviet socialist, face the consequences of the scientific and technological changes which are revolutionizing social structure." *The Coming of Post-Industrial Society*, p. 41.

93. Touraine asked whether the working-class movement was still at the center of conflicts in society, and answered that "in the programmed society, the working class is no longer a privileged historic agent . . . simply because the exercise of power within a capitalist firm no longer places one at the center of the economic system and its social conflicts." Neither firms nor unions are today's chief actors in the struggle over social power. Their conflicts "do not come to grips with real social power—in the United States, the Western social democracies, or in the Soviet bloc." The most highly organized sectors of the working class have not provided the leadership in support of new themes of social conflict; it has appeared instead "in the economically advanced groups, the research agencies, the technicians with skills but no authority, and, of course, in the university community. . . . Tomorrow's struggle will not be a repetition or even a modernization of yesterday's." Alain Touraine, *The Post-Industrial Society: Classes, Conflicts and Culture in the Programmed Society*, Leonard F. X. Mayhew, trasl., 1st American ed. (New York: Random House, 1971), pp. 17–18.

94. J. Rogers Hollingsworth and Robert Boyer, eds., *Contemporary Capitalism: The Embeddedness of Institutions* (Cambridge: Cambridge University Press, 1997).

95. *Ibid.*, p. 477.

96. David C. Korten, *The Post-Corporate World: Life After Capitalism* (West Hartford, CT: Kumarian Press, 1999), p.1.

97. *When Corporations Rule the World* (West Hartford, CT: Kumarian Press, 1995).

98. *The Post-Corporate World*, p. 2, and Chapters 7–10.

99. Earlier, reindustrialization challenged postindustrialization as a dominant trend, and some of the prevailing notions about group relationships under conditions of advanced social complexity were being reexamined. For examples, refer to Amatai Etzioni, "Who Killed Postindustrial Society?," *Next* 1, No. 1 (March/April 1980): 20; and Clarence N. Stone, "Conflict in the Emerging Post-Industrial Community: A Reassessment of the Political Implications of Complexity," 44 pp. mimeographed, prepared for the 1982 Annual Meeting of the American Political Science Association. More recent expressions of uncertainty as to the shape of the society said to be emerging have already been cited.

100. Seitz, *The Politics of Development*, p. 181.

101. Mittelman and Pasha, *Out from Underdevelopment Revisited*, pp. 106–107.

102. *Ibid.*, pp. 173, 179.

103. *Ibid.*, p. 183.

104. *Ibid.*, pp. 213, 214.

105. *Ibid.*, pp. 238–250.

106. Julie Fisher, *Nongovernments: NGOs and the Political Development of the Third World* (West Hartford, CT: Kumarian Press, 1998).

107. Paul Cammack, *Capitalism and Democracy in the Third World: The Doctrine for Political Development* (London: Leicester University Press, 1997), p 7.

108. *Ibid.*, p. 256.

109. Refer, for example, to Daniel Patrick Moynihan, *Pandaemonium: Ethnicity in International Politics* (New York: Oxford Paperbacks, 1993); and Gidon Gottlieb, *States-Plus-Nations: A New Approach to Ethnic Conflicts, the Decline of Sover-*

eignty, & the Dilemmas of Collective Security (New York: Council on Foreign Relations Press, 1993).

110. A Brazilian social scientist who came to the United States in 1966, Ramos was on the faculty of the University of Southern California until his death in 1982. Initial statements of his views are summarized in a "Brief Note on Social Systems Delimitation," 6 pp. mimeographed, prepared for the 1976 National Conference of the American Society for Public Administration, and in "Theory of Social Systems Delimitation: A Preliminary Statement," *Administration and Society* 8, No. 2 (1976): 249–272. The definitive formulation of his views is a landmark work, *The New Science of Organizations: A Reconceptualization of the Wealth of Nations* (Toronto: University of Toronto Press, 1981). W. N. Dunn of the University of Pittsburgh has presented similar points of view. See his paper, "The Future Which Began: Notes on Development Policy and Social Systems Delimitation," 63 pp. mimeographed, prepared for the 1976 National Conference of the American Society for Public Administration; and W. N. Dunn and B. Fozouni, *Toward a Critical Administrative Theory* (Beverly Hills, CA: Sage Publications, 1976).

111. *The New Science of Organizations*, pp. 135–136.

112. *Ibid.*, p. 168.

113. Rosemary E. Galli, ed., *Rethinking the Third World: Contributions Toward a New Conceptualization* (New York: Taylor & Francis, 1992).

114. *Ibid.*, pp. ix, xii.

115. On this issue, see J. D. B. Miller, "The Sovereign State and Its Future," *International Journal* 39, No. 2 (Spring 1984): 284–301.

116. For these reasons, I have tried as much as feasible to avoid the term, but I recognize that it is built into the literature of the past, and is still frequently used in current books and articles, although often somewhat apologetically and for the protection of a prior publishing investment. For example, in her introduction as series editor to a contribution in an ongoing series of monographs on "Issues in Third World Politics," Vicky Randall reviews arguments for and against continued use of what she calls "the well-worn phrase." While not insisting on "the continuing usefulness of the notion of a Third World," she ends up deciding not to retitle the book or the series; Robert Pinkney, *Democracy in the Third World* (Boulder, CO: Lynne Rienner Publishers, 1994), "Series editor's introduction," pp. vii, viii. Similarly, in her introduction as editor to *Rethinking the Third World*, at p. xv, Rosemary Galli admits that "the term *Third World* appears in the text for convenience only. It is problematic because it groups together social formations from Asia, Africa, and Latin America that have less in common than is generally assumed."

4

Historical Antecedents of National Administrative Systems

Each of today's nation-states has an administrative heritage combining in various proportions historical antecedents from the geographic region in which the contemporary nation-state is located, and from external sources through either imposition or importation of administrative concepts and institutions.

The need for an awareness of historical antecedents is self-evident, but providing historical background adequate to understanding is a difficult task. Sorting out and weighting the complex elements of any nation's administrative inheritance must be on a judgmental rather than a scientific basis. Such an effort is also handicapped by the relatively slight attention given to administrative history either by professional historians or by students of government and public administration.[1] In any case, only a brief, cursory, and highly selective treatment is possible here, focusing primarily on the political and administrative evolution of Western European countries because of their own importance and their global influence. Some attention is given to historical systems only remotely linked to this Western cultural tradition, but we will be more concerned with ancient and medieval civilizations which have contributed directly to evolution of the nation-state as the dominant model for ordering society, and bureaucracy as the most common form of large-scale organization.

ORGANIZING CONCEPTS FOR
HISTORICAL INTERPRETATION

Given the tremendous time span of human history and the enormous variety of human experience to be taken into account, any effort at summarization and explanation must be based on some interpretive theme or themes. Some leading students of administrative history have advanced various concepts intended to serve this purpose, and we will review several that are particularly suggestive.

The best known generalized attempt at interpretation summarizes the process as one of demystification, rationalization, and bureaucratization. Associated primarily with the historical studies of Max Weber, this view is that mankind has endeavored more or less continuously to move from myth to reason as a way of understanding phenomena, and that rational methods of operation have led gradually to more complex forms of organized effort, culminating in fully developed bureaucracies which approximate the characteristics of Weber's "ideal type." This explanation is closely echoed in Jacoby's book, *The Bureaucratization of the World.*[2] "Bureaucratic systems developed," he says, "in all instances where large groups of men existed in large areas creating the need for a central agency to deal with problems."[3] Modern all-encompassing bureaucratic organizations are the culmination of a long process of centralization and accumulation of power. Weber spoke with concern of the "overtowering" power of fully developed bureaucracy. Jacoby amplifies this concern, stating that the basic problem of our times is the concept of bureaucracy and what it entails by way of regulation, manipulation, and control. Mankind simultaneously demands, depends on, and deplores the apparatus of bureaucracy. Our age is characterized, according to Jacoby, by "the forceful transformation of rational administration into the irrational exercise of power, the lack of clearly defined limits to coercion, and the increasing competence of a state which arrogates independence to itself."[4] This interpretation centers on the paradox that bureaucracy is necessary and indeed inevitable on the one hand, but dangerous and potentially usurpative on the other. The seeds for this predicament were sown early, when historical civilizations found it necessary to create and then rely on the prototypes of present-day bureaucracies.

Nash has suggested a less disturbing theme in his monograph, *Perspectives on Administration: The Vistas of History.*[5] He is primarily concerned with the historical relationship between civilization and administration, using the term civilization to refer to the "achievement levels" of a society and administration to refer to its "organizational structures and techniques." His thesis is that "civilizations have flourished and maintained themselves only as they were able to effect a satisfactory balance between cultural achievement and the development of an organizational framework for society."[6] Closely related from the dawn of history, civilization and administration have helped determine the rise and fall of societies by the balance or lack of balance between them at various periods of time. Nash cites numerous examples of success by societies in making progress toward higher levels of culture because of supporting achievements in administration, and corresponding instances of societal decline when administrative systems have not been adequate to sustain existing civilizations at previously attained levels of complexity. He illustrates from the history of ancient Egypt and China, Greek city-states, Imperial Rome, Byzantium, Europe during the Middle Ages, mercantilist regimes of post-Renaissance absolutist monarchies, and nation-states of the last two centuries, among others.

In summary, Nash argues that past and present experience

> underscores the nexus between cultural progress and the attainment of administrative rationality. For better or worse, civilization and organization have been mutually dependent. . . . some form of balance between cultural accomplishments and administrative organization is desirable. Undue emphasis on one may undermine the very existence of a society. For example, the Athenians were preoccupied with intellectual accomplishments and neglected administration; in the case of Sparta, there was undue concentration on administrative rationality at the expense of creative cultural endeavors. A subtle blending of the two components, such as Rome achieved during the period of her greatness, as the Catholic Church maintained in the Middle Ages, and as the Atlantic civilization seems to have developed during the last 150 years, may promise the most enduring progress.[7]

Karl A. Wittfogel's main historical interest has been to explore the combination of circumstances in the past leading to the growth of complex bureaucratic systems as aspects of despotic patterns in society and government. His *Oriental Despotism: A Comparative Study of Total Power*[8] is the product of a lengthy and wide-ranging study which led him to the conclusion that such systems evolved in what he terms "hydraulic" societies. These were Oriental river valley civilizations which took advantage of opportunities to cultivate large areas of potentially fertile soil by supplying water not provided directly by nature. He distinguishes between small-scale irrigation farming when on-the-spot rainfall was not available, which he calls hydroagriculture, and hydraulic agriculture, requiring extensive construction of facilities to provide enough but not too much water. Realization of the possibility of hydraulic society depended not only on a natural setting combining an ample supply of water and sufficient fertile soil, but also cooperative human action on a large scale. The necessary degree of highly organized effort to construct the required irrigation and flood control works could only be obtained through governmental institutions capable of planning and executing such projects. The long-range consequence of the growth of these early hydraulic societies at various locations in the ancient world was "Oriental despotism" involving the claim to and exercise of "total power" by the rulers of such societies.

Wittfogel explores in great detail many aspects of this type of society, including the natural setting, the economy, the state and its despotic system of power, property patterns, and the class structure. Of special interest to us is his treatment of the reliance of the rulers of hydraulic societies on bureaucratic officialdom. The monopoly of societal leadership exercised by the masters of hydraulic society was dependent on their control of a complex governmental machinery. Hydraulic rulers permitted "no conspicuous and bureaucratically organized rivals," and exerted "exclusive leadership by ruthlessly and continually operating as a genuine monopoly bureaucracy."[9]

In Wittfogel's view, hydraulic society has two major subdivisions. "The masters and beneficiaries of this state, the rulers, constitute a class different from, and superior to, the mass of the commoners—those who, although personally free, do not share the privileges of power. The men of the apparatus state are a ruling class in the most unequivocal sense of the term; and the rest of the population constitutes the second major class, the ruled."[10] The ruling class in turn is divided into several subgroups. Atop the vertical structure is the sovereign ruler with his court, including the members of his personal entourage and perhaps a vizier or other official who shares authority operationally with the sovereign. Next are the ranking officials, both civil and military, who serve the ruler by exercising the limited decision-making power entrusted to them and who enjoy the status conferred by their stations. Below them in the bureaucratic hierarchy are large numbers of scribes and menial aides who carry on the routine work of administration. Horizontally, the ruling network of officials often covered a wide territorial area, but with central dynastic authority firmly maintained except in periods of disruption or dynastic decline, when greater local autonomy could be asserted. Despite obvious and significant differences among members of the ruling class, Wittfogel asserts that "there can be little doubt that the masters of hydraulic society, who enjoyed extraordinary privileges of power, revenue and status, formed one of the most class-conscious groups in the history of mankind." In all hydraulic societies "the potential and the actual rulers are deeply aware of their superiority to, and difference from, the mass of the ruled—the commoners, the 'people.'"[11]

Naturally, in such a society there were many social antagonisms—between the masses of the ruled and the rulers, among subgroups of the ruling class, and to some extent among different groups of commoners, but the monopolistic claims of societal leadership in the "total apparatus state" succeeded in hydraulic society in keeping the level of antagonisms under control while such a society persisted.

Wittfogel sheds much light on the historical origins of large-scale bureaucratic organizations in these early river valley civilizations with many shared characteristics, which evolved not only in Asia and the Middle East, but elsewhere under similar circumstances, such as in the Inca civilization of South America. His monumental study also attempts, much more controversially, to extend the concepts of "Oriental despotism" and the "Asiatic mode of production" to the USSR as the heir of hydraulic society in the twentieth century, but we do not need to describe or evaluate this aspect of his work here.

Our last and most significant example of a thesis for historical interpretation is presented by S. N. Eisenstadt in *The Political Systems of Empires*.[12] His interest is centered on a particular type of political system, which he considers of great importance for comparative purposes because these polities stand between "traditional" and "modern" political regimes, combining features of both and having had to contend with problems similar to those being faced by "new states."

Eisenstadt calls these examples "centralized historical bureaucratic empires" or "historical bureaucratic societies." This major type of political system is only one of seven which he suggests as a basis for classifying the most common forms of political systems in human history. Others include primitive political systems, nomad or conquest empires, city-states, and feudal systems. Modern societies, whether democratic, autocratic, or totalitarian, are grouped together as a type.

Polities with this label show great variety in their historical and cultural settings, but are claimed to share some fundamental characteristics which distinguish them from patrimonial and feudal societies on the one hand, and from modern political systems on the other. They achieved a limited differentiation of political activities, organizations, and goals, but not to the extent common in modern contemporary societies. "Thus," as Eisenstadt states, "in these political systems—*within the framework of the same political institution*—traditional, undifferentiated types of political activities and organizations coexisted with more differentiated and autonomous ones, all closely interwoven in the major aspects of political activity."[13]

Among these institutions were "distinct and separate organs devoted specifically to fulfilling various administrative and governmental functions."[14] They had such attributes as recruitment based mainly on criteria such as skill, wealth, achievement, or political loyalty rather than membership in a kinship or local-territorial group, internal organizational autonomy tending toward task centralization and specialization, hierarchical authority, and abstract rules for regulating work. They showed growing staff professionalization indicated sometimes by salaried personnel and usually by an ideology stressing service to the polity as represented by the ruler rather than personal service to the ruler. In other words, these were centralized *bureaucratic* empires.

A tremendous range of examples is offered by Eisenstadt as meeting these requirements. Ancient Egyptian, Chinese, Hindu, and Persian empires are included, and possibly those of the Incas and Aztecs as well. The later Roman,

Byzantine, and Ottoman empires also qualify. Perhaps more surprising is that the absolutist empires of Europe after the fall of feudalism are also put in this category, as are the colonial empires of European countries established in other parts of the world by conquest. Admittedly, these polities differ tremendously in geography, history, and culture, but Eisenstadt argues that they share political attributes which justify grouping them together. The place of the bureaucracy in the political process is fully explored,[15] with special emphasis on two paradoxical features. Bureaucracies were crucial for success to the rulers of such empires. Only through the development of bureaucratic institutions could the necessary degree of societal control and regulation be achieved following the growth of differentiation and the increase of "free-floating" resources. Also bureaucratic institutionalization helped provide stabilization of relations among groups in the society. The result was a considerable degree of dependency on the bureaucratic apparatus for the survival of these political systems. At the same time, the bureaucracy was in a position to achieve substantial autonomy because of its crucial role in perpetuation of the regime, and this presented possibilities for the bureaucracy to stray from the desired service orientation to the rulers and other major social groups. The resulting tendency was often for the bureaucracy to become self-oriented and displace service goals with goals of bureaucratic aggrandizement, and to escape from effective political control. This was a potential danger that would not always materialize because, as Eisenstadt says, "the conditions that gave rise to the extension of the bureaucracy's technical and service activities were not necessarily compatible with those which made its usurpation of political control and its displacement of service-goals possible."[16]

Thus Eisenstadt's analysis of the political systems of historical bureaucratic empires reaches the conclusion that in these polities can be found partial and ambivalent manifestations of two tendencies which continue to offer alternatives for modern political systems—either toward the growth of "latent despotic and totalitarian power" or toward realization of "the potentialities for the fuller free participation of different social groups in the political process."[17]

With these interpretive themes as points of reference, we will embark on a survey of the historical background for the contemporary nation-state political system and its administrative subsystem.

ANCIENT WORLD ORIGINS

Long before the time of any written historical records, mankind had laid the groundwork for the civilizations of recorded history. Administration in its basic sense of cooperative human endeavor aimed at achieving identified objectives obviously began very early. During Paleolithic and Neolithic times (extending roughly to 5000 B.C.), the discovery of fire and the development of a variety of stone weapons and tools paved the way for later technological advances. Belief in magic and the rise of primitive religious beliefs probably led to one of the earliest instances of specialization or professionalization in the *shaman* or religious practitioner. The antecedents of writing appeared in painting, sculpture, carving, engraving, and other artistic accomplishments. Even nomadic civilizations were dependent on considerable cooperation, the use of hunting weapons produced by skilled craftsmen, and other rudimentary forms of division of labor, specialization, and hierarchy.

More settled societies were made possible by the domestication of animals and the cultivation of crops, permitting transition from a food-gathering to a food-producing economy and the growth of communities with permanent sites and sizable populations. Beginning around 5000 B.C., in several parts of the world where conditions were favorable, river valley civilizations developed independently of one another, but sharing the attributes of "hydraulic society" as described by Wittfogel. The earliest of these civilizations is now generally conceded to be that of the Sumerians in the valleys of the Tigris and Euphrates rivers leading into the Persian Gulf, settled by emigrants from central Asian plateaus between 5000 and 4000 B.C., who gradually formed urbanized communities surrounded by agricultural lands made fruitful by irrigation and protected from flooding by large-scale public works, all of which was accomplished only because of Sumerian contributions in agriculture, engineering, mathematics, government, and other areas.

Finer comments on how amazing it is that here, "at the very dawn of recorded history, we should find not states with few functions and feeble means of execution, but the very opposite: states that are organized and administered, so it would seem, to the last degree. It is as if government as we conceive it today had already arrived, fully fledged, at the first moment the records begins to speak."[18]

Rather than trace chronologically similar developments elsewhere, it will serve our purposes better to mention briefly the chief examples of such river valley civilizations, widely separated geographically, which had little or no impact on the more interconnected chain of civilizations contributing directly to the Judaic-Greco-Roman cultural tradition of Western Europe, and then turn to the historical antecedents of that tradition.

In the Eastern Hemisphere, these autonomous examples are the ancient empires of China and India, and in the Western Hemisphere, the pre-Columbian civilizations located in present-day Mexico, Central America, and the northern parts of South America.

Chinese civilization has been marked by continuity and autonomy from very early times to the recent past, with Imperial China extending into the twentieth century. Finer refers to the Chinese state as "a wholly self-sufficient civilization and polity" that evolved "in total independence of the Mediterranean world."[19] Although no doubt having considerably earlier origins, Chinese culture can be traced only to about 1500 B.C., when the Shang dynastic system was already established in the Yellow and Yangtze river valleys, with what appears to have been a strong centralized government organized into ministries and staffed by powerful officials. Shortly before 1000 B.C., the Shang people were conquered by the Chou, ushering in the classical period of Chinese history under the Chou dynasty, which lasted until 247 B.C. Under the monarch, known as the Son of Heaven, a hierarchy of officials extended from a chief minister to functional ministers in areas such as agriculture, public works, and military affairs, and then to officials with territorial jurisdiction in areas ruled directly. A much wider control was exercised through feudal lords owing allegiance to the emperor but because of distance and other factors able to maintain considerable autonomy in handling local affairs. Literature and culture flourished during the Chou period, which produced the great philosophers Confucius, Mencius, and Lao Tsu. A system of education emerged which provided lengthy programs of study for those preparing for official careers and opened government officialdom to individuals chosen by ability rather than by birth.

Despite the length of the Chou dynasty, there were ups and downs in political stability and in the extent and degree of territorial hegemony, with numerous semi-independent states contending with one another during its later centuries. Out of this struggle came the brief Ch'in (256–207 B.C.) and longer Han (206 B.C.–A.D. 200) dynasties, which created what is usually considered China's golden age. Ch'in ruler Shih Huang Ti was known as the Great Unifier. He replaced feudal institutions with a system of prefectures whose administrators were frequently transferred, and in other ways undertook to standardize and centralize administration. He strengthened military defenses, and improved agricultural production. Chinese society became more highly stratified into five main classes (i.e., scholars, farmers, artisans, merchants, and soldiers).

After a brief interlude of resistance to centralism following the death of Shih Huang Ti, the Han dynasty built upon and extended his empire, organizing it eventually into a three-tiered system of provinces, prefectures, and districts. The Han rulers, following Confucian philosophy, undertook to shape an officialdom capable of governing such a large and complex empire. They perfected a method of selection based on competitive examinations, and revamped the educational system to prepare candidates according to their abilities rather than birth. These reforms, building on earlier similar efforts, succeeded in producing a stable and competent civil service which set the pattern for many centuries. Along with its good points, this strongly hierarchical system also carried the seeds of subsequent internecine struggles and a tendency toward overemphasis on stereotyped literary preparation for official careers.

Over three centuries of division into several separate states followed the weakening of the Han regime soon after A.D. 200, before the Sui dynasty restored order and undertook massive public works, including canals, palaces, and extension of the Great Wall in the north. These large-scale projects were accompanied by an overhaul of the administrative system, including improvements in the examination scheme and its supporting library facilities, and creation of a corps of traveling inspectors to check on the performance and loyalty of officials. Sui rule was brief, with the T'ang dynasty taking over in A.D. 618 for a period of almost 300 years to A.D. 907. This dynasty made no drastic break with the past, but gave special attention to agricultural production and grain storage, and to improvement of the system of schooling and examinations. Printing was introduced during this period, making an advance with widespread ramifications on administration in China and elsewhere later on.

Following the downfall of the T'ang dynasty early in the tenth century, China was split for most of the following three centuries into the Liao empire in the north, founded by nomad invaders, and the Sung empire in the south. Liao ruling practices were a peculiar combination of nomadic conquering power and Chinese administrative institutions adapted to the regime's purposes, with the empire divided into two regions, one more nomadic and the other more settled, each with its own set of governmental offices and officials.

The contemporary Sung dynasty in the south reached what Gladden calls China's "pinnacle of culture and science."[20] The governmental system was based on earlier Han and T'ang models adapted to new circumstances but not fundamentally changed. In external affairs, the concern was mainly with centers of power to the north—the Liao regime until it was overthrown in 1125, and then the Chin empire until 1234. A greater threat arose from the rapid expansion out of central Asia of the Mongols, who by 1280 had conquered all of China and had founded the Yuan dynasty, which in turn after less than a century was replaced by a Chinese regime, the Ming, which concentrated on restoration and consolidation of traditional Chinese civilization, succeeding at the task until the quality of its rulers fell and opened the way for yet another barbarian invasion by the Manchus in 1644. The Ch'ing dynasty of the Manchus lasted until the Chinese revolution of 1910 brought an end to this remarkable Imperial Chinese legacy.

The Chinese civil service, which evolved in ancient times and retained its basic characteristics through two millennia, is notable in two respects. First, as Gladden points out, the Chinese bureaucracy as an institution was "the one steadying factor that contributed more than anything else to the remarkable staying power of the Chinese civilization."[21] Second, by carrying over to modern times, it eventually exercised great influence on the development of modern civil service systems in the West.[22]

The Indian subcontinent, in contrast, neither produced as much continuity in its civilizations nor had as much impact on the West. Wittfogel's hydraulic society thesis does seem to be applicable, however. Between 2500 and 1500 B.C., the river valleys of the Indus and the Ganges had produced flourishing civilizations, before there occurred stagnation and decline probably due to neglect of irrigation systems and denuding of the forests. This process was reversed for a relatively brief period under the Mauryan dynasty which lasted from 322 to 184 B.C. Founded by Chandragupta, a military leader who ousted the occupation garrisons left a few years earlier by Alexander the Great, this kingdom included much of what is now Afghanistan and northern India. Essentially despotic and military, the regime nevertheless was highly organized, with a departmental structure staffed by officials hierarchically arranged and responsible for a pervasive network of state enterprises and monopolies as well as extensive health and welfare facilities. In the administration of this realm, Chandragupta was assisted by his vizier, Kautilya, reputed to be the author of a surviving Sanskrit treatise on statecraft, the *Arthasastra*.

Aside from this brief interlude, the history of India has revealed no ancient regimes comparable in extent or degree of complexity to those of China. Not until the rise of the Mughal empire in the sixteenth century did India produce a rival to the Mauryan regime of a millennium and a half earlier.

The civilizations of early America were in their origins contemporaneous with but of course completely autonomous from the ancient civilizations of the Old World. The cultures of the Mayas, the Incas, and the Aztecs, which are of most interest to us because of their impact on contemporary Latin American countries, trace their beginnings at least as far back as the second millennium B.C., although they peaked much later. We will comment on each briefly, discussing them roughly in the chronological order in which they reached their apex, and in ascending order as to their influence on currently existing nations.[23]

The territory inhabited by the Mayas consisted of the Yucatan Peninsula and adjacent areas, including present-day Guatemala, Belize, and parts of Mexico, Honduras, and El Salvador. The Mayan culture, dating back to at least 2000 B.C., was at its height during the period 500 B.C. to A.D. 900, and was in decline for several centuries before arrival of the Spaniards soon after 1500. Mayan society consisted of a widely scattered group of autonomous cities. Societal ties were not primarily political, since during most of Mayan history there was no capital city and no centralized empire. The cities were bound together not only by common language, and religious and cultural ties, but also were linked by an efficient road network which permitted extensive trade. Soil and climate combined to provide amply for the population, which was able to attain a high standard of living. Massive construction projects were undertaken, including temples and other public buildings, warehouses, and reservoirs and canals for water conservation. This was all accomplished despite the absence of work animals, the wheel, and metal tools.

This city-state system had a two-class society of nobles and farmers. Governance was headed by an official who combined civil and religious functions. Ordinarily, this office was filled by descent from father to son but another blood relative might be chosen. A council of members of the ruling family made this decision, as well as authenticating the exercise of power by the head of state. Elaborate ritual controlled appearance, adornment, dress, and performance, with religious significance being pervasive.

The Mayas are famous for their accomplishments in astronomy and mathematics, linked no doubt to their emphasis on religion and their support of a priestly class who acted as official astrologers. The only written record was in documents with pictorial glyphs, most of them destroyed by the Spanish. Little is known about their administrative structures and processes, but presumably these were relatively simple and confined mostly to each city-state. Only late in Mayan history, after 1200, is there evidence of a league among the city-states in northern Yucatan, with Mayapan as the capital, and this unusual experiment ended in 1441, before arrival of the Spanish.

Although descendants of the Mayas survive in large numbers today, the Mayan impact on colonial and contemporary society has been relatively slight, owing to such factors as less interest on the part of the conquering Spanish and a slower rate of conquest, the remoteness and scattered nature of the Mayan cities, and the fact that Mayan culture was on the decline after A.D. 1000.

The Incas of South America dominated an area stretching along the Pacific coast from modern Ecuador through Peru and into Chile. Pre-Inca cultures in the area can be traced to 1200 B.C., but these were later absorbed by the Incas, who suppressed information about them in order to build up the oral Inca tradition. Inca dominance came rather late, around A.D. 1250, resulting from successful expansion from the Cuzco Valley into surrounding areas. The organizational skill of the Incas seems to be largely responsible for their prominence. Life in Inca society was highly controlled. The basic social unit was the *ayllu*, a group of families varying in size from inhabitants of a small area to a large city. Land was owned by the *ayllu* and loaned out to members. A council of elders and an elected leader controlled the *ayllu*. These units were then combined into districts and other higher levels in a hierarchical system culminating in the *Sapu*, or Lord Inca, as a combination of supreme ruler and god. This position was hereditary, with the Lord Inca choosing his successor from among his sons. A sun-worshiping religion was closely linked to the state under a state-supported priesthood.

The organizational skills of the Incas were reflected in their management of public services. Power was centralized over a large geographic area through a hierarchy based on a span of control of ten for each level of supervision, leading from the individual worker to the Lord Inca at the apex of the hierarchy. Despite the lack of a system of writing, methods of communication, reporting, and recording were impressive, relying to a large extent on the *quipu*, which was a cord of threads of different colors which could be knotted so as to record statistical information. In addition, a road network, including bridges, provided an empire-wide means of communication and trade. There were no wheeled vehicles, but the llama was used as a beast of burden. Irrigation systems were built and extensive terracing aided in stimulating agricultural production and the cultivation of numerous foods now known worldwide, including the potato. The whole economic system was under state direction and control. Gladden sums up this way: "Authority and religious acceptance were at the root of the Inca system of government, but without the superb sense of organization which permeated their administrative arrangements and procedures their empire could not have functioned so efficiently as it did."[24]

When Cortez arrived in Mexico in 1519, he found a situation in which the Aztecs, from their base in the city of Tenochtitlan, where Mexico City now stands, had established a tributary system which enabled them to control most of the central plateau and the coastal area on the Gulf of Mexico. Aztec dominance was relatively recent, having been achieved only in the twelfth and thirteenth centuries. The Aztecs were preceded by and built upon the cultures of the Olmecs on the coast who dated back to 800 B.C., the Zapotecs inland to the south who centered at Monte Alban from 500 B.C., and the Toltecs on the central plateau who, beginning about 200 B.C., built the ceremonial city of Teotihuacan northeast of Mexico City. Arriving in the area of the Toltec civilization 500 years after it had mysteriously gone into decline, the warlike Aztecs combined a theocratic political system with an efficient military machine to conquer and then maintain control over a large number of tribes through indirect rule based on extraction of tribute.

Although the Aztecs inherited the cultural achievements of their predecessors rather than being innovators themselves, they did improve on what they found and contributed a talent for efficiency in both warfare and civil administration. The Aztec social system was based on clans, each with an elected leader, and an interclan council, which chose the Aztec ruler from among the brothers or nephews of the previous ruler. This overlord combined state, religious, and warfare leadership roles, all conducted according to elaborate customary ritual.

Aztec power was based on military prowess. Aztec administration was effective without being highly centralized, since subject tribes were allowed considerable local autonomy provided they remained submissive and met their tribute obligations. This decentralized system was feasible because of well-maintained roads that allowed rapid movement of warriors and messengers.

The nature of the Aztec empire also made it vulnerable, helping to explain its rapid overthrow by the Spanish, who were able to gain allies from subject tribes to combine with their advantages in weaponry and ruthlessness, with the result that Aztec civilization was systematically destroyed, not to be extolled again until recently following the 1910 revolution, as a manifestation of Mexican nationalism.

Although all these historical societies have had some influence on contemporary Western systems, either through peripheral contacts during their heyday or because of more recent borrowings from their experience, the mainstream of

Western development resulted from the convergence in the Roman Empire of three cultural currents—those from Fertile Crescent, Egyptian, and Mediterranean city-state civilizations.

The Sumerian civilization was only the first of a series of great empires that rose and fell in the Fertile Crescent area over a time span of 3000 years. The successor Babylonian, Assyrian, Chaldean, and Persian empires flourished for varying periods of time from different geographical bases, with overlaps, borrowings, and adaptations by the later from the earlier cultures. From this Middle East region came some of the most noteworthy contributions to technology and statecraft. To mention just a few examples, these included the first use of the wheel; the first instances of urbanization on a large scale; the coming of the written record, produced initially on sunbaked brick, later on clay tablets, and leading from pictographs to cuneiform signs and eventually to the development of a written alphabet; and the promulgation of comprehensive law codes, the most famous being the Laws of Hammurabi of about 1000 B.C. in Babylon. This era provides some of the most impressive cases both of Wittfogel's "hydraulic society Oriental despotisms" and Eisenstadt's "centralized historical bureaucratic empires." Governments were generally despotic with minimum popular participation, but they recorded remarkable accomplishments in material undertakings made possible by administrative systems which could harness and direct the immense manpower resources available for exploitation.

Ancient Egypt, although now thought to have been antedated by Sumer as the birthplace of civilization, reached a similar level at nearly the same time, and thereafter sustained a distinctive and homogeneous culture for at least 3000 years to 332 B.C. The Nile provided the setting for a river valley civilization without parallel. Long and narrow, with desert on each side, the Nile offered the ideal combination of fertile land which could be dependably and amply irrigated, and natural defenses against external invasion. Village settlements sprang up first in the delta of the lower Nile during the fourth millennium B.C., with communities spreading up the valley as time passed, leading initially to separate political institutions in the lower and upper halves. Integration of northern and southern Egypt is credited to Menes, the first Pharaoh, in about 3200 B.C.

Subsequent Egyptian rulers are grouped into thirty-one dynasties, with Egyptian political history divided into four major epochs: the Old Kingdom (to 2180 B.C.), the Middle Kingdom (2080–1640 B.C.), the New Kingdom (1570–1075 B.C.), and the Late Period (1075–332 B.C.). Before the end of the Old Kingdom, several developments closely identified with Egypt had already taken place, including the use of papyrus as a writing material and the construction of tomb pyramids and other monumental edifices. Following a century of division, the country was again united, power was centralized, new construction projects were completed, and expansion by conquest and trade was accomplished during the Middle Kingdom.

The Middle and New Kingdoms are separated by a seventy-year period of rule by the Hyksos people from the southern uplands, before a liberation war ushered in a 500-year golden age of glory and territorial expansion which reached as far as Palestine and Syria. Then began a long era of gradual decay, economic decline, social unrest, and retraction of boundaries, with invasions once by the Assyrians in 670 B.C. and twice by the Persians in 525 and 341 B.C., during the so-called Late Period.

Despite vicissitudes, the hallmarks of ancient Egyptian history are stability and continuity. Rule by the Pharaohs, firmly sanctioned by religious beliefs, was an absolutism generally touched by benevolence. The idea of life after death was a powerful motivator, accounting for lavish use of resources in preparation for the afterlife, and incidentally responsible for the preservation of so much information about Egyptian lifestyles.

Clearly one of the reasons for Egyptian institutional longevity was the high level of administrative services achieved, ranking the Egyptians with the Chinese as creators of the most impressive bureaucracies in the ancient world. The pattern was set under the Old Kingdom, which was extensive enough to call for delegation and specialization. The practice of appointing a deputy to the Pharaoh in the position of vizier was adopted early, as was a system of functional central officers including a treasurer, a chief architect, a superintendent of public works, and a chief justice. Territorial jurisdiction for local government purposes was through units called *nomes*, each under a *nomarch* appointed by the Pharaoh. The *nomarch* was an all-purpose official, whose responsibilities included irrigation and agricultural production, care of temples and other public structures, tax collection, control of the local militia, and local administration of justice. Royal deputies posted as aides to the *nomarch* were in fact inspectors acting in behalf of the central authorities.

Egyptian officialdom was a mixture of members of the royal family, priests, holders of sinecures, scribes, architects, engineers, and craftsmen of various kinds. There was no single public service organized along standardized lines. Offices had a tendency to become hereditary and sometimes were subject to purchase. For important posts, knowledge of hieroglyphics was needed, requiring lengthy training to master reading, writing, and arithmetic, and leading to a degree of professionalization and shared interests among those with such skills.

Along with what must have been competent performance by many officials, evidence of abuse and inefficiency also exists. Over-standardization, bribery, duplication of offices, excessive red tape, extortion, and laziness were all complained against. The ebb and flow of administrative performance no doubt helps explain the peaks and valleys in Egyptian political history. Gerald Nash uses the Egyptian experience as a prime example of his thesis that cultural achievement and organizational framework must be balanced. Attributing the long gradual decline during the Late Period in large measure to the administrative system's decreasing efficiency, he summarizes:

> The decrease in the effectiveness of royal administration led to the decline of agricultural innovation and development. The inability of the central government to protect the nation from foreign invaders hastened decay. Similarly, the preoccupation of royal administrators with religious formalism led to the gradual deterioration of the communications systems and of engineering projects in which the Egyptians had once pioneered. The belief in magic retarded scientific and artistic work and helped to slow cultural advance. Thus, the level of Egyptian civilization was closely related to its organizational framework."[25]

The ancient societies which most influenced later developments in Western Europe were situated in the land areas surrounding the Mediterranean basin. Several Fertile Crescent empires extended their domains to the eastern fringes of the Mediterranean, and of course Egypt, from its very beginnings in the Nile Delta, was a Mediterranean society.

Geography also helps to explain the impact of the Hebrew people of the Old Testament, whose promised land was found at the eastern end of the Mediterranean after their exile in Egypt. Relatively insignificant in contrast to the great ancient empires in terms of territorial power, as shown by the Babylonian captivity and other historical evidence, the Hebrew kingdom was nevertheless the source of the Judaic-Christian religious tradition which became so central to Western development after the Christianization of the Roman Empire.

None of these societies, however, provided the distinctive political contribution of the Mediterranean borderlands. The Mediterranean city-state, which evolved here, was a dramatically different political entity from the ancient Oriental despotisms and bureaucratic empires. Finer views the classical Greek *polis* as antithetical to most preceding polities, and as revolutionizing the theory and practice of governing.[26]

The city-state apparently took shape independently, or by colonization, in various locations in the Mediterranean basin, in response to conditions which facilitated emigration, communication, and trade by sea among widely scattered Mediterranean communities. Earliest among these city-state societies were the Phoenicians of the eastern coast, the Mycenaeans and Minoans of mainland Greece and the island of Crete, and the Etruscans of the Italian peninsula. Their colonizing efforts, particularly those of the Phoenicians, reached throughout the circumference of the Mediterranean over a long period extending back into the second millennium B.C. The principal successors to these earlier city-state civilizations were Carthage in North Africa (originally a Phoenician colony), the city-states of classical Greece (notably Athens and Sparta), and Rome as a city-state and republic prior to establishment of the empire by Augustus in 27 B.C.

These city-states characteristically had a central metropolis surrounded by a rural hinterland, with the whole area relatively small as compared to either earlier ancient empires or modern nation-states. Usually they were located on or near the sea, and dependent on water routes for communication and trade. City-state autonomy was highly valued, with confederations among even friendly neighboring communities shifting and usually short-lived. Although several such city-states (including Carthage, Athens, and Rome) eventually developed into extensive empires, they tended to retain their basic political configuration, with only Rome eventually deliberately abandoning the old forms and turning to an imperial regime.

The city-state did not have a standardized set of political institutions, but a common tendency was to move from early kingships linked to a class system of nobles and lesser groups toward a governmental pattern which provided for political control by the free male citizens of the city-state through mechanisms which emphasized, in various degrees of combination, seniority and rotation in office. Sparta and Athens offered contrasting examples. Sparta retained more elements from the monarchic era, had a more rigidly stratified social structure, and was much more highly organized. A dual kingship survived representing the two royal houses from which the city-state had emerged. The two kings and twenty-eight nobles who had to be at least sixty years old formed a Council of Elders, with their selection being formally approved by an assembly of Spartan citizens over thirty years of age. Over time the principal governmental authority became centered in the ephorate, consisting of five citizens originally chosen by lot for one-year terms, but who later became eligible for reelection and began to serve for extended periods of time. Service to the state was the paramount value of the Spartan citizenry, but participation was barred to a large proportion of the population, the Helots, who were held in a condition of serfdom.

In Athens a more flexible and participative system evolved, but it also was predicated on a social system which reduced half the population to a status of subservience. By 500 B.C., under reforms sponsored by Cleisthenes, a Council of Five Hundred had been established, representing Athenian freemen, as the chief governing authority, under the Ecclesia or general assembly. Selection of council members was done annually by lot, on the basis that this method represented the impartial judgment of the gods, thus theoretically providing equal access to all Athenian citizens. To facilitate the conduct of state business under such an unwieldy council, the practice evolved of dividing the membership into ten committees, each with fifty members functioning on behalf of the council for a tenth of the year.

Rome also was under a king originally, with political leadership in the hands of aristocratic families who formed the patrician class, with tribal units serving as the basis for governmental operations. Joint meetings of tribal groups constituted the first popular assembly, which gave formal ratification to the choice of new kings, but had no actual authority. A council of elders, or Senate, made up of members of patrician families, served in an advisory capacity, but had the crucial responsibility of selecting a new king in case of a vacancy, since the office was not hereditary.

Gradually the kingship gave way to a system in which two consuls held office jointly for a year, with the Senate continuing as an advisory body but really the source of power because of its responsibility to choose the consuls annually. This republican system evolved slowly, with the most important development being the organization of the plebeian class and creation of a new set of institutions with an assembly, and officers called tribunes to represent the plebeians with the Senate and consuls. Numerous other offices emerged in connection with this involved dual system, which permitted patrician dominance but protected strongly held plebeian interests in a complex, flexible, and slowly shifting set of institutions. This highly traditional system survived long after Rome had expanded from its city-state base to control first the Italian peninsula and by the last century B.C. an empire which included nearly all the territory surrounding the Mediterranean Sea.

Public administration in the Mediterranean city-state was neither clearly differentiated nor amply staffed. Public officials held office for short intervals and were amateurs rather than professionals. Being generally wealthy, with high social status, they were expected to and were able to contribute to the state from their personal resources and to rely for help on family members and household slaves. Nothing comparable to a permanent civil service was created. Only minor posts with routine functions such as policing, record-keeping, providing messenger services, and performing other minor administrative tasks were held on a semipermanent basis, often by either public or private slaves. Administrative functions, initially simple and manageable using this approach, gradually outgrew the capability of the available administrative machinery, with grave consequences for survival of the city-state as a political entity. The decline of the classical Greek city-states is frequently linked to this deficiency in coping with political and administrative demands. Nash observes, for example, that "the relatively brief span of Greek supremacy may in part be attributed to the failure of the Greeks, despite their great cultural contributions, to develop an administrative system within which their culture could flourish."[27] Argyriades states that "the growing inability of the ancient city state to resolve those problems satisfactorily would soon lead to its demise and incorporation in the large empires of the Hellenistic and later Roman periods."[28]

The Roman response was slow and deliberate, but it was sufficient. J. H. Hofmeyr mentions three reasons to explain the long delay in adjusting the governmental system to the fact of empire.[29] Foremost were the power of tradition and the inherently conservative nature of the Roman people, who preferred to adapt old institutions rather than create new ones. Next was the circumstance that most of the territory conquered by the Romans up to the end of the republic contained settled communities organized usually on a city-state basis, so that the government in place could continue to be used. Finally, Rome did not deliberately set out to become an imperial power, and hence did not plan for an administrative system suited to empire.

As military successes multiplied and boundaries expanded, Rome began to experience increasing difficulties at the center, with unrest and inaction leading to repeated seizures of power from early in the second century B.C., by leaders such as the Gracchi brothers, Marius, and Sulla, none of whom succeeded in maintaining power or bringing about lasting reforms. By 70 B.C., Pompey had established himself as the most prominent leader, only to be challenged by Julius Caesar, who eventually forced the Senate to recognize him as a constitutional dictator. Caesar's efforts at overhaul were cut short by his assassination in 44 B.C., leading to the triumvirate of Lepidus, Mark Antony, and Octavian (who was Julius Caesar's adoptive son). In the ensuing struggle for supremacy, Octavian won out. He returned to Rome in 29 B.C. firmly in control, and in 27 B.C. the Senate conferred upon him the title Augustus, paving the way for him to undertake the conversion of Rome from a republic to an imperial empire.

IMPERIAL ROME AND BYZANTIUM

The Roman Empire persisted from 27 B.C. to A.D. 476 in the West, centered in Rome, and for a much longer period, to A.D. 1453, in the East, with the capital in Byzantium (renamed Constantinople). The heritage of the Roman Empire, in combination with the Catholic church, clearly provides the dominant historical influence on development of Western European political and administrative institutions. We can mention only a few of the most important features from a system which changed over centuries of time, and took distinctly different shapes in the western and eastern segments after breakup of the unified empire.

As the principal architect of the imperial structure which replaced the republic of the Roman city-state, Augustus proceeded in a slow step-by-step manner which suited both his own personality and the temperament of the Roman people. As Hofmeyr puts it, he succeeded because he made the Romans believe that he was not really founding anything at all. Originally, he rejected the title Emperor, preferring Princeps or first citizen. The arrangement he arrived at with the Senate was to create a diarchy under which he and that body ruled as two concurrent authorities, dividing legislative powers, supervision of executive agencies, and governance of provinces of the empire between them. His obvious intent, however, was for the diarchy to move toward monarchy. That is in fact what happened, to a major degree under Augustus himself, and by stages under his successors, until imperial rule was eventually legally sanctioned after it had been established in practice. By the time of Diocletian, who ruled from A.D. 284

to 305, the last traces of republican institutions disappeared, and the emperor became an absolute monarch. Nevertheless, as Brian Chapman points out, Roman law continued to embody two legal principles which have a direct bearing on the modern state. The first was that the head of state received his powers from the people, even though the ruler might be invested with all-embracing authority. "Even the virtually all-powerful Roman Emperors," Chapman says, "remained the representatives of the state, and held and exercised their powers in the name and interests of the state."[30] The second was that a distinction must be made between the private and public personalities of the head of state, meaning in practical terms a differentiation between the resources of the state itself, and the personal resources of the head of state. Acknowledged by Augustus and many of his successors, these principles later became eroded and sometimes even rejected, but remained as Roman legal concepts to be revived as precedents long after the Roman Empire had itself dissolved.

Among the reforms initiated by Augustus, improvement of the administrative system was most important. Gradually the transition was made from unpaid amateur short-term officials drawn from the privileged classes to a paid professionalized civil service with more open access and offering the prospect of lifetime careers. Faced with the necessity of broadening recruitment of officials beyond the nobility as represented by the Senate, Augustus drew upon two elements of the population. Members of the Equestrian order became the source for filling many important posts below the highest levels, which continued to be reserved for representatives of the Senate. The Equites were originally the cavalry arm of the Roman army, made up of citizens wealthy enough to provide horses when they entered military service. Later these military connotations disappeared, but the Equestrian class remained as an upper middle class in Roman society, barred from the privileged circle of the Senatorial order, but distinguished by their wealth from the bulk of the population. Augustus reserved most of the posts in his sphere of administration for members of the Equestrian class, and used them effectively as a counterweight to the Senate, with the result that over time they provided the core of the imperial bureaucracy. The other element was the extensive slave segment of the population, including many highly educated and cultured slaves from the eastern portions of the empire, as well as skilled artisans and other specialists who could provide a variety of much needed services, at minimal cost. The use of household slaves by public officials in carrying out their duties was a long-standing practice which could be followed by reliance upon imperial household slaves, with the distinction between private and public status becoming blurred gradually, so that the slave ranks eventually produced the bulk of the civil service. Slavery in this context did not necessarily mean abject servitude in menial tasks. Often slaves were freed in recognition of their services, and many slaves or ex-slaves came to occupy influential posts.

To bring order to this expanding bureaucracy, steps were taken to clarify hierarchical relationships and to set up grades for purposes of establishing salary levels for both the Senatorial and Equestrian career categories (with six and four stages, respectively). Less elaborate organizational arrangements were worked out for the lower grades.[31]

Augustus also undertook a rationalization of the administrative structure to provide more adequate machinery for centralized control and to engage directly in activities which had formerly been contracted out. For example, the practice of collecting taxes through tax-farming arrangements was largely replaced by the use of new revenue-collecting agencies. Provincial officials generally were subjected to much closer scrutiny and were made more accountable. Great emphasis was placed on the development and codification of legal rights and duties applicable to inhabitants throughout the empire.

Along with these efforts to improve capabilities for direction from the center, the administrative system of the early Roman Empire continued to rely heavily on the pre-existing city-states which had been brought within the sphere of Roman rule. A high degree of devolution of administrative functions not requiring uniformity had the twin advantages of reducing unrest among the subject population and lessening the demands on the imperial bureaucracy.

Later developments both improved upon and detracted from the accomplishments initiated by Augustus. His successors continued with the process of expanding, organizing, and professionalizing the imperial civil service. This process peaked in the regime of Hadrian (A.D. 117–138). By that time, the administrative system was at its most effective level, as evidenced by the generally prosperous condition of the empire and the impressive accomplishments in road-building, aqueduct and drainage works, monument construction, provision of hospitals and libraries, and many other state-sponsored activities. Later on, in the view of most historians, the bureaucracy became too large, overcentralized, inflexible, and oppressive, contributing significantly to the eventual decline. How much blame should be placed on bureaucratic excesses and how much on intractable problems such as threat of invasion, civil disorder, pestilence, and economic stagnation is of course hard to unscramble. At any rate, it seems clear that by A.D. 300, during the reign of Diocletian, the bureaucracy was most highly organized on hierarchical lines patterned after the military but was also beyond its prime as an effective instrument for preserving the empire.

In A.D. 330, Emperor Constantine moved the capital of the empire to Byzantium, which became the center first for a weakened unified empire and then for an eastern realm which lasted for 1000 years. The division of the empire took place in A.D. 395, at the death of Theodosius the Great. After a losing struggle against barbarian invasions and internal decay, the western empire succumbed late in the fifth century. After one final unsuccessful attempt to regain the west by Justinian the Great in the middle of the sixth century, the Byzantium Empire became the inheritor of the Roman tradition, modified in two basic aspects. From Constantine on, Christianity became the official religion, and culturally Byzantium was highly influenced by Oriental civilizations. The resulting mix was a complicated and intricate amalgamation of political institutions similar to those of Rome during the later empire, overlaid by a state religion with a worldly quality, and borrowing many features from nearby cultures in the East. Resiliency and adaptability were prime characteristics, permitting an accordion-like expansion and contraction of boundaries as the fortunes of the regime rose and fell, until its final overthrow by the Ottoman Turks in 1453.

The keystone to governmental power was the absolutism of the emperor. The incumbent chose his successor whose coronation was by church officials. The prerogatives of office were dramatized by elaborate Oriental court ceremonial. The pattern was set under Justinian in the sixth century. The Justinian Code restated and revised Roman law for the needs of Byzantium. The royal court in Constantinople included high officials who functioned as a central executive, heading the various administrative offices. Military and civil hierarchies were kept separate, in order to strengthen imperial control. The civil administration was organized under a tight hierarchical system of provinces and several lower administrative levels, all closely accountable to the central administration. The approach to government was comprehensive and paternalistic, with the state regulating the economy closely, operating a variety of industrial enterprises directly, supporting an elaborate educational system, and providing at least rudimentary social services.

The extensive bureaucracy required to carry out these multiple functions seems to have been generally competent, chosen with merit considerations foremost and trained for specialized roles. A ranking system and corresponding titles conferred by the emperor provided an orderly framework for management of bureaucratic careers and identified officials as servants of the emperor. The longevity of the Eastern Roman Empire is at least in part accounted for by the performance record of the Byzantine administrative machinery.

Byzantium certainly had widespread influence, not only in political and administrative matters, but in art, architecture, religion, and other fields. The impact on Western Europe was somewhat muted and indirect as compared to the Byzantine inheritance of imperial Russia and other countries of Eastern Europe, as channeled not only through their political institutions but through the Eastern Orthodox church.

For our purposes, the main reason for interest in administration in the Roman Empire, as manifested in both East and West, is its attraction centuries afterward to the builders of postfeudal governmental institutions in Europe. Chapman puts it this way: "The longlasting success and the logical clarity of the administrative structure could not fail to impress the statesmen and jurists of later generations when once again the achievements of the Roman Empire came to be known." He also points out that in the Roman administrative system, four of the five "main pillars of administration" can already be identified in the administrative pattern: military affairs, finance, justice, and police. Modern systems follow this basic model, with the "police" function broken into its component parts, and with the fifth "pillar," foreign affairs, becoming more institutionalized than it was under the Roman Empire as the direct responsibility of the head of state or his personal representatives.[32] Finer offers a similar positive assessment of the Roman contribution, asserting that its legacy was ideational, and that without it "neither Europe, nor after Europe the entire world, could ever have been remotely like it is today."[33]

To summarize, the main legacies of Roman law and administration are (1) the principle that the head of the state receives his powers from the people, (2) a distinction between the private and public personalities of the head of state, (3) the hierarchical nature of the administrative structure, and (4) the division of government into major constituent parts which are still recognized for purposes of administration.

EUROPEAN FEUDALISM

"For 500 long years after the last emperor of the Roman Empire in the West had been deposed its provinces slid deeper and deeper into anarchy and decay. Indeed, it is only with the benefit of hindsight that one can discern around the year 1000 the turning-point towards a new political and social order."[34] The breakdown of the Roman Empire, and the centuries of feudalism that followed, drastically disrupted the Roman concepts of government administration and reduced the provision of public services to a rudimentary level. The result, as Bendix points out, is that "the overall similarity of the Western European experience" arose "from the common legacies of European feudalism," rather than from the influences of an earlier time.[35] The dominant authority relationship in feudalism was between lord and vassal, with reciprocal ties providing an element of stability. In Western Europe these relations between ruler and vassals were "consecrated through the affirmation of rights and duties under oath and before God."[36] Legal rights were personal rather than territorial; each man belonged to a jurisdictional group, which determined his rights and duties for him. "Accordingly," says Bendix, "medieval political life consists in struggles for power among more or less autonomous jurisdictions, whose members share immunities and obligations that are based on an established social hierarchy and on a fealty relation with the secular ruler whose authority has been consecrated by a universal church."[37]

These characteristics of feudalism emerged very slowly as Western Europe adjusted its social system to the circumstances of the dissolution of Roman authority. Weakened Roman institutions crumbled gradually, not all at once, as their support from the center faded and their effectiveness dropped. Roman ways of life had been absorbed by inhabitants of the empire, and were assimilated by the infiltrating barbarians and mixed with their tribal customs and patterns of authority. Withdrawal of Roman legions therefore did not mean an immediate transition to feudalism. Indeed, the initial successor regimes were extensive kingdoms, such as those of the Visigoths in the Iberian peninsula and the Merovingian Franks in Gaul and Germany. These kingdoms soon had to develop governmental capabilities beyond the reach of tribal institutions. Political control was highly personalized in the king, who offered protection in return for obedience. The king, as described by Gladden,

> exercised paternal rights over his subjects and could issue orders and interdicts as any Germanic leader, but he also exercised certain powers rooted in Roman practice, such as the right to create currency and levy taxes. The shadow of the Empire manifested itself in the adoption of the doctrine of *lese-majeste* as a protection of the royal person but the ruler's despotic sway was greatly diminished by the restricted nature of the governmental means at his disposal. The *Palatium,* or Royal Household, was a mere shadow of its imperial prototype: it consisted of councillors, officers and bodyguards, but there were no offices, or bureaux to form a central administration. It was just the ruler's mobile household.[38]

By the end of the seventh century Merovingian rule had declined, but was revived by Charles Martel, who repelled the Arabs at Tours in A.D. 732. Later his grandson Charlemagne was able to extend his control south of the Pyrenees, to Rome and beyond in Italy, and north to the Elbe and the Danube. In A.D. 800, Charlemagne was crowned by the pope in Rome, and the Holy Roman Empire was born, claiming to be the legitimate successor to the Roman Empire, with the duty of protecting the universal church. It combined the Merovingian pattern between ruler and subjects with a close relationship with the church and an attempt to identify with the imperial tradition of Rome. As an idea, the Holy Roman Empire continued to receive lip service for centuries, but as a political reality it was short-lived. Charlemagne's realm declined rapidly under his successors into a number of power centers, which in turn gave way to the network of contractual relationships which became known as the feudal system, under which comprehensive political jurisdiction essentially disappeared. The only ordered hierarchical entity which continued to function throughout what had been the Western Roman Empire came to be the Church of Rome. It established temporal power in the Papal State based in Rome and surrounding areas, and elsewhere it not only provided spiritual bonds but also acquired extensive property holdings and became the provider of administrative services that in other times would have been the responsibility of civil authorities.

With the fall of the Carolingian empire, responsibility had to be localized for such measures as could be marshalled for defense purposes and protection of public order. As Chapman says, "Communal self-help rather than organized administration was the key to early feudal society. . . . Men were forced back on one of the most primitive forms of association, the search for a chief who would protect them at the price of personal homage and fealty. . . . The very concept of the state disappeared together with the concept of the public service."[39]

The feudal system was able to accomplish the minimum that was necessary, which was to allow the basically agrarian society to survive. Feudal lords, in return for vassalic fealty, undertook to offer protection, dispense justice, and provide rudimentary services. Governing power was fragmented among numerous small entities constantly in conflict with one another and requiring increasing resources for defensive and offensive purposes. The long-range consequence during the period up to roughly the eleventh century was declining population, diminished agricultural production, and generally a reduction in the level of social interaction.

Feudal society also contained, however, the seeds for its eventual transformation. The key was gradual development of a money economy to replace the barter economy of the middle feudal period, which led to wealth not based solely on landed property and broke the economic monopoly of the feudal nobility. A self-sufficient agricultural economy began to give way in connection with what Eisenstadt refers to as "the development of free-floating resources" and "the emerging predominance of non-ascriptive rural and urban groups."[40] The new wealth based on exchange of commodities was centered in medieval towns which were able because of their growing economic power to loosen the hold on them of feudal lords and establish their own spheres of power. Municipal burgesses began to gain experience in the handling of matters of trade, finance, and the provision of minimal administrative services. The guild approach to organization of craftsmen provided a way of mobilizing specialized skills, although in a static and rigid way which limited competition and innovation.

Feudalism fostered continuous efforts by medieval kings and princes to extend their domains and to increase the dependence of the notables of the realm on the ruler and his immediate entourage, with the local notables in turn trying to exact guarantees of rights or extension of privileges for the services demanded of them. This process during the later medieval period produced kingships with greater territorial claims and with a greater power differential over the lesser nobility. Emergence of the autonomous medieval cities with their new middle class populations offered an opportunity for alliance between these aspiring monarchs and urban interests against the old aristocracy. Mutually advantageous to the rising monarchies and the growing cities, this alliance hastened the breakup of feudal patterns of political authority, to be replaced eventually by absolutist monarchical regimes organized on national lines.

RISE OF EUROPEAN ABSOLUTIST MONARCHIES

The conversion of medieval political patterns into such national monarchies took place gradually, over a period of centuries, at different rates in different places.[41] After 1200 A.D., consolidation of royal power was achieved at intervals in England, France, Spain, and Central Europe. This occurred earlier in England than on the Continent, partly as a consequence of the Norman conquest. On the other hand, the prompt growth of countervailing power in England resulted in a balance that was not achieved in the continental countries, where either the absolutist regimes brought a greater ascendancy of royal power, as in France, or many principalities arose at the expense of overall unity, as in Germany.

During the 400 years required for transformation of feudal monarchies into the absolutist monarchies of the sixteenth to eighteenth centuries, the most important changes of interest to us were (1) vesting sovereignty in the monarch, (2) securing resources for support of the monarchy, (3) adopting mercantilism as state policy for controlling social and economic activity, and (4) expanding and centralizing governmental administration.

In the feudal order, the king was the first among peers rather than standing apart from other feudal nobility. Royal decrees were issued on the authority of the king and his royal council, made up of barons of the realm, who in turn bore major responsibility for their execution. This basically contractual conception of kingship came to be replaced by claims of royal prerogatives referring back to the Roman imperial tradition.

The lead in this reorientation was taken by *legistes* in the royal service who cited Roman law precedents for their arguments on behalf of kingly power. As early as the thirteenth century, a claim could be made such as the following: "The King is sovereign over all the nobility; only he can issue edicts, he is in overall charge of the churches, and all worldly justice is in his hands."[42] Monarchical claims to political power were bolstered by a succession of jurists who reinterpreted concepts of Roman law by transferring the Roman imperium to the monarch and identifying the imperium of the monarch with the individual's private property.

> The "right" of sovereignty, they argued, was vested in the monarch. The state then was "owned" by the monarch, and sovereignty belonged to him personally; he alone could legally exercise it, transmit it to his heirs, or otherwise dispose of it. . . . Sovereignty was the right to command, and those commanded had a duty to obey. Laws were the tangible expression of the will of the monarch, and there was no higher authority to which further appeal could be made.[43]

The king shared his powers only with the oligarchic estates, and such political struggle as took place was between king and estates, with the former establishing greater and greater ascendancy.

The material resources available to the monarchy had to be increased in order to fulfill the claims to sovereignty. This was a long and arduous process, in which royal efforts to raise revenue were strenuously resisted, both by the feudal lords and by the towns. In the feudal order, each fiefdom stood on its own financially. Feudal kings could obtain revenues for unusual expenses, including even defensive warfare, only by convoking an assembly of the general estates to give consent. Feudal lords demanded a share of any taxes imposed, and the towns, where most of the readily available wealth was concentrated, tried to protect what they had, with the wealthiest towns also being able to maintain the most autonomy.

A centralized system of government required a centralized system of taxation. Aspiring monarchs realized this, and strove to establish their taxing authority as a major step in breaking down feudal society. In France, for example, a royal decree of 1439 forbade collection of taxes by feudal lords without the king's permission. In the absence of an administrative mechanism for collecting royal revenues, the levying of taxes was initially leased out to the highest bidder, but before the end of the sixteenth century financial officials had been stationed around the realm acting directly on behalf of the crown. Revenues raised from these newly exploited tax sources soon far surpassed income from the king's own holdings. Success in establishing the taxing prerogative of the crown had the twin advantage of providing the material resources necessary for carrying out royal policies and at the same time further weakening the autonomy of the nobility and the towns.

As monarchical power grew, so did the monarchical policy of increasingly extensive control of economic and social activities. The initial thrust was to seek the security of the realm and foster conditions conducive to trade and economic expansion. These common objectives were the basis for the alliances between crown and town common toward the end of the feudal period. The eventual outcome was the mercantile system of the later absolutist regimes in the sixteenth and seventeenth centuries. Jacoby describes how under centralized monarchy the state "made it its business to protect the wealth of the middle class. Systems of coinage and measurement were developed. The exportation of raw material and the importation of finished goods were forbidden. Subsidies were given to certain enterprises and trade monopolies were distributed. Guild regulations, forbidding the expansion of businesses, were discontinued. Roads and canals were built, improved and maintained. Mercantilism was born."[44]

Mercantilism as an economic concept considered wealth as the basis of state power. State policy was aimed at economic arrangements which were designed to achieve an excess of exports over imports in foreign trade. A favorable balance of trade would be reflected in payments enabling the state to build up its wealth by acquiring the precious metals, gold and silver. Encouragement of domestic manufacturing required both subsidies and detailed controls. High tariff barriers reduced reliance on imported goods. Overseas colonies, as they were acquired, became a source of additional revenue for the benefit of the colonizing power.

The policy objectives of mercantilism in its various national manifestations could only be realized by installing an intricate network of laws and regulations, which in turn called for specialized administrative officials capable of harnessing available sources of strength for the maximum buildup of the mercantilist state's potential wealth.

These developments—in the legitimacy base, the resources, and the economic and social policies of European monarchies—were therefore all accompanied, and indeed made possible, by far-reaching revamping of the simple governmental apparatus available as the feudal period drew to a close.

An early significant move toward this end was the gradual conversion of the feudal *curia regis*, or royal council, into the king's privy council. This process began by admitting royal officials, in addition to the nobility. Dependent on the monarch, and more regular in their participation than the aristocratic members, who had to journey from their respective parts of the realm to attend, these officials provided the king with a source of support to counterbalance the nobility and enhance royal authority. As the councils became more controllable and more secret in their operations, responsibility for administration on behalf of the crown became the responsibility of privy-council committees. Spain, France, Prussia, England, and other countries evolved their own versions of such privy-council committee systems for supervising administration as the absolutist monarchies consolidated their authority.

Meanwhile, the scope of public services and the number of public functionaries grew dramatically. Defense and justice had been the primary concerns of the king during the Middle Ages. In addition, the crown now assumed responsibilities for a range of activities which had been left to local regulation since the breakup of the Roman Empire.[45] The administrative apparatus which made this expansion and centralization possible was achieved by a conversion, put in simplest terms, of the royal household into the royal service. In Weberian terminology, the change was from patrimonial to bureaucratic administration.

The medieval king, engaged in a constant struggle to maintain and extend his domain, protect his prerogatives against competing claims of the nobility and the church, manage his own extensive estates, preserve a minimum of order in the realm, and free himself from administrative minutiae, depended on his own corps of officials. Servants of the crown, with training and duties entitling them to be thought of as professional administrators, go far back in medieval European history. H. F. Tout has traced the growth of centralized administration in England in fascinating detail. He points out that these early public administrators, like all early public officials, were simply members of a king's house-hold. The king's clerks, accountants, and administrators belonged to the same category as the king's cooks, scullions, grooms, and valets. The public service of the state then was hopelessly confused with the domestic service of the court. . . . The time was still far distant when the modern distinction was made between the king in his private and public capacities, between the royal officers who ruled the king's household, and those who carried on the government of the country.[46]

Max Weber used the concept of patrimonialism to characterize this pattern of authority relationships. In the patrimonial structure of authority, the royal household and the royal domains are managed by the king's personal servants. In principle, grants of power to these officials are arbitrary decisions made by the ruler which can be altered by the ruler as he sees fit. Of course, under patrimonialism, even the ruler is subject to the dictates of tradition.

Turning claims of absolutist supremacy into reality depended on success in professionalizing, directing, and controlling a royal service which could be identified mainly with the monarchy as an institution rather than with the reigning monarch as an individual. This required thoroughgoing reform efforts which fitted differing circumstances but had similar overall results. As Leonard D. White puts it in citing notable examples, "Richelieu in France, Henry VIII and Elizabeth in England, and the Great Elector (Father of Frederick William I of Prussia) are among the chief architects who reconstructed the concept of the State, of office, of civil life, and of permanent officials out of the debris of the feudal system."[47]

Experience in France and Prussia is especially relevant because of the influence of these absolutist administrative systems on subsequent nation-state bureaucracies and on later bureaucratic theory as formulated by Weber and others.

Although France eventually produced the most centralized European monarchy, under Louis XIV in the seventeenth century, this came only after a long period of struggle to assert the supremacy of the crown against centrifugal forces. As early as the thirteenth century, a hierarchical administrative system designed to enforce the king's authority had begun to operate through officials in each province specializing in military, legal, and financial matters. Difficulties of communications and control also led to efforts before 1300 by King Philippe le Bel to send out royal emissaries to tighten supervision, investigate complaints, and try to reduce the growing number of officials. As the territorial boundaries of France expanded by conquest, marriage, and treaty, subsequent rulers made similar attempts to strengthen the powers and curb the excesses of officialdom.

It remained for Richelieu, as principal minister under Louis XIII from 1624 to 1642, to consolidate the system through the office of intendant, which he converted from its earlier function as an intermittent agent of the king. He made the intendant a continuing provincial representative of royal authority, concentrating in his hands "very considerable powers covering taxes, tutelage, war supplies, recruitment, public works, and so on."[48] During the reign of Louis XIV later in the seventeenth century, Colbert improved the effectiveness of the intendant system and brought the French monarchy to its point of greatest strength.

Nevertheless, these royal reforms were only partially successful. Part of the problem was continuing resistance from local sources, but the main deficiency was the failure to create a body of competent officials adequate to cope with the burdens placed upon it. The intendants themselves had legal training which was not particularly suited to administrative tasks, but the principal fault was that generally posts in the royal service were obtained through influence and intrigue rather than merit, and could then be transferred by sale or inheritance. The result was a centralized administrative apparatus firmly under royal direction but staffed by officials of uncertain and unequal quality with their own vested interests in office-holding, which they regarded almost as private property. Favoritism and venality rather than competence became the touchstones for obtaining positions in the French royal service.

Meanwhile, a different approach toward recruitment for administrative careers was being taken beginning during the seventeenth century in Prussia. Previously one of the poorest and most backward of the German states, Prussia at the end of the Thirty Years War in 1648 entered a period of reconstruction and rapid progress, under a succession of four kings who ruled from 1640 through 1786 and who devoted much of their attention to creation and maintenance of a professionalized state service. Frederick William of Brandenburg (the Great Elector) began the process by undertaking to centralize and militarize the country. He worked through his Privy Council, which he converted from an advisory to an executive body supervising specialized administrative departments. The king appointed officials assigned to local provinces with duties in economic, fiscal, and social matters on behalf of the central authority.

Recognizing the importance of a professionally trained corps of royal servants to staff the centralized state he was creating, Frederick William began to expand and improve the civil service. Reforms which he started gradually became more formalized, particularly under Frederick William I (1713–1740), who created chairs in cameralism, or administrative science, at German universities, and made a university diploma the usual prerequisite for office. Examinations were then given for ranking candidates who had good academic records and had completed a period of practical field training. "Certainly Prussia has the distinction," says Gladden, "of being the first modern state to introduce and develop a system of entrance examinations for the public service in which both the central administration and the individual departments were involved, and which comprised both written and oral tests, in subjects of a practical as well as an academic nature."[49]

Similar measures were taken to regularize and control the conduct of public business. According to Herman Finer,

Various instructions settled exactly the hours of work, procedure, and official secrecy. Employment outside the official service was prohibited, the acceptance of presents was prohibited, excise officials were forbidden to buy confiscated goods, and from those who handled money a guarantee was required. The officials who came into direct contact with the public were ordered to be polite. . . . Residence in the neighborhood of the work was exacted, and the conditions of leave were rigidly regulated. For breaches of the regulations there was a series of heavy fines, which were imposed. A Spartan quality was introduced into the service.[50]

Finer goes on to summarize the significance of these reforms as follows: "The administration of the state had been professionalized: that is to say, it now depended upon a body of men permanently employed upon special work, their activities being uniquely at the service of the state and being purposively regulated and disciplined to accomplish its specific ends."[51]

The Prussian civil service reached its peak during the reign of Frederick the Great (1740–1786), declining after that from excessive militarization in an increasingly militarized state, and from over-dependence on personal leadership from the king, which was no longer provided by his successors. By the end of the eighteenth century, the positive features of the elite administrative corps created by Prussian monarchs had been overshadowed by tendencies toward caste status, aloofness, exclusiveness, and inflexibility. Although extensive reforms were carried out by Baron vom Stein in 1808 following the collapse of Prussia under attacks from Napoleon's armies, the Prussian bureaucracy never again attained its earlier level of performance, which had made it the most notable example of absolutist monarchical administration.

EMERGENCE OF THE NATION-STATE

The French Revolution and the subsequent advent of Napoleon brought about vast changes in the nature of the state and in the conduct of public administration. Out of this period of drastic transformation at the end of the eighteenth and the beginning of the nineteenth centuries emerged the nation-state as the dominant form of political system and the modern public bureaucracy as the vehicle for conducting the nation's business.

S. E. Finer declares the French Revolution to be "the most important single event in the entire history of government." He goes on to say: "It was an earthquake. It razed and effaced all the ancient institutions of France, undermined the foundations of the other European states, and is still sending its shock-waves throughout the rest of the world."[52] Probably the most important legacy of the French Revolution was that it depersonalized the concept of the state. "The

French theorists took over one version of the patrimonial state and replaced the king by the nation. The country was no longer the patrimony of the king but the patrimony of the nation, and the state was the machinery which the nation set up for its own government and to organize its public services."[53]

Under Napoleon, the state did not cease to be authoritarian and centralized, but the allegiance of the public official shifted from the monarch to the nation.

> The status of the public official changed at once. He was no longer the servant of the Crown or the prince, he was the servant of the state, and indirectly of the nation. He became an instrument of public power, not the agent of a person. He acted according to the law, and not according to the wishes of the individual, and his allegiance was to the law because the law was the expression of the will of the nation.[54]

Thus the royal service was converted into the public service. The change was primarily in allegiance and purpose rather than being a transformation from amateurism to professionalism. The tradition that a career as a public official was one of the most honorable professions had already been established in France before the Revolution, and did not result from the administrative reforms of Napoleon.

The Napoleonic approach to administration stressed order, hierarchy, specialization, and accountability. As emperor, he incorporated many military-like features into a tightly knit command structure which assigned duties clearly and demanded personal responsibility for performance. He created the Conseil d'Etat to act in a general staff capacity, revamping the former king's council for this purpose. Having only advisory functions to the emperor, the Conseil d'Etat nevertheless exerted considerable influence by making studies and recommending policies, and it gradually developed into a control agency exercising general supervision over the work of administrative agencies.

The administrative structure of the central government consisted of five basic ministries (finance, foreign affairs, war, justice, and interior) closely resembling the much earlier Roman model, with other units being added later by breaking out functions from the comprehensive Interior Ministry. Each ministry was subdivided into divisions and bureaus for purposes of specialization, some with field offices outside Paris. The hierarchy of territorial governmental units was revised into a three-tiered system under the Minister of Interior. The department became the major jurisdictional subdivision, headed in each case by a prefect who was the principal representative of central authority and the conduit for representing local interests at the center. Each department was divided into arrondissements under subprefects, and at the base were communes with mayors as chief executive officers. Although representative councils existed at each level, they did not participate in the conduct of administrative affairs, which were handled under a pattern of authority firmly managed from above.

Among Napoleonic administrative reforms, none surpassed his insistence on competence in the selection of higher public service personnel. His own capacity for work was prodigious, and he expected devotion to duty and productive results from his subordinates. He apparently participated directly in the selection of many officials, and later personally judged their records of performance. The stress was on talent wherever it could be found, with particular emphasis on training in science, mathematics, and engineering. He had available specialists from the former royal regime with civil engineering experience in the public works field. He created a new specialist corps in mining and explosives. To provide a continuing source of competent officials, the Ecole Polytechnique was established. Since its graduates possessed "a prestige of quite a different kind from that conferred by caste or social class," and it promised prospects of the highest posts in the state, "it attracted not only the brightest of the middle class but also those members of the upper class who happened to be both ambitious and able." As a result, from its graduates came, according to Chapman, "many of the most prominent administrators, scientists, scholars and generals in the nineteenth century."[55]

As Gladden observes,

> Napoleon's object of shaping a highly authoritarian system and of furnishing it with an efficient administration was a remarkable achievement considering the magnitude of the task and the short time he had at his disposal. By a judicious selection of ancient institutions, modified to the purposes of the world he was moulding right across Europe, he brought order out of chaos and achieved a level of administrative efficiency far above that of the preceding era. . . . But it had the defects of all systems that depend ultimately upon the selective favouritism of the leader and upon decisions from above that cannot be modified except through the initiative of the leader himself.[56]

With both its virtues and its faults, it is the system of governmental administration in the type of modern Western nation-state which appeared first in France that Weber characterized as bureaucratic in contrast to the earlier patrimonial pattern of administration in Western Europe. He shows point by point the way in which the two types vary. According to Weber's definition, as given in abbreviated form by Bendix, a bureaucracy tends to be characterized by (1) defined rights and duties, which are prescribed in written regulations; (2) authority relations between positions, which are ordered systematically; (3) appointment and promotion, which are regulated and are based on contractual agreement; (4) technical training (or experience) as a formal condition of employment; (5) fixed monetary salaries; (6) a strict separation of office and incumbent in the sense that the employee does not own the "means of administration" and cannot appropriate the position; and (7) administrative work as a full-time occupation.

This combination of characteristics is generally regarded as common to the public service systems of the nation-states of Western Europe. "Each of these characteristics," says Bendix, "stands for a condition of employment in modern government administration. The process of bureaucratization may be interpreted as the manifold, cumulative, and more or less successful imposition of these employment conditions since the nineteenth century."[57]

NOTES

1. The first comprehensive historical account of public administration was published, in two volumes, less than three decades ago: E. N. Gladden, *A History of Public Administration* (London: Frank Cass, 1972), vol. I, *From the Earliest Times to the Eleventh Century*; vol. II, *From the Eleventh Century to the Present Day*. Since then, S. E. Finer has written an even more comprehensive three volume general history of government or polities, not published until a few years after his death: *The History of Government from the Earliest Times* (Oxford: Oxford University Press, 1997), vol. I, *From Ancient Monarchies to the Han and Roman Empires*; vol. II, *The Intermediate Ages*; vol. III, *Empires, Monarchies, and the Modern State*. Together, these works provide a remarkable overview of polities, defined by Finer as "the structures of government under which groups of men live, and its relationship towards them" (*The History of Government*, vol. I, p. 1) and public administration, described by Gladden as "essentially a subordinate or supporting factor in government" (*A History of Public Administration*, vol. I, p. vii). A valuable recent contribution is Jos C. N. Raadschelders, *Handbook of Administrative History* (New Brunswick, NJ: Transaction Publishers, 1998).
2. Henry Jacoby, *The Bureaucratization of the World* (Berkeley, CA: University of California Press, 1973). This is a translation of the original, published in Germany in 1969.
3. *Ibid.*, p. 9.
4. *Ibid.*, p. 2.
5. Gerald D. Nash, *Perspectives on Administration: The Vistas of History* (Berkeley, CA: Institute of Governmental Studies, University of California, 1969).
6. *Ibid.*, p. 4.
7. *Ibid.*, p. 23.
8. Karl A. Wittfogel, *Oriental Despotism: A Comparative Study of Total Power* (New Haven, CT: Yale University Press, 1957).
9. *Ibid.*, p. 368.
10. *Ibid.*, p. 303.
11. *Ibid.*, pp. 320–21.
12. S. N. Eisenstadt, *The Political Systems of Empires* (New York: Free Press, 1963).
13. *Ibid.*, p. 23.
14. *Ibid.*, p. 21.
15. *Ibid.*, Chap. 10, pp. 273–299.
16. *Ibid.*, p. 299.
17. *Ibid.*, p. 299.

18. Finer, *The History of Government*, vol. I, p. 104.
19. *Ibid.*, p. 442.
20. Gladden, *A History of Public Administration*, vol. I, p. 172.
21. *Ibid.*, vol. II, p. 227. For a description of Chinese bureaucracy during the Ch'ing dynasty, see Lawrence J. R. Henson, "China's Imperial Bureaucracy: Its Direction and Control," *Public Administration Review* 17, No. 1 (1957): 44–53. Reprinted in James W. Fesler, ed., *American Public Administration: Patterns of the Past* (Washington, DC: American Society for Public Administration, 1982), pp. 41–56.
22. For details, refer to Y. Z. Chang, "China and English Civil Service Reform," *American Historical Review* 47 (1942): 539–544; and Ssu-yu Teng, "Chinese Influence on the Western Examination System," *Harvard Journal of Asiatic Studies* 7 (1943): 267–312.
23. For information concerning the later Spanish colonial period, refer to Jack W. Hopkins, "Administration of the Spanish Empire in the Americas," in Ali Farazmand, ed., *Handbook of Bureaucracy* (New York: Marcel Dekker, 1994), Chap. 2, pp. 17–27.
24. Gladden, *A History of Public Administration*, vol. II, p. 119.
25. Nash, *Perspectives on Administration*, pp. 8–9. Finer renders an even more negative judgment, saying that even when the Egyptian polity was at its zenith, "despite the appearance of meticulous organization and efficiency, the Egyptian administration was, in fact, a monument of laxity, procrastination, ineptitude, corruption, and petty brutality." *The History of Government*, vol. I, p. 199.
26. See *The History of Government*, vol. I, pp. 316–317.
27. *Perspectives on Administration*, p. 10.
28. Demetrios Argyriades, "Administrative Legacies of Greece, Rome, and Byzantium," 17 pp. mimeographed, prepared for the 1990 Annual Meeting of the American Society for Public Administration, at p. 17.
29. J. H. Hofmeyer, "Civil Service in Ancient Times: The Story of Its Evolution," *Public Administration* 5, No. 1 (1927): 76–93. Reprinted in Nimrod Raphaeli, ed., *Readings in Comparative Public Administration* (Boston: Allyn and Bacon, 1967), pp. 69–91.
30. Brian Chapman, *The Profession of Government* (London: George Allen & Unwin, 1959), pp. 9–10.
31. Gladden, *A History of Public Administration*, vol. I, pp. 121–123.
32. Chapman, *The Profession of Government*, p. 12.
33. Finer, *The History of Government*, vol. I, p. 604.
34. *Ibid.*, vol. II, p. 855.
35. Reinhard Bendix, *Nation-Building and Citizenship* (New York: John Wiley & Sons, 1964), p. 101.
36. *Ibid.*, p. 37.
37. *Ibid.*, p. 39.
38. Gladden, *A History of Public Administration*, vol. I, p. 202.
39. Chapman, *The Profession of Government*, pp. 13–14.
40. Eisenstadt, "Bureaucracy and Political Development," in Joseph La Palombara, ed., *Bureaucracy and Political Development* (Princeton, NJ: Princeton University Press, 1963), p. 106.
41. For informative accounts of this process, see Joseph R. Strayer, *On the Medieval Origins of the Modern State* (Princeton, NJ: Princeton University Press, 1970), and

James W. Fesler, "The Presence of the Administrative Past, " in Fesler, *American Public Administration: Patterns of the Past*, pp. 1–27, especially pp. 1–16.

42. Philippe de Remi, sire de Beaumanoir, in 1283. Quoted by Jacoby, *The Bureaucratization of the World*, pp. 14–15.
43. Chapman, *The Profession of Government*, pp. 15–16.
44. Jacoby, *The Bureaucratization of the World*, p. 18.
45. "For the first time since the Romans, finance, justice, foreign affairs, internal affairs and defense were clearly distinguished from each other with specialized administrative services." *Ibid.*, pp. 16–17.
46. H. F. Tout, "The Emergence of a Bureaucracy," in Robert K. Merton, ed., *Reader in Bureaucracy* (Glencoe, IL: Free Press, 1952), p. 69.
47. Leonard D. White, *The Civil Service in the Modern State* (Chicago: University of Chicago Press, 1930), p. xi.
48. Chapman, *The Profession of Government*, p. 21.
49. Gladden, *A History of Public Administration*, vol. II, p. 163.
50. Herman Finer, *The Theory and Practice of Modern Government*, rev. ed. (New York: Holt, Rinehart and Winston, 1949), p. 731.
51. *Ibid.*, p. 733.
52. Finer, *The History of Government*, vol. III, p.1517.
53. Chapman, *The Profession of Government*, p. 25.
54. *Ibid.*, p. 26.
55. *Ibid.*, p. 29.
56. Gladden, *A History of Public Administration*, vol. II, p. 297.
57. Bendix, *Nation-Building and Citizenship*, p. 109. For an enlightening discussion as to how the development of the modern nation-state has affected contemporary public administration, see Nolan J. Argyle, "Public Administration, Administrative Thought, and the Emergence of the Nation State," in Farazmand, *Handbook of Bureaucracy*, Chap. 1, pp. 1–16.

5

Administration in More Developed Nations

General Characteristics and "Classic" Administrative Systems

Given the historical background of the dominant lines of evolution in the process of political and administrative development, as this process is identified with the Western European experience, we need to consider more closely the current leading characteristics of these particular polities and of others like them. Also, we should try to identify some of the attributes of the bureaucracies in these polities which may be shared despite substantial individual divergences, and which may distinguish them as a group from those countries that are less developed politically. Then we can proceed to examine in more detail some of the more important representative individual countries. Public administration in the countries we have called developed does not suffer from lack of attention. Much is known and much has been written about these administrative systems. Our task is briefly to characterize administration in a few of these countries, to show differences among them, and to distinguish them as a group, with respect to public administration, from the developing countries. This does not permit the qualifications and amplifications a fuller treatment would demand.

SHARED POLITICAL AND
ADMINISTRATIVE CHARACTERISTICS

The characteristics shared by the developed polities of Western Europe and elsewhere have been described with substantial agreement by a number of students of comparative politics.[1]

1. The system of governmental organization is highly differentiated and functionally specific, and the allocation of political roles is based on achievement rather than ascription, reflecting general characteristics of the society. Among other things, this means a bureaucracy with a high degree of internal specialization and with competence or merit as a standard for bureaucratic recruitment.

2. Procedures for making political decisions are largely rational and secular. The power position of traditional elites has been eroded and the appeal of traditional values greatly weakened. A predominantly secular and impersonal system of law reflects this orientation.

3. The volume and range of political and administrative activity are extensive, permeating all major spheres of life in the society, and the tendency is toward further extension.

4. There is a high correlation between political power and legitimacy, resting on a sense of popular identification with the nation-state which is widespread and effective. Such a system makes a prolonged discrepancy between power and legitimacy less likely, and is more efficient "in the sense that power relationships are more often translated into legitimations and less frequently left outside the political sphere."[2]

5. Popular interest and involvement in the political system are widespread, but this does not necessarily mean active participation by the citizenry in general in political decision-making. The concept of political development is not linked with any particular regime or ideology; it does not imply, for example, democracy and representative government. Nevertheless, one of the characteristics shared by modernizing societies is that commonly "modernization begins under autocracy or oligarchy and proceeds toward some form of mass society—democratic or authoritarian."[3] In the mass society, the range of effective popular participation in the process of political decision-making may be extensive or it may be drastically curtailed by the dominance of a relatively small elite group.

Counterpart characteristics may be anticipated in the bureaucracies of these polities, despite substantial variations in the pattern of the bureaucracy from one country to another.

1. The public service of a developed political system will be large scale, complex, and instrumental in the sense that its mission is understood to be that of carrying out the policies of the political decision-makers. In other words, it will tend to have the attributes Weber specified for his "ideal type" bureaucracy,

including both the structural prerequisites and the behavioral tendencies mentioned by him.

2. The bureaucracy will be highly specialized and will require in its ranks most of the occupational and professional categories represented in the society. This is a reflection both of the range of governmental activities in a developed polity and of the technical requirements for success in carrying out governmental programs.

3. The bureaucracy will exhibit to a marked degree a sense of professionalization, both in the sense of identification with the public service as a profession and in the sense of belonging to a narrower field of professional or technical specialization within the service, such as law, nuclear engineering, or social work. This professional outlook springs from a combination of such factors as the standards of competence applied in recruitment and the common background in education and training that this implies for various specialties, pride in the work being done and in the manner of its performance, and career orientation to the public service as against private sector careers. The positive values for the public service associated with professionalization are apt to be accompanied by tendencies toward bureaucratic self-protection. Such behavior has been variously referred to as dysfunctional, latent, expedient, self-defeating, and pathological. It is the opposite side of the coin of professionalism in bureaucracy.

4. Because the political system as a whole is relatively stable and mature, and the bureaucracy is more fully developed, the role of the bureaucracy in the political process is fairly clear. The desirability of a line of demarcation between the bureaucracy and other political institutions is generally accepted, although the line may be somewhat blurred. Some indicators point toward a double transfer of power in recent years—from the legislature to the executive, and from the executive to the top civil service—which has resulted in a partial merger of political power and administrative action in the careers of higher ranking bureaucrats who have been dubbed "the Western mandarins,"[4] but this has not meant the replacement of politicians by bureaucrats. In functional terms, the bureaucracy continues to be primarily involved in the output function of rule application, to a lesser extent in the output function of rule-making, and to a quite limited degree in such input functions as interest aggregation.

5. The bureaucracy in a developed polity will be subject to effective policy control by other functionally specific political institutions. A major study of relationships between bureaucrats and politicians confirms that "most descriptions of policymaking in Western nations concur that policy must be acceptable to the top political leadership, as embodied in the ruling party or parties." Civil servants need endorsements from political leaders for their actions. "Constitutionally, politicians are everywhere empowered to reject the counsel of bureaucrats, although such rejection is infrequent in practice. Policymaking is thus a kind of

dialectic, in which the 'law of anticipated reactions' normally governs the behavior of bureaucrats. Consequently, in broad political and ideological terms most major policies reflect the preference of party and parliamentary majorities."[5] This situation is partly due to the specialized orientation of bureaucrats. Morstein Marx has advanced the general proposition that "present-day Western bureaucracies have grown more multiminded than they were before. In turn, they are less capable of staging their own campaigns over general issues of public policy. Activation is likely to be broader only when policy ends impinge on the immediate occupational interests of the career service as a whole."[6] Even more important is the fact that the bureaucracy and its competitor institutions in the political system have developed more or less simultaneously over a considerable period of time. Political growth is more likely to have been balanced. If there is imbalance, it is not probable that the bureaucracy is the political institution that has the upper hand in a developed polity; such a situation is much more likely in a developing country. Fred Riggs has placed unusual emphasis on this matter of imposing effective policy control over the bureaucracy, making it a necessary condition for positive political development. In his earlier formulation, he stated that such development occurs "only if these functionally specific institutions actually succeed in imposing policy control over the bureaucracy—if their effective control matches their formal authority. Otherwise, we have negative political development."[7] Later, he applied the term "constitutive system" to these institutions of control, but he continued to stress their importance.[8] It should be noted, in line with the earlier rejection of the idea of identifying political development with either democracy or totalitarianism, that effective policy control over the bureaucracy need not come from the sources considered proper in a Western political democracy. The mark of bureaucratic control in a developed political system is not the source from which the control comes but the fact that it exists.

"CLASSIC" ADMINISTRATIVE SYSTEMS

The writings of Max Weber have sometimes been referred to as "classic" bureaucratic theory. It is in the sense that the bureaucracies of France, Germany, and a number of other continental European nations conform most closely to Weber's description of bureaucracy that they are called here "classic" administrative systems. We center our attention on contemporary France and Germany.

German and French political cultures are similar in two basic respects. One is that during the preceding two centuries and more each country has been the victim of continuing political instability; successive regimes have often had drastically different political orientations, and political change has been abrupt, drastic, and frequent. In France it meant the violent overthrow of the monarchy brought about by the French Revolution, followed by the era of Napoleon, experiments with constitutional monarchy alternating with republican government to 1870, and a succession of crises during the Third and Fourth Republics, culminating in the Fifth Republic of De Gaulle in 1958. Since 1789 France has been a constitutional monarchy three times, an empire twice, a semidictatorship once, and a republic five times, with most of the transitions taking place as the result of violence. Germany has gone through even more extreme and disruptive changes. The rise of Prussia eventually led to the establishment of a unified reich under Bismarck in 1871, the German Empire to 1918, the Weimar Republic after World War I, Nazi dictatorship, the post–World War II division between West and East Germany, and reunification again in 1990. The German political heritage is one of disunity, frustration, and the absence of any well-established political culture.

In contrast to discontinuity in politics, both France and Germany have had remarkable administrative and bureaucratic continuity. Prussian administration, acknowledged to be the forerunner of modern bureaucracy, became the core of government in a unified Germany, and this pattern of administration remains essentially unchanged. In France, the administrative apparatus that had been created to serve the *ancien regime* transferred and maintained its allegiance to the nation, after the brief interruption of the Revolution late in the eighteenth century, whether its government took the form of empire or republic. Stability in administrative affairs has been a phenomenon as marked in these two countries as political instability.

The recent and current consequences of this historical inheritance for bureaucratic operating characteristics, for the scope of bureaucratic activity, and for the maintenance of controls over the bureaucracy will be explored next, first in contemporary France and then in the German Federal Republic (before and since reunification).

Fifth Republic France

France under the Fifth Republic is evolving a governmental system which combines old and new features in a pattern which is still fluid.[9] The state remains unitary and centralized, but major changes have occurred both in the central government and in central-local relations.

At the center, the multiparty parliamentary system with frequently changing coalition cabinets of the Third and Fourth Republics has been replaced by a mixed presidential-parliamentary system. Gaullist-Centrist parties were in control from 1958 to 1981. The Socialists then took over the presidency until 1995, electing Francois Mitterrand to consecutive seven-year terms. During these years, however, there were two short periods of "cohabitation" (with a Socialist president and a Gaullist-Centrist coalition in control of the National Assembly) from 1986 to 1988 and again from 1993 to 1995. Jacques Chirac, heading a center-right coalition, then took over from Mitterrand as president, inheriting a National Assembly controlled by his coalition. In 1997, Chirac made a political miscalculation by dissolving the National Assembly and calling for legislative elections a year ahead of when they were scheduled. The result was a left wing parliamentary majority led by the Socialists, and a return to cohabitation, with Chirac as president and Socialist Lionel Jospin, whom he had defeated two years earlier in the run-off for the presidential election, as prime minister. This power sharing arrangement is the prospect as the century ends, pending the presidential and legislative elections scheduled for 2002, leading commentators to remark that the French are making a habit of cohabitation.

The president of the French Fifth Republic, directly elected since a constitutional amendment in 1962, is an extremely powerful chief executive, able (except during cohabitation) to nominate the premier and Council of Ministers in the mixed system. In various ways, the powers of the National Assembly have been curtailed to shift the balance of authority from the legislature to the executive and to separate the two branches, including a prohibition against cabinet ministers holding parliamentary seats. Structurally, the central government is divided into ministries, ranging in recent years from eleven to twenty-two, each in turn subdivided into *directions* as the principal operating units, plus a ministerial *cabinet* or secretariat with staff assisting the minister, and various consultative and control organs.

Since the Napoleonic era, ninety-six *departments* have constituted the most important units of local government, each with a prefect as the principal representative of the central government. In a series of reforms culminating in 1982, efforts at decentralization have been put in place, with the result, as viewed by Meny, that "decision-making processes are becoming more complex, even more cumbersome, but also more democratic."[10] Fourteen regions have been interposed between the central government and the *departments*, each with a Commissioner of the Republic responsible for coordinating the field services of most but not all ministries. More power has been given to local government authorities in relation to field service officials of the central ministries. The field services of these ministries continue to be extensive, however, with 95 percent of the total work force located outside of the central offices in Paris.

The French higher level bureaucrats, who provide direction for this still relatively centralized administration, are the direct successors of the "corporate body that does not die" which Napoleon wanted to create, and which was in turn linked to the royal service of the *ancien regime*. The most notable characteristic of the French administrative elite is that they are considered members of a corps or cadre representing and closely identified with the state, in a polity long considered as exhibiting a high degree of "stateness."[11] The bureaucrat views himself and is viewed as a public official rather than as a public servant. Speaking for the state and acting on its behalf, he tends to consider himself as possessing a bit of sovereignty which entitles him to respectful attention, and this view is at least partly shared by the citizenry.

The civil service is a career service, ordinarily chosen early in life and pursued to retirement, with slight movement of individuals into and out of the administrative corps in mid-career. Entrance to the bureaucracy, particularly to the higher levels, is difficult and through prescribed channels. The recruitment system is closely geared to the educational system, so that access to the higher civil service is effectively restricted to those who also have access to higher education.

A unique feature of the French bureaucracy is the existence of an administrative superelite, made up of members of groupings known as the *grands corps*, tracing their origins in most cases to the Napoleonic period. Included are major technical corps (such as Corps des Mines and Corps des Pontes et Chaussees) and nontechnical corps (such as Conseil d'Etat, Cours des Comptes, and Inspection des Finances). The number in each corps is quite small: for instance, in 1970 it was only 229 in the Conseil d'Etat and 364 in the Inspection des Finances. "Each corps has its own jurisdictions, and has a particular sphere of activity."[12] Members of the prestigious corps are not confined to assignments in these specialized spheres of activity, however. They are frequently placed on detached duty in other influential positions throughout the administrative system. As many as one-third of the members of a corps such as the Conseil d'Etat may be on such assignments at a given time. In the case of the Inspection des Finances, members often take other assignments after an initial tour of regular duty and may never return to the specialized work of the corps. The Corps des Mines retains its prestige among technical corps despite the decline of mining engineering as a field of activity, with membership serving as a springboard to important administrative posts not requiring this particular specialization. Such practices mean that these corps in effect serve as a way to confer status and prestige on those individuals fortunate enough to be chosen for membership at the time of entrance into bureaucratic careers.

Prior to World War II, recruitment into the higher civil service was on a fragmented basis, with each of the *grands corps* making its own selections and individual ministries doing their separate screening of other civil administrators. Extensive reforms undertaken in 1945 were aimed at broadening the recruitment base and bringing more uniformity into the selection process. Because of the direct tie-in with the system of higher education, this in turn meant educational reforms. For nontechnical administrators, the first steps were to nationalize the private political science school in Paris where most future officials had for decades received their formal higher education, and then in addition to create a series of similar institutions at locations spread across the country. The most significant innovation was to establish a National School of Administration (ENA) as a common training center for future higher administrators, with entry through a common examination open to university graduates. The intent was to open up the service to a broader spectrum of applicants, screen them through an intensive three-year postselection curriculum, and then parcel them out to the *grands corps* and the ministries on the basis of matching the most promising young administrators with the most desirable career opportunities. Coupled with these moves, for the first time a central civil service directorate was established and a uniform code dealing with rights and responsibilities of civil servants was enacted.

The consensus is that these reform efforts have accomplished much less than was anticipated.[13] Democratization of the civil service has not occurred, mainly because access to higher education continues to be primarily confined to students from upper-social-class origins, with a heavy concentration of graduates from metropolitan Paris rather than from the provinces.[14] About 40 percent of the entrants into the *grands corps* continue to come from family backgrounds in the civil service, mostly in the higher ranks. A provision designed to permit entry of a limited number of civil servants with prior executive experience into the ENA has not in fact opened up many such opportunities. In 1983, the Socialist government of President Mitterrand undertook a reform designed to reserve up to one-fifth of each ENA entering class for trade union members and elected local officials with ten years or more of experience, but this effort at further diversification did not succeed and has since been dropped.

ENA graduates have access to the *grands corps* and the ministries according to a well-established pecking order of desirability. All aspire to membership in a prestigious corps, but only about the top 20 percent of the graduates can qualify for one of the *grands corps*. The others enter the corps of particular ministries, with finance and interior being the most attractive, and others such as agriculture, labor, and justice having less drawing power. The result is an uneven distribution of talent among program areas of government operation. Although only partially successful, the postwar reforms nevertheless led to significant changes. The aim of instilling a more common outlook among the administrative elite gained headway through the replacement of separate examinations by a common examination for entry into the ENA, and the sharing of a three-year training program by newly selected recruits for the higher administrative service, which combined internship for practical experience, concentrated study in one of four fields (general administration, economic and financial administration, social administration, and foreign affairs), and placement for a brief period in private industry to provide insight into industrial management. The result has undoubtedly been to reduce separatist tendencies, despite the continued prevalence of the corps tradition within the bureaucracy.

The postwar period also saw an almost total replacement in the ranks of higher level bureaucrats, due in part to wartime manpower losses and purges at the time of liberation, opening up opportunities for younger products of the administrative reform movement. Moreover, the Fifth Republic political leadership has stressed national renewal to be gained by technological expertise provided by technicians in the bureaucracy, which has brought many higher civil servants into prominent positions as ministerial advisors and frequently as ministers themselves. Suleiman has perceptively pointed out that this elite does not stress a technical expertise that is narrowly specialized, but that instead its success "lies in its profound belief in generalized skills, which are the only kind of 'skills' that enable one to move from one sector to another without prior technical training for a particular post."[15] Opportunities for the meaningful use of administrative skills continue to be abundant, undiminished by political transitions. As summarized by Ridley and Blondel, the civil service "is still the reservoir of talented and enterprising men, the best training ground for many careers outside the public service, and the source of much power. Its economic, social and even cultural influence has probably increased over the years. It has been one of the main driving forces, if not *the* driving force, in French life—and it is likely to remain so."[16]

Recent years have also brought about a clearer definition of the relationship between the state and civil servants. In theory, the French civil servant has always been subject to employment conditions determined unilaterally by the state, as distinguished from the contractual relationship between private employees and employers. This basic concept has been unaffected by the shift from monarchy to nation, or by variations in political regimes. In practice, this meant during the nineteenth century that although civil servants were given such advantages as security of tenure and generous salaries and fringe benefits, they were also denied rights extended to private employees in such matters as union recognition, collective bargaining, and resort to strikes.

The civil service statute of 1946, although reaffirming the concept that conditions of public employment are to be set by the state and can be unilaterally changed by state action, in fact retained prior privileges while recognizing rights previously denied. Consequently, the French civil servant continues to enjoy security of tenure on a lifetime basis, subject only to the unlikely loss of job on the basis of redundancy (in which case compensation must be provided), or dismissal as a disciplinary action available only in accordance with detailed procedures by special disciplinary tribunals on which officials are represented. Salaries are intended to maintain status and recognize the public obligations of the official rather than to pay for actual work performed, and the remuneration is adequate although not lavish. Comprehensive fringe benefits include family allowances, various social security programs, and generous retirement pensions. Promotions and other changes in status are controlled in large measure by the civil service itself.

The 1946 law gave formal recognition of the right of civil servants to organize trade unions, following decades of uncertainty as to legality. Strikes by civil servants had been ruled as illegal earlier, and the 1946 reforms did not clearly define whether a right to strike exists. In the absence either of a prohibition or a positive authorization, decisions of the Conseil d'Etat have held that disciplinary action cannot be taken against civil servants solely because they have gone on strike, but with reservations that essential services must be maintained and that higher civil servants cannot strike. The civil service union movement has grown markedly in the postwar period, and strikes by civil servants have in fact become commonplace.

Participation in political activities has also been clarified. Most civil servants are free to join political parties and take part in party activities. Those in positions of responsibility are not barred but are not supposed to disclose their civil service status or make use of information acquired because of their official assignments. Civil servants may become candidates for elective office, and may serve in most local offices without giving up active duty, but if they run and are elected to the national legislature they must go on inactive status during the term of service, with a right to return later.

Successive French governments have continued to introduce changes aimed toward modernization of the administrative system. Since the mid-1980s, these measures share four goals, as viewed by Alain Guyomarch: "increasing the speed, effectiveness and efficiency of service provision, giving to individual units defined objectives and responsibility for achieving those targets, providing both civil servants and citizens with clear definitions of standards expected in public services and mobilizing civil servants by better training, career management and job involvement."[17] Many of these reforms appear to be based on imported "new public management" doctrines, and Guyomarch agrees that they are, but argues that these concepts have hybrid characteristics as they have been modified by the French national context, and that missing elements from the usual "paradigm" of new public management include shifts to greater competition in the public sector and the adoption of private management practices in hiring, firing, promoting and paying civil servants.

Within this legal framework, French bureaucratic behavioral traits as related to more general French cultural characteristics have been analyzed thoroughly and perceptively by various scholars, most notably by Michel Crozier and Ezra N. Suleiman.

Crozier sees the bureaucratic pattern of decision-making as well fitted to basic French cultural traits in stressing the qualities of rationality, impersonality, and absoluteness.[18] Crozier views France as essentially a "stalemate society," reflecting his conclusion as to the consequences of two deep-seated yet contradictory attitudes: an urge to avoid as much as possible direct face-to-face authority relationships, and a prevailing view of authority in terms of universalism and absolutism. The bureaucratic system provides a means of reconciling these contradictory attitudes through impersonal rules and centralization, which combine an absolutist conception of authority with the elimination of most direct dependence relationships. "In other words," he says, "the French bureaucratic system of organization is the perfect solution to the basic dilemma of Frenchmen about authority. They cannot bear the omnipotent authority which they feel is indispensable if any kind of co-operative activity is to succeed."[19]

Although suited to the basic requirements of a stalemate society, the French administrative subsystem suffers, according to Crozier, from inherent dysfunctions. One is that decisions are inadequate because those making decisions are too far removed from those affected by the decisions. A second is that coordination is difficult. Fears of conflict and face-to-face relationships lead to organizational self-restraint to avoid overlapping, about which French higher civil servants have "a sort of panicky fear" caused, Crozier suggests, "by their conception of authority as an absolute that cannot be shared, discussed, or compromised."[20] The final "overall and recurrent" problem is that of adjusting to change. Crozier believes that the usual response of a bureaucratic organization to change shows a pattern of routine and crisis, with long periods of routine alternating with short periods of crisis—a pattern especially pronounced in France.[21]

In Crozier's judgment, the *grands corps* offer the most promise as agents of change, being remote from pressure and capable of cushioning at least minor crises. However, such intervention has only limited possibilities. The direction of reform is usually toward more centralization, because this has resolved earlier crises. Citizen participation is minimal or nonexistent. "Peace, order, and harmony" are the objectives, rather than "experimentation and innovation." Hence the *grands corps* "cannot really play the role of prime mover," and major issues of change must be referred by the bureaucracy to higher level policy-makers.[22]

Suleiman's later study of the French administrative elite supports Crozier on most basic matters, offers some different interpretations, and deals with additional questions. He concurs as to the rigid centralizing tendencies in French administration and the urgency of far-reaching administrative reforms. He also confirms the pivotal role of the *grands corps* in the apparatus of administration, essentially undisturbed by postwar reform efforts. However, he challenges Crozier's suggestion that these corps function as agents of change within the bureaucracy. Rather than mediating between the bureaucracy and the environment in times of crisis, he interprets the available evidence as indicating that these corps are an integral part of a system that is resistant to change, and concludes that "the existence of numerous corps is indissolubly linked with a centralized State."[23] He cites a case study of the Corps des Mines showing how members of this corps have succeeded in stationing themselves in a variety of key administrative positions despite the declining importance of the mining sector. Such corps networks, Suleiman argues, set the standards by which the desirability and pace of change are judged. Moreover, since numerous networks exist and often work at cross-purposes, policy formulation is "reduced to the lowest common denominator between the rival corps."[24] As a result, internecine rivalry takes precedence over public policy issues, tending to dampen change. Suleiman does hypothesize that although the corps as organized entities do not serve as change agents, an individual corps member can initiate change when occupying an important agency post outside the corps, and may use the corps network to which he belongs to support the innovative policy, provided the interests of the corps itself are not threatened. In summary, Suleiman seems to be even less optimistic than Crozier about the prospects for change to be initiated from within the bureaucracy, except in special circumstances.

An interesting question explored by Suleiman is whether the social class origins of members of the administrative elite affect their attitudes and behavior as bureaucrats. After confirming that the higher civil servants continue to come predominantly from the middle and upper-middle classes, he compiles and analyzes available data as to the degree of correlation between socioeconomic background and bureaucratic performance.[25] His tentative conclusion is that the attitudes and behavior of the higher civil servants included in his study were not determined by their social origins, in view of the lack of evidence of division on issues and attitudes along class lines, but were more likely due to the training of higher civil servants, the administrative structure itself, and the work environment. Hence, Suleiman cautions against the expectation that proportional representation of societal classes in the French administrative elite would bring about radical transformation.

From what has already been said about the role of the state in French society and about the role of higher civil servants as agents of the state, it is apparent that members of the French administrative elite are involved in a wide range of activities extending well beyond the function of rule application. Two principal features of the French bureaucracy account for this: the permanence of bureaucratic structures and the ubiquity of bureaucratic personnel. Administrative continuity, particularly through the *grands corps*, has already been examined. We need also to review the extent to which members of the bureaucratic elite occupy positions of power and influence both inside and outside the administrative agencies of government.

As would normally be expected, members of one of the *grands corps* or a ministry corps almost invariably serve as directors of the *directions*, or operating divisions, of each ministry, although this is not a legal requirement. For practical purposes, the minister's choice is not only limited to the civil service, but in some instances to members of a particular corps which has "colonized" that sector of the administration. These factors, plus others, greatly circumscribe the actual range of choice and firmly retain these pivotal positions in the hands of the civil service, making the transitory minister greatly dependent on the key professional administrators heading up the *directions*.[26]

Service in the uniquely French institution of the ministerial *cabinet* offers another channel for input from civil servants. The *cabinet* is the product of custom rather than statute (except for an unsuccessful effort to place a limit of ten on the number of members), consisting of staff associates of the minister chosen by him and serving at his discretion. Its role has shifted over time and may vary from ministry to ministry, but the *cabinet* is usually viewed as a buffer or intermediary between the minister and external political figures on the one hand, and the permanent internal administrative apparatus on the other. The *cabinet* has its own hierarchy despite its small size, with a director who is the key official in the ministry after the minister himself, several members who act as links to particular *directions*, and a lesser number who deal with external matters or have a close personal working relationship with the minister.

Assessments as to the value of these ministerial *cabinets* vary, some commentators viewing the *cabinet* as a positive creation making administration more effective, and others looking on it as a device designed to cope with inadequacies in the ministerial system although in practice aggravating them; there seems to be agreement, however, that the role of the *cabinet* is crucial, that it has been growing, and that it engenders conflict. The author of one report says that ministerial *cabinets* "are simultaneously the product and reflection of the French administrative system as a whole," and that their members "occupy a choice position in the French government because of the advice they lavish, the decisions they prepare, and the implementation they supervise."[27]

If such a view is accurate, the fact that civil servants predominate in these assignments is important evidence as to the sphere of activity of higher administrators. During the Fifth Republic, before 1981, 90 percent of the members of ministerial *cabinets* were civil servants, as compared to 60 percent during the Third Republic. The proportion declined somewhat during the Mitterrand era,[28] but continues to be high. The average length of service is about three years. At least one such tour has become part of the normal career pattern of an aspiring bureaucrat, with approximately half of the members of several of the *grands corps* having had such experience, usually in relatively early stages of their careers.

Suleiman has analyzed carefully the conflict and tension between members of ministerial *cabinets* and directors of *directions* within ministries, which exists despite the similarities in background and training of individuals in the two groups. He found a marked hostility on the part of the directors toward the *cabinet* and a reciprocal lack of confidence in the directors by *cabinet* members, reflecting greatly divergent views between the two groups as to what their degree of authority should be, and as to the relationship between politics and administration. The power of *cabinet* members tends to be exercised in the name of the minister and with due regard for general governmental policies. The sphere of authority of the directors is more narrowly defined and is little concerned with overall policy questions. The directors regard politics and administration as "distinct domains that only infrequently come into contact with one another, and which, in any case, ought always to remain strictly separate." *Cabinet* members believe that "the two domains cannot be separated at the highest levels of the administrative system, where decisions are prepared for and alternatives submitted to the minister."[29]

Although Suleiman considers that this conflict reflects two diametrically opposed role perceptions, he also stresses that the occupants who assume these seemingly incompatible roles at different stages in their careers nearly always come from the civil service. "They are the same people; they merely alternate positions and, hence, roles." He concludes that it is dangerous to speak of an administrative "mind" or "mentality" when such diversity of role perceptions exists even among higher civil servants who have "shared a common socialization experience." Loyalties can shift with relative ease. *Cabinet* members who become directors "adopt a view totally at odds with the view they held while in the cabinet. . . . Evidently a civil servant's interests change with the position he occupies in the politico-administrative hierarchy, and his perception of his role changes too."[30]

Not only do civil servants have a virtual monopoly on the important positions in the *directions* and in the ministerial *cabinets*, but in recent years, particularly since the beginning of the Fifth Republic, they also have been appointed in increasing numbers to key ministerial posts, with over one-third of the ministers in some recent governments being drawn from the ranks of the civil servants. The Socialist shift in 1981 did not change this trend, but only substituted some elite administrators for others more attuned politically to the Mitterrand government. Similar moves have occurred since during cohabitation when the premier and the president are not political allies. The Fifth Republic has been referred to as *La Republique des fonctionnaires*, and Mattei Dogan says that its hallways have become "the paradise of the modern mandarins."[31]

Finally, it should be noted that French civil servants, particularly those who have achieved membership in one of the *grands corps*, hold numerous influential posts outside the governmental ministries. Girling describes former pupils of the ENA as having a "monopoly of French political life," and states that "France remains the only country where the notion of an all-powerful elite preoccupies political analysis."[32] Included in this elite group have been four out of five presidents of the Fifth Republic, and all of the Fifth Republic premiers between 1958 and 1984. Members of the national parliament are being drawn in increasing numbers from the ranks of former civil servants, with the proportion reaching nearly half of the membership of the National Assembly after the 1981 Socialist victory, and standing currently at about forty percent. Leadership in most of the nationalized industries is in the hands of civil servants.[33] Frequently higher civil servants have moved at mid-career into private sector positions. This diffusion, greatest under the Fifth Republic, justifies Suleiman's reference to "the ubiquity of civil servants in all the crucial institutions in France,"[34] and explains Ashford's judgment that "France is probably among the more skilled administrative systems in blending entrepreneurial and administrative talents."[35]

In view of the prevalence of French bureaucrats, the question must be addressed as to what this means in terms of the long-run "political" role of the bureaucracy and the effectiveness of controls over the bureaucracy. Various interpretations are offered by different authorities. The most common generalization, one that plainly has much to support it historically, is that the bureaucracy has been able to compensate by its own competence and continuity for the fragile and shifting political leadership, and has taken measures to keep its own house in order. As Alfred Diamant has put it, "The Republic passes but the administration remains."[36] Certainly prior to the Fifth Republic, executive control of the bureaucracy was weak, and legislative control was sporadic and fragmented, often directed toward obtaining favors or blocking programs rather than guiding bureaucratic efforts. In the absence of effective external controls, mechanisms of internal control were developed as an "inner check" on the bureaucracy. The Conseil d'Etat gradually became the most important such agency, by taking on the judicial function of evaluating administrative acts for the protection of citizens' rights, by advising on bill drafting and executive decrees, and by consulting with ministries on administrative problems and suggesting remedial measures.

This hypothesis of political instability offset by administrative stability has come under increasing attack. Crozier objects to a simplified contrast between "permanent and efficient administrative bureaucracy" and "unstable governments unable to choose and carry out consistent policy." He regards this situation not as a paradox but as a reflection at the organizational level of basic French traits of rationality, impersonality, and absoluteness which are present in the decisions produced by a decision-making pattern in which the administrative system is dominant. He maintains that as long as this dominance persists, the whole political system will remain unbalanced.[37]

Suleiman's study of the French administrative elite, being more recent, is able to devote fuller attention to the evolution of political control over the bureaucracy during the Fifth Republic. He sharply criticizes the theme that under the Third and Fourth Republics power was shifted from the politicians to the civil servants because of ministerial instability, and raises doubts about assertions that long-range policies were largely the work of permanent officials rather than politicians, maintaining instead that they were usually the product of shifting alliances between the two groups. He does argue that the Fifth Republic has brought significant changes in political control over the bureaucracy. The impact of parliamentary supervision has definitely weakened, a by-product of the relative impotence of the legislative branch under the mixed presidential-parliamentary system. Executive control has been considerably strengthened, particularly since the 1962 constitutional changes which enhanced the powers of the presidency. Ministerial direction has been assisted by the somewhat longer average term in office of ministers.

It is becoming increasing clear that the most crucial consideration affecting the operation of the mixed presidential-parliamentary system of the Fifth Republic is whether or not a dominant political party or coalition controls both the presidency and the National Assembly. John A. Rohr has presented evidence that the framers of the current constitution intended to place the prime minister at the head of the executive power, but that the 1962 amendment providing for direct election of the president led to a more dominant role for the president, except for periods of cohabitation.[38] As a consequence, it is realistic to talk of presidential government and of prime ministerial government, depending on the relative power relations of the president and the prime minister. As Robert Elgie has pointed out, "the peculiarities of the French constitutional arrangement have institutionalized rivalry within the executive," thus creating "a situation of constant tension between the two institutions as each one tries to increase its control over the policy process at the expense of the other."[39]

The current political system in France, as accurately characterized by Suleiman, continues to combine "the chief elements of the British parliamentary system and the American presidential system."[40] When the presidency and the legislature have been in the hands of a single political party, it has been able to govern effectively, with a strong hold over state institutions, including the bureaucracy. Transfers of party dominance have not led to massive purges of the civil service, but have brought the replacement in key positions of some civil servants by others. When this happened after the Socialist victory in 1981, Suleiman concluded that "the true politicization of the administration" had begun, and predicted accurately that just as the Socialists were not averse to rewarding their adherents with critical appointments, neither would the Right be when it returned to power.[41] Fortin agreed that such alternations in power would make "some redeployment of officials almost automatic."[42]

In summary, the usual conclusion by students of the French system is that although French bureaucrats take an active and crucial part in public policy making, ultimate control lies outside the bureaucracy as an institution. "The higher civil service in France," according to Quermonne and Rouban, "has been so closely involved with top-level government policy making, social reforms, and economic development that the political and administrative worlds are now merging."[43] Vernardakis concurs, stating that during the Fifth Republic "the role of higher civil servants in the making of public policy has reached a new plateau. Yet," he goes on to say, "the assertion of executive control over the bureaucracy in the face of weak parliamentary control . . . does not suggest the appropriation of power by the public bureaucracy itself. On the contrary, its effective subordination to the dual executive has weakened its relative autonomy."[44] Without being basically threatened as to its role in the political system, the French administrative elite, despite its impressive capabilities for self-protection, has faced and adjusted under the Fifth Republic to a greater challenge to its autonomy than it has been accustomed to in the past.

Reunified Germany

The political and administrative institutions of Germany differ in some basic respects from those of France.[45] After unification of the Reich under Bismarck, Germany had a federal system of government until the period of Nazi rule. With the division of the country at the end of World War II, West Germany (the German Federal Republic) reverted to the federal system, whereas East Germany (the German Democratic Republic) retained under its Communist bloc regime a unitary centralized structure much like the Nazi pattern.

Reunification took place rapidly after the fall of the Berlin Wall in 1989. The process was essentially absorption of East by West through official confirmation of the accession of East Germany to the Federal Republic in October, 1990.[46]

In the German federal system, the constituent unit is the *Land*. With reunification, five additional *Laender* were added from what had been the German Democratic Republic, bringing the total to sixteen. Each *Land* has extensive administrative and adjudicative responsibilities delegated to it, but the national or Reich government dominates in the legislative arena. Essentially the division of functions in this federal system is that most important legislative decisions on policy are made by the central government, but the *Laender* are relied on primarily as the vehicles for administration of the programs legislated. As a consequence, only 10 percent of the bureaucracy is attached to the national government, with the bulk of the bureaucrats being in the administrative services of the *Laender*.

The Bonn constitution of 1949 also provided for a parliamentary government, with a bicameral legislature, a chancellor as the chief executive officer, and a president functioning essentially as an elected constitutional monarch with very limited powers, chosen for a term of office of five years. The chancellor was designed to be a strong executive. Elected by the Bundestag, or lower house of the legislature, every four years at the beginning of a new Bundestag, the chancellor can be removed only by a motion of no confidence coupled with election of a successor by an absolute majority of the Bundestag members. This has occurred only once, in 1982, when a shift in party coalitions led to the ouster of Helmut Schmidt as chancellor and the election of Helmut Kohl as his replacement. Moreover, the chancellor can ask for a vote of confidence any time he chooses, and if he is defeated, he can request the president to dissolve the Bundestag and hold new elections. The chancellor appoints cabinet ministers to serve at his discretion.

The executive structure under the chancellor includes the chancellor's office and a variable number of ministries as determined by him. The chancellery consists of about 100 higher civil servants, with a supporting staff more than three times as large, and is headed by a director whose powers are second only to those of the chancellor. Under Konrad Adenauer, from 1949 to 1963, tight control was exercised over the ministries by the chancellor's office, which set program priorities, prepared cabinet agendas, and served as a communication channel between the executive and the legislature. Under later coalition governments, control from the chancellor and his office has been somewhat diluted. The more highly personalistic leadership style of Kohl as compared to Schmidt, his predecessor, also decreased the role of the office during Kohl's long tenure heading a Christian–Free Democrat coalition. His successor, Gerhard Schroder, elected in September, 1998, as leader of a coalition of Social Democrats and Greens, has not been in office long enough to leave his mark. The overall image of executive leadership which has emerged has been described as "a focused network rather than a pyramid."[47]

The number of ministries has varied in the past from a high of nineteen to a low of twelve, and now stands at eighteen. The typical German ministry is quite small as compared to those in most other countries, with a range of from about 1800 down to about 300 employees, due to reliance in most instances on *Laender* officials to provide the necessary administrative infrastructure. As Mayntz and Scharpf point out, "most federal ministries should be regarded primarily as fairly large policy-making staffs rather than as administrative line organizations."[48] In contrast to France, higher civil servants are not appointed as ministers. "Federal ministers are politicians, not bureaucrats. The career ladder of the higher civil service does not lead to these political offices."[49] However, ministers are ordinarily experts in their sectoral fields as well as professional politicians, and rotation among ministries is rare.

The typical ministerial structure is organized along lines that emphasize hierarchical authority but also allow for considerable decentralization in operation. Staff capability around the minister at the top is relatively limited, but this small staff is selected by the minister and usually leaves office when he does, so that personal loyalty to the minister is its hallmark. The staff consists of a personal assistant and a press or public relations assistant, a bureau to perform routine clerical and administrative tasks, and one or two state secretaries. The latter, usually picked from among the permanent civil servants in the ministry, provide the strongest element of continuity and may continue in office from one minister to another, although they have no claim to do so. In recent years, an additional role of parliamentary secretary has been created, designed to deal with parliamentary relations for the ministry, and filled by a member of parliament who usually is a close political associate of the minister.

Below the level of the minister and state secretaries, the typical structural breakdown is into divisions, which in turn are subdivided into sections as the basic working units. The divisions and sections are ordinarily set up on the basis of programs provided or clienteles served. An exception is a division in each ministry where management or housekeeping functions are centralized, such as budgeting, personnel administration, and provision of legal services. Most of the operating sections are quite small, but the working capacity of the ministry, as Mayntz and Scharpf point out,[50] is almost entirely concentrated at this lowest hierarchical level. Policy-making is decentralized, with limited capacity for policy direction from the top.

The bureaucrats of the German Federal Republic are the modern-day offspring of the Prussian officialdom of earlier centuries, which has been accurately described as "a social elite recruited on the basis of competitive examination and dedication both to efficiency and to the principle of autocracy."[51] This bureaucracy, consisting of university-trained professionals, held a dominant position in the industrialization of Germany during the nineteenth century. Nominally responsible during the Second Reich to the prime minister and the monarchy, the federal bureaucracy in practice made most domestic policy decisions, relying for their administration on the bureaucracies of the *Laender*, which were in turn patterned on the same model. This bureaucratic system became famous for its competence and integrity and earned high prestige, although it also must bear some of the responsibility for the slow development of institutions of popular self-governance in Germany.

The harmony between the bureaucratic elite and the dominant political leadership was disrupted during the Weimar Republic and the Nazi Third Reich. Many higher level bureaucrats were unsympathetic to the republic and were not trusted by its political leaders. Later, under the Nazis, the bureaucrats were made subservient to the party leaders, who were suspicious of them at the same time they were dependent on them.

After World War II, the occupying powers made efforts to reform the German public service, with very little lasting impact. The tendency has been to revert to many of the bureaucratic patterns which had been altered temporarily by the political turmoil earlier in the century. Hence the lines of continuity are strong with the Prussian bureaucracy, despite the fact that most of the area that had been Prussia was not within the German Federal Republic before reunification, and even though a successful transition to a parliamentary political regime has been made since World War II.

The public service sector in Germany is extensive. Prior to reunification, employees of the Federal Republic constituted almost 8 percent of the population and about 20 percent of the gainfully employed in the country. In the former GDR, 12 percent of the population worked officially as state employees, a proportion that has been significantly reduced.

Less than 10 percent of German public employees are in the federal bureaucracy, because of reliance on the *Laender* for program administration, and the rate of growth is lower for the federal bureaucracy than for such areas as health and education at the *Laender* level.

These German public employees are divided into three principal categories: permanent members of the civil service (*Beamte*), salaried employees (*Angestellte*) who do not have the same tenure and pension privileges, and wage-earning manual laborers (*Arbeiter*) employed on short-term contracts. The *Beamte* have higher status and theoretically are assigned to the more responsible positions. They account for about 45 percent of the total number of public servants, and their ranks include judges, teachers, and managerial personnel in the railroad and postal systems as well as most of the occupants of higher level positions in other ministries. Although the status and prestige of the *Beamte* still set them apart, the differences between this group and the salaried employees have been diminishing in recent years, both as to responsibilities assigned and employment conditions. Identical functions are now often performed by members of the two groups, and job security and retirement provisions are not markedly different in actual practice, although handled under separate systems. The remaining significant differences have more to do with career training, recruitment, and patterns of advancement. Proposals for unification into a single uniform public service of all persons employed full time have been made recently, but do not seem likely to be adopted soon.

Vertically, the civil service is divided into four classes—lower, medium, intermediate, and higher. Each class is in turn broken into numerous functional categories, such as general administration, finance, teaching, health, and other technical fields. Each functional category within a class normally consists of five ranks constituting a career ladder, with entrance of new recruits at the bottom rank of the category for which they qualify, only rare horizontal movement later between functional categories, and very slight opportunity for advancement upward into the next higher class. As evaluated by Mayntz and Scharpf, this system has advantages in ease of comprehension, easy comparability of positions, and equality of promotion chances, but has features that present "serious handicaps for a flexible system of personnel management."[52]

The *Beamte* in the higher civil service continue to characterize the German bureaucracy, but they no longer receive the special deference and respect accorded to them in the past, especially in Prussia. According to Mayntz, "German higher civil servants of today do not possess a special elite status on the basis of social origin, recruitment, or occupational prestige." Their social background is usually middle or upper-middle class, "in no way superior to that of other functional elite groups, such as managers in industry, university professors, or free-practicing professionals including lawyers."[53]

Recruitment to the higher civil service is on a career basis, with a high proportion of the recruits continuing to come from families of former civil servants. During their careers, these recruits are expected to be prepared for assignment to positions covering a wide variety of duties, particularly in the functional category of general administration.

Access to these policy-making positions in the higher civil service is along a well-defined path open ordinarily only to holders of a university degree. Traditionally, a legal education has been preferred, and 60 percent of the higher civil servants today have had legal training, but more diversification is occurring gradually, particularly in fields of technical specialization. Even so, top positions in the federal bureaucracy are still filled mostly by individuals with legal training.

University graduates who are selected on the basis of general examinations enter a three-year period of further training within the service, combining academic and on-the-job instruction. Those who are successful in a second examination at the end of this period then enter the higher civil service on a career basis. Owing to the extended preparatory steps, entrance is rarely possible earlier than age twenty-five. In addition to screening through university curricula and examinations, a self-selective tendency is indicated in recent studies pointing toward attraction to the civil service of students who emphasize occupational values such as job and old-age security, tasks that are clearly structured, and well-circumscribed demands on abilities and time, rather than values such as work that is interesting and autonomous, or that leads to more than average success in terms of income and position. Dogmatism, rigidity, and intolerance of ambiguity are among the personality traits of the typical recruit, who is at the same time performance-motivated to a high degree. "The higher civil service still seems to attract those who are by disposition a typically bureaucratic version of organization man," with a self-selective tendency which "appears dysfunctional from the viewpoint of personal characteristics favorable to the needs of active policy-making."[54]

Advancement within the system after entry seems to depend on a combination of two sets of criteria. Most important are the traditional civil service considerations such as seniority, professional competence, loyalty, and good working relationships with colleagues. There are indications that other criteria of a more political nature are now being given more weight as well, including "partisan affiliation, political skills, the political support someone can muster or enjoys, and a record of good relations to one or more important client groups."[55] Officially criteria in the first category continue to be the ones recognized, and periodic evaluations are intended to be the instruments for measuring them, but such criteria are difficult to operationalize, and the subjective judgment of superiors is clearly an influential factor, so that it is not easy to measure the actual mix of these competing sets of criteria.

For the individual higher civil servant, promotion is crucial if he is to gain the benefits of higher salary, old-age pension, and social benefits which are tied in with the rank system. In addition to these material benefits, promotion also opens up opportunities for moving into more influential and responsible positions with corresponding autonomy, prestige, and authority. However, this kind of incentive is somewhat muted by the lack of strict correlation between the hierarchy of formal ranks and the hierarchy of positions, with advancement in rank and in position not necessarily coinciding. The result is a tendency for the civil servant in his own material self-interest to emphasize primarily promotion in rank. Since seniority and experience are more important here and present fewer risks than the exercise of initiative, some commentators think that the consequence is a tendency by federal bureaucrats to take a passive rather than an active stance in policy-making.

Normally, the higher civil service continues to be a career pursued to retirement by those who succeed in getting in during early maturity, but as in France instances of departure at mid-career to accept lucrative opportunities in the professions or in the private sector have been on the increase, causing concern as to the long-range impact on the quality of the higher civil service.

Based on the historical background of the German bureaucracy, its structural features, and the pre-entry experiences and views of those who enter it, one might naturally expect that German senior civil servants would hold attitudinal values conforming closely to those of classical Weberian bureaucrats. This has been the accepted view, and undoubtedly it continues to be accurate for large numbers of German bureaucrats. However, empirical studies made in the early 1970s indicated that a growing number of them did not fit this classical image. Robert D. Putnam, reporting on results of a cross-national research project on the political attitudes of senior civil servants,[56] concluded that German federal bureaucratic respondents did not, as had been anticipated, cluster heavily toward the "classical bureaucrat" type in a continuum postulating this and the "political bureaucrat" as polar syndromes. The distinction between these types has to do with attitudes toward politics and political actors, with the classical bureaucrat believing that public issues can be resolved in terms of impartial and objective standards, and distrusting political institutions such as parliaments, political parties, and pressure groups. The political bureaucrat, on the other hand, has a more pluralistic concept of the public interest, recognizes the need to bargain and compromise, and is more willing to accept the legitimacy of political influences on policy-making.

Contrary to expectations, the German respondents proved to be as "political" in orientation and to hold the associated attitudes at least as much as their colleagues in Great Britain, and to a much greater extent than the Italian respondents.

These findings, supported by related research, point toward significant ongoing attitudinal shifts among German bureaucrats. Although part of the explanation may be interview bias and the turnover in top positions which took place in 1969 when the Social Democratic party came to power, the age structure of the respondents offers what Putnam calls the "essential clue" to interpretation of his data. A rapid generational change seems to have taken place during the 1960s. Since age turns out to be the best predictor of political attitudes, this transition from older to younger bureaucrats has meant an overall shift away from "classical" bureaucratic attitudes in the bureaucracy as a whole. This interpretation is bolstered by the fact that German respondents showed a much greater diversity of attitudes than did their British counterparts, reflecting an ambivalence that is associated with the wider age spread in the German group. Of course, it is possible that the correlation between attitude and age is due, as Putnam puts it, to "the temporary effects of being a particular age," rather than "the permanent effects of being in a given historical generation," but he argues that the generational change more likely accounts for the correlation, and observes that "as Germany has finally come to terms with the age of democracy, her bureaucracy seems likely to continue to move toward greater responsiveness, at least insofar as this is a function of the norms and values of senior bureaucrats."[57] Mayntz and Scharpf concur that the evidence indicates that "federal bureaucrats involved in policy-making are by and large characterized by attitudes favorable to the fulfillment of their function." The authors add that this is so, however, "not because of, but rather in spite of the current civil service system with its typical patterns of training, recruitment, and promotion."[58]

Given the historical precedent of bureaucratic initiative, augmented by current inclinations to work cooperatively with the political leadership, the implication would be that the current German bureaucracy is actively and extensively engaged in policy-making functions, and this is corroborated by available evidence. In their analysis of the process of policy-making, Mayntz and Scharpf absolve the bureaucracy from any deliberate intent to usurp political control, saying that "the federal bureaucracy does not attempt actively to circumvent executive control and to impose upon the political executive a course of action developed to its own preferences."[59] However, they conclude that much policy is initiated on a decentralized basis and that the executive does not direct the policy-making process systematically by formulating explicit policy goals and closely controlling new program development. This in turn reflects unusual difficulty in obtaining political consensus among divergent interests. Acknowledging that this is a problem "characteristic of all ideologically heterogeneous, socio-economically pluralistic, and politically differentiated Western democracies," they nevertheless argue that "institutional conditions in the Federal Republic increase these difficulties beyond the level that is characteristic of either the classical parliamentary systems or the American presidential system."[60] Elections do not usually reduce interest complexity requiring consideration, governments tend to be coalition governments, Germany's "peculiar type of federalism adds to the range of interests that must be taken into account," and the federal government itself "consists of a plurality of semi-independent actors" with the chancellorship lacking unifying potential. The resulting decision-making deadlocks often mean that policy issues are left unresolved or are dealt with in the bureaucracy by default.

Despite political turbulence and the variety of political regimes in German national history, the record is one of effective external political controls over the bureaucracy. During the Second Reich, direct controls were few but, as Herbert Jacob comments, "the confluence of interests and values among all participants in the political process almost automatically produced responsiveness," with dissenters from the conservative consensus simply being excluded from the political arena. The Weimar Republic resorted to more stringent hierarchical controls, and the Nazi Third Reich placed even more emphasis on direct hierarchical controls plus exerting various other external pressures to keep the bureaucracy in line. The German Federal Republic uses a mixture of hierarchical and political controls. "In retrospect," Jacob summarizes, "each German regime commanded a loyal enough administration so that not once in the last century did a breakdown of the administrative process lead to the collapse of a regime. . . . To an amazing extent the civil service identified with whatever regime possessed power and served it ably."[61]

A closer look at the mix of controls existing in the period since World War II underlines the strong element of continuity with the past. The German civil service is to a considerable extent self-regulating out of necessity, because of political regime instability. Certainly the comment that governments come and go but the bureaucracy remains is at least as applicable to Germany as to France. With its elite composition, shared professional perspective, and public prestige, the German bureaucracy has acknowledged an obligation and has had the means to police itself in many respects.

Parliamentary control through the chancellor and the ministers conforms basically to standard practice in a parliamentary system, although there are obstacles to effective clear-cut directives from these political sources, as has already been mentioned. As a result, "the dominant pattern is one of checks and countervailing powers," making "more for a stable than for a very powerful government."[62] Hierarchical controls within the ministries, strong in the past, tended to be weaker during the early years of the German Federal Republic, but have been reinforced in recent years. One device has been more effective utilization of a special category of "political civil servants" (*politische Beamte*), who hold the ranks of state secretary and division chief in federal ministries. Career civil servants ordinarily move into this category by being promoted to these ranks. These *politische Beamte* may be replaced and temporarily retired by the minister at any time, without any reason needing to be given. The political executive is thus able "to get rid of persons in functionally important top positions who do not enjoy his or her full trust," mitigating the clash "between the functional needs of the political executive on the one hand and the career principles of the civil service on the other hand," as Mayntz explains in commenting favorably on this arrangement, which in her judgment has resulted in only a very limited politicization of the federal bureaucracy.[63]

An important contrast between the situation in Germany and in France is that political and administrative career paths are distinctly different. In Germany, career crossovers of individuals from the bureaucracy into politics or from politics into administration are rare, with one exception. Traditionally, civil servants have been strongly represented in German parliamentary bodies, taking leave from their civil service duties temporarily and resuming their bureaucratic careers later if they wish. Even during the postwar period, public employees have made up about 20 percent of the members of the Bundestag, but the proportion seems to be decreasing. This overlapping of membership probably has helped somewhat to ease relationships between the parliament and the bureaucracy as institutions.

The federal structure of German government also affects bureaucratic control. The Bundesrat, which is the upper chamber of the legislature, represents the interests of the *Laender* and has constitutional powers designed to protect the integrity of the federal system. Membership of the Bundesrat consists of representatives of the *Laender*, chosen by the *Land* governments, with the number varying from five to three depending on *Land* population. All constitutional amendments require Bundesrat approval, as does all legislation affecting *Land* administrative, tax, and territorial interests—amounting to more than 50 percent of all laws passed. Even "ordinary" legislation outside of these categories is subject to a limited veto power by the Bundesrat, which can be overruled only by an equivalent majority in the Bundestag, or lower house. If a two-thirds majority rejects a proposal in the Bundesrat, for example, it must be passed by a two-thirds majority of the Bundestag to become law. The threat of a Bundesrat veto is a consideration which must be taken into account by federal government officials, including both politicians and bureaucrats.

Finally, Germany has a well-articulated system of administrative courts which have jurisdiction over acts of administrators at both the federal and *Land* levels. Decisions of the supreme administrative courts of the *Laender* are subject to appeal to the federal administrative court, which also has exclusive jurisdiction over cases that arise at the federal level. Rulings of the administrative courts provide uniform interpretations for policies mandating administrative action and in other ways ensure responsive administration.

The overall result, as summarized by Mayntz, is that "while high German civil servants in central government play a crucial role in policy development and planning, it cannot be said that in doing so they have escaped political control." The reason is not so much stability and cohesion in the political sector, but more "the willingness of high bureaucrats . . . to take political constraints seriously, to anticipate them correctly and to avoid conflict and confrontation with those in a strategically superior position."[64] The record shows that German bureaucrats have obediently and even subserviently responded to whatever political leaders have gained power. Even the Nazis encountered little difficulty in converting the civil service of the Weimar Republic to their own ends. The bureaucratic tradition is one of professional identity, of service status and prerogative, and of maintaining continuity in the management of governmental affairs, but it is also one of service to the state, whatever masters the state may have.

Other "Classic" Systems

Several other countries of western and southern Europe share many of the attributes found in France and Germany, so that they can also be considered as "classic" systems. Included are Italy, Spain, Austria, Switzerland, Belgium, the Netherlands, and Ireland (even though it is not a continental country). To a somewhat lesser extent, this is true also of the Scandinavian countries of northern Europe (Norway, Denmark, Sweden, and Finland). Unfortunately, nation-by-nation variations cannot be explored here, but the literature on these systems is extensive and current, and there are valuable comparative analyses of both similarities and contrasts.[65]

Together with France and Germany, all of these countries have systems of public administration "molded by history and tradition" that have "kept an amazing continuity, even in view of changes in the political system."[66] This is not the same as saying that they are uniformly alike. Distinctive features appear in almost every instance. Innovation and experimentation are most common in the Nordic countries. Sweden, for example, has evolved its own unique pattern of relationships between the cabinet ministries and semi-independent organs of program implementation,[67] and has pioneered the office of Ombudsman (now widely copied around the world) as a device for protection of citizens' rights against administrative abuses.

Nevertheless, as Siedentopf has pointed out, these European countries do conform consistently to two basic Weberian conceptual features of bureaucracy. One is the existence of a professional public service produced by specialized training, and the other is recognition by this bureaucracy of its constitutional obligation to the law as formulated in the political sphere.[68] The bureaucratic elite is actively involved in the conduct of governmental affairs, including intimate participation in policy-making and program planning, but it does not lay claim to becoming the political elite as well.

NOTES

1. These include Herman Finer, "The Civil Service and the Modern State," *The Theory and Practice of Modern Government*, rev. ed. (New York: Henry Holt and Co., 1949),

Chap. 27, pp. 709–723; Leonard Binder, *Iran: Political Development in a Changing Society* (Berkeley, CA: University of California Press, 1962), pp. 46–48; Joseph LaPalombara, "Bureaucracy and Political Development: Notes, Queries, and Dilemmas," pp. 34–61, at pp. 39–48, and S. N. Eisenstadt, "Bureaucracy and Political Development," pp. 96–119, at pp. 98–100, in Joseph LaPalombara, ed., *Bureaucracy and Political Development* (Princeton, NJ: Princeton University Press, 1963); Robert E. Ward and Dankwart A. Rustow, eds., *Political Modernization in Japan and Turkey* (Princeton, NJ: Princeton University Press, 1964), pp. 3–7; Stanley Rothman, Howard Scarrow, and Martin Schain, "Bureaucracy and the Political System," *European Society and Politics* (St. Paul, MN: West Publishing Co., 1976), Chap. 16, pp. 322–325; Mattei Dogan, "The Political Power of the Western Mandarins: Introduction," in M. Dogan, ed., *The Mandarins of Western Europe* (New York: John Wiley & Sons, 1975), pp. 3–24; Joel D. Aberbach, Robert D. Putnam, and Bert A Rockman, "Introduction," *Bureaucrats and Politicians in Western Democracies* (Cambridge, MA: Harvard University Press, 1981), pp. 1–23; Ezra N. Suleiman, "Introduction," in E. N. Suleiman, ed., *Bureaucrats and Policy Making: A Comparative Overview* (New York: Holmes & Meier, 1984), pp. 7–9; and James W. Fesler, "The Higher Public Service in Western Europe," in Ralph Clark Chandler, ed., *A Centennial History of the American Administrative State* (New York: The Free Press, 1987), Chap. 16, pp. 509–539.

2. Binder, *Iran*, p. 47.
3. Ward and Rustow, *Political Modernization*, pp. 4–5.
4. "The top civil servant who plays an important role has a hybrid personality: half-political, half-administrative. Like Janus the Roman god, he has two faces. He is a kin to the mandarins of old Imperial China." Mattei Dogan, "The Political Power of the Western Mandarins: Introduction," in Dogan, ed., *The Mandarins of Western Europe*, pp. 3–24, at p. 4.
5. Aberbach, Putnam, and Rockman, *Bureaucrats and Politicians in Western Democracies*, p. 248.
6. Fritz Morsten Marx, "The Higher Civil Service as an Action Group in Western Political Development," in LaPalombara, ed., *Bureaucracy and Political Development* (Princeton, NJ: Princeton University Press, 1963), pp. 73–74. Copyright 1963 by Princeton University Press.
7. Fred W. Riggs, *Administration in Developing Countries—The Theory of Prismatic Society* (Boston: Houghton Mifflin, 1964), p. 422.
8. Fred W. Riggs, *Prismatic Society Revisited* (Morristown, NJ: General Learning Press, 1973), pp. 28–29.
9. Major sources on the French system include Finer, *The Theory and Practice of Modern Government*, Chaps. 29 and 32; Rothman, Scarrow, and Schain, *European Society and Politics*, Chap. 16, pp. 332–342; Alfred Diamant, "The French Administrative System: The Republic Passes but the Administration Remains," in William J. Siffin, ed., *Toward the Comparative Study of Public Administration* (Bloomington, IN: Department of Government, Indiana University, 1957), pp. 182–218; F. Ridley and J. Blondel, *Public Administration in France* (London: Routledge & Kegan Paul, 1964); Michel Crozier, *The Bureaucratic Phenomenon* (Chicago: University of Chicago Press, 1964), and *Strategies for Change: The Future of French Society*

(Cambridge, MA: MIT Press, 1982); Ezra N. Suleiman, *Politics, Power, and Bureaucracy in France: The Administrative Elite* (Princeton, NJ: Princeton University Press, 1974), and *Elites in French Society: The Politics of Survival* (Princeton, NJ: Princeton University Press, 1978); Jerzy S. Langrod, "General Problems of the French Civil Service," in Nimrod Raphaeli, ed., *Readings in Comparative Public Administration* (Boston: Allyn and Bacon, 1977), pp. 106–118; Douglas E. Ashford, *Policy and Politics in France* (Philadelphia: Temple University Press, 1982); Ezra N. Suleiman, "From Right to Left: Bureaucracy and Politics in France," in E. N. Suleiman, ed., *Bureaucrats and Policy Making: A Comparative Overview*, pp. 107–135; Patrick McCarthy, ed., *The French Socialists in Power, 1981–1986* (Westport, CT: Greenwood Press, 1987); Sonia Mazey and Michael Newman, eds., *Mitterrand's France* (London: Croom Helm, 1987); Yves Meny, "France," in Donald C. Rowat, ed., *Public Administration in Developed Democracies* (New York: Marcel Dekker, 1988), Chap. 17, pp. 273–292; Yvonne Fortin, "Country Report: Reflections on Public Administration in France 1986–87," *Governance* 1, No. 1 (January 1988): 101–110; David Wilsford, "Running the Bureaucratic State: The Administration in France," in Ali Farazmand, ed., *Handbook of Comparative and Development Public Administration* (New York: Marcel Dekker, 1991), Chap. 43, pp. 611–624; William Safran, *The French Polity*, 3rd ed. (New York: Longman, 1991), Chap. 8; James F. Hollifield and George Ross, eds., *Searching for the New France* (New York: Routledge, 1991); James Corbett, *Through French Windows: An Introduction to France in the Nineties* (Ann Arbor, MI: The University of Michigan Press, 1994), Chap. 15; Maurice Larkin, *France Since the Popular Front: Government and People 1936–1996*, 2nd ed. (Oxford: Oxford University Press, 1997); Philip Thody, *The Fifth French Republic: Presidents, Politics and Personalities* (London and New York: Routledge, 1998); and John Girling, *France: Political and Social Change* (London and New York: Routledge, 1998).

10. Meny, "France," in Rowat, *Public Administration in Developed Democracies*, p. 279. For a full analysis, see Alfred Diamant, "French Field Administration Revisited: The Beginnings of the Mitterrand Reforms," in Robert T. Golembiewski and Aaron Wildavsky, eds., *The Costs of Federalism* (New Brunswick, NJ: Transaction, 1984), Chap. 7, pp. 143–164.

11. See Pierre Birnbaum, "France: Polity with a Strong State," in Metin Heper, ed., *The State and Public Bureaucracies: A Comparative Perspective* (Westport, CT: Greenwood Press, 1987), Chap. 6, pp. 73–88.

12. Ezra N. Suleiman, *Politics, Power and Bureaucracy in France: The Administrative Elite*, p. 241. "For example," he continues, "that of the Inspection des Finances consists of the verification of the State's finances and expenditures; that of the Conseil d'Etat consists of its dual role as advisor to the government and as an administrative court; and that of the Cour des Comptes in its role as a court that verifies all public accounts. In performing these tasks the corps are fiercely independent institutions: they have their own statutes, by which all members are bound, and they are subject to little interference by the State. They have thus come to be regarded as being at once an integral part of the State apparatus and the State's means of checking its own excesses." Copyright 1974 by Princeton University Press. Reprinted by permission of the Princeton University Press.

13. For recent assessments, see George Vernardakis, "The National School of Administration and Public Policy-Making in France," *International Review of Administrative Sciences* 54 (1988): 427–451; and Jean-Luc Bodiguel, "Haute Fonction Publique et Traditions Administrative et Politique," 24 pp. mimeo., prepared for the XIVth World Congress of the International Political Science Association, Washington, DC, 1988.

14. For a description of the complex French system of higher education and how its institutions contribute to elite formation, refer to Suleiman, *Elites in French Society*, especially Chaps. 2, 3, and 4.

15. *Ibid.*, p. 163.

16. Ridley and Blondel, *Public Administration in France*, p. 54.

17. Alain Guyomarch, "'Public Service,' 'Public Management' and the 'Modernization' of French Public Administration," *Public Administration* 77, No. 1 (1999): 171–193, at p. 176.

18. "Frenchmen do not dislike change; they dislike disorder, conflict, everything that may bring uncontrolled relationships; they cannot move in ambiguous, potentially disruptive situations. . . . What they fear is not change itself, but the risks they may encounter if the stalemate that protects them (and restricts them at the same time) were to disappear." Crozier, *The Bureaucratic Phenomenon*, p. 226.

19. *Ibid.*, p. 222.

20. *Ibid.*, p. 253.

21. "The difference between France and other Western countries concerns much more the way change is achieved than the actual degree of change. To obtain a limited reform in France, one is always obliged to attack the whole 'system,' which is thus constantly called into question. This explains why the rules of the game can never be completely accepted. Reform can be brought about only by sweeping revolution. . . . On the other hand, revolutionary utterances tend to have only a symbolic value, and they suffer a constant erosion." *Ibid.*, p. 287.

22. *Ibid.*, p. 255. Crozier's views as to how French reforms should be undertaken are set forth in *Strategies for Change* (originally published in France in 1979, with English translation issued in 1982).

23. Suleiman, *Politics, Power, and Bureaucracy*, p. 271.

24. *Ibid.*, p. 274.

25. *Ibid.*, "Social Class and Administrative Behavior," Chap. 4, pp. 100–112.

26. Suleiman asserts that under a parliamentary regime such as that of the Fourth Republic, the real power of civil servants lay in obstruction, and he quotes the observation of one director that "when a minister wanted something unfeasible done, we only had to say 'fine,' and chances were that we would hear no more of it." *Ibid.*, p. 167.

27. Jeanne Siwek-Pouydesseau, "French Ministerial Staffs," in Dogan, *The Mandarins of Western Europe*, pp. 208–209.

28. See Suleiman, "From Right to Left: Bureaucracy and Politics in France," p. 122.

29. Suleiman, *Politics, Power, and Bureaucracy*, p. 222.

30. *Ibid.*, "The Cabinet and the Administration: Political and Administrative Roles in the Higher Civil Service," Chap. 9, pp. 201–238, particularly pp. 202, 233, and 234.

31. Dogan, *The Mandarins of Western Europe*, p. 11.

32. Girling, *France: Political and Social Change*, pp. 82, 83. For another recent summary

of this elite system, see Thody, *The Fifth French Republic*, Appendix C, "A note on the French civil service," pp. 156–160.

33. Daniel Derivry, "The Managers of Public Enterprises in France," in *The Mandarins of Western Europe*, pp. 210–225.

34. Suleiman, *Politics, Power, and Bureaucracy*, p. 374.

35. Ashford, *Policy and Politics in France*, p. 78.

36. Diamant, "The French Administrative System," pp. 182–218.

37. Crozier, *The Bureaucratic Phenomenon*, pp. 251–263.

38. John A. Rohr, "Executive Power and Republican Principles at the Founding of the Fifth Republic," *Governance* 7, No. 2 (April 1994): 113–134.

39. Robert Elgie, "The Prime Minister's Office in France: A Changing Role in a Semi-presidential System," *Governance* 5, No. 1 (January 1992): 104–121, at p. 113. Elgie identifies three types of presidential-prime ministerial relations under the Fifth Republic: (1) "pure presidential leadership, . . . where the president is the dominant political force and where the prime minister is little more than a loyal presidential servant," (2) "limited presidentialism," where the prime minister "tries to foster a certain independence, but he is still constrained by the political situation which operates in the president's favor," and (3) "prime ministerial leadership," where "the prime minister is the primary political force and the president plays a secondary role." *Ibid.*

40. Suleiman, *Politics, Power, and Bureaucracy*, p. 358.

41. "From Right to Left: Bureaucracy and Politics in France," p. 131.

42. "Country Report: Reflections on Public Administration in France 1986–87," p. 103.

43. Jean-Louis Quermonne and Luc Rouban, "French Public Administration and Policy Evaluation: The Quest for Accountability," *Public Administration Review* 46, No. 5 (1986): 397–406, at p. 398.

44. "The National School of Administration and Public Policy-Making in France," p. 447.

45. Refer to Finer, *The Theory and Practice of Modern Government,* Chaps. 28 and 31; Rothman, Scarrow, and Schain, *European Society and Politics*, Chap. 16, pp. 343–347; Herbert Jacob, *German Administration Since Bismarck* (New Haven, CT: Yale University Press, 1963); Arnold J. Heidenheimer and Donald P. Kommers, *The Governments of Germany*, 4th ed. (New York: Thomas Y. Crowell Company, 1975); Renate Mayntz and Fritz W. Scharpf, *Policy-Making in the German Federal Bureaucracy* (Amsterdam: Elsevier, 1975); Renate Mayntz, "Executive Leadership in Germany: Dispersion of Power or 'Kanslerdemocratie'?," in Richard Rose and Ezra N. Suleiman, eds., *Presidents and Prime Ministers* (Washington, DC: American Enterprise Institute for Public Policy Research, 1980), Chap. 4, pp. 139–170; Nevil Johnson, *State and Government in the Federal Republic of Germany: The Executive at Work*, 2nd ed. (Oxford: Pergamon Press, 1983); Klaus Konig, H. J. von Oertzen, and F. Wagener, eds., *Public Administration in the Federal Republic of Germany* (Antwerp: Kluwer-Deventer, 1983); Renate Mayntz, "German Federal Bureaucrats: A Functional Elite between Politics and Administration," in Suleiman, ed., *Bureaucrats and Policy Making*, pp. 174–205; Heinrich Seidentopf, "Western Germany," in Rowat, ed., *Public Administration in Developed Democracies*, Chap. 19; Hellmut Wollman, "Policy Analysis in West Germany's Federal Government: A Case of

Unfinished Governmental and Administrative Modernization?" *Governance* 2, No. 3 (July 1989): 233–266; Phyllis Berry, "Country Report: The Organization and Influence of the Chancellory during the Schmitt and Kohl Chancellorships," *Governance* 2, No. 3 (July 1989): 339–355; Karl Kaiser, "Germany's Unification," *Foreign Affairs* 70, No. 1 (1991): 179–205; H. G. Peter Wallach and Ronald A. Francisco, *United Germany: The Past, Politics, Prospects* (Westport, CT: Greenwood Press, 1992); Michael G. Huelshoff, Andrei S. Markovits, and Simon Reich, eds., *From Bundesrepublik to Deutschland: German Politics after Unification* (Ann Arbor, MI: The University of Michigan Press, 1993); M. Donald Hancock and Helga A. Welsh, *German Unification: Process & Outcomes* (Boulder, CO: Westview Press, 1994); David P. Conradt, *The German Polity*, 6th ed. (New York: Longman, 1996); Alan Watson, "Choices Change for Germany," *World Today* 54 (August/September, 1998): 212–215; David P. Conradt, "Germany," in M. Donald Hancock, David P. Conradt, B. Guy Peters, William Safran, and Raphael Zariski, *Politics in Western Europe*, 2nd ed. (Chatham, NJ: Chatham House Publishers, 1998), Part Three, pp. 215–323; and John Grimond, "The Berlin Republic: A Survey of Germany," *Economist* 350 (February 6, 1999), 18-page section following p. 56.

46.   Reunification has meant a process of rebuilding the governmental and administrative institutions of what had been East Germany according to the Federal Republic model. This has required drastic institutional transformations in the former GDR, and has imposed burdensome obligations on the resources of the German Federal Republic (particularly because of the "elite transfer" of administrative personnel from West to East)—problems which cannot be examined here. For detailed analyses, refer to Klaus Konig, "Bureaucratic Integration by Elite Transfer: The Case of the Former GDR," *Governance* 6, No. 3 (July 1993): 386–396; "Transformation of Public Administration in Middle and Eastern Europe: The German Case," 24 pp. mimeo., prepared for the 54th National Training Conference of the American Society for Public Administration, July 17–21, 1993, San Francisco; and "Administrative Transformation in Eastern Germany," *Public Administration* 71, Nos. 1/2 (Spring/Summer 1993): 135–149.

47.   Mayntz, "Executive Leadership in Germany," p. 144.

48.   Mayntz and Scharpf, *Policy-Making in the German Federal Bureaucracy*, p. 46. Reprinted by permission of the publisher, copyright 1975 by Elsevier Science Publishing Co., Inc.

49.   Mayntz, "Executive Leadership in Germany," p. 150. Former civil servants may and do become ministers, but only after they have renounced their civil service careers, and have been elected to, and served in, the federal parliament.

50.   Mayntz and Scharpf, *Policy-Making in the German Federal Bureaucracy*, p. 64.

51.   Rothman, Scarrow, and Schain, *European Society and Politics*, p. 342.

52.   Mayntz and Scharpf, *Policy-Making in the German Federal Bureaucracy*, p. 52.

53.   "German Federal Bureaucrats," pp. 180, 181.

54.   Mayntz and Scharpf, *Policy-Making in the German Federal Bureaucracy*, pp. 53–54.

55.   *Ibid.*, p. 55.

56.   Robert D. Putnam, "The Political Attitudes of Senior Civil Servants in Britain, Germany, and Italy," in *The Mandarins of Western Europe*, pp. 87–127. [Reprinted from *British Journal of Political Science* 3 (1973): 257–90.] This and other recent

studies are summarized by Mayntz and Scharpf in *Policy-Making in the German Federal Bureaucracy*, pp. 57–62.

57. Robert D. Putnam, "The Political Attitudes of Senior Civil Servants in Britain, Germany, and Italy," in Dogan, ed., *The Mandarins of Western Europe*, pp. 113 and 116. Copyright 1975, reprinted by permission of the publisher, Sage Publications, Inc. (Beverly Hills/London).

58. Mayntz and Scharpf, *Policy-Making in the German Federal Bureaucracy*, p. 62.

59. *Ibid.*, p. 95.

60. *Ibid.*, p. 171.

61. Jacob, *German Administration Since Bismarck*, pp. 198, 202.

62. Mayntz, "Executive Leadership in Germany," pp. 169–170.

63. Mayntz, "German Federal Bureaucrats," pp. 183, 184.

64. *Ibid.*, p. 202.

65. The best single source of information continues to be Rowat, *Public Administration in Developed Democracies*. This volume has separate country chapters, plus comparative overviews on Western Europe by Heinrich Siedentopf, and on the Nordic countries by Lennart Lundquist. See also Walter J. M. Kickert, Richard J. Stillman II, Jacques Chevallier, Wolfgang Seibel, Christopher Pollitt, and Torben Beck Jorgensen, "Changing European States; Changing Public Administration," *Public Administration Review* 56, No. 1 (January/February 1996): 65–103. This symposium contains articles on the Netherlands and Scandinavia, as well as France, Germany, and the United Kingdom.

66. Heinrich Siedentopf, "A Comparative Overview," in Rowat, ed., *Public Administration in Developed Democracies*, Chap. 20, at p. 352.

67. For an explanation and analysis, see Olof Ruin, "The Duality of the Swedish Central Administration: Ministries and Central Agencies," in Farazmand, ed., *Handbook of Comparative and Development Public Administration*, Chap. 6, pp. 67–79.

68. Siedentopf, "A Comparative Overview," pp. 340–343.

6

Administration in More Developed Nations
Some Variations in Administrative Systems

Although developed nations as a group constitute only a small proportion of the total number of existing nation-states, there are too many of them to permit individualized treatment. A choice must be made designed to illustrate significant variations among them, even though this means omission of many large and important countries and scanty attention to innovative features that have evolved in some of the smaller ones.

In addition to France and Germany, we have selected five other administrative systems for primary attention—those of Great Britain, the United States, and Japan as examples of "first tier" countries on a developmental continuum, and the Russian Federation in the Commonwealth of Independent States and the People's Republic of China as "second tier" examples. The first two countries share a common political heritage, exhibit many similarities in their systems of administration, and have been unusually influential as models for developing nations. Japan is the outstanding and possibly the only non-Western nation which clearly has achieved recognition as highly developed, whatever scale for measuring development might be used. The former USSR, as one of the world's superpowers and the primary model for developing nations in the Communist bloc, was also generally considered as belonging in the most developed category. It is doubtful that any of the successor states to the USSR qualify. The Russian Federation would be the strongest contender, but as of now probably fits in the "second tier." Communist China also deserves to be considered here, based on a combination of current measures of achievement and future probabilities.

ADMINISTRATION IN "THE CIVIC CULTURE"

The political characteristics which to a large extent are shared by Great Britain, the United States, and a few other countries that were formerly British colonies have been called "the civic culture" by Almond and Verba. They describe it as a political culture that is participant and pluralistic, "based on communication and persuasion, a culture of consensus and diversity, a culture that permitted change but moderated it."[1] Since the political culture and political structure are congruent, the political system is relatively stable and its legitimacy well established. The Almond and Verba study tested certain hypotheses concerning the diffusion of democratic culture, through studies in five operating democratic systems, including Germany, Italy, and Mexico, as well as the United States and Great Britain. They found that the latter two countries have the civic culture to the greatest degree, with basically similar patterns in each but with somewhat different dimensions, reflecting differences in national histories and social structures. They summarized these differences by labeling Great Britain a "deferential" and the United States a "participant" civic culture.

Despite the differences between them, and the close relationship that each (particularly Great Britain) has to the political systems of continental Europe, we have chosen to group Great Britain and the United States together as examples of "civic culture" systems. In contrast to Germany and France, the history of their political development is one of relative stability. Circumstances permitted them for the most part to take an incremental approach to the problems of political change, and to develop their political institutions without violent discontinuities and abrupt changes of direction. Great Britain achieved political integration by the early seventeenth century, and the political heritage of the United States is largely British. Both countries have been able to establish stable democratic political systems and to maintain them over considerable periods of time.

This gradualist pattern of political development led to decidedly contrasting formal political characteristics, with Great Britain retaining a figure-head monarchy linked with a unitary and parliamentary system, and the United States opting for a federal system with an elected president as chief executive. The greatest consequence of gradualism on public administration was that the administrative system also was able to take shape feature by feature in a way that reflected the political changes and was consonant with them. Political and administrative adaptations were concurrent and fairly well balanced, but the political theme was dominant. At no time has the administrative apparatus been called upon to assume the whole burden of government because of a breakdown of the political machinery.

This background has had profound effects on the composition, behavioral characteristics, and political role of the British and American bureaucracies, accounting both for their similarities and for the differences between them. One similarity, as compared to France and Germany, is that the civil service in Great Britain and the United States was markedly slow in becoming professionalized and in acquiring other important characteristics of Weberian-style bureaucracy. It was not until the middle of the nineteenth century that the British reformed their civil service by putting recruitment on a merit basis. Earlier, most appointments were filled on patronage considerations and many posts were sinecures requiring very little work, although some use was made of qualifying examinations before appointment. Reform of the defects of the civil service came about as the result of the famous Northcote-Trevelyan Report of 1854, which in turn was strongly influenced by personnel practices which had been adopted by the Indian Civil Service during the previous two decades. The principal recommendations which were put into effect included the abolition of patronage and the substitution of appointment on a career basis at an early age through a system of competitive examinations to a unified service which drew a clear distinction between intellectual and routine work, with subsequent promotion also to be based on merit rather than nepotism, connections, or political considerations. These British reform measures provided the model—with important adaptations—for a civil service reform movement in the United States, where the spoils system had been carried to excess during the middle part of the nineteenth century, eventually leading to enactment of the Pendleton Act by Congress in 1883. Although substantial, this reform measure was limited in its impact, applying only partially to the federal civil service and not at all to state and local levels of government service. However, it did start a process, still not completed throughout the American public service, of putting selection and advancement on a merit rather than a patronage basis.

A bureaucracy of competence, it should be noted, did not appear in either country until representative political organs decided that it was needed and provided for it. This has basically influenced the conception the bureaucracy has had of itself and of its relationship to political leaders and to the public at large. In political cultures such as these, where the participative role is highly developed, the citizenry regards the bureaucracy as performing in a service capacity and being properly subjected to firm political control, however expert the bureaucrat may be, and however intimately he may be involved in the consideration of policy alternatives. Partial myth though it is, the bureaucracy is viewed as the neutral agent of the political decision-makers.

These similarities should not be allowed to obscure the distinctive ways in which British and American bureaucracies vary. For example, the British service seems to have a clear advantage over the American service in terms of prestige and status. This reflects general patterns of deference toward governmental and other forms of authority in the society, as well as more specific historical factors such as timing of conversion from a spoils to a merit service, the tradition in the United States of political party reliance on public service patronage, and the relative standing of governmental as against business careers. Some evidence indicates that the gap is narrowing, as simultaneously the British service loses and the American gains prestige, but the difference is still there. Another important difference pointed out by Crozier is that in Great Britain administrative organizations "maintain their effectiveness by relying on the old patterns of deference that binds inferiors and superiors within the limits of the necessary cohesion." In the United States, on the other hand, organizations "must use many more impersonal rules in order to achieve the same results."[2] The differences are also reflected in the choices the two countries have made in arranging for staffing and operating the bureaucracy. As Sayre summarizes it, the British responses have produced "a more orderly and symmetrical, a more prudent, a more articulate, a more cohesive and more powerful bureaucracy." The American choices have produced "a more internally competitive, a more experimental, a noisier and less coherent, a less powerful bureaucracy within its own governmental system, but a more dynamic one."[3] With this background, we can now examine in more detail some of the specifics of each of these systems.

Great Britain

The setting in which the British public bureaucracy operates is unitary and parliamentary.[4] Ministries are the basic administrative units, supplemented by nationalized industries and public corporations outside the ministerial framework. Decisions as to executive organization are considered a prerogative of the crown, meaning that they can be made by the government of the day. Changes in the lineup of ministries are relatively frequent. The standard arrangement is for each ministry to be headed by a minister who is responsible before Parliament for all ministry affairs, and who heads the ministerial hierarchy. Directly under the minister is the uniquely British office of permanent secretary, held by a senior civil servant with the obligation to serve any minister and any government with equal skill and devotion. One or more deputy secretaries assist the permanent secretary, each in charge of several sections. Undersecretaries and assistant secretaries head up lower echelon divisions, with principals and assistant principals in turn heading up smaller units within these divisions. The pattern is orderly and symmetrical, with the prime minister and cabinet able to make adjustments which the government considers timely.

Traditionally the British Treasury, along with its many other important functions, had responsibility for supervising the civil service, including recruitment, training, promotion, and compensation. Only within the last few years has responsibility for personnel management been shifted from the Treasury and placed directly under the control of the prime minister. In staffing the civil service, the British have shown a preference for recruiting candidates with general capacity to serve on a career basis. During most of its history, the British civil service was divided into three major classes—clerical, executive, and administrative—in an ascending order of responsibilities and qualifications. The elite of the service were in the administrative class, comprising fewer than 3000 members in 1968, or less than 0.5 percent of the total civil service. This select group had responsibility for policy initiation and implementation and dealt directly with political officials. In 1971, as recommended earlier by the Fulton Committee, these three classes were merged in a new administrative group as part of a system of occupational groupings, but it appears that a small select cadre continues to bear similar responsibilities, although no longer identified as members of a distinct administrative class.[5]

Entry into the British higher service until the end of World War II was based on competitive examinations in a variety of subjects paralleling the courses of study offered in the universities and open only to recent university graduates. Some common test subjects were required, such as ability in written expression and knowledge of contemporary affairs, but most stress was placed on performance in subjects chosen from a wide range of possibilities not necessarily having anything directly to do with later work assignments.[6] An alternative approach, called Method II, was provided at the end of World War II, primarily for the benefit of returning war veterans, with emphasis placed mainly on a series of individual and group interviews, in addition to performance on the usual required examinations. The 1971 reforms involved a shift to a system of selection of administrative trainees for careers in the new administrative group. Candidates are put through a series of examinations and interviews along Method II lines. Most of the successful candidates continue to come from honors graduates of the universities, but an increasing number are being chosen from persons already in the service with a minimum of two years of experience. Those chosen enter a probationary period which includes several weeks of training at the Civil Service College established in 1970. During succeeding years further assessment and training leads to "streaming" into ability groupings of those considered promising for high level posts in their later careers and those deemed more suitable for middle management positions, thus resulting apparently in career patterns corresponding roughly to the old administrative and executive classes. Sophie Watson reported in 1992 that the "fast track stream" continued to be the route for a successful civil service career, with the vast majority of individuals reaching the top three grades coming up this way, and with only three permanent secretaries during the century coming from the executive officer route.[7]

The social background of higher civil servants in Great Britain has in the past shown very little diversity. The administrative class before World War II came almost exclusively from upper class graduates of Oxford or Cambridge, who earlier had attended public schools such as Eton and Harrow. During recent years, however, several factors have helped broaden the social and educational base from which higher civil servants are being drawn. Scholarship assistance to talented students from lower class backgrounds has diversified the student composition at "Oxbridge" universities. The less prestigious "Redbrick" universities have gained in stature and now provide more graduates who succeed in the competition for entry into the civil service. Opportunities for promotion into the former administrative class were broadened for individuals with experience in the executive class. Age restrictions for entry have largely been abolished, and females now make up a third of those entering the "fast stream."[8] Further diversification of background can be anticipated from ongoing recruitment and training reforms.

Career-staffing in Great Britain, with entry usually barred except at an early age, has meant a minimum interchange of personnel between governmental and nongovernmental careers. Even today, as Christoph reports,

> . . . the higher civil service does not serve as an instrument for systematically recruiting talent into other elites, whether they be members of parliament, political executives, local government officials, or managers in the private sector. However attractive their skills may appear at the middle or ends of their careers, few civil servants trade their places in Whitehall for ones elsewhere.[9]

Guarantees of civil service status are substantial in Great Britain, but they depend more on a protective tradition than on elaborate legal provisions. The civil service is an establishment of the crown, and its affairs are almost exclusively controlled by orders-in-council or other executive action. High-ranking British bureaucrats play substantial roles in governmental decision-making, but the specifics are difficult to discover. The British operate under a convention that imposes upon the official and the minister clearly understood mutual obligations based on the principles of impartiality and anonymity. The civil servant is expected to offer his advice to the minister, who has political responsibility, but he is obligated to carry out loyally whatever decision is reached. The principle of anonymity means that the career official is to be protected by the political leadership from disclosure of the advice given, and is not to be brought into the limelight of the political arena.

This system is supposed to and does keep out of the public eye the extent and nature of the involvement of civil servants in policy-making, but it certainly permits the higher-ranking officials to initiate and choose among policy proposals, subject to ministerial discretion. Apparently, there are considerable variations in the powers actually exercised by civil servants, depending on the characteristics of individual ministers. Both Brian Chapman and James B. Christoph have pointed out how the attention of British civil servants is highly concentrated on the minister as the key political referent in their lives as officials. In some respects, ministers are much alike. For example, they must be members of Parliament, and they usually are experienced members, with the average length of service in recent governments being fifteen years, which means that their skills are associated mainly with parliamentary success. More than likely, the minister will not have expertise that is relevant to the work of the ministry. Tenure is often brief; the average in recent governments has been only 26 months. Individuals are frequently shifted from one cabinet post to another with widely differing functions. All are extremely busy, putting in work weeks of sixty hours or more, and are limited in the time they can devote to ministerial policy-making.

Within this common frame of reference, ministers do differ in the ways in which they approach their tasks, including relations with top civil servants. Christoph and others have contrasted "strong" and "weak" ministers. A strong minister views the role of civil servants as "largely one of informing the minister fully, analyzing his choices in terms of their technical feasibility, freeing him from trivial paper work, and ensuring that his policies are put into effect swiftly and positively. Because they are left in no doubt over what their minister wants, civil servants act as handmaidens rather than brakes."[10] Weak ministers lack focus as to mission, show little strength in dealing with cabinet colleagues and permanent officials, are passive on policy issues, and become preoccupied with routines and trivia, thus enhancing opportunities for civil servants to engage in independent policy-making.

Bruce W. Headey has carried such analysis further by suggesting a fivefold typology of ministers, based on interview data from both current and former ministers and civil servants.[11] His five types are policy initiators, policy selectors, executive ministers, ambassador ministers, and minimalists. The policy initiators emphasize that their role is to state objectives and priorities. They initiate the search for appropriate policy programs, with the role of the civil servant being essentially responsive. Policy selectors as a group have a quite different view of the minister-civil servant relationship. Their main emphasis is on the necessity of choice by the minister, who must make decisions and not delay or vacillate. This seems to be a more commonly accepted role, and is viewed favorably by most civil servants. Executive ministers have a management textbook view of their jobs, believing it is a mistake to divorce questions of policy from questions concerning cost, structure, and personnel management. They are few in number and usually have a background of business experience. Their role conception is an ambitious one, involving large time commitments, and infringing on what has been generally considered the management function of the permanent secretary. Ambassador ministers give high priority to their role in dealing with outside groups. Civil servants tend to have policy matters devolve on them under such a minister, but they do not regard this ministerial role favorably, because it often causes delays in decisions which need to be taken at the minister's level. Ministers who are minimalists, as the term suggests, do no more than is necessary, such as formal acceptance of responsibility for departmental decisions, putting up a respectable effort to win support for departmental measures, and avoiding parliamentary trouble. Civil servants express disapproval of minimalists on two grounds: a poor standing by a minimalist minister reflects unfavorably on the whole department; and officials are forced to formulate policy objectives as well as advise on alternatives.

Headey summarizes by stating that constitutional theory regarding the minister-civil servant relationship

> is highly misleading. Civil servants are not always restricted to advisory and administrative roles in relation to policies laid down by ministers. . . . A realistic picture of relations between ministers and their officials needs to recognize that ministers have markedly different role conceptions and that time constraints mean that giving high priority to one role is likely to mean that other roles are downgraded and, implicitly, delegated to civil servants.[12]

Although recognizing that different types of ministers are needed, depending on time and circumstances, Headey concludes that only the political initiator and policy selector types actually exert much influence over policy, and expresses concern about the undesirable consequences of failure by ministers to define policy objectives and priorities, since proposals generated by civil servants are apt to be status quo-oriented rather than innovative.

Christoph offers a useful summary of the political role now commonly played by higher civil servants in Great Britain, cautioning that the exact mix will depend on the functions of the ministry and the orientation and skills of its minister. The traditional and still pre-eminent role is substantive policy implementation, which involves a wide range of discretion because of the general terms of much legislation and the volume of delegated legislative powers. The offering of political advice to the minister as a basis for policy decisions is a second crucial and exacting role, requiring sensitization to the political implications of actions recommended. Third is a symbiotic relationship with the minister of providing mutual political protection, through which civil servants, "in return for their protection and enhancement of their minister's reputation . . . are shielded by him from direct political interference from parliament, the press, and the public." Advancement of clientele claims in various arenas, and efforts to reconcile pressure group claims, are the final two related roles in this analysis. Christoph also mentions several "non-roles," activities engaged in only marginally, if at all, as clues to understanding the system. British civil servants do not have to try to substitute for ineffectual party or electoral machinery, as has been the case historically in Germany and France, for example. They do not usually deal directly with the public by providing goods and services. Direct control of the populace or of subordinate governmental units is likewise untypical. Finally, higher civil servants usually do not leave their careers for service in other elites in the society or actively participate in partisan politics. Taking these "do's and don'ts" into account, Christoph says that "the higher bureaucracy in Britain will continue to be called on to carry a substantial share of political decision-making. . . . It is still a share, though, not a monopoly. By temperament, socialization, situation, and resources, top civil servants are well placed to strongly influence the outcome of policy, but not to transform it into a sole proprietorship."[13]

Responsiveness to political authority is not only given lip service but is genuinely accepted as appropriate by career officials, reflecting the historical fact that representative institutions antedated a modern civil service and have established the legitimacy of their authority. Putnam's report on the political attitudes of senior British civil servants confirmed that they continued to tend toward the "political" rather than the "classical" model of bureaucrat in acceptance of responsiveness to political institutions. The data indicated that this was less characteristic of specialist and technical officials in the sample than of generalists in what was then the administrative class, indicating that a bureaucracy led by such officials might be less responsive. On the other hand, British "high-fliers" (younger officials considered likely to be assigned major responsibilities later) were "the most politically conscious, the most programmatically committed, the most egalitarian, and the most tolerant toward politicians and pluralism" of any of the groups interviewed.[14]

Although in the past political leaders from different parties had expressed confidence in such responsiveness to policy changes by high ranking bureaucrats, there is considerable evidence that in recent years, beginning in the early 1980s during the Conservative government of Margaret Thatcher, distrust of the civil service has grown and steps have been taken to exercise more direct control over the assignment of civil servants to top posts on the basis of loyalty, to reduce the policy-making role and emphasize more the managerial role of civil servants, to take vigorous disciplinary action against officials suspected of leaking information, and to encourage departure from the service of those not considered sufficiently committed to current policy objectives. The basic question asked by the Thatcher government of senior officials was: "Is he one of us?" The responses available to these officials, as expressed by Richard Rose, became more and more a choice among "loyalty, voice, or exit."

Reform of the civil service, initiated by Margaret Thatcher, has continued as an objective of her Conservative successor John Major, and of the current Labour government of Tony Blair, so that this is no longer a matter of dispute between the major parties. "The outcome," as summarized by Sylvia Horton, is that the civil service "is smaller, its structure has radically altered, its methods of delivering services have been transformed and it is now staffed by a new cadre of public managers."[15] The changes have resulted from a series of reform efforts. The first was an "efficiency initiative" during the 1980s designed to bring about immediate savings and change the administrative culture of the service. The second stage was aimed at separating policy and service delivery responsibilities. This led to the restructuring of departments and the creation of Next Step Agencies (NSAs) headed by chief executives charged with day-to-day operations within policy and resources boundaries determined by a parent department to which the NSA was attached. Over 150 such agencies have been created since 1988 and nearly 80 percent of civil servants now work in them. This devolved management pattern is intended to make these public agencies more like their private sector counterparts. The third stage, beginning in the early 1990s, has involved several moves intended to steer public management further toward a market orientation. The consequences for the public service have been significant. Its size is about 35 percent smaller, having been reduced from 742,990 in 1979 to 481,000 in 1998. The approach to personnel management has shifted to what is known as "new people management" based on ideas imported from the private sector.

Despite these reforms, the governments of the last twenty years have remained committed to sustaining the key principles on which the British civil service is based—integrity, political impartiality, objectivity, selection and promotion on merit, and accountability to Parliament through ministerial responsibility. The Blair Labour government, while endorsing the aims of its Conservative predecessors, has reemphasized its intention to strengthen political control and reaffirm full ministerial responsibility. It has also stressed a commitment to "joined-up government," which puts a priority on coordination rather than decentralization as the most promising strategy for achieving modernization.

Opinions differ as to the ultimate impact of these reform efforts. Perhaps the most balanced appraisal is offered by Francis R. Terry, who says that the relationships of bureaucrats and politicians in the United Kingdom have been "fundamentally altered," with the control of civil servants over policy being eroded, but that "the values that civil servants should espouse have been thrown into doubt without any clear replacements being identified." He summarizes by observing that as these changes progress, "policy civil servants seem to be holding on to their traditional place in government administration," whereas "agency civil servants meanwhile are increasingly developing the habits of private sector managers, although they remain generally lower in status and less well paid."[16] Undoubtedly evaluation of these changes will continue to be the subject of speculation and controversy.[17]

As already mentioned, legislative oversight over administration in Great Britain relies mainly on the doctrine of ministerial responsibility. Taking shape during the nineteenth century, this doctrine was intended as a parliamentary check on the powers of ministers and civil servants. "The doctrine required," as explained by Christoph, "that all actions of civil servants be taken in the name of the minister, who would be held accountable by the Commons for such actions, and in cases where evidence of malfeasance in the performance of duties came to light, censured or made to resign."[18] Christoph and others now contend that as British government has evolved, the doctrine of ministerial responsibility has been warped so that it no longer serves the intended purpose, but instead makes it difficult for Parliament to deal with bureaucratic operations. The argument is that two developments in British politics in the twentieth century have brought about this result. Governmental activities have expanded to the point that ministers no longer can reasonably be expected to have full awareness or give active approval to every action taken by civil servants in their ministries, and this has led to a weakened application of the doctrine when civil service abuses or blunders have been revealed. The other change is the growth of party and cabinet power over Parliament, which overlays the earlier precept of ministerial responsibility with "the politics of collective responsibility," making it hard for opposition members of Parliament or even government party "backbenchers" to penalize a minister if he is supported by the prime minister and his colleagues in the cabinet. As a consequence, the doctrine is alleged to strengthen the hand of the executive rather than the legislature, by making it impossible for Parliament to summon civil servants because only the minister is supposedly accountable, by throwing a cloud of secrecy over minister-civil servant relationships as well as over negotiating with outside groups, and by reinforcing "the centralized and hierarchical nature of British administration by channeling controls from above."[19]

Attempts to modify the doctrine of ministerial responsibility or to increase the number and strengthen the expertise of specialized parliamentary committees as a means of control have made little headway up till now. A partial response is found in the office of the British Parliamentary Commissioner, created in 1967 as a modified version of the Scandinavian Ombudsman to deal with citizen grievances against administrators. However, this official can act only if a complaint is received through a member of Parliament, and can only investigate and report back to Parliament as to defects of procedure in administration. Christoph correctly judges that this mild reform "does not impinge greatly on the behavior of higher civil servants and must be considered at best a minor influence on their overall political role."[20]

Finally, it should be noted that a separate system of administrative courts, along continental European lines, to review allegations by citizens of administrative excesses, has not been appealing in Great Britain. "The common-law courts, plus the efficacy of external political controls, were seen as sufficient bulwarks against the misuse of public authority."[21]

To sum up, recent trends seem to point toward a lessening somewhat of bureaucratic participation in the making of policy and to a gradual weakening of overall legislative control over administrative action, with the beneficiaries being the ministers in the cabinet collectively, and particularly the prime minister. The civil service has gradually become more competent in its composition and more professional in its outlook, in response to the demands placed upon government for performance, but the service orientation remains and responsiveness to the political organs of government, centered in the cabinet, is generally accepted in theory and largely recognized in practice.

The United States

The American political framework in which the public administration system operates has as dominant features constitutionalism (with a written constitution conferring and limiting governmental powers), federalism (which divides functions between the central government and the states as constituent units), and presidentialism (with an elected chief executive heading the executive branch).[22] Although these features have not been fundamentally altered since 1789, each has been modified constantly. The constitutional base has been amended formally occasionally, and modified informally repeatedly by judicial interpretation. The balance of power between the central government and the states in the federal system has undergone marked adjustments in the past and is still shifting.[23] The presidency as an institution has had its ups and downs, depending on the impact of such factors as the individual characteristics of particular presidents, and movements back and forth between times of crisis which enhance and times of uncertainty or ambivalence which diminish the role of the executive in relation to the legislative and judicial branches.

Taken together, these institutional arrangements have exhibited a low degree of "stateness" in the sense used by Heper and others as discussed in Chapter 1. Indeed, Ronald M. Glassman refers to the United States as "the anti-statist society,"[24] and Richard J. Stillman goes even further by characterizing the American situation as one of "statelessness," by which he means that until about the turn of this century the United States was lacking basic features "which by that time characterized much of Europe—namely, centralized power, rationalized authority, and developed administration."[25] Certainly, the American inclination has been to denigrate any claims of state prerogatives, and to place strict limits on the powers delegated to governmental institutions.

With regard to organizational specifics in the central government, executive departments are the major entities of administration, but included in the executive branch are a plethora of regulatory commissions, government corporations, and other units. Decisions as to executive reorganization are basically matters of legislative action. Congress has retained control over the creation or abolition of executive departments (currently there are fourteen), but has been willing to delegate limited discretion to the president to make less major organizational changes. These were usually subject to congressional review and potential disapproval through use of a "legislative veto" until 1983, when that device was held by the U. S. Supreme Court to violate the constitutional separation of powers between the legislative and executive branches. Issues of executive reorganization are recurring agenda items for Congress and the president.

Departmental internal structure follows a less standard pattern than in the British ministry. The department secretary at the head is a political appointee of the president (subject to Senate confirmation) and serves at his pleasure. Usually a department has an undersecretary and several assistant secretaries, who are also political executives with such short tenure on the average that they have been characterized by Heclo as "a government of strangers." No equivalent to the British permanent secretary exists, although all departments now have an official (usually an assistant secretary for administration or management) with much more limited functions of a housekeeping nature. The successive program units by level are most commonly called bureaus, divisions, and sections, but the terminology is not uniform. Beginning at the bureau level, career civil servants are likely to be in charge, but this is not necessarily so and the incumbent has no tenure claim on the office.[26]

The central personnel agency for the federal government from 1883 through 1978 was the Civil Service Commission, a three-member board with statutory powers designed to guarantee the integrity of the merit system. Its functions have now been divided between the Office of Personnel Management and the Merit Systems Protection Board, as one feature of civil service reforms initiated by President Jimmy Carter.

From the beginning, the American preference has been for program-staffing of the civil service through recruitment of candidates with specialized capacity. The approach has been to emphasize the position held and the requirements for satisfactory performance of the duties connected with it, rather than assessment of individual potential for placement in an appropriate rank category. As a result, there has been no clear-cut grouping equivalent to the British administrative class. In the American system of grades reflecting levels of responsibility in the system, the top three "supergrades" were considered to constitute the elite of the civil service prior to the 1978 reforms. In contrast to the "professional amateurs" of the British administrative elite, the occupants of these posts were experts in a professional specialty, leading Frederick C. Mosher to suggest "the professional state" as an appropriate way to designate this clustering of professional elites.[27] Just as recent modifications in the British system have moved toward American concepts, the idea of a "senior civil service" with similarities to the British administrative class was recommended in several versions beginning with that of the Second Hoover Commission in the 1950s, but was not adopted until 1978, when a Senior Executive Service (SES) was authorized, becoming operational in 1979. In a significant departure from the program-staffing tradition, SES members are selected on the basis of demonstrated competence during their careers rather than their suitability for particular positions. After two decades of experience, the SES has received mixed evaluations, and there is considerable doubt that it is producing a service-wide category of administrative generalists with more clear-cut lines for promotion to positions of high level administrative responsibility.

Beginning in 1980 with the election of President Ronald Reagan, and continuing during the successive presidencies of Bush and Clinton, civil service reform efforts have emphasized reorganizing, downsizing, reengineering, and devolution.[28] "Reinventing government," derived from the title of a book by Osborne and Gaebler,[29] is the label most commonly used to describe these reforms. A National Performance Review report issued on 1992 soon after Clinton was elected emphasized the need "to cut rules and regulations wherever possible, to decentralize and/or delegate both authority and program delivery, to empower employees and customers and to eliminate any services and programs that were no longer necessary."[30] Accountability was to be redirected to employees and customers, and product and performance were to replace process as governmental bywords. By 1997 a substantial downsizing of 12.2 percent had taken place in the federal workforce, with the largest cutbacks taking place in civilian employment in the Department of Defense. The Government Performance and Results Act of 1993, a congressional initiative, is intended to impose pressure for improvement by linking annual performance plans and reports to budget and personnel requests. The long-term impact of these efforts is not yet clear. Many commentators are skeptical that the results will live up to expectations.[31]

Although the American preference in civil service recruitment has continued to be the offering of specialized and practical examinations on an open competitive basis to those meeting prescribed minimum qualifications, entry-level general subject matter examinations were made available to university graduates beginning in the late 1930s. These examinations were designed to bring promising young people into the government service, but they were abandoned in the early 1980s because of allegations that they discriminated against minority groups, and similar examinations designed to be non-discriminatory were not offered again until 1990.[32]

Increasingly, students preparing for administrative careers in the public service pursue undergraduate or graduate curricula in public administration or public affairs in preparation for a variety of civil service examinations. The result has been the recruitment of large numbers of potential higher level administrators, but the channels for their career advancement are much less planned and more haphazard than in the British system, with its clearer demarcation of those civil servants who occupy, or are in training to occupy, the posts of higher managerial responsibility.

Because the United States is a relatively open society without pronounced class distinctions, and because of appointment and advancement methods used in the civil service, the upper echelons of the bureaucracy have been reasonably representative of the society, without much of a caste or elite quality. Although public executives have been better educated than the general population and have tended to come from families with business and professional backgrounds, a study made in the 1960s indicated that nearly one-fourth of them had fathers who were blue-collar workers. The distortion has been on the basis of sex and ethnic background, with disproportionate numbers of white males, particularly in the higher brackets, leading to extensive programs of "affirmative action" which have made some progress in improving the representation of women and men from black and other minority ethnic groups. Compared to most national public services, the American record is certainly better than average, despite these group deficiencies in representation.

Again by way of contrast with Great Britain and continental Europe, in the United States movement by individuals back and forth at various levels between governmental and nongovernmental careers has been and continues to be quite feasible and even encouraged under existing personnel practices in both the public and private sectors, leading to proposals aimed to achieve a more closed civil service system for greater expertise, continuity, and stability, but little actual change in that direction.

As in Great Britain, the merit bureaucracy depends more on a protective tradition than on legal safeguards. The executive and legislative branches share in regulating the bureaucracy, so that it has a partial statutory base, but there is no constitutional protection for the national civil service. On the other hand, American civil servants are subjected to significant restrictions as to their participation in partisan political activities, beyond the basic rights to vote and to express political opinions.

In the American setting, there is probably no dramatic contrast from other systems in the overall impact on policy-making of higher ranking civil servants, but the rules of the game are quite different. Bureaucratic policy-makers in the United States must operate much more in the public eye, which gives greater leeway but also involves greater risks. The relationship between the top career man and his political superior is more ambiguous. The civil servant has an obligation either to render loyal service or to resign or transfer, but he is likely to be linked with his policy preference in any event, and he may very well be called on to defend the agency's policy position in a legislative hearing, whatever his own position. The system is less closed and more competitive. Contesting elements must seek allies not only elsewhere in the government but outside it as well. Many of these characteristics result from the lack of a definite or inviolable demarcation between bureaucratic and political officialdom. Heclo notes that in this "dual structure" the "basic organizing principle—more unintentional than planned—of the higher civil service is horizontal," with the lines of authority running "outward through programs and policies rather than upward to bureaucratic or political superiors."[33] Mainzer sums up the American situation this way: "no clear line between career and political executives exists in law, regulations, policy, or tradition. . . . The mixture of career administrators and outsiders in high executive posts which are not sharply differentiated as to their political or administrative character has been our pragmatic solution to the management of political bureaucracy."[34]

Instead of behind-the-scenes activity protected by a carefully preserved veil of secrecy, as has been the British practice, the American expectation is that bureaucratic participation in policy-making will be much more in the public view, with the inevitable reactions that follow, whether favorable or unfavorable, to the individual concerned. Moreover, movement across the vague line between career and political activity is easy and frequent. Indeed, as Sayre remarks, "The American civil servant who earns high and lasting prestige in his society is usually one who most completely breaks the mask of anonymity and becomes a public figure."[35]

Administrative accountability in the United States is exerted through a variety of channels with diffuse consequences. For reasons already mentioned, executive supervision through hierarchical channels leading to the president is partial and shared, as compared to the prerogatives of the prime minister and cabinet in a parliamentary system. Fred Riggs has presented a well-documented argument that the professional/functionalist orientation of American public servants has resulted in a "centrifugal" and "semi-powered" bureaucracy which helps explain the longevity of the American presidentialist system as compared to experience elsewhere.[36]

In the final analysis, Congress is the most potent source of control, because of its constitutional grants of power, but its oversight functions tend to be fragmented by primary reliance on legislative committees with limited jurisdictions and more interest in programmatic than managerial issues. Congress has shown little inclination, however, to alter this pattern, except for recent attempts, only partially successful, to consolidate budgetary policy decisions. Proposals for an Ombudsman, for example, have been considered but never adopted, because of apprehension that such an office would interfere with the rapport between legislators and their constituents.

As in Great Britain, judicial control is in the hands of the regular courts, rather than a separate set of administrative courts. The judicial role, always important because of the ultimate authority that courts have for constitutional interpretation, has been enhanced in recent years by a more activist stance toward intervention in matters that have been dealt with by administrative action. Judicial controls are limited, however, to issues raised in particular cases, and litigation is expensive and time consuming as an instrument of administrative accountability.

These controls, plus those exercised more indirectly through clientele groups and elections, provide an armory of potential but competitive control mechanisms, making evaluation of their specific contributions and overall effectiveness difficult. One result is a "love-hate" or "dependency-resentment" relationship between the American public and American public administrators. Despite recent evidence of a decline of confidence in government,[37] I continue to hold this overall view of the situation: "Americans are not really apprehensive about or dissatisfied with public administration and public administrators, but they don't want to admit it. Bureaucratic usurpation or unresponsiveness is less a reality than a complaint voiced to help remind administrators that they are public servants rather than officials of an omnipotent state."[38] The bureaucracy enjoys the benefit of a widespread although somewhat skeptical acceptance of the job it is doing, but it must be prepared to fit into its proper niche in the political system. Major political innovation or transformation, therefore, is not likely to have a bureaucratic source.

ADAPTIVE MODERNIZING ADMINISTRATION—JAPAN

In only a century and a quarter since the Meiji restoration of 1867–1868, Japan has undertaken a mammoth program of modernization which has converted an Asian kingdom with its own type of feudalism, long isolated by its own choice from outside contacts, into the only major Asian society that ranks as highly modernized and developed. In this transformation, the bureaucracy, both civil and military, has played a leading part, one which makes the Japanese experience unique in important respects.[39]

The so-called "centralized feudalism" of the Tokugawa shogunate, which began in 1603, developed a civil bureaucracy which had basic patrimonial characteristics. Bureaucrats were recruited from specified feudal family ranks, and great emphasis was placed on status distinctions among classes in the hierarchy. "Appointments to office, promotions and dismissals were made at the discretion of superiors. The powers and responsibilities of offices were poorly defined, and there was a great deal of room for inefficiency, imbalance, and the personal interpretation of official duties."[40]

Edwin Dowdy has examined historical evidence, particularly during the Tokugawa period, concerning elements within this outwardly patrimonial Japanese bureaucracy before the Meiji restoration which facilitated modernizing processes. He concludes that Japanese society had long provided some of the prerequisites for the development of a modernized country, among them "a central if somewhat patchy administration operating within mass obedience, elaborate and rational local administrations, large-scale commercial networks, industrial undertakings in both urban and rural areas, and a high standard of literacy."[41] Moreover, the samurai class provided a source for modernizing bureaucrats. Traditionally warriors, the samurai had to substitute a bureaucratic function for a military one in order to preserve a useful role during the long period of peace after 1600. Among them developed "a kind of professional bureaucratic ethic" which included dedication to duty, self-reliance, and resoluteness, along with attitudes concerning merit, mobility, duty rotation, and various aspects of rationality which facilitated the transition to a modernized bureaucracy. With characteristics such as these extending far back into Japanese history, Dowdy argues that "Japanese modernization continued organically from traditional sources, certainly with increased tempo but without any serious break." Much imitation of other societies certainly occurred over a considerable period of time, "but that imitation was selectively adapted to home conditions. Spontaneous growth was more important than any policy of quick imitation. The Meiji bureaucracy was not a break with the past but rather a modified continuation of it."[42]

The arrival of Commodore Perry in 1853 precipitated a crisis for the Tokugawa shogunate which triggered the vast changes leading within a few years to the Meiji restoration. One of the immediate results was modification of the ascriptive pattern for appointment of officials. Talented individuals, including many of relatively low social status, were appointed to staff new offices that were created in response to the crisis situation. They became part of an intellectual aristocracy of talented individuals who were exposed to and had respect for Western learning in the years prior to the restoration, and who took part in the overthrow of the shogunate under the guise of restoring the emperor to his rightful place. "The spiritual motive force of modern Japan," says Inoki, was the set of beliefs that members of this new intellectual aristocracy held in common, combining "national loyalty, symbolized by loyalty to the emperor, and respect for achievement."[43]

The wielders of political power who brought about the restoration and directed the governmental experimentation leading to the Meiji constitution of 1889 were a modernizing oligarchy. The system they devised provided for a sharing of political power among several competing groups during a period of several decades until the authoritarian resurgence of the 1930s. One of these groups consisted of the higher ranking civil bureaucrats, along with holders of the top civilian governmental positions, the professionalized military bureaucracy, leaders of the important conservative political parties that developed, representatives of big business, and the hereditary peerage. This oligarchy was a modernizing one, but it was not designed to encourage the establishment of a democratic political system. Its principal foreign model was imperial Germany, with which it shared a preference for monarchical institutions and a tradition of aristocratic control. It successfully curbed for a significant period of time tendencies toward popular participation in government and it kept political order while the country was advancing economically at a rapid rate.

The bureaucratic establishment was well suited to take a leading part in this type of modernization. The social background of the Meiji bureaucrats was predominantly lower samurai, since this group had been dislocated by the transition from feudalism and its members had skills that could be utilized in the bureaucracy. As bureaucratic growth and reform took place, recruitment by examination was introduced in the 1880s, and graduates were drawn from the rapidly expanding educational institutions, particularly Tokyo Imperial University. The higher civil bureaucracy thus created was cohesive and professionally trained, but it was not indoctrinated in a tradition in which the bureaucrat was viewed as a public servant. Instead, the bureaucrat was "officially viewed as a chosen servant of the Emperor, a politically and socially superior being who derived status and privileges from his Imperial connection."[44] The bureaucrat's attitude toward the public continued to be well expressed by an old Tokugawa adage: "officials honored, the people despised." The legal framework for the bureaucracy reflected this orientation. All regulation of the civil bureaucracy prior to the end of World War II was by means of imperial ordinance and beyond the reach of parliamentary controls.

Japan's defeat and surrender at the end of World War II, followed by the Allied Occupation from 1945 to 1952, led to new patterns in Japanese politics and administration, embodied in a new constitution which became effective in 1947. The monarchy was preserved, but the emperor was stripped of any claim of divine right, and the institution was transformed into a constitutional monarchy. The peerage was abolished. Legislative authority was vested in a bicameral parliament or Diet, designated as "the highest organ of state power," with little resemblance to its prewar counterpart. The House of Representatives is dominant, with the upper chamber, or House of Councillors, having only limited power to delay legislation. Executive power is vested in a prime minister and cabinet collectively responsible to the Diet. At least a majority of the cabinet ministers are required to be members of the Diet. In case of a no-confidence vote in the House of Representatives, the cabinet must resign unless the House is dissolved and a new election held.

The cabinet consists of the heads of the ministries (currently twelve), plus several ministers "without portfolio." Units not given ministerial status (including those responsible for such important functions as defense and economic planning) are parceled out among this latter group of cabinet members or assigned to the prime minister's office. The ministries have quite similar internal structures. The cabinet minister is assisted by one or two parliamentary vice-ministers, who like the minister are political appointees although the incumbents may be former career civil servants. An administrative vice-minister occupies the highest career position in the ministry. Each ministry has one secretariat and a number of bureaus. The bureaus are usually further subdivided into divisions and sections, headed at each level by senior career officials.

The postwar Japanese civil service blends the prewar bureaucracy with efforts during the occupation period to reform and democratize it. Article 15 of the 1947 constitution declared: "All public officials are servants of the whole community and not of any group thereof." A new civil service law enacted also in 1947 detailed the reform provisions and established a National Personnel Authority with a guaranteed semiautonomous status. Commentators generally agree that these efforts have had an impact but have not fundamentally altered the bureaucratic system.[45]

The Japanese civil service grew remarkably during the period from 1940 to 1975, when there was an eightfold increase, but the level of public employment has leveled off in recent years, partly as a result of prolonged and broadly based administrative reform efforts undertaken during the 1980s. These reforms were aimed at a general shrinkage or "decrementalism" in the role of government, involving not only structural reorganization and personnel controls, but also deregulation, devolution of functions from the central to local units of government, and privatization of services formerly provided by government corporations.[46] The total number of public employees was reduced to the neighborhood of five million, with slightly over one million of them in the national government service. With public servants making up approximately 9 percent of the total labor force (at 45 public employees per 1,000 people), this is a proportion far below the level in other industrialized nations, as has already been noted in Chapter 2.[47]

The higher civil service in Japan, as in other countries, is a relatively small group with somewhat indeterminate boundaries. The occupants of the senior administrative posts in ministry and agency headquarters total about 2500. When others in the lower levels of the bureaucratic elite or *kanryo* are added, the number reaches approximately 10,000, or about one percent of the civilian employees of the national government.

The present-day government service continues to be a career that attracts Japanese youth, hence it has been possible to restrict access to the upper ranks of the bureaucracy to those able to survive a hazardous series of qualifying steps. With an annual replenishment rate of 300 to 400, competition is intense among those who pass the higher civil service examinations. The educational base for successful candidates has been very narrow. "The proportion of higher administrators with a university education is remarkably high, even in comparison with major Western bureaucracies."[48] Graduation with honors from one of the leading universities has been a prerequisite to success in the examinations, and this in turn has been restricted to those who had earlier done superior work in the better elementary and secondary schools. Thus, in practice, only the exceptional sons of families able to afford such educational preparation have ordinarily been able to enter the higher bureaucracy.

In content, the tests have largely been under the control of law school faculties and designed for law school graduates. Although this has meant continued stress on legal technicalities, a fairly broad range of subject matter is covered, reflecting the fact that law faculties generally offer work in political science and economics and to a more limited extent in management skills.[49] The remarkable extent of dominance of this academic specialization is highlighted by the fact that more than two-thirds of postwar higher civil servants are law school graduates. Even more exceptional is the extent to which one institution, Tokyo Imperial University, has been the source of entrants to the bureaucracy. Kubota and Kim both report that about 80 percent of postwar higher civil servants attended and in most cases graduated from this one university. Another 13 percent have come from five other government universities. The four major private universities supplied less than 3 percent. "The extent of this dominance by graduates of a single university is staggering," as Kubota says, "even in comparison with the combined share for Oxford and Cambridge in the British bureaucracy."[50]

This domination by Tokyo Imperial University, particularly from its faculty of law, has led to widespread charges of favoritism in appointments and promotions based on school cliques, or *gakubatsu*. Kubota examines the evidence as to the pervasiveness of the *gakubatsu* system, with mixed conclusions. With regard to Tokyo University graduates, he states that the fact of their great numbers "made ingroup favoritism not only probable but also less provable, since there were always many Tokyo University graduates who did not rise as fast as others." He believes that school tie favoritism is practiced subtly, but doubts that Japanese higher administrators are apt to choose subordinates "solely on the basis of school background and without regard to competence." He points out that Tokyo University attracts and graduates the most able students. He also notes that a common university background does not necessarily mean shared attitudes and values, and that Tokyo University graduates show wide variations in outlook. On the positive side, the existing system has made possible the recruitment of many of the brightest Japanese youth, and has contributed to the stability and success of the bureaucracy. A negative aspect is the group homogeneity that results. "The narrow educational base in the recruitment of postwar higher civil servants resembles in some ways the narrow social base of recruitment in the Tokugawa and early Meiji governments."[51]

Available data as to the social origins of postwar bureaucrats point, however, toward a much more heterogeneous higher civil service than was the case historically in Japan, despite the relatively narrow educational base for recruitment. All parts of Japan are represented, although with disproportionately large numbers from towns and cities, particularly Tokyo. A majority come from middle class origins. Eminent families are somewhat over-represented also, but the data did not show any one social or political group providing a dominant share of higher administrators, or any significant number of families supplying higher civil servants in successive generations. Kubota attributes this current diversity to the cumulative effects of the disappearance of most traditional forms of social stratification, and opportunities for greater social mobility through the modern educational system and the system of examinations for the higher civil service. Noting that the Japanese people are remarkably homogeneous ethnically, linguistically, and religiously, he does point out that the factor of heterogeneous social origins does not have the importance in Japan that would be attached to it in other nations with more diversified populations.[52]

Sex discrimination, however, continues to deny women in Japan equal opportunities in employment generally, including entry into the higher civil service. Kim reports that although annually some female university graduates pass the required examinations and enter the bureaucracy, their chances for advancing to higher positions remain very restricted, with a survey conducted in 1982 showing that women represented only 4.6 percent of the total pool of qualified personnel, with very few having expectations of rising above the rank of section chief,[53] but the appointment of women to senior posts is expected by Sakamoto to increase in the near future.[54]

Career patterns for those who enter the higher civil service are highly particularized. The successful candidate tries to be accepted where his prospects for promotion, access to power, and postretirement opportunities would seem to be greatest. He is likely to remain with whatever ministry he enters, since lateral movement between ministries is limited. A study conducted in 1969 showed that approximately a third of those who entered a given ministry remained with it throughout their careers; another third began and ended careers in the same ministry, with interim transfers elsewhere. A later study indicated that in the early 1970s two-thirds of those in top posts had served in only one ministry, and less than 9 percent had served in three ministries or more.[55] Such low interministerial mobility promotes loyalty to a particular ministry rather than to the public service as a whole, and tends toward compartmentalism rather than coordination among different bureaucratic units. On the other hand, it does permit a buildup through long experience of specialized knowledge about the ministry in which the typical bureaucrat makes his career home.

Promotion within the system is also along a standardized path, and demotion is virtually nonexistent. The principal factors that are taken into account for promotions are university attended, field of academic specialization, and years since graduation—all of course settled matters at the start of a civil servant's career. Educational background and seniority are what count, making the timing and nature of promotions generally well known in advance. An interesting incidental fact, confirming the school clique phenomenon, is that those promoted most rapidly and in closest conformity with seniority have proved to be law graduates of Tokyo Imperial University.

A most unusual feature of the Japanese civil service is the early age of retirement. Until 1985, there was no compulsory retirement provision. It was then set at 60 years for most employees, and is now in the process of being increased to 65 gradually. Historically, the actual retirement age has been in the neighborhood of fifty years, although this varies somewhat from ministry to ministry. This means that the typical retiree is in the prime of life, can expect to live at least another twenty years, and is very likely to seek a postbureaucratic career of some kind. Kubota attributes this massive outflow at such a relatively early age to the rapid movement of civil servants from post to post during their careers, the promotion system based mainly on seniority, pressures from junior bureaucrats who want to be promoted into vacated higher positions, and the availability of alternatives to government service.[56] Although there seems to be a slow long-term trend toward a slightly higher average retirement age, there are no indications of a sharp movement away from this aspect of standardization in career patterns.[57]

In essence, the record shows that continuity and stability are the chief features of the postwar higher civil service in Japan, despite the reform measures instituted during the occupation and the tremendous changes which have taken place generally in Japanese life. After temporary adjustments which were unavoidable in the early postwar period, the tendency has been to follow what has been called the "reverse course" of returning to earlier practices stressing generalist training, seniority, ministerial loyalty, and early retirement.

When we turn our attention to multifunctionalism in Japanese bureaucratic operations, the most striking observation is that political activism has long been, and continues to be, an accepted part of the bureaucratic tradition. The Japanese bureaucrat is likely to be deeply absorbed in making political decisions and may become involved in active political life. This is partly explained by the blurring in Japan historically of the distinction commonly made in Western theory between the politician and the bureaucrat. As Dowdy observes: "In Japan at the higher levels this distinction has not always been evident, for often both the political and bureaucratic functions were discharged by the same official."[58] In more recent times, this has helped account for the persistent role of the bureaucracy as one of the prime sources of policy initiative as the society has modernized. "Approximately 90 percent of all legislation passed since 1955 was drafted within a government agency," according to Pemple, and

> top-level bureaucrats typically serve as behind-the-scenes managers of these bills once they are up for parliamentary consideration. It is most often the civil servant, rather than the minister, who undergoes the meticulous questioning and browbeating that passes for parliamentary interpellation in Japan. And once a bill is passed, it frequently includes a proviso that allows the specifics of implementation to be regulated by bureaucratically generated ordinances.[59]

Not only do active career bureaucrats often hold positions and carry out functions usually reserved for political appointees in other countries, but also perhaps of more importance is the prevalence of former bureaucrats in a wide variety of influential positions both inside and outside of government. The elitist status of higher civil servants is retained after they retire, giving them better prospects for postretirement placements than are usually available to their counterparts in Great Britain or the United States. With early retirement as the norm, this means that an individual can make and carry out career plans that include a second phase after leaving active service which frequently is even more lucrative, influential, and prestigious. Kubota's estimate is that about three out of ten retiring higher civil servants go into semiautonomous public corporations, another three move into business enterprises (often as directors of major private corporations), and the remaining four enter a wide variety of professional and governmental activities. Substantial numbers of them have run successfully for elective political office and often they have served as members of postwar cabinets. For example, in 1959 a total of 165 former career bureaucrats made up 18 percent of the total membership of the lower house and 32 percent of the upper house in the Diet. In 1986, ex-bureaucrats held seventy of the seats of the ruling Liberal Democratic party in the lower house and forty-nine in the upper house, or 30 percent of the party's total membership. Former bureaucrats have made up approximately 20 percent of postwar cabinet ministers, and the proportion has been higher during shorter time periods. The most impressive statistic demonstrating this phenomenon of bureaucratic political prowess is that professional politicians held the office of prime minister only five years during the period between 1955 and 1980, and that half of all the postwar Japanese prime ministers have been former civil servants.[60]

From a long-range perspective, the resilience and adaptability of the Japanese bureaucracy are exceptional. As Kubota comments,

> the effectiveness and efficiency of the higher civil service appear to be independent of political ideology. The bureaucracy has functioned with at least relative success under the Meiji oligarchy, under political parties of the prewar type, under militarist and ultranationalist control, under the Allied Occupation, and now under parliamentary democracy based upon the 1947 Constitution.[61]

This record has not been built on the basis of bureaucratic neutrality toward the existing political regime, but rather of conformance to changes in the political climate.

During nearly the whole postwar period, this meant a close identification between the higher bureaucracy and the ruling Liberal Democratic party (actually conservative in its political orientation), which exerted parliamentary control without a break, although with diminishing margins in later years, until it was deprived of a controlling majority in the crucial lower house in the mid-1993 parliamentary election, after having lost its majority in the less important upper house in 1989.

This landmark development ushered in a new era of uncertainty in Japanese politics. Within a single year following the 1993 election, Japan had four different governments. Following ouster of the LDP leadership after its election defeat, a seven party coalition chose Morihiro Hosokawa, founder and leader of the Japan New Party, as premier, although the Social Democratic (formerly Socialist) party controlled twice as many seats in the Diet. The Liberal Democratic party became the opposition, but it still held 223 seats in the 511 member lower house. Hosokawa managed to maintain his post until the following April, when he quit because of failure to push through his political reform program and because of charges of corruption lodged against him based on activities when he was a provincial governor a decade earlier. His deputy premier and foreign minister, Tsutomo Hata, who had founded the Renewal Party after leaving the LDP the previous year, was elected premier in his place by the same coalition, but was almost immediately left without a legislative majority when the Social Democratic party withdrew, leading to his resignation in June to avoid a vote of no-confidence. Then came an unlikely linkup between the Liberal Democratic and Social Democratic parties, which were historical enemies and differed on most major policy issues but allied in opposition to political reform. This new coalition elected as premier Tomiichi Murayama, the Social Democratic leader, although his party held only about a third as many parliamentary seats as the LDP.

The fragility of this coalition made another political realignment highly likely, and in 1994, after only one year in opposition, the LPD returned to power. Ryutaro Hashimoto became prime minister, remaining in office until he resigned in mid-1998 following LDP losses in elections to the upper house of the Diet. He was replaced as LPD leader and as premier by Keizo Obuchi, who continues to head the government, which since early in 1999 has been a coalition between the LPD and the small Liberal Party, entered into to give the coalition more seats in the upper house.

These changes in the political landscape, and the resulting questions as to future party prospects, means also that the relationships between political leaders and the higher bureaucracy must be reexamined. The long period of political dominance by the Liberal Democratic party brought about a close identification between the higher bureaucracy and the ruling party. This tendency toward fusion of high civil servants and Liberal Democratic leaders received much attention from commentators on the Japanese system,[62] with differences of opinion as to the consequences. Inoki argued that it undermined civil service neutrality, made civil service careers less attractive to able university graduates, and contributed to a steady decline in the formerly high prestige of the civil service. Others (including Ward, Kubota, and Pempel) seemed to regard it as further evidence of the strength and unity of the bureaucracy, which continued to seize its opportunities by moving into any partial power vacuums that existed.

Obviously, the end of LDP political domination is leading to a reorientation of political-bureaucratic relations, but the outcome is not yet clearly discernible.

The prevailing view at first was that instead of curtailing the bureaucratic role, an era of shifting coalition governments would offer higher civil servants new opportunities for asserting themselves in the making of policy.[63] Later, following a concerted administrative reform effort while Hashimoto was prime minister, Mishima gave this assessment of the current relationship between the LPD and the bureaucracy: "The LPD has become more assertive with respect to the bureaucracy and more suspicious about bureaucratic intentions. The bureaucracy has become more conciliatory and less willing to take the leading role in policy formation."[64] In the opinion of Jun and Muto, resistance to administrative reform has come from both the bureaucrats and politicians in the dominant political party, and it has been generally successful.[65]

Certainly members of the bureaucratic class still belong to the political elite of Japan, and the bureaucracy continues to be an integral part of the governing power structure. The situation legitimately raises questions as to the adequacy of controls over the bureaucracy, at least when viewed in relation to European parliamentary democracies. The Japanese Diet, despite its constitutional status and obvious political centrality as compared to the prewar period, conspicuously lacks the historical record of power and prestige of legislative bodies such as the British House of Commons or the French Chamber of Deputies. Its membership, as already indicated, includes a large segment of recently retired higher civil servants, who are unlikely to disturb the prerogatives of career bureaucrats. For its part, the bureaucracy as a political institution seeks to keep the legislature weak or at least sympathetic to bureaucratic interests.

Characteristics of postwar Japanese political parties have helped perpetuate this pattern of relationships. Leadership in the Liberal Democratic party has tended to be multifactional, shifting, semisecretive in its methods, without widespread mass appeal, and decidedly conservative in its orientation. The other parties, although differing in political orientation, have not yet demonstrated that they have developed mass membership bases of support or the capacity for strengthening the effectiveness and reputation of the legislative branch.

At least until recently, factionalism and jockeying for position within Liberal Democratic ranks were also reflected in the composition and tenure in office of cabinet ministers. Although highly educated, they have tended to be elderly, with the average age close to sixty. Pressures for factional representation and personal recognition have led to frequent cabinet changes, with a resulting high rate of turnover which has distracted from the ability of ministers to gain the knowledge and time needed to exert firm control over their agencies. The office of prime minister has provided the only conspicuous focal point of political and administrative leadership, but with the average life of a cabinet during recent years being less than a year, the powers of the office are meager compared to those of chief executives in the other developed polities we have considered. There is no indication yet of improvement in any of these characteristics.

Judicial controls over administration in Japan are minimal. The 1947 constitution included sweeping reforms of the legal system and the judiciary, introducing Anglo-American common-law principles and a judicial branch with independent status and powers of judicial review. The earlier legal system had been largely derived from European sources, with the courts being administered by the Ministry of Justice of the national government. The existing court network possesses powers to hold government servants accountable in much the same manner as in the United States. No separate system of administrative courts now exists. The traditional attitude in Japan has been to avoid rather than seek litigation, and there is little indication of resort to the courts for controlling the bureaucracy.[66]

The degree of bureaucratic self-control in Japan is problematical. The constitutional provision converting bureaucrats from "the Emperor's aides" to "servants of the people" is given lip service but whether basic bureaucratic attitudes have altered correspondingly is more questionable. Kubota, as part of his comprehensive survey of the postwar bureaucracy, found that the public is more openly critical of the civil service than it has ever been, indicating citizen skepticism about the conversion. However, his own view is that the bureaucracy, "whether from conviction or from expediency," has responded to the postwar changes "by making a greater effort to create harmonious relations with the general public and to adjust itself to the new political environment."[67] Perhaps the best assessment to make is that Japanese higher bureaucrats are prepared to conduct themselves in a way which will fit them acceptably into the current political scheme of things, without impairing their traditional power position. Now that the long period of Liberal Democratic party dominance has ended and has been replaced by an era of coalition governments, the bureaucracy will have to confront a new challenge to its resilience.

The Japanese bureaucratic system owes its unusual strength to certain basic features of Japanese development. Modernization in Japan was internally stimulated and led by the ruling groups themselves, including the bureaucracy. The governing elite enjoyed relative solidarity and its leadership was accepted by the population, so that, as Bendix remarks, here a modernizing autocracy "succeeded for a significant period of time in advancing a country economically while containing her political conflicts within manageable limits."[68] The transition and the role played in it by the bureaucracy reflected in part the pervasiveness of respect for authority in Japanese society generally. This in turn has affected the operating characteristics of the bureaucracy. Crozier comments that in Japan a strong authoritarian pattern of hierarchy "has been internalized and conflicts are handled more by subservience than by avoidance," and that the problem of controlling the behavior of subordinates in the Japanese system of organization "is centered on a model of stratification which presents some similarities to the French system." However, he adds that unlike French bureaucracy, "whose main function is to maintain law and order in a rebellious society, Japanese bureaucratic power has a decisive role as prime mover."[69]

This common assessment of the past record is well expressed by Pempel, who says: "What is most striking about the case of Japan is that, for most of its modern history, the political weight of the civil service has been extremely high and broadly comprehensive. Bureaucratic influence has typically been greater than that of other political actors, including Parliament, parties, and interest groups."[70] Williams is even more emphatic. "Since the war," he states, "the bureaucracy has normally dominated the legislative process, and in this narrow sense can be said to have ruled while the Diet reigned."[71] Tsurutani asserts that, in Japan, "the higher civil service is still endowed with an aura of intrinsic authority and natural competence as the authentic guardian of the common-weal."[72] Looking ahead, Kubota predicts that the bureaucracy's role will continue to be decisive. "For years to come Japanese higher civil servants are likely to exert a degree of influence that is impressive by any comparative standards."[73] Thus in the past, currently, and for at least the near future, the Japanese higher bureaucracy has had conferred upon it a position of central political power outstripping that accorded to the bureaucracies of other developed countries.

"SECOND TIER" EXAMPLES

Ranking somewhat below the countries already reviewed as to their level of development are a sizable number of "second tier" cases, from which we have chosen one example (the Russian Federation) of recent movement downward into this group and another (the People's Republic of China) of movement upward toward and actually or shortly into it. Most of the remaining instances are countries of southern and eastern Europe and a few of the upwardly mobile smaller nations along the eastern fringe of Asia.

The Russian Federation

As the largest and most important remnant of the USSR, one of the post–World War II global superpowers, and the leading member of the successor Common-wealth of Independent States, the Russian Federation is in the midst of an uncertain societal transition, including transformation of both its political and administrative systems, making a current assessment of the situation and specu-lation about the future equally difficult.[74]

On December 25, 1991, Mikhail Gorbachev resigned as President of the Soviet Union (USSR), and the following day the Soviet parliament formally dissolved itself. Boris Yeltsin, as President of the Russian Federation (RSFSR), took over what remained of the central government, including control of the nuclear weapons of the former Soviet Union. The Russian Federation inherited the USSR role in international affairs, and replaced the Soviet red hammer and sickle flag with its own. Only a loose and feeble Commonwealth of Independent States (without Lithuania, Estonia, Latvia, and Georgia) remained from what had been the fifteen-republic Soviet Union, founded after the Russian Revolution of 1917.

The Russian Federation was by far the largest of the Soviet Union republics, consisting of almost three-quarters of its landmass, having over half of its total population, and possessing a high proportion of its raw materials, energy resources, heavy industry, and scientific/engineering personnel. Nevertheless, the Russian Federation is considerably weaker and less developed than the USSR had been, embracing as it does numerous smaller nationalities with different ethnic backgrounds seeking greater autonomy within the federation, and having to contend with the social, economic and political fallout of the collapse of the Soviet Union.

Before the current Russian politico-administrative system is examined, some attention must be given to the Soviet system before the rise of Gorbachev, to the Gorbachev reform efforts, and to the transition after they failed.

During the decades between 1917 and 1985, although there were several distinct stages in its evolution, the Soviet system had two basic distinctive characteristics. One was that political power was concentrated in the Communist party as the "vanguard of the Revolution," with the state apparatus playing a secondary role. The other was that this reality of one-party rule was disguised behind an elaborate facade which borrowed the phraseology of liberal democracy and pretended to be a constitutional federal system—with elections, legislative and executive organs, and agencies of state administration.

The Communist revolutionaries confronted early on the dilemma of reconciling the expectations of Marxist doctrine concerning "the withering away of the state" with the hard reality of having to govern using the administrative machinery inherited from imperial Russia. Lenin's original hope that a professional civil service could be dispensed with soon was replaced with recognition that the existing bureaucracy could not be eliminated wholesale but would have to be reshaped. The strategy adopted was to utilize the old bureaucrats as long as this could not be avoided, while surrounding them with controls, and to train a new generation of Soviet administrators as soon as possible. The initial stance of the regime toward the bureaucracy was one of forced reliance coupled with distrust.

This ambivalent attitude toward bureaucracy and bureaucrats continued to be a feature of the Soviet polity, with Lenin shortly before his death expressing worry about the dangers of "bureaucratization," and Stalin later during his long period of dominance using ruthlessness and terror to enforce proper bureaucratic behavior, even after the bureaucracy was staffed with products of the massive

Soviet educational program. The emergence of a managerial elite was fostered and encouraged by the core party leadership, but at the same time viewed with apprehension and kept under firm control.

One resulting feature of the system which became solidified during the Stalinist era was consistency in maintaining the Communist party and the state apparatus as separate instrumentalities. The party had a major concern with state affairs, was intimately involved in administration, and was ultimately dependent on bureaucratic machinery to preserve its political control, but it nevertheless avoided amalgamation of the party and state bureaucratic organizations. Party control was assured through a network of interlocking directorates at each hierarchical level.

The product was two elaborate sets of institutional arrangements. The more important but less formal one consisted of the organs of the Communist party, including the party Congress, meeting at infrequent intervals, the Central Committee, the Politburo (usually made up of about fourteen regular and eight candidate members), and the party Secretariat headed by the general secretary. Theoretically, a process of election operated for the selection of representatives at each successive level of the party pyramid, but Lenin's doctrine of "democratic centralism" as a way of reconciling democratic participation with the need for firm leadership meant in practice that decisions taken at the higher levels were absolutely binding on lower levels.

The formal state structure was a federal union of Soviet Socialist Republics, with the highest organ of state power being the Supreme Soviet of the USSR, a bicameral legislature made up of the Soviet of the Union and the Soviet of Nationalities. Between sessions of the Supreme Soviet, formal authority was exercised by a Presidium of about forty members, including the heads of the fifteen Union Republics and members elected by the Supreme Soviet. The Supreme Soviet also appointed the chairman and other members of the Council of Ministers, with jurisdiction over the state administrative apparatus. As an instrumentality of the Soviet polity, the Council of Ministers was primarily concerned with the execution rather than the formulation of policy, except as its members participated as policy-makers in their overlapping party capacities. The ministries consisted of two types: "all-Union" ministries operating directly throughout the Soviet Union, and "Union Republic" ministries operating indirectly through corresponding ministries in each of the Union Republics. Over two-thirds of these units had functions falling in the economic management category, with responsibility for agriculture, transportation, communications, or a branch of industry or construction. Less than one-third accounted for the whole range of other state functions, including military and police agencies. The state bureaucracy staffing these ministries was immense, since the almost monopolistic nature of state employment meant that public service of some kind had to be the career ambition of most Soviet youth. The path toward the higher-ranking posts was long and arduous, but it did lead to a professionalized bureaucracy, with behavioral traits reflecting the pressure packed and intimidating environment in which it operated.

The usual interpretation by foreign observers of the system in place when Stalin died in 1953 was that the USSR was a "totalitarian directed society," with the state bureaucracy and all other institutions intervening between the Communist party and the people being basically subservient to the party. The most widely accepted image of Soviet bureaucracy, consistent with such a "directed society" model for the whole system, characterized it as subject to unavoidable outside controls leading to the adoption of protective measures resulting in formalism and inefficiency, but nevertheless capable of bringing about massive societal changes.

During the three decades between Stalin and Gorbachev, there were some substantial shifts in approach and policy, without fundamental alterations. In 1956 Khrushchev denounced Stalin's despotism, and embarked on a policy of "de-Stalinization" which included moves toward "competitive coexistence" in foreign policy as well as numerous internal reforms. During Brezhnev's long tenure from 1964 to 1981, steps were taken to reaffirm the dominant role of the party and to hail Soviet progress by including in a new constitution adopted in 1977 provisions identifying the party as "the leading and guiding force of Soviet society," and claiming that the USSR had evolved into a "developed socialist society."[75]

These changes were sufficient to bring about a shift during the 1970s in the prevalent interpretation by foreign observers as to power relationships in the Soviet system. Jerry F. Hough, for example, suggested a model of "institutional pluralism" as an alternative way of analysis. He found increasing evidence of pluralistic tendencies within the system. He pointed out that Soviet administrative hierarchies contained specialties covering a vast spectrum, with the professional orientations going with these specializations. This in turn implied multiple and diversified organizational goals rather than monolithic and universal ones. He argued that the Soviet Union should be viewed "as a total bureaucratic system in which the leaders themselves rose through the bureaucracy and are part of it rather than a parliamentary system in which a cabinet of generalist political leaders gives direction to a pliable bureaucracy." In a broader context, he proposed that the "directed society" paradigm be replaced by one taking greater account of characteristics of the Soviet political system that had evolved bearing a close resemblance to "classic pluralism" as understood in the West, with such features as recognition of the legitimacy of group interests and conflict, recognition of accommodation, bargaining, and brokerage, and expectation that political change normally would be incremental rather than drastic and abrupt. He recognized that a pluralist model for the USSR would have to exclude several key features of pluralism in the West, such as competitive elections, formation of pressure groups or parties to advance political interests, or criticism of societal fundamentals. The assumption of this conceptualization was that political institutions in the

Soviet Union (most importantly the Communist party) had become more receptive to input from societal groups which did not challenge the system.[76]

Foreign interpreters, nevertheless, continued during these decades to rely basically on a bureaucratic model to explain Soviet society, because of the existence in the USSR of the network of bureaucracies already described. Alfred G. Meyer, for example, stated that the USSR "is best understood as a large, complex bureaucracy comparable in its structure and functioning to giant corporations, armies, government agencies, and similar institutions . . . in the West. It shares with such bureaucracies many principles of organization and patterns of management."[77] Developments at the time Khrushchev was replaced by Brezhnev were labeled by Zbigniew Brzezinski as a "victory of the clerks," as rule by an "ossified bureaucracy," resulting from a tendency of "bureaucratic politics . . . to elevate nonentities," and meaning the dominance of "bureaucratic conservatism."[78] Hough summed up the common judgment when he said that "Soviet society quite literally is a 'bureaucracy writ large' with all large-scale organizations ultimately being subordinated to a single political institution."[79] Ulam similarly stated that "the Soviet state has been, because of the size and complexity of its administrative structure, *the* administrative state of recent times."[80]

The selection in 1985 of Mikhail Gorbachev as general secretary of the Communist party ushered in a new political era for the USSR. Although their specific meanings were not entirely clear, *glasnost* (openness) and *perestroika* (restructuring) gained worldwide notice as key indicators of his reform objectives. The greatest stress was placed on changes in political power relationships in the system, designed to consolidate his leadership role within the party, and in the state structure. In both sets of institutions, numerous members were replaced by Gorbachev supporters, and in 1988 Gorbachev himself was elected as chairman of the Presidium while continuing as general secretary of the Communist party.

Meanwhile, Gorbachev advocated and put into place major structural reforms. New legislative organs replaced the old bicameral Supreme Soviet, with a Congress of People's Deputies consisting mostly of members elected on a district basis by secret ballot created as the highest organ of government, meeting once a year. This body in turn chose members of a reconstituted bicameral Supreme Soviet, which became a standing body with frequent meetings. By 1990 the office of president had been created, and Gorbachev was elected by the Congress of People's Deputies for an initial five-year term, after which the president was to be chosen by popular vote. The role of the Communist party changed drastically. A constitutional amendment ended its claim to be "the leading and guiding force in Soviet society," its officials were subjected to direct election, it was effectively removed from day-to-day involvement in government operations, and the way was opened for competition among parties in a quasi-presidential political system.

Reform in policy and administration proceeded at a much slower pace. The prime minister, appointed by the president, headed a streamlined Council of Ministers (with the number of ministries reduced by 30 percent to fifty-seven by 1989). A revamping of the state bureaucracy was undertaken, with stress on hierarchical authority exercised by official state agencies replacing party controls, a deemphasis on centralized state planning, introduction of limited private enterprise, and greater exposure of the economy to market forces, but the results were not very impressive.[81]

These Gorbachev reform efforts were undertaken without a commitment on his part to abandon the basic system or break his own allegiance to the Communist party. His intent was to reform Soviet society through a reformed Communist party. Ultimately, he failed both to convert the party into a vanguard of reform and to preserve the Soviet Union itself.

In this process, leadership was transferred from Gorbachev to Boris Yeltsin during the years 1990 and 1991. Elections were held in March 1990 for the People's Congresses in the USSR republics, and two months later Yeltsin was elected chairman of the Russian Federation (RSFSR) Supreme Soviet, thus becoming Russia's head of state and providing him with a political base from which he could challenge his principal rival, USSR President Gorbachev. In July, Yeltsin left the Communist party, and the battle was joined with the power elite of the party, with which Gorbachev became increasingly identified. Yeltsin then embarked on a threefold strategy to enlarge his institutional power base. First, he initiated a referendum to create an elected Russian Federation presidency. After this proposition was approved by the voters, Yeltsin was elected in June 1991 to the newly created office on the first ballot, with a 57.3 percent majority, thus becoming the first democratically elected Russian political leader, giving him an advantage in legitimacy over Gorbachev, who had not been elected by popular vote to the USSR presidency. His second move was to convert the chief administrative positions in the major cities of Moscow and Leningrad into elective offices as well. Thirdly, he fulfilled a campaign promise to eliminate the Communist party apparatus paralleling official state agencies by a decree banning organized political activity in workplaces throughout the Russian republic.

The climactic event was the failed coup d'etat of August 19 to 21, 1991, undertaken while Gorbachev was on vacation away from Moscow by a group of conservative Communist party leaders seeking to end the reformist programs. Yeltsin took a prominent public role in foiling this attempted putsch, and followed up by vigorous action over Gorbachev's protests to ban the Russian Communist party, seize its assets, and oust its personnel from state agencies. Before the end of 1991, the USSR had disintegrated, Gorbachev had resigned, and Yeltsin as president of the Russian Federation had taken his place as the leading figure in the ongoing political transition.

Late in 1991, the Russian People's Congress granted special powers to President Yeltsin for a thirteen month period, including appointment of the prime minister, members of the cabinet, and regional, district and municipal administrative heads (subject to approval of their respective councils), plus authority to issue decrees amending existing legislation (subject to legislative veto within seven days). Using these powers, Yeltsin appointed himself as acting prime minister, reduced the number of cabinet ministers from forty-six to twenty-three (appointing reformist supporters to the most crucial posts), and sought by administrative appointments to establish a vertical power structure over regional and local levels of government. Many of these moves were resisted, and by the end of 1992 two competing power centers had emerged in the People's Congress, led by Yeltsin and Ruslan Khasbulatov, chairman of the Congress. This standoff was based on constitutional uncertainty as to the division of powers between the president and the legislature, and it led to a prolonged and complicated struggle eventually brought to an end when Yeltsin broke the deadlock by forcibly dissolving the legislature in September 1993, and scheduling the election of a new one, as well as a referendum on a new constitution, held on December 12. The outcome was adoption of a constitution granting extremely broad powers to the president, and election of a badly splintered but essentially conservative legislature, with the party of ultranationalist Vladimir Zhirinovsky holding the largest bloc of seats.

Despite this stalemated situation, President Yeltsin was able to serve out his term, and in 1996 was reelected to a second five-year term by a margin of 53.7 percent in a runoff ballot. His second term was impaired by a succession of serious health problems, and was unstable because of frequent shuffles in the premiership and the cabinet. He was unable to muster reliable majority legislative support, and narrowly escaped impeachment in May, 1999. Then he abruptly announced his resignation on the last day of 1999, naming as acting president Vladimir Putin, who had been Yeltsin's premier since the previous August. In an election held on March 26, 2000, Putin was elected president with 53 percent of the vote. Initially he had widespread backing because of Yeltsin's support and the popularity of his stand in favor of the military campaign against the separatist Chechnya republic, and he was able to obtain legislative approval of some minor reform proposals, but in August he received widespread criticism because of the loss of life in the sinking of the nuclear submarine Kursk. As a result, widespread speculation continues as to the governability of the Russian polity.

This chaotic and unpredictable political scene has been matched by disarray in economic and administrative matters. The only clear change is that the highly bureaucratized institutional arrangements of the pre-Gorbachev period have disappeared. Instead, the Russian Federation and other successor entities in the Commonwealth of Independent States have been "de-statized," exhibiting an exceptionally low level of state bureaucratic activity. Richard Rose aptly describes the resulting situation as "getting by without government."[82]

This is the consequence of several factors. One is the intended impact of policies aimed at privatization and movement toward a market economy in lieu of a system of centralized planning. Another, more important, is the massive tendency of former or incumbent civil servants to take advantage of opportunities to appropriate state resources for their own advantage in what has been called "nomenklatura capitalism." Lesage gives specifics of such misdeeds uncovered by official investigations during 1991 and 1992, numbering in the thousands each year.[83] A third factor is the growing impact of incursions by organized crime groups, often linked to allies in the state bureaucracy, which profit from the emerging market economy through coerced payoffs.[84]

Government efforts to cope with these problems in the civil service and to upgrade bureaucratic performance have been abortive or ineffective. A General Directorate was established by decree in 1991 with the mission of training educated and qualified specialists for various levels of administration and of improving administrative performance. One of its actions was to establish seven centers for incoming trainees. In 1992 a draft civil service law was considered by the Supreme Soviet. It proposed to establish fourteen ranks in the civil service, organized into four groups (A—higher civil servants, with ranks 1–5; B—principal civil servants, with ranks 6–8; C—responsible civil servants, with ranks 9–12; and D—junior civil servants, with ranks 13–14). The draft was rejected, however, and basic legislation remains to be enacted to bring about civil service reform.[85]

Efforts to explain the demise of the Soviet Union and to predict the future of the Russian Federation and other members of the Commonwealth of Independent States are legion and contradictory, but one combination of explanations linked to the transition from high to low levels of stateness and bureaucratization is particularly interesting and persuasive. These views are represented by Philip G. Roeder, Charles H. Fairbanks, Jr., and Richard Rose. Roeder's thesis[86] is that political relationships fostered by the Soviet system produced policies suited to transformation of early twentieth-century Russian society, but that these relationships were highly resistant to reform, leading to breakdown rather than adaptation when extensive change was attempted by new leadership. Fairbanks concurs that Russia is trying to deal with the disintegration of the state. The lack of "a working constitutional order and economic system" has resulted in "the absence of any genuine politics at all," with the void being filled by a "politics of resentment" that clouds prospects for progress.[87] Rose anticipates that political and administrative trends in the present system of Russian government will extend indefinitely into the future rather than be replaced by alternatives such as military or strong man rule, or government by technocratic experts. "Pluralist politics are likely to continue," he says,

> because the present fragmentation of power serves many interests. Former Party bosses in the provinces and managers, entrepreneurs, and kleptocrats in former state enterprises have an interest in preventing the government from becoming strong enough to take away what they have carved out for themselves in the past few years. A broken-backed regime offering freedom, disorder, and ineffective government is not a noble goal, but in a society under stress it may be preferred as a lesser evil.[88]

McAuley aptly describes the current scene in Russia as "the politics of uncertainty," resulting from such factors as "the reassertion of the executive, the failure of the representative assemblies to hold their ground, and the inability of political movements or parties to sustain themselves or to attract a following."[89] There is no consensus as to what the future holds, only varying degrees of optimism and pessimism as to whether there will be a "rebirth of politics" in Russia, which in turn might lead to administrative reform.

The People's Republic of China

China's claim to be included in the "second tier" of more developed countries is based on a combination of actuality and potential. Mainland China (the People's Republic) contains an area slightly larger than the United States, with approximately 1.2 billion people, about one out of every five in the world. In 1997, Hong Kong was absorbed, and later perhaps an accommodation will be reached with Taiwan (the Republic of China), bringing significant additional area, people, and economic resources. Annual economic growth in the People's Republic since the late 1970s has been averaging about nine percent, and in 1993 the increase in gross domestic product (GDP) over 1992 was 13.4 percent, faster than that of any other country. The International Monetary Fund already lists the People's Republic as the world's third largest economy, and World Bank forecasts are that greater China (consisting of the People's Republic, Hong Kong, and Taiwan) will have by 2002 a gross domestic product greater than that of the United States, making it first in the world. Official statistics as to per capita gross national product (GDP) indicate that China is still a poor country, but the data are unreliable and not very meaningful. As Kristof comments, "the only thing that is certain is that the Chinese live much better than the official statistics would suggest."[90]

The People's Republic of China is the contemporary manifestation of a long Chinese political history traceable through the revolutions of 1949 and 1910 to the dynasties of Imperial China. After the Chinese Communists gained control of the mainland and established the People's Republic in 1949, the new regime had a remarkable continuity in its top leadership until 1976. With the deaths of Mao

Zedong, Zhou Enlai, and other revolutionary veterans, however, the last two decades have brought major changes in the political order, the dimensions of which have been unclear since the 1989 upheaval centered in Beijing's Tiananmen Square.[91]

The main political structures during the entire period since 1949 have been the Chinese Communist party (CCP), the official state institutions centering on the National People's Congress (NPC), and the People's Liberation Army (PLA). The CCP's highest formal organ is the National Party Congress, which elects the Central Committee, which in turn elects the Politburo and its Standing Committee. Theoretically, the Party Congress members are elected every five years and meet annually, but in practice meetings have been much less frequent. The actual decision-makers are the members of the Standing Committee of the Politburo, usually numbering fewer than ten individuals, including the chairman. The official state structure parallels this party structure, with the NPC electing a Standing Committee and the chairman of the People's Republic (a position which had been abolished in 1975, but was restored in 1983). The chief administrative organ in the state structure is the State Council, which brings together all ministry and commission heads. The role of the PLA as the third major political structure does not rest on any constitutional grant of special status, but on the intimate involvement of the PLA in the whole history of the Communist movement in China beginning in the late 1920s. Formally, the PLA is now controlled by a Central Military Commission within the State Council, but actually direction over military policy has often been closely held by the CCP Military Affairs Committee. This political chain of command is carried through at each level within the PLA hierarchy by means of a political commissar or officer who is stationed alongside the military commander of the unit. These three structures of party, state, and army are thus interlocking hierarchies dominating the Chinese political system.

During its half century of existence, Communist China has gone through several stages in its political development, reflecting shifts in program objectives and power relationships. In the early years from 1949 to 1957, the emphasis was on reconstruction following the long years of warfare, and the launching of projects for rapid economic development with special stress on heavy industry. The Soviet model was influential, and the state apparatus was mainly relied on for results. During 1957 a complicated intraparty debate led to the movement known as the "Great Leap Forward," with what proved to be overly ambitious objectives for rapid movement on all fronts. The CCP took a more commanding role using the slogan "politics takes command," and the state apparatus was downgraded as overbureaucratized. Soviet-style economic planning was dropped in favor of a decentralized effort to stimulate agricultural production through rural communes without sacrificing industrial development. A breakdown in this campaign, resulting in a severe economic crisis from 1959 to 1961, ushered in a period of retrenchment and consolidation which lasted through 1965, and which involved extensive criticism of Mao's leadership because of his identification with the Great Leap Forward.

Mao resumed the political offensive again in 1966 by launching the "Great Proletarian Cultural Revolution," aimed at rectifying what were charged to be deviations by the CCP from Maoist policies. The widespread internal turmoil which was spearheaded by Red Guard revolutionary groups loyal to Mao had two important consequences on the institutional balance of power. The CCP leadership was purged and its organizational effectiveness vastly reduced; the People's Liberation Army emerged as the primary power center. By 1969 the Cultural Revolution had subsided. The CCP had been thoroughly revamped with military figures in a plurality on the CCP Central Committee, and with Mao's major opponents purged. From 1969 to Mao's death in 1976, an unstable equilibrium was maintained, during which the military influence was sharply curtailed, and "moderate" and "radical" factions jockeyed for position within the CCP. Glorification of Mao increased as his actual participation in governance declined. The official state structure, which like the party had suffered during the Cultural Revolution, regained authority and responsibilities. The long anticipated power showdown triggered by Mao's death late in 1976 brought about a victory for the more moderate and pragmatic elements in the CCP, as evidenced by the appointment of Hua Guofeng as premier and chairman of the CCP Central Committee, and the ouster of the so-called Gang of Four, one of them Mao's widow, Jiang Qing.

The ascendancy of Hua Guofeng proved to be short-lived, however, as he lost out in a struggle with Deng Xiaoping, who had been stripped of all posts by the Politburo shortly before Mao's death but was reinstated in mid-1977 as a vice chairman and a member of the Standing Committee of the Politburo. Deng gradually asserted his influence and replaced Hua's supporters with his own in crucial posts, leading eventually in 1981 to Hua's "resignation" as CCP Chairman. Deng continued after that as undisputed leader and elder statesman until his death in 1997 at age 92, although the only official position he held in later years was chairman of the Central Military Commission, and he relinquished that in 1987.

During the early 1980s, Deng's ally Hu Yaobang served as general secretary of the CCP until he was forced to resign in 1987 because of conservative opposition to relaxation of controls over political activities. In the resulting shakeup, Zhao Ziyang became CCP general secretary, and Li Peng was designated as premier. Hu's death in April 1989 triggered the student demonstrations that eventually led in June to the military crackdown at Tiananmen Square and elsewhere in China. A showdown between Zhao and Li as to how to deal with the political unrest led to Zhao's ouster and replacement as general secretary by Jiang

Zemin, the CCP party chief in Shanghai. Behind the scenes, Deng made the crucial decisions, and then called upon the military forces to carry them out.

In 1993 Jiang and Li consolidated their formal official roles. Jiang was elected president for a five-year term, while continuing as CCP general secretary and chairman of the Central Military Commission, thus combining the top state, party, and military posts for the first time since the 1970s. Li, although he faced some open opposition, was elected as premier for a second five-year term. When that term ended in 1998, Li was replaced as premier by Zhu Rongji, but continues in an influential leadership role.

Up to now, even after Deng's death, there has been no significant shift from the "pragmatic" policy he advocated while he was the acknowledged paramount leader. His program combined economic liberalization with continued and increasing restraints on political activity. This economic policy has placed stress on efforts toward rapid progress in promoting a program of "four modernizations": of industry, agriculture, science and technology, and the military. A new constitution approved in 1993 contains the phrase "socialist market economy" as a description of these capitalistically oriented economic reforms. Deng's political program clearly drew the line against any challenge to the ultimate exercise of power by him and his associates. This intent was reemphasized by a purge of the military command early in 1993, during which half of those with the rank of general were replaced, apparently to weaken the influence of the incumbent president, who had close military ties and was shortly afterward passed over for reelection in favor of Jiang. The current party leaders, as represented by the membership of the Central Committee, have been characterized by Xiaowei Zang as "a political-technocratic leadership," younger and better educated than their predecessors, but dedicated to an insistence on "the dominance of the Communist Party over society while pursuing economic development."[92]

David Shambaugh predicted before Deng's death that he would bequeath a "robust economy and rejuvenated society," but an "antiquated political system."[93] With rising expectations having been stimulated, the uncertainty is whether economic progress can be sustained while the CCP leadership responds sufficiently to demands for more political participation and copes adequately with strong socio-economic centrifugal forces.[94]

These system-wide political upheavals form a backdrop for an examination of the operation of the state bureaucracy, which has varied with changes in the political climate. In general, treatment of the official state bureaucracy in the Chinese Communist regime reflects a basic distrust of bureaucratic responsiveness and a desire to curb bureaucratic power, combined with reluctant acceptance of the inevitable need to maintain a state bureaucratic apparatus. The outcome of this ambivalence has been an alternating pattern of expansion and contraction, depending on general political conditions. Bureaucratic power peaked during the mid-1950s, rose again in the early 1960s, had another resurgence after Mao's death, and currently is at an intermediate level. The low points of bureaucratic status have coincided with the Great Leap Forward of the late 1960s and the Cultural Revolution a few years later.

Some consistent themes have persisted during the entire period since 1949. One is a determination to politicize the bureaucracy and make it responsive to party direction, using various devices. Most fundamental is the practice of putting party members in most of the important government positions. Another is to recognize a party "fraction" in each organizational unit, as the vehicle for making sure that party policies are being carried out. Backing up these measures is the existence of a hierarchy of party committees at each level of the state administrative hierarchy, with oversight functions designed to assure the supremacy of politics. As a consequence of these multiple controls, Barnett concluded early on that party dominance of the government bureaucracy "operates not only at the upper levels of leadership in the hierarchy, it also reaches effectively to the lowest levels of all organizations in the bureaucracy."[95]

The second theme is decentralization by the transfer of administrative powers to the lowest feasible level. This diffusion strategy is designed to prevent the buildup of a nonproductive administrative superstructure and at the same time strengthen local initiative and responsibility. Carried to an extreme during the Great Leap Forward, the central ministries essentially lost control over lower administrative levels, and local party committees became the effective decision-makers. A by-product of this involvement turned out to be a bureaucratization of politics as the CCP organs themselves became identified with administrative specifics, leading later during the Cultural Revolution to charges that the CCP itself had become overbureaucraticized. Despite this and other problems, and despite the fact that "decentralization and antibureaucratism are considered Maoist themes, the post-Mao leadership has continued to inveigh against the evils of bureaucratism and to experiment with decentralization."[96]

The product of this campaign to ensure subordination of the state administrative apparatus to CCP control is what Dittmer calls a "mass line" bureaucracy. The term is borrowed from Mao's "mass line" principle that there should be a pattern of reciprocal communications between citizens and party leaders, with the masses presenting ideas to the party for consideration and carrying out decisions rendered, but with the right of decision-making reserved to the party. Such a mass line bureaucracy is described by Dittmer as "a combination of an activist Central organization and extensive mass participation, the two coordinated by an evolving ideological consensus."[97] He rates it as an authority system having a high level of elite power combined with a high level of mass participation.

Criteria for recruitment into the Chinese bureaucracy, as in other Communist regimes, have varied in the stress placed on political loyalty versus competence, on being "red" as against being "expert." During mobilization and rectification campaigns, the former factor has been more important, with the latter gaining in times of comparative quiet and stability. Vogel points out that in case of direct conflict, the "red" or political considerations have taken priority, finding expression in the slogan "politics takes command." He also notes that bureaucratic career patterns "reflect the mixture of political and rational bureaucratic considerations." Generally career patterns have followed "a fairly regular progression much as one might expect in an ordinary bureaucracy, with some striking exceptions that have occurred for political reasons. The exceptions are concentrated at the time of rectification campaigns when political considerations take on greater primacy." In such circumstances, "the politically vulnerable are attacked and sacrificed. At the end of a rectification campaign, new openings are available as a result of the removal of the politically vulnerable, and the politically reliable . . . are promoted." At all times, political reliability has been a must. Disciplinary action to ensure it was institutionalized in the "semi-purge" rather than through resort to the violent purge methods of Russia in the 1930s, with offenders being sent away for study and labor and then returning to work but often at a lower level. This practice tended "to maintain a high degree of responsiveness to political pressures from above" even if it derived "more from anxiety than from spontaneous enthusiasm."[98]

The post-Maoist leaders, especially Deng Xiaoping, have viewed reform of the bureaucracy as necessary for realization of the "four modernization" policy goals, and have taken steps toward greater bureaucratic rationalization and professionalization. In a speech delivered as early as 1980, Deng referred to the relationship between "red" and "expert" in these words:

> Expert does not mean red, but red requires expert. If you are not an expert, and don't know much, but blindly take command . . . you will only delay production and construction. Unless we resolve this question we cannot realize four modernizations. . . . From now on, in the selection of cadres we should pay special attention to expert knowledge.[99]

Later specific measures sponsored by Deng included opening up access to advanced education at home and abroad; greater stress on technical qualifications for initial recruitment; replacement of aging bureaucrats by de-emphasizing seniority in favor of expertise; structural streamlining which sharply reduced the number of ministries and agencies in the State Council (from 86 to 59 in 1993) and the size of their staffs (a reduction of one million bureaucrats or twenty percent of the total within a year was announced in 1993); and renewed emphasis on direct public controls over lower level officials through the ballot, public opinion polls, and other devices. Jean C. Robinson summed up this new emphasis by saying that bureaucratic personnel "are now expected to be revolutionary, well-educated, and professionally competent." She cautioned, however, that the evidence available was "insufficient for proclaiming that fundamental institutional, leadership, and ideological changes have taken place in China." By combining Maoist and more technocratic principles, Deng hoped "to achieve stability, marked by efficiency and production."[100]

The post-Deng leaders have continued these efforts to establish a more modern civil service system, while retaining the essential features required for continued ultimate control by the dominant party. The reform process has extended over more than a decade, and it has been incremental in nature, with numerous changes in direction and emphasis. Clearly it has emphasized the values of accountability and efficiency as keys to economic growth and development. This has called for the adoption of Western principles of personnel management, such as recruitment by examination, position classification, and performance evaluation. At the same time, the concept of political neutrality is rejected and loyalty to the CCP is stressed as a basic requirement.

Recent analyses have detailed some of the results of these reforms, such as the streamlining of ministries and other administrative organs by reduction in the number of units, the separation of government functions from those of economic enterprises, and the downsizing of staff. There is no doubt as to the significance of these changes. Neither is there disagreement that the reforms are designed to create a civil service system combining Western personnel techniques and Chinese characteristics. Commentators differ, however, as to which element is most important. For example, Worthley and Tsao, along with Aufrecht and Li, stress the similarities of these reforms to the "reinventing government" phenomenon elsewhere and see it as a Chinese manifestation of the new public management movement. Others, such as Lam and Chan, stress that the intent is to distance the Chinese civil service from those of Western democracies, and to place more importance on its Chinese characteristics.

Premier Zhu Rongji, who took office in 1998, has indicated that he intends to give renewed attention to administrative reform, but it is too early to evaluate what redirection may take place due to his influence. Meanwhile, I concur with the view of Liou that "the most important challenge to the fate of China's civil service system is the future role of the Chinese Communist Party." He points out that Chinese reformers have not adopted the value of political neutrality and that "there has never been a clear-cut line between Party leaders and government bureaucrats. Party leaders at all levels are administrative officials at the same time, and in order to be a successful bureaucrat one has to become a Party member first."[101] Party control of administration continues to be demonstrated in many ways, indicating that the overriding consideration of the regime has not changed. It is to make sure that the bureaucracy remains safely politicized.

NOTES

1. Gabriel A. Almond and Sidney Verba, *The Civic Culture* (Princeton, NJ: Princeton University Press, 1963), p.8.
2. Michel Crozier, *The Bureaucratic Phenomenon* (Chicago: University of Chicago Press, 1964), p. 233.
3. Wallace S. Sayre, "Bureaucracies: Some Contrasts in Systems," *Indian Journal of Public Administration* 10, No. 2 (1964): 219–229, at p. 223. [Reprinted in Nimrod Raphaeli, ed., *Readings in Comparative Public Administration* (Boston: Allyn and Bacon, 1967), pp. 341–354.]
4. Selected sources on the British system include: H. R. G. Greaves, *The Civil Service in the Changing State* (London: Harrap and Co., 1947); Herman Finer, *The Theory and Practice of Modern Government*, rev. ed. (New York: Henry Holt and Company, 1949), Chap. 30; R. A. Chapman, *The Higher Civil Service in Britain* (London: Constable & Co., 1970); James B. Christoph, "High Civil Servants and the Politics of Consensualism in Great Britain," pp. 25–62, Bruce W. Headey, "A Typology of Ministers: Implications for Minister-Civil Servant Relationships in Britain," pp. 63–86, and Robert D. Putnam, "The Political Attitudes of Senior Civil Servants in Britain, Germany, and Italy," pp. 87–126—all in Mattei Dogan, ed., *The Mandarins of Western Europe: The Political Role of Top Civil Servants* (New York: John Wiley and Sons, 1975); Stanley Rothman, Howard Scarrow, and Martin Schain, *European Society and Politics* (St. Paul, MN: West Publishing Company, 1976), pp. 325–332; Richard Rose, "British Government: The Job at the Top," pp. 1–49, in Richard Rose and Ezra N. Suleiman, eds., *Presidents and Prime Ministers* (Washington, DC: American Enterprise Institute for Public Policy Research, 1980), pp.1–49; Richard Rose, "The Political Status of Higher Civil Servants in Britain," in Ezra N. Suleiman, ed., *Bureaucrats and Policy Making: A Comparative Overview* (New York: Holmes & Meier, 1984), pp. 136–173; Rosamund Thomas, "The Duties and Responsibilities of Civil Servants and Ministers: A Challenge Within British Cabinet Government," *International Review of Administrative Sciences* 52, No. 4 (December 1986): 511–538; Dennis Kavanaugh, *Thatcherism and British Politics: The End of Consensus?* (Oxford: Oxford University Press, 1987); Geoffrey Fry, Andrew Flynn, Andrew Gray, William Jenkins, and Brian Rutherford, "Symposium on Improving Management in Government," *Public Administration* 66 (Winter 1988): 429–445; Geoffrey J. Gammon, "The British Higher Civil Service: Recruitment and Training," prepared for XIVth World Congress of the International Political Science Association (1988), 20 pp. mimeo.; Ian Budge, David McKay, Rod Rhodes, David Robertson, David Sanders, Martin Slater, Graham Wilson with the collaboration of David Marsh, *The Changing British Political System: Into the 1990s,* 2nd ed. (London and New York: Longman, 1988); Gavin Drewry and Tony Butcher, *The Civil Service Today* (Oxford: Basil Blackwell, 1988); Brian Smith, "The United Kingdom," in Donald C. Rowat, ed., *Public Administration in Developed Democracies: A Comparative Study* (New York: Marcel Dekker, 1988), Chap. 4, pp. 67–86; Richard Rose, "Loyalty, Voice or Exit? Margaret Thatcher's Challenge to the Civil Service," in T. Ellwein, J. J. Hesse, Renate Mayntz, and F. W. Scharpf, eds.,

Yearbook on Government and Public Administration (Boulder, CO: Westview Press, 1990); Sophie Watson, *Is Sir Humphrey Dead? The Changing Culture of the Civil Service* (Bristol: SAUS Publications, 1992); Robin Butler, "The Evolution of the Civil Service—A Progress Report," *Public Administration* 71 (Autumn 1993): 395–406; R. A. W. Rhodes, "From Institutions to Dogma: Tradition, Eclecticism, and Ideology in the Study of British Public Administration," *Public Administration Review* 56, No. 6 (November/December 1996): 507–516; Francis R. Terry, "Getting on in Government: Political Priorities and Professional Civil Servants," in Ali Farazmand, ed., *Modern Systems of Government: Exploring the Role of Bureaucrats and Politicians* (Thousand Oaks, CA: Sage Publications, Inc., 1997), Chap. 11, pp. 255–271; Sylvia Horton, "The Civil Service," in Sylvia Horton and David Farnham, eds., *Public Management in Britain* (New York, NY: St. Martin's Press, Inc., 1999), Chap. 9, pp. 145–161; and R. A. W. Rhodes, "Transforming British Government: An Interpretative Guide to the ESRC's Whitehall Programme," prepared for the 1999 National Conference of the American Society for Public Administration, mimeographed, 61 pp.

5. "The selection, training, and streaming of the administrative trainees is still designed to produce a class of senior civil servants that can serve ministers by synthesizing the contributions of specialists, placing these in the context of political realities, and by formulating policy alternatives. If the new administrator turns out not quite to fit the old model of the 'talented amateur,' it is even less likely that he will fit the model of the narrow specialist." Rothman, Scarrow, and Schain, *European Society and Politics*, p. 331.

6. "From the British point of view," as a distinguished Nigerian put it, "a first-class brain, particularly if produced by Oxford or Cambridge, can, without any special training, govern anybody and anything in the world." S. O. Adebo, "Public Administration in Newly Independent Countries," in Burton A. Baker, ed., *Public Administration: A Key to Development* (Washington, D.C.: Graduate School, U.S. Department of Agriculture, 1964), p. 22.

7. "Fast streamers are likely to become assistant secretaries in their mid to late thirties, if not earlier, compared to around their fifties, which is the approximate age for promotion to assistant secretary from the mainstream." Watson, *Is Sir Humphrey Dead?*, p. 57.

8. Butler, "The Evolution of the Civil Service," p. 403.

9. James B. Christoph, "High Civil Servants and the Politics of Consensualism in Great Britain," in Dogan, ed., *The Mandarins of Western Europe*, p. 50. c 1975. Reprinted by permission of the publishers, (Beverly Hills/London) Sage Publications, Inc. 1975.

10. *Ibid.*, p. 40.

11. See Headey, "A Typology of Ministers: Implications for Minister-Civil Servant Relationships in Britain," in Dogan, ed., *The Mandarins of Western Europe*, Chap. 2, pp. 63–86.

12. *Ibid.*, p. 82.

13. Christoph, "High Civil Servants," pp. 47, 49, 59.

14. Putnam, "The Political Attitudes of Senior Civil Servants," p. 117.

15. Horton, "The Civil Service," p. 145.

16. Francis R. Terry, "Getting on in Government: Political Priorities and Professional Civil Servants," p. 270.

17. For example, Drewry and Butcher have expressed concern that the greater emphasis on commitment to government policies "conflicts with traditional notions of neutrality and impartiality, and that the traditional objectivity of the civil service will be eroded by a process of 'creeping politicization.' One result is that there is a danger that civil service advice will be tailored to what ministers want to hear, with civil servants offering 'honest and unpalatable advice' being either tight-lipped or offering ministers only the advice they wish to hear." *The Civil Service Today*, p. 170. On the other hand, Robin Butler, former Secretary of the Cabinet and Head of the Home Civil Service, after reviewing the reforms that have taken place, argued that these constitute an agenda for continuity, retaining "a permanent civil service recruited by open competition, and promoted by merit, rather than by patronage or political affiliation," and "a clear separation of tenure, functions and responsibilities between civil servants and politicians." "The Evolution of the Civil Service—A Progress Report," p. 403. For additional discussions of these issues, see James B. Christoph, "The Remaking of British Administrative Culture: Why Whitehall Can't Go Home Again," *Administration and Society* 24, No. 2 (August 1992): 163–181, and "A Traditional Bureaucracy in Turbulence: Whitehall in the Thatcher Era," in Ali Farazmand, ed., *Handbook of Bureaucracy* (New York: Marcel Dekker, 1994), Chap. 37, pp. 577–589; David L. Dillman, "The Thatcher Agenda, the Civil Service, and 'Total Efficiency'," in Farazmand, ed., *Handbook of Bureaucracy*, Chap. 14, pp. 241–252; and Christopher Pollitt, "Antistatist Reforms and New Administrative Directions: Public Administration in the United Kingdom," *Public Administration Review* 56, No. 1 (January/February 1996): 81–87.

18. Christoph, "High Civil Servants," p. 33.

19. *Ibid.*, p. 35.

20. *Ibid.*, p. 56.

21. Rothman, Scarrow, and Schain, *European Society and Politics*, p. 331.

22. Selected sources on the United States include Finer, *The Theory and Practice of Modern Government*, rev. ed., Chap. 33; Paul P. Van Riper, *History of the United States Civil Service* (Evanston, IL: Row, Peterson, and Company, 1958); David T. Stanley, *The Higher Civil Service* (Washington, DC: The Brookings Institution, 1964); Frederick C. Mosher, *Democracy and the Public Service* (New York: Oxford University Press, 1968); Lewis C. Mainzer, *Political Bureaucracy* (Glenview, IL: Scott, Foresman, 1973); Samuel Krislov, *Representative Bureaucracy* (Englewood Cliffs, NJ: Prentice-Hall, Inc. 1974); James A. Medeiros and David E. Schmitt, *Public Bureaucracy: Values and Perspectives* (North Scituate, MA: Duxbury Press, 1977); O. Glenn Stahl, *Public Personnel Administration*, 7th ed. (New York: Harper & Row, 1977); Hugh Heclo, *A Government of Strangers: Executive Politics in Washington* (Washington, DC: The Brookings Institution, 1977); James W. Fesler, *Public Administration: Theory and Practice* (Englewood Cliffs, NJ: Prentice-Hall, Inc., 1980); Hugh Heclo, "In Search of a Role: America's Higher Civil Service," in Suleiman, ed., *Bureaucrats and Policy Making*, pp. 8–34; John Rohr, *To Run a Constitution: The Legitimacy of the Administrative State* (Lawrence, KS: University Press of Kansas, 1986); Ralph Clark Chandler, *A Centennial History of the Ameri-*

can Administrative State (New York: Macmillan, 1987); Ferrel Heady, "The United States," in Rowat, ed., *Public Administration in Developed Democracies*, Chap. 23, pp. 395–417; James Q. Wilson, *Bureaucracy: What Government Agencies Do and Why They Do It* (New York: Basic Books, 1989); Richard J. Stillman, *Preface to Public Administration: A Search for Themes and Direction* (New York: St. Martin's Press, 1991); James W. Fesler and Donald F. Kettl, *The Politics of the Administrative Process* (Chatham, NJ: Chatham House Publishers, 1991); Charles T. Goodsell, *The Case for Bureaucracy: A Public Administration Polemic*, 3rd ed. (Chatham, NJ: Chatham House Publishers, 1994); Donald F. Kettl, Patricia W. Ingraham, Ronald P. Sanders, and Constance Horner, *Civil Service Reform: Building a Government That Works* (Washington, DC: Brookings Institution Press, 1996); Morris P. Fiorina, *Divided Government*, 2nd ed. (Boston: Allyn & Bacon, 1996); Carolyn Ban, "Reinventing the Federal Civil Service: Drivers of Change," *Public Administration Quarterly* 22, No. 1 (Spring 1998): 21–34; and Gillian Peele, Christopher J. Bailey, Bruce Cain, and B. Guy Peters, eds., *Developments in American Politics 3* (New York: Chatham House Publishers, 1998).

23. For recent examinations of such issues, see Alice M. Rivlin, "A New Vision of American Federalism," *Public Administration Review* 52, No. 4 (July/August 1992): 315–320, and James Edwin Kee and John Shannon, "The Crisis and Anticrisis Dynamic: Rebalancing the American Federal System," *Ibid.*, pp. 321–329.

24. Glassman, "The United States: The Anti-Statist Society," in Metin Heper, ed., *The State and Public Bureaucracies: A Comparative Perspective* (New York: Greenwood Press, 1987), Chap. 3, pp. 27–39.

25. Stillman, *Preface to Public Administration*, p. 15. He elaborates on this theme in "The Peculiar 'Stateless' Origins of American Public Administration Theory," Chap. 2, pp. 19–41.

26. For a revealing study of the role of bureau chiefs, refer to Herbert Kaufman, *The Administrative Behavior of Federal Bureau Chiefs* (Washington, DC: The Brookings Institution, 1981).

27. Mosher, *Democracy and the Public Service*, Chap. 4, pp. 99–133.

28. For a succinct summary of these changes, see Patricia Ingraham, "The Federal Bureaucracy," in Peele, Bailey, Cain, and Peters, *Developments in American Politics 3*, Chap. 5, pp. 97–113.

29. David Osborne and Ted Gaebler, *Reinventing Government* (Reading MA; Addison-Wesley, 1992).

30. Ingraham, "The Federal Bureaucracy," p. 101.

31. For example, see the assessments by Kettl, Ingraham, Sanders, and Horner in *Civil Service Reform: Building a Government That Works*. Their view is that the current civil service system was designed for direct delivery of most public services, and is not well adapted to management of the increasing number of partnerships with private companies, nonprofit organizations, and state and local governmental agencies.

32. For an account of this situation, see Fesler and Kettl, *The Politics of the Administrative Process*, pp. 119–122.

33. Heclo, "America's Higher Civil Service," p. 21.

34. Mainzer, *Political Bureaucracy*, pp. 107, 112.

35. Sayre, "Bureaucracies: Some Contrasts in Systems," p. 228.

36. See his article, "Bureaucracy and the Constitution," *Public Administration Review* 54, No. 1 (January/February 1994): 65–72, and others listed among the references. Bureaucrats in the United States "do exercise substantial power, but normally only within the niches defined by the programs and policies of the agencies within which they work. They are neither willing nor able to consolidate bureaucratic power across the board. . . . American bureaucrats (including military officers) have neither the motivation nor the capacity to stage a coup and seize power." Riggs, "Bureaucracy and the Constitution," p. 67.

37. See Susan J. Tolchin, *The Angry American: How Voter Rage is Changing the Nation* (Boulder, CO: Westview Press, 1996), and Joseph S. Nye, Jr., Philip D. Zelikow, and David C. King, eds., *Why People Don't Trust Government* (Cambridge, MA: Harvard University Press, 1997).

38. Heady, "The United States," pp. 415, 416. Charles Goodsell states the situation accurately: "As a traditional bete noire in our society, bureaucracy is often thought of as some kind of alien force. It is imagined as a 'they' that opposes us and hence is apart from us. Actually, bureaucracy is very close. It is public institutions operating within our communities. It is public employees living in our neighborhoods. It is programs mandated by government officials for whom we personally voted. It is collective action in our behalf. In a meaningful sense, then, bureaucracy is *ours.*" *The Case for Bureaucracy*, pp. 183–184.

39. Sources on Japan include: Robert E. Ward, "Japan," in Robert E. Ward and Roy C. Macridis, eds., *Modern Political Systems: Asia* (Englewood Cliffs, NJ: Prentice-Hall, 1963), pp. 17–114; Masamichi Inoki, "The Civil Bureaucracy," in Robert E. Ward and Dankwart A. Rustow, eds., *Political Modernization in Japan and Turkey* (Princeton, NJ: Princeton University Press, 1964), Chap. 7, pp. 283–300; Reinhard Bendix, "Preconditions for Development: A Comparison of Japan and Germany," *Nation-Building and Citizenship* (New York: John Wiley & Sons, 1964), Chap. 6, pp. 177–213; Akira Kubota, *Higher Civil Servants in Postwar Japan* (Princeton, NJ: Princeton University Press, 1969); Edwin Dowdy, *Japanese Bureaucracy: Its Development and Modernization* (Melbourne: Cheshire, 1973); Robert E. Ward, *Japan's Political System*, 2nd ed. (Englewood Cliffs, NJ: Prentice-Hall, 1978); B. C. Koh and Jae-On Kim, "Paths to Advancement in Japanese Bureaucracy," *Comparative Political Studies* 15, No. 3 (1982): 289–313; a collection of articles on Japanese public administration and administrative law, in *International Review of Administrative Sciences* 48, No. 2 (1982): 115–262; Kiyoaki Tsuji, ed., *Public Administration in Japan* (Tokyo: Institute of Administrative Management and University of Tokyo Press, 1984); T. J. Pempel, "Organizing for Efficiency: The Higher Civil Service in Japan," in Suleiman, ed., *Bureaucrats and Policy Making*, pp. 72–106; Deil S. Wright and Yasuyoshi Sakurai, "Administrative Reform in Japan: Politics, Policy and Public Administration in a Deliberative Society," *Public Administration Review* 47, No. 2 (March/April 1987): 121–133; Paul S. Kim, *Japan's Civil Service System: Its Structure, Personnel, and Politics* (Westport, CT: Greenwood Press, 1988); Gerald L. Curtis, *The Japanese Way of Politics* (New York: Columbia University Press, 1988); Ku Tashiro, "Japan," in Rowat, ed., *Public Administration in Developed Democracies*, Chap. 22, pp. 375–394; Masaru

Sakamoto, "Public Administration in Japan: Past and Present in the Higher Civil Service," in Ali Farazmand, ed., *Handbook of Comparative and Development Public Administration* (New York: Marcel Dekker, 1991), Chap. 9, pp. 101–124; T. J. Pempel, "Bureaucracy in Japan," *PS: Political Science and Politics* 25, No. 1 (March 1992): 19–24; Karel van Wolferen, "Japan's Non-Revolution," *Foreign Affairs* 72, No. 4 (September/October 1993): 54–65; David Williams, *Japan: Beyond the End of History* (London: Routledge, 1994); C. Johnson, *Japan: Who Governs? The Rise of the Developmental State* (New York: W. W. Norton, 1995); Taketsugu Tsurutani, "The National Bureaucracy of Japan," *International Review of Administrative Sciences* 64 (1998): 181–194; Jong S. Jun and Hiromi Muto, "The Politics of Administrative Reform in Japan: More Strategies, Less Progress," *International Review of Administrative Sciences* 64 (1998): 195–202; Takashi Nishio, "Arts and Symbols in the Japanese Public Personnel Management," *International Review of Administrative Sciences* 64 (1998): 261–273; Ko Mishima, "The Changing Relationship Between Japan's LDP and the Bureaucracy," *Asian Survey* 38, No. 10 (October 1998): 968–985; Yasuo Takao, "Participatory Democracy in Japan's Decentralization Drive," *Asian Survey* 38, No. 10 (October 1998): 950–967; and L. William Heinrich Jr., "Political and Economic Challenges for Japan in the Twenty-First Century," *American Asian Review* 16, No. 3 (Fall, 1998): 7–41.

40. Inoki, "The Civil Bureaucracy," p. 288.
41. Dowdy, *Japanese Bureaucracy*, p. xii.
42. *Ibid.*, pp. 156, 181–182.
43. Inoki, "The Civil Bureaucracy," p. 288.
44. Ward, *Japan's Political System*, p. 163.
45. For a recent assessment along these lines, see Nishio, "Arts and Symbols in the Japanese Personnel Management."
46. For details, see Wright and Sakurai, "Administrative Reform in Japan," and Tashiro, "Japan," pp. 379–392.
47. For more specifics, refer to Tsuji, *Public Administration in Japan*, Chap. 6; Pempel, "The Higher Civil Service in Japan," pp. 98–101; Tashiro, "Japan," pp. 378–379; and Sakamoto, "Japan's Civil Service," pp. 107–114.
48. Kubota, *Higher Civil Servants in Post-War Japan: Their Social Origins, Educational Backgrounds, and Career Patterns* (copyright 1969 by Princeton University Press), p. 58. Reprinted by permission of Princeton University Press.
49. "In terms of objectives . . . a Japanese faculty of law more nearly resembled a combination of a political science department and a business administration school in an American university than it did a law school." *Ibid.*, p. 78.
50. *Ibid.*, pp. 70, 162. Even today, roughly 35 percent of the entrants continue to be Tokyo University graduates. Pempel, "Bureaucracy in Japan," p. 22. The Oxford/Cambridge total in Great Britain totaled slightly over 47 percent in 1950.
51. *Ibid.*, pp. 85–91, 165–168.
52. *Ibid.*, pp. 27–57, 160–161. The impact of Japanese cultural homogeneity in the operation of business organizations has received much attention because of Japan's success in global competition. See William G. Ouchi, *Theory Z: How American Business Can Meet the Japanese Challenge* (Reading, MA: Addison-Wesley, 1982). For an exploratory discussion of similar factors in public administration, see Jong

S. Jun and Hiromi Muto, "The Hidden Dimensions of Japanese Administration: Culture and Its Impacts," 32 pp. mimeo., prepared for the 54th National Training Conference of the American Society for Public Administration, July 17–21, 1993, in San Francisco, CA. Linda Weiss argues that the agent of transformation which produced the main features of the Japanese employment system was the Japanese state, particularly the bureaucratic agencies charged with labor affairs. See "War, the State, and the Origins of the Japanese Employment System," *Politics & Society* 21, No. 3 (September, 1993): 325–354.

53. Kim, *Japan's Civil Service System*, pp. 38–40.
54. "Japan's Civil Service," pp. 116–119.
55. Pempel, "The Higher Civil Service in Japan," pp. 96–97. Sakamoto reports that there is some evidence of a recent increase in interdepartmental mobility. "Japan's Civil Service," pp. 119–120.
56. Kubota, *Higher Civil Servants in Post-War Japan*, p. 140.
57. For a full review of the Japanese retirement system, see Kim, *Japan's Civil Service System*, Chap. 4.
58. Dowdy, *Japanese Bureaucracy*, p. xiv.
59. Pempel, "The Higher Civil Service in Japan," p. 85.
60. Ward, *Japan's Political System*, p. 166; Pempel, "The Higher Civil Service in Japan," p. 88; and Kim, *Japan's Civil Service System*, p.59.
61. Kubota, *Higher Civil Servants in Post-War Japan*, p. 173.
62. See Inoki, "The Civil Bureaucracy," pp. 299–300; Ward, *Japan's Political System*, p. 84; Pempel, "The Higher Civil Service in Japan," p. 87; and Tashiro, "Japan," p. 391.
63. See, for example, Karel van Wolferen, "Japan's Non-Revolution," in which he contended that even during the LDP years effective political oversight over bureaucratic decision-making was lacking, and that this absence of political accountability would probably be intensified under shortlived coalition governments.
64. Mishima, "The Changing Relationship Between Japan's LPD and the Bureaucracy," p. 969.
65. Jun and Muto, "The Politics of Administrative Reform in Japan: More Strategies, Less Progress," p. 195.
66. For reviews of the situation, refer to Ichiro Ogawa, "Outline of the System of Administrative and Judicial Remedies Against Administrative Action in Japan," *International Review of Administrative Sciences* 48, No. 2 (1982): 247–252; and "Administrative and Judicial Remedies against Administrative Actions," in Tsuji, *Public Administration in Japan*, Chap. 15, pp. 217–227.
67. Kubota, *Higher Civil Servants in Post-War Japan*, p. 174.
68. Bendix, *Nation-Building and Citizenship*, p. 200.
69. Crozier, *The Bureaucratic Phenomenon*, p. 231n.
70. Pempel, "The Higher Civil Service in Japan," p. 78. Karel van Wolferen goes further, saying that "Japanese ministries come closer to being states unto themselves than any other government institutions in the industrialized world. Besides their responsibilities for administration, they also monopolize the lawmaking capacities and jurisdiction within their own bailiwicks. For all practical purposes they themselves are not subject to the rule of law." See "Japan's Non-Revolution," p. 58.

71. Williams, *Japan: Beyond the End of History*, p. 20.
72. Tsurutani, "The National Bureaucracy of Japan," p. 183.
73. Kubota, *Higher Civil Servants in Post-War Japan*, p. 176.
74. For an excellent overview, refer to Geoffrey Ponton, *The Soviet Era: Soviet Politics from Lenin to Yeltsin* (Oxford: Blackwell Publishers, 1994). For analyses of the Soviet Union before the Gorbachev era, see Jerry F. Hough and Merle Fainsod, *How the Soviet Union is Governed* (Cambridge, MA: Harvard University Press, 1979); John N. Hazard, *The Soviet System of Government*, 5th ed., rev. (Chicago: The University of Chicago Press, 1980); Donald R. Kelley, *The Politics of Developed Socialism: The Soviet Union as a Post-Industrial State* (Westport, CT: Greenwood Press, 1986); and other sources cited in the fourth edition of this work. Selected sources on developments in the USSR, the Commonwealth of Independent States, and the Russian Federation during the Gorborchev era and more recently include citations in the fourth edition [especially Moshe Lewin, *The Gorbachev Phenomenon* (Berkeley, CA: University of California Press, 1988); Thomas H. Naylor, *The Gorbachev Strategy: Opening the Closed Society* (Lexington, MA: D. C. Heath and Company, 1988); Dawn Oliver, "'Perestroika' and Public Administration in the USSR," *Public Administration* 66 (Winter 1988): 411–427; B. M. Lazarev, "Improvement of the Administrative Machinery in the USSR: Vital Questions," *International Review of Administrative Sciences* 55 (1989): 7–13; D. Richard Little, *Governing the Soviet Union* (White Plains, NY: Longman, 1989); and Jerry F. Hough, "Gorbachev's Politics," *Foreign Affairs* 68, No. 5 (Winter 1989/90): 26–41]; plus Michael Mandelbaum, "Coup de Grace: The End of the Soviet Union," *Foreign Affairs* 71, No. 1 (1992): 164–183; Eugene Huskey, ed., *Executive Power and Soviet Politics: The Rise and Decline of the Soviet State* (Armonk, NY: M. E. Sharpe, 1992); Gregory Gleason, "The Federal Formula and the Collapse of the USSR," *Publius* 22, No. 3 (Summer 1992): 141–163; Philip G. Roeder, *Red Sunset: The Failure of Soviet Politics* (Princeton, NJ: Princeton University Press, 1993); John B. Dunlop, *The Rise of Russia and the Fall of the Soviet Empire* (Princeton, NJ: Princeton University Press, 1993); Denis J. B. Shaw, "Geographic and Historical Observations on the Future of a Federal Russia," *Post-Soviet Geography* 34, No. 8 (1993): 530–540; Michel Lesage, "The Crisis of Public Administration in Russia," *Public Administration* 71 (Spring/Summer 1993): 121–133; Helmut Wollman, "Change and Continuity of Political and Administrative Elites from Communist to Post-Communist Russia," *Governance* 6, No. 3 (July 1993): 325–340; Jonathan Steele, *Eternal Russia: Yeltsin, Gorbachev and the Mirage of Democracy* (London: Faber and Faber, 1994); Charles H. Fairbanks, Jr., "The Politics of Resentment," *Journal of Democracy* 5, No. 2 (April 1994): 35–42; Richard Rose, "Getting By Without Government: Everyday Life in Russia," *Daedalus* 123, No. 3 (Summer 1994): 41–62; Nikolai Biryukov and Victor Sergeyev, *Russian Politics in Transition: Institutional Conflict in a Nascent Democracy* (Brookfield, VT: Ashgate Publishing Company, 1997); Karen Dawisha and Bruce Parrott, eds., *Democratic Changes and Authoritarian Reactions in Russia, Ukraine, Belarus, and Moldova* (Cambridge: Cambridge University Press, 1997); Mary McAuley, *Russia's Politics of Uncertainty* (Cambridge: Cambridge University Press, 1997); and Michael

Urban, with Vyacheslav Igrunov and Sergei Mitrokhin, *The Rebirth of Politics in Russia* (Cambridge: Cambridge University Press, 1997).

75. For a detailed analysis, published in 1986, of the characteristics associated with this concept of "developed socialism in a post-industrial state," see Kelley, *The Politics of Developed Socialism.*

76. Hough, "The Bureaucratic Model and the Nature of the Soviet System," *Journal of Comparative Administration* 5, No. 2 (August 1973): 134–167. Pluralism in the Soviet Union was discussed more fully in Hough and Fainsod, "The Distribution of Power," in *How the Soviet Union is Governed*, Chap. 14, particularly pp. 547–555.

77. Alfred G. Meyer, *The Soviet Political System* (New York: Random House, 1965), pp. 477–478.

78. Quoted in Hough, "The Bureaucratic Model," pp. 135–137.

79. *Ibid.*, p. 135.

80. Adam B. Ulam, *The Russian Political System* (New York: Random House, 1974), p. 75.

81. The best sources are Oliver, "'Perestroika' and Public Administration in the USSR," and Lazarev, "Improvement of the Administrative Machinery in the USSR."

82. Rose, "Getting By Without Government: Everyday Life in Russia."

83. "The Crisis of Public Administration in Russia," p. 131.

84. For more details, see Stephan Handelman, "The Russian 'Mafiya'," *Foreign Affairs* 73, No. 2 (March/April 1994): 83–96.

85. See Lesage, "The Crisis of Public Administration in Russia," pp. 131–132.

86. Roeder's "new institutionalist approach to authoritarian institutions" is elaborated in *Red Sunset: The Failure of Soviet Politics.*

87. "The Politics of Resentment," at pp. 36 and 41.

88. "Getting By Without Government: Everyday Life in Russia," p. 57.

89. McAuley, *Russia's Politics of Uncertainty*, p. 11.

90. Nicholas D. Kristof, "The Rise of China," *Foreign Affairs* 72, No. 5 (November/December 1993): 59–74, at p. 63.

91. For recent generalized treatments of the Chinese political system, refer to Lucian Pye, *The Dynamics of Chinese Politics* (Cambridge, MA: Oelgeschlager, Gunn, & Hain, 1981); Jurgen Domes, *The Government and Politics of the PRC: A Time of Transition* (Boulder, CO: Westview Press, 1985); Harry Harding, *China's Second Revolution: Reform after Mao* (Washington, DC: The Brookings Institution, 1987); Victor C. Falkenheim, "The Limits of Political Reform," *Current History* 86 (September 1987): 261–265, 279–281; Benedict Stavis, *China's Political Reforms: An Interim Report* (New York: Praeger, 1988); John Gittings, *China Changes Face* (Oxford: Oxford University Press, 1989); James T. Myers, "Modernization and 'Unhealthy Tendencies,'" *Comparative Politics* 21 (January 1989): 193–213; John P. Burns, "China's Governance: Political Reform in a Turbulent Environment," *The China Quarterly* 119 (September 1989): 481–518; Richard Baum and Stanley Rosen [special eds.] "China's Post-Mao Reforms in Comparative Perspective," *Studies in Comparative Communism* 22, Nos. 2 and 3 (Summer/Autumn 1989): 111–264; Ross Terrill, *China in Our Time: The Epic Saga of the People's Republic, from the Communist Victory to Tiananmen Square and Beyond* (New York: Simon & Schuster, 1992); Weizhi Xie, "The Semihierarchical Totalitarian Nature of

Chinese Politics," *Comparative Politics* 25, No. 3 (April 1993): 313–330; Suzanne Ogden, "The Chinese Communist Party: Key to Pluralism and a Market Economy?," *SAIS Review* 13, No. 2 (Summer/Fall 1993): 107–125; David Shambaugh, "Assessing Deng Xiaoping's Legacy," *The China Quarterly*, No. 135 (September 1993): 409–411; June Teufel Dreyer, *China's Political System: Modernization and Tradition* (New York: Paragon House, 1993); Gerald Segal, "China's Changing Shape," *Foreign Affairs* 73, No. 3 (May/June 1994): 43–58; and Richard Baum, *Burying Mao: Chinese Politics in the Age of Deng Xiaoping* (Princeton, NJ: Princeton University Press, 1994). More specialized studies dealing with Chinese bureaucracy include A. Doak Barnett, "Mechanisms for Party Control in the Government Bureaucracy in China," pp. 415–436, and Ezra R. Vogel, "Politicized Bureaucracy: Communist China," pp. 556–568, both in Fred W. Riggs, ed., *Frontiers of Development Administration* (Durham, NC: Duke University Press, 1970); Franz Schurmann, *Ideology and Organization in Communist China*, 2nd ed., enlarged (Berkeley, CA: University of California Press, 1968); Chalmers Johnson, "The Changing Nature and Locus of Authority in Communist China," in John M. H. Lindbeck, ed., *China: Management of a Revolutionary Society* (Seattle: University of Washington Press, 1971), pp. 34–76; Lowell Dittmer, "Revolution and Reconstruction in Contemporary Chinese Bureaucracy," *Journal of Comparative Administration* 5, No. 4 (1974): 443–486; Harry Harding, *Organizing China: The Problem of Bureaucracy 1949–1976* (Stanford, CA: Stanford University Press, 1981); Jean C. Robinson, "De-Maoization, Succession, and Bureaucratic Reform," prepared for the 1982 Annual Meeting of the American Political Science Association, 34 pp. mimeo.; Anne Freedman and Maria Chan Morgan, "Controlling Bureaucracy in China (1949–1980)," in Krishna K. Tummala, ed., *Administrative Systems Abroad* (Washington, DC: University Press of America, 1982), pp. 229–264; Monte R. Bullard, *China's Political-Military Evolution* (Boulder, CO: Westview Press, 1985); June Teufel Dreyer, "Civil-Military Relations in the People's Republic of China," *Comparative Strategy* 5, No. 1 (1985): 27–49; King W. Chow, "Public Administration as a Discipline in the People's Republic of China: Development, Issues, and Prospects," in Farazmand, *Handbook of Comparative and Development Public Administration*, Chap. 14, pp. 185–197; Xiaowei Zang, "The Fourteenth Central Committee of the CCP: Technocracy or Political Technocracy?," *Asian Survey* 33, No. 8 (August 1993): 787–803; Ting Gong, *The Politics of Corruption in Contemporary China* (Westport, CT: Praeger, 1994); King K. Tsao and John Abbott Worthley, "Chinese Public Administration: Change with Continuity During Political and Economic Development," *Public Administration Review* 55, No. 2 (March/April 1995): 164–174; Steven E. Aufrecht and Li Siu Bun, "Reform with Chinese Characteristics: The Context of Chinese Civil Service Reform," *Public Administration Review* 55, No. 1 (March/April 1995): 175–182; Tso-chiu Lam and Hon S. Chan, "China's New Civil Service: What the Emperor is Wearing and Why," *Public Administration Review* 56, No. 5 (September/October 1996): 479–486 (including responses by Aufrecht and Li, and Worthley and Tsao); Koutsai Tom Liou, "Issues and Lessons of Chinese Civil Service Reform," *Public Personnel Management* 26, No. 4 (Winter 1997): 505–514; Jiang Xianrong, "An Overview of the Reform of China's Administrative System and Organizations and Its Prospects," *International*

Review of Administrative Sciences 63 (1997): 251–256; and John Abbott Worthley and King K. Tsao, "Reinventing Government in China: A Comparative Analysis," *Administration & Society* 31, No. 5 (November 1999): 571–587.

92. Xiaowei Zang, "The Fourteenth Central Committee of the CCP: Technocracy or Political Technocracy?," p. 803.

93. Shambaugh, "Assessing Deng Xiaoping's Legacy," p. 410.

94. Among the analysts cited in Note 91, Suzanne Ogden is relatively optimistic, feeling that the gradualist approach of the Chinese Communist Party, although not leading soon to democracy, may create sufficient pluralism, along with economic growth, to make the Chinese transition less painful than has been the case in Eastern Europe or the former Soviet Union. Gerald Segal is not as sanguine, saying that the basic question over China's future "revolves around the degree to which Beijing's authority will give way to the centrifugal pull of China's increasingly dynamic periphery." Segal, "China's Changing Shape," p. 43.

95. Barnett, "Party Control in the Government Bureaucracy in China," p. 429.

96. Townsend, "Politics in China," p. 403.

97. Dittmer, "Revolution and Reconstruction in Contemporary Chinese Bureaucracy," p. 480.

98. Vogel, "Politicized Bureaucracy," pp. 561, 563.

99. Quoted in Freedman and Morgan, "Controlling Bureaucracy in China," at p. 248. One byproduct of efforts to revitalize the administrative system has been the rapid growth of public administration as a field of study and research. For details, see King W. Chow, "Public Administration as a Discipline in the People's Republic of China: Development, Issues, and Prospects."

100. Robinson, "De-Maoization, Succession, and Bureaucratic Reform," pp. 2, 15, 29. A continuing problem is widespread corruption in the system. For a recent examination of corruption issues, refer to *The Politics of Corruption in Contemporary China*, by Ting Gong, who concludes that for corruption to be contained, "China needs not only bold economic innovations toward a market economy, but also comprehensive political reforms to install effective control over power holders." *Ibid.*, p. 162.

101. Koutsai Tom Liou, "Issues and Lessons of Chinese Civil Service Reform," p. 510.

7

Administration in Less Developed Nations

Potentially the most significant political fact of the twentieth century has been the closing out of the colonial era and the emergence, in most cases as newly independent states, of the nations of Africa, Asia, Latin America, and the Middle East. We have chosen the term "developing" or "less developed" as most appropriate to describe these countries as a group, recognizing that any adjective is inadequate to such a task, and that the one selected has shortcomings as noted in Chapter 3. Alternative descriptive labels, such as "emerging" or "modernizing" in earlier and "Third World" or "the South" in more recent usage, have at least equivalent deficiencies for our purposes. Admittedly no single word or phrase can cope with the diversities of such disparate nations as Iraq, Ghana, India, and Mexico, to mention only a few countries that do not represent the extremes of contrast but do suggest the variety that exists in location, resources, population, history, culture, religion, and a multitude of other factors. Just as the more developed nations can be sorted into "first tier" and "second tier" categories, the less developed can be considered as falling into "third tier" and "fourth tier" groupings, reflecting the differences between such contrasting cases as Brazil and Haiti in the western hemisphere, South Korea and Bangladesh in Asia, or the Republic of South Africa and Zaire in sub-Saharan Africa.

Despite their differences, all of these countries are caught up in a process of drastic and rapid social change, not just the continuous change that any society undergoes, but change that is critical and disruptive. Put in terms of "models" of societies which have often in the past been used for purposes of analysis, they are moving from the traditional toward the modern type. They are all in transition, no longer traditional and not yet modern, either as they view themselves or as others view them. To the extent that "modernity" itself is losing its attractiveness for some of these countries, the alternatives being considered differ markedly from the "postindustrial" society often forecast as the future of countries which have been considered more developed. In sum, we are concerned here with a large group of nation-states whose current status and future prospects have produced a commonality among them in their own self-perceptions, which also provides a basis for our consideration of their political regimes and administrative systems.

THE IDEOLOGY OF DEVELOPMENT

Despite recent misgivings, most of these developing countries continue to share a generalized consensus of the objectives toward which change should be directed. Since this "ideology of development" is crucial to an understanding of politics and administration in these countries, we need to look at its major elements.

The twin goals of development are nation-building and socio-economic progress.[1] Agreement on the desirability of these goals is found even among political leaders who show wide variation in political orientation, political strategy, social origin, and opportunity for success in goal attainment. To the extent that they are politically motivated at all, the rank and file of the population in these countries share the belief that these are proper objectives, and will tend to bring pressure on political leaders who may be tempted to give precedence to more immediate and selfishly motivated aims. These paired values seem to explain to a substantial degree the accepted ideological commitment in these developing countries.

Esman has described nation-building as "the deliberate fashioning of an integrated political community within fixed geographic boundaries in which the nation-state is the dominant political institution."[2] Nationhood, said Rustow in 1967, "now has become the vocal aspiration of 130 peoples all linked tightly through modern means of communication and transport," whereas earlier it was "the proud achievement of a few people isolated from the rest of humanity."[3]

It is somewhat paradoxical that the concept of the nation-state has gained so in appeal to the rest of the world at the same time that the nation as a political unit and nationalism as a doctrine have been increasingly questioned in the West where the nation-state system originated. The urge to seek a national identity is probably in part a reaction to escape from colonialism, expressing a desire to emulate the nationhood of the former colonial power once independence has been gained.

Actual achievement of nationhood in most of the emerging areas is not an easy task. It calls for success in meeting the challenge of political development, requiring the creation, as summarized by Palmer, of "a system of political institutions capable of controlling the state's population, of mobilizing the state's human and material resources toward the ends of economic and social modernization, and of coping with the strain of social, economic, and political change without abdicating its control and mobilization roles."[4]

In the case of Europe, this process was indigenous and slow. Kautsky calls it "the politics of modernization from within." He reviews the gradual transformation of society in Western Europe from beginnings as far back as the eleventh century, pointing out that it was brought about by natives of the society and was in a sense organic to the society, thereby allowing more time for adjustment to different strata of the population and reducing the shock of sudden transformation. The developing countries, on the other hand, face the trauma of "modernization from without," which involves "a rather sudden break with the hitherto traditional past and can be brought to a society either by foreigners or by some of its own natives or by both."[5] Although this distinction is not, of course, clear-cut, since both internal and external factors will always be present, the matter of preponderance is an important point, and emphasizes the difficulties and hazards of rapid "modernization from without," which is the typical prospect for developing nations.

Also in the case of Europe, the movement toward nationalism was largely one of uniting under one government people already speaking a single language. Most of the developing states are artificial entities in the sense that they are the products of colonial activity rather than of a pre-existing political loyalty. Their boundaries likewise were often drawn by imperial powers without regard to ethnic groupings, excluding people with close cultural ties and including minority groups opposed to assimilation. The situation leads Kautsky to remark that whatever nationalism in underdeveloped countries may be, it commonly lacks this key language element.[6] Such problems, although prevalent throughout the developing world, are especially acute in Africa. "An old recipe has it that, to make rabbit pie, you must first catch the rabbit. By the same token, to engage in nation-building, you must first find the nation. In the African setting, this is likely to be a more hazardous and uncertain venture than anywhere else."[7]

Still another dilemma has been investigated in detail by Inkeles and Smith in their study of individual change in selected developing countries. Observing that many new states were "actually only hollow shells, lacking the institutional structures which make a nation a viable and effective socio-political and economic enterprise," they emphasized that nation-building is an empty exercise "unless the attitudes and capacities of the people keep pace with other forms of development." Independence does not necessarily bring about such articulation, as mounting evidence indicates. "A modern nation needs participating citizens, men and women who take an active interest in public affairs and who exercise their rights and perform their duties as members of a community larger than that of the kinship network and the immediate geographical locality."[8] The authors explore the process of movement of individuals from being traditional to becoming modern personalities, using a concept of "modern man" which they formulate as a research tool. Their thesis is that the essence of national development is the diffusion through the population of the qualities of the modern man, and their study, intended as an aid to the process of modernization, is addressed to explaining how men become modern.

Such obstacles to nation-building as have been mentioned understandably lead to expressions of pessimism about the future. Historian Joseph R. Strayer, for example, predicted in the 1960s that since building a nation-state is a slow and complicated affair, "most of the polities created in the last fifty years are never going to complete the process." The new states to which he gave the best chance of success were "those which correspond fairly closely to old political units; those where the experience of living together for many generations within a continuing political framework has given the people some sense of identity; those where there are indigenous institutions and habits of political thinking that can be connected to forms borrowed from outside."[9] Whatever their prospects, the new states put a premium on establishing their nationhood, and give this priority in political action.

The related goal of social and economic progress in the ideology of development may be equally hard to achieve, but it is somewhat more tangible and measurable. Esman identifies it as "the sustained and widely diffused improvement in material and social welfare."[10] The desire to triumph over poverty and to distribute the benefits of industrialization generally in the society are powerful motivations to people just becoming aware of what is possible as demonstrated by the developed nations, including both those with democratic and those with more authoritarian orientations.

The ideology of development sets the sights for political and administrative action, but it does not specify the exact form of the machinery for either politics or administration. As Merghani observes, "there is a general inclination toward a strong government, a strong executive, and high degree of centralization," on the assumption that "without a strong government and a strong leadership the task of national unity and rapid economic and social transformation becomes difficult if not impossible."[11] Beyond this, the mood is one that favors experimentation and adaptation from the successful experience of developed countries, whatever may have been the political paths followed.[12] Shils puts the situation neatly: "The elites of the new states have lying before them, not the image of a future in which no one has as yet lived or of a living and accepted past, but rather an image of their own future profoundly different from their own past, to be lived along the lines of the already existent modern states, which are their contemporaries."[13]

In essence, the distinctive quality of the developmental ideology is the agreement on the desirability of the joint goals of nation-building and material progress combined with a sense of movement toward fulfillment of a long-delayed destiny, underlying which is a nagging uncertainty concerning the prospects for eventual success.[14] The combination is a volatile one, mirrored in the political systems of most of these countries.

THE POLITICS OF DEVELOPMENT

Knowledge of the political process in the developing world is understandably still fragmentary and tentative. It is nevertheless possible on the basis of recent studies of the political experience of developing nations,[15] supplemented by more speculative formulations of political activity in such societies,[16] to identify some of the more obvious and common features of the politics of development. The principal ones appear to be these: (1) a widely shared developmental ideology (discussed above) as the source of basic political goals; (2) a high degree of reliance on the political sector for achieving results in the society, coupled often with ineffectiveness in actual accomplishment; (3) widespread incipient or actual political instability; (4) modernizing elitist leadership, accompanied by a wide "political gap" between the rulers and the ruled; and (5) an imbalance in the growth of political institutions, with the bureaucracy among those in the more mature category.

Developmental aims and the urgency with which they are sought inevitably mean that state action is the principal vehicle for accomplishment. Neither time nor means is available for gradualness or for primary reliance on private enterprise, as was possible in the Western countries, which developed earlier. The political element almost automatically assumes a central importance in the developing society. Some version of "socialism" tended to be the dominant preference until recently, and a philosophy with a Marxist label, emphasizing industrial expansion and social welfare and denouncing the evils of foreign capitalism, was commonly given lip service, although one commentator remarked that it was "an ideology resembling that of Ataturk more than Marx—an ideology of development and industrialization based on national culture and tradition and related to local conditions."[17] At any rate, the state was and is seen as the main hope for guiding the society toward modernization.

Paradoxically, such reliance on political responses is coupled with widespread political alienation and antipathy toward politicians. Shils calls this "the oppositional mentality." He traces it to the fact that prior to independence most political activity was directed toward gaining freedom from the colonial power. Politics was agitational and remonstrative rather than constructive and responsible. The oppositional attitude has carried over and is strong not only among the leaders in the movement for independence, but also among the new intellectuals, and among students in the younger generation. The resulting distrust of politicians and low esteem for them, according to Shils, "is a striking feature of the outlook of the people of the new states. Politicians are frequently thought to be timid, compromising, indecisive, dishonest, wasteful, selfish, etc."[18] At the same time that unprecedented demands are being made for political performance, active political participation does not appeal to many in the most promising recruitment groups, and those who do engage in political careers are apt to lose rather than gain in prestige. This probably is a carryover from the colonial period, as well as one expression of the recognition that the task of reconciling expectations with prospects is an exceedingly difficult one, and the outlook for success uncertain.

Christopher Clapham, in his 1985 survey of politics in these countries, places special emphasis on state fragility. The rulers of these "weak and artificial states, only too aware of the feebleness of the instrument on which they have to rely," often try unsuccessfully to suppress opposition, with resulting violence. Even more common is inefficiency and exploitation. As a result, even though the state can claim credit for success in the achievement of national independence, it generally has a poor record in the maintenance of effective political institutions that can attain national goals.[19] Joel Migdal views the common predicament as one in which strong societies hinder the emergence of strong states, leading to a pathological "politics of survival" strategy on the part of state leaders which converts the focus of state activities to an "arena of accommodations," further perpetuating patterns of fragmented social control.[20]

Political instability is another closely related prominent characteristic. In his 1969 survey of approximately 100 countries, von der Mehden found that in almost two-thirds of them there had been either successful coups or serious attempts to overthrow the government. In eleven of the fourteen colonies that achieved independence from 1945 through 1955, the governments had been either overthrown or attacked. Extraconstitutional governments had been imposed in twenty-six states in the Afro-Asian area alone. He concluded that the maintenance of stable governments is plainly one of the major problems of the emerging nations, and that such figures are "not such as to give the early optimists much comfort."[21] Writing in the mid-1970s, Gerald Heeger concurred that in the preceding years almost every underdeveloped state had experienced "political instability in one form or another—military coups and mutinies, insurrections, political assassinations, rioting, chaotic factional conflict among leaders, and so forth."[22] Writing in the late 1980s, Andrain confirmed the continuance of this common pattern for bringing about political change.[23] Although there has been some improvement in recent years, contemporary news reports indicate the persistence of such conditions. As compared to the more developed polities, the typical situation in less developed countries is one of political uncertainty, discontinuity, and extra-legal change.

Heeger's explanation for the politics of instability is that consolidation of the political system in a new state is difficult for any regime, regardless of its characteristics, because of the segmental and amorphous nature of these polities.

Independence brings "a political center in the form of central government and political institutions," and political conflict focuses on "gaining access to and control of the various strategic roles within the new political center." The search for dominance leads to efforts at coalition among groups not strong enough to capture the machinery of government without allies. Successful coalitions then try to expand and consolidate by using their power resources. Usually the stability sought is not attained, because the available political institutions "lack the capability to deal with the consequences of social and economic change" in these societies, such as the highly unbalanced effects of modernization, the rapid escalation of demands by groups upon which the new political system depends, and the exacerbation of communal divisions because of competition for scarce resources.[24]

Political leadership is concentrated in a minute segment of the population in most developing countries. The governing elite, in the sense of those wielding major decision-making power in the political system, tends not only to be small in numbers but also separated socially and culturally, as well as politically, from the bulk of the citizenry. The elitist group is not the same everywhere, although there are some common characteristics. During the past half-century, according to von der Mehden, the new nations have experienced four types of political leadership: colonial, traditional, nationalist, and economic. The common pattern has been for the colonial elite, who often worked during the colonial period indirectly through traditional and economic elite groups, to give way after independence to a nationalist elite which holds almost complete power for a time, and is then generally replaced by a "reinfusion of traditional elements into the leadership as memories of the independence struggle wane and recognition of long-term local power relationships increases."[25] In former colonies, the old colonial elite and the economic elite, which frequently consists of resident foreigners, have now been largely excluded from positions of power. In the few independent states that never experienced colonialization, traditional elites have generally been able to retain power longer, although increasingly challenged by modernizing elements pushing for recognition. In Thailand, for example, traditional elements remain strong, as they were in Ethiopia until the mid-1970s.

Whatever the elitist combination in a particular country, the political elite is almost certain to be out of touch with the masses of the population. The gap "is not a gap of inherited traditional status, but one of modern achievement."[26] The peasant majority in most of the new states has been little disturbed from the traditional ways, and still holds the old attitude that the best way to deal with government is by avoidance and noncommitment. Even the desire of political participation is rare, and its practice is rarer. Apathy and withdrawal are common, and efforts to bring about modernizing change may be actively opposed or, just as effectively, resisted. Except in those nations in which a sizable middle class with basic education has emerged, the task of the elite in establishing adequate political communication is immense. The single mass party, a common phenomenon in developing countries, is justified in part as offering the best hope of bridging the gap between the elite and the masses. Even where strenuous efforts are made to involve the people in the villages, they remain, as Shils pointed out, "the 'objects' of modernization and the political activities which seek to bring it about, rather than initiators in the process. Their preferences and responses are of much concern to the political elite, but they do not participate in the dialogue of rulers and ruled."[27]

The isolated position of elitist leadership is emphasized by increasing evidence that in the developing countries, in contrast to the situation in late eighteenth and early nineteenth century Europe, pressures of nonelite groups to be admitted to the elite are often not great, even when the modernizing elite may be open for recruitment and trying to recruit.[28] A permeable elite may not be permeated because eligible candidates cling to traditional values and acquired status in preference to the hazards of political leadership during transition.

Imbalance in political development is another characteristic consequence of past events in the developing countries. Traditional cultural patterns, colonialism, and the telescoping of change have produced political systems that are askew as judged by experience in the more developed polities, particularly those with a representative democratic political framework. Means for interest articulation and aggregation, through such instrumentalities as an informed electorate, organized associational groups, competing political parties, and representative legislative bodies, are either weak or absent except in the most rudimentary form. On the other hand, the executive agencies of government are dominant, under the control of an elitist leadership. This leadership may take various forms, among them the continued rule of an absolutist monarchy, such as in several Arabic countries and in Ethiopia until a few years ago, the emergence of a highly nationalistic mass-mobilization regime, such as that of Egypt, and the takeover of power by one or a group of "strongmen," usually after a military coup, as in Indonesia in 1966 and Chile in 1973. The stability of the regime is likely to be highly dependent on the loyalty and competence of the civil and military bureaucracies, giving these groups with a professional orientation toward government a uniformly influential role, and often making them dominant.

Three trends impacting on this underlying tendency toward imbalance have appeared in sequence during the post–World War II period. Given our primary concern with the civil bureaucracy, each has special relevance and deserves attention. These three trends are: the movement soon after independence away from competitive party systems; the subsequent shift toward military intervention and control of the machinery of government; and the contemporary tendency toward redemocratization.

Movement away from Competitive Party Systems

One element of the Western political heritage that gained almost universal acceptance in the developing countries was the institution of the political party. If party is defined in the broad way suggested by von der Mehden as "an organized group which seeks the control of the personnel and policies of government—a group that pays at least lip service to a principle or set of principles, including the electoral process,"[29] then the formal structure of party government was introduced in most of the new states. Von der Mehden's 1969 survey revealed, however, the extent to which party competition had either disappeared or never actually developed. Of the ninety-eight states classified, he found that only twenty-four, or one-quarter of them, had a party system in which there existed "a reasonable chance for a peaceful change of office." No effective party government was found at all in two-fifths of them, or thirty-eight countries. In five there were Communist one-party systems, in sixteen other forms of one-party governments, and in sixteen, one-party dominant systems.[30] Von der Mehden concluded that with the passage of time political competition had lessened rather than increased, and that the emphasis on unity and cohesion would continue to foster noncompetitive political systems.[31]

Some of the reasons for this trend away from political competitiveness are clear enough. The colonial system contained "the intellectual germs of the one-party state,"[32] with the claim of the dominant-party bureaucracy to represent all segments and interests of the population being directly descended from the claims of colonial bureaucratic rule. In addition, the natural inclination of those who led the battle for independence was to think of themselves as "identified with the nation and, after their accession to power, with the state." Those who disagreed with them were thus viewed "not merely as political opponents but as enemies of the state and nation."[33] A demand for a one-party state may be motivated not only by an urge to safeguard power but also as the only feasible way to push ahead on economic and social fronts and to conserve national unity after the threat of a common external enemy has disappeared.[34] The political doctrine apt to be developed in the new nations was one favoring monopolistic claims to authority in the society by government—what Apter called a "political religion."[35] When such a doctrine becomes a key feature of the polity, the outcome is likely to be some kind of mobilization system "profoundly concerned with transforming the social and spiritual life of a people by rapid and organized methods."[36] Such a "new theocracy" will be inclined to operate through a party as its chosen instrument.

Naturally any mass-mobilization regime, in connection with its drive to monopolize political power and the means of physical coercion, will seek to keep the civil bureaucracy, as well as the army and the police, firmly in check. This is not a milieu in which bureaucratic officials can safely compete for political power, although Apter suggests that civil servants may be excused from some of the pressures for conformity placed on other significant groups. He believes, in some instances, at least, that "a kind of 'positive neutralism' within the state may surround the bureaucratic role, with the effect of exempting them from ritualized practices and religious observances."[37] The higher bureaucracy could anticipate being within the governing elite in such a regime, provided it did not aspire to senior partnership.

Even during the period of low competitiveness among political parties in the less developed countries, Vicky Randall argued in 1988 that there was a need to correct the tendency to dismiss these parties as "of only marginal importance either as distinct institutions or in terms of their impact."[38] She pointed out the clear trend away from the proliferation of single-party mass-mobilization regimes that had been so prominent during the 1960s and 1970s, and she emphasized the variety of these parties, noting that most developing states "have produced political parties at some stage and a good majority have parties of some kind at the present time." She suggested that the frequent reinstatement of some form of party politics following intervals of military rule meant that the political party "performs certain tasks that Third World states cannot easily dispense with or substitute for."[39] Their main importance, Randall concluded, was that they "provide governments with mechanisms of support, whether in building sustaining coalitions or imparting some degree of popular legitimacy; they provide people outside government with a way of influencing and even of overthrowing existing governments." By "bringing together people and government," she observed, they acted as vehicles of new adjustments and hence were likely to be "a recurring element in the politics of modernizing societies."[40] This prediction that the significance of such political parties might show an upswing has since been vindicated by the recent and current redemocratization movement.

Military Intervention and Control

With the decline of competitive political parties, the phenomenon of military intervention in developing polities became so marked that it became the subject of much analysis and speculation.[41] During most of the three decades from the early 1960s through the 1980s the statistics showed an increasing tendency toward military regimes. In 1969 von der Mehden reported that approximately 40 of the 100 nations he surveyed had experienced a military takeover since the end of World War II, and that in half of these there had been more than one successful coup. Among fifty-six states which had gained independence following World War II, one-third had been overthrown by the military since independence.[42] According to Welch, more than a third of the member states of the United Nations were ruled in the mid-1970s by governments installed by military intervention,[43] and Kennedy correctly pointed out in 1974 that military government had become "the most common form of government in the Third World."[44] Finer found that during the eighteen-year period from 1962 through 1980 a total of 152 military coups occurred, bringing the number of "hard core" cases of countries "governed by men who came to power as a result of military intervention" to thirty-seven.[45] Later instances of military takeover or interference added to these numbers. Sivard, using more inclusive criteria, reported that at the end of the 1980s the military held the reins of political power in 64 of 113 Third World countries, the largest number in over a decade.[46] This was 56 percent of the total, according to her measures, as compared to only 26 percent in 1960.

Political action by the military since World War II has usually been related to the tensions that go with major social change, rather than a simple bid for power by an ambitious military leader or clique. Existing political structures, whether indigenous or imposed by a former colonial power, have succumbed to the pressures resulting from unsuccessful efforts to cope with expectations as to political stability and attainment of developmental goals. Military regimes have replaced other political systems of various types. Most frequently they have supplanted short-lived parliamentary competitive systems installed by a colonial power in a newly independent nation, as in Pakistan or Burma. Occasionally they have ousted traditional monarchies, as in Ethiopia and in Afghanistan before the Russian intervention in 1979. The most pronounced tendency has been for military regimes to supersede mass party dominance in the polities of numerous Afro-Asian countries. The largest Communist party outside of the Communist world existed in Indonesia before it was decimated by a military takeover. In Ghana the Convention People's Party and in Mali the Sudanese Union were examples of dominant mobilization parties which gave way to the military. For whatever reasons, Communist regimes seem to have been most immune from this movement toward enhanced political involvement by the military in developing countries.

Military involvement is, of course, a relative matter; it occurs in every political system. Amos Perlmutter has offered a general analysis of the major types of military roles which have evolved in the modern nation-state.[47] The classical professional soldier type is characteristic of stable political systems of the kind usually considered politically developed, with civilian officials maintaining political control over the military. Military activities at this minimum level are confined to what Janowitz has termed "the mark of sovereignty."[48] A second type is what Perlmutter calls the revolutionary soldier, "linked to a political order that is stable despite its origins in an unstable, decaying, or new political system."[49] With this orientation, the military views itself as a partner in a major revolutionary movement. Perlmutter presents Communist China and Israel as prime examples.

Perlmutter's praetorian soldier type is the most prevalent in the political systems of developing countries. Thriving in an environment of political instability, military praetorianism expands military participation until it becomes military intervention, which asserts control of the political process and succeeds in establishing some form of military regime.

Numerous authors have suggested classifications of the varied intensified roles characteristically played by the military in such regimes.[50] The mildest form is what von der Mehden calls "tacit coercion," where the military "does not directly assume power but remains as a major factor in the political environment, setting the conditions for the performance of civilian government." Clapham and Philip call these "veto" regimes. Finer distinguishes between "indirect-limited," "indirect-complete," and "dual rule" regimes, depending on whether the military intervenes "only from time to time to secure various limited objectives," is fully in charge but with puppet civilians in formal leadership positions, or is in alliance with civilian elements with both being essential for survival.

Probably the most common pattern is for the military to take action seizing effective power as what von der Mehden calls a "constitutional caretaker," because it deems "marked crisis, confusion, or corruption to be paralyzing political institutions," with the avowed purpose being "to establish the conditions under which political authority may eventually be returned to a civilian government through constitutional procedures." Finer calls this "open direct" military rule, with the military admittedly in control of important decisions. Clapham and Philip distinguish between "moderator" and "factional" regimes, depending on whether the military professionals involved have a high or a low degree of unity among themselves. Janowitz labels as "civil-military coalitions" both instances in which civilian leadership remains in power, but "only because of the military's passive assent or active assistance," and instances in which the military establishes a caretaker government with the intention of returning power soon to civilian political groups.

A third possibility is for the military, as the spearhead of basic reform or revolution, to regard its role as one, in von der Mehden's words, of creating "new political institutions that, in the long run, will provide for effective civilian government." Janowitz says that this is a "military oligarchy," because the military has taken the political initiative, setting itself up as "the political ruling group," under which "civilian political activity is transformed, constricted, and repressed." Clapham and Philip call these "breakthrough" regimes, because rather than defending "an existing social order with which its own interests are identified, the military seeks to attack a social order which presents a threat" to military interests. Finer prefers to call this "quasi-civilianized direct" military rule because, although the military remains in firm control, an effort is being made to provide more legitimacy for the arrangement even though the earlier civilian regime has been supplanted and the intent is to perpetuate and institutionalize this supplantment. "With quasi-civilianization," he says, "the regime moves out of the realm of the provisional, and purports to be a regime in its own right."[51]

Variations in the role of the military among different geographic regions have been quite noticeable. The tradition of military intervention has been long established in Latin America, and is not primarily a post–World War II phenomenon there. It goes back to the period of the wars of independence of the 1820s and 1830s and the postindependence years, when military control was justified on the basis that qualified civilian leadership was not yet available. Later the situation deteriorated to the point at which strongman government under a military caudillo became the most characteristic form of political leadership in Latin America during the latter part of the nineteenth and early part of the twentieth centuries. In general, the military was a conservative force allied with the church and the landed aristocracy for preservation of the status quo. Early in the 1950s, twelve of the twenty Latin American republics still were under the rule of military men who had originally come to power by force. Then followed a period of antimilitarism which led by 1961 to the elimination (by deposition, assassination, or election of a civilian successor) of all but one of these—General Alfredo Stroessner of Paraguay. The military appeared to be shifting to a mediating role and to the preservation of order and stability, leading to predictions that Latin America had purged itself of military regimes and was entering a phase when civilian rule would be the norm.[52] This lull in military activity proved to be brief, with seven military coups occurring during the early 1960s, deposing presidents who had been duly elected under constitutional processes. This resurgence of militarism subsided later, but several Latin American countries were still under military rule at the end of the 1980s, and a survey of regime transitions in Latin America concluded in 1987 that probably "the basic cyclical swing between authoritarian and democratic modes will continue."[53]

Second only to Latin America, the area with the most extensive historical political involvement of the military has been the Middle East and North Africa. In 1964 four of the twelve states with modern professional armies had a military oligarchy. During the 1960s and the 1970s at least half of the nations in this regional group had extended periods of military rule, and about one-third still have either open military regimes or regimes in which the military is highly influential. As a consequence of the numerous successful military coups in recent years, "by far the most important single factor in Arab politics is the army; by far the most important type of regime is military."[54] The success of military rule here seems also to be linked with the past, with the military groups benefiting from a political tradition of military involvement and sharing some of the attributes of the administrative services of earlier empires. In South and Southeast Asia, six of eighteen countries had regimes in which the military was dominant in 1973.[55] Since then, Cambodia (now renamed Kampuchea) and South Vietnam have been taken over by Communist revolutionary regimes. During the 1980s, two other countries in the region (Bangladesh and Pakistan) were governed under martial law for considerable periods,[56] and in the Philippines political activity was sharply curtailed by Marcos from 1972 until his ouster in 1986.

In sub-Saharan Africa, a colonial history of substantial demilitarization, the relative ease with which independence was granted to many countries without resort to widespread violence, and the newness of most of the African states led to predictions in the early 1960s that political roles for the military would continue to be minor,[57] despite some concern about proclivities for governmental intervention.[58] By the mid-1970s, after a decade of coups, one such optimist reluctantly concluded that it was by then "statistically justifiable to regard military rule as a norm rather than a deviant,"[59] in view of more than a score of successful coups from 1963 through 1974. Military intervention took place in countries which previously had various political systems (competitive parties, mobilization single-parties, authoritarian personal rule), which represented extremes of poverty and relative affluence, and which offered a range of ethnic homogeneity, polarization, and fragmentation. The armed forces of many African states shifted "from political bystanders to political participants."[60] After being a rarity until the early 1960s, military coups d'etat seemed to have become almost systemic in the region, leading Harbison to conclude in 1987 that the military had played "a prominent, even dominating role in African politics during the continent's first generation of independence."[61]

The literature on military intervention addresses numerous controversial issues, only two of which are touched on here: (1) assets and liabilities of the military in governing and (2) the effects of military rule on social change.

The prevailing view as to the political capability of the military has been succinctly expressed both by Janowitz and by Clapham and Philip in these statements: "While it is relatively easy for the military to seize power in a new nation, it is much more difficult for it to govern."[62] "The basic problem about military regimes is one not of how they can gain power, but of what they can do with it."[63]

The basis for this judgment that the seizure of power is usually easy is that the military is made up of professionals in the art of violence and has control over the instruments of violence, making effective opposition difficult or impossible. Edwin Lieuwen put the matter bluntly: "In terms of political institutions, there is no civilian political force or combination of forces able to compete with the armed forces. Once that institution makes up its mind on a given issue, nothing can prevent it from having its way."[64]

Others would apparently consider this an overstatement and would stress the societal prerequisites for success in military takeover, rather than innate characteristics of the military as an institution. Samuel Huntington asserts that "the most important causes of military intervention in politics are not military but political and reflect not the social and organizational characteristics of the military establishment, but the political and institutional structure of the society." These causes particularly relate to "the absence or weakness of effective political institutions in the society."[65] The opportunity to intervene in domestic politics if the military decides to do so is frequently present in the semichaotic conditions of emerging societies, but can be lessened by extending the scope of political participation and by the growth of vigorous political parties and other political instrumentalities.

Having seized or been presented the opportunity, the military has certain positive traits which suit it for political participation. In many of the developing countries, modernization and exposure to Western techniques came earlier to the officers in the armed forces than to other groups in society. The army often provided one of the most feasible routes to status and power for upwardly mobile individuals from the lower and middle social classes. The indoctrination given to the officer corps furnished a professional ideology that combined a strong sense of nationalism with a "puritanical" outlook, an acceptance of "collectivist" forms of economic enterprise, and hostility toward civilian politicians and political groups.[66] These themes fit very well with the prevalent ideology of development in the new states, make military intervention aimed at national unity and progress more likely, and help a military regime to be accepted. The military offers a professional outlook, dedication, and an action orientation. In a transitional society, the situation may well be, as Brown asserts, that the army is a "more supple instrument of modernization" than the civil service, embodying to a greater degree the qualities of "dynamism, empiricism and 'know-how.'"[67]

The armed forces also face some typical handicaps in governing, which may outweigh these advantages. Military professionals lack training and may lack interest in economic planning and the administration of civilian programs, leading to dependency on the civil bureaucracy and the necessity usually of working out a modus vivendi with the higher civil servants. A more basic obstacle is military distrust of the give-and-take of politics, despite the lip service given to the ultimate goal of extensive political participation, and the limited supply in the military profession of "those leadership skills in bargaining and political communications that are required for sustained political leadership."[68] These attitudes and deficiencies inhibit the formulation of clear ideological doctrines or the launching of systematic efforts to educate the public politically. They create a basic problem of establishing sufficient rapport with the national community to retain support, or at least acquiescence. Building a mass base of popular support is crucial for assured continuity in power, but this calls for a political apparatus. The political skill of military leadership is strained to meet such a requirement, although it seems to have been done in Turkey under Ataturk and more recently in Egypt under Nasser, Sadat, and Mubarak.

S. E. Finer has stressed as a flaw of the military in politics that in the rare cases in which it is prepared to disengage, it does not know how to do so. "In most cases," he says, "the military that have intervened in politics are in a dilemma: whether their rule be indirect or whether it be direct, they cannot withdraw from rulership nor can they fully legitimize it. They can neither stay nor go."[69] As a result, they tend to become "transit regimes" which run up and down the scale of intervention.[70]

The usual overall evaluation, therefore, is that although a military regime can meet a need in bringing political stability and reform to societies in which they cannot be provided under other auspices, this is likely to be only a temporary and transitional pattern in political development, leading sometimes to a viable competitive political system under civilian leadership, but more often to some variant form of military oligarchy or to single-party authoritarianism.

On the issue of the effects of military rule on social change in developing countries, consensus is far from achieved and available empirical evidence is inconclusive. Three distinctive points of view have been expressed on this matter during the past forty years, one portraying the military as a positive modernizing force,[71] one regarding military regimes as inhibitors of modernizing social change,[72] and the third (advanced by Huntington) hypothesizing that the impact of military governments varies according to the levels of economic development of the countries concerned.[73]

Some major efforts have been made to test these divergent views, utilizing empirical data from many developing countries in different geographical regions, with somewhat contradictory results, but with slight support for claims that military regimes have an impressive record as modernizers. The first study, by Eric Nordlinger, analyzed data collected earlier on seventy-four developing non-Communist countries. He essentially confirmed Huntington's third hypothesis, with the qualification that "only at the very lowest levels of political participation and only in the context of a minuscule middle class" do military officers sponsor modernizing policies.[74] Two later studies discounted all three of the points of view summarized earlier, including Huntington's. McKinlay and Cohan, utilizing data on all the independent states of the world except Communist ones, concluded that there was no clear evidence to differentiate the economic performance of their three regime types—military, civilian, and hybrid.[75] In the most recent study, which used the data analyzed by Nordlinger plus a new set of data for seventy-seven countries covering the decade from 1960 to 1970, Robert H. Jackman found that "military intervention in the politics of the Third World has no unique effects on social change, regardless of either the level of economic development or geographic region."[76] According to Jackman, observers who have attributed unique political skills to the military are probably mistaken. Also he finds no support for the proposition that military regimes "assume different mantles" as countries move between levels of development.

Even if we accept Jackman's conclusion that "blanket statements portraying military governments in the Third World as either progressive or reactionary are without empirical foundation,"[77] this does not mean, of course, that no military regime at a particular time in a particular country will ever have any effect on what happens with regard to social change. Certainly doubt has been cast on any anticipation that military rule guarantees modernization, even in the more backward and traditional countries. However, it is still a matter of interest and importance as to what stance is taken on issues of social change by the leadership of a given military regime.

In closing this summary of military intervention and governance, I want to reiterate a point agreed upon by commentators who differ on other matters—namely, that collaboration at the operating level with civilian bureaucrats is absolutely essential for the maintenance over any substantial period of time of every variety of military regime, whether it rules directly, indirectly, or on a clear-cut dual basis in a partnership arrangement with the civil bureaucracy.[78]

Redemocratization

The current tendency in these polities, as well as globally, is a pronounced movement toward greater political competition, which has received a great deal of attention during recent years.[79] Perhaps the best known presentation is Huntington's argument that the world is in the midst of a "third wave" of democratic expansion.[80] By the early 1990s, using a rather generous standard for defining democracy, a count on a global basis by Freedom House classified as democracies eighty-nine or well over half of the 171 countries rated, twice the number counted twenty years earlier. With thirty-two countries considered in some form of democratic transition, this meant that seventy percent of all countries were rated as already democratic or moving in that direction.[81]

Such estimates, of course, include countries (from the old Soviet Union, southern and central Europe, and elsewhere) that would not be among the less developed categories that are our central concern. Robert Pinkney, who concentrated more closely on this group, confirmed that they conformed to this overall pattern. He pointed out in 1994 that nearly all of the governments in Latin America had been chosen by means of competitive election. In Africa, with a total of forty-one nations, contested elections had been held within the past five years or are scheduled for the near future in twenty-five of them. In Asia, countries that had emerged from or had weakened military or personal rule included South Korea, Pakistan, Bangladesh, Thailand, and Nepal, with the dominant one-party systems of Singapore and Taiwan in a borderline category. Authoritarian rule still prevailed, in his judgment, principally in the Asian cases of Burma and Indonesia, and in much of North Africa and the Middle East. This transformation, "over so much of the world in so short a time," was considered by him to be "remarkable by any standards."[82] The last several years have brought a few additional instances of moves toward greater democratization, with Nigeria in Africa and Indonesia in Asia as prominent examples.

In Pinkney's view, three factors account for the pressure to continue democracy where it exists or to restore it where it had been suspended. First is the negative experience from authoritarian rule, "which generally failed to deliver the promised material benefits yet was frequently more repressive, especially in Latin America, than anything experienced in the recent past." The second factor is that there is "no longer any long-term claim to legitimacy, in most parts of the world, other than pluralist democracy. Outside the Middle East, we no longer have societies that can sustain monarchies or theocracies, and there are no longer communist or fascist regimes in Europe to offer a vision of popular mobilization under the banner of a single party. In the absence of any plausible alternative, the debate is no longer about whether pluralist democracy is desirable, but about how quickly it should be attained and in what form." Finally, with the end of the Cold War, "there are fewer pretexts for supporting authoritarians as bulwarks against communism," and "Western aid is increasingly tied to a commitment to pluralism."[83] Taken together, although with impacts varying from country to country, these factors have accounted for the trend toward political pluralism combined with a mixed economy.

Despite the progress of this redemocratization movement, nearly all of the commentators on it also voice concern as to its long run viability. Huntington speculates about the possibility of a third reverse wave, similar to the reverse waves that ended the two earlier periods of democratic expansion.[84] Diamond and Plattner note that in Latin America, the region in which third wave democratic progress has been most extensive, many of the new democracies have poorly developed and generally ineffective political institutions, have been unable to deal adequately with economic problems, have not settled the issue as to the proper role of the military, and have weak records in protecting human rights. Moreover, Latin America already has a history of pendulous swings back and forth in its experience with democratic governance. As for Africa, they assert that progress toward democracy is even more fragile, with the democratic trend springing primarily from the pervasive failures of authoritarian regimes, and with most of the democratic transitions yet to be completed while the new regimes face daunting challenges. Both Joseph and Ihonvbere are also skeptical about democratization in Africa, with the former pointing out that ostensibly reformist regimes in sub-Saharan Africa are more virtual that real, and the latter stating that "the general feeling is that no real transition is taking place."[85] Munch and Leff emphasize the importance of modes of transition toward democracy and their differential impacts, using seven countries in South America and East Central Europe as examples.[86]

The overall conclusion of Diamond and Plattner is that although globally opportunities for democratization are greater than ever before in modern history, time is of the essence, with "wise leadership and intelligent institution-building" required to "consolidate tentative and fragile democracies around the world."[87]

Hence Diamond's prediction is that "for the near term, democracy is likely to continue to expand and to manifest itself as a global phenomenon; nevertheless, in most of the world throughout the 1990s, democracy will remain insecure and embattled."[88] Schutz and Slater are somewhat less optimistic, stating that "Third World instability will persist. Shifting demographic patterns such as intensifying urbanization, further decreases in the already imperiled quality of social and economic life, the political emergence and activism of ethnic minorities (in some cases majorities), and continuing endemic violence ensure the likelihood of more revolutionary activity. . . . Outside interests, already a factor in the emergence of revolutionary movements, will likely become even more intensive as global interdependence intensifies. The diminution of superpower rivalry . . . may in the long run exacerbate, rather than inhibit, revolutionary challenges to Third World regimes."[89]

A realistic assessment thus must be that despite the evidence of extensive redemocratization during the last decade or so, these less developed nations exhibit continuing persistent traits of political instability and imbalance.

POLITICAL REGIME VARIATIONS

Attempts to identify patterns of political resemblance among developing countries should not be allowed to obscure what differentiates them. Students of the comparative politics of development have turned more and more to the task of compiling and correlating data on a large number of variables for cross-national comparisons,[90] and to suggestions for classifying political systems into regime types.[91]

Regime classifications which have been proposed show great similarity but little uniformity. This reflects mainly the difficult and tentative nature of the enterprise, although it also demonstrates individual differences in perspective and perhaps even a proprietary interest in having a scheme of one's own. The most significant point of agreement is that the groupings should not be made on the basis of geographical propinquity or common colonial background, important though these factors concededly are. Criteria for classification which cut across locational, historical, and cultural lines are used. A regime type may and usually does include polities from several of the major regional segments of the developing world. Particular categories suggested also frequently match up from one scheme to another, even though the overall systems are not identical and the category labels differ.

No classification system of this variety can claim to be definitive; these categories are not "ideal types" in the Weberian sense. Instead they are modal types which seek to simplify reality for heuristics purposes, serving as guides for better understanding. A decision as to the optimal number of types to be used must be a matter of judgment, taking into account S. E. Finer's advice that "the categories must be neither so many as to make comparison impossible nor so few as to make contrasts impossible."[92] No attempt need be made to fit every existing developing nation into one of the categories used. Such an undertaking would be extremely hazardous. Borderline or mutating cases are difficult to classify,[93] and these are apt to be numerous. A few countries may not be well described by the characteristics of any one or a combination of types. For example, this may be the case currently for some of the successor states to the Soviet Union, Haiti, and the Republic of South Africa as they pass through rapid and drastic transitions.

Since the classification system we use draws heavily on some of the proposals made by others, a sampling of them may be useful for background purposes. These systems differ considerably as to their principal focus for comparative purposes. Coleman's pioneering effort, which in turn was based on earlier work by Shils, ranks the political systems of developing nations along two dimensions, based on their degree of competitiveness and their degree of political modernity, and then presents functional profiles grouping them into six types, including among them traditional oligarchy, modernizing oligarchy, tutelary democracy, and political democracy. Diamant uses the dimension of political system style, referring to "the manner in which power is exercised and the manner in which decisions on public policy are made in the system,"[94] leading to four types: traditional-autocratic, limited polyarchy, polyarchy, and movement regime. Along similar lines, Andrain concentrates on modes of decision-making in the formulation and implementation of public policies, in turn reflecting basic societal characteristics, and elaborates an earlier typology suggested by Apter classifying Third World political systems as folk, bureaucratic-authoritarian, reconciliation, or mobilization. Riggs presents a neo-institutional typology, with a major three-way breakdown into bureaucratic polities, monarchies, and republics, plus a sub-breakdown of the republics into single-party, parliamentary, and presidentialist regimes.

Esman's primary purpose in formulating his classification scheme was to assess the relative capacities of different countries to perform developmental tasks successfully by utilizing "the criteria of purposeful leadership, a developmentally relevant doctrine, and capacity to create and effectively to deploy a variety of action and communication instruments."[95] On the assumption that regimes sharing common structural and behavioral characteristics would approach the tasks of nation-building and socioeconomic progress in similar ways, he designated five political regime types with this objective in mind: (1) conservative oligarchies, (2) authoritarian military reformers, (3) competitive interest-oriented party systems, (4) dominant mass party systems, and (5) Communist totalitarian systems.

The criterion of classification used by Merle Fainsod is "the relationship of bureaucracies to the flow of political authority," making his breakdown into types of particular interest to us. He also distinguishes five different alternatives:

(1) ruler-dominated bureaucracies, (2) military-dominated bureaucracies, (3) ruling bureaucracies, (4) representative bureaucracies, and (5) party-state bureaucracies. Each occurs in the context of a particular political system.[96] On the assumption that the political system type would be the most crucial standard for distinguishing among the public bureaucracies of developing countries, I adopted during the mid-1960s in the original version of this study a classification plan that was designed to place special emphasis on the relationship between the basic political characteristics of the regime and the political role of the bureaucracy in the system. Although influenced by other classification proposals, it most closely resembled those of Esman and Fainsod. The following categories were chosen: (1) traditional-autocratic systems, (2) bureaucratic elite systems—civil and military, (3) polyarchal competitive systems, (4) dominant-party semicompetitive systems, (5) dominant-party mobilization systems, and (6) Communist totalitarian systems.

With modifications responding to subsequent shifts in political arrangements, this approach is still well suited to our needs. As mentioned above, a comprehensive classification including every developing country would be difficult to achieve. However, for our purposes, complete classification is unnecessary. We try merely to identify some of the countries in each category used, and offer illustrative cases to examine the impact on bureaucratic characteristics and behavior of the political features of the regime type.

In recent years, the regime categories which have undergone the most significant alterations, either in regime characteristics or number of country examples, are those with traditional and with bureaucratic political elites. These changes can be taken into account in either or both of two ways. One is to subdivide the regime type into additional more discriminating types. The other is to give special attention, in the selection of illustrative countries for a regime type, to the importance of including representatives of the most notable existing orientations contained within the type.

With regard to what I referred to earlier as traditional-autocratic systems, my choice has been to make a slight change in the designation and to identify two major orientations among nation-states with such regimes, without adding another regime type. Now labeled traditional elite systems, illustrative countries within the type are identified as being either ortho-traditional or neo-traditional. The distinction between these orientations is explained below.

The problem of dealing with the array of bureaucratic elite systems is more complicated and its resolution more debatable. In the mid-1970s, I concluded that a single category for all bureaucratic elite regimes was no longer adequate, in view of the dramatic spread of such regimes on almost a global basis and increasingly pronounced variations in the characteristics of regimes in this category. Numerous polities had already moved from other categories into this one—especially from the traditional, polyarchal competitive, and dominant-party mobilization groupings. I also identified several factors which appeared to deserve special emphasis in selecting the most useful categories for subdividing bureaucratic elite regimes, and with these factors in mind substituted five differentiated types for the single broader bureaucratic elite category. These were not mutually exclusive groupings, however, and they did not differentiate among all possible combinations of the key factors. They were selected on the assumption that they accounted for the most common possibilities among developing countries at that time.

Although these factors all continued to be important, my view a decade later in the mid-1980s was that only one of them should be used as the basis for placement of bureaucratic elite regimes into distinct types, and that the other factors should be taken into consideration as orientations in the choice of illustrative country examples.

The essential criterion for separation into types was the familiar distinction between regimes which are headed by one powerful individual and collegial regimes where authority is shared more or less equally by a group of individuals. In Latin American politics since the nineteenth century, the caudillo has represented the first option, and the junta the second. In the states of contemporary Africa, Claude E. Welch, Jr. suggests a contrast between "personalist" and "corporatist" regimes, with the former centering on "the head-of-state/commander-in-chief," and the latter being collegial rather than hierarchical in nature.[97] My choice of terminology is to call one category "personalist bureaucratic elite systems," and the other "collegial bureaucratic elite systems."

In most instances, both personalist and collegial bureaucratic elite regimes will have military officials in leadership positions; however, there have been examples both of civilian-headed personalist regimes and of collegial regimes in which civilians and military officers share the top leadership posts. A secondary consideration is the pattern of participation by civilian bureaucrats in governance below the uppermost level. In the terminology used both by Janowitz and by Perlmutter, a military oligarchy exists if the military leaders are clearly in control and civilians have been co-opted in plainly indicated subordinate capacities. In what Janowitz calls a civil-military coalition and Perlmutter labels authoritarian praetorianism, there is much more equality in actual influence and a mutual interdependency of the two elements, whose combined participation in governance is crucial.

After again reviewing in 1990 the current adequacy of this roster of political regime types, I decided to add one additional category. This regime type admittedly has a basis varying somewhat from the others, because its distinctive characteristic is frequent movement back and forth between two other regime categories. Of course, the possibility of transition from one regime type to another has been assumed, and a variety of such transitions have occurred historically. The record shows clearly, however, that the most common type of shift has been back and forth between bureaucratic elite regimes (usually but not necessarily collegial rather than personalist) and polyarchal competitive regimes. When it happens several times within a relatively short period, this phenomenon may constitute the most important political factor affecting the public bureaucracy, thus justifying recognition of this set of relationships as constituting a separate political regime category. One aspect of such political circumstances is that the bureaucracy, particularly the military branch of it, is continually in a position to reassert dominance, even if it is currently subordinated to party control. I use the label "pendulum regimes" to identify this category. Examples are provided from a wide range of less developed nation-states, representing various geographical locations, colonial backgrounds, cultural and religious settings, and so forth, thus satisfying the expectation that a regime type should include a cross-section of developing countries.

The differences in orientation referred to above continue to be pertinent not only to bureaucratic elite regimes but to many of these pendulum regimes as well. The most common orientation is a pervasive emphasis on the maintenance of political stability, or its restoration if disorder has become widespread. This law-and-order orientation provides a justification for legitimacy by a bureaucratic elite regime, but it also usually brings a claim that circumstances have compelled an intervention in the political process, that this intervention is temporary, and that political competition will be normalized as soon as conditions permit. When the pendulum has swung temporarily toward more political competition, the polyarchal competitive regime must be primarily concerned with its capacity to preserve law and order as a means of avoiding another shift of the pendulum back toward bureaucratic elitism.

Other orientations needing to be highlighted are instances in which the current regime has recently replaced either an indigenous traditional elite system, or a colonial power which had been dominant for an extended period leaving a distinctive imprint on both the military and civil bureaucracies. In each case, the current regime is preoccupied with carry-over forces from the earlier era, usually with the intent of eradication in the first situation and with the objective of preservation with adaptations in the second. Neither of these possibilities exists in Latin America, but each of them can be found in Asia and Africa.

Finally, regimes may differ in orientation with regard to the role they attribute to the state as a corporate entity representing functional interest groupings in the society and in the extent of their reliance on technical expertise for the attainment of regime goals. Elites with a pronounced corporate-technocratic orientation have appeared in Latin America and to some extent elsewhere. They show a marked contrast in their makeup and methods of operation to instances where the concern is mainly with gaining political control, imposing order, and preserving the existing social and economic arrangements.[98]

The consequence of corporatism and technocracy as a composite ideological rationale is a determination to extend the power of the state over major societal forces coupled with acceptance of the goal that the polity should be depoliticized.[99]

This revised scheme for dealing with political regime variations produces a classification plan with eight categories, which provide the basis for exploration in the next two chapters of political-bureaucratic relationships in selected developing countries. Primary emphasis is given to the shared characteristics within each type, but countries are chosen for case studies to show important variations in orientation among them. A secondary interest is how the various types relate to one another.

In this last context, two broad groupings among the eight types immediately suggest themselves. As Lee Sigelman has pointed out,[100] there is a "fundamental divergence" of the traditional elite and bureaucratic elite (both personalist and collegial) systems from the last four categories. In these three regime types, bureaucracies are, as he says, "squarely at center stage in the play of political power." Traditional elites are heavily dependent on the bureaucracy as the instrument of political action. With rare exceptions, both personalist and collegial bureaucratic elite regimes center political power in the hands of military or civil bureaucrats, with military professionals usually being the senior partners. In the case of pendulum regimes, even during periods when party political competition is operative for the time being, there is a constant threat that bureaucratic prerogatives will again be reasserted to take over political control.

In the remaining four regime types, on the other hand, political power is channeled through the instrumentality of the political party. In well-rooted polyarchal competitive systems, power is dispersed among two or more competing parties. One party has a power monopoly in regimes with dominant or single parties. The bureaucracy is constricted in its access to political power in either case when vigorous parties are operating.

These two sets can be conveniently labeled as "bureaucratic-prominent" and "party-prominent" political regime groupings and arranged in tandem for discussion. This system for regime groupings and regime classes is summarized in Table 1.

TABLE 1   Political Regime Variations in Developing Countries

Regime groups	Regime classes
Bureaucratic-prominent regimes	Traditional elite regimes
	Personalist bureaucratic elite regimes
	Collegial bureaucratic elite regimes
	Pendulum regimes
Party-prominent regimes	Polyarchal competitive regimes
	Dominant-party semicompetitive regimes
	Dominant-party mobilization regimes
	Communist totalitarian regimes

COMMON ADMINISTRATIVE PATTERNS

Before turning to differences flowing from political regime variations, to which the two chapters that follow are devoted, let us try to identify some of the principal features that may be considered "typical" of administration in developing countries, in the sense of their prevalence or recurrence rather than their uniform and identical existence in all of these polities.

The importance of administration is almost universally recognized among commentators on the problems of development.[101] Usually an effective bureaucracy is coupled with a vigorous modernizing elite as a prerequisite for progress. Nearly as unanimous is the view that administration has been a neglected factor in development and that the existing machinery for the management of developmental programs is grossly inadequate. Most of the recurring features found in these administrative systems bolster the charge of grave administrative deficiencies alleged to be common in development-oriented nations. Our purpose at this point, however, is to be descriptive rather than prescriptive. If these administrative tendencies seem to point toward serious problem areas, it should be remembered that we are concerned with societies caught in the midst of tremendous social change, striving to reach social goals of demanding complexity, and working under great pressure for early accomplishment.[102]

The following five points are indicative of general features of administration currently found in countries of the developing world:

1. The basic pattern of public administration is imitative rather than indigenous. All countries, including those that escaped Western colonization, have consciously tried to introduce some version of modern Western bureaucratic administration. Usually it is patterned after a particular national administrative model, perhaps with incidental features borrowed from some other system. A country that was formerly a colony almost certainly will resemble the parent administratively, even though independence was forcibly won and political apron strings have been cut. Kingsley has vividly described how

> the organization of offices, the demeanor of civil servants, even the general appearance of a *bureau*, strikingly mirror the characteristics of the bureaucracies of the former colonial powers. The *fonctionnaire* slouched at his desk in Lome or Cotonou, cigarette pasted to his underlip, has his counterpart in every provincial town in France; and the demeanor of an administrative officer in Accra or Lagos untying the red tape from his files would be recognizable to anyone familiar with Whitehall or, more specifically, with the Colonial Office.[103]

Of course some countries have been more fortunate than others, depending on whether the colonial power was distinguished or otherwise for its skills in administration, and whether or not it systematically undertook to tutor its colonials in these skills. An ex-colony of Great Britain, France, or the United States has an advantage over a former possession of Spain, Portugal, Belgium, or the Netherlands. The British record of successful administrative institution-building is probably the best. Britain showed more permissiveness than did France; according to a Frenchman, French administrators could view natives "only as unsuccessful or promising Frenchmen."[104] The mark of the United States is much more restricted, but shows up well where it exists, as in the Philippines.

The colonial administrative heritage includes one incidental feature that has lasting effects. The colonial version of British, French, or any other system of administration was suited to the requirements of colonial government rather than government at home. It was more elitist, more authoritarian, more aloof, and more paternalistic. Remnants of these bureaucratic traits have inevitably carried over to the successor bureaucracies in the new states.

The fact that precedents from outside have largely shaped the developing bureaucracies does not mean that they are less suitable than they would be if fully homegrown, but it does emphasize the importance of making adaptations after independence as conditions change, particularly to enhance the legitimacy of these bureaucracies and to point them toward the accomplishment of developmental goals.

2. The bureaucracies are deficient in skilled manpower necessary for developmental programs. The problem is not a general shortage of employable manpower; actually, the typical developing country has an abundance of labor in relation to other resources—land and capital. Unemployment and underemployment are chronic in the rural economy and in many urban areas among the unskilled labor force. The public services are almost universally conceded to be overstaffed in the lower ranks with attendants, messengers, minor clerks, and other supernumeraries.

The shortage is in trained administrators with management capacity, developmental skills, and technical competence. Although this usually reflects an inadequate educational system, it is not necessarily equivalent to a deficit in holders of university degrees. A number of countries, for example India and Egypt, have sizable pockets of seemingly highly educated unemployed, who either have been educated in the wrong subjects or are the products of marginal institutions.

This gap between supply and demand for responsible administrative posts in newly independent countries is probably unavoidable and can only be remedied by strenuous training efforts which require time. At the critical early stages of nationhood the shortage is accentuated by the urgency with which "nativization" of the bureaucracy is pushed even in the face of continuing availability of trained foreign personnel during the transition and a desperate absence of suitable local replacements. A Nigerian has given the understandable reasons for such a policy.

The decision was taken by our leaders that the British officials should be replaced, not because they hated or distrusted them, but because they felt that political independence was a sham unless you had also a great measure of administrative independence. You just could not be politically independent and remain administratively dependent, over a long period of time, without misunderstanding and tensions arising between the expatriate administrator and his indigenous political master.[105]

Other factors may complicate the task of staffing from local sources. In countries such as Burma and Indonesia administrators who served during colonial days were unwilling to stay or had their effectiveness impaired by charges that they had been "tools of imperialism." Requirements leading to facility in a new national language or the policy of reserving civil service posts for certain minority groups, as in India, have also restricted access to otherwise qualified candidates.

Given the disparity between minimum needs and maximum possibilities for meeting them, there is no short-range solution to the problem of administrative capacity in most new countries. Even if the public bureaucracy succeeds in recruiting most of the available talent, this only diminishes the available supply for political parties, interest groups, and other organizations in both the public and private sectors.

3. A third tendency is for these bureaucracies to emphasize orientations that are other than production-directed; that is, much bureaucratic activity is channeled toward the realization of goals other than the achievement of program objectives. Riggs refers to this as a preference among bureaucrats for personal expediency as against public-principled interests. It may take a variety of forms, most of which are not unique by any means to these bureaucracies, but which may only be more prominent in bureaucratic behavior in a transitional setting.

The most prevalent of these practices are evidence of the carry-over of deep-seated values from a more traditional past, which have not been modified or abandoned despite the adoption of nontraditional social structures. The value attached to status based on ascription rather than achievement explains much of this behavior. Studies of the Thai bureaucracy emphasize that status and status relationships are the prime motivating factors in the system, rather than the urge to reach program goals, hence, one of the important ways to bring about change is to link status with program accomplishment.

Personnel processes may be deeply affected by these considerations, even though the forms of a merit system are outwardly observed. Riggs refers, for example, to "bureaucratic recruitment," where the choice of the official dominates. "Using the pretext of eligibility based on examination, he chooses from the certified those whose personal loyalty he trusts. The same criterion enables him to choose from his family and friends those in whom he has confidence. He helps them gain schooling, certificates, and examination ratings which make them eligible."[106] Similar nonmerit considerations may greatly influence promotions, assignments, dismissals, and other personnel actions within the service, as well as the conduct of business with agency clientele on the outside.

Corruption, on a scale ranging from payments to petty officials for facilitating a minor transaction to bribes of impressive dimensions for equally impressive services, is a phenomenon so prevalent as to be expected almost as a matter of course. Sanctioned by social mores, semi-institutionalized corruption may serve a useful purpose, but it is at best an indirect and undependable way to carry out governmental programs.[107]

Still another common and socially significant practice is that of using the public service as a substitute for a social security program or as a way to relieve the problem of unemployment. Without question, this is one of the reasons for maintaining a surplus of rank and file employees on the public payroll. Paring down the work force cannot be seriously considered until alternative means have been found for handling such threatening social problems as unemployment.[108]

4. The widespread discrepancy between form and reality is another distinguishing characteristic. Riggs has labeled this phenomenon "formalism."[109] It seems to follow naturally from features already mentioned, reflecting an urge to make things seem more as they presumably ought to be rather than what they actually are. The gap between expectations and actualities can be partially masked by enacting laws that cannot be enforced, adopting personnel regulations that are quietly bypassed, announcing a program for delegation of administrative discretion while keeping tight control of decision-making at the center, or reporting as actually met production targets which in fact remain only partially fulfilled. These tendencies are not absent in such developed countries as France, Japan, and the United States; however, the risk of making judgments about substance from what the formal record shows—hazardous enough in trying to understand any administrative system—is much greater in most transitional situations.

5. Finally, the bureaucracy in a developing country is apt to have a generous measure of operational autonomy. This can be accounted for by the convergence of several forces usually at work in a recently independent modernizing nation. Colonialism was essentially bureaucratic rule with policy guidance from remote sources, and this pattern persists even after the bureaucracy has a new master in the nation. The bureaucracy has a near monopoly on technical expertise. It also benefits from the prestige that goes to the professional expert in a society aiming toward industrialization and economic growth. Military bureaucrats have access to weaponry for coercion. Few groups are capable of competing for political influence or of imposing close controls over the bureaucracy, so that often it is able to move into a partial power vacuum.

The political role of the bureaucracy varies from country to country and is intimately related to variations in political system types among the developing countries. To these relationships we turn next.

NOTES

1. See Paul E. Sigmund, Jr., *The Ideologies of the Developing Nations* (New York: Praeger, 1963); Karl W. Deutsch and William J. Foltz, eds., *Nation-Building* (New York: Atherton Press, 1963); Milton J. Esman, "The Politics of Development Administration," in John D. Montgomery and William J. Siffin, eds., *Approaches to Development: Politics, Administration and Change* (New York: McGraw-Hill, 1966); Dankwart A. Rustow, *A World of Nations: Problems of Political Modernization* (Washington, DC: The Brookings Institution, 1967); John H. Kautsky, *The Political Consequences of Modernization* (New York: John Wiley & Sons, Inc., 1972); Monte Palmer, *Dilemmas of Political Development* (Itasca, IL: F. E. Peacock Publishers, Inc., 1973); and Alex Inkeles and David H. Smith, *Becoming Modern: Individual Change in Six Developing Countries* (Cambridge, MA: Harvard University Press, 1974).

2. Esman, "The Politics of Development Administration," p. 59.

3. "Sometime in the nineteenth century in Europe," he goes on to say, "modernization was wedded to the nation-state, and in Asia and Africa that alliance is being consummated anew in the present day. . . . For the present, throughout Asia, Africa, and Latin America, nationalism and the drive for modernity are parts of the same dual revolution." Rustow, *A World of Nations*, pp. 2, 3, 31.

4. Palmer, *Dilemmas of Political Development*, p. 3.

5. Kautsky, *The Political Consequences of Modernization*, pp. 44–45.

6. "Indian nationalism is not an attempt to unite people speaking Indian, Nigerian nationalism is not an attempt to unite people speaking Nigerian, for there are no such languages. . . . Virtually nowhere . . . do so-called nationalists in underdeveloped countries seek to redraw the boundaries of their countries to unite all people speaking a single language. Consequently, the creation of numerous new states and the occurrence of 'nationalist' revolutions in old as well as new ones in the past few decades have resulted in almost no boundary changes, even though the present boundaries of most underdeveloped countries were originally drawn by colonial powers or . . . by earlier conquerors, without regard to linguistic or cultural divisions among the natives." *Ibid.*, p. 56.

7. Rupert Emerson, "Nation-Building in Africa," in Deutsch and Foltz, *Nation-Building*, p. 95.

8. Inkeles and Smith, *Becoming Modern*, pp. 3–4.

9. Joseph R. Strayer, "The Historical Experience of Nation-Building in Europe," in Deutsch and Foltz, *Nation-Building*, p. 25.

10. Esman, "The Politics of Development Administration," p. 60.

11. Hamzeh Merghani, "Public Administration in Developing Countries—The Multilateral Approach," in Burton A. Baker, ed., *Public Administration: A Key to Development* (Washington, DC: Graduate School, U. S. Department of Agriculture, 1964), p. 28.

12. Hence the Soviet model of industrial development had a strong appeal although there may have been only a slight understanding of the price being paid in stringent totalitarian controls to follow the Soviet example. Merle Fainsod, "Bureaucracy and Modernization: The Russian and Soviet Case," in Joseph La Palombara, ed.,

Bureaucracy and Political Development (Princeton, NJ: Princeton University Press, 1963), p. 265.

13. Edward A. Shils, *Political Development in the New States* (The Hague: Mouton & Co., 1962), pp. 47–48.

14. Monte Palmer has expressed well the mood of foreboding: "The road from traditionalism to modernity is not an easy one. Such forces of change as colonialism, war, technology, and mass communications have been more than adequate to assure the steady and apparently irreversible erosion of traditional institutions. The erosion of traditional institutions, unfortunately, does not produce modernity. Disintegration and reintegration are diverse processes. Disintegration involves reducing the utility and effectiveness of traditional institutions, beliefs, and behavior patterns. Reintegration involves inducing individuals to accept a new set of institutions, beliefs, and behavior patterns radically different from the old. . . . Indeed there can be no certainty that those states in or entering the development process must inevitably attain their goal of achieving parity with the world's most economically developed states. . . . The prospects for rapid development in the Third World, then, are not particularly bright." *Dilemmas of Political Development*, pp. 4, 199.

15. In addition to works cited in note 1, leading sources are Gabriel A. Almond and James S. Coleman, eds., *The Politics of the Developing Areas* (Princeton, NJ: Princeton University Press, 1960); Samuel P. Huntington, *Political Order in Changing Societies* (New Haven, CT: Yale University Press, 1968); Shils, *Political Development in the New States*; Fred R. von der Mehden, *Politics of the Developing Nations*, 2nd ed. (Englewood Cliffs, NJ: Prentice-Hall, 1969); Andrew J. Sofranko and Robert C. Bealer, *Unbalanced Modernization and Domestic Instability* (Beverly Hills, CA: Sage Publications, 1972); Gerald A. Heeger, *The Politics of Underdevelopment* (New York: St. Martin's Press, 1974); Christopher Clapham, *Third World Politics* (London: Croom Helm, 1985); and Charles F. Andrain, *Political Change in the Third World* (Boston: Unwin Hyman, 1988).

16. Notable examples are Fred W. Riggs, *Administration in Developing Countries—The Theory of Prismatic Society* (Boston: Houghton Mifflin Company, 1964) and *Prismatic Society Revisited* (Morristown, NJ: General Learning Press, 1973); and more recently, Joel S. Migdal, *Strong Societies and Weak States: State-Society Relations and State Capabilities in the Third World* (Princeton, NJ: Princeton University Press, 1988).

17. Sigmund, *The Ideologies of the Developing Nations*, pp. 39–40.

18. Shils, *Political Development in the New States*, pp. 34–35.

19. Clapham, *Third World Politics*, pp. 182–186.

20. See Migdal, *Stong Societies and Weak States*, especially Chap. 8.

21. von der Mehden, *Politics of the Developing Nations*, p. 1.

22. Heeger, *The Politics of Underdevelopment*, p. 75.

23. "An incumbent regime faces greater instability if the political cohesion of social groups supporting the existent government is weak, if government leaders have neither the will nor the ability to exercise effective coercion and to form a coalition, and if the ruling political elites demonstrate a waning commitment to an ideological cause." Andrain, *Political Change in the Third World*, p. 4.

24. Heeger, *The Politics of Underdevelopment*, pp. 49–51, 75–78.

25. von der Mehden, *Politics of the Developing Nations*, p. 72.

26. Emerson, "Nation-Building in Africa," p. 118.

27. Shils, *Political Development in the New States*, p.25.

28. See Alfred Diamant, *Bureaucracy in Developmental Movement Regimes: A Bureaucratic Model for Developing Societies* (Bloomington, IN: CAG Occasional Papers, 1964), pp. 42–43, and sources cited therein.

29. von der Mehden, *Politics of the Developing Nations*, p. 49.

30. *Ibid.*, p. 60.

31. *Ibid.*, pp. 68–70. This view was shared by others, including Bernard E. Brown, *New Directions in Comparative Politics* (New York: Asia Publishing House, 1962), p. 23.

32. Victor C. Ferkiss, "The Role of the Public Services in Nigeria and Ghana," in Ferrel Heady and Sybil L. Stokes, eds., *Papers in Comparative Public Administration* (Ann Arbor, MI: Institute of Public Administration, The University of Michigan, 1962), p. 175.

33. Shils, *Political Development in the New States*, p. 42.

34. Emerson, "Nation-Building in Africa," p. 111.

35. David E. Apter, "Political Religion in the New Nations," in Clifford Geertz, ed., *Old Societies and New States* (New York: Free Press, 1963), pp. 57–104.

36. *Ibid.*, p. 63.

37. *Ibid.*, p. 100.

38. Vicky Randall, ed., *Political Parties in the Third World* (London: Sage Publications, 1988), p. 1. The volume contains case studies of political parties in Zambia, Ghana, Iraq, India, Mexico, Brazil, Jamaica, and Cuba.

39. *Ibid.*, p. 3. Nevertheless, the eight country studies included in this survey reinforced the generalization that the roles of these parties usually differed from expectations at the time of national emergence from colonialism. Among other things, they faced persistent organizational, leadership, and financial problems; they often suffered from a lack of institutional autonomy which blurred the boundary between the ruling party and the government bureaucracy; and they had difficulties in marshalling and maintaining public sources of support.

40. *Ibid.*, p. 190.

41. Selective comprehensive studies, listed in chronological order, include John J. Johnson, ed., *The Role of the Military in Underdeveloped Countries* (Princeton, NJ: Princeton University Press, 1962); Morris Janowitz, *The Military in the Political Development of New Nations* (Chicago: The University of Chicago Press, 1964); Henry Bienen, ed., *The Military Intervenes: Case Studies in Political Development* (New York: Russell Sage Foundation, 1968); Henry Bienen, ed., *The Military and Modernization* (Chicago: Aldine-Atherton, 1971); Catherine McArdle Kelleher, ed., *Political-Military Systems: Comparative Perspectives* (Beverly Hills, CA: Sage Publications, 1974); Gavin Kennedy, *The Military in the Third World* (London: Duckworth, 1974); Claude E. Welch, Jr. and Arthur K. Smith, *Military Role and Rule: Perspectives on Civil-Military Relations* (North Scituate, MA: Duxbury Press, 1974); Claude E. Welch, Jr., ed., *Civilian Control of the Military: Theory and Cases from Developing Countries* (Albany: State University of New York Press, 1976); Henry Bienen and David Morell, eds., *Political Participation under Military Regimes* (Beverly Hills, CA: Sage Publications, 1976); Morris Janowitz, *Military*

Institutions and Coercion in the Developing Nations (Chicago: University of Chicago Press, 1977); Amos Perlmutter, *The Military and Politics in Modern Times* (New Haven, CT: Yale University Press, 1977), *Political Roles and Military Rulers* (London: Cass, 1980), and "The Comparative Analysis of Military Regimes: Formations, Aspirations, and Achievements," *World Politics* 33 (October 1980): 96–120; Christopher Clapham and George Philip, eds., *The Political Dilemmas of Military Regimes* (Totowa, NJ: Barnes & Noble Books, 1985); S. E. Finer, *The Man on Horseback: The Role of the Military in Politics*, 2nd edition, revised and updated (Boulder, CO: Westview Press, 1988); and Ruth Leger Sivard, *World Military and Social Expenditures 1989*, 13th ed. (Washington, DC: World Priorities, 1989).

42. von der Mehden, *Politics of the Developing Nations*, p. 92.

43. Welch, *Civilian Control of the Military*, p. 34.

44. Kennedy, *The Military in the Third World*, p. 3.

45. Finer, *The Man on Horseback*, p. 223.

46. Sivard, *World Military and Social Expenditures 1989*, pp. 21–22.

47. Perlmutter, *The Military and Politics in Modern Times*, especially the preface and Chap. 1, which explain his typology.

48. Janowitz, *The Military in the Political Development of New Nations*, pp. 5–7.

49. Perlmutter, *The Military and Politics in Modern Times*, p. 9.

50. Refer to von der Mehden, *Politics of the Developing Nations*, pp. 92–100; Janowitz, *The Military in the Political Development of New Nations*, pp. 7–8; Clapham and Philip, *The Political Dilemmas of Military Regimes*, pp. 8–11; Finer, *The Man on Horseback*, pp. 149–167; and Perlmutter, "The Comparative Analysis of Military Regimes."

51. Perlmutter, in "The Comparative Analysis of Military Regimes," supplemented these earlier classification systems with a suggested fivefold typing of modern military regimes in developing countries. These types (with illustrative examples as of 1980 in each case) are corporative (Brazil), market-bureaucratic (South Korea), socialist-oligarchic (Burma), army-party (Cuba), and tyrannical (Zaire). His treatment emphasizes that these regimes are not purely military, but are fusionist or military-civil regimes. It also underscores the lack of agreement as to what should be considered a military regime, since he includes in his army-party and socialist-oligarchic categories such countries as Cuba, Egypt, Syria, and Iraq, which are viewed by other authorities as dominant-party rather than military regimes.

52. For example, see Edwin Lieuwen, *Arms and Politics in Latin America*, rev. ed. (New York: Frederick A. Praeger, 1961), p. 171.

53. James M. Malloy and Mitchell A. Seligson, eds., *Authoritarians and Democrats: Regime Transitions in Latin America* (Pittsburgh, PA: University of Pittsburgh Press, 1987), p. 256. For other descriptions of the recent trend away from military rule, see Martin C. Needler, "The Military Withdrawal from Power in South America," *Armed Forces and Society* 6, No. 4 (1980): 614–624; and Howard Handelman and Thomas G. Sanders, eds., *Military Government and the Movement Toward Democracy in South America* (Bloomington, IN: Indiana University Press, 1981). For a fuller treatment over time, refer to Brian Loveman and Thomas M. Davies, Jr., eds., *The Politics of Antipolitics: The Military in Latin America* (Lincoln, NE: University of Nebraska Press, 1978).

54. Gabriel Ben-Dor, "Civilianization of Military Regimes in the Arab World," in Bienen and Morell, eds., *Political Participation under Military Regimes*, pp. 39–49.

55. Robert N. Kearney, ed., *Politics and Modernization in South and Southeast Asia* (New York: John Wiley & Sons, 1975), p. 25.

56. For details, see Craig Baxter, "Democracy and Authoritarianism in South Asia," *Journal of International Affairs* 38, No. 2 (Winter 1985): 307–319.

57. For example, W. F. Gutteridge stated that Africa was "different," and incapable of being "Latin-Americanized." *Military Institutions and Power in the New States* (New York: Praeger, 1965). Quoted in Finer, *The Man on Horseback*, p. 223.

58. Janowitz, *The Military in the Political Development of New Nations*, p. 65.

59. W. F. Gutteridge, *Military Regimes in Africa* (London: Methuen & Co., Ltd., 1975), p. 5.

60. Claude E. Welch, Jr., "Personalism and Corporatism in African Armies," in Kelleher, *Political-Military Systems*, pp. 125, 141.

61. John W. Harbeson, ed., *The Military in African Politics* (New York: Praeger, 1987), p. 1.

62. Janowitz, *The Military in the Political Development of New Nations*, p. 1.

63. Clapham and Philip, *The Political Dilemmas of Military Regimes*, p. 1.

64. Edwin Lieuwen, *Generals vs. Presidents: Neomilitarism in Latin America* (New York: Praeger, 1964), p. 97.

65. Huntington, *Political Order in Changing Societies*, pp. 194, 196. Welch concurs, writing that the strongest base for civilian control of the military "comes through the legitimacy and effectiveness of government organs." *Civilian Control of the Military*, p. 35.

66. Janowitz, *The Military in the Political Development of New Nations*, pp. 63–67.

67. Brown, *New Directions in Comparative Politics*, pp. 60–61.

68. Janowitz, *The Military in the Political Development of New Nations*, p. 40. Esman perhaps overstates the point when he says that military reformers "usually reject politics with revulsion. They put a moratorium on political expression. Politics to them are wasteful, corrupt, hypocritical, and above all, inefficient." "The Politics of Development Administration," p. 95.

69. Finer, *The Man on Horseback*, p. 221.

70. *Ibid.*, pp. 167–173, 279–283.

71. During the 1950s and early 1960s, the prevailing judgment, held mainly by regional specialists in the Middle East (including North Africa) and Southeast Asia, was that military rule was reformist and promised to speed up economic growth and other modernization processes. This interpretation was presented by Lucien Pye, "Armies in the Process of Political Modernization," pp. 69–89, and by Manfred Halpern, "Middle Eastern Armies and the New Middle Class," pp. 277–315, both in Johnson, *The Role of the Military*.

72. This judgment came mainly from area specialists in Latin America and East Asia, based mostly on analysis of military regimes into the mid-1960s. For examples, see Edwin Lieuwen, *Generals vs. Presidents*; Martin Needler, "Political Development and Military Intervention in Latin America," *American Political Science Review* 60 (September 1966): 616–626; Jae Souk Sohn, "Political Dominance and Political Failure: The Role of the Military in the Republic of Korea," in Bienen, ed., *The*

Military Intervenes, pp. 103–121; and Henry Bienen, "The Background to Contemporary Study of Militaries and Modernization," in Bienen, ed., *The Military and Modernization*, pp. 1–33.

73. Samuel Huntington has been the primary advocate of the thesis that the actual impact of the military in power depends on the level of backwardness or advancement of the particular society. "As society changes, so does the role of the military. In the world of oligarchy, the soldier is a radical; in the middle-class world he is a participant and arbiter; as the mass society looms on the horizon he becomes the conservative guardian of the existing order. Thus, paradoxically but understandably, the more backward a society is, the more progressive the role of its military; the more advanced a society becomes, the more conservative and reactionary becomes the role of its military." *Political Order in Changing Societies*, p. 221. Since Latin American polities as a group are older, have a more significant middle class, and are generally more "advanced" and less "backward" than their counterparts in other regions, Huntington's hypothesis offers the interesting possibility of reconciling the other two opposing views. His concept would confirm the view, mainly held by students of Latin America, that military regimes are apt to be more conservative in these polities, while at the same time backing the expectation that in other regions military governments hold greater promise as societal reformers, as postulated by observers familiar mainly with these societies.

74. Eric Nordlinger, "Soldiers in Mufti: The Impact of Military Rule upon Economic and Social Change in the Non-Western States," *American Political Science Review* 64 (December 1970): 1131–1148, at pp. 1143–1144.

75. R. D. McKinlay and A. S. Cohan, "Performance and Instability in Military and Nonmilitary Regime Systems" *American Political Science Review*, 70, No. 3 (September 1976): 850–864.

76. Robert H. Jackman, "Politicians in Uniform: Military Governments and Social Change in the Third World," *American Political Science Review* 70 (December 1976): 1078–1097, at p. 1096. According to Jackman, the contradiction between Nordlinger's analysis and his is explainable in methodological terms.

77. *Ibid.*, p. 1097. Perlman agrees that other studies have strengthened Jackman's findings. "The Comparative Analysis of Military Regimes," p. 117.

78. As Finer points out, this is an essential but not always a sufficient condition to ensure success. *The Man on Horseback*, p. 280. The case studies in *Political Participation under Military Regimes*, edited by Henry Bienen and David Morell, demonstrate that it is an oversimplification to draw a sharp distinction between military and civilian regimes. More accurately, various types of mixed regimes have emerged, with the military generally retaining final authority but developing civil alliances under which limited political participation is permitted. Perlman confirms this, as indicated above.

79. These studies include: Barry M. Schutz and Robert O. Slater, eds., *Revolution & Political Change in the Third World* (Boulder, CO: Lynne Rienner, 1990); Samuel P. Huntington, *The Third Wave: Democratization in the Late Twentieth Century* (Norman, OK: University of Oklahoma Press, 1991); Zehra F. Arat, *Democracy and Human Rights in Developing Countries* (Boulder, CO: Lynne Rienner, 1991); Rosemary E. Galli, *Rethinking the Third World: Contributions Toward a New*

Conceptualization (New York: Taylor & Francis, 1991); Carlos Barra Solano, Jose Luis Barros Horcasitas, and Javier Hurtado, Compiladores, *Transiciones a la Democracia en Europa y America Latina* (Mexico, DF: Miguel Angel Porrua, 1991); Kenneth E. Bauzon, *Development and Democratization in the Third World: Myths, Hopes, and Realities* (Washington, DC: Taylor & Francis, 1992); Constantine P. Danopoulos, *Civilian Rule in the Developing World: Democracy on the March?* (Boulder, CO: Westview Press, 1992); Larry Diamond, ed., *The Democratic Revolution: Struggles for Freedom and Pluralism in the Developing World* (New York: Freedom House, 1992); Dietrich Rueschemeyer, Evelyne Huber Stephens, and John D. Stephens, *Capitalist Development and Democracy* (Chicago, IL: University of Chicago Press, 1992); Paul Cammack, David Pool, and William Tordoff, *Third World Politics: A Comparative Introduction*, 2nd ed., (Baltimore, MD: The John Hopkins University Press, 1993); Larry Diamond and Marc F. Plattner, eds., *The Global Resurgence of Democracy* (Baltimore, MD: The Johns Hopkins University Press, 1993); Robert W. Jackman, *Power without Force: The Political Capacity of Nation-States* (Ann Arbor, MI: The University of Michigan Press, 1993); Robert O. Slater, Barry M. Schutz, and Steven R. Dorr, eds., *Global Transformation and the Third World* (Boulder, CO: Lynne Rienner, 1993); Robert Pinkney, *Democracy in the Third World* (Boulder, CO: Lynne Rienner, 1994); Juan J. Linz and Alfred Stepan, *Problems of Democratic Transition and Consolidation: Southern Europe, South America and Post-Communist Europe* (Baltimore: Johns Hopkins University Press, 1996); Adam Przeworski, "Democratization Revisited," *Items—Social Science Research Council* 51, No.1 (March 1997): 6–11; Lisa Anderson, ed., "Transitions to Democracy: A Special Issue in Memory of Dankwart A. Rustow," *Comparative Politics* 29, No. 3 (April 1997): 253–405 (especially Gerardo L. Munch and Carol Skalnik Leff, "Modes of Transition and Democratization: South America and Eastern Europe in Comparative Perspective," pp. 343–362, and Richard Joseph, "Democratization in Africa after 1989: Comparative and Theoretical Perspectives," pp. 363–382); Julius O. Ihonvbere, "Democratization in Africa," *Peace Review* 9, No. 3 (September 1997): 371–378; Lars Rudebeck and Olle Tornquist, eds., *Democratization in the Third World: Concrete Cases in Comparative and Theoretical Perspective* (New York: St. Martin's Press, Inc., 1998); Jean-Germain Gros, ed., *Democratization in Late Twentieth-Century Africa* (Westport, CT: Greenwood Press, 1998); and Laurence Whitehead, "The Drama of Democratization," *Journal of Democracy* 10, No. 4 (October 1999): 84–98.

80. Samuel Huntington, *The Third Wave*. The first of these waves, in his view, began in the 1820s with the expansion of democratic suffrage in the United States and lasted until the 1920s; the second began after World War II and continued until the early 1960s; and the third started with the 1974 overthrow of dictatorship in Portugal, becoming during the 1980s a global phenomenon that still continues.

81. See Larry Diamond, "The Globalization of Democracy," in Slater, Schutz, and Dorr, *Global Transformation and the Third World*, Chap. 3, pp. 31–69, particularly pp. 31, 40, and 41.

82. Pinkney, *Democracy in the Third World*, p. 1.

83. *Ibid.*, pp. 170–172.

84. See *The Third Wave*, pp. 290–293.

85. Ihonvbere, "Democratization in Africa," p. 374.
86. The modes include "reform from below" (Chile), "reform through transaction" (Brazil, Poland), "reform through extrication" (Hungary), "reform through rupture" (Argentina, Czechoslovakia), and "revolution from above" (Bulgaria). See Munck and Skalnik, "Modes of Transition and Democratization," Figure 1, p. 346.
87. Diamant and Plattner, *The Global Resurgence of Democracy*, pp. xxiv–xxvi.
88. Diamond, "The Globalization of Democracy," p. 61.
89. Schutz and Slater, *Revolution and Political Change in the Third World*, p. 250.
90. The pioneering works are Arthur S. Banks and Robert B. Textor, *A Cross-Polity Survey* (Cambridge, MA: MIT Press, 1963); and Bruce M. Russett et al., *World Handbook of Political and Social Indicators* (New Haven, CT: Yale University Press, 1964). For more recent contributions, refer to Arthur S. Banks, *Cross-Polity Time-Series Data* (Cambridge, MA: MIT Press, 1971); Charles L. Taylor, ed., *Indicator Systems for Political, Economic & Social Analysis* (Cambridge, MA: Oelgeschlager, 1980); and Charles Lewis Taylor and Michael C. Hudson, *World Handbook of Political and Social Indicators*, 3rd ed. (New Haven, CT: Yale University Press, 1983).
91. Leading examples may be found in James S. Coleman, "Conclusion: The Political Systems of the Developing Areas," in Almond and Coleman, eds., *The Politics of the Developing Areas*, pp. 532–576; Shils, *Political Development in the New States*; Esman, "The Politics of Development Administration," pp. 59–112; von der Mehden, *Politics of the Developing Nations*; Alfred Diamant, "Bureaucracy in Developmental Movement Regimes," in Fred W. Riggs, ed., *Frontiers of Development Administration* (Durham, NC: Duke University Press, 1970), pp. 486–537; Andrain, *Political Change in the Third World*, pp. 7–9 and Chap. 2; and Anton Bebler and Jim Seroka, eds., *Contemporary Political Systems: Classifications and Typologies* (Boulder, CO: Lynne Rienner, 1990), particularly Fred W. Riggs, "A Neoinstitutional Typology of Third World Politics," Chap. 10.
92. Finer, *The Man on Horseback*, p. 249.
93. John Rehfuss has understandably criticized such classification systems as being "very weak at the boundaries" and presenting problems of appropriate placement of individual countries. *Public Administration as a Political Process* (New York: Scribners, 1973), p. 208.
94. Diamant, "Bureaucracy in Development Movement Regimes," p. 490.
95. Esman, "The Politics of Development Administration," p. 105.
96. This classificatory scheme is presented in Fainsod, "Bureaucracy and Modernization," pp. 234–237.
97. Welch, "Personalism and Corporatism in African Armies," in Kelleher, ed., *Political-Military Systems*, pp. 125–145.
98. For a brief presentation of the "corporate-technocratic" state as an emerging type, see Jorge I. Tapia-Videla, "Understanding Organizations and Environments: A Comparative Perspective," *Public Administration Review* 36, No. 6 (1976): 631–636. For a more comprehensive compilation of essays on the subject, refer to James M. Malloy, ed., *Authoritarianism and Corporatism in Latin America* (Pittsburgh, PA: University of Pittsburgh Press, 1977). This orientation is composed of two complementary elements: "corporatism" and "technology." Corporatism refers to a

particular pattern of relationships between the state and civil society which is the product of a longstanding traditional view that the state should play the central role in mediating among competing groups and interests in society. The result is "a system of interest and/or attitude representation, a particular model or ideal-type institutional arrangement for linking the associationally organized interests of civil society with the decisional structures of the state." Philippe C. Schmitter, "Still the Century of Corporatism?" *The Review of Politics* 36 (January 1974): 85–131, at p. 86. Robert R. Kaufman describes these corporatist systems as "vertically segmented societies, encapsulating individuals within a network of legally-defined guilds and corporations which derive their legitimacy from and in turn are integrated by a dominant bureaucratic center." *Transitions to Stable Authoritarian-Corporate Regimes: The Chilean Case?* (Beverly Hills, CA: Sage Publications, 1976), p. 7. For a historical account of the corporate tradition, see Howard J. Wiarda, "Corporatism and Development in the Iberic-Latin World: Persistent Strains and New Variations," *The Review of Politics* 36 (January 1974): 12–24. The element of technocracy consists of recognition of "the need to cope with the larger questions of development, conflict, and change from a technical and/or scientific perspective," with the technocratic argument becoming "the very source of legitimation for political control and domination in the name of expertise and science." Tapia-Videla, "Understanding Organizations and Environments," p. 634. For a recent comprehensive treatment of the concept of corporatism, see Howard J. Wiarda, *Corporatism and Comparative Politics: The Other Great "Ism"* (Armonk, NY: M. E. Sharpe, 1997).

99. The dominant ruling elite in such a corporate-technocratic state is ordinarily a combination of military and civilian officials, with the former usually but not necessarily having the upper hand. Whatever the mix, strong ties must exist between the military and civilian bureaucracies to provide the regime with the necessary mastery of scientific and technical knowledge and with the means to maintain the power required for institutionalizing the state's expanded scope of control. The higher civil bureaucracy, particularly in areas of technocratic expertise, occupies a strategic position. The technocrat becomes the center of attention, being relied on by the regime not only for success in the pursuit of developmental goals but also as a valuable source of legitimacy.

100. Lee Sigelman, "Bureaucratic Development and Dominance: A New Test of the Imbalance Thesis," *Western Political Quarterly* 27, No. 2 (June 1974): 308–313, at pp. 310–311.

101. For a comprehensive treatment, see the collection of essays in Kenneth J. Rothwell, ed., *Administrative Issues in Developing Economies* (Lexington, MA: D. C. Heath, 1972).

102. For a perceptive analysis of some of these problems, see Randall Baker, "The Role of the State and the Bureaucracy in Developing Countries Since World War II," in Ali Farazmand, ed., *Handbook of Comparative and Development Public Administration* (New York: Marcel Dekker, 1990), Chap. 26, pp. 353–363.

103. J. Donald Kingsley, "Bureaucracy and Political Development, with Particular Reference to Nigeria," in LaPalombara, *Bureaucracy and Political Development*, p. 303.

104. Michel Crozier, *The Bureaucratic Phenomenon* (Chicago: University of Chicago Press, 1964), p. 269.

105. S. O. Adebo, "Public Administration in Newly Independent Countries," in Baker, ed., *Public Administration*, p. 20. The problems of Nigerianization are well treated in Kenneth Younger, *The Public Service in New States* (London: Oxford University Press, 1960), pp. 12–52. For discussion of this process in a broader context, see Fred G. Burke and Peter L. French, "Bureaucratization and Africanization," in Riggs, ed., *Frontiers of Development Administration*, pp. 538–555.

106. Riggs, *Administration in Developing Countries*, pp. 230–231.

107. For reviews of corruption as a social phenomenon, including references to the problem in developing countries, see Gerald E. Caiden and Naomi J. Caiden, "Administrative Corruption," *Public Administration Review* 37, No. 3 (May/June 1977): 301–309; David J. Gould, "The Zairianization of the World: Bureaucratic Corruption and Underdevelopment in Comparative Perspective," 20 pp. mimeographed, prepared for the 1980 annual conference of the American Society for Public Administration; and David J. Gould, "Administrative Corruption: Incidence, Causes, and Remedial Strategies," in Farazmand, ed., *Handbook of Comparative and Development Public Administration*, Chap. 34, pp. 467–480.

108. For discussions of some of these constraining factors, see Jean-Claude Garcia-Zamor, "Problems of Public Policy Implementation in Developing Countries," in Farazmand, ed., *Handbook of Comparative and Development Public Administration*, Chap. 31, pp. 435–444; John D. Montgomery, "The Strategic Environment of Public Managers in Developing Countries," *Ibid.*, Chap. 36, pp. 511–526; and Joseph W. Eaton, "The Achievement Crisis: The Management of Unanticipated Consequences of Social Action," *Ibid.*, Chap. 37, pp. 527–537.

109. Riggs, *Administration in Developing Countries*, pp. 15–19.

8

Bureaucratic-Prominent Political Regimes

In several of the political regime types identified in Chapter 7, professional bureaucrats either wield the preponderance of political power directly, or are indispensable to the nonbureaucratic elites who are in the highest political leadership roles. Most of the key policy-making positions are apt to be occupied by career government officials—military or civilian, or more often a combination of both. These are societies in which traditional elites may in some cases still be actively exercising power or exerting significant political influence through a reigning monarch or leaders with aristocratic or religious credentials, but more likely traditional elitist groups will have been displaced from the hub of political power, and monarchy as an institution either eliminated or reduced to a figurehead role. Modernizing goals are usually officially proclaimed, although with varying degrees of commitment and considerable divergence as to content. The general populace is usually not actively engaged in the political arena, often because political participation is severely limited. A competitive party system with related instrumentalities for representation and political decision-making either has never developed, has been superseded, or is in jeopardy. On the other hand, no dominant mass party has emerged capable of engaging in a program of mobilizing general support for the regime. The current political elite group has often moved in to fill a partial political vacuum, and is generally motivated by the announced twin objectives of preserving law and order, and of providing guardianship for the presumably unprepared masses during a period of tutelage toward fuller participation in government. A more hidden secondary motive that may grow in importance with time is the desire of the guardian class to consolidate and perpetuate control.

TRADITIONAL ELITE SYSTEMS

The dominant political elites in these regimes owe their power position to a long-established social system, which usually emphasizes inherited monarchic or aristocratic social status, but may also have a religious legitimizing base. As a group, these countries have not undergone drastic societal transformation, but they show considerable variation in the extent to which change has been permitted or encouraged. The range is from the Arabian peninsula monarchies (which have changed least) to Jordan, Morocco, and Iran (in which major modifications have taken place).

Countries in this category are shrinking in number. Within recent years, traditional elite regimes have been replaced in Afghanistan, Ethiopia, Libya, Kampuchea (Cambodia), and Laos. Successor regimes have been installed either as the result of military coups or Communist takeovers. In the spectacular instance of Iran, one traditional elite regime has been ousted by another with a decidedly different orientation. Clearly the prospects for survival are precarious for such regimes. Those that remain tend to be located in the Near East or North Africa, and are predominantly Islamic. Most of them are large in area and have a widely scattered rural population, often including tribal groupings alienated from the national government.

Two orientations deserve recognition in differentiating among traditional elite regimes. Ortho-traditional regimes are more common, have longer historical continuity, are more static, and have a lower prospect for survival. The political elite is commonly a ruling family relying on a monarchical claim for legitimacy. Although such a regime will probably be committed to modernizing goals, these are likely to be limited in scope and designed not to jeopardize the political status quo. The emphasis will instead be on rapid industrialization and provision of public services, particularly if the country is fortunate enough to have extensive oil reserves which can be exploited, as in the Arabian peninsula states. These elites, as Esman says, are "seldom political risk takers, but rather cautious reformers."[1] In such a setting, political activity is severely curtailed. Competitive politics is usually not permitted. Political parties and associational interest groups with diverse programs are not tolerated or are weak. On the other hand, the political elite does not attempt to mobilize the mass of the population in any official political movement, and little interest is shown in articulating a political ideology. A political attitude of acquiescence and conformity in the community suits the dominant elite, and it is not inclined to invite trouble by pushing hard for programs to increase literacy or otherwise stimulate political awareness and activity. The ruling family or cluster of families is such a regime must rely on the army and civil bureaucracy both as instrumentalities of change which has been invoked as desirable and as inhibitors of unwanted change. The administrative machinery is the principal vehicle for action, but its ability to operate effectively is hampered by its own traditional characteristics, by its embryonic condition, and by the difficulties it faces in penetrating the community. Reforms to remedy these handicaps are undertaken reluctantly and tentatively, if at all.

Neo-traditional regimes are more recent, are more likely to increase in number even though they are less common, are much more activist in the pursuit of announced goals, and face uncertain futures. The political elite is drawn from traditional legitimizing sources which are religious rather than monarchic or aristocratic, and a campaign for religious orthodoxy is apt to be an overriding public policy objective, with more usual modernizing goals being of secondary importance. Religious leaders, although dominant, must rely on trustworthy laymen for occupying many of the formal political offices and for staffing the military and civil bureaucracies. The prospects for survival of such a neo-traditional regime, after the fervor of the initial takeover has subsided, would appear to be as dependent in the long run on the competence and effectiveness of bureaucratic officials as it is in the case of ortho-traditional regimes.

As prime examples of traditional elite regimes, Saudi Arabia exhibits an ortho-traditional and Iran a neo-traditional orientation.

Ortho-Traditional Regimes: Saudi Arabia

Saudi Arabia is a most exceptional society, combining the extension into the late twentieth century of what has been termed a "patriarchal desert state" with immense wealth in the form of the world's largest known petroleum reserves.[2] Wenner has described Saudi Arabia as retaining "the essential elements of a value system, a set of behavior patterns for both elite and mass alike, and a political system which is in most respects an anachronism in the modern world."[3] The political framework barely qualifies to be labeled a territorial nation-state in the usual sense. The ruling Saudi dynasty has, however, been able to sustain a society with internal solidarity resting on the traditional bases of custom, heredity, and religion. The royal family has sought to retain the pattern of personal patriarchal government to the extent possible while embarking on mammoth economic development projects and social reform measures.

Although the governmental machinery now includes a standard roster of about twenty ministries, most of them have been created only within the last thirty five years, and the Council of Ministers itself did not begin to function in a meaningful way until the mid-1950s. Even today, members of the royal family hold nearly all of the important posts, and members of the traditional upper class occupy most higher echelon positions. However, a "new" middle class of secularly educated Saudis is coming into increasing prominence in "modern" sector ministries such as commerce, health, and communications.[4] The Saudi political system continues to be largely traditional, under aristocratic leadership, and without differentiated political institutions, although a Consultative Assembly of sixty appointed members with very limited powers was created in 1992 and began to function late in 1993.

The rudimentary Saudi bureaucracy, although it has grown rapidly in numbers and has assumed new obligations in formulating and administering development programs, is still lacking in capability to meet demands put upon it. Government is the main employer, and the ratio of civil servants to the total population has been growing; however, the major increase has been in the lower levels of the administrative hierarchy, where overstaffing is apparent. Managerial, technical, and scientific expertise, on the other hand, continues to be scarce. Despite unusual efforts to recruit non-Saudis for such positions, reaching over 30 percent at one time, many vacancies cannot be filled. Administrative reform efforts, including enactment of a public personnel law in 1970 which enunciated the merit principle in public employment and adopted concepts of position classification, have exhibited a great deal of formalism as they have actually been put in practice. An evaluation of the developmental capacity of the Saudi bureaucracy across six dimensions (psychological drive, flexibility, communications, client relations, impartiality, and job satisfaction) showed it to be very low, with poor marks in every one of these areas, suggesting that the bureaucracy "is likely to be of minimal use to the Saudi government in its strenuous efforts to provide services to the Saudi population or in its equally strenuous efforts to escape from the trap of rentierism and external dependency."[5] Recent studies indicate that most Saudi executives are "predisposed against developmental programs that might engender social conflict or value change," that they "feel responsible only to their superiors, and not to situational or environmental demands," and that they are "ill-disposed to generate innovation among their subordinates."[6] Osman sums up the situation by saying that "the rapid growth of wealth has created an over-optimistic environment without taking into consideration the capacity of the bureaucracy. . . . Saudi Arabia is a country with unlimited wealth but very limited human resources."[7]

Neo-Traditional Regimes: Iran

Iran presents a more complex, changeable example of a traditional elite regime.[8] Binder asserted nearly forty years ago that Iran recapitulated "within living memory most of the varied political experience of all the Middle East," and that "the variety of coexisting and competing legitimizing formulae and patterns of political activity" testified to the impermanent nature of the Iranian political system.[9] This variability has been amply demonstrated since, with the overthrow of the Pahlavi monarchy in 1979 and its replacement by the Islamic Republic of the Ayatollah Ruhollah Khomeini, substituting one variety of traditional elite regime for another.

Among other historical differences from most of the Middle East, Iran escaped from ever being a colony of a Western power directly subject to foreign control, with resulting benefits in national self-esteem and in experience in diplomacy as an independent power, which have been of aid both to the monarchy and to the Islamic Republic. Avoidance of colonial status also had its costs, however, as Zonis has pointed out. During the monarchy, "Iran never gained the experience of having a palpable enemy with tangible symbols of that enemy's control. There was never . . . the rallying point for national aspirations that independence or anticolonial struggles provided other nations."

Myths of national unification or bases of national identity failed to develop. The Iranians did not develop a sense of the concept of Iranian "citizenship."[10] The monarchical tradition was the main unifying and legitimizing force, the state was identified with the institution of monarchy, and people were considered subjects of the monarch. Monarchical legitimacy proved to be insufficient. The ouster of the shah led for the first time to a massive national motivating energy based on religious values incorporated in the Islamic Republic. Another consequence of escape from colonial status was that Iran never had a colonial bureaucracy which could provide a later model for structuring an indigenous bureaucracy or for the behavior of indigenous bureaucrats. This has complicated administrative performance in both the earlier ortho-traditional and the current neo-traditional regimes.

The focus of attention here is on contrasts in political and administrative characteristics between the shah's regime and the Islamic Republic during its formative years. The Pahlavi monarchy was typical of ortho-traditional regimes in its emphasis on what James Bill described as "the politics of system preservation," rather than aiming at any fundamental alteration of the existing system.[11] The shah's "White Revolution" involved massive expenditures from dramatically expanded oil revenues for infrastructure investments to improve production and communication facilities and to expand the size and capability of the armed forces, but Iran as a society was characterized by a minimal "trickle down" flow of these phenomena to the mass of the population, leading Marvin Zonis to label Iran as a society "characterized by far more growth than development."[12]

Political power was highly centralized in the person of the shah, and the total political elite consisted of a very small group, estimated by Zonis to total only slightly over 300 individuals, even including a "second stratum" of the ruling class "located structurally between the shah and the non-elite,"[13] and functioning to put the shah's policies into action. Members of this select political elite were also almost invariably members of the official elite, occupying formal positions within the governmental structure. This structure, however, was fragmented and unwieldy. Operational coordination had to be provided by influential officials with access to the shah. The bureaucracy that served this regime was also segmented along agency lines rather than uniformly structured. After years of effort, a law was finally passed in 1966 which attempted to install a merit system based on position classification and the concept of equal pay for equal work, but these reforms apparently ran counter to Iranian values and norms, and as a result either had unfortunate effects or became inoperative.

Within this unusual political and administrative environment, members of the political elite and of the career bureaucracy exhibited some shared characteristics. One was the gradually broadening social base from which they were recruited, leading to emergence of what Bill described as a "new class,"[14] consisting of individuals possessing skills and talents acquired through access to modern educational opportunities in Iran and abroad. Members of this growing professional-bureaucratic intelligentsia were deliberately recruited by the shah for major governmental posts in order to improve the level of competence, weaken his dependence on the traditional social elite, and enhance his political position generally. Along with their shared technical training, however, this intelligentsia also became a focus for criticism, both voiced and hidden, of the regime. They shared attitudinal characteristics such as "political cynicism, personal distrust, manifest insecurity, and interpersonal exploitation" making up a syndrome of covert resistance which was prevalent among the political elite and higher ranking bureaucrats in response to the political environment.[15]

The Pahlavi monarchy thus well exemplified the type of traditional elite regime which deliberately discourages widespread popular participation in political affairs, and relies on a balanced rivalry among subservient groups to retain power. This situation, however, had profound consequences for governance in Iran. The shah's regime was placed in increasing jeopardy, and inefficiency became the hallmark of the administrative system.

By the late 1970s, Western specialists on Iran were in agreement as to the lack of stability and the likelihood of drastic political change, but typically predicted, as did Bill, that the political future of Iran would involve "either a continuation of some kind of Pahlavi rule or a government led by a radical-progressive military group."[16]

A momentous political transition did indeed take place, but it was of a character quite dissimilar to that anticipated by most Western observers. The successor regime in Iran was not a military dominated bureaucratic elite, nor was it some other distinctly different type of political regime. Instead, it turned out to be another traditional elite regime with a drastically changed orientation—inspired and dominated by the ascetic Islamic religious leader of the Shi'ite sect, the Ayatollah Ruhollah Khomeini.

The turmoil, bloodshed, and recurring domestic and foreign relations crises which took place need not be detailed here. Suffice it to say that the outcome has been the emergence of a regime which is formally an Islamic Republic but in essence was ruled until his death in 1989 by Khomeini and associated religious leaders. Occupants of key official positions have come and gone, eliminated by loss of support by Khomeini, by exile, or by death. The revolution devoured many of its early supporters. With the passage of time, more and more clerics moved directly into government offices, including the presidency, parliament, cabinet positions, and other important posts. Behind the curtain of repression, however, deep political cleavages have continued to exist, with the spectrum running from the extremist right represented by Khomeini and the Islamic Republic Party, to a moderate center of bazaar merchants and secular intelligentsia which gradually lost ground before Khomeini's death, and then to a number of groups in the radical left differing as to ideology and tactics but promoting the most determined opposition to the regime and providing its principal targets for arrests and executions.

Infighting among the elite of the Islamic Republic has remained as a source of uncertainty, with differences of judgment as to its impact. Bill's view in 1982 was that the social and political fabric of Iran had "continued to unravel in the face of government factionalism, personal rivalry, ethnic cleavages, religious fanaticism, ideological confrontation, and economic malaise," and he anticipated the advent of some kind of military rule.[17] By 1987 Akhavi conceded that power had been successfully consolidated, but concluded that factionalism among the elite had prevented the evolution of consistent public policy.[18] Most observers anticipated that the test of survivability would come with the creation of a power vacuum upon the death of Khomeini. When this actually occurred in mid-1989, the transition was remarkably easy. Ali Khamenei, who had served as President since 1981, was named as supreme religious leader the day after Khomeini died. Later in the summer of 1989 Hashemi Rafsanjani, who had been presiding officer of the unicameral legislature, was the winner by an 85 percent majority in a new presidential election. Rafsanjani had long been considered a moderate among the elite group. He was reelected in 1993 to a second four year term, but with a much lower percentage of the vote than before, presaging a period in the mid-1990s of public unrest and a behind the scenes power struggle between Khamenei and Rafsanjani, who was ineligible for a third term. The 1997 presidential election, which produced an unusually high voter turnout, resulted in the victory by a wide margin of Muhammad Khatami, considered to be a moderate cleric with a reformist agenda. Khatami has followed an internal policy of greater tolerance for divergent political and religious views, and has made overtures for more cordial relations with the United States and other Western powers through a "dialogue of civilizations." Clawson evaluates the Khatami record to date as a paradox, stating that he "campaigned on domestic issues while saying little on foreign and security policy, but his first year in office saw progress on the latter front while domestic policy has been a continuing struggle," and predicts more of the same as

Khatami's term proceeds.[19] Meanwhile, the staying power of the current regime seems to have been demonstrated, at least for the near future.

In the long run, the role of the bureaucracy—civil and military—may turn out to be a key factor, as it was in deciding the fate of the shah. According to Hooshang Kuklan, "the administrative system in Iran played an active, aggressive and involved role in the revolution. It did not prove to be the guardian of the status quo. It, in fact, was militantly engaged in immobilizing the Shah's regime and facilitating the opposition's success."[20] With the gradual spread of work stoppages and strikes, vital activities such as tax collection, power distribution, transport, and oil production were crippled, paralyzing the government's capacity to function.

The Islamic Republic from the beginning has had to balance its concern with loyalty to its leadership and objectives against the necessity of keeping the machinery of government in operation. Indications are that the old regime collapsed sooner than the revolutionary forces expected, and they were caught unprepared to install a new governance system when they actually came to power. Farazmand reported that during the first year little change was made in the administrative structure or the public service. Then came a period of about three years when a strong priority was to scrutinize the public sector for disloyalty to the revolution, using a network of purge committees. Kuklan estimated that 5 percent of the total work force lost their jobs or were retired, with many of them facing prosecution before revolutionary committees. The purge rate was much greater among higher ranks and in sensitive agencies. Bill reported that Iran was stripped of its top three or four layers of technocrats. The Ministry of Foreign Affairs apparently lost 40 percent of its total staff, and the turnover on university faculties was at least 10 percent. Certainly the preexisting shortages in technical, managerial, and other types of expert manpower were made more acute by the purge campaign, and the problem was further complicated by the loss of various professionals who chose voluntarily to leave the country in search of more settled conditions.

Despite formal adoption of such concepts as political neutrality, merit recruitment, and rank in job as part of administrative reforms during the 1960s and 1970s, the public bureaucracy had in fact been politicized under the shah. During the period from late 1979 through 1982 the Islamic Republic repoliticized it to a higher degree for the purpose of gaining acceptance and support of Islamic religious values and the political ideology espoused by the new regime. One device was the assignment by the leadership to each government agency of a cleric who functioned independently of the official agency head for the stated purpose of upholding Islamic principles, but apparently had wide-ranging control responsibilities. Along with these loyalty obligations, the bureaucracy faced substantial additions to its administrative tasks. The scope of governmental activity was expanded by the nationalization of private banks, insurance companies, large-scale industries, and foreign trade. Various new "revolution-rooted institutions" were created for safeguarding the regime, such as a revolutionary guard separate from conventional military forces, revolutionary tribunals, and neighborhood public safety and protection centers. All these augmented both the numbers and responsibilities of public servants, as the private sector shrank and the public sector grew.

Since 1983 there has been, according to Farazmand, a major shift "in the direction of moderation, a relaxation of radical positions in domestic and international affairs, and a standardization of societal arrangements."[21] This has meant for the public bureaucracy a renewed acceptance of the importance of expertise, and relatively greater job security for professional bureaucrats. The lessening of stressful circumstances may have led to better performance capabilities, but has also revived some of the earlier emphasis on enhancement of bureaucratic self-interest, with resulting public dissatisfaction with bureaucratic operations. "The Iranian bureaucracy has not been abolished by the Revolution. On the contrary, it has survived and prevailed as a well-entrenched institution of power."[22] Hence the prospects for success by this unusual neo-traditional political elite regime in consolidating its position further will depend to a considerable extent on whether or not it can curb these tendencies and put in place and maintain a responsive and capable public bureaucracy.

PERSONALIST BUREAUCRATIC ELITE SYSTEMS

Among bureaucratic elite systems, some are characterized by what is essentially one-man rule, with a single individual clearly in a dominant position, although dependent on a professional bureaucracy for regime continuity. The leader in most cases comes from a military background, heading what are commonly referred to as caudillo or strongman regimes, but there have been rare instances when the personalist leadership has come from a civilian.

Caudillo or strongman regimes have occurred most often in Latin American countries during the nineteenth and twentieth centuries and in recent years in countries of sub-Saharan Africa. The Spanish word *caudillo*, meaning leader or chief, was applied during the nineteenth century to what became a characteristic form of political leadership in Latin America. Caudillos, usually of mestizo or Indian origin, assumed power to fill the void left by the disappearance of colonial governments and the widespread constitutional failures following independence. The resulting geographical fragmentation of political power led to the rise of caudillo-led armies which often consisted of nothing more than an armed band led by a self-designated "general." Gino Germani and Kalman Silvert observe that in this Latin American tradition of caudillismo "the geographical fragmentation took the form of a 'federal' state, the absolute rule of the caudillo that of the 'president' and, at the same time, 'general' of the army."[23] This alternative frequently seemed preferable to continuing factional rivalries. The most common pattern was for caudillo-style dictatorships to replace intervening periods of political chaos, but occasionally caudillos succeeded in maintaining themselves in power over long stretches of time, notable examples being Rodriguez de Francia, known as "El Supremo," who ruled in Paraguay from 1814 to 1840, and General Porfirio Diaz, who served as Mexican president from 1877 to 1910.

Less typical in Latin America since early in this century, political regimes with caudillo or strongman characteristics have appeared since World War II in numerous recently independent countries in Africa. In his classification of sub-Saharan political regimes with a high degree of military involvement in politics, Claude E. Welch, Jr. contrasts "personalist" and "corporatist" categories, with the former closely corresponding to the strongman or caudillo model. According to Welch, personalist regimes focus on the head of state or commander-in-chief and exhibit characteristics which include an act of intervention usually initiated by the ranking officer in the armed forces, who identifies himself closely with their interests, names both officers and civilians to cabinet positions, and may propagate a national "ideology" stressing the head of state.[24] In these personalist regimes, as Welch points out, the head of state becomes "the focus, the prime mover," evoking the image of "the benevolent, modernizing leader" who can promote national unity. With power so centered in the head of state, cabinet instability almost invariably results. The personalist leader ensures that important governmental positions will be distributed to those he considers his most dependable and avid supporters. The vagaries of such leadership are illustrated by a comment quoted by Welch concerning one ruling general in the Central African Republic that only his cabinets changed even more frequently than his policies.[25]

The life span of these personalist regimes is unpredictable. With power resting basically on the claims of hierarchy, any breakdown in military discipline and cohesion raises the threat of further intervention. The ranking officer and his close associates cannot avoid the obvious fact that their political power is derived from the use of coercion. These are continually vulnerable regimes.

It may safely be assumed that in such a regime there will be a distinctive impact on the characteristics of the administrative system. For example, with the bulk of administrative power centralized in the leader, he is the one who makes most major administrative decisions. Higher-ranking bureaucrats are personally scrutinized by him; the bureaucracy resembles a patriarchal community headed by the caudillo. Those bureaucrats who are loyal to the leader and supportive of him are amply rewarded with increased pay, promotion, or other recognition. Those officials who do not display these attributes are promptly punished by demotion, dismissal, or perhaps even death. In general, high-ranking administrative officials will be appointed by the caudillo based on his own self-defined criteria, with personal loyalty and adherence to regime ideology usually given primary emphasis. It may also be assumed that merit recruitment criteria such as the possession of technical skills, degree of education, past work experience, or professional competence will be held in low regard, if considered at all.

The military strongman or caudillo personalist style of rule has been represented frequently in Latin America during this century. The lengthiest example was that of General Alfredo Stroessner in Paraguay, who was in power from 1954 to 1989. Other instances occurred in Nicaragua prior to 1979, and in Guatemala prior to 1944,[26] and again briefly in 1982–1983 (when General Efram Rios Montt, after deposing his junta partners, named himself president before being ousted in turn by another coup). The following African countries are among those with existing or recent such personalist regimes: Algeria, Benin (formerly Dahomey), Burkina Faso (formerly Upper Volta), Burundi, Central African Republic, Equatorial Guinea, Liberia, Nigeria, Sudan, Togo, Uganda, and the Democratic Republic of the Congo (formerly Zaire).

Personalist regimes with a nonmilitary leader are less common, but there have been some recent examples. From 1957 to 1986, the Caribbean nation of Haiti was under one-man rule, first by Francois "Papa Doc" Duvalier until his death in 1971, and then by his son, Jean-Claude "Baby Doc" Duvalier, until he fled the country. Both governed in a repressive strongman style. After independence in 1966, Guyana (formerly the colony of British Guiana), on the northern coast of South America, was headed by Forbes Burnham, first as prime minister and then in 1980, after adoption of a new constitution and conduct of a controlled election, as "executive president." Burnham ruled with virtually unlimited powers, including authority to appoint and dismiss vice presidents and to veto any legislative enactment. After Burnham died in 1985, Hugh Desmond Hoyte succeeded him for a five-year term in the same office after another controlled election. Guyana did not shift to a more competitive system until 1992, when the candidate of another party succeeded Hoyte after a fair election. In the Philippines, President Ferdinand Marcos headed a civilian personalist regime from 1972, when he proclaimed martial law, until his ouster in 1986. Marcos, who had been elected in 1965 and reelected in 1969, imposed martial law as a means of setting up a personalist regime which combined political repression, law-and-order objectives, and a decidedly corporate/technocratic orientation.

Reliable information concerning the public bureaucracies and their operational characteristics in these personalist polities is understandably hard to obtain while the regime is still operating, particularly when a military strongman is in control. For this reason, we use past examples to illustrate—from Latin America with Paraguay under General Stroessner, and from Africa with Uganda under the now defunct regime of General Amin.

Paraguay (1954–1989)

The thirty-five year period of strongman rule by Alfredo Stroessner in Paraguay was the longest in a country with a historical record of numerous authoritarian regimes since achievement of independence in 1811.[27]

Following a period lasting more than four decades (1904–1947) of relatively open political competition between the Colorado and Liberal parties, conditions deteriorated at mid-century to the point that the stage was set for a return to authoritarianism. The strongman who emerged to take advantage of the opportunity was General Alfredo Stroessner. In May, 1954, he led a successful coup that ousted the incumbent and led to the naming of a figurehead provisional president. Meanwhile, Stroessner was preparing to take over. He was nominated by the Colorado party as its candidate in the presidential election already scheduled for July 11, 1954, and easily won the election, the first of eight such victories, always with a margin of at least eighty percent, before his eventual ouster in 1989.

Miranda describes Stroessner as "an atypical ruler, not the flamboyant caudillo-style dictator characteristic of other Latin American nations," who "masterfully reorganized Paraguayan politics to fit his own script," demonstrating an ability to maintain personal control that was matched by his skill in manipulating constituencies.[28] Contrasting him with Fidel Castro, Sondrol classifies Stroessner as an "authoritarian" rather than a "totalitarian" dictator, "lacking ideological vision and employing tyrannical power for essentially private ends," but sharing with Castro "a common, Latin American *caudillo* heritage buttressing their power."[29]

Stroessner's "distinct brand of authoritarianism" was based on two goals of modernization delineated by him: "eradicating domestic chaos and providing the people with some degree of political participation."[30] He was able to take advantage of several features of the existing political environment, including the precedents set by earlier dictators, the tendency toward submissiveness by the peasantry derived from Guarani Indian culture and the impact of religious conversion and colonialism, and provisions in the 1940 Constitution then in force which gave extraordinary powers to the executive (including authority to dissolve Congress, dictate laws, and command the armed forces, which had a constitutional obligation to guarantee order and respect for the Constitution).

From such ingredients, Stroessner fashioned a stable long-lasting regime with several interlinking features which came to be known as *stronista* political doctrine. One was conversion of the Colorado party into the dominant party under his leadership, with competing parties confined to non-threatening roles. Another was bureaucratic co-optation. The armed forces were catered to but kept under firm control. Public employment was greatly expanded, more than doubling between 1972 and 1982, absorbing large numbers from the middle class that might otherwise have been alienated. Great stress was placed on economic development efforts (especially in agriculture, industry, and hydroelectric projects), resulting in yearly increases in per capita income during the 1970s that were among the highest in Latin America. *Stronista* doctrine "emphasized the role of the leader as a crucial element of the new political system. . . . All acts of government, all ideological constructs, all material well-being were said to come from the work and the creative thinking of the leader" resulting in "a demicult of total and complete adulation" centered on Stroessner.[31]

After these impressive results in consolidating his regime during the 1960s and 1970s, Stroessner's dominance began to deteriorate during the 1980s. Contributing factors were cleavages within the Colorado party; rumors about possible contenders for the presidency from among military leaders; serious economic problems leading to a recession which by 1983 drove unemployment to fifteen percent, resulted in a decrease in the country's GDP, and greatly increased foreign debt; new points of friction between the regime and the Catholic church hierarchy; external pressures for greater democratization; and growing public discontent and disillusionment with the system. Despite these setbacks, Stroessner won re-election in February, 1988, and appeared able to weather the storm, at least for the near future.

This expectation was shattered a year later, when General Andres Rodriguez, who was second to Stroessner in the line of command and one of his most likely heirs apparent, launched a coup on February 2, 1989. By the next day, Stroessner had been taken into custody and Rodriguez had taken over the presidency, closed down Congress, and installed his choice as leader of the Colorado party. Elections held in May marked the end of the Stroessner era. In what was apparently a relatively free election, General Rodriguez won the presidency, opening up the prospect of a more democratic period in Paraguayan politics. Rodriguez was followed by other Colorado party candidates elected in 1993 and 1998. Early in 1999 the vice president was assassinated by men in military uniforms, leading to suspicion of possible involvement by the incumbent president, Raul Cubas Grau, who resigned and was succeeded by the president of the Senate, Luis Gonzalez Macchi, to serve out the remainder of the presidential term, until 2003. Thus the eventual success of the transition is still problematic.[32]

Miranda perceptively points out both the short run advantages and long run disadvantages of such personalist bureaucratic elite regimes with these words summing up the record of the Stroessner era in Paraguay:

> The quick pace of Stroessner's leavetaking confirms that authoritarian regimes based on the distribution of ill-gotten gains, corruption, and fear cannot sustain themselves in power forever. On the other hand, his longevity at the top shows that when enough resources are available to the elite, that when enough repression ensures a weak and ineffective opposition, and that when a cult of personality is built around the persona of a leader, authoritarian regimes can take tenacious hold.[33]

Uganda (1971–1979)

A striking example of African strongman personalist regimes was Uganda under General (later Field Marshal) Idi Amin Dada.[34] In 1971, when he was commander-in-chief of the armed forces, General Amin led a successful coup, which ousted President Milton Obote. He soon installed a personalist regime with himself as president, assumed full governmental powers, and suspended all political parties. After eight years in power, he was in turn ousted early in 1979, and replaced soon afterward again by Obote.[35]

Uganda under Amin is not easily classifiable, being a unique product of historical forces in the area and personality traits of the individual in charge. Mazrui refers to developments after the 1971 coup as the making of a "military ethnocracy," combining the warrior tradition in Africa with ethnocracy as a basis for political organization, and as a "military theocracy," likewise having its origins in the historical politicization of religion in Uganda. In essence his themes are that the warrior tradition, which connected physical virility and martial valor, and which had been in decline during the colonial period, was revived; that ethnocracy, in the sense of a system of distributing political power primarily on the basis of kinship, which had persisted in African society, became stronger than ever; and that Amin and the military as rulers succeeded earlier Christian missionaries in claiming a monopoly on the setting of standards of personal conduct and the legitimate use of spiritual sanctions.

Whether or not this approach to interpretation of events is correct, clearly there were dramatic changes in both the political and administrative systems in Uganda following the military takeover. Originally, General Amin adopted a conciliatory stance, engaged in various well-publicized efforts to consult with representatives of divergent groups, encouraged political participation by civilians, retained a largely civilian cabinet, seemed to rely heavily on the professional bureaucracy, and in other ways indicated an intent to follow a course of moderation aimed at his own version of a military-intellectual coalition. This indicated partnership between the military and the intelligentsia soon dissipated, however, with military dominance becoming more and more evident and being expressed through the personal actions of General Amin. Decalo notes that "the very same characteristics that had helped Amin move up in the ranks in the armed forces were to become features of his military regime," with primary reliance on "the use or manipulation of brute force." Amin soon "ruled in the style of an oriental potentate," with the result that

> Uganda became the personal fiefdom of a brutal despot, within which there was no semblance of law and order, established administration, or set policy guidelines. This was a tyranny where personal whims dictated policy, expertise played no role in government and administration, the economy was but a source of plunder for the ruling elite, and foreign policy was rooted in the whims and biases of the paramount leader.[36]

With the replacement of most of the civilian cabinet members by military men, who then occupied the critical posts, Welch's list of characteristics for a personalist military regime was closely matched by Amin's government. The impact of this personalist style of rule on the bureaucracy parallels but exceeds what was reported in Paraguay under Stroessner. In the case of Uganda, at the time of independence the country had in place a bureaucratic elite similar to that in other British African colonies, staffed at the top by the British but including Ugandans in subordinate and apprenticeship roles. As in other nations gaining independence, rapid Africanization took place soon afterward, displacing most of the non-Ugandans. The criteria for selection to these higher civil service posts placed a major emphasis on command of English and a modern Western education. As a consequence, Ugandan bureaucratic elite members were more highly educated than members of the political elite, particularly after the military takeover occurred, since upward mobility in the armed forces was not nearly as dependent on fluency in English or a high level of general education.

The higher civil service also began with the advantages of tenure status and high social prestige associated with the British colonial pattern. Entry into the civil service became the career ambition of most of the ablest Ugandan university graduates, because of its promise of a secure career as against the risks of either political or entrepreneurial activity.

This privileged position was maintained during the Obote period and the early part of the Amin regime, but then was almost completely wiped out, placing civil bureaucrats in a role of dependence upon and subservience to the military ruler. This destabilization of the civil service was accomplished mainly by eliminating guarantees of security of tenure. General Amin announced soon after taking over that inadequate performance would lead to dismissal, and dramatically drove the point home during the second year of his rule by ousting twenty-two senior civil servants, who were "pensioned off," with some receiving retirement benefits subsequently and some not. Soon afterward similar action was taken affecting a group of police officers. The vulnerability of public service careers became increasingly obvious as time passed, with more and more unpredictability as to what whim of General Amin might lead to sudden dismissal, often with dire consequences following, including exile, imprisonment, or sudden disappearance. The deterioration in professional qualifications and performance capabilities of what had been a well-developed civil service was devastating. Uganda under Amin thus offers a dramatic example of a military bureaucratic elitist regime with power highly concentrated in the hands of a single individual whose access to political control was made possible by his military background, but whose excesses led to his downfall after a few years, and have cast a pall over the country's prospects for the indefinite future.

COLLEGIAL BUREAUCRATIC ELITE SYSTEMS

The distinctive feature of these regimes is that a group of individuals, usually composed exclusively of professional bureaucrats who are military officers, exercises political leadership. The collegial bodies, or juntas, have in a few instances in Central America, with Nicaragua after the ouster of Somoza being a leading example, included civilians as well as military members, but our primary interest is in the more typical case where rule is in the hands of what Morris Janowitz and others refer to as a "military oligarchy." Welch calls them "corporatist" regimes, contrasting them with "personalist" or "strongman" regimes. Generally, the members of a junta which establishes such a regime come from the same or adjacent military ranks. Collegiality rather than hierarchy is stressed as the means of maintaining cohesion, but as Welch points out, it is not easy to maintain collegiality.[37] The leader of a coup which brought the group to power is likely to enjoy a position of preeminence in the group, and later this leader or some other individual may emerge as dominant in the junta.

The rationale for military intervention is usually put in terms of protecting the country from some internal or external threat, and the basic thrust as to policy objectives is reduction of disorder and violence and establishment of law and order. The military establishment is viewed as having a special obligation to take action to protect the national interest. As Lieuwen puts it, with special reference to the Latin American context, "The armed forces hold that they have a legitimate political mission above that of the government. Their first allegiance is to the nation and to the constitution, as they interpret it, rather than to the ephemeral civilian politician who happens to occupy the presidential chair at a given moment. Thus, the military's custodianship of the national interest . . . makes its political involvement inevitable."[38]

Martin Needler, who has closely examined the internal dynamics of coups that have brought military juntas to power, points out two common phenomena—collaboration with civilian politicians, and the role of the "swing man." He observes that military coups are not made solely by the military.

> Almost invariably, the conspirators are in touch with civilian politicians and respond to their advice, counting on their assistance in justifying the coup to public opinion and helping to run the country afterwards. This relationship not infrequently takes the form of a coup only reluctantly staged by the military at the insistence of civilian politicians, who appealed to the officers' patriotism, the historic role of the army in saving the country at its hour of need.[39]

The swing man phenomenon refers to the fact that often the "critical margin of support" before a coup is provided by an individual or group decision to collaborate with the original conspirators. The initiators of the plans for the coup tend to be in strongest opposition to the current regime, "while other officers of different political orientations and a greater commitment to constitutional procedures have higher thresholds to intervention." The last adherent or set of adherents is likely to come from this latter group, often providing a swing man who may be extremely important for success of the coup for reasons such as his high rank or critical position within the armed forces, and/or his high prestige with the public. Frequently such a swing man will be selected to head the postcoup military junta or provisional government, even though he may be an individual "who was least committed to the objectives of the coup, whose threshold to intervention was the highest of all the conspirators, and who was a last minute addition to the conspiracy. . . ." The presence of a moderate swing man often leads to a conflict situation later on, if he initiates plans for a return to civilian rule and constitutional normalization while "the original instigator of the coup and the group around him . . . resist this tendency and instead urge the necessity for the military to keep power for a longer period."[40] The position of the swing man as junta leader may eventually become untenable, leading to an internal reorientation.

If a junta regime retains power very long, some kind of redistribution of political authority is almost certain to occur. It may simply take the form of internal shifts within the coalition, such as replacement of some or all of the original junta members. As time passes, even though political direction by the military is still manifest, the military junta is likely to take steps toward gradual civilianization intended to mask the fact of continued military control.

> This shift of emphasis is both symbolic (e.g., wearing civilian clothing) and constitutional. The new constitution is supposed to redefine the separation of functions and power among the military and other executive branches of government. It also should forbid soldiers and officers on active duty to participate in politics. The civilianized military elite itself takes over (with different degrees of success) the leadership of a civilian-political movement.[41]

As long as members of the military elite continue to dominate the polity, however, even though they have donned civilian garb, there is no essential shift in the basic regime characteristics. The most difficult problem of possible reclassification is under circumstances in which civilianized military leaders choose to emphasize the instrumentality of a dominant party as the principal vehicle for governance, while retaining ultimate control options. Egypt presents such an instance, with the choice being to continue considering the regime to be a military oligarchy in disguise, or to classify it as having shifted to the dominant-party mobilization category with former military leaders occupying crucial party posts. Indonesia is another such borderline case. Our choice, as detailed below, has been to put Egypt on one side of this line and Indonesia on the other.

A third type of power reallocation, of course, is transfer from direct military rule to what is clearly rule by a civilian elite, even though the possibility of future military intervention remains. Such "abdication" or "return to the barracks" occurs when a ruling military junta voluntarily or involuntarily returns power to civilians. In this eventuality, there is no doubt about the necessity for a political regime reclassification, either to the pendulum category or one of the party-prominent categories, depending on the degree of risk of early reimposition of military control.

Any military junta is certain to devote attention to a revamping of the civil bureaucracy, but it will at the same time be limited in what can be done by its dependency on the nonmilitary administrative system. Civil bureaucrats are likely to be one of the targets of a newly installed military regime, accused of corrupt practices, wasteful and ineffective performance, and inadequacies as an instrument of social change. Some program of administrative reform is apt to be launched, and it may involve substantial structural changes along with efforts to modify patterns of bureaucratic behavior. However, at most a military regime can hope to bring about changes in the bureaucratic apparatus; it cannot be supplanted. "The military elite can run a country only with the collaboration of the civil service. Even though it denounces, purges, and transforms it, the elite will inevitably be forced into a coalition with the civil service; they can only supervise it, check it, interfere with it, and, at best, penetrate and dominate it."[42]

Under a collegial military regime, the strategic position of the civil bureaucracy is intermediate as between the situation under a military strongman and the situation in a civilian-military coalition bureaucratic regime. While a personalist regime lasts, its leader can make bureaucrats subservient and force responsiveness to his whims because of their vulnerability to reprisal for incurring his disfavor. In a coalition regime, equality or near equality in the partnership arrangements offers more leverage to the civil bureaucracy for participation in political decision-making and for protection of group interests. A military junta can subordinate civilian officials but cannot avoid relying on their cooperation to keep the regime intact.

Law-and-Order Regimes: The Example of Indonesia

Among numerous recent or current examples of collegial military regimes primarily oriented toward the maintenance of political stability, notable examples are Argentina from the ouster of Isabel Peron to late 1983, Chile from the 1973 coup which eliminated Salvador Allende to the relinquishment of power by General Pinochet and his associates early in 1990, South Korea from 1961 to 1992, when a gradual transition from military to civilian political leadership was completed,[43] and Indonesia from 1966 to the end of the century. Depending mainly on the length of time since the beginning of military rule, these regimes range from orthodox juntas composed of active duty military officers with one of them perhaps designated as president or head of state (as in Argentina and Chile), to instances in which the leader of the junta which gained power through a military coup subsequently had his claim to political leadership ratified by an election process of some kind (as with President Suharto in Indonesia and President Park and his successors until recently in South Korea).

Experience in Indonesia from the mid-1960s until very recently manifested several of the characteristics commonly found in a military dominated regime with an emphatic law-and-order orientation. The country is currently undergoing a significant political transition, with the outcome still uncertain.[44]

The Republic of Indonesia is an archipelago of more than 13,600 islands (fewer than a thousand of which are inhabited) stretching nearly 5,000 kilometers west to east between Southeast Asia and Australia. Its population in the early 1990s (almost two-thirds of them concentrated on the island of Java) was approaching two hundred million, making it the fourth most populous nation in the world. Most Indonesians are of Malay origin, but there are nearly four hundred different ethnic groups with indigenous languages. This linguistic diversity has led to the development of new national language, *Bahasa Indonesia*. Indonesia is the largest Muslim nation in the world, with 90 percent of the population adhering in some form to Islam, but there are substantial Christian, Hindu, and Buddhist minorities, and an Islamic state has not been established.[45] With abundant natural resources (especially in oil, natural gas, forests, minerals, rubber, tin, tea, and coffee), Indonesia has enjoyed an annual average growth rate of six percent in recent years, making it the world's eighth fastest growing economy.

Before gaining independence from the Netherlands after World War II, Indonesia had gone through a long period of European colonization, beginning with explorations by the Portuguese at the end of the fifteenth century, primarily aimed at monopolizing the spice trade. After about a century, the Portuguese were ousted by the Dutch, who in 1602 chartered the United East India Company, based in Jakarta (also know as Batavia during the colonial period), with authority not only as a trading company but also as a governing entity on behalf of the Netherlands. From the early seventeenth to the middle of the eighteenth century, the United East India Company led Dutch expansion in Java, interrupted by British occupation from 1811 to 1816 as a byproduct of the Napoleonic wars in Europe. Gradually direct Dutch government rule replaced company control, resulting in expansion of Dutch imperialism beyond Java to other parts of the archipelago, and bringing together the territory that later became independent Indonesia after Japanese occupation during World War II and the successful postwar struggle against the Dutch between 1945 and 1949.

Indonesian political history from independence to the late 1990s can be divided into three periods. From 1950 to 1957, Indonesia was a unitary state with a parliamentary system of government vesting primary power in parliament and the cabinet, but with a president (Sukarno, the leading nationalist leader of the movement for independence) holding important reserve powers. During these years, Indonesian politics consisted of a series of government coalitions and constant cabinet changes, leading eventually to a proclamation of martial law by Sukarno and establishment of his system of "Guided Democracy," based on a repromulgation of an earlier 1945 "revolutionary" Constitution based on a strong presidential system.

The Guided Democracy era, which lasted until 1966, was dominated by Sukarno, in alliance with military leaders, particularly General Abdul Haris Nasution, who advocated a "middle way" which would concede to the armed forces an obligation to preserve national unity, without actually assuming political power. The political party system was revised drastically, with some parties being outlawed and only ten surviving, the strongest of which was the Indonesian Communist Party (PKI). Moreover, half the seats in the new parliament were allocated to functional groups, among which the military was included. By 1963, Sukarno had been proclaimed president-for-life, with support from the PKI, but with increasing hostility from Islamic groups and the military.

With internal antagonisms deepening, and external confrontations increasing, the political crisis led in October, 1965, to the displacement from power of Sukarno. An abortive coup d'etat led by procommunist elements in the armed forces succeeded in killing army commander General Yani and five of his close associates, but was quelled quickly by Major General Suharto, Yani's deputy. During the following six months, Suharto took a firm grip on power, pro-Sukarno elements in the armed forces were purged, and the PKI was eliminated in a violent anticommunist reaction in which hundreds of thousands were killed. In March, 1966, Sukarno was forced to transfer political authority to Suharto, while remaining president formally, but by a year later he had been stripped of all power, and was then kept under house arrest until his death in June, 1970. These events ushered in the "New Order" under General Suharto, which retained control in Indonesia for over three decades. This was a collegial military bureaucratic elite regime, even though there was no change in leadership at the very top. Suharto served six full terms as president, and was elected to a seventh term early in 1998, but was forced to resign less than three months later.

Suharto's most important accomplishment during these years was "to make the military the loyal, unquestioning pillar of his power." He astutely shifted his associates as circumstances changed, but consistently maintained the objective of maintaining "order and political calm," even though, as Sundhaussen commented, "many critics would regard it as the calmness of a cemetery, stifling political debate through press censorship, control of the electronic media, and, when necessary, massive intimidation and even arrests of opponents or mere critics."[46]

An elaborate doctrinal and institutional framework was erected to support the regime. Legitimacy was bolstered by Suharto's adoption as state ideology of Sukarno's *Pancasila* (Five Pillars), promulgated in 1945 at the beginning of the movement for independence.[47] The constitutional structure as a unitary republic with a presidential system of government was retained. Among other advantages, this permitted the president to choose ministers who are not members of the legislature but came from military, intellectual, or technocratic backgrounds. Legislative authority was shared by the People's Consultative Assembly (MPR) and the House of People's Representatives (DPR). The DPR, a body of 500 members, met annually, with 400 of the seats filled by elections in which the authorized political parties competed, and the remaining 100 seats were allocated to representatives of the armed forces. The MPR met every five years following the parliamentary elections, with its principal function being to elect the president and vice president for a five-year term. The MPR was made up of the 500 members of the DPR, plus another 500 individuals holding seats reserved for members of professional groups appointed by the president, delegates elected by provincial legislatures, and representatives of political parties proportional to their membership in the DPR.

The political party system was strictly circumscribed to avoid what was considered disruptive competition. The Communist party continued to be banned, and in 1973 the nine existing parties were forced to regroup into two coalitions— Muslim parties into the United Development Party (PPP), and Christian and secular parties into the Indonesian Democratic Party (PDI). The most important political action entity, however, was GOLKAR (Functional Groups), which functioned as the government "party." It was a federation of societal groups (such as peasants, workers, and women) firmly under the control of senior officers of the armed forces, cabinet ministers, and technocrats. GOLKAR dominated elections, receiving more than 73 percent of the vote in 1987 and 68 percent in 1992 (compared to 17 percent for PPP and 15 percent for PDI), preventing the emergence of an opposition majority.

In Indonesia's strong presidential system, the president was responsible to the MPR for the execution of state policy, had concurrent legislative power with the DPR, served as supreme commander of the armed forces, and appointed the cabinet. During the latter years of the Suharto era, there were twenty-one departments headed by ministers grouped under three coordinating ministers, plus eight ministers of state and six junior ministers, making a total of thirty-eight members. Moreover, three other high-ranking officials are accorded ministerial rank.

Attached to these ministries in various ways were a wide variety of public enterprises, which were relied on for the fulfillment of many government objectives. The 1945 Constitution provided for state control of "economic activities essential to the nation and the life of the people." This was interpreted to mean either ownership by the state or control by the state, with the priority shifting over time from one to the other, but with Suharto's New Order generally leaning toward control rather than direct ownership, partly because a contributing factor to Sukarno's downfall was that "political and economic conditions were aggravated by the excessive numbers of public enterprise personnel, which had grown due to patronage, and the low productivity and mismanagement of public enterprises which caused continual economic losses."[48] Reforms grouped continuing public enterprises into three types: department agencies (public service corporations, such as the railways, attached to a ministerial department and headed and staffed by civil servants); public corporations (having mixed functions generating income while providing public services, such as public utilities, with operations supervised by a technical minister and with employees not regarded as civil servants); and government/state companies (commercial corporations with shares wholly or partly government owned, and managed by a Board of Directors appointed by the Ministry of Finance). These formal categories were not always observed in practice, however, leading Mardjana to conclude that public enterprises continued to have problems of inefficiency due to excessive government intervention.

The bureaucracy staffing these ministries and public enterprises was a varying mix of civilians and military officers, with the latter dominating. Donald K. Emmerson made extensive studies of these combinations, concurring in the general conclusion that "the military as an oligarchy or an institution holds power and exercises it through the bureaucracy."[49] In 1981, a tabulation on the distribution of officers vs. civilians in the upper echelons of seventeen ministries showed a variation in military penetration from a high of one hundred percent in Defense and Security to a low of twelve percent in Public Works, and that the minister was from the military in nine instances as against eight civilians.[50] He found in 1986 that officers filled two-fifths of the posts in the higher central bureaucracy, "including presidential aides, ministers and top ministerial staff," had been named as "ambassadors, governors and district heads," had replaced "village heads purged in the anti-communist sweep of the 1960s," and occupied appointed seats in parliament, thus implementing "what the armed forces call their 'dual function': to shape the state while defending it."[51] While agreeing that "the New Order has transformed a previously polycentric bureaucracy into a military instrument for internal security and economic growth," Emmerson accepted the notion of "limited bureaucratic pluralism" as best describing "the roles within the bureaucracy of relatively civilian organizations with characteristic policy positions that reflect programmatic mandates," and he emphasized that the New Order "is not a homogenized antithesis of the nation it claims to represent. While the regime is certainly repressive, and it has sponsored a pattern of non-egalitarian growth, it is not anti-national."[52]

As long as the economic news continued to be good, rifts between President Suharto and elements in the armed forces leadership did not deepen,[53] and Suharto remained healthy, prospects appeared to be excellent for the regime to continue. Leifer observed in 1990 that "the wave of democratization now sweeping the world has left Indonesia surprisingly untouched, prompting neither a more assertive opposition nor a more open and accommodating government." Since the armed forces "are probably Indonesia's only truly national institution," political succession, he predicted, "will depend on the cohesion of its senior echelons and the extent to which they share a sense of common purpose in keeping Indonesia on the political and economic course set by Suharto since the mid-1960s."[54]

Then a rapid succession of unanticipated events in 1998 brought about the downfall of Suharto. The economic crisis that spread throughout East Asia during the last half of 1997 reached Indonesia, leading to soaring inflation, widespread unemployment, and demands for reform led by student activists in demonstrations on university campuses and elsewhere which caused widespread disorder and loss of life. The resulting chaos resulted in a growing demand for the ouster of Suharto, and to withdrawal of support for him from key military leaders. He resigned on May 21, and Vice President B. J. Habibie immediately took over as president.

During the ensuing two years, Indonesia has experienced a major political transformation, but the outlook for the future remains unclear. Habibie pledged political reformation and took steps to stabilize the economy, but immediately faced resistance because of his long association with Suharto. Late in 1998, the government announced that elections for the national parliament would be held in June, 1999, with the reconstituted body convening later in the year to elect a new president. This schedule was carried out. In the June elections, the Indonesian Democratic Party of Struggle, led by Megawati Sukarnoputri, daughter of founding President Sukarno, gained the most support, followed by Habibie's Golkar party. In the October presidential election, Habibie dropped out at the last minute, and the winner over Sukarnoputri was Abdurrahman Wahid, a noted Islamic leader who had formed the National Awakening Party after the fall of Suharto. The following day Sukarnoputri was elected vice president. President Wahid soon appointed a "national unity" cabinet, including for the first time a civilian as minister of defense. Wahid is in frail health, and the outlook for close collaboration between him and Sukarnoputri is uncertain, so that it is too early to know whether Indonesia is successfully following South Korea along the path toward greater democratization.

From Traditional to Collegial Regimes: The Example of Thailand

In a small number of instances, a collegial bureaucratic elite regime has directly replaced a traditional elite regime without a substantial intervening period of colonialism, although the country may have been for a time in the status of a protectorate or mandated territory under one of the major powers. These regimes have in common a necessity to adapt to their modernizing objectives the political and administrative structures which they inherited, but their approaches to doing this may vary considerably.

In Afghanistan (1973) and Ethiopia (1974), monarchies with traditional characteristics were overthrown by military coups and replaced by governments with collective military leadership, showing little inclination to share power with civilian elements, and facing immediate threats to their viability. By 1978, Afghanistan had succumbed to a Soviet-backed revolutionary regime which remained in power following the withdrawal of Soviet troops early in 1989, but by 1993 had given way to a coalition government with Islamic leadership. In Ethiopia, the military regime—beset with continuing problems of shifts within the core leadership group, internal disorder, famine, and revolt in the province of Eritrea—eventually was replaced in 1991.

Iraq in 1958, Syria in 1963, and Libya in 1969 likewise have all deposed monarchs, replacing them with military regimes with have espoused revolutionary ideology, advocated Arab unity and opposition to Israel, sponsored official parties which appear to be largely window dressing, and engaged in a moderate sharing of power with nonmilitary officials.

Thailand is an outstanding example of regimes of this type, with some features that are unique.[55] One of the very few ancient kingdoms managing to survive without being colonized, Thailand has at the same time borrowed heavily from the Western powers. The closest parallel is probably Japan. The resulting amalgam is best described as a bureaucratic polity under "predatory military rule," with a figurehead monarchy which serves a legitimizing role. "Among Third World countries," according to Welch and Smith, "the Thai polity and its participation pattern of civilian-military relations are in many ways highly anomalous." This praetorian political system is one in which "military factions and personal rivalries constitute the crucial factors in governmental change," with political competition limited to a narrowly restricted elite group while the mass of the population remains politically passive.[56]

The Chakkri reformation which took place in what was then Siam during the middle and late nineteenth century was primarily a response to the threat of British and French colonialism. This movement of adaptive modernization was led by two remarkable Siamese kings, Mongkut (Rama IV) and Chulalongkorn (Rama V). They sponsored programs of education abroad for young Thais, including commoners as well as members of the nobility. Military personnel were among those receiving foreign training. As a result, by the 1930s "a surplus of able young men, imbued with Western liberal thinking and anxious for a more influential role in government" had materialized. They "had absorbed much of Western liberalism and democracy and had become increasingly discontent with the anachronism of absolute monarchy."[57] Finding upon their return home that members of the royal and princely families continued to hold a monopoly on top posts and to control the decision-making process, these Western-trained civilian and military officials were ripe for bringing about political change.

In 1932 the absolute monarchy was overthrown by a bloodless coup d'etat, a constitutional monarch was substituted, and political power passed from the king and a small number of royal princes to a middle class group of military men and civilians. This new political elite has now maintained control for almost seven decades despite a bewildering succession of coups and countercoups as factional strength has shifted. The coup d'etat has become the usual means for transferring political power.[58]

The monarchy continues to serve a legitimizing function, despite being reduced to symbolic rather than active participation. "The continuing importance and inherent power of the monarchy in Thai politics," according to Morell, "place distinct constraints on the military, limiting the degree to which a military leader can exercise national charisma and rendering the armed forces liable to the palace for continuing recognition of their legitimate political role."[59] However, Neher notes that the direct impact of the monarchy on politics has been slight, as evidenced "by the king's inability to prevent coups d'etat and by his silence on issues before the government. . . . Thai leaders have not been willing to precipitate a confrontation between themselves and the monarchy, and in that sense the king acts as a moderating influence."[60]

During most of the period since 1932, Thailand has had a constitutional facade of a parliamentary system with occasional elections in which political parties are allowed to compete. Elections in Thailand, however, usually are not held for the purpose of permitting changes in the government, but "are held when the ruling groups become convinced that elections will enhance their power."[61] Political parties have been generally ineffectual and at times outlawed. Few nongovernmental interest groups exist.

Except for brief intervals, the longest being from 1973 to 1976, and again most of the time from late 1992 to the present, the ruling military-civilian establishment has remained firmly in control, although there have been tentative steps toward experimentation with a less authoritarian style of government. For example, under a new constitution promulgated in 1968 martial law was lifted and limited parliamentary government was permitted, but early in 1971 Prime Minister Thanom Kittikachorn, because of aggressive parliamentary activity on a number of fronts, brought this more open period of political competition to an abrupt end by suspending the constitution, dissolving the legislature, and banning all political parties except for a new government-sponsored party.

The most significant attempt to expand popular control over the bureaucratic elite came as the aftermath of student demonstrations late in 1973 which led to the downfall of the Thanom government and the appointment as prime minister of the rector of Thammasat University. These events led to the calling of a constitutional convention and the promulgation of another constitution in 1974 followed by elections in 1975 in which a large number of highly fragmented parties competed. Two short-lived coalition governments followed before another election was held early in 1976, which again failed to reduce the multiplicity of parties represented in the legislature or provide a base for a governing coalition acceptable to the military.

Late in 1976, another coup again installed a military-dominated government and reinforced the pattern of power transfer by coup. The leading military figures in the following years were General Kriangsak Chamanon, who was prime minister from 1977 to 1980, General Prem Tinsulanonda, who succeeded Kriansak and continued as prime minister despite various cabinet crises and abortive coups until he retired in 1988, and Major General Chatchai Choonhaven, who served until he was ousted by a coup early in 1991 which led to the installation of a interim junta called the National Peacekeeping Council (NPC) and the drafting of yet another new constitution which was promulgated later that same year. An election held in March, 1992, gave a legislative majority to four leading pro-military parties, leading to the appointment as prime minister, after he resigned his military posts, of General Suchinda Kraprayoon, the army commander. Suchinda was not an elected official, however, and although his appointment was constitutionally valid, it resulted in massive opposition, the adoption of a constitutional change banning such an appointment in the future, and Suchinda's resignation. In another election later in 1992, four non-military parties, with 51.4 percent of the vote, won a bare majority in the legislature, but felt it necessary to enter into a coalition with the conservative Social Action Party. Nevertheless, Chuan Leekpai, leader of the Democratic Party, became the first non-military leader since the mid-1970s to be named prime minister. From 1995 to late 1997, several coalition governments were in office briefly, before Chuan was appointed again as prime minister of a multiparty governing coalition which is currently still in power. Meanwhile, following extensive consideration, a new constitution was adopted in 1997 which among other provisions reduced the powers of the previously military dominated Senate and provided for direct election of its members.

Despite these constitutional changes and the current civilian leadership, the coup seems to have become institutionalized as a device for seeking to replace one clique with another, without moving decisively toward an alternative to elitist military rule. At least for the near future, political competition in Thailand is likely to follow the pattern described by Welch and Smith, "restricted to a very narrow elite, whose members share a substantial consensus regarding the political structures and values that uphold the status quo," and with cleavages within the elite tending to be based on "struggles between personal cliques for power, wealth, and status, rather than on conflicting political goals or differences in ideology."[62] Dissident political forces will continue to be subject to firm government controls, with those attempting to organize opposition to the government being repressed through harassment or withholding of favors, or more harshly through imprisonment or exile. Whatever prospects there may be for gradual transition from military rule seem to be dependent on two conditions: the strengthening of civilian institutions to reduce the factionalism and bickering which result in political instability, and arrangements which will allow the military leaders who are accustomed to political roles to continue as participants in policy formulation although in a less dominant capacity.[63] Whether or not the military's political authority gradually diminishes, the Thai political leadership is almost sure to maintain a paternalistic attitude toward the public, with few channels of accountability to the society as a whole.

The pattern of Thai administration within this political environment was determined more by reforms set in motion by King Chulalongkorn in 1892 than by changes following the 1932 revolution. He undertook to transform the traditional system by creating functionally specialized ministries in the European manner and by shifting to a salaried officialdom carefully selected from noble families, trained at home and abroad, and systematically assigned during their service careers. Lines of continuity to the existing administrative structure and the current bureaucracy are remarkably direct.

The executive branch of the Thai government is headed by the prime minister, who wields immense authority as leader of the military as well as the cabinet, and who himself has been a military officer in most instances. Under the prime minister in the cabinet are a dozen or more ministers heading the major government agencies, the most important of which are the Defense Ministry and the Ministry of Interior (controlling local administration and the police force). Each ministry has an undersecretary, who is the top ranking civil service official. Directors general in turn are in charge of departments within each ministry, which are further subdivided into divisions and sections in a highly rationalized scheme of organization. Nevertheless, observers report that administrative coordination has proved difficult to achieve. The system continues to be plagued by "ministerial and departmental competition, duplication of effort, and lack of cooperation in long-term planning."[64] This is in part due to the operation of the clique phenomenon in Thai politics, which places a premium on solidification of the power position of the dominant clique. Confidants of the clique leader are appointed to the important cabinet posts and then given considerable autonomy in operation. This process of clique solidification, "amounts to a 'feudalization' of the government administration, with each important member of the clique being conceded a virtual free rein in directing the affairs of his particular sector of the bureaucracy."[65]

The Thai civil service staffing these ministries is organized into hierarchical levels, with the top levels including those serving as section chiefs, undersecretaries, or even in a few instances as cabinet ministers. Except for those in the lowest class, these officials are usually college graduates, selected on a competitive basis. The prestige of the service remains high. Advancement depends very much on the approval of an official's superior in the administrative hierarchy. The adequacy of pay rates has been severely depressed by inflation, but fringe benefits are good. Disciplinary action against an official is rare. A civil service career offers status and security, plus the remote chance of breaking into the inner circle of the political elite.

Behavior patterns in the Thai bureaucracy reflect general cultural traits in the society such as deference to authority and stress on proper superior-subordinate relationships. Siffin suggests that the bureaucracy should be viewed as a social system which provides a framework for the behavior of its members. The dominant value orientations of the Thai bureaucrats are not productivity, rationality, and efficiency. He identifies them as hierarchical status; personalism, or "the reliance upon personal relationships and personal concerns as primary bases for behavior within the system"; and security, or "the desire to preserve one's membership in the system."[66] Bureaucratic actions are intended to support these primary values, not the secondary ones of providing goods and services for the general public in an efficient manner. The procurement, allocation, and utilization of resources by the bureaucracy take place in a context which emphasizes the primary rather than the secondary values.

Authority in such a system does not conform closely to impersonal legal-rational patterns; it "remains essentially personal and status-derived."[67] Siffin stresses that authoritativeness in the Thai bureaucracy is hierarchical, that status in the system is expressed by rank, and that these concepts do not necessarily conform to expectations taken from classical models of bureaucracy.

> Authority goes with rank, and rank is to a very great degree a personal thing. Thus subordinates are subject to superiors in a range of relationships not limited to "official business." They may serve drinks at his parties; they may even help him make money through non-official talents or connections . . . ; certainly they may play mirror to the Narcissism of the boss to a degree uncommon in an egalitarian context.[68]

At the same time, the authority of rank is limited in many ways that protect the subordinate against demands not socially acceptable. The total pattern of behavior is more concerned with maintenance of proper personal relationships in the social system than with productive output. Hence, there is "little of the tension between the formal and the informal which is characteristic of output-oriented Western systems."[69] The Thai bureaucracy is not subject to great internal stress; it is well adapted to its environment.

Generally civil bureaucrats in Thailand have been successfully brought under control by the military. This has been accomplished "by assignment of military officers to crucial positions of authority over civilians and by the continual process of coopting the bureaucrats to work amiably and effectively for the military regime," as well as "through the assignment of supporters or relatives to important subordinate positions, through periodic rotation of potential civilian competitors, and through fragmentation of power and responsibility among various civil agencies."[70] Civilians have normally administered the nation for the military, but they have also shared in the advantages that accrue to the ruling bureaucratic elite in the absence of effective external controls.

In his study of political development in Thailand, Riggs concludes that here is an almost classical case of a "bureaucratic polity." The interest of the bureaucrats themselves shape the organization of government so as to reflect their needs and purposes as its official beneficiaries.[71] Morell and Chai-anan assert that the Thai bureaucrat "views his position as his personal possession that can be used to advance his and his clique's interests."[72] Welch and Smith agree that there is a "distinctly amoral character to the pattern of elite competition in Thailand. The government's civil and military bureaucracies exist essentially to serve their own interests, since no outside social forces are powerful enough to threaten the government with political sanctions and thereby force it to recognize a larger moral purpose for its existence."[73]

Despite the tensions which have built up in recent years, the evidence still backs up the prediction made by Riggs that "the Thai political system will continue without major change as a relatively well-integrated and hence stable bureaucratic polity, a prismatic society in equilibrium, at a low level of industrialization and economic growth and an intermediate level of power distribution between the democratic and authoritarian extremes."[74] The process of modernization has permitted successful response to the impact of the West, but in the transition the official class has become the ruling class, largely self-recruited from the upper reaches of the military and civilian bureaucracies. This pattern of development has not been balanced; a rapid increase in bureaucratic capabilities has not been accompanied by a compensatory growth of institutions, outside the bureaucracy, able to control it. The resulting polity corresponds closely to Riggs' model of "prismatic" society.

The Influence of Colonialism: The Example of Ghana

In other regimes with collegial bureaucratic elites, a pervasive background factor has been a prolonged colonial era during which the colonial power was able to implant its political and administrative institutions in the subject territory so firmly as to provide the decisive point of reference for developments following national independence, even though over time significant modifications may have been made in the initial institutional framework. In most of these cases, continuity has proved to be greater in the administrative than in the political sphere, with bureaucratic elites formed during the colonial period gradually taking over political control in what were immediately after independence polyarchal competitive political regimes. Several former British colonies, such as Burma, Pakistan, and Ghana, best fit this description, but it applies also to some former French colonies such as Chad, Mali, Niger, and the Republic of the Congo. We use Ghana as an illustrative case.

The political history of Ghana in the postindependence era features a succession of political regime types, with the military and civilian bureaucracies playing crucial roles in all of them.[75] The first West African country to gain independence, Ghana started in 1957 with a parliamentary political system on the British model. Kwame Nkrumah, who had led the struggle for national autonomy, became prime minister under a cabinet system of government, with opposition parties well represented in parliament. Within five years, a "cult of personality" had emerged which bestowed the title of "Osagyefo the President" upon Nkrumah under a republican constitution, and a one-party system was in operation. Every aspect of social life became politicized in support of the Convention People's Party, which had for its main objectives "work and happiness for all the people." Apter viewed the effort as a uniquely Ghanaian blend, consisting of a national form of traditionalism in the name of socialism. "The nation replaced the ethnic community. The Presidential-monarch replaced the chief. . . . Ideology became a political religion increasingly intolerant of all other religions, monopolistic, expressed through the militant elect of the party."[76]

Gradually Nkrumah lost his charisma and the party fell apart. "By 1965," according to Apter, "the party consisted of vast networks of committees which did not meet, organizations which failed to function, and personal manipulations which aroused mutual suspicion, mistrust, and recrimination."[77] Despite the fact that Nkrumah was made party chairman for life, held a national referendum that made Ghana officially a one-party state, and in various ways attempted to increase his authority, political opposition grew and the economic situation worsened. The outcome was a skillfully planned and well-executed bloodless coup staged by army and police leaders in 1966 when Nkrumah was out of the country. An eight-man National Liberation Council (NLC) was set up, headed at first by Major General Ankrah and later by Brigadier Afrifa.

The military regime discredited Nkrumah, purged his followers, launched an austerity economic program, sponsored the drafting of a new constitution, and promised a prompt return to civilian rule. This was done following elections in 1969, which resulted in the designation of Kofi A. Busia, a civilian, as prime minister, first under a three-man presidential commission of NLC members and later under another civilian as head of state. The Busia government lasted only two-and-a-half years, however, before it was ousted following another seizure of control by the military early in 1972. The leader of this coup was then Colonel (later General) I. K. Acheampong, who served as head of state and chairman of the Supreme Military Council. This military regime dissolved the National Assembly, formally banned all political parties, and suspended the constitution. Acheampong in turn was forced to resign in mid-1978. His replacement, Lieutenant General Fred W. Akuffo, pledged on behalf of the ruling supreme military council that power would be handed over to a popularly elected government on July 1, 1979.

This election did in fact occur, but it led only to the temporary interruption of military rule in Ghana. Less than a month before the scheduled election, a mutiny launched by junior officers in the air force and army ousted the Akuffo regime and installed Flight Lieutenant Jerry Rawlings, then thirty-two years old, as head of a new Armed Forces Revolutionary Council (AFRC). Its main targets were senior military officers, eight of whom were executed (including three former heads of state). The AFRC then allowed the election to be held, and surrendered power later in 1979 to an elected civilian government led by President Hilla Limann and the People's National Party (PNP). As Bjorn Hettne remarks, this military regime "must be unique in the history of military politics. It took power from a military regime and handed it over to a civilian, after having executed a number of high military officers and put many more in jail."[78]

The interlude of civilian government was short, however. "In handing over power in the National Assembly in 1979," Jon Kraus reports, "Rawlings had warned the assembled politicians that if they used their offices to pursue their own self-interests, they would be resisted and removed from power."[79] Late in 1981, slightly more than two years later, Rawlings did indeed oust the Limann/PNP government is what Kraus aptly calls his "second coming," returning Ghana to rule by a military oligarchy which continues in power, giving it the longest survival record in Ghana since independence.

The main instrument for control during most of this period was the Provisional National Defense Council (PNDC), chaired by Rawlings, with authority to "exercise all the powers of government." Both military officers and civilians were members of the PNDC and served as cabinet ministers under it, but the military provided the key power base. Local government institutions were replaced early on by regime support councils, designated in 1984 as Committees for the Defense of the Revolution (CDRs).

After more "participatory democracy" had been promised for years, elections for district assemblies were held in late 1988 and early 1989, and early in 1993 a new Constitution of the Fourth Republic revamped the central government. It provided for a directly elected president, a presidentially appointed vice president, a military-civilian Security Council headed by the president, and a directly elected unicameral legislative body. The PNDC was formally disbanded. Under the new constitution, after a disputed election in which he received 58.3 percent of the vote, Rawlings was elected president for a four-year term beginning in 1993. He was reelected for a second four-year term starting in 1997, thus consolidating his power for the indefinite future.

In all of these civilian and military regimes in Ghana since independence, the civil bureaucracy in place when British colonialism ended has maintained a stance of indispensability but not dominance. The British civil service model still formally characterizes public administration in Ghana, referred to by Price as an exceptional instance of "institutional emulation."[80] Many of the senior bureaucrats in Ghana began their careers in the British colonial civil service, and were trained under the British. Even after independence, many British expatriates continued to man the upper echelons of the civil service, which was not fully "Africanized" until the mid-1960s.

The civil service has been able to retain much of its inherited status and prestige, despite efforts to curb it, especially when civilian politicians have controlled the government. A split between the political and bureaucratic elites began in Ghana before independence was finally won and continued into the period of single-party dominance, when one observer wrote that "The people who staff the bureaucracy are not representative of those who control or support the party that controls the government."[81] The bureaucrats came from higher social status groups, were more Westernized, and were less reform-minded than the leaders of the Convention People's Party (CPP). Accordingly, the CPP leadership viewed the higher civil service, along with the university community, as a possible source of disaffection, and took precautionary steps. A British-modeled public service commission was replaced by a civil service commission with largely advisory powers. The 1960 constitution vested full control of the civil service in the president, including "appointment, promotion, transfer, termination of appointment, dismissal, and disciplinary control." The CPP program called for a complete revamping of the civil service to release it from colonial restraints and mentality and relate its methods to Ghanaian needs and conditions, but there was more rhetoric than accomplishment. The actual steps taken were not drastic. A new school for civil servants was set up, partly to instill new attitudes, but also in recognition of the mounting need for managerial personnel. Membership in the government-sponsored trade union organization was made mandatory for all but the higher civil servants, but they were denied the right to strike and the government was not bound by an agreement made with their unions.

The basic fact seems to have been that the party and the civil service needed one another, and Nkrumah needed them both. "What kept the system going," as Apter comments, "was the quiet alliance between two often hostile forces, the party bureaucracy and the civil service. If they had mutual contempt for one another, both recognized that they were essential for the running of day-to-day affairs."[82] During the time Nkrumah maintained firm control of the state and party apparatus, the career officials remained politically passive and obeyed their political masters, but they retained essential governmental powers.

During its brief time in power, the Busia government ousted several hundred public servants for what appeared to be political and ethnic considerations rather than faults in administrative conduct. The military regimes preceding the current one, although sporadically displaying their power to humiliate or discipline civil servants incurring the displeasure of military officials, did not undertake to disturb civil service prerogatives, which seemed to be firmly established. Indeed, Price stated as his belief in 1975 that it was "doubtful whether the contemporary political leadership in Ghana . . . would have sufficient political support to engage in a drastic restructuring of the existing 'scheme of service' in public bureaucracy, even if it were so inclined."[83]

Under Rawlings, the civil bureaucracy seems to have been facing a more precarious situation without ceasing to be influential. When the AFRC seized power in 1979, it dismissed many high-ranking civil servants simultaneously with its purge of senior military officers. When Rawlings took over again in 1981, however, his power base was unstable and he has since undertaken to build support from a broad coalition which has included civilians as cabinet ministers and as occupants of other important positions. He has recruited professional managers and technocrats both for the ministries and state corporations. Higher wages were provided for lower level workers, with a resulting compression between the lowest and highest wage levels, which in turn required adjustments at the higher levels.[84] Nevertheless, in the opinion of Donald Ray, the shortage of qualified personnel has meant that "there has been little effective political supervision of the civil service, whose senior levels have been in large measure unsympathetic and whose junior levels have been demoralized by the inability of their salaries to meet the ravages of inflation."[85]

Ghana, like other new states in Africa, is still operating basically with inherited colonial administrative institutions.[86] The civil service, as the most significant of these institutions, has retained the aura of the colonial service, but there is doubt that it has conformed to reasonable expectations as to performance in the new national setting. In his study of Ghanaian bureaucracy, Price concludes that "administrative performance suffers . . . because of institutional malintegration, the existence of structurally differentiated organizations in an unsupportive sociocultural environment."[87] He argues that "status" institutionalization has taken place much more thoroughly than "role" institutionalization, with the result that "organizationally dependable role behavior" by Ghanaian civil servants is unlikely because of the social pressures placed on them. Behavior that leads to the accomplishment of organizational goals is not apt to bring social approval in the environment of a traditional African society.

The recurring issue of corruption, for example, may be explainable by social expectations based on the "exalted status" inherited by contemporary Ghanaian senior bureaucrats from their British predecessors, which implies "great expectations" as well. A senior civil service post "brings with it greatly increased influence, obligation, and responsibility within one's extended family. The obligations and responsibilities carry a heavy material burden. Not only will the African civil servant be expected to provide financial assistance to his family . . . but . . . he is also likely to be expected to maintain the material aspects of a European 'life-style.'" These socially appropriate symbols of status and family financial obligations "will entail great expense and will tend to outdistance what is financially available to the civil servant through his salary,"[88] leading to widespread administrative corruption. This has been one of the factors motivating military intervention, without resulting in elimination or significant reduction of the problem.[89]

Despite being, according to Apter, "the one African country with a genuine parliamentary experience,"[90] despite presenting two of the rare instances of voluntary relinquishment of military for civilian rule, and despite the political liberalization beginning with the 1993 election of Rawlings as president, Ghana still seems to be firmly set in a pattern of bureaucratic elite governance. The power mix between civilian and military elements is real but blurred. As Hettne points out, however, once the military intervenes in politics, "this tends to become a politicizing experience which makes a repetition likely, and in consequence, when military rulers leave power to civilians it is seldom unconditionally."[91]

PENDULUM SYSTEMS

As explained in Chapter 7, the most significant feature of the political environment in some developing countries may be that a pattern has been established swinging the political system periodically back and forth between bureaucratic elite and polyarchal competitive regime categories. Whatever the current situation, the pendulum is likely to swing again in the other direction in the near future. Because of the actual or potential political power position of the bureaucracy, these need to be viewed as bureaucratic-prominent regimes.

Any specification as to what qualifies as a pendulum system will necessarily be somewhat arbitrary. Other things being equal, of course, the longer a country has been independent, the more opportunities it will have had for political regime transitions. Our interest is primarily in what has happened during recent decades and what may happen during the next decade or so. Hence, for our purposes, the essential requirement will be that at least three swings of the pendulum have taken place during the period since the end of World War II (or since independence if that came later), and that the likelihood of still another movement of the pendulum within the next decade remains high.

Because independence came earlier to the countries of Latin America than to those in other regions of the Third World, some of these nations have compiled astonishing records of political changeability, with Bolivia standing out. Bolivia's current constitution, adopted in 1967 and suspended intermittently since, was its sixteenth following independence in 1825. Two hundred chief executives have been in office since independence, thirteen of them during the brief period from 1969 to 1982. Bolivia easily qualifies as a pendulum system, using any time scale, long or short. So do numerous other Latin American nations. Some additional important examples, based on the more restricted criteria mentioned earlier, are Argentina, Brazil, and Peru.

Drawing from different regions for illustrations of pendulum systems, we use Brazil from Latin America, Nigeria from sub-Saharan Africa, and Turkey from the Middle East.

Brazil

Beginning in 1964, Brazil was governed by a military elite in collaboration with civilian bureaucrats, with a gradual opening up of political competition during the 1970s, leading to restoration of civilian political leadership (through indirect election in 1985 and direct election in 1989) which has continued through the 1990s.[92] The political history of Brazil after independence from Portugal in 1822 has included a lengthy period of monarchy during most of the nineteenth century, followed by a federal constitutional republic under which elected presidents have alternated with presidents who have been installed as the result of military intervention. In 1930 Getulio Vargas began a fifteen-year authoritarian presidency after a coup d'etat, giving way in 1945 to a period of almost two decades during which elected presidents again held office, the last being Joao Goulart, who had been elected as vice president and took over as president in 1961 when President Quadros resigned. The Goulart administration came under increasing attack for pervasive governmental corruption, pro-Communist sympathies, and inflationary economic policies, and was overthrown in 1964 by the military in a nearly bloodless coup.

Although the military in Brazil had long been recognized as a moderating force in Brazilian society and had frequently intervened politically, military retention of political power for a lengthy and indeterminate time span did not conform to the military's traditional role as a "moderator" among competing political factions. Backed by language in several Brazilian constitutions designating the military as a "permanent national institution specifically charged with the tasks of maintaining law and order in the country and of guaranteeing the normal functioning" of the executive, legislative, and judicial branches, it was generally conceded, according to Einaudi and Stepan, that the military "had sanction to overthrow the elected President, but not to assume political power."[93] Drury concurred that the military as an institution had considered itself "the final authority in political conflicts, charged specifically with preventing the imposition of radical solutions to political problems."[94]

Political intervention of such a limited nature, with control being passed back to civilians after military imposition of an effective compromise, was no longer considered sufficient by the post-1964 regime, which acted on the belief that "the crisis which confronted the political system could be resolved only by an extended period of military rule during which the system would be rebuilt."[95]

This period turned out to be over twenty years, with five generals succeeding one another as president, the last being President Figueiredo, inaugurated in 1979 for a six-year term. As time passed, minor and temporary concessions were made toward a partial restoration of normal constitutional government, but the presidency remained subject to indirect election by an electoral college considered to be firmly under control by the political elite, and only two political parties were authorized-one progovernment and one in opposition. Figueiredo was identified with a faction of the higher-ranking military leadership favoring a further "opening" or "decompression" in the Brazilian political system, leading in the 1982 elections to significant gains by the opposition group, which garnered 62 percent of the vote, and gained control of ten states and the national House of Representatives, while the ruling party won in thirteen states and maintained control of both the Senate and the electoral college (scheduled to elect a new president in 1985).

The pace of political change then picked up such momentum that in 1985 the progovernment party nominated a civilian for president instead of a general, and he was in turn defeated in the electoral college by Tancredo Neves of the Party of the Brazilian Democratic Movement (PMDB). Unfortunately, illness prevented Neves from assuming office, and his vice presidential running mate, Jose Sarney, became acting president and then president after Neves died. During Sarney's term in office, a new constitution was adopted providing for direct election of the president for a nonrenewable five-year term, but Sarney himself proved to be ineffective and unpopular. As a result, the victor in the 1989 election was a political newcomer, Fernando Collor de Mello, who campaigned on an anti-Sarney platform focusing on the punishment of corruption in high places. Inaugurated as president early in 1990, Collor instead of leading a reform movement soon became the object of corruption charges involving himself, his wife, and close associates. After prolonged investigations and controversies, by late 1992 Collor had been impeached and had resigned, being replaced by Vice President Itomar Franco. The winner in the 1994 election was Fernando Enrique Cardoso, a centrist who had been serving as finance minister. Inaugurated at the beginning of 1995, Cardoso has headed a center-right coalition government. After securing approval of a constitutional amendment permitting him to seek reelection, Cardoso won a second four-year term in 1998, despite having to contend with a severe economic crisis. Thus, Brazil's fragile transition to democracy has taken place, but its staying power remains to be proved, with the pendulum poised to swing back again toward bureaucratic elitism should civilian leadership falter.

How has the nature of the Brazilian administrative system been affected first by the two decades of the military regime and more recently by the movement toward democratization, and what will its role be in future Brazilian political development?

One of the most striking features of the period of military rule beginning in 1964 was its strong corporate-technocratic orientation. More than any other region, Latin America has provided examples of regimes with corporatist-technocratic tendencies. As Tapia-Videla has pointed out, this requires that emphasis must be placed on "the critical role of expertise, depersonalized leadership, and the development of a new bureaucratic ethos: one stressing the corporate ideology that aims at achieving a balanced interdependence between competing policy and issue areas."[96] Partial political demobilization and increased reliance on an overhauled bureaucracy become prime objectives. The intent is to "form strong and relatively autonomous governmental structures that seek to impose on the society a system of interest representation based on enforced limited pluralism," and to "eliminate spontaneous interest articulation and establish a limited number of authoritatively recognized groups that interact with the government in defined and regularized ways."[97]

Motivated by such values, the Brazilian military elite, in cooperation with civilian technocrats, tried to attain both political stability and economic development. The approach taken was to adopt corporatist strategies for controlling the political process and to rely on *tecnicos* for progress on the economic front. Corporatism concentrated on the dampening of lower class protest by setting up a government-manipulated system of labor organizations, or *sindicatos*, to channel labor interest-group representation. The aim of the elite for more rationalized policy-making led to an increase in numbers and authority of technically trained administrators or *tecnicos* in decision-making posts where they were expected to act on technical criteria.[98] The civilian technocrats were able to enter into the ruling elite, and even constituted "a kind of aristocracy within the public service,"[99] but the condition of admission was "complete loyalty to the ideology of the regime."[100] The political and economic goals were attained in part, but at the price of severely restricted political competition and without a widespread sharing of economic gains among the nation's people,[101] contributing to the eventual weakening of the regime.

Robert Daland, a longtime student of the Brazilian administrative system, described this ruling elite as "an essentially technocratic alliance of convenience between the old civil bureaucracy and the military bureaucracy," with the two proving compatible because they shared "the same basic attitudes toward the business of government."[102] However, he concluded that although the military government desired an administrative machine that was strong and efficient, it did not succeed in achieving one. He found that there had been too few experts to recruit, that bureaucratic career paths did not effectively utilize talent that was available, and that "patterns of administrative culture and administrative behavior in Brazil are buried deeply in the history and culture of the society and will not easily be changed." He asserted that the Brazilian bureaucracy had indeed become increasingly "the motor for economic development," but a motor that was towing a very large anchor, which could be reduced in size only by adoption of a long-range strategy for management modernization.[103]

Such modernization was not accomplished under the military, and for understandable reasons it has not been a high priority during the difficult transition to civilian political control. As Reis comments, "the rectification of public bureaucracies has not ranked high on the political agenda."[104] President Collor did signal interest in administrative matters early in his term by streamlining the number of ministries from twenty-five to twelve and by announcing plans to cut public employment by twenty to twenty-five percent. Collor's attention soon was diverted to other matters, however, and up to now deficiencies in the civil bureaucracy continue to be a serious problem.[105]

Meanwhile, most observers agree that the Brazilian armed forces continue to play a crucial political role. Perhaps Juan de Onis is correct in saying that "there is no hint that the military has the desire to reimpose an authoritarian system," and only wants to guard public order and resist revolutionary violence,[106] but William C. Smith cautions that "the repressive apparatus remains intact, the armed forces' underlying interventionist posture is largely unchanged, and the military's institutional presence in the state has not been significantly affected by civilian rule."[107] Pointing out that the institutional prerogatives of the military "in effect since the end of the Brazilian Empire . . . were extended during the authoritative regime and remain untouched by the civilian government," Maria do Carmo Campello de Souza pessimistically predicts that the most probable outcome is that "the Brazilian democratization effort will be slowly debilitated by the suffocating weight of the military's presence."[108] Given the combination of military advantages, civil bureaucratic weaknesses, and inexperienced political leadership, the outlook for the current democratic regime in Brazil is at best doubtful.

Nigeria

Nigeria has had a turbulent political history since gaining independence from Great Britain in 1960.[109] As a political entity, Nigeria was invented by the British, and in the early years Nigerian nationhood was less a reality than a possibility. Constituted at the beginning as a federation of three regions, with the initial civilian government patterned after the British parliamentary model, Nigeria soon faced intractable regional and tribal tensions which led first in 1966 to overthrow of the civilian government and imposition of military rule, and later to a civil war which resulted in defeat of the attempt of the eastern region to assert its independence as the republic of Biafra.

During the 1970s, a succession of military regimes struggled with problems of national consolidation, constitutional revision, and setting of a timetable for resumption of civilian rule. By 1979, a remarkable political transformation had taken place, offering one of the rare instances of a voluntary planned military withdrawal from political power. This transition was preceded by the adoption of a new constitution which restructured the Nigerian federation into a system of nineteen states, and substituted a modified presidential form of government for the parliamentary form inherited from the British. The president was elected by a nationwide constituency for a four-year term under a complicated voting formula designed to assure that the winning candidate not only had support from the largest number of voters but in addition had backing spread geographically among the states. The American model was followed also by constitutional provision for a bicameral national legislature and an independent judiciary.

The turnover of power came at the end of a four-year transition schedule which was adhered to precisely. Five presidential candidates competed in elections won by Alhaji Shehu Shagari of the National Party of Nigeria (NPN), who took over from General Olusegun Obasanjo in October, 1979. Shagari was re-elected for a second term in 1983, again meeting the constitutional requirement for widespread support, as well as receiving the most votes (47 percent of the total) in a field of six candidates. Nigeria apparently had emerged into an era of relative political stability following the devastating civil war of the late 1960s and the continued turmoil of the 1970s.

On the last day of 1983, however, a bloodless military coup led by a group of senior military officers overthrew Shagari, on the grounds that his administration was inept (as shown by public unrest, diminished oil income and a declining economy), and corrupt. As chairman of a new Supreme Military Council, Major General Muhammadu Buhari suspended portions of the constitution, banned political parties, and launched a campaign against corruption and lack of discipline. Plagued by worsening economic conditions and resistance to political repression, Buhari was in turn ousted in mid-1985 by Major General Ibrahim Babangida, who in 1987 set in motion a five-year schedule for another restoration of civilian government. The agenda called for constitutional revision, a lifting of the ban on political parties (although only two parties were later sanctioned), elections to unicameral state legislatures in 1990, and federal presidential and legislative elections in 1992.

This plan for a return to civilian rule was never implemented. Two attempts to conduct presidential primaries in the fall of 1992 were aborted, presumably because of fraud. After a new series of primaries, a presidential election was finally held in June, 1993, with the apparent winner being a millionaire businessman, Moshood Abiola. Babangida then suspended the election results, leading to Abiola's declaring himself president, but then being charged with treason by Babangida, who also fired the army and navy commanders. Later in 1993, Babangida stepped aside and was replaced by an interim civilian president.

This interim government was soon forced out by Defense Minister General Sani Abacha, who late in 1993 took over as head of state and in the other roles that had been occupied by Babangida. Abacha dissolved all legislative assemblies, banned political parties and political activity, and announced that the military would rule, although he later chose a cabinet made up in part of civilians, and announced plans to turn authority over to an elected civilian government on October 1, 1998. Despite continuing political turmoil, Abacha maintained a tenuous hold on power while facing increasing international criticism, until his death in June, 1998, of an apparent heart attack. His replacement, General Abdulsalam Abubakar, soon approved a revised timetable for a series of elections starting at the local level, then gubernatorial, and finally legislative and presidential. The culmination of this process was that General Obasanjo, who had given way to Shagari in 1979, returned to power as the candidate of the People's Democratic Party in a direct election held in February, 1999, and in May took office for a four-year term.

Thus the pendulum phenomenon is an integral feature, retrospectively and prospectively, of the Nigerian political scene. "This alternation of civilian and military regimes," in William Graf's opinion, "must now be seen as the norm, rather than an aberration, of Nigerian politics." Moreover, he adds, "this pendulum-movement may be the adequate (or least inadequate) political 'form' of system maintenance."[110] Larry Diamond has suggested that, given the Nigerian experience, the path to political stability and the way out of "Nigeria's ruinous political cycles" may in fact require "institutionalization of a role for the military," and he has sketched the outlines of a "diarchy" of shared civilian and military rule, which would assign to the military "those regulatory and administrative functions vital to democratic stability and highly vulnerable to political abuse at Nigeria's current stage of political and economic development." These supervisory powers would include the monitoring and punishment of corruption, the conduct of elections, control over police officers, appointments to judicial posts, and the collection of census data.[111] He points out that such a scheme could be put in place either by a civilian government providing a permanent institutional role for the military, or by the creation and gradual enlargement by the military of institutional roles for civilians. This "reverse implementation" may turn out to be the strategy of the current move toward greater civilianization of the political system.

The Nigerian civil bureaucracy has played a prominent role both during periods of military and civilian rule, in part because of the frequent regime oscillations. Nigeria provides another instance of greater stability and continuity in administration than in politics. The British bequeathed to the new nation a functioning bureaucracy well suited to colonial needs but inadequate after independence. Nigerian reshaping and restaffing began immediately at a rapid pace which has been maintained to the present, explaining Peter Koehn's summary comment that ". . . expansion and extension constitute the most striking and consistent forms of bureaucratic development in Nigeria."[112]

Initial stress was put on speeding up the process of Nigerianization of the public service which had begun before independence. Early in the 1960s, Nigerians already occupied a majority of senior posts, but there was considerable regional variation, with expatriates continuing to be employed on a contract basis, especially in the northern region. Indicative of the difficulties involved were the reported vacancies in almost one-fifth of the senior posts in the country as a whole and the fact that in the eastern region, where Nigerianization had occurred at a rapid rate, the median age of administrative officers was thirty-three, and the average officer had a background of only three-and-a-half years of any kind of government experience. Personnel shortages were aggravated by the practice of giving priority in employment in the regions of the federation to individuals from the region; this preference apparently continues in the present more numerous states.

British administrative practices have been retained, but substantially modified. The ministerial system, including the permanent secretary's role, is still in place, but a distinction is made between "administrative" and "technical" ministries; in the former group the permanent secretary continues to serve as chief administrator and advisor to the minister, but in the technical ministries there is more of a sharing of executive responsibilities between the permanent secretary and directors of technical services within the ministry.

Other carry-over tendencies from the colonial period are the preference for generalists over specialists both in assignment of responsibility and status recognition, and the maintenance of a sharp distinction between senior and junior officer groupings in the public service, with the former having much higher salaries and emoluments. As a consequence, as in other former British colonies, high-ranking civil servants have been able to inherit the role and status of their predecessors in the British colonial service.

The most important overall trend, however, has been a cumulative expansion in government employment at both central and state government levels and in a growing number of public enterprises. This in turn is a reflection of what most observers regard as the overweening role of the state in Nigerian affairs. "Nigerian society is characterized," according to Marenin, "by an overpowering statism which inextricably intertwines political and economic power."[113] Diamond contends that "the primary source of economic crisis and political decay in Nigeria today is the lengthening shadow of the state over every other realm of society."[114] An incidental and detrimental effect of this high degree of statism is a bloated and ineffectual public bureaucracy and a low level of private entrepreneurship.

Another related feature of the postindependence period has been the spread of corruption, which is now acknowledged to be "all-pervasive," at a level "as great or greater than anywhere else in the world."[115] Koehn asserts that "the salaries and fringe benefits of public servants pale in significance by comparison with the more indirect opportunities for individual enrichment that government service provides . . . ," and he claims that most civil servants "have principally devoted their ample social prestige and political power to reaping personal or corporate group benefits."[116] Ronald Cohen notes that the gaining of a "blessed job" is the common goal of university graduates, who then jealously guard the perquisites that come with the job and are drawn into the pattern of corruption which is deeply ingrained into the system itself. In his view, the Nigerian bureaucracy is "a partially-separate sociocultural system set into, and articulated with, a wider, culturally plural, national entity. In this sense the bureaucracy is a set of new social structures grafted on top of what were in the recent past a set of forcibly subjugated, previously autonomous, African societies." The resulting maladaptive patterns, including corruption, mean that "the very infrastructure created to carry out development is, in fact, one of the main obstacles to its achievement."[117] Koehn also raises the question as to whether the Nigerian bureaucracy is a participant in national underdevelopment rather than development.

Under these circumstances, it is not surprising that Nigerian civil bureaucrats have played a major role in public policy-making, supported both by colonial tradition and postcolonial practice. Koehn asserts that "higher civil servants have been central, and often dominant participants in the policymaking process throughout Nigeria's history."[118] He traces shifts in the degree of their involvement during the various regimes since independence, finding it to be substantial under the original civilian government, increasing with the onset of military rule, and reaching its zenith during the regime of General Gowon, which ended in 1975. Ensuing military and civilian regimes have tried in various ways to establish firmer control over the civil bureaucracy, but with generally ineffective results. Despite these variations, Adamolekun is probably correct in reaching the overall conclusion that "changes in regime types have had minimal impact. The roles of political leaders and administrators in the policy process did not change significantly from one regime type to another. The key determinant was the continued attachment to the concept of a career civil service which ensured that civil servants had primary responsibility for policy advice and the implementation of settled policies under successive regime types."[119] A political setting with frequent shifts back and forth from transient military to weak civilian governments thus can offer an optimal environment for civil career bureaucrats to participate in policy-making and to profit personally and corporately from their opportunities.

Turkey

Modern Turkey is the product of a modernizing military leadership which surrendered power to civilian hands but has stood nearby to intervene as necessary.[120]

Emerging after World War I as the nation-state remnant of the old Ottoman Empire, Turkey experienced rapid and pervasive modernization under the leadership of Mustafa Kemal Ataturk until his death in 1938. Ataturk eliminated the political influence of the religious hierarchy, removed the military from direct participation in politics, and created the Republican People's Party (RPP) as the vehicle for carrying out national modernization. The political domination of the RPP continued after Ataturk's death under his successor and associate Ismet Inonu. During the late 1940s, the Democratic party was organized and grew rapidly. In the 1950 election, it succeeded in ousting the RPP after twenty-seven years in office, ushering in a period of political competition which was maintained, with one major interruption, until 1980.

During the first decade of this thirty year period, the ruling Democratic party embarked in the 1950s on a program of increased agricultural production, economic development, improved communication and transportation facilities, and other reforms designed to bring the traditional peasant masses more actively into the economic and political arenas. The changes which took place, however, also had profound consequences for inter-elite relationships, because the new political elite "adopted policies that adversely affected the position of the military, the bureaucracy and the intellectuals. . . . The result was acute polarization."[121] Military intervention in May 1960 was the outcome, with power being seized by a junta called the National Unity Committee, which tried and convicted leaders of the Democratic party, hanging former Prime Minister Menderes and imprisoning others. This military regime announced its intention to restore civilian rule promptly and actually did so in 1961. During the 1960s and 1970s political cleavages continued to be evident, with most governments consisting of multiparty coalitions. The RPP functioned as the leading party in a series of these coalitions, mostly under Inonu as prime minister, until 1965. In the general election that year, the Justice party (which had replaced the outlawed Democratic party) won a major victory and was able to maintain a shaky unity within its ranks until another crisis came to a head in 1971, resulting in the formation of "non-party" governments during 1971 and 1972 after the imposition of martial law in several provinces. Following an inconclusive election in 1973 and continuing to the end of civilian rule in 1980, the political situation remained stalemated with contention between two major parties—the moderately left RPP led by Bulent Ecivit, and the moderately right Justice party by Suleyman Demirel, neither of which could form a government without working out a coalition involving one or more minor parties, and neither of which could maintain itself in a dominant position for long.

Eventually in late 1980 a junta led by General Kenan Evren took over, suspended the 1961 constitution, disbanded the parliament, and imposed martial law restrictions on political statements and activity. After a two-year interval, the junta in 1982 submitted a revised constitution to a referendum by the voters, who ratified it by a wide margin. It authorized parliamentary elections, which were held in November 1983, with the Motherland party headed by Turgut Ozal winning by a two-to-one margin over the National Democracy party favored by the military. Ozal was installed as prime minister in December, with a cabinet consisting mostly of members of parliament from the Motherland party. The new constitution automatically continued Evren as president for a seven-year term, and it extended restrictions on political freedom, including the ten-year ban from political life imposed in 1980 on both Ecevit and Demirel, leaders of what had been the two main political parties.

Under a system of proportional representation designed to penalize minor parties, the Motherland party in 1987 increased its majority to 251 in the 400-member National Assembly. Also in 1987, the constitutional ban on pre-1980 political leaders was repealed, enabling both Demirel and Ecevit, among others, to resume their political careers. Late in 1989, when President Evren's term ended, Ozal was elected by parliament (with opposition parties boycotting the vote) to replace him for a seven-year term, and a moderate member of the Motherland party took over from Ozal as prime minister. Midway through his term, in early 1993, President Ozal died suddenly of a heart attack, leading to the election of Demirel as president for a seven-year term ending in 2000. Shortly afterward, Tansu Ciller of the True Path Party was selected as the first woman to serve as prime minister. In 1995, after being defeated on a confidence motion in the National Assembly, Ciller entered into a center-right coalition, which broke up in 1998, leading to another short-lived coalition, which collapsed a few months later. President Demirel then invited Ecevit of the Democratic Left Party to form a new government early in 1999, and it remains in power despite being another shaky three-party coalition.

Thus, in 2000 the current era of civilian government, although troubled, was almost two decades in length, with no immediate change in prospect. Nevertheless, the Turkish military remains poised on the sidelines. As James Brown points out, the armed forces, having endowed the nation with civilian institutions, later ventured with reluctance into the political arena, but "they have reserved the right to intervene, if necessary, to protect these institutions." Today the military is "the most potent group in society, with the mission to defend the nation from both internal and external threats."[122] George S. Harris concurs. "Little on the Turkish political scene," he says, "can rival the potential importance of the military establishment. Yet little presents so many imponderables. To delve into the future course of the political role of Turkey's military is to leap into the unknown and even the unknowable."[123] Whatever the odds may be, another swing of the political pendulum must be anticipated as distinctly possible, in view of Turkey's historical record.

Among developing countries with a substantial record of political competition, Turkey is unusual in the solid bureaucratic base upon which the present-day nation-state could build. Modern Turkey inherited the centuries-old tradition of the Ottoman "ruling institution" comprising the sultan's military and administrative establishments, as well as the benefits of a series of efforts during the nineteenth century to reform the civil bureaucracy, including a training school for the civil service, founded in 1859, which has been in almost continuous operation since. The Kemalist regime therefore was able to start after World War I with a bureaucracy which had been professionalized for generations. The public service has continued to be attractive and prestigious for educated young Turks, although its appeal is no longer unchallenged, and the tradition of familial identification with the bureaucracy is still strong, son following in the father's footsteps.

Although the Turkish bureaucracy is not a by-product of colonialism, Western models have had an impact, with French influence being strongest. For example, Turkey has followed the French example in leaving management of the bureaucracy primarily to the individual ministries and agencies, subject to general policy guidelines, rather than relying heavily on a central personnel agency. The extent to which behavioral patterns in the Turkish bureaucracy deviate from performance norms is hard to measure accurately, but commentaries stress the prevalence of tendencies such as exceptional deference to persons with higher hierarchical status, reluctance to accept responsibility, centralization of authority, procedural complexity, emphasis on security and protection of civil service tenure, personalized value-premises underlying administrative action, and other "prismatic" or transitional characteristics.

In Turkey, the bureaucracy has been intimately involved in the policy-making process, and subject to relatively weak external controls. Political modernization can be accurately described as the joint handiwork of the civil and military bureaucracies. The new nation-state emerged under the leadership of a military officer, Mustafa Kemal, but he found support for his policies among the civil bureaucrats and he used them to put these policies into effect. As Chambers points out, the bureaucratic class and the military officer corps provided the major reservoir of talent available, and individuals with bureaucratic backgrounds provided a considerable proportion of the parliamentary leaders and cabinet ministers until they were substantially displaced following the free elections of 1950. He reports that at least until that time there was "considerable community of social, educational, and occupational background among parliamentary deputies and cabinet ministers on the one hand and the upper levels of the civil bureaucracy on the other," with a sort of closed corporation composed of "professional public servants who, acting as politicians, passed laws which they and their colleagues administered as bureaucrats."[124]

As already noted, during the 1950s the strength of both the civil and military bureaucrats within the national elite diminished markedly. The military intervention of 1960 reasserted the claim of the armed forces for a primary political role in case of necessity to maintain stability, a claim which was reaffirmed with greater emphasis in 1980, and continues to be made today. The civil bureaucracy, on the other hand, has never regained its former key importance, although higher civil servants still are members of the governing elite. The process of political modernization in Turkey has brought in additional elements to the current elite mix, without eliminating earlier participants. As a consequence, the Turkish civil bureaucracy can be expected to retain its involvement in the exercise of political power but with a decreasing likelihood as time passes that it will regain its prerogatives of either the Ottoman or Kemalist periods.

In pendulum systems such as Turkey, with frequent shifts in political regime type over relatively short time periods, it might be anticipated that the relationship between current regime type and the political role of the public bureaucracy would be more tenuous than in a polity where a particular regime type has been evident for a prolonged period, and that the impact of other factors on bureaucratic characteristics would be greater. The Turkish case provides some confirming evidence, as indicated in studies conducted by Metin Heper, which have stressed the importance in Turkey of both "the historical bureaucratic tradition"[125] and a relatively high degree of "stateness" during Turkish political development from the Ottoman era to the present.[126] Although each case must be examined individually, the normal expectation would be that in pendulum systems the bureaucracy is in a favorable position over time to play a prominent political role.

NOTES

1. Milton J. Esman, "The Politics of Development Administration," in John D. Montgomery and William J. Siffin, eds., *Approaches to Development: Politics, Administration and Change* (New York: McGraw Hill, 1966), p. 88.
2. The limited available sources on Saudi Arabia include Richard A. Chapman, "Administrative Reform in Saudi Arabia," *Journal of Administration Overseas* 13, No. 2 (1974): 332–347; Manfred W. Wenner, "Saudi Arabia: Survival of Traditional Elites," in Frank Tachau, ed., *Political Elites and Political Development in the Middle East* (Cambridge, MA: Schenkman Publishing Company, 1975), pp. 157–191; Osama A. Osman, "Formalism v. Realism: The Saudi Arabian Experience with Position Classification," *Public Personnel Management* 7, No. 3 (1978): 177–181, and "Saudi Arabia: An Unprecedented Growth of Wealth with an Unparalleled Growth of Bureaucracy," *International Review of Administrative Sciences* 45, No. 3 (1979): 234–240; Abdelrahman Al-Hegelan and Monte Palmer, "Bureaucracy and Development in Saudi Arabia," *The Middle East Journal* 39, No. 1 (Winter 1985): 48–68; M. Al-Tawail, *Public Administration in the Kingdom of Saudi Arabia* (Riyadh, Saudi Arabia: Institute of Public Administration, 1986); Mordechai Abir, "The Consolidation of the Ruling Class and the New Elites in Saudi Arabia," *Middle Eastern Studies* 23 (April 1987): 150–171; Monte Palmer, Abdelrahman Al-Hegelan, Mohammed Bushara Abdelrahman, Ali Leila, and El Sayeed Yassin,

"Bureaucratic Innovation and Economic Development in the Middle East: A Study of Egypt, Saudi Arabia, and the Sudan," *Journal of Asian and African Studies* 24, No. 1–2 (January–April 1989): 12–27; Ayman Al-Yassini, "Saudi Arabia," in V. Subramaniam, ed., *Public Administration in the Third World: An International Handbook* (Westport, CT: Greenwood Press, 1990), Chap. 8; Adnan A. Alshiha and Frank P. Sherwood, "The Need for a Concept in Executive Personnel Systems and Development: Saudi Arabia as an Illustrative Case," in Ali Farazmand, ed., *Handbook of Comparative and Development Public Administration* (New York: Marcel Dekker, 1991), Chap. 32; Peter W. Wilson and Douglas F. Graham, *Saudi Arabia: The Coming Storm* (Armonk, NY: M. E. Sharp, 1994); Kathy Evans, "Shifting Sands at the House of Saud," *The Middle East* (February, 1996): 6–9; Mamoun Fandy, *Saudi Arabia and the Politics of Dissent* (New York: St. Martin's Press, 1999).

3. Wenner, "Saudi Arabia: Survival of Traditional Elites," p. 167.

4. Wenner asserts that "it is possible to document the rise and increasing influence of what has been called a 'new middle class' among whom are to be found the predominance of rationalist, universalist and secular value systems. On the other hand, one cannot yet point in Saudi Arabia to the beginnings of a political system dominated by mass participation, populist ideologies, much less the prominent role which a modernized and rationalist military structure is often expected to play in the 'drive for modernization.'" *Ibid.*, pp. 177–179.

5. Al-Hegelan and Palmer, "Bureaucracy and Development in Saudi Arabia," p. 67.

6. See Palmer et al, "Bureaucratic Innovation and Economic Development in the Middle East," pp. 26–27; and Alshiha and Sherwood, "Executive Personnel Systems: Saudi Arabia," p. 453.

7. Osman, "Saudi Arabia: An Unprecedented Growth of Wealth," pp. 237, 239.

8. Sources on Iran before the fall of the shah include Richard W. Gable, "Culture and Administration in Iran," *Middle East Journal* 13, No. 4 (1959): 407–421; Leonard Binder, *Iran: Political Development in a Changing Society* (Berkeley, CA: University of California Press, 1962), pp. 127–144; James Alban Bill, *The Politics of Iran: Groups, Classes, and Modernization* (Columbus, OH: Charles E. Merrill Publishing Co., 1972); Marvin Zonis, "The Political Elite of Iran: A Second Stratum?" pp. 193–216, in Tachau, ed., *Political Elites*; Marvin Zonis, *The Political Elite of Iran* (Princeton, NJ: Princeton University Press, 1976); Hooshang Kuklan, "Civil Service Reform in Iran: Myth and Reality," *International Review of Administrative Sciences* 43, No. 4 (1977): 345–351; James A. Bill, "Iran and the Crisis of '78," *Foreign Affairs* 57, No. 2 (Winter 1978/79): 323–342; and M. Reza Ghods, *Iran in the Twentieth Century* (Boulder, CO: Lynne Rienner Publishers, 1989). For information on the Islamic Republic of Iran, refer to Eric Rouleau, "Khomeini's Iran," *Foreign Affairs* 59, No. 1 (Fall 1980): 1–20; Hooshang Kuklan, "The Administrative System in the Islamic Republic of Iran: New Trends and Directions," *International Review of Administrative Sciences* 47, No. 3 (1981): 218–224; James A. Bill, "The Politics of Extremism in Iran," *Current History* 81, No. 471 (January 1982): 9–13; Elaine Sciolino, "Iran's Durable Revolution," *Foreign Affairs* 61, No. 4 (Spring 1983): 893–920; Shahrough Akhavi, "Elite Factionalism in the Islamic Republic of Iran," *Middle East Journal* 41, No. 2 (Spring 1987): 181–201; Ali Farazmand, "The Impacts of the Revolution of 1978–1979 on the Iranian Bureaucracy and Civil

Service," *International Journal of Public Administration* 10, No. 4 (1987): 337–365; Charles F. Andrain, "Political Change in Iran," in *Political Change in the Third World* (Winchester, MA: Allen & Unwin, 1988), Chap. 8, pp. 252–283; Fouad Ajami, "Iran: The Impossible Revolution," *Foreign Affairs* 67, No. 2 (Winter 1988/89): 135–155; R. K. Ramazani, ed., "The Islamic Republic of Iran: The First 10 Years [Symposium]," *Middle East Journal* 43, No. 2 (Spring 1989): 165–245; Ali Farazmand, *The State, Bureaucracy, and Revolution in Modern Iran* (New York: Praeger, 1989); Shireen T. Hunter, "Post-Khomeini Iran," *Foreign Affairs* 68, No. 5 (Winter 1989–1990): 133–149; Ali Farazmand, "Iran," in Subramaniam, ed., *Public Administration in the Third World*, Chap. 7; Ali Farazmand, "State Tradition and Public Administration in Iran in Ancient and Contemporary Perspective," "Bureaucracy, Agrarian Reforms, and Regime Enhancement: The Case of Iran," and "Bureaucracy and Revolution: The Case of Iran," in Farazmand, ed., *Handbook of Comparative and Development Public Administration*, Chaps. 19, 39, and 55; Shireen Hunter, *Iran after Khomeini* (New York: Praeger, 1992); Mahnaz Afkhami and Erika Friedl, eds. *In the Eye of the Storm: Women in Post-Revolutionary Iran* (Syracuse, NY: Syracuse University Press, 1994); Hazhir Teimourian, "Iran's 15 years of Islam," *The World Today* 50, No. 4 (April 1994): 67–70; and Patrick Clawson, Michael Eisenstadt, Eliyahu Kanovsky, and David Menashri, *Iran Under Khatami: A Political, Economic, and Military Assessment* (Washington, DC: The Washington Institute for Near East Policy, 1998).

9. Binder, *Iran*, pp. 59–60.
10. Zonis, "The Political Elite of Iran," in Tachau, *Political Elites*, p. 203.
11. Bill, *The Politics of Iran*, pp. 133–156.
12. Zonis, "The Political Elite of Iran," p. 207.
13. *Ibid.*, pp. 195–196.
14. Bill, *The Politics of Iran*, pp. 53–72.
15. Zonis, *The Political Elites of Iran*, pp. 11–14.
16. Bill, "Iran and the Crisis of '78," p. 341.
17. Bill, "The Politics of Extremism in Iran," pp. 9, 36.
18. Akhavi, "Elite Factionalism in the Islamic Republic of Iran," p. 182.
19. Patrick Clawson, "The Khatami Paradox," in *Iran Under Khatami*, Chapter 1, pp. 1, 2.
20. Kuklan, "The Administrative System in the Islamic Republic of Iran," p. 218.
21. Farazmand, "Iranian Bureaucracy and Civil Service," p. 345.
22. *Ibid.*, p. 355.
23. Gino Germani and Kalman Silvert, "Politics, Social Structure and Military Interventions in Latin America," in Wilson C. McWilliams, ed., *Garrisons and Government* (San Francisco: Chandler, 1967), at pp. 230–231.
24. Claude E. Welch, Jr., "Personalism and Corporatism in African Armies," in Catherine McArdle Kelleher, ed., *Military Systems: Comparative Perspectives* (Beverly Hills, CA: Sage Publications, 1974), p. 131. Refer also to Robert H. Jackson and Carl G. Rosberg, *Personal Rule in Black Africa: Prince, Autocrat, Prophet, Tyrant* (Berkeley, CA: University of California Press, 1982); and Samuel Decalo, *Psychoses of Power: African Personal Dictatorships* (Boulder, CO: Westview Press, 1989).
25. *Ibid.*, pp. 132–133.

26. For more information concerning Guatemala during the rule of General Jorge Ubico from 1930 to 1944, refer to earlier editions of this book.

27. Selected sources include: George Pendle, *Paraguay: A Riverside Nation* (London: Royal Institute of International Affairs, 1956); Joseph Pincus, *The Economy of Paraguay* (New York: Praeger, 1968); Paul H. Lewis, *Paraguay Under Stroessner* (Chapel Hill, NC: University of North Carolina Press, 1980); Paul H. Lewis, *Socialism, Liberalism and Dictatorship in Paraguay* (Chapel Hill, NC: University of North Carolina Press, 1982); Luis Valdes, *Stroessner's Paraguay: Traditional vs. Modern Authoritarianism* (San German, PR: Centro de Investigaciones del Caribe y America Latina, 1986); Virginia M. Bouvier, *Decline of the Dictator: Paraguay at a Crossroads* (Washington, DC: Washington Office on Latin America, 1988); Carlos R. Miranda, *The Stroessner Era: Authoritarian Rule in Paraguay* (Boulder, CO: Westview Press, 1990); Paul C. Sondrol, "Totalitarian and Authoritarian Dictators: A Comparison of Fidel Castro and Alfredo Stroessner," *Journal of Latin American Studies* 23, No. 3 (October 1991): 599–620; Nancy R. Powers, *The Transition to Democracy in Paraguay: Problems and Prospects*, Working Paper #171 (Notre Dame, IN: Helen Kellogg Institute for International Studies, University of Notre Dame, 1992); and Peter Lambert and Andrew Nickson, eds., *The Transition to Democracy in Paraguay* (New York: St. Martin's Press, 1997).

28. Miranda, *The Stroessner Era*, p. 1.

29. Sondrol, "Totalitarian and Authoritarian Dictators," p. 601.

30. Miranda, *The Stroessner Era*, p. 4.

31. *Ibid.*, p. 69.

32. For an expression of "qualified optimism" that the regime "will continue liberalizing and not return to dictatorship," see Powers, *The Transition to Democracy in Paraguay*, p. 39. However, Peter Lambert points out that there remain serious obstacles to democratic consolidation, such as "the retention of power by political elites from within the authoritarian regime, the power of the military, the prevalence of authoritarian patterns of political domination (including clientelism, patronage, corruption and electoral fraud) and the blocking of measures to alleviate socio-economic inequalities." Lambert, "Assessing the Transition," in Lambert and Nickson, *The Transition to Democracy in Paraguay*, Chap. 16, p. 201.

33. Miranda, *The Stroessner Era*, pp. 144–145.

34. In addition to the military rank, "dada" was an honorific title adopted by Amin, with the meaning of patriarch or father.

35. For information on political events in Uganda during the Amin regime, with incidental reference to administrative matters, refer to Ali A. Mazrui, "Piety and Puritanism under a Military Theocracy: Uganda Soldiers as Apostolic Successors," in Catherine McArdle Kelleher, ed., *Political-Military Systems*, pp. 105–124, and *Soldiers and Kinsmen in Uganda* (Beverly Hills, CA: Sage Publications, 1975); Nelson Kasfir, "Civil Participation under Military Rule in Uganda and Sudan," in Henry Bienen and David Morell, eds., *Political Participation under Military Regimes* (Beverly Hills, CA: Sage Publications, 1976), pp. 66–85; Jackson and Rosberg, *Personal Rule in Black Africa*, pp. 252–265; and Samuel Decalo, *Psychoses of Power: African Personal Dictatorships*, Chap. 3, pp. 77–127.

36. Decalo, *Psychoses of Power*, pp. 96, 98, 104.

37. Welch, "Personalism and Corporatism in African Armies," in Kelleher, ed., *Political-Military Systems*, p. 135.

38. Edwin Lieuwen, *Generals vs. Presidents* (New York: Praeger, 1964), p. 98.

39. Martin Needler, "Political Development and Military Intervention in Latin America," in Henry Bienen, ed., *The Military and Modernization* (Chicago: Aldine/Atherton, 1971), p. 83.

40. *Ibid.*, pp. 87–90.

41. Moshe Lissak, *Military Roles in Modernization: Civil-Military Relations in Thailand and Burma* (Beverly Hills, CA: Sage Publications, 1976), p. 33.

42. Edward Shils, "The Military in the Political Development of the New States," in John R. Johnson, ed., *The Role of the Military in Underdeveloped Countries* (Princeton, NJ: Princeton University Press, 1962), p. 57.

43. South Korea was used as an example of a law-and-order regime in previous editions of this study, which contain numerous citations to sources on the thirty-year period when South Korea had a collegial bureaucratic elite system. For excellent reviews of the current situation, refer to Hagen Koo, ed., *State and Society in Contemporary Korea* (Ithaca, NY: Cornell University Press, 1993); and Jong S. Jun, "Enhancing Professional Roles and Ethical Responsibility: A Means for Creating Democratic Administration in Korea," in Farazmand, ed., *Handbook of Comparative and Development Public Administration*, Chap. 15.

44. Sources on Indonesia include Herbert Feith, *The Decline of Constitutional Democracy in Indonesia* (Ithaca, NY: Cornell University Press, 1962); Donald K. Emmerson, *Indonesia's Elite: Political Culture and Cultural Politics* (Ithaca, NY: Cornell University Press, 1976); Hamish McDonald, *Suharto's Indonesia* (Honolulu, HI: University of Hawaii Press, 1982); Ulf Sundhaussen, *The Road of Power: Indonesian Military Politics, 1945–1967* (Kuala Lumpur: Oxford University Press, 1982); Donald K. Emmerson, "Understanding the New Order: Bureaucratic Pluralism in Indonesia," *Asian Survey* 23 (1983): 1220–1241, and "Invisible Indonesia," *Foreign Affairs* 66, No. 2 (Winter 1987/88): 368–387; Ulf Sundhaussen, "Indonesia: Past and Present Encounters with Democracy," in Larry Diamond, Juan J. Linz, and Seymour Martin Lipset, eds., *Democracy in Developing Countries*, Vol. 3, *Asia* (Boulder, CO: Lynne Rienner Publishers, 1989), Chap. 11, pp. 423–474; Mochtar Lubis, *Indonesia: Land under the Rainbow* (Singapore: Oxford University Press, 1990); Michael Leifer, "Uncertainty in Indonesia," *World Policy Journal* 8, No. 1 (Winter 1990): 137–159; IKetut Mardjana, "Policy Changes in Indonesian Public Enterprises during the Old Order and New Order Governments," *ASEAN Economic Bulletin* 9, No. 2 (November 1992): 187–206; Michael R. J. Vatikiotis, *Indonesia under Suharto: Order, Development, and Pressure for Change* (London: Routledge, 1993); William H. Frederick and Robert L. Worden, eds., *Indonesia: A Country Study* (Washington, DC: Federal Research Division, Library of Congress, 1993); Andrew MacIntyre, "Indonesia in 1993: Increasing Political Movement?" *Asian Survey* 34 (1994): 111–118; Anders Uhlin, *Indonesia and the "Third Wave of Democratization": The Indonesian Pro-Democracy Movement in a Changing World* (New York: St. Martin's Press, 1997); Michael R. J. Vatikiotis, "Indonesia: A Guide to Succession," *Washington Quarterly* 20 (Autumn 1997): 191–210; John McBeth and Michael Vatikiotis, "The Endgame," *Far Eastern Economic Review* 161 (May

28, 1998): 12–15; Martha G. Logsdon, "The Development of Indonesia's Civil Service, 1974–1994," *Journal of Political and Military Sociology* 26 (Summer 1998): 3–22; Dwight Y. King, "Qualifications of Indonesia's Civil Servants: How Appropriate to the Dynamic Environment?" *Journal of Political and Military Sociology* 26, No. 1 (Summer 1998): 23–38; George Aditjondro, "Corruption Continues: More of the Same in Habibie's Indonesia," *Multinational Monitor* 19 (September 1998): 25–27; and "Indonesia's Second Chance," *Economist* 351 (June 9, 1999): 37–39.

45. For an informative analysis of the coexistence in Indonesia of Islam and secular authority, refer to Garth N. Jones, "*Musjid* and *Istana*: Indonesia's Uneasy Calm in Its Developmentalist Age," prepared for the Conference on The Muslim World held at Georgia Southern University, Statesboro, GA, October, 1991, 25 pp. mimeo. Jones concludes that "Islam in Indonesia is unlike that found in any other so-called Islamic country—Iran, Pakistan, Bangladesh, Egypt, Malaysia, or even the Muslim enclave in the Southern Philippines. Indonesia is a pluralistic nation in which regional ethnic and linguistic groups are the paramount socio-political factors." *Ibid*, p. 3.

46. Sundhaussen, "Indonesia," pp. 439, 441.

47. These pillars or principles are: "belief in one supreme God; just and civilized humanitarianism; nationalism as expressed in the unity of Indonesia; popular sovereignty arrived at through deliberation and representation or consultative democracy; and social justice for all Indonesian people." Frederick and Worden, *Indonesia: A Country Study*, p. 427.

48. Mardjana, "Policy Changes in Indonesian Public Enterprises during the Old Order and New Order Governments," p. 192.

49. "Understanding the New Order," p. 1222.

50. *Ibid.* p. 1227.

51. "Invisible Indonesia," pp. 384–385.

52. "Understanding the New Order," p. 1238.

53. For details on some of these tensions, see MacIntyre, "Indonesia in 1993: Increasing Political Movement?" pp. 111–115.

54. "Uncertainty in Indonesia," pp. 137, 158.

55. Sources on the political system of Thailand include David A. Wilson, "The Military in Thai Politics," in Johnson, ed., *The Role of the Military in Underdeveloped Countries,* pp. 253–275; Kenneth P. Landon, *Siam in Transition* (Westport, CT: Greenwood Press, 1968); Fred R. von der Mehden, "The Military and Development in Thailand," *Journal of Comparative Administration* 2, No. 3 (1970): 323–340; Henry Bienen and David Morell, "Transition from Military Rule: Thailand's Experience," in Kelleher, ed., *Political-Military Systems*, pp. 3–26; Claude E. Welch, Jr. and Arthur K. Smith, *Military Role and Rule: Perspectives on Civil-Military Relations* (North Scituate, MA: Duxbury Press, 1974), Chap. 4, pp. 81–111; Clark D. Neher, "Thailand," in Robert N. Kearney, ed., *Politics and Modernization in South and Southeast Asia* (Cambridge, MA: Schenkman Publishing Co, 1975), pp. 215–252; David Morell and Chai-anan Samudavanija, *Political Conflict in Thailand: Reform, Reaction, Revolution* (Cambridge, MA: Oelgeschlager, Gunn & Hain, Publishers, 1981); Clark D. Neher, ed., *Modern Thai Politics*, rev. ed.

(Cambridge, MA: Schenkman Publishing Co., 1981); John L. S. Girling, *Thailand: Society and Politics* (Ithaca, NY: Cornell University Press, 1981); Clark D. Neher, "Thailand in 1986: Prem, Parliament, and Political Pragmatism," *Asian Survey* 27, No. 2 (February 1987): 219–230; Clark D. Neher, "The Transition to Democracy in Thailand," *Asian Perspective* 20 (Fall/Winter, 1996): 301–321; and Peter Eng, "Thai Democracy: Let the People Speak," *Washington Quarterly* 20 (Autumn 1997): 169–189. The Thai bureaucracy has received an unusual amount of study. The standard works are Fred W. Riggs, *Thailand: The Modernization of a Bureaucratic Polity* (Honolulu: East-West Center Press, 1966); and William J. Siffin, *The Thai Bureaucracy* (Honolulu: East-West Center Press, 1966). Other helpful sources include Bidhya Bowornwathana, "Public Policies in a Bureaucratic Polity," prepared for the 1988 World Congress of the International Political Science Association, 17 pp. mimeo., "Transfers of Bureaucratic Elites by Political Bosses: The Question of Political versus Bureaucratic Accountability," prepared for the 1987 Conference of the Eastern Regional Organization for Public Administration (EROPA), 25 pp. mimeo., "Three Decades of Public Administration in Thailand," prepared for the 1985 Conference of the Eastern Regional Organization for Public Administration (EROPA), 20 pp. mimeo., and "Multiple Superiors in the Thai Public Health Bureaucracy," prepared for the 1982 National Conference of the American Society for Public Administration, 84 pp. mimeo.; Suchitra Punyaratabandhu-Bhakdi, "Development Administration in Thailand: Changing Patterns?" prepared for the 1986 National Conference of the American Society for Public Administration, 30 pp. mimeo.; Ronald L. Krannich, "The Politics of Personnel Management: Competence and Compromise in the Thai Bureaucracy," prepared for the 1977 National Conference of the American Society for Public Administration, 48 pp. mimeo.; James N. Mosel, "Thai Administrative Behavior," in Siffin, ed., *Toward the Comparative Study of Public Administration*, pp. 278–331; Edgar L. Shor, "The Thai Bureaucracy," *Administrative Science Quarterly* 5, No. 1 (1960): 66–86; William J. Siffin, "Personnel Processes of the Thai Bureaucracy," in Ferrel Heady and Sybil L. Stokes, *Papers in Comparative Public Administration*, pp. 207–228 (Ann Arbor, MI: Institute of Public Administration, The University of Michigan, 1962); and Kasem Udyanin and Rufus D. Smith, *The Public Service in Thailand: Organization, Recruitment and Training* (Brussels: International Institute of Administrative Sciences, 1954).

56. Welch and Smith, *Military Role and Rule*, pp. 81, 106.

57. Mosel, "Thai Administrative Behavior," pp. 296–297.

58. Neher suggests several reasons for the coup phenomenon. "Since high political posts are held by only a very few people and since governmental participation is concentrated in the bureaucracy, it is possible to dominate the entire political system merely by controlling the bureaucratic structure. And, since extra bureaucratic institutions have been inconsequential, they are easily bypassed. In addition, the fact that Bangkok is the nation's only major city considerably eases the logistical problems in carrying out a coup. Finally, Thailand has been independent of foreign influence that opposes the means or the results of coups d'etat." Neher, *Thailand*, p. 244.

59. Morell, "Alternatives to Military Rule," p. 10.

60. Neher, "Thailand," p. 239.

61. *Ibid.*, p. 241.

62. Welch and Smith, *Military Role and Rule*, p. 102.

63. Morell, "Alternatives to Military Rule," p. 22.

64. von der Mehden, "The Military and Development in Thailand," pp. 334–335.

65. Welch and Smith, *Military Role and Rule*, p. 103.

66. Siffin, *The Thai Bureaucracy*, pp. 161–162.

67. *Ibid.*, p. 165.

68. Siffin, "Personnel Processes of the Thai Bureaucracy," p. 222.

69. *Ibid.*, p. 220.

70. Bienen and Morell, "Transition from Military Rule," pp. 18–19.

71. Riggs, *Thailand*, p. 348.

72. Morell and Chai-anan, *Political Conflict in Thailand*, p. 48.

73. Welch and Smith, *Military Role and Rule*, p. 104.

74. Riggs, *Thailand*, p. 395. In *Thailand: Society and Politics,* Girling accepts the view that Thailand continues to be a bureaucratic polity.

75. Principal sources on Ghana include Victor D. Ferkiss, "The Role of the Public Services in Nigeria and Ghana," in Heady and Stokes, *Papers in Comparative Public Administration*, pp. 173–206; Kofi Ankomah, "Reflections on Administrative Reform in Ghana," *International Review of Administrative Sciences* 36, No. 4 (1970): 299–303; Clyde Chantler, *The Ghana Story* (London: Linden Press, 1971); David E. Apter, *Ghana in Transition*, 2nd rev. ed. (Princeton, NJ: Princeton University Press, 1972); Robert Pinkney, *Ghana under Military Rule 1966–1969* (London: Methuen & Co. Ltd., 1972); Robert M. Price, *Society and Bureaucracy in Contemporary Ghana* (Berkeley, CA: University of California Press, 1975); Dennis Austin, *Ghana Observed* (Manchester: Manchester University Press, 1976); Leonard Kooperman and Stephen Rosenburg, "The British Administrative Legacy in Kenya and Ghana," *International Review of Administrative Sciences* 43, No. 3 (1977): 267–272; Bjorn Hettne, "Soldiers and Politics: The Case of Ghana," *Journal of Peace Research* 17, No. 2 (1980): 173–193; Donald Rothchild and E. Gyimah-Boadi, "Ghana's Return to Civilian Rule," *Africa Today* 28, No. 1 (1981): 3–15; Jon Kraus, "Rawlings' Second Coming," *Africa Report* 27, No. 2 (March/April 1983): 59–66; Donald I. Ray, *Ghana: Politics, Economics and Society* (Boulder, CO: Lynne Rienner Publishers, 1986); Jon Kraus, "Ghana's Shift from Radical Populism," *Current History* 86, No. 520 (May 1987): 205–208, 227–228; Victor T. Le Vine, "Autopsy on a Regime: Ghana's Civilian Interregnum 1969–72," *Journal of Modern African Studies* 25, No. 1 (1987): 169–178; Baffour Agyeman-Duah, "Ghana, 1982–6: the Politics of the P.N.D.C.," *Journal of Modern African Studies* 25, No. 4 (1987): 613–642; Richard C. Crook, "Legitimacy, Authority and the Transfer of Power in Ghana," *Political Studies* 35, No. 4 (December 1987): 552–572; Simon Baynham, *The Military and Politics in Nkrumah's Ghana* (Boulder, CO: Westview Press, 1988); Colleen Lowe Morna, "A Grassroots Democracy," *Africa Report* 34 (July/August 1989): 17–20; E. Gyimah-Boadi and Donald Rothchild, "Ghana," in Subramaniam, ed., *Public Administration in the Third World*, Chap. 10; Jeffrey Herbst, *The Politics of Reform in Ghana, 1982–1991* (Berkeley, CA: University of California Press, 1993); Youry Petchenkine, *Ghana: In Search of Stability, 1957–*

1992 (Westport, CT: Praeger, 1993); E. Gyimah-Boadi, "Ghana's Uncertain Political Opening," *Journal of Democracy* 5, No. 2 (April 1994): 75–87; Terrence Lyons, "Ghana's Encouraging Elections," *Journal of Democracy* 8 (April 1997): 65–91; Robert Pinkney, *Democracy and Dictatorship in Ghana and Tanzania* (New York: St. Martin's, 1997); and Ho-Won Jeong, "Strategies for Reform in Ghana: The State, Interest Groups, and International Financial Institutions," *21st Century Afro Review* 3 (Fall 1997): 67–102.

76. Apter, *Ghana in Transition*, p. 358.
77. *Ibid.*, p. 377.
78. Hettne, "Soldiers and Politics," p. 184.
79. Kraus, "Rawlings' Second Coming," p. 59.
80. Price, *Society and Bureaucracy in Contemporary Ghana*, p. 150.
81. Ferkiss, "The Role of the Public Services in Nigeria and Ghana," p. 178.
82. Apter, *Ghana in Transition*, p. 360.
83. Price, *Society and Bureaucracy*, p. 216.
84. Kraus, "Ghana's Shift from Radical Populism," pp. 206–207, 227.
85. Ray, *Ghana: Politics, Economics and Society*, p. 155.
86. See Fred G. Burke, "Public Administration in Africa: The Legacy of Inherited Colonial Institutions," *Journal of Comparative Administration* 1, No. 3 (1969): 345–378.
87. Price *Society and Bureaucracy*, p. 206.
88. *Ibid.*, pp. 150–151.
89. Kraus, "Ghana's Shift from Radical Populism," p. 227.
90. Apter, *Ghana in Transition*, p. xxi.
91. Hettne, "Soldiers and Politics," p. 190.
92. Recent sources on politics and administration in Brazil include Luigi R. Einaudi and Alfred C. Stepan III, *Latin American Institutional Development: Changing Military Perspectives in Peru and Brazil* (Santa Monica, CA: The Rand Corporation, 1971); Robert T. Daland, "Attitudes toward Change by Brazilian Bureaucrats," *Journal of Comparative Administration* 4, No. 2 (1972): 167–203; Barry Ames, *Rhetoric and Reality in a Military Regime: Brazil Since 1964* (Beverly Hills, CA: Sage Publications, 1973); Alfred Stepan, ed., *Authoritarian Brazil* (New Haven, CT: Yale University Press, 1973); Bruce Drury, "Civil-Military Relations and Military Rule: Brazil Since 1964," *Journal of Political and Military Sociology* 2 (Fall 1974): 191–203; Georges-Andre Fiechter, *Brazil Since 1964: Modernisation under a Military Regime* (London: Macmillan, 1975); Henry H. Keith and Robert A. Hayes, eds., *Perspectives on Armed Forces in Brazil* (Tempe, AZ: Center for Latin American Studies, Arizona State University, 1976); Kenneth S. Mericle, "Corporatist Control of the Working Class: Authoritarian Brazil Since 1964," in Malloy, ed., *Authoritarianism and Corporatism in Latin America*, pp.303–338; Jean-Claude Garcia-Zamor, ed., *Politics and Administration in Brazil* (Washington, DC: University Press of America, 1978); Jan Knippers Black, "The Military and Political Decompression in Brazil," *Armed Forces and Society* 6, No. 4 (Summer 1980): 625-637; Peter McDonough, "Development Priorities among Brazilian Elites," *Economic Development and Cultural Change* 29, No. 3 (1981): 535-559; Robert T. Daland, *Exploring Brazilian Bureaucracy: Performance and Pathology* (Washing-

ton, DC: University Press of America, 1981); Scott Mainwaring, *The Transition to Democracy in Brazil* (Notre Dame, IN: Helen Kellogg Institute for International Studies, University of Notre Dame, 1986); William C. Smith, "The Travail of Brazilian Democracy in the 'New Republic,'" *Journal of Interamerican Studies and World Affairs* 28 (Winter 1986/87): 39-73; Frances Hagopian, *The Traditional Political Elite and the Transition to Democracy in Brazil* (Notre Dame, IN: Helen Kellogg Institute for International Studies, University of Notre Dame, 1987); Thomas E. Skidmore, *The Politics of Military Rule in Brazil, 1964–85* (New York: Oxford University Press, 1988); Maria Helena Moreira Alves, "Dilemmas of the Consolidation of Democracy from the Top in Brazil: A Political Analysis," *Latin American Perspectives* 15, No. 3 (Summer 1988): 47–63; Timothy J. Power, "Political Landscapes, Political Parties, and Authoritarianism in Brazil and Chile," *International Journal of Comparative Sociology* 29 (September/December 1988): 251–263; Alfred Stepan, ed., *Democratizing Brazil: Problems of Transition and Consolidation* (New York: Oxford University Press, 1989); Thomas R. Rochon and Michael J. Mitchell, "Social Bases of the Transition to Democracy in Brazil," *Comparative Politics* 21 (April 1989): 307–322; Barbara Geddes and John Zaller, "Sources of Popular Support for Authoritarian Regimes," *American Journal of Political Science* 33, No. 2 (May 1989): 319–347; Juan de Onis, "Brazil on the Tightrope toward Democracy," *Foreign Affairs* 68, No. 4 (Fall 1989): 127–143; Elisa P. Reis, "Brazil: The Politics of State Administration," in H. K. Asmeron and R. B. Jain, eds., *Politics, Administration and Public Policy in Developing Countries: Examples from Africa, Asia and Latin America* (Amsterdam: VU University Press, 1993), Chap. 3, pp. 37–51; Frances Hagopian, *Traditional Politics and Regime Change in Brazil* (Cambridge: Cambridge University Press, 1996); Lincoln Gordon, "Assessing Brazil's Political Modernization," *Current History* 97 (February 1998): 76–81; and David J. Samuels, "Incentives to Cultivate a Party Vote in Candidate-centric Electoral Systems: Evidence from Brazil," *Comparative Political Studies* 32, No. 4 (June 1999): 487–518.

93. Einaudi and Stepan, *Latin American Institutional Development*, p. 73.

94. Drury, "Civil-Military Relations and Military Rule," p. 191.

95. *Ibid.*

96. Jorge I. Tapia-Videla, "Understanding Organizations and Environments: A Comparative Perspective," *Public Administration Review* 36, No. 6 (1976): 631–636, at pp. 633–634.

97. James M. Malloy, ed., *Authoritarianism and Corporatism in Latin America* (Pittsburgh, PA: University of Pittsburgh Press, 1977), p. 4.

98. Ames, *Rhetoric and Reality in a Military Regime*, p. 9.

99. Reis, "Brazil: The Politics of State Administration," p. 45.

100. C. Neale Ronning and Henry H. Keith, "Shrinking the Political Arena: Military Government in Brazil Since 1964," in Keith and Hayes, *Perspectives on Armed Politics in Brazil*, pp. 225–251, at p. 227.

101. Mericle, "Corporate Control of the Working Class," p. 306.

102. Daland, "Attitudes toward Change by Brazilian Bureaucrats," p. 199.

103. Daland, *Exploring Brazilian Bureaucracy*, pp. 431–432.

104. "Brazil: The Politics of State Administration," p. 47.

105. "Unfortunately," as Stepan said in 1989, "as the first three years of civilian rule have made painfully clear, the Brazilian State apparatus was in such a stage of decomposition that the attempt to utilize it, without making serious changes in its structure, values, and responsiveness, served only to deepen developmental crises." Stepan, *Democratizing Brazil*, p. xi. These changes have not occurred, and Brazilian public administration retains its "long-standing reputation for being too centralized, inefficient, parasitic, and oversized." Reis, "Brazil: The Politics of State Administration," p. 40.

106. Juan de Onis, "Brazil on the Tightrope toward Democracy," p. 136.

107. Smith, "The Travail of Brazilian Democracy," p. 62.

108. Maria do Carmo Campello de Souza, "The Brazilian 'New Republic': Under the 'Sword of Damocles'," Chap. 11, in Stepan, *Democratizing Brazil*, at pp. 381–382.

109. Selected sources on Nigerian politics and administration include Taylor Cole, "Bureaucracy in Transition: Independent Nigeria," *Public Administration Review* 38, No. 4 (Winter 1960): 321–337; Victor C. Ferkiss, "The Role of the Public Services in Nigeria and Ghana," in Heady and Stokes, *Papers in Comparative Public Administration*, pp. 173–206; J. Donald Kingsley, "Bureaucracy and Political Development, with Particular Reference to Nigeria," in Joseph LaPalombara, ed., *Bureaucracy and Political Development*, pp. 301–317 (Princeton, NJ: Princeton University Press, 1963); D. J. Murray, ed., *Studies in Nigerian Administration*, 2nd ed. (London: Hutchinson & Co., 1978); Jean Herskovits, "Democracy in Nigeria," *Foreign Affairs* 58, No. 2 (Winter 1979/80): 314–335; Ronald Cohen, "The Blessed Job in Nigeria," in Gerald M. Britan and Ronald Cohen, eds., *Hierarchy and Society: Anthropological Perspectives on Bureaucracy*, pp. 73–88 (Philadelphia: Institute for the Study of Human Issues, 1980); Paul Collins, ed., *Administration for Development in Nigeria* (New Brunswick, NJ: Transaction, 1981); Peter Koehn, "Prelude to Civilian Rule: The Nigerian Elections of 1979," *Africa Today* 28, No. 1 (1st Quarter, 1981): 17–45; Stephen Wright, "Nigeria: A Mid-Term Assessment," *The World Today* 38, No. 3 (March 1982): 105–113; Lapido Adamolekun, *Public Administration: A Nigerian and Comparative Perspective* (New York: Longman, 1982); Peter H. Koehn, "The Evolution of Public Bureaucracy in Nigeria," in Tummala, ed., *Administrative Systems Abroad*, pp. 188–228; Larry Diamond, "Nigeria in Search of Democracy," *Foreign Affairs* 62, No. 4 (Spring 1984): 905–927, and "Nigeria Update," *Foreign Affairs* 64, No. 2 (Winter 1985/86): 326–336; Lapido Adamolekun, *Politics and Administration in Nigeria* (Ibadan: Spectrum Books, 1986, in association with Hutchinson of London); Larry Diamond, "Nigeria Between Dictatorship and Democracy," *Current History* 86, No. 520 (May 1987): 201–224, and *Class, Ethnicity and Democracy in Nigeria: The Failure of the First Republic* (Syracuse, NY: Syracuse University Press, 1988); Otwin Marenin, "The Nigerian State as Process and Manager: A Conceptualization," *Comparative Politics* 20 (January 1988): 215–232; Claude S. Philips, "Political versus Administration Development: What the Nigerian Experience Contributes," *Administration and Society* 20, No. 4 (February 1989): 423–445; Celestine O. Bassey, "Retrospects and Prospects of Political Stability in Nigeria," *African Studies Review* 32, No. 1 (April 1989): 97–113; William D. Graf, *The Nigerian State* (Portsmouth, NH: Heinemann, 1989); Peter H. Koehn, *Public Policy and Administration in Africa:*

Lessons from Nigeria (Boulder, CO: Westview Press, 1990); Lapido Adamolekun and Victor Ayeni, "Nigeria," in Subramaniam, ed., *Public Administration in the Third World*, Chap. 11; Peter H. Koehn, "Development Administration in Nigeria: Inclinations and Results," in Farazmand, ed., *Handbook of Comparative and Development Public Administration*, Chap. 18, pp. 239–254; Amadu Sesay and Charles Ugochukwu Ukeje, "The Military, the West, and Nigerian Politics in the 1990s," *International Journal of Politics, Culture and Society* 11 (Fall 1997): 25–48; and Kaye Whiteman, "Nigeria: End of the Nightmare?" *African Business* (January 1999): 8–10.

110. Graf, *The Nigerian State*, p. 234.

111. See Diamond, "Nigeria in Search of Democracy," pp. 916–921, and "Nigeria Update," pp. 333–336.

112. Koehn, "The Evolution of Public Bureaucracy in Nigeria," p. 188.

113. Marenin, "The Nigerian State as Process and Manager," p. 221.

114. Diamond, "Nigeria in Search of Democracy," p. 915.

115. Graf, *The Nigerian State*, p. 205.

116. Koehn, "The Evolution of Public Bureaucracy in Nigeria," pp. 212–213.

117. Cohen, "The Blessed Job in Nigeria," pp. 73–77.

118. Koehn, "The Evolution of Public Bureaucracy in Nigeria," p. 209.

119. Adamolekun, *Politics and Administration in Nigeria*, p. 178. "Real achievements can be credited to the Nigerian public service system in general and the civil service has successfully maintained the continuity of the machinery of government, in spite of all the changes in regime type and the high degree of political instability." Adamolekun and Ayeni, "Nigeria," p. 284.

120. Selected useful sources on Turkey include Joseph B. Kingsbury and Tahir Aktan, *The Public Service in Turkey: Organization, Recruitment and Training* (Brussels: International Institute of Administrative Sciences, 1955); A. T. J. Matthews, *Emergent Turkish Administrators* (Ankara, Turkey: Institute of Administrative Sciences, Faculty of Political Science, University of Ankara, 1955); Lynton K. Caldwell, "Turkish Administration and the Politics of Expediency," in William J. Siffin, ed., *Toward the Comparative Study of Public Administration* (Bloomington, IN: Department of Government, Indiana University, 1957), pp. 117–144; Richard L. Chambers, "The Civil Bureaucracy—Turkey," in Robert E. Ward and Dankwart A. Rustow, eds., *Political Modernization in Japan and Turkey* (Princeton, NJ: Princeton University Press, 1964), pp. 301–327; George L. Grassmuck, *Polity, Bureaucracy and Interest Groups in the Near East and North Africa* (Bloomington, IN: CAG Occasional Papers, 1965); Frederick T. Bent, "The Turkish Bureaucracy as an Agent of Change," *Journal of Comparative Administration* 1, No. 1 (1969): 47–64; Ersin Onulduran, *Political Development and Political Parties in Turkey* (Ankara, Turkey: Ankara University Press, 1974); Ilkay Sunar, *State and Society in the Politics of Turkey's Development* (Ankara, Turkey: Ankara University Press, 1974); Joseph S. Szyliowicz, "Elites and Modernization in Turkey," in Frank Tachau, ed., *Political Elites and Political Development in the Middle East* (Cambridge, MA: Schenkman Publishing Company, 1975), pp. 23–66; Metin Heper and A. Umit Berkman, *Development Administration in Turkey: Conceptual Theory and Methodology* (Istanbul: Bogazici University Press, 1980); Metin Heper, Chong Lim Kim, and

Seong-Tong Pai, "The Role of Bureaucracy and Regime Types: A Comparative Study of Turkish and South Korean Higher Civil Servants," *Administration and Society* 12, No. 2 (August 1980): 137–155; Walter F. Weiker, *The Modernization of Turkey: From Ataturk to the Present Day* (New York: Holmes & Meier Publishers, 1981); I. Atilla Dicle, "Public Bureaucracy in Turkey," in Tummala, ed., *Administrative Systems Abroad*, pp. 265–302; Mehmet Yasar Geyikdagi, *Political Parties in Turkey* (New York: Praeger, 1984); Robert Bianchi, *Interest Groups and Political Development in Turkey* (Princeton, NJ: Princeton University Press, 1984); John H. McFadden, "Civil-Military Relations in the Third Turkish Republic," *Middle East Journal* 39, No. 1 (Winter 1985): 69–85; Ilter Turan, "The Recruitment of Cabinet Ministers as a Political Process: Turkey, 1946–1979," *International Journal of Middle East Studies* 18 (1986): 455–472; Metin Heper, "State, Democracy, and Bureaucracy in Turkey," in Metin Heper, ed., *The State and Public Bureaucracies: A Comparative Perspective* (Westport, CT: Greenwood Press, 1987), pp. 131–145; James Brown, "The Military and Politics in Turkey," *Armed Forces & Society* 13, No. 2 (Winter 1987): 235–253; Metin Heper and Ahmet Evin, *State, Democracy and the Military: Turkey in the 1980s* (Berlin: Walter de Gruyter, 1988); and Metin Heper, "Turkey," in Subramaniam, ed., *Public Administration in the Third World*, Chap. 9, and "The State and Bureaucracy: The Turkish Case in Historical Perspective," in Farazmand, ed., *Handbook of Comparative and Development Public Administration*, Chap. 48, and "Islam and Democracy in Turkey: Toward a Reconciliation?" *Middle East Journal* 51 (Winter 1997): 32–45; Ben Lombardi, "Turkey: The Return of the Reluctant Generals?" *Political Science Quarterly* 112 (Summer 1997); 191–215; Christopher de Bellaigue, "Turkey: Into the Abyss?" *Washington Quarterly* 21 (Summer 1998): 137–148; James H. Meyer, "Politics as Usual: Ciller, Refah and Susurluk: Turkey's Troubled Democracy," *East European Quarterly* 32 (January 1999): 489–502; William Hale, "In Deep Trouble," *World Today* 55 (January 1999): 22–25; and Jeremy Salt, "Turkey's Military 'Democracy,'" *Current History* 98 (February 1999): 72–78.

121. Szyliowicz, "Elites and Modernization in Turkey," pp. 43–47.
122. Brown, "The Military and Politics in Turkey," pp. 248–249.
123. George S. Harris, "The Role of the Military in the 1980s: Guardians or Decision-Makers?" pp. 177–200, in Heper and Evin, *State, Democracy and the Military*, at p. 178.
124. Chambers, "The Civil Bureaucracy-Turkey," pp. 325–326.
125. Metin Heper, Chong Lim Kim, and Seong-Tong Pai, "The Role of Bureaucracy and Regime Types: A Comparative Study of Turkish and South Korean Higher Civil Servants."

9

Party-Prominent Political Regimes

The political party as an institution is pivotal in some manner in the operation of the political regimes in this broad grouping, although the party or parties involved may differ greatly in number, organization, ideology, membership, and other important respects, including relationships with the public bureaucracy. For our purposes, these political regimes are classified as polyarchal competitive systems, dominant-party semicompetitive systems, dominant-party mobilization systems, and Communist totalitarian systems.

As indicated by the last three of these four types, political regimes characterized by a dominant mass party of some kind have become quite common in the developing countries. They differ markedly in the kind and degree of political competition permitted. Various suggestions have been made for describing and analyzing these regimes, and for identifying specific varieties and subtypes. Tucker labels the general category as a "revolutionary mass-movement regime under single-party auspices," with a revolutionary ideology, a base of mass participation and involvement, and leadership by a militant centralized elite.[1] Apter speaks of a "mobilization system which has as its object the transformation of the society." It recognizes certain secular values, such as "equality, opportunity, and the unfolding of the individual personality in the context of the unfolding society," and downgrades others, such as "individual liberty, popular representation, pluralism, and the like."[2] Esman prefers "dominant mass party" to identify the general type, with varieties according to the degree of competitiveness permitted, and he distinguishes it as a type from Communist totalitarian systems.[3]

The three-way breakdown used here for political regimes with a dominant political party can be justified for other reasons as well, but the principal consideration in making this choice is that the role of the bureaucracy seems to differ in each of these kinds of political systems.

POLYARCHAL COMPETITIVE SYSTEMS

The states in this category have political systems that conform most closely to the parliamentary and presidential models of Western Europe and the United States. As used here, the category does not require complete adherence to a model that assures regular free elections with an informed electorate, interest-oriented political parties, unrestricted political expression, and a balanced division of functions among representative institutions. The essential is political competition, in the sense that well-organized political groupings are engaged in an active rivalry for political power, with the probability of a significant shift in power relationships taking place without disrupting the system. The competing units need not be necessarily or exclusively Western-style political parties. Countries with viable competitive interest-oriented party systems are in the group, but it also includes other countries where in recent years temporary military intervention has occurred, or where there have been other interruptions to competition which can be considered as at least intended to be transitory. At least until recently, as Esman rightly points out, the more idealized model has been a fragile one, "tried in the majority of the transitional societies, abandoned in many, reinstated in few."[4] We are concerned here with the countries that still maintain or have reinstated it, or have only partially and temporarily modified it.

Even using this less restrictive definition, the number of nations with polyarchal competitive regimes diminished extensively during the 1960s and 1970s, before increasing considerably again in the 1980s and early 1990s. Argentina, Brazil, Chile, Greece, Pakistan, the Philippines, Turkey, and Uruguay are among countries that lapsed from the competitive category after 1960 but more recently have restored competitive conditions, although some of them, as already discussed, can best be considered as pendulum systems. Lebanon has recovered only partially from a prolonged period of social disorder which disrupted a unique competitive system based on a complicated distribution of political power among religious sects.

Numerous countries have been able to maintain polyarchal competition over considerable periods of time, in some instances from the beginning of nationhood. They include Costa Rica, Colombia, and Venezuela from Latin America; Botswana, Gambia, and Zimbabwe from Africa; Papua New Guinea, the Philippines, Singapore and Sri Lanka from the Far East; Cyprus, Israel, and Malta from the Mediterranean area; a cluster of Caribbean polities (including Antiqua and Barbuda, the Bahamas, Barbados, St. Lucia, St. Vincent, and

Trinidad and Tabago); and several small island states widely scattered around the world (such as Fiji, Maldives, Mauritius, the Solomon Islands, and Vanuatu).

These polyarchal competitive polities obviously exhibit a wide range of political characteristics. One important difference among them, now being subjected to intensive scrutiny, is that some are parliamentary and some are presidential systems. For the most part, the choice between these options can be traced to the pre-independence period. The emerging polity normally followed the pattern inherited from the colonizing power (usually parliamentary, but presidential in the case of the Philippines), except that most Latin American countries and a few countries elsewhere, as they gained independence during the nineteenth century or later, adopted the presidential pattern of the United States. A continuing debate among political scientists focuses on the relative rates of success of polities starting as parliamentary or presidential systems in avoiding later transition to bureaucratic elitism or some other form of non-competitive regime, with the usual assumption having been that the record of parliamentarianism is better than that of presidentialism.[5] The matter is receiving increased attention and provoking a growing debate.[6] The analysis of the data by Riggs, which he concedes is complicated by such factors as state size and date of independence, indicates that the survival rate against breakdown among developing countries is highest for one-party regimes, followed by parliamentary regimes, with presidentialist regimes ranking lowest, and he examines some of the presumed reasons for the relative success of parliamentarianism over presidentialism. Shugart and Carey, on the other hand, in their analysis of data on the frequency of breakdowns during the twentieth century as a whole, conclude that about the same number of breakdowns have occurred in each type of system, with newer democracies more likely than older ones to suffer such crises, which accounts for the greater number of recent breakdowns in the currently more popular presidential option. All analysts seem to agree that the issue is complicated by the existence of numerous institutional variations within each system type, and by hybrid mixtures between the two. Although the possibility of regime breakdown is obviously high in developing countries as a group, my assessment of the evidence is that both major options have demonstrated their viability, and that most political crises are due primarily to other factors than the choice between them. Nevertheless, this issue will be an ongoing topic for study, with not only theoretical but also possibly practical implications. Up to now, there has been little indication of serious consideration of country shifts from one system to the other, except in Brazil, where the issue of a move from presidentialism to parliamentarianism was debated at length when the constitution was being revised in 1987 and 1988. The new constitution continued the presidential system, but it also provided for a later plebiscite, held in 1993, which resulted in the retention of presidentialism over the alternatives of replacement with either a parliamentary or monarchical form of government.

Taken together, these polyarchal polities share some important characteristics. Generally, they have less clearly defined and cohesive political elites than the other regime types. Political power tends to be dispersed. Urban merchants, landlords, military leaders, and representatives of other well-established interests share the stage with entrepreneurs, labor leaders, professionals, and other emerging leaders from newer interests in the society. Social mobility exists, and this permits and promotes competition.

Since participation in regular elections by the citizenry occurs in practice, or is at least recognized as the normal expectation, political leaders must direct appeals to public opinion and must make commitments in return for political support. This leads to a search for "the widest possible political consensus" and to political doctrine that is "pragmatic and melioristic."[7] It also makes politicians vulnerable to pressures from particular interest groups for special consideration. The resulting governmental programs emphasize short-range objectives in fields such as education, welfare, and health which can be easily understood and appreciated. Longer-range goals involving major social and economic reform are less apt to be formulated and are much harder to effectuate. Mobilization of mass support for a developmental program is not likely to be attempted. For reasons such as these, the capacity of such a system to initiate and sustain government-sponsored measures for basic reform is doubtful; major transformation is more likely to come from entrepreneurial and allied professional groups acting primarily in the private sector. Political leadership determined to undertake far-reaching economic development measures or primarily concerned about maintaining public order and stability is tempted to abandon political democracy in favor of some alternative offering greater potential for decisive governmental intervention.

These prevailing conditions in polyarchal competitive systems indicate that the hand of government will be weak when it attempts to collect taxes, impose regulations, or otherwise exert pressures that affect private interests. Public administration must be carried on without consistent political support even from the political instrumentalities that have previously made the formal policy decisions being administered. The bureaucracy itself may become one of the focuses for competition among contending political groups in such a polyarchal system. Although their professional caliber is of a relatively high order among developing countries, these bureaucracies have internal weaknesses and suffer from inconsistent backing from political policy-makers. External controls over the bureaucracy are sufficient but sometimes work at cross-purposes. The danger is less of usurpation by these bureaucracies than of bureaucratic inadequacy to meet the demands placed upon them.[8]

Three examples of these regimes, drawn from different areas and with different historical backgrounds, will be examined in more detail: the Philippines, Sri Lanka, and Colombia.

The Philippines

In Southeast Asia, the Republic of the Philippines exhibits features that reflect its unusual fused or hybrid character resulting from the exposure of an Asian population to prolonged Spanish and American colonialism, followed by a half-century of independence under an operative functioning democracy which was interrupted in 1972 by martial law rule imposed by President Ferdinand Marcos and reinstituted in 1986 under President Corazon Aquino.[9]

Between 1946 and 1972, when political competition was unrestricted, the contending Filipino political parties were personality-oriented and shifting in their leadership, but political changeover following electoral victory was a reality, with incumbent presidents usually being beaten in bids for reelection. The Philippine president during this period exerted strong leadership, but the national congress was a legitimate legislative body, not a facade, and interest groups as well as political parties were active and well organized. The civil service, although presumably protected by a comprehensive constitutional merit provision, was in fact operating under a modified patronage system. Higher civil servants were not members of a separate administrative class with cohesive traditions, common indoctrination, or a sense of corporate identity. The bureaucratic contribution to policy formulation was relatively minor, and came more from expertise in a program field of specialization, such as agriculture or public health, than from membership in an elitist bureaucratic in-group. Bureaucratic allegiances were primarily to particular subject-matter specialties or government agencies, or to political sponsors or patrons, rather than to a centralized core political leadership.

The martial law regime proclaimed late in 1972 by President Marcos, who had been elected in 1965 and reelected in 1969, brought drastic alterations. The political transformation was styled by him as "constitutional authoritarianism," designed to bring about a "New Society" for the Philippines. The actual outcome was described by Rosenberg as "highly personalistic rule"[10] by Marcos, so personalistic that no provisions were made for presidential succession until late 1983. This civilian personalist regime combined political repression, law-and-order objectives, and a decidedly corporate/technocratic orientation. Despite token gestures from time to time, little progress was made under Marcos toward the restoration of democratic processes which he promised. The suspended national legislature was replaced in 1978 by a virtually powerless interim national assembly. Early in 1981, martial law was formally lifted, but wide-ranging authoritarian controls continued and decrees issued under martial law remained in effect. Soon afterward, constitutional amendments were adopted by the interim national assembly and ratified in a plebiscite which established a presidential-parliamentary system along the lines of the French Fifth Republic, but also authorized the president to continue to rule by decree. In June 1981, another in a series of token elections to help legitimize the regime was held, resulting in another six-year term for Marcos, which he did not complete before his ouster.

The policy objectives of the Marcos regime emphasized the imposition and maintenance of political order, coping with Moslem rebels on the southern island of Mindanao and leftist militants elsewhere, and the attainment of economic development goals (which included land reform, self-sufficiency in rice production, promotion of tourism, increased production for export, and construction of infrastructure facilities). The operating methods of the Marcos government in trying to reach such goals displayed strong corporate-technocratic tendencies.

Corporatism under Marcos was somewhat different than the Latin American variety. Sympathetic commentators, such as Filipino political scientist Remigio Agpalo, saw it as consistent with an "organic hierarchical paradigm" long characteristic of politics in the society, with interest groups and government departments operating as arms of the political leader of the nation.[11] Critics such as Robert Stauffer viewed it as a strategy to counteract and control rival centers of influence.[12] Whatever the motivation, Marcos attempted "to draw interest groups of a certain type together in industry-wide umbrella organizations" designed to "rationalize communication channels for administration policy and theoretically serve as a conduit of opinion to the government."[13] Closely linked to the regime's corporatist ideology was placement of great stress on the importance of technocratic and professional skills in the selection of appointees for important positions concerned with policy implementation.[14] This technocratic orientation was also reflected in measures designed to strengthen bureaucratic capabilities. The civil service system was revamped to make it more inclusive and more responsive to presidential direction. Summary disciplinary action, including dismissal, was taken early in the martial law period against numerous officials charged with corruption, incompetence, or disloyalty to the regime. In 1976, a new civil service law in the form of a presidential decree restructured the central personnel agency, reaffirmed a merit approach to personnel administration, and created the Career Executive Service. As indicated by this last feature, special attention was directed at higher-level civil servants, intended to enhance their professionalism and make them more "development-oriented." Patterned after the British administrative class, the Career Executive Service was designed to provide a pool of career administrators available for government-wide service, with a common training program required through a newly established Development Academy. Various attempts were made to introduce improved management and budgeting techniques, usually borrowed from the United States, and to promote regionalization and decentralization of administration, often with formalistic rather than effective results. Linda Richter's overall judgment, nevertheless, was that "problems of scarcity, skilled expertise, public apathy or a lack of informed executive ability which are so frequently the cause of development plans going awry" were not major obstacles in the Philippines during the Marcos era.[15]

The problems of the regime were much more fundamental, linked to longstanding tendencies in Filipino politics toward abuse of public office, the unrestrained rapaciousness of Ferdinand and Imelda Marcos and their cronies, and the prolonged stifling of political opposition. The vulnerability of the regime was drastically increased by the assassination of Benigno Aquino, the chief political rival of Marcos, when Aquino returned to Manila from abroad in August 1983. Demonstrations against the regime grew in volume and intensity, leading to widespread speculation that there might be a military takeover. Faced with mounting opposition and hoping to restore confidence in his administration, Marcos announced a premature presidential election to be held early in 1986. His opponent was Corazon Aquino, running as a replacement for her slain husband. The election results were disputed, with both Marcos and Aquino claiming victory. The tide was turned by a combination of "people power" and a declaration of allegiance to Aquino from two key military figures under Marcos— Minister of Defense Juan Ponce Enrile and General Fidel Ramos, acting chief of staff. After Marcos and his closest associates went into exile in the United States, Aquino as the new chief executive consolidated her position by suspending the 1973 constitution, dissolving the national assembly provided for by it, supporting a new constitution approved in 1987 which restored the presidential system and extended her term in office to 1992, and gaining control of both legislative houses after nationwide elections. Her political position remained precarious, however. She survived several coup attempts from disaffected military factions, continued to combat leftist and Moslem insurgencies, faced numerous aspirants who hoped to take over the presidency, and failed in pushing through to completion several promised fundamental social and economic reforms.[16] Nevertheless, she completed her term as scheduled, and was succeeded after the 1992 election by Fidel Ramos, who had served as minister of defense in the Aquino cabinet and who was backed by her. Ramos was one of seven candidates, and won with a plurality of only 23.4 percent of the vote, so had to govern with a weak political base. Nevertheless, he completed his five-year stint in office, and even explored the possibility of amending the constitution so that he could run for a second term. When this drew widespread opposition, he abandoned the effort. In the 1998 presidential election, the winner was Vice President Joseph E. Estrada, who had formed a three party electoral coalition called the Struggle for the Nationalist Filipino Masses (LAMMP), gaining 39.9 percent of the vote in a field of ten candidates. The vice presidency went to Gloria Macapagal-Arroyo, who was backed by Ramos. Previously, Estrada had been best known as a popular film actor, but had also served in several elective positions. His coalition also gained control of both houses of the legislature, establishing for Estrada a firmer base of support than had been enjoyed by Ramos. Thus a competitive political system has been in operation in the Philippines most of the time since independence. It lapsed, however, during the Marcos years and its prospects after restoration a decade and a half ago under Aquino, although encouraging, continue to be uncertain.

A major concern of the Aquino government was reform of the bureaucratic apparatus inherited from Marcos. As Richter observed, "the bureaucracy has been singled out for rebuke, purges, and restructuring since Corazon Aquino took power."[17] Understandably, the civil service was regarded as an institution that had collaborated with the discredited regime, even though many individual civil servants were recognized as being victimized by and opposed to it. Moreover, the civil service had greatly expanded in size under Marcos, growing from under 600,000 in 1973 to 1.3 million in 1985. The reform efforts, including "summary dismissals, early retirement, reorganization, use of non-governmental groups, exhortation, and various incentives," have been reviewed in detail by Carino, who viewed them as "strongly punitive" overall, contrasting sharply with the policy of reconciliation pursued toward the military, political prisoners, and insurgent groups.[18] An early step was to remove tenure security rights of incumbents. Although the basic problem of overstaffing was not been dealt with comprehensively, a sizable number of career civil servants were purged through dismissals, forced resignations, and retirements.[19] The greatest impact on the service as a whole was probably demoralization resulting from uncertainty, but there were major changes in top level staffing. Although the existing Career Executive Service for high-ranking officials was retained, 35 percent of the incumbents were separated, others were reassigned or promoted, and only 43 percent were untouched.[20]

Along with these personnel shifts, efforts were made to improve salary levels, curb corruption, and make organizational adjustments. Resource scarcities, inbred practices, and inconsistencies in implementation have led to disappointing results, however. As Varela reports, the Civil Service Commission has taken the lead in recent years in pursuing a strategy of professionalization, but she cautions that this strategy relies too much on controls over the recruitment and utilization of personnel, and warns that "policies and action measures, properly calibrated to avoid and deflect the pitfalls of excessive bureaucratization, must be found if the program thrust toward professionalization is to be successfully achieved."[21]

The current Philippine public bureaucracy unavoidably reflects general societal characteristics. On the plus side, as Richter states, the bureaucracy "has in place the reservoir of talent and commitment, skills and procedures to operate effectively in most policy sectors."[22] Its record is excellent, for example, with regard to levels of education of personnel and provision of employment opportunities for women. On the negative side, it reflects the tensions generated by external influences exerted in an Asian cultural context. Ledivina Carino, one of the most knowledgeable observers of the Philippine scene, explains the situation perceptively:

> Existing within a nation still in crisis, the administrative system manifests rather than resolves the contradictions of Philippine society. . . . In other words, the seeds toward a bureaucracy that can provide more effective servants of the people or more efficient masters over them have both been sown. The bureaucracy alone cannot choose which direction will win out. Its fate cannot be independent of the conflicting forces struggling in the Philippine society in which it is embedded.[23]

Sri Lanka

Sri Lanka represents another variant among polyarchal competitive systems.[24] After more than four centuries of colonial domination under the Portuguese, the Dutch, and the British, Sri Lanka (then Ceylon) gained independent status within the British Commonwealth in 1948. During over five decades since independence, Sri Lanka has succeeded in maintaining a competitive political system, despite being a country of marked ethnic and religious diversity and having to cope with escalating inter-group violence beginning in the 1980s. The dominant racial group, making up approximately 74 percent of the population, consists of Sinhalese who originated in northern India. The Tamils, most of who have arrived more recently from southern India, constitute about 18 percent with the remaining 8 percent consisting of smaller minority groups. Although two-thirds of the people of Sri Lanka are Buddhists, there are also sizable numbers of Hindus, Christians, and Muslims. Similar diversity exists in language and cultural patterns.

The intensification of ethnic violence has disrupted political stability in Sri Lanka, and even led to intervention by Indian troops in 1987 in an unsuccessful effort to bring about a cease-fire and negotiate a political settlement between the dominant Sinhalese and minority Tamil factions. Although no accord has been reached to end dissension and Tamil rebels have been responsible for the assassination of several prominent political leaders, the continuing unrest has not caused abandonment of competitive politics on a national scale, or forceful usurpation of political power. Transitions in party control have occurred periodically, first under a parliamentary system patterned after the British model, and more recently under a mixed presidential-parliamentary system. The United National Party and the Sri Lanka Freedom Party alternated in power for two decades until 1977. Then the United National Party controlled the government for seventeen years, until it was displaced in the 1994 parliamentary elections by the People's Alliance, led by Chandrika Bandaranaike Kumaratunga, who had taken over leadership of the party after the assassination of her husband in 1988. She then became prime minister and in the presidential election held later in 1994 she was the People's Alliance candidate, winning a six year term in a landslide (partly because the United National Party candidate had been assassinated less than a month before the election and replaced on short notice by his widow). President Kumaratunga promptly appointed her own mother, Serimavo Bandaranaike, as prime minister, a post the older woman had held in the 1960s and 1970s before adoption of the mixed presidential-parliamentary system. Soon after the election, President Kumaratunga also initiated a truce with the Tamil rebels, and proposed constitutional changes to eliminate the presidency and go back to a more orthodox parliamentary system. This change was still being debated in 1999, but had not been adopted. Thus, as a new century begins, Sri Lanka is in the process of trying once more to deal with internal problems and experimenting again with institutional reform.

Although continued Sinhalese-Tamil conflict has led to short periods during which a state of emergency has been declared, and to a ban on parties advocating a separate state within Sri Lanka territory, the record shows that the practice of peaceful transfer of power after a shift in electoral support appears to be firmly established.

As in the case of other former British colonies in South and Southeast Asia, Sri Lanka began independence with the legacy of an ongoing administrative system which had been established under British rule. Although not the subject of much detailed analysis, apparently the bureaucratic apparatus has been able to transfer its services rather successfully from the colonial power to the political leadership of the new nation-state. This pattern of accountability seems to have been maintained with the shift from the orthodox British parliamentary political pattern to the mixed presidential-parliamentary system, and is not likely to be disturbed if there is a return to the parliamentary model.

Colombia

After an earlier political history in which periods of stability alternated with unrest and occasional warfare, since 1958 Colombia has provided a Latin American example of polyarchal competition, limited in nature until 1974 and more open since then.[25]

Colombia is the fourth largest nation in Latin America, with a predominantly mestizo or mulatto population of about 40 million, making it the most populous country in South America after Brazil. Both positive and negative consequences flow from its strategic location in the northwestern part of the South American continent and its geographic variety (with flat coastal areas, highland mountain ranges and valleys, and tropical eastern plains). For instance, its proximity to the United States has assisted in the growth of the nation's economy, but has also made Colombia the leading world center for illegal drug traffic. The geography accounts for an amazing multiplicity of life forms in a relatively small area and promotes economic diversification, but it also impedes the development of adequate transportation and communication networks and hampers the control of subversive groups.

Colombia has a checkered political history. Independent from Spain since 1819, what is present-day Colombia was part of a larger Gran Colombia until 1830, then became New Granada until it was renamed in 1863. Under pressure from the United States, Colombia was forced in 1903 to recognize the independence of Panama. During the nineteenth century, a bidimensional pattern of political competition between the Conservative and Liberal parties became entrenched, with its sources in the differing political philosophies of the nation's founding fathers, Simon Bolivar and Francisco de Paula Santander, with the former advocating centralism and unification and the latter decentralization and federalism. Until almost the middle of this century, the two parties alternated in power, with the Conservatives enjoying a long period of hegemony from 1886 to 1930, giving way to the Liberals from 1930 to 1946.

After this protracted era of relative political stability, broken by minor insurrections and brief but bloody internal fighting at the turn of the century, tensions erupted into a destructive civil war in 1948, leading in 1953 to a forced pacification following military intervention by General Gustavo Rojas Pinilla. After an atypical four-year military dictatorship, the two major parties entered into a pact in 1957 to alternate the presidency every four years and otherwise to share equally in government at all levels. This National Front was successful in paving the way for a resumption of open political competition beginning with the 1974 presidential election and continuing up to the present. During this time the Liberals have controlled the presidency except for the years 1982 to 1986, when the occupant was Conservative Belisario Betancur, and since 1998, when Andres Pastrana was elected for a four-year term. He succeeded Ernesto Samper, elected in 1994 to succeed fellow Liberal Cesar Gaviria. In 1998, the Liberals were badly split in losing the presidential election, but retained legislative majorities in both houses of the national legislature.

Powerful inhibiting factors have slowed development in Colombia during recent decades. Two of them have deep historical roots: continuing inequality between groups in Colombian society, reflected in a severe maldistribution of wealth, high rates of unemployment and inflation, declining markets for exports, and upper class dominance in the leadership of both major political parties; and the longtime prevalence of *la violencia* as a feature of everyday life in both the public and private spheres.[26]

Beginning with the years of civil conflict at mid-century, Colombia has also had to contend with two additional troubling phenomena: persistent insurgencies by radical guerrilla groups and the emergence of powerful cartels engaged in illegal drug trafficking.

Restrictions on political participation during the military dictatorship and the National Front era led to the emergence of dissident groups who had gained experience in guerrilla warfare during the more violent civil war years. Sharing a leftist political philosophy but never united under a common leadership with a cohesive plan of action, three of these groups remain active as insurgents—the Colombia Revolutionary Armed Forces (FARC), the National Liberation Army (ELN), and the Popular Army of Liberation (EPL). A fourth, the April 19 Movement (M-19), was demobilized in 1990 and its former members now form a party which has placed representatives in the national legislature and the cabinet, and provided the third place finisher in both the 1990 and 1994 presidential elections. Despite repeated efforts by the government to negotiate with and pacify the remaining insurgents, they continue to engage in costly destruction of infrastructure facilities and to terrorize and massacre ordinary citizens, particularly in rural areas.

Illegal international trafficking in drugs (primarily cocaine and marijuana) is the second source of lawless and violent activity. Colombia has emerged as a global center for the drug business because of its location between the United States as the main consumer and producers within its own borders and in neighboring countries such as Bolivia and Peru. The cities of Medellin and Cali, the second and third largest metropolitan centers in the country, became headquarters for the major drug cartels. The Medellin cartel was headed by the notorious and vengeful Pablo Escobar until he was finally cornered and killed in 1993.

Despite these impediments, Colombia has undertaken during these same years to achieve an impressive array of political and administrative reforms. The most significant was adoption of a new constitution, which went into effect in mid-1991. Following a referendum held in 1990, the much-amended 1886 constitution was extensively revised by a constituent assembly which operated without limits as to what could be considered. The basic presidential system was retained, but a number of less fundamental changes were accepted. Several of these reforms affected existing institutions (including the legislature, the office of attorney general, the supreme court of justice, and the constitutional court). Others added new features which had been previously considered but not adopted, such as elimination of reference to the traditional two-party system and recognition of a multiparty system, removal of the last constitutional vestiges of the defunct National Front political arrangements, recognition of legal equality for all religious sects, and adoption of a set of mechanisms for direct citizen participation in the making of policy decisions through devices such as referenda and initiatives. Finally, a number of reforms were made that had not been seriously considered earlier. These included election of all members of the Senate by popular vote, a runoff if needed in the election of the president, adoption of a bill of rights, creation of an office of public defender, introduction of the "tutela" as a form of legal action to secure guaranteed rights, and formalization of constituent assemblies for future constitutional reforms.

Administrative improvement efforts had been made earlier, in the 1960s and 1970s, with disappointing results, as reported by Vidal Perdomo and Ruffing-Hilliard.[27] The 1991 constitutional revision has laid the foundation for a renewed program of administrative reforms, some already in place and some still in the planning stage.[28]

A major thrust of the new constitution and of current government policy is toward greater privatization and decentralization of programs now administered by the central government, but not much has actually been accomplished along these lines. Structural reform of the administrative machinery is another objective. The constitution called for the establishment of a study commission for reorganizing public administration and for the adoption within fourteen months (by early 1993) of plans to eliminate, merge, or restructure executive branch entities. This reorganization has been only partially accomplished. There are as of now seventeen ministries plus several administrative departments, which include, for example, the Administrative Department of the Public Service.

The constitution also declared the public service to be a career service unless otherwise provided in the constitution or by law, and created a National Civil Service Commission for its protection. Several preliminary steps have been taken toward this end, including reorganization of the existing center operated by the government for public service education and training (Escuela Superior de Administracion Publica); issuance of a presidential decree specifying functions, setting minimum requisites, and fixing salaries and emoluments of central government employees; and compilation by the new National Civil Service Commission of the existing standards for personnel administration.

In summary, Colombian public administration has in the past exhibited and continues to suffer from maladies common in polyarchal competitive countries generally, and particularly in Latin America, but is making a concerted effort at improvement. It is too early to evaluate the results.

DOMINANT-PARTY SEMICOMPETITIVE SYSTEMS

In a dominant-party semicompetitive system, one party has held a monopoly of actual power for a substantial period of time, but other parties are legal and do in fact exist. The dominant party has a record of overshadowing all other parties and is victorious in virtually all elections. It is nondictatorial, however, and a condition for classification in this regime type is the presumption that the dominant party can be displaced in competition at the polls by the successful challenge of a rival.

The number of qualifying polities is obviously small. Until very recently, the most clear-cut example of such a dominant party has been Mexico's Partido Revolucionario Institucional (PRI). India presents a somewhat more debatable illustration. India's Congress party has been similarly dominant during most of the period since independence in 1947, but it was displaced between 1977 and 1980, from 1989 to 1991, and again since 1998. The third example is Malaysia, where the Alliance (now renamed the National Front), a "holding company" type of political party formed by communal organizations representing the country's three major ethnic groups, has dominated political life and controlled the government continuously since the first federal elections in 1955. Each of these instances is examined in more detail.

Mexico

In Mexico, the Partido Revolucionario Institicional (PRI) can be traced to the revolution of 1910, and over the years it has claimed to be the official party of the revolution.[29] As a result, the PRI has been able until recently to monopolize the electoral process "by preempting and institutionalizing the revolutionary myth and by creating for itself an image as the key component of an indissoluble trinity composed of Party, government, and political elite."[30] After controlling all branches of the federal government and most of the state governments for decades, the PRI has rapidly lost ground since 1976, when its presidential candidate obtained 94.4 percent of the popular vote. In 1982, with a total of seven candidates competing, the PRI elected its candidate, Miguel de la Madrid, with 71 percent. By 1988, in an election widely considered to have been manipulated and fraudulent, PRI presidential candidate Carlos Salinas de Gortari received in the official count a bare 50.39 percent of the popular vote against three competitors, with substantial support also going to the nominees of the leftist National Democratic Front (31 percent) and the conservative National Action Party (16.8 percent). Moreover, the PRI managed to retain control of the Chamber of Deputies by a scant 52 percent, and lost four seats in the Senate. In the face of these setbacks, newly elected President Salinas announced the day after the 1988 election that the era of the "virtual one-party system" had ended, leading to a period of "intense political competition," and he pledged a thoroughgoing reform of the PRI apparatus, which was soon set in motion.[31] In 1994, after a hectic campaign marred by the assassination of PRI candidate Luis Donaldo Colosio, who was replaced by Ernesto Zedillo, the PRI again won the presidency (in an election generally evaluated as fair), with just over 50 percent of the vote as compared to slightly under 27 percent for the PAN and 17 percent for the PRD candidates. The PRI also obtained substantial majorities in both houses of the national legislature, but in 1997 for the first time lost control of the Chamber of Deputies. Despite threats posed by the 1994 Zapatista rebellion in Chiapas, by the financial crisis early in 1995, by the conviction in 1999 of former president Salinas for ordering the assassination in 1994 of the PRI general secretary, and by other signs of political and economic unrest, the PRI continued as Mexico's dominant party until the presidential election held on July 1, 2000, supervised by the new Federal Election Institute. Vicente Fox, the PAN candidate, with 42.71 percent of the vote, defeated Francisco Labastida, the PRI nominee (35.78 percent) and Cuauhtemoc Cardenas of the PRD (16.52 percent), with 64 percent of registered voters casting ballots. However, the PAN did not gain a plurality of seats in either legislative chamber, and the PRI retained the governorship in 20 of the 31 states, so that no party has clear political control.

The long-term strategy of the PRI in the past has been to seek a consensus to avoid a splintering away of party factions on either the right or the left; it has been a coalition party of the center. The Mexican political system has been described as "center-dominant,"[32] and "monistic," because it has involved "the centralization and control of potentially competing interests."[33] In such a regime, the most significant political competition takes place among ideological, regional, and interest-oriented factions within the dominant party. This has been officially recognized to some extent by the sectoral form of organization within PRI, put into effect by President Lazaro Cardenas when he reorganized the party in 1938, and based in recent years on three distinct sectors—labor, agrarian, and "popular"—with the latter being a catch-all category including representation for civil and military bureaucrats, among others. Without abandoning the basic strategy of consensus building over a wide spectrum of political interests, the current party restructuring efforts have been aimed at changing the basic relationship between the PRI and its constituency to de-emphasize or even eliminate these sectoral blocs and stress a more direct relationship between the party and individual citizens. The biggest problem faced by President Salinas in this effort, according to one analysis, was "to gain sufficient control over his own house—the ruling party, the government bureaucracy, and the government-affiliated 'mass' organizations—to force its most retrograde occupants to accept fundamental changes that will inevitably diminish their power, security, and wealth."[34]

The prospects for success were bolstered by a secondary key feature of the Mexican regime—the preeminence of executive leadership in both the political and administrative spheres. Needler calls this "executivism," pointing out that the president is "by far the dominant figure in the Mexican political system,"[35] with other chief executives occupying somewhat comparable positions at the state and local levels. Legislative and judicial bodies do not operate in a way that can effectively check executive supremacy. The reins of control over the PRI, as well as the official governmental apparatus, have been held by the Mexican president, subject to limits imposed by the requirements for protecting the centralist nature of the regime. In the opinion of Raymond Vernon, recent Mexican presidents, in their concern "to achieve unanimity, . . . to extend the reach of the PRI the full distance to both the right and the left," have been held to "a course of action which is zigzagging and vacillating when it is not blandly neutral."[36] The political process in this kind of dominant-party regime under executive leadership apparently tends over time toward a policy orientation that stresses consensus at the price of boldness and decisiveness.

During the presidency of Salinas, limited reforms were indeed undertaken, sufficient to be referred to by Centeno as *salinastroika*. Included were changes toward democratization of the PRI, but Centeno notes that it was clear that Salinas and his associates "wanted to retain control of the process." He quotes Salinas as declaring that criticism of the party amounted to treason, and as admonishing some who spoke of democratization as instead actually promoting division.[37] Another reform, the National Solidarity Program (PRONOSOL), was aimed at providing more local controls over development programs, but it likewise placed severe limits on authority delegated, and its critics asserted that it was designed to bolster electoral support for the government.[38] Both Centeno and Mendez agree that Salinas was more interested in implementing his program of neoliberal macro-economic reforms than in political reforms.[39] This probably helps explain the difficulties that he left to be faced by Zedillo as his successor.

Turning to administrative capacities and performance, Mexican experience has been traumatic because of the almost complete breakdown of the administrative machinery during the revolutionary period of 1910–1917. Rebuilding has taken place on a gradual and piecemeal basis. The structure of the executive branch currently includes a bewildering complexity of units, ranging from almost a score of ministries to a myriad of interministerial committees, administrative commissions, and decentralized institutions in commercial, financial, and industrial fields.

Recruitment into the Mexican bureaucracy has been described as the outcome of "continuing struggle between the needs of the political system and the requirements for technically qualified personnel."[40] The formal personnel system does not include a central personnel agency. Each department has its own personnel office, with considerable variation in their operation. A basic personnel law, enacted in 1941, dealt primarily with the legal rights of employees. It divided them into two basic categories—"workers of confidence" and "ordinary workers"—with the former group corresponding roughly to an expanded administrative class and containing about one-third of the total number of employees. Our principal concern is with these "confidence" officials. Writing in the late 1940s, Wendell Schaeffer listed these factors as important in the selection of confidence personnel: personal and political relationships, family ties, contributions to the PRI, and expertise.[41] Greenberg asserted in 1970 that the balance seemed to have shifted by then from other considerations toward expertise because of technological developments which made professional training more important than before.[42]

Confidence personnel have been denied unionization and strike rights granted to the "ordinary" or "base" workers. Official salaries have been notoriously low, and only moderate progress has been made in raising salary rates.

Multiple jobholding and "institutionalized" corruption are common conse-quences. One observer refers to the continued practice of "undiluted, unambigu-ous corruption," sanctioned in part by an "enduring Mexican attitude of resignation and cynicism,"[43] and requiring fifteen Mexican terms to denote "graft." Another states that the reasons for corruption can be found

> both in the nature of the society and in the demands of the personnel system. The prevalence in the society of personalism and *amistad*, with primary loyalties being directed toward one's family and friends rather than toward the government or administrative entity, has an important effect on the level of corruption. . . . In addition, the predicament of the bureaucrat, with no real union protection, no job security, and no guarantee of future income, causes him to turn to corrupt practices.[44]

Lack of information makes an assessment of the current level of perfor-mance of the Mexican bureaucracy risky. Some encouraging signs can be seen. An economist asserted as long ago as the 1960s that Mexico was a nation with

> a well-developed public sector, consisting of its government agencies and its government-controlled enterprises, which by now have acquired a sense of continuity and of effective performance. . . . The men who design the dams, roads, and factories of the country, direct its business and financial institutions, plan its educational system, provide its ad-vanced training, and guide its agricultural research are principally Mex-ican nationals.[45]

Based on a case study of the Ministry of Hydraulic Resources, a student of public administration concluded in 1970 that "government agencies *can* operate effi-ciently within a structure which on the surface appears to be inefficient."[46] Martin Needler, a political scientist, probably makes a realistic assessment when he observes that the Mexican public service

> contains people of a wide range of capabilities. Many of the people at the top levels of the system are intelligent, well educated, and dynamic political entrepreneurs with well-developed conceptions of the public interest; but, frequently, in his dealings with government, the citizen encounters only corrupt, self-serving, time-wasting incompetents. Be-tween these extremes are many dedicated public servants, especially among the technically trained; but there are also others, particularly among middle- and lower-level administrative personnel, such as office managers, who are primarily interested in their bank accounts, who take kickbacks from lower-level employees, divert supplies, and pocket fees on purchases and contracts.[47]

The extent to which political power has been diffused in the Mexican system has been obscured by the "monolithic facade" provided by the institution of the presidency.[48] Scott has suggested the term "government by consultation" to describe the mechanism by which the Mexican chief executive has used "all of the formal and informal, legal and extra-legal agencies of the presidency" to hear and consider "the competing needs and desires of all the major functional interests concerned in any given policy decision."[49] Although the arbiter in policy disputes is the president, he must engage in a complex consultative process in order to seek a national consensus and maintain the hegemony of the PRI. One of the groups consulted consists of the technicians within the bureaucracy, particularly the economic technicians who are integrally involved in decision-making related to development. The line between the *tecnicos* and the *politicos* is still reasonably clear, but the strength of the technicians has been growing. It "lies not so much in their powers to shape policy directly as in their capacity to choose the technical alternatives which are presented to their political masters."[50] This range of proposals, however, is not likely to extend to a drastic refashioning of governmental programs.

Bureaucratic access to political power opportunities has been increasing due to the emergence of a "new class" of career political administrators, who have become the dominant element in the ruling political elite.[51] They are not "simple bureaucrats," but have "combined progress through ever-higher administrative, subcabinet, and cabinet appointments with periods as state governors, members of the national legislature, or officials in the party apparatus."[52] The most striking indication of this phenomenon is that none of the last five presidents had ever held an elective office before running as the PRI candidate for the presidency. They represent the tip of the pyramid of "a ruling administrative class—recruited partly on the basis of academic performance, partly on family connections, and promoted on technical merit and clique membership—which has subsumed the political roles of popular representative, orienter of policy direction, and leader of mass opinion into its role as governor."[53]

The basic fact to remember, however, in understanding the relationship between the political system and the bureaucracy in Mexico up to now has been the primacy of politics and the PRI. The dominant force in the lives of bureaucrats has been "politics in the form of party ties." The multiplicity of roles played by Mexican bureaucrats, often including also involvement in private financial and economic enterprises, means that "the decision-making process in the agencies must therefore cope with often conflicting needs engendered by the system, with the result that technical considerations often take a back seat to political and personally based economic factors."[54]

The persistence of these political and professional networks, known as *camarillas*, is emphasized by recent commentators.[55] Centeno says that they may be viewed "as either the curse of Mexican politics or the savior of the system," on one hand causing use of nonmeritocratic criteria in personnel selection, nonoptimal resources distribution and massive corruption, while on the other providing an element of stability for individuals and for the political class as a whole.[56]

The Mexican bureaucracy, therefore, although playing an important role in the political arena, including institutional recognition within the PRI organizational structure and access by the most successful "political administrators" to key leadership roles, has been effectively sealed off as a separate entity from mounting a challenge to the PRI's historically established claim to political dominance. If the political future in Mexico brings a transition toward the type of party dominance represented by the Congress party in India, or even if a system of party parity evolves, the Mexican bureaucracy is unlikely to move into a primary role as policy-maker.

India and Malaysia

India and Malaysia, as Asian examples of dominant-party regimes, show similarities between them and together offer some contrasts to the Mexican case. The similarities include a common British colonial past with its legacy of political and administrative institutions, dominant parties with many shared characteristics, comparable working relationships between political leaders and professional bureaucrats, and established effective external controls over the bureaucracy.[57]

During the lengthy period of British colonialism in these areas, the British institutional imprint was firmly fixed. "Gradually under British rule," according to Kochanek, "a model of government evolved which was ultimately to be accepted as the structure of government for independent India." One key element in this model was "the creation of a unified central administration based on the emerging principle of a merit bureaucracy recruited on the basis of open competition and merit."[58] Similarly, Means says that the British impact on Malaysia has been "so pervasive it is impossible to trace all its manifestations," but with one feature being the British administrative system, representing "an institutional embodiment of the values of rational organization designed to provide certain social services for the benefit of society as a whole."[59] In both instances, the inherited administrative pattern has been retained relatively intact since independence.

More noticeable adjustments have been made in the British parliamentary and party systems, particularly in the substitution of a dominant party for the British dual-party tradition. Founded in 1885, the Congress party had no serious rival for leadership in the campaign for Indian independence or after 1947 in the postindependence government until the mid-1970s. This record of dominance, much like that of the PRI in Mexico, was based on "strong leadership, a long history marked by a high level of institutionalization, an ability to manage internal conflict generated by competing demands, an integrative political style, and an ability to preempt the middle ground of the Indian political spectrum."[60] During these years, the Congress was regularly able to secure massive majorities in Parliament and also controlled nearly all of the state governments, despite the existence of several other major political parties, arrayed both to the right and to the left.

More recently, domination by the Congress has weakened. In 1975, deterioration of the political situation led to the declaration of a state of emergency by Prime Minister Indira Gandhi, and to a decisive defeat for the Congress party under her leadership in the general elections which she eventually called for in March 1977. The victorious Janata party was a coalition of disparate elements, consisting of splinters from the Congress party, and most of the non-Communist opposition parties, including the Socialist party and the Indian People's Union, a right-wing nationalist Hindu party. Events proved that this coalition could not be held together or retain popular support for very long. Early in 1980, the Congress-I (for Indira) party swept back into power with an overwhelming electoral victory which gave it a top-heavy majority in Parliament, and Mrs. Gandhi again became prime minister. Domestic disturbances mounted, however, focusing on demands by Sikhs in Punjab for autonomy, leading in 1984 to the assassination of Indira Gandhi by two Sikh members of her bodyguard. Her younger son, Rajiv, was immediately sworn in as prime minister, and later in the year won an unprecedented victory in parliamentary elections, with the Congress-I party gaining 415 of the 523 seats. Nevertheless, by 1989 the Rajiv Gandhi government had suffered such a deterioration in public support that the Congress-I party won only 176 seats (more than any other party but far short of a majority) and Gandhi was forced to resign as prime minister. The resulting coalition government, with Vishwanath Pratap Singh of the National Front as prime minister, was supported by the right-wing Indian People's Party and by four leftist parties, combining for a working majority of 283 seats. This shaky coalition had already encountered a crisis by mid-1990, leading to the resignation by Prime Minister Singh, and the return to power of a Congress-I government, headed by P. V. Narasimha Rao, which in turn was ousted in early 1996 after the Congress-I party suffered heavy losses in parliamentary elections. Weak coalition governments then alternated in office for brief periods until late 1999, when the Bharati Janata Party sharply defeated the Congress-I. A coalition was installed with a solid parliamentary majority of 303 out of 543 seats, with Atal Bihari Vajpayee as prime minister. Whether or not the Congress party will be able in the future to regain its longstanding role of dominance is an unsettled issue.[61]

The dominant-party counterpart in Malaysia is the National Front. Formed in 1952 as the Alliance party and later renamed, it is a coalition of groups representing the three major ethnic components of the population. The United Malays National Organization has occupied the leading role in this coalition because of Malay numerical superiority, with Chinese and Indian communal organizations in secondary roles. In continuous control of the government since independence, the National Front currently holds 163 of the 192 seats in the House of Representatives, the power wielding chamber in the bicameral legislature. Despite recent friction within the United Malays National Organization, its main component group, the National Front appears to face no serious challenge to its well-established role of political dominance. As Means points out, its success depends "upon its ability to preserve intact a political coalition which bridges the basic communal cleavage within the country." On the most important communal issues, the National Front "has worked out fairly moderate compromises, but with a distinct pro-Malay bias." To function smoothly, it "needs communal moderates in leadership positions of the constituent communal parties, and it relies upon the support of communal moderates at the polls."[62] Future dominance is dependent on avoiding crises serious enough to break up the unstable coalition.

Both India and Malaysia have benefited from unusually advanced higher public bureaucracies. Indeed, India could legitimately lay claim to producing the forerunner of the modern civil service in Great Britain itself, due to the influence of the British East India Company experience during the nineteenth century. The preindependence Indian Civil Service (ICS) has gradually been replaced by the new Indian Administrative Service (IAS) as the apex of this system, supplemented by a series of other service categories staffing the central government and the state governments. The emphasis continues to be on the very selective annual recruitment (the intake is 125 or slightly more per year) of exceptionally intelligent university graduates. A system of competitive examinations is administered by the Union Public Service Commission, an independent body that is also responsible for training new recruits. There is no question that those selected for the IAS are able. Critics claim, however, that the recruitment policy is overly exclusive and that the IAS has a law-and-order orientation not well suited to a welfare state. Tummala reported in the early 1980s that nearly 70 percent of the higher civil servants continued to be drawn from 10 percent of the population— "the middle class, urban professional group"—and that nearly half of those recruited were offspring of civil servants.[63] Maheshwari confirmed this pattern a decade later, despite partial success from educational opportunity and affirmative action efforts to broaden the recruitment base, and reported that "no great attitudinal changes are manifested by the civil servants coming from the newly opened social groups, the young being socialized in the values of their seniors."[64] The system as a whole was rated in the 1950s by an American observer, Paul H. Appleby, as among the dozen or so most advanced in the world, but he also pointed out that it was "designed to serve the relatively simple interests of an occupying power," was not adequate for an independent India, and required systematic improvement.[65] Similar comments continue to be made. Kochanek has recommended that the bureaucracy "must be made more innovative, less subject to rapid expansion as a way of creating employment and must exercise self-restraint in its demands for higher incomes."[66] Maheshwari recognizes that "public administration in India has absorbed many changes," but asserts that "the apparent conflict between the needs of development in all spheres of life and the colonial attributes of an overly cautious bureaucracy continues to plague the system."[67] Attempts from the political leadership to shake things up, such as Indira Gandhi's call in the 1970s for a "committed bureaucracy," and occasional transfers in the upper echelons of the civil service to obtain greater compliance with current government policies, have drawn mixed reactions. "The net result," according to Tummala, "is that the civil servant not only remains entrenched but also threatened; hence very cautious."[68] Jain, on the other hand, feels that there is now greater politicization, with the bureaucracy "regarded not a value-free but a value-laden instrument of political power," with political influences tending to "pervade every nook and corner of Indian national life," so that loyalty to the party in power has become part of the award structure of the civil service.[69]

The higher civil service in Malaysia likewise has evolved directly from the colonial bureaucratic system, with little change in the institutional arrangements or the social status attached to membership. The most significant transformation has been the substitution of national for expatriate personnel by the process of Malayanization, which had been substantially completed by the early 1960s. Selection for entry continues to be made primarily from university graduates by an autonomous public service commission, based mainly on previous academic performance. A feature of the postindependence recruitment process has been a legally imposed quota approach favoring Malay over non-Malay applicants in the population at a four-to-one ratio for appointment to the Malaysian Administrative and Diplomatic Service (MADS). Such preferential treatment for Malays is confined to this small administrative elite group, however, and the ethnic composition varies in different sectors of the Malaysian civil service as a whole. Milne and Mauzy generalize that Malays predominate in the services requiring a general educational background, but that "in those requiring substantial professional qualifications there is proportionately a preponderance of non-Malays."[70] In general, the legitimacy inherited from colonial times by the bureaucracy has been retained, and its level of competence continues to be impressive. Writing in 1964, Tilman concluded that the administrative system was not working precisely as it had in the colonial environment, but that it was effectively serving the current needs of the society.[71] A few years later Esman reported that the Malaysian bureaucratic cadres had "maintained their integrity, discipline, and organizational coherence" and remained competent "in the discharge of routine service and control activities." Echoing the criticism made by others of the Indian higher bureaucrats, however, he contended that the "attitudes, role definitions, and operational capabilities" of Malaysian bureaucrats were not adequate to meet development administration requirements.[72] The problem again is adaptation from the needs of colonialism to those of nationalism.

A cherished part of the political tradition in both India and Malaysia is that there should be a separation between the politicians who make policy and the administrators who carry them out. In practice, working relationships between the political leaders and the professional bureaucrats have generally conformed to the tradition, and have proceeded smoothly, but with Malaysian bureaucrats playing a more active policy role than their Indian counterparts.

In India, this cooperative pattern has no doubt been fostered by the lengthy political dominance of the Congress party, and by the similarity in background and outlook of leaders in the party and the higher bureaucracy. The policy role of the bureaucracy seemed to grow as the Congress party moved toward its pro-claimed dedication to establish "the socialist pattern of society" and government programs tried to achieve welfare state objectives. Through the process of defining and explaining alternatives of social and economic reform, and giving advice for choosing among them, the expert tended to be brought into more active participation. The IAS probably has had a policy role equal to that of the British administrative class and one of equally low visibility. The general impression, nevertheless, has been that the professional bureaucrats have been effectively subordinated to the political leadership in the cabinet and in Parliament.[73] In recent years more concern in the opposite direction has been expressed, based on allegations of undue political interference in administrative matters and a resulting politicization or semi-politicization of the bureaucracy.[74]

In Malaysia, according to Esman's analysis, high-ranking bureaucrats form an integral part of the governing elite, which is composed of "two sections which maintain a symbiotic pattern of relationships: the . . . politicians who head the political section and the senior administrators who operate the bureaucracy. Despite tensions between them, their relationships are mutually supportive."[75] Many of the senior politicians were formerly administrators, which helps explain the collaboration. In a polity where communal pluralism is the basic reality, the dominant political party is compelled to rely on the relatively neutral bureaucracy as a partner in keeping the system going. Indeed, Esman goes so far as to claim that Malaysia's senior officials "have been the indispensable steel frame which has held this precarious state together even when political processes failed."[76]

DOMINANT-PARTY MOBILIZATION SYSTEMS

Important differences separate countries in this group from those just discussed. Permissiveness in politics is less; actual or potential coercion is greater. The dominant party is usually the only legal party. If other parties are permitted to operate openly at all, they are surrounded by restrictive controls designed to keep them weak and only symbolic of opposition. Ideology is more doctrinaire and more insistently proclaimed, although it may be adjusted for purposes of expediency. Greater stress is placed on mass demonstration of loyalty to the regime. The elite tends to be relatively young, urbanized, secularized, and well educated, with a strong commitment to developmental nationalism. Often a single charismatic leader holds a commanding position dominating the movement he heads. Such a regime is likely to have acceded to power during the post-World War II period of independence from colonialism, and is most commonly found in new African nations. It may have replaced some earlier regime in a recently independent state, or it may have altered its own character markedly since taking over the government at the time of independence. Its own political future may be precarious, thus emphasizing the urgency of building a strong base of mass support and of assuring the loyalty of key groups in the society. The leadership may feel a strong tutelary obligation to a population not yet considered ready for self-government. For the national mobilization effort to succeed, the dominant party must insist on the allegiance and support of the public bureaucracy, while being dependent on it for adequate performance.

The viability of these dominant-party mobilization systems has not been as high as was generally anticipated a couple of decades ago. Several countries formerly in this category turned to bureaucratic elite regimes under military leadership, including Algeria after the 1965 coup which overthrew Ben Bella, Bolivia most of the time since 1969 when the National Revolutionary Movement leadership was ousted, Ghana (except for a brief interval) since the downfall of Nkrumah, Guinea since 1984, Liberia, Mali, Mauritania, and some of the other new states carved out of former French West Africa. Numerous nations continue to have one-party regimes, with considerable variation, however, as to the party role in governance and with several instances recently of movement toward more party competition. Among them are Egypt, Gabon, Ivory Coast, Malawi, Mozambique, Senegal, Tanzania, and Zambia. Egypt and Tanzania offer contrasting examples of dominant-party mobilization systems, the former having derived from a military reformist regime which sponsored the party and harnessed it to support the regime, and the latter evolving as the dominant party after serving as the vehicle for winning independence under civilian leadership.

Egypt

During the almost five decades since the 1952 coup which ousted King Farouk, the Egyptian regime in power has had unusual continuity in leadership, first under Gamal Abdel Nasser until his death in 1970, then under Anwar el-Sadat until his assassination in 1981, and currently under Hosni Mubarak. Beginning as a radical interventionist military regime, this government has endeavored to enhance its legitimacy and mobilize popular support for its foreign and domestic programs by combining charismatic appeal with the buildup of a single broadly based mass political party, but with limited political competition permitted in recent years.[77]

The 1952 revolution was started by the "Free Officers," a group of young army officers who were able to depose an unpopular monarch but who were politically inexperienced and lacked a well-defined revolutionary program. Their coup was triggered as a protest against the support failures they believed had led to the defeat of Egyptian armed forces by the Israelis in the Palestinian conflict. Beyond that they aimed at elimination of the monarchy and the introduction of agrarian reform.

This initial uncertainty was reflected in various ways. For a brief period after the coup a civilian prime minister was installed in office before the Free Officer group took over directly, under the title of Revolutionary Command Council. General Muhammad Naguib was nominal head of the group for a while before being replaced by Nasser, who had actually engineered the takeover, and emerged by 1954 as the strongman and regime leader. Gradually Nasser and his colleagues turned toward a program of "Arab socialism," encompassing a far-reaching program of social and economic reforms. This brand of socialism was defended as being in accord with Islamic principles; it rejected the Marxist belief in the inevitability of the class struggle, and in theory favored a mixed economy, although it involved the nationalization of most major business enterprises. Beginning in 1974, however, an "open door" policy, initiated by Sadat and continued by Mubarak in a modified form, has encouraged foreign investments and partially restored a free market economy.

In consolidating its power, the regime first abolished the monarchy, purged the military officer corps, and dissolved existing political parties. Then it undertook to create an official party as the vehicle for realization of its program of Arab socialism. The first two experiments along this line were unsuccessful, in 1953 with the National Liberation Rally and in 1957 with the National Union. Disappointment with both of these organizations in mobilizing mass support led in 1962 to establishment of the Arab Socialist Union (ASU), which continued as the dominant party until 1978, when another conversion substituted the National Democratic Party (NDP) as the principal government party in a limited multi-party system.

The intention was to develop a "socialist vanguard" which would mobilize Egyptian society behind the revolution, borrowing many features from the practices of Communist party regimes. These included a nationwide pyramidal form of organization which would parallel the official governmental structure, interlinking of party and governmental personnel culminating in designation of the president of the republic also as chairman of the party, and restriction of party membership to individuals considered completely loyal to the political regime. On paper the dominant party has developed along the lines planned, but its actual role is obscure. Most commentators are skeptical that it in fact fulfills its proclaimed function as "the supreme popular authority which assumed the leadership role in the people's name," exercising "popular political control on the government organism."[78] However sincere the intent of the revolutionary military leadership to constitute the party as a vehicle for moving toward mass political participation, less has been accomplished than projected.[79]

Despite these setbacks, the Egyptian leadership has continued to seek ways to utilize the reconstituted National Democratic Party as a means of increasing political awareness and extending political competition within carefully controlled limits. This opening up process was started in 1976 by President Sadat, who authorized the formation of three political groups or subparties within the framework of the Arab Socialist Union, each of which nominated candidates for the unicameral national legislature, the People's Assembly. An overwhelming majority of those elected came from the centralist ASU faction with which Sadat himself was identified, but a few members were elected from each of the other two groups, one to the left and the other to the right of the dominant ASU core segment. In the 1979 elections, three officially authorized opposition parties participated, but only two of them won seats in the People's Assembly, totaling 32 seats against 330 for the National Democratic Party. Mubarak has continued this process of providing, in his words, "doses of democracy in proportion to our ability to absorb them."[80] In elections held in 1987, opposition parties won 108 seats out of 448 in the People's Assembly, with the largest opposition contingents coming from a coalition headed by the Socialist Labor Party and from the New Wafd Party. In the popular vote, the NDP had about 70 percent, as compared to 17 percent for the SLP alliance and 11 percent for the New Wafd, with other groups unable to gain the minimum of 8 percent required to gain legislative representation. The failure of the electoral process to engage popular interest is shown by the low turnout of eligible voters—about 25 to 30 percent nationwide and as low as 14 percent in the Cairo area. In the most recent election, held in 1995, the NDP won 317 of the 454 seats (ten of which are filled by presidential appointees). Under this "contrived multiparty system" the NDP is clearly still the dominant party,[81] but it has never succeeded in its intended mission of popular mobilization.

With the future of party politics uncertain, and with a continuing threat from Islamic fundamentalist groups, for the present at least Egypt appears to be firmly in the hands of political leaders representing a variety of interests, but with military components deriving from the 1952 revolutionary cadre at the inner core. Analysis of the composition of government cabinets, of the dominant party executive committee, of provincial governorships, and of other important posts during the period from 1952 to the early 1970s indicated that military officers or former military officers had a representation ratio high enough to assure their control, although the percentages declined under Sadat.[82] The regime in Egypt, in the judgment of Welch and Smith, "increasingly seems a civil-military coalition, one based on the middle-class technocracy, skilled workers, medium landholders, and (of course) officers."[83] Another view as to actual political processes in Egypt is that the party is

> a facade behind which the constituent groups in Egypt's elite may operate. These groups include the military, the civil bureaucracy, political party leaders, and, to some extent, leaders of economic interest groups such as trade unions. Competition among these groups is amorphous and difficult to discern. However, there is in Egypt . . . a difference of opinion over important policy among different groups within the elite. This leads to a kind of disguised factionalism, which constitutes the essence of politics in Egypt. . . . Decisions are made by an insulated elite behind closed doors and are enforced by a civil bureaucracy responsible to the elite and not to the public.[84]

The dominant party and competing parties in this complex and evolving political system play an ambiguous part, but one which seems more likely to grow than to diminish.

The contemporary Egyptian civil bureaucracy, which plainly is one of the actors on the political stage, has impressive historical antecedents. In embarking on its national reform program, the regime has benefited from administrative advantages derived from Egypt's past, going back to a system of large-scale administration existing as early as 1500 B.C., which Weber called the historical model of all later bureaucracies. More recent are the administrative traditions resulting from successive conquests of the country, beginning with the Ottoman Empire in the sixteenth century, followed by the period of French influence after the Napoleonic invasion of 1798, and the seventy years of British control which ended in 1952. The Egyptian bureaucratic tradition is thus ancient, cumulative, and mixed.

In the 1800s, Lord Cromer initiated improvements in administration, but these did not include the recruitment in large numbers of Egyptians for the more responsible civil service posts. As late as 1920 only one-fourth of the higher positions were held by Egyptians, but this changed rapidly after 1922, when the Egyptians assumed control of the civil service. That same year a classification system was installed, relating rank to salary following a French format. It was not until 1951, just before the revolution, that a merit system based on open competitive examinations was adopted and a civil service commission created, following a survey by a British expert. This system was activated by the new regime as part of its program for administrative reform. It follows Western patterns of selection, conduct, and discipline of civil servants.

A career in the middle or upper levels of the bureaucracy has always had great attraction for the educated elite in Egypt, and the educational system is geared to this occupational expectation. Competitive outlets have developed, but the demand for civil service jobs far exceeds the number available, particularly in the case of university graduates in the fields of law and commerce. This creates heavy pressures for overstaffing in the higher ranks as well as in the lower levels of the service. As a result, rapid expansion of the bureaucracy has been a continuing trend, both before and after the adoption of an "open door" economic policy in the mid-1970s. The rate of bureaucratic growth was about 8.5 percent annually during the 1960s and 10 percent in the late 1970s and early 1980s. By 1986/1987 public employment totaled five million out of a labor force of thirteen million, or at least 40 percent of the civilian labor force resident in the country. The bureaucracy has grown at a much faster rate in the central government than at local government levels, and increases have been proportionately larger in the top echelons than in the lower ranks.[85]

Accompanying this expansion in numbers, which is several times the rate of population growth, the Egyptian bureaucracy shows persistent behavioral traits that limit its effectiveness. Modern Egypt was described by Walter Sharp as inheriting from its long past "a highly personalized pattern of administration in which the inter-play of religious, class, and family interests was, and to a considerable extent still is, the most distinctive behavior trait." He reported that a sense of status insecurity, resulting from favoritism "related to family connections, religion, social position, or political belief" stifled initiative and induced fear of exercising discretion. "There is thus a high premium on rigid conformity to formal procedural rules. This psychology also tends to discourage delegation of authority down the hierarchy."[86]

Available empirical evidence is discouraging with regard to changes in traditions, attitudes, and work methods, even after over four decades of remolding under a mobilization regime, and with special emphasis being given to public sector reform by President Mubarak. Responsiveness to political leadership has clearly improved. The appointment of army personnel to key administrative positions is one way in which this has been accomplished. Recognized opponents of the regime in the civil bureaucracy have long since been purged. Senior officials in Egypt have not traditionally taken the initiative in policy-making and have been subservient to holders of political power. Certainly the present regime wants to confirm such a relationship, and appears to have done so.

The military leaders have recognized that their plans for social and economic reform depend on competent professionals, and have turned to technically trained civilians for help. The caliber of civilians in key positions is reported to be excellent, and a growing professionalism seems to be altering work habits and codes of conduct among middle-management officials, but as individuals they are vulnerable unless they satisfy their superiors, who are likely to be military officers. "In many ways," according to Akhavi, the individuals serving on the administrative staff are exceptional for their intelligence and their motivation for achievement. In examining the biographies of some of them, one comes away feeling that they embody a kind of Renaissance-man ideal. However, . . . the energies and capabilities of these persons seem to have been sublimated in the interests of compliance.

Indications are that "the non-military members of the Egyptian political elite are a service bureaucracy," under an urgent obligation to supply "technical and managerial proficiency."[87] McLennan concurs that "these new modern bureaucrats have increased in influence," mainly because of their technical expertise, but also points out that "if they wish to climb the hidden hierarchy to power, they have to impress the modernizing segment of the Egyptian elite—the military and nationalist politicians."[88] This setting makes it difficult to emulate the Western rational model of administration; instead, since authority granted to these Egyptian administrators is "always conditioned on loyal service to the state," they have a tendency to administer "as though their respective domains of activity were fiefdoms."[89] Program initiative and interagency cooperation are difficult to achieve under these circumstances.

Probably a more serious problem is conversion of the rank and file in the civil service from a traditional to a revolutionary perspective. Historically, Egyptian bureaucrats were representatives of the king's authority, expected to be completely subservient to the ruler, and in turn taking advantage of their opportunities to extract from taxpaying subjects gains for themselves in the process of collecting the royal revenues. Many long-standing habits persist.

The Egyptian bureaucracy remains a generally conservative force within a regime that is outwardly revolutionary. Traditionally subservient and never a great source of legislative initiative, the civil service in Egypt has been slow to transform itself into a revolutionary force. . . . Egypt has really not attacked many old institutions (including the bureaucracy) because of a basic commitment of the leadership to Egyptian nationalism. . . . Similarly, the personnel of the bureaucracy has been 'Egyptianized' . . . , but the manner of business itself is not very different from before.[90]

The most recent study of the developmental capabilities of the Egyptian bureaucracy, based on survey data collected in 1983 from civil servants in three representative government sector agencies, reaches the pessimistic conclusion that "it is now apparent that the Egyptian bureaucracy is a major obstacle to the economic and social development of Egyptian society."[91] More specifically, Egyptian bureaucrats are charged with being "lethargic, inflexible, noninnovative, and lacking in rapport with the masses."[92] Relatively speaking, senior- and middle-level officials were found to be far more productive and far more innovative than lower-level officials, but the overall profile was a negative one. Moreover, although improvements in productivity and decision-making patterns were regarded as subject to improvement through education and training, the traits of inflexibility, resistance to innovation, and low regard for mass relations were found to have deep roots in Egyptian culture and hence much more difficult to change.

Tanzania

The East African nation of Tanzania was formed in 1964 by the union of Tanganyika on the mainland and the island of Zanzibar, both of which had gained independence within the British Commonwealth early in the 1960s.[93] The union is not a close one, and the mainland component is by far the senior partner. Colonialism for what is now Tanzania had included both German and British rule, with British control coming later and exerting a much greater post-independence influence. The Tanzanian population is mostly African, rural, and poor. The economy is primarily agricultural, with few natural resources to be exploited. With a low per capita income, a high rate of population growth, and only limited industrial development, economic prospects are not promising. On the other hand, the nation does not have serious internal rivalries among racial or tribal groups, or great disparities between rich and poor. Although tensions between the mainland and Zanzibar have escalated in recent years, Tanzania's relative political stability has been a rarity among new African states.

Tanzania's successful campaign for independence and most of its subsequent political development took place under a single political leader heading a single political party. Julius Nyerere came into political prominence during the 1950s as the chief advocate of freedom from British rule, using an organization then known as the Tanganyika (later Tanzania) African National Union (TANU), which had been originally an association of African civil servants before expanding into a vehicle for political action. After independence was peacefully obtained, there was a brief period of political competition between TANU and the much weaker United Tanganyika party before Tanzania became officially a one-party state in 1965. Until 1977, the Afro-Shirazi Party (ASP) was the counterpart single party in Zanzibar for TANU on the mainland. Since then, the Revolutionary Party of Tanzania (CCM—based on its name in Swahili), formed from a merger of these two groups, has been the dominant party.

Nyerere was elected as the country's first chief executive, and was reelected at five-year intervals until 1985. At that time, he stepped down and was replaced by Ali Hassan Mwinyi, who had been vice president and prime minister. Nyerere also served continuously as chairman of CCM, the government party, until 1990, when he retired and was replaced by Mwinyi in this post also, a move that had been expected in 1987, but was apparently delayed by policy differences between the two leaders.

Nyerere's political program was one he described as African socialism or *ujamaa* (meaning "brotherhood" in Swahili). Rejecting capitalism as a colonial inheritance exploitative in operation, Nyerere advocated African socialism as an egalitarian concept based on traditional African views that society is an extension of the basic family unit. A one-party system was preferred, as part of this political philosophy, on the ground that two-party or multiparty systems foster divisive factionalism within society, whereas a single party could identify with the interests of the nation as a whole.

The differences between Nyerere and Mwinyi had more to do with economic issues than the role of the party. Without questioning the aim of becoming a socialist country, Mwinyi sought to deal with Tanzania's economic and debt problems by entering into agreements with the International Monetary Fund which Nyerere had not been willing to accept while he was head of state. President Mwinyi insisted, however, that "in our country, the party is supreme and the government is only an instrument which implements the party's positions."[94]

Unlike some other dominant parties, the CCM has not been highly centralized structurally. Building on local party cells, the levels of party organization extend through branch, district, and regional committees to a National Executive Committee, but detailed supervision from the center has not been attempted. The party's National Conference, held every two years, has been mainly ceremonial. Major policy-making functions have in fact been exercised by the party head and his key advisors. As in other single-party systems, individuals have often simultaneously held both party and governmental positions, but in contrast to the situation commonly found elsewhere, in Tanzania government posts have, at least until recently, been considered more powerful and prestigious than party assignments.

In elections for the unicameral National Assembly, Tanzania has gradually been moving toward more political competition. CCM began by fostering a two-way competition in each of the single-member constituencies by having party agencies review the records of candidates and decide which two will be permitted to run. The two selected were both certified as acceptable to the party, and each was provided with equal access to campaign resources. Neither was supposed to claim to be favored by either the party or the president. This procedure resulted in hotly contested elections in many constituencies and a considerable turnover in membership at five-year intervals after each election. The level of popular participation was relatively high for a country at Tanzania's level of development, indicating that the party functioned well as an instrument for building up a sense of national loyalty and identity. Perry described it in 1974 as the most important political structure in Tanzania and its successes and failures, problems and prospects, are of vital concern to the country's political development. It has mobilized voters and party activists, organized the economic activities of Tanzania's peasantry, and served as a major recruitment source for governmental and quasi-governmental agencies as well as for more explicitly political positions.[95]

In 1992, the government and the party endorsed the introduction of a multiparty system, with municipal and local elections to be held first, leading to national elections in 1994 or 1995. In June 1993, however, a few months before they were scheduled, the national electoral commission cancelled the first round, and the first nationwide multiparty elections did not take place until October 1995. With Mwinyi being ineligible for a third term, the Revolutionary Party of Tanzania elected one of his cabinet members, Benjamin William Mkapa, as its presidential nominee. Thirteen opposition parties contested the election, but only four won legislative representation, and they gained less that a quarter of the seats. On the eve of national elections scheduled for late in 2000, CCM continues as the dominant party and Tanzania is still essentially a single-party regime.

Although Tanzania after independence chose a constitutional system with an elected president and a single established party, it stayed closer to the British model in arrangements for executive organization and the civil service, and in subordinating the military to civilian control. A cabinet of about twenty ministries is headed by a prime minister appointed by the president. Within each ministry, a permanent secretary from the career civil service functions in the British tradition as chief aide to the minister. The civil service as an institution continues along much the same line as before independence, with the main changes being the substitution of Africans for the British in the senior posts. Although civil servants can and do hold party membership, the service has not been heavily politicized. Also, Nyerere carried out a commitment to keep the civil service open to any Tanzanian citizen, whatever the individual's racial background. Particularly with regard to specialized manpower needs for national planning programs, a central recruiting agency has been authorized to seek qualified personnel from any available source, pending the availability of qualified Tanzanian citizens. Technical competence has had high priority. At the same time, Nyerere tried to avoid the emergence of a civil service elite such as happened in other African nations, by keeping firm control over salary levels and other benefits. Goran Hyden reports that the mode of policy-making adopted by Tanzania's political leadership compels public sector employees to work "in a context where public expectations constantly exceed what can actually be attained . . . ," and that "sudden and bold policy initiatives . . . have forced the civil servants into a defensive posture." As a result, the civil bureaucracy as an institution does not possess much autonomy, enjoy a high degree of security, or have an influential impact in the making of major policy decisions.[96] The main unsolved problems have been keeping restraints on expansion of the size of the civil service, and dealing with growing evidence of corruption.[97]

Also in sharp contrast to most new states in Africa, the military has not played a significant role in political affairs.[98] An antimilitary tradition before independence in Tanganyika led to serious consideration being given to the issue of whether or not a national army should be maintained at all after independence. The decision was to have an army, but it has been kept small and under tight rein. The only serious threat from the armed forces came in 1964, when a mutiny occurred reflecting discontent with status and pay, and with the rate at which British officers were being replaced by Tanzanians. This uprising was not politically motivated, and received little public support. It was quickly and decisively suppressed, with its leaders being imprisoned and many of the soldiers who took part being dismissed.

> As with other cases of organized group dissatisfaction, the government decided on a mixture of co-optation and infiltration. Members of the army and police were admitted to TANU, and party members were given important posts in the army and police bureaucracies. Ordinary soldiers were ordered to take part in "nation-building" projects (such as road construction and agricultural improvement) and to receive political indoctrination.[99]

Again early in 1983 there was a small conspiracy involving both soldiers and civilians which likewise was detected promptly and easily suppressed.

The Tanzanian political experience to date, therefore, resulted in the establishment of a one-party state under a political leader who until his retirement dominated the governmental scene since before independence. External controls are effectively in operation over both the civil and military bureaucracies. Tanzania's prospects for a stable polity appear to be excellent, whether the Revolutionary Party remains dominant or multiparty competition increases.

COMMUNIST TOTALITARIAN SYSTEMS

Among more developed countries, only the People's Republic of China, which now deserves to be included in this category because of its size and global potential, has retained the single-party and totalitarian characteristics which it earlier shared with former Communist regimes in the old USSR and in Eastern Europe.

In contrast, other Afro-Asian and Latin American countries with Communist regimes, which like their non-Communist counterparts are at a lower level of development, have up to now deviated very little from these characteristics. Included in this group are Cuba, Laos, North Korea, and Vietnam. Cambodia (renamed Kampuchea from 1976 to 1990) is currently in a stage of transition, having installed an interim coalition regime in 1993, which was retained in office after elections in 1998. These Communist systems of the developing world retain their common commitment to Marxist-Leninist ideology and a totalitarian political style, with political power monopolized in the hands of a single party. The party does not recognize the legitimacy of open opposition, because it "seeks to dominate every sphere of life and to annul every center of previously independent authority."[100] Mobilization of the masses is diligently sought, but only for participation in approved activities; participation will be secured to the extent necessary by coercion or the threat of coercion.

The administrative apparatus required by such a regime is enormously complex, and it must be subjected to reliable party supervision, which in turn calls for a control network responsive to the narrow circle of elitist leadership in the party. The state bureaucracy must be paralleled by an interlocking party bureaucracy. This is an arduous obligation in a society plagued by a shortage of skilled manpower, but it cannot be avoided without risking the security of the regime. These dual hierarchies are held together by the unquestioned right of the party to exercise control as it sees fit and by the common devise of dual office-holding which makes most members of the state administrative hierarchy also subject to the party hierarchy and its discipline.

A perennial problem in staffing the state administrative apparatus is the relative stress put on the need to be "red" and to be "expert." Apparently the general tendency has been to emphasize class background and political loyalty while the regime is being installed and secured, and then to pay more attention to expert knowledge later on. Along the way, there may be short-range alternations. Of course, the ultimate objective is to ensure that the system produces officials who will be both "red" and "expert." Hence, strenuous efforts are made to train a younger generation of industrial and technical intelligentsia and thus transform the party-versus-bureaucracy problem into more of an intraparty struggle.

Administration in these countries encounters all of the problems faced in other societies urgently engaged in rapid industrialization and economic development that have inadequate resources for the scheduled pace of accomplishment. The insistent emphasis on responsiveness of the official state administrative machinery to the party apparatus introduces an additional set of complications. It leads in practice to continuous conflicts between party units and the official government agencies held accountable for the administration of particular programs, with resulting losses in organizational efficiency. It also poses problems of individual choice to the person who is both a public official and a disciplined party member, reducing his initiative and willingness to experiment because of apprehension about being caught between competing obligations.

Available up-to-date reliable information on the state bureaucracies in these Communist regimes is regrettably but understandably scarce. The most systematic analysis was done on the Communist countries of Eastern Europe and is now obsolete because of the changes that have occurred. Our choices for case examples are North Korea from Asia, and Cuba as the only Communist nation in Latin America.

North Korea

The Democratic People's Republic of Korea, occupying the northern half of the Korean peninsula in northeastern Asia, was formally organized in 1948, soon after establishment of the Republic of Korea in the south, replacing a provisional People's Republic set up in 1946 under Soviet auspices. For almost half a century, until his death in July 1994, Kim Il Sung was the undisputed leader of both of these entities, shaping during these years a unique example of Communist totalitarianism.[101]

Born in 1912, Kim Il Sung as a young man was a guerrilla fighter against Japanese occupation and later went to the Soviet Union, which sponsored him to head the new North Korean government. From this base, he developed close ties not only with the USSR but also with the People's Republic of China, while at the same time maintaining a position of relative independence from domination by either. Up to about 1960, Kim's main emphasis was on consolidating his power against internal and external pressures. Then he turned to cultivation of the Kim Il Sung personality cult which became the hallmark of his regime. Bruce Cumings describes the product as "corporatist socialism," closely linked to Korean traditions.

> The style is always paternal, with Kim depicted as the benevolent father of the nation, and the nation compared with one big family. The strongest of emotional bonds in Korea is that of filial piety, and Kim and his allies sought to weld the nation together by drawing on vast reservoirs of duty and obligation towards one's parents, seeking to have them transferred to the state through Kim's auspices.[102]

According to Cumings, there are eight main elements in this system: the leader (who functions as a charismatic source of legitimacy and ideology and as a father figure); the family (society's core unit, with the leader's family as the model); the party (core of the body politic, linking the nation together); the collective (mediating social organization between party and family); the idea (*Juche*, North Korea's official ideology, symbol of the nation and the leader); the revolution (the biography of the leader and his family, showing how to apply *Juche*); the guide (the leader's progeny, establishing the principle of family-based succession); and the world (structured with the leader as "the Sun" at the center, spreading its rays outward).[103] Similarly, Sung Chul Yang lists eight "main themes of North Korea's political indoctrination: loyalty to Kim Il Sung; *Juche* ideology; revolutionary tradition; class consciousness; anti-imperialism; communist morality; collectivism; and socialist patriotism," pointing out that the first three themes are unique, and that the others are similar to the main themes of former East European socialist states.[104]

One key feature of this system has been the expectation that Kim Il Sung's successor would be a member of his family, and since at least the early 1980s his son Kim Jong Il was groomed to take over. With his father's death, this did indeed happen on a de facto basis, but was not formally proclaimed until 1998, when he was reconfirmed by the Supreme People's Assembly as chairman of the National Defense Commission and as head of state. Kim Jong Il now seems to be firmly in power.

As a single-party state, North Korea has been dominated by the Korean Workers' Party as the core of an umbrella grouping which includes other authorized political mass organizations. The state apparatus includes a unicameral Supreme People's Assembly elected from a single slate of nominees endorsed by the party. Kim Il Sung during his lifetime served both as secretary general of the party and as president of the republic. In 1998 a constitutional change abolished the presidency in deference to his memory, and his son has not taken over as head of the party, apparently reflecting his preference to maintain a lower public profile.

Much as in Communist China, the power centers in North Korea have been the party, the military, and the official state civil institutions. The Korean Workers' Party from its beginning has been considered "a mass party of a new type," with a large membership rather than a small vanguard group. Its membership has fluctuated between 12 and 14 percent of the population, the highest in any Marxist-Leninist regime. In addition, an extensive network of mass organizations exists for youths, workers, women, and peasants who are not party members.

Recognizing that control of the military was the key to maintaining his totalitarian regime, Kim Il Sung took steps to consolidate that control. He designated his son and announced successor Kim Jong Il as commander of the people's army, and assigned political commissars representing the Workers' Party of Korea to each level of the military, to make sure that it was thoroughly politicized.

Although information is scanty, the agencies of civilian government and civil bureaucrats appear to be the least important of these power wielders. Cumings quotes approvingly a study done in the early 1960s terming the relationship between Kim and his closest allies as "a semi-chivalrous, irrevocable and unconditional bond . . . under iron discipline," a "deeply personal" system, "fundamentally hostile to complex bureaucracy." He goes on to say that Kim and his associates were "generalists, Jack-of-all trades who could run the government or command the army, show a peasant how to use seeds or cuddle children in a school; Kim would dispatch them as loyal observers of officials and experts or specialists outside the inner core, i.e. in the realm of impersonal bureaucracy." As a result, there arose "a plodding, dense bureaucracy that manages the day-to-day administration." In contrast, he concludes, "at the commanding heights this was a charismatic politics, its legitimacy resting in an overblown history and a trumpeted mythology about men with superhuman qualities."[105]

Some key features of this unusual regime have been identified, but in view of the recent change in leadership, the ongoing negotiations with the United States over nuclear matters, and the tentative explorations with South Korea as to possible reunification, it would be hazardous to venture predictions about the future.

Cuba

Cuba under Castro has gone through several stages during the revolutionary period since the overthrow of the Batista regime in 1959, even though there has been no significant change in the top leadership.[106]

After a couple of years devoted to consolidation of the regime and liquidation of prerevolutionary institutions, late in 1961 the system was avowed to be Communist, based on a claimed adaptation of Marxism-Leninism to Latin American circumstances. This led during the early 1960s to severance of diplomatic relations with the United States, increasing reliance on the Soviet Union, and vigorous efforts to export the revolution to other Latin American countries. Toward the end of the decade, emphasis shifted to internal economic development based primarily on agriculture, international revolutionary activity declined, and the strategic goal became the "building of socialism in one island." Beginning about 1970, the dominant theme turned to "institutionalization of the revolution," leading to efforts at depersonalizing political leadership, strengthening the Cuban Communist party (PCC), and revamping the governmental apparatus. The advent of *perestroika* in the USSR and in Eastern Europe brought no corresponding response in Cuba, despite a state visit by Gorbachev early in 1989. Instead, Castro reaffirmed that the PCC would retain its absolute political control, and rejected moves toward a market-oriented economy.

Despite the changes that have taken place, political leadership in Cuba has continued to be highly concentrated. Fidel Castro, his brother Raul, and a limited group of associates from the revolutionary takeover have dominated the regime.

> Castro exerted a charismatic, personalistic type of government characterized by the concentration of power in the "Maximum Leader" and his inner circle of loyalists and by the lack of institutionalization. . . . In practice, Castro and his small circle occupied the top positions in the administration, the party, and the army; he was the best example combining the jobs of prime minister, first secretary of the party, and commander-in-chief of the armed forces.[107]

This pattern helps explain some unusual features of the Cuban regime as compared to other Communist systems: a relatively weak Communist party; a high rate of participation by the military in the top elite; and a lack of clear institutional differentiation among the party, military, and administrative hierarchies. In each of these respects, recent reforms have been undertaken.

The PCC as it now exists is the descendant of a series of earlier organizational manifestations going back to the 26th of July Movement which was formed to support Castro's opposition to Batista. In its present form, the PCC was not established until 1965, and the party as an entity has played a symbolic rather than a central role in political affairs. With Fidel Castro as first secretary and a central committee of about 150 members, the PCC has been tightly controlled despite an extensive organizational network. The party membership has never been large. Only 55,000 in 1969, it increased to over 200,000 in 1975, and reached almost 524,000 in 1986 (still only about 5 percent of the population). The party machinery has been relatively inactive. The first PCC party congress was not held until 1975, following numerous postponements; the second occurred in 1980 after another five-year interval. A third was held in 1986, bringing with it major personnel changes, with approximately one-third of the central committee and nearly one-half of the politburo members being replaced. Subsequent party congresses were held in 1991 and 1997. Despite these modest measures to enhance the party's stature, expand participation in its activities, and bring in new blood to its leadership, the PCC remains peripheral as compared to other Communist polities.

On the other hand, the military role has been crucial. Castro's rebel army brought him to power, and veterans of the revolution have continued to occupy many of the important positions in both the party and the state administration. When the PCC was formed in 1965, two-thirds of the members of its central committee came from military ranks. Most cabinet ministers and heads of other central agencies were drawn during the early years of the regime from individuals with military backgrounds. The army as an institution was assigned a wide variety of nonmilitary as well as military duties, including active participation in the much publicized sugar cane harvest campaigns. As a consequence, Dominguez maintained that the key political role in Cuba was that of the "civic soldier." He asserted that Cuba was largely governed by the civic soldiers—

> military men who actually rule over large sectors of military and civilian life, who are held up as symbols to be emulated by all military and civilians, who are the bearers of the revolutionary tradition and ideology, who have civilianized and politicized themselves by internalizing the norms and organization of the Communist Party and who have educated themselves to become professionals in military, political, managerial, engineering, economic and educational affairs. Their civic and military lives are fused.[108]

Unlike China, where the role of the People's Liberation Army has expanded and contracted over time and where party-military conflict has frequently surfaced, in Cuba military participation in central decision-making was "more stable and institutionalized," without an alternative civilian elite available to replace the civic soldiers. Dominguez argued that this degree of reliance upon military personnel reflected failures in handling labor supply and economic production problems, and that the political use of the military had "stifled criticism from the bottom of the system, . . . shut off the upward flow of political communication, and . . . curtailed the adaptability of the political system."[109]

Perhaps in recognition of these consequences, a reorientation of the armed forces has taken place in recent years. "During the 1980s," according to Juan del Aguila, "Cuba's armed forces became more professional and modern, in keeping with the institutionalization process. The duties of the military became separate from those of civil sectors, and its functions and responsibilities distinct from those of the state and the Communist party."[110] This trend away from the earlier political mission and more toward modernization and professionalization was helped extensively during the 1970s and 1980s by the Soviet Union, which provided sophisticated weaponry and trained military personnel.[111] Military men continue to occupy high government and party positions, but by the time of the third PCC congress in 1986 their number on the PCC central committee had fallen to its lowest level ever, both in absolute numbers and in the military proportion of the total membership. Partly because of these measures to assert more strongly the civilian leadership role, and partly because of the aging of the revolutionary generation, military prominence in the Cuban version of communism is on the decline although still a distinctive feature.

Institutionalization of the revolution also meant a revamping of the official government structure during the 1970s, bringing it closer to the then existing Soviet Union model. A new constitution, approved by the PCC congress in 1975 and adopted by popular referendum early in 1976, established for the first time since the revolution a unicameral national assembly. Its members were indirectly elected for five-year terms from the membership of popularly elected municipal assemblies until 1993, when they were directly elected for the first time. However, the only option for opposition is to reject nominees, and none were rejected. The National Assembly in turn formally designates from among its members a state council, whose president serves as head of state. Executive and administrative responsibilities are assigned to a council of ministers. Fidel Castro serves both as president of the State Council and president of the Council of Ministers, in addition to continuing as first secretary of the PCC, so the institutionalization has not disturbed his undisputed place as "Maximum Leader." The Council of Ministers also currently includes Raul Castro as first vice president, and five other vice presidents. After administrative restructuring during the 1990s there are now thirty-one cabinet ministers.

These measures probably have not altered the actual pattern of political leadership much, although they may help to ease a later transfer of power from Fidel Castro, who is now in his seventies, to a successor. "The image projected . . . by Castro's promised reform was of a decentralized, democratic, independent, and mass-participation movement," wrote Mesa-Lago in 1978, but in actuality "there has been an institutionalization trend characterized by central controls, dogmatism, and administrative-bureaucratic features resembling the Soviet system."[112]

In this milieu, civilian administrators have obviously not been in positions of crucial importance, and professional competence has been a secondary consideration. Administration in this revolutionary setting has been carried out by what Petras called "ambulating bureaucrats," who recognize that "decisions are made at the top and carried out on the bottom."[113] Most bureaucrats have been generalists who frequently change positions and rarely carve out a career in any particular area of administration. Political reliability has been the foremost criterion in recruitment and advancement, with little attention paid to professional preparation for administrative careers. In the face of acute shortages of technical and managerial personnel, a higher priority has been given recently to economic planning and to the training of administrators who combine political reliability and expertise, but with mixed and generally negative assessments as to results.[114]

In the early 1980s, at the beginning of its third decade, Dominguez stated that "the principal achievement of the Cuban revolutionary government has been sheer survival."[115] George Volsky made a more positive assessment that "Socialist Cuba can claim to have attained revolutionary authenticity and maturity, a degree of international respect, and a standing in the Communist bloc and the rest of the world far in excess of her size, population and economic wealth."[116] At the beginning of its fifth decade, in view of domestic and international developments, Castro's Cuba now faces what appears to be a much more uncertain future. As viewed by Mazarr, it

> has remained a politically repressive, economically stagnant, militarily adventuristic state. The legitimacy of the Cuban regime depends, in many ways, on the persona of Fidel Castro; when he dies, the government will face by far its severest test to date and, most probably, at a time when a potentially deadly economic and systemic crisis continues to threaten the Cuban polity. Revolutionary or reformist elements will almost certainly emerge to demand change.[117]

Although Jorge Dominguez points out reasons that Castro may survive for "many more years,"[118] Susan Purcell agrees with Mazarr's prediction, saying that it is "only a matter of time before Cuban communism collapses. While the date of its demise is obviously unknown in advance, it can be expected sooner rather than later."[119] Most other recent commentators concur.

NOTES

1. Robert C. Tucker, "Towards a Comparative Politics of Movement-Regimes," *American Political Science Review* 60, No. 2 (1961): 283. See also his "On Revolutionary Mass-Movement Regimes," *The Soviet Political Mind: Studies in Stalinism and Post-Stalin Change* (New York: Praeger, 1963), Chap. 1, pp. 3–19.

2. David E. Apter, *Ghana in Transition* (New York: Atheneum Publishers, 1963), p. 330.

3. Milton J. Esman, "The Politics of Development Administration," in John D. Montgomery and William J. Siffin, eds., *Approaches to Development: Politics, Administration and Change* (New York: McGraw Hill, 1966), pp. 96–97.

4. *Ibid.*, p. 91.

5. This was the dominant view expressed in a special roundtable on comparative presidentialism at the Fourteenth World Congress of the International Political Science Association held in Washington, D.C. August 28–September 1, 1988, with reports presented on Brazil, Chile, Colombia, and other countries.

6. For leading presentations of the two points of view, refer to Fred W. Riggs for arguments favoring the parliamentary option, "A Neoinstitutional Typology of Third World Politics," in Anton Bebler and Jim Seroka, eds., *Contemporary Political Systems: Classifications and Typologies* (Boulder, CO: Lynne Rienner Publishers, 1990), Chap. 10, pp. 205–239, especially "Survivability of Regime Tyes," pp. 219–224; and for arguments favoring the presidential alternative refer to Matthew Soberg Shugart and John M. Carey, *Presidents and Assemblies: Constitutional Design and Electoral Dynamics* (New York: Cambridge University Press, 1992).

7. Esman, "The Politics of Development Administration," p. 92.

8. Because of the impermanence of many of these regimes, some of the most valuable information about typical bureaucratic behavior patterns in polyarchal competitive regimes comes from countries where earlier more open regimes were extensively described and analyzed before political competition was later stifled. For example, two revealing studies deal with Chile during the lengthy period of political competition prior to the ouster of President Allende in 1973. These are Charles J. Parrish, "Bureaucracy, Democracy, and Development: Some Considerations Based on the Chilean Case," in Clarence E. Thruber and Lawrence S. Graham, eds., *Development Administration in Latin America* (Durham, NC: Duke University Press, 1973), pp. 229–259; and Peter S. Cleaves, *Bureaucratic Politics and Administration in Chile* (Berkeley, CA: University of California Press, 1974).

9. For sources on the Philippines prior to martial law, refer to Edwin O. Stene and Associates, *Public Administration in the Philippines* (Manila: Institute of Public Administration, University of the Philippines, 1955); Onofre D. Corpuz, *The Bureaucracy in the Philippines* (Manila: Institute of Public Administration, University of the Philippines, 1957), and *The Philippines* (Englewood Cliffs, NJ: Prentice-Hall, 1965); Ferrel Heady, "The Philippine Administrative System—A Fusion of East and West," in William J. Siffin, ed., *Toward the Comparative Study of Public Administration* (Bloomington, IN: Department of Government, Indiana University, 1957), pp. 253–277; Raul P. DeGuzman, ed., *Patterns in Decision-Making: Case Studies in Philippine Public Administration* (Manila: Graduate School of Public

Administration, University of the Philippines, 1963); Jean Grossholtz, *Politics in the Philippines* (Boston: Little, Brown and Company, 1964); Ledivina V. Carino, "Bureaucratic Norms, Corruption, and Development," *Philippine Journal of Public Administration* 19, No. 3 (1975): 278–292; and Thomas C. Nowak, "The Philippines before Martial Law: A Study in Politics and Administration," *American Political Science Review* 71, No. 2 (June 1977): 522–539. For the martial law period, refer to Beth Day, *The Philippines: Shattered Showcase of Democracy in Asia* (New York: M. Evans and Company, 1974): Sherwood D. Goldberg, "The Bases of Civilian Control of the Military in the Philippines," in Claude E. Welch, Jr., ed., *Civilian Control of the Military* (Albany, NY: State University of New York Press, 1976), pp. 99–122; Raul P. DeGuzman and Associates, *Citizen Participation and Decision-Making Under Martial Law: A Search for a Viable Political System* (Manila: College of Public Administration, University of the Philippines, 1976); David A. Rosenberg, ed., *Marcos and Martial Law in the Philippines* (Ithaca, NY: Cornell University Press, 1979); and Linda Richter, "Bureaucracy by Decree: Public Administration in the Philippines," in Krishna K. Tummala, ed., *Administrative Systems Abroad* (Washington, DC: University Press of America, 1982), pp. 76–95. Sources on the post-Marcos period include: A. James Gregor, "After the Fall: The Prospects for Democracy after Marcos," *World Affairs* 149, No. 4 (Spring 1987): 195–208; Sandra Burton, "Aquino's Philippines: The Center Holds," *Foreign Affairs* 65, No. 3 (1987): 524–537; Carl H. Lande, ed., *Rebuilding A Nation* (Washington, DC: The Washington Institute Press, 1987); Linda K. Richter, "Public Bureaucracy in Post-Marcos Philippines," *Southeast Asian Journal of Social Science* 15, No. 2 (1987): 57–76; Raul P. DeGuzman and Mila A. Reforma, eds., *Government and Politics of the Philippines* (Singapore: Oxford University Press, 1988), especially Raul P. DeGuzman, Alex B. Brillantes, Jr., and Arturo G. Pacho, "The Bureaucracy," Chap. 7; David Wurfel, *Filipino Politics: Development and Decay* (Ithaca, NY: Cornell University Press, 1988); Ledivina V. Carino, "Bureaucracy for a Democracy: The Struggle of the Philippine Political Leadership and the Civil Service in the Post-Marcos Period," Occasional Paper No. 88-1 (Manila: College of Public Administration, University of the Philippines, 1988), and "The Philippines," in Subramaniam, ed., *Public Administration in the Third World*, Chap. 5; A. B. Villanueva, "Post-Marcos: The State of Philippine Politics and Democracy During the Aquino Regime, 1986–1992," *Contemporary Southeast Asia* 14, No. 2 (September 1992): 174–187; Amelia P. Varela, "Personnel Management Reform in the Philippines: The Strategy of Professionalization," *Governance* 5, No. 4 (October 1992): 402–422; W. Scott Thompson, *The Philippines in Crisis* (New York: St. Martin's Press, 1992); Jose V. Abueva and Emerlinda R. Roman, eds., *Corazon C. Aquino: Early Assessments of Her Presidential Leadership and Administration and Her Place in History* (Manila: University of the Philippines Press, 1993); Ledivina V. Carino, "A Subordinate Bureaucracy: The Philippine Civil Service Up to 1992," in Ali Farazmand, ed., *Handbook of Bureaucracy* (New York: Marcel Dekker, 1994), Chap. 39, pp. 603–616; A. B. Villanueva, "Parties and Elections in Philippine Politics," *Contemporary Southeast Asia* 18 (September 1996): 175–192; David G. Timberman, ed., *The Philippines: New Directions in Domestic Policy and Foreign Relations* (New York Asia Society, 1998); and John L. Linantud, "Whither Guns,

Goons, and Gold? The Decline of Factional Election Violence in the Philipppines," *Contemporary Southeast Asia* 20 (December 1998): 298–318.

10. Rosenberg, *Marcos and Martial Law in the Philippines*, p. 28.

11. Agpalo, *The Organic-Hierarchical Paradigm and Politics in the Philippines* (Manila: University of the Philippines Press, no date).

12. Stauffer, "Philippine Corporatism: A Note on the New Society," *Asian Survey* 17, No. 4 (April 1977): 393–407.

13. Richter, "Bureaucracy by Decree," p. 86.

14. Jose V. Abueva gave this summary assessment: "Alongside the officers of the armed forces, civilian technocrats exercise delegated presidential authority as cabinet members and heads of departments, agencies, and government corporations. Drawn from the University of the Philippines and other educational institutions, as well as from business firms and the military, the technocrats act as presidential advisors, government executives, drafters of presidential decrees, and advocates and defenders of the New Society. Responsible only to the president and appointed by him, they serve at his pleasure. They assist him in the exercise of his tremendous executive and legislative powers, uninhibited by elected representatives or by a critical press." Abueva, "Ideology and Practice in the 'New Society,'" in Rosenberg, ed., *Marcos and Martial Law in the Philippines*, pp. 33–84, at p. 40. A dramatic and significant example of this pattern was the appointment by President Marcos in 1981 as the first prime minister under the newly installed presidential-parliamentary system of Cesar Virata, who had been the most prominent of these technocrats, having served previously as finance minister and as dean of the business school at the University of the Philippines. Virata was still in this post when Marcos was ousted.

15. Richter, "Bureaucracy by Decree," p. 89.

16. For details, refer to Emerlinda R. Roman, "Assessing President Aquino's Policies and Administration," in Abueva and Roman, eds., *Corazon C. Aquino*, Chap. 4, pp. 185–235.

17. Richter, "Public Bureaucracy in Post-Marcos Philippines," p. 63.

18. Carino, "Bureaucracy for a Democracy," p. 39.

19. Reports vary as to the extent of turnover. Carino mentioned initial estimates ranging as high as 300,000. Richter said more than 200,000, mostly in local and regional governments. However, Carino stated that by mid-1987 fewer than 30,000 had actually been removed.

20. Carino, "The Philippines," p. 116.

21. "Personnel Management Reform in the Philippines," p. 421.

22. Richter, "Public Bureaucracy in the Philippines," p. 71.

23. Carino, "The Philippines," p. 123. She was discouraged that under Ramos the civil service was becoming even more a "simple acquiescent instrument worried only about its wages and working conditions." See Carino, "A Subordinate Bureaucracy," p. 614.

24. Limited available resources include James Jupp, *Sri Lanka: Third World Democracy* (London: Frank Cass, 1978); Tissa Fernando and Robert N. Kearney, eds., *Modern Sri Lanka: A Society in Transition* (Syracuse, NY: Maxwell School, Syracuse Univeristy, 1979); Tissa Fernando, "Political and Economic Development in Sri

Lanka," *Current History* 81, No. 475 (May 1982): 211–214, 226–228; S. J. Tambiah, *Sri Landa: Ethnic Fratricide and the Dismantling of Democracy* (Chicago: The University of Chicago Press, 1986); Sujit M. Canagaretna, "Nation Building in a Multiethnic Setting: The Sri Lankan Case," *Asian Affairs* 14 (Spring 1987): 1–19; Chelvadurai Manogaran, *Ethnic Conflict and Reconciliation in Sri Lanka* (Honolulu: University of Hawaii Press, 1987); A. Jeyaratnam Wilson, *The Break-Up of Sri Lanka: The Sinhalese-Tamil Conflict* (London: C. Hurst & Company, 1988); Shantha K. Hennayake, "The Peace Accord and the Tamils in Sri Lanka," *Asian Survey* 29 (April 1989): 401–415; Shelton U. Kodikara, "The Continuing Crisis in Sri Lanka," *Asian Survey* 29 (July 1989): 716–724; and William McGowan, *Only Man Is Vile: The Tragedy of Sri Lanka* (New York: Farrar, Straus and Giroux, 1992).

25. Refer to Robert H. Dix, *Colombia: The Political Dimensions of Change* (New Haven, CT: Yale University Press, 1967), and *The Politics of Colombia* (New York: Praeger, 1987); Jorge P. Osterling, *Democracy in Colombia: Clientelist Politics and Guerrilla Warfare* (New Brunswick, NJ: Transaction Publishers, 1989); Stephen J. Randall, *Colombia and the United States: Hegemony and Interdependence* (Athens, GA: University of Georgia Press, 1992); David Bushnell, *The Making of Modern Colombia* (Berkeley, CA: University of California Press, 1993); Angel Maria Ballen Molina, *La Democracia Participativa en Colombia* (Bogota: Unidad Editorial UNINCCA, 1993); Fernan E. Gonzalez et al., *Violencia en la Region Andina: El caso Colombia* (Bogota: Cinep, 1993); Ferrel Heady, "Dilemmas of Development Administration in the Global Village: The Case of Colombia," in Jean-Claude Garcia-Zamor and Renu Khator, eds., *Public Administration in the Global Village* (Westport, CT: Praeger, 1994), Chap. 6, pp. 121–135; Jaime Buenahora Febres-C., "Democracia Tropical: Conflicto de Poderes," *Economia Colombiana* (April/May 1997): 46–49; John D. Martz, *The Politics of Clientelism: Democracy and the State in Colombia* (New Brunswick, NJ: Transaction Publishers, 1997); Gary Hoskin and Gabriel Murillo, "Can Colombia Cope?," *Journal of Democracy* 10, No. 1 (January 1999): 36–50; and Daniel L. Neilson and Matthew Soberg Shugart, "Constitutional Change in Colombia: Policy Adjustment Through Institutional Reform," *Comparative Political Studies* 32, No. 3 (May 1999): 313–341.

26. "Violence appears as a nationwide phenomenon; almost all of the nation's municipalities and most rural and urban areas experience it. It touches virtually all sectors of the population, without distinction as to socioeconomic class, profession, race, or ethnic group. Almost everybody is a potential victim." Osterling, *Democracy in Colombia*, p. 265.

27. See J. Vidal Perdomo, "La reforma administrativa de 1968 en Colombia," *International Review of Administrative Sciences* 48, No. 1 (1982): 77–84; and Karen Ruffing-Hilliard, "Merit Reform in Latin America," in Farazmand, ed., *Handbook of Comparative and Development Public Administration*, pp. 301–312.

28. For details, see Heady, "Dilemmas of Development Administration," pp. 123–125; Comision Presidencial para la Reforma de la Administracion Publica del Estado Colombiano, *Informe Final* (Bogota: Centro de Publicaciones, Escuela Superior de Administracion Publica, 1991); "Decreto 643," *Carta Administrativa, Revista del Departamento del Servicio Civil* 69 (Marzo-Abril, 1992): 51–60; and Departamento

de la Funcion Publica, *Compilacion de Normas sobre Administracion de Personal al Servicio del Estado* (Bogota: Oficina de Comunicaciones del Departmento Administrativo de la Funcion Publica, 1994).

29. For some general treatments of Mexican politics, refer to William P. Tucker, *The Mexican Government Today* (Minneapolis: University of Minnesota Press, 1957); Raymond Vernon, *The Dilemma of Mexico's Development* (Cambridge, MA: Harvard University Press, 1963); Robert E. Scott, *Mexican Government in Transition*, rev. ed. (Urbana: University of Illinois Press, 1964); L. Vincent Padgett, *The Mexican Political System*, 2nd ed. (Boston: Houghton Mifflin Company, 1976); Roderic A. Camp, *Mexico's Leaders: Their Education and Recruitment* (Tucson: University of Arizona Press, 1980); Jorge I. Dominguez, ed., *Mexico's Political Economy: Challenge at Home and Abroad* (Beverly Hills, CA: Sage Publications, 1982); Martin C. Needler, *Mexican Politics: The Containment of Conflict* (New York: Praeger, 1982); Roderic A. Camp, ed., *Mexico's Political Stability: The Next Five Years* (Boulder, CO: Westview Press, 1986); Judith Gentleman, ed., *Mexican Politics in Transition* (Boulder, CO: Westview Press, 1987); George Philip, "The Dominant Party System in Mexico," in Vicky Randall, ed., *Political Parties in the Third World* (Beverly Hills, CA: Sage Publications, 1988), Chap. 5; Paul Cammack, "The 'Brazilianization' of Mexico?" *Government and Opposition* 23 (Summer 1988): 304–320; Kevin J. Middlebrook, "Dilemmas of Change in Mexican Politics," *World Politics* 41 (October 1988): 120–141; Diane E. Davis, "Divided over Democracy: The Embeddedness of State and Class Conflicts in Contemporary Mexico," *Politics & Society* 17, No. 3 (September 1989): 247–280; Wayne A. Cornelius, Judith Gentleman, and Peter H. Smith, eds., *Mexico's Alternative Political Futures* (San Diego: Center for U.S.-Mexican Studies, University of California, San Diego, 1989); Roderic Ai Camp, "Political Modernization in Mexico: Through a Looking Glass," in Jaime E. Rodriguez O., ed., *The Evolution of the Mexican Political System* (Wilmington, DE: SR Books, 1993), pp. 245–262, and *Politics in Mexico* (New York: Oxford University Press, 1993); Jose Luis Mendez, "Mexico Under Salinas: Towards a New Record for One Party's Domination?," *Governance* 7, No. 2 (April 1994): 182–207; Miguel Angel Centeno, *Democracy Within Reason: Technocratic Revolution in Mexico* (University Park, PA: The Pennsylvania State University Press, 1994); Kathleen Bruhn, *Taking on Goliath: The Emergence of a New Left Party and the Struggle for Democracy in Mexico* (University Park, PA; Pennsylvania State University Press, 1997); David Masci, "Mexico's Future: Is It on the Path to True Democracy?," *CQ Researcher* 7 (September 19, 1997): 819–839; Carlos Baez Silva, "Mexico: Instituciones, Democracia y Cambio," *Revista Mexicana de Ciencias Politicas y Sociales* 41 (October/December 1997): 201–222; Denise Dresser, "Mexico After the July 6 Election: Neither Heaven nor Hell," *Current History* 97 (February 1998): 55–60; and George Philip, "Democratization and Social Conflict in Mexico," *Conflict Studies* (May 1999): 1–21. More specialized studies dealing with Mexican administration include William Ebenstein, "Public Administration in Mexico," *Public Administration Review* 5, No. 2 (1945): 102–112; Martin H. Greenberg, *Bureaucracy and Development: A Mexican Case Study* (Lexington, MA: D. C. Heath, 1970); Roderic A. Camp, "The Political Technocrat in Mexico and the Survival of the Political System," *Latin American Research Review* 20, No.

1 (1985): 97–118; Lawrence S. Graham, "The Implications of Presidentialism for Bureaucratic Performance in Mexico," prepared for the annual meeting in Miami of the American Society for Public Administration, 1989, 24 pp. mimeo.; and Jose Luis Mendez, "La Reforma del Estado en Mexico: Alcances y Limites," *Gestion y Politica Publica* 3, No. 1 (1994): 185–226.

30. Evelyn P. Stevens, "Mexico's PRI: The Institutionalization of Corporatism?" in Malloy, *Authoritarianism and Corporatism in Latin America*, pp. 227–258, at p. 227.

31. For details, see Cornelius, Gentleman, and Smith, "Overview: The Dynamics of Political Change in Mexico," pp. 21–36, and Lorenzo Meyer, "Democratization of the PRI: Mission Impossible?," pp. 325–348, both in Cornelius, Gentleman, and Smith, eds., *Mexico's Alternative Political Futures*.

32. Kaufman, "Corporatism, Clientelism, and Partisan Conflict," pp. 120–121.

33. Glen Dealy, "The Tradition of Monistic Democracy in Latin America," in Howard J. Wiarda, ed., *Politics and Social Change in Latin America: The Distinct Tradition* (Amherst: University of Massachusetts Press, 1974), pp. 73, 83.

34. Cornelius, Gentleman, and Smith, "Overview," pp. 30–31. The most conspicuous step in this direction was the arrest early in 1989 of the longtime head of the oil workers union on charges of smuggling arms.

35. Needler, *Politics and Society in Mexico*, p. 42.

36. Vernon, *The Dilemma of Mexico's Development*, p. 189.

37. Centeno, *Democracy Within Reason*, p. 223.

38. *Ibid.*, p. 224. For more details on PRONOSOL, see Camp, *Politics in Mexico*, pp. 143 and 169, and Mendez, "Mexico Under Salinas," pp. 191–192.

39. Mendez comments that Salinas "lacked a deep or at least well-planned program of political reforms." *Ibid.*, p. 198.

40. Greenberg, *Bureaucracy and Development*, p. 98.

41. Wendell Schaeffer, "National Administration in Mexico: Its Development and Present Status" (unpublished Ph.D. dissertation, University of California, 1949), pp. 183–184. Quoted by Greenberg, *Bureaucracy and Development*, p. 100. For a later version in Spanish, refer to Steven Goodspeed, William Ebenstein, Wendell Schaeffer, and William Glade, *Aportaciones a la Administracion Publica Federal* (Mexico City: Secretaria de la Presidencia, 1976).

42. Greenberg, *Bureaucracy and Development*, p. 98.

43. Vernon, *The Dilemma of Mexico's Development*, pp. 151–152.

44. Greenberg, *Bureaucracy and Development*, pp. 70–71.

45. Vernon, *The Dilemma of Mexico's Development*, pp. 5–6.

46. Greenberg, *Bureaucracy and Development*, p. 138.

47. Needler, *Mexican Politics*, p. 92.

48. For a fuller discussion, see Kenneth M. Coleman, *Diffuse Support in Mexico: The Potential for Crisis* (Beverly Hills, CA: Sage Publications, 1976).

49. Scott, *Mexican Government in Transition*, p. 279.

50. Vernon, *The Dilemma of Mexico's Development*, pp. 136–137.

51. Roderic A. Camp has been a leading student of Mexican leadership recruitment patterns. See his *Mexico's Leaders: Their Education and Recruitment*, and "The Political Technocrat in Mexico and the Survival of the Political System."

52. Needler, *Mexican Politics*, p. 72.

53. *Ibid.*, p. 82.

54. Greenberg, *Bureaucracy and Development*, p. 45.

55. See Camp, *Politics in Mexico*, pp. 103–107, and Centeno, *Democracy Within Reason*, pp. 146–149.

56. Centeno, *Democracy Within Reason*, p. 147.

57. Selected sources on India's political system include Norman D. Palmer, *The Indian Political System* (Boston: Houghton Mifflin Company, 1961); Stanley A. Kochanek, "The Indian Political System," in Robert N. Kearney, ed., *Politics and Moderniza- tion in South and Southeast Asia* (Cambridge, MA: Schenkman Publishing Co., 1975), pp. 39–107; Richard L. Park and Bruce Bueno de Mesquita, *India's Political System*, 2nd ed. (Englewood Cliffs, NJ: Prentice-Hall, 1979); Yogendra K. Malik and Dhirendra K. Vajpeyi, eds., "India: The Years of Indira Gandhi," *Journal of Asian and African Studies* 22 (July/October 1987): 135–282; Paul H. Kreisberg, "Gandhi at Midterm," *Foreign Affairs* 65, No. 5 (Summer 1987): 1055–1076; Vicky Randall, "The Congress Party of India: Dominance with Competition," in Randall, ed., *Political Parties in the Third World*, Chap. 4; C. P. Bhambhri, *Politics in India 1947–1987* (New Delhi: Vikas Publishing House Pvt. Ltd., 1988); Atul Kohli, *India's Democracy* (Princeton, NJ: Princeton University Press, 1988); Bharat Wariavwalla, "India in 1988: Drift, Disarray, or Pattern?" *Asian Survey* 29, No. 2 (February 1989): 189–198; F. Tomasson Jannuzi, *India in Transition: Issues of Political Economy in a Plural Society* (Boulder, CO: Westview Press, 1989); Arthur G. Rubinoff, "India at the Crossroads," *Journal of Asian and African Studies* 28, Nos. 3–4 (July-October 1993): 198–217; P. K. Das, "The Changing Political Scene in India: A Comment," *Asian Affairs* 25, No. 1 (February 1994): 24–29; Shashi Tharoor, *India: From Midnight to the Millennium* (New York: HarperCollins, 1997); Ashutosh Varshney, "Why Democracy Survives," *Journal of Democracy* 9 (July 1998): 36–50; Sudha Pai, "The Indian Party System Under Transformation: Lok Sabha Elections 1998," *Asian Survey* 38 (September 1998): 836–852; and Pradeep K. Chhibber, *Democracy Without Associations: Transformation of the Party System and Social Cleavages in India* (Ann Arbor, MI: University of Michigan Press, 1999). For more specific information on Indian administration, refer to A. R. Tyagi, "Role of Civil Service in India," *Indian Journal of Political Science* 19, No. 4 (1958): 349–356; R. Dwardakis, *Role of the Higher Civil Service in India* (Bombay: Popular Book Depot, 1958); Krishna K. Tummala, "Higher Civil Service in India," in Tummala, ed., *Administrative Systems Abroad*, pp. 96–126; O. P. Dwivedi and R. B. Jain, *India's Administrative State* (New Delhi: Gitanjali Publishing House, 1985); R. B. Jain, "Role of Bureaucracy in Policy Development and Implementation in India," prepared for World Congress of the International Political Science Associa- tion in Washington, DC, 1988, 27 pp. mimeo.; Shriram Maheshwari, "India," in Subramaniam, ed., *Public Administration in the Third World*, Chap. 3; R. B. Jain, "Political Executive and the Bureaucracy in India," in H. K. Asmeron and R. B. Jain, eds., *Politics, Administration and Public Policy in Developing Countries: Examples from Africa, Asia and Latin America* (Amsterdam: VU University Press, 1993), Chap. 7, pp. 134–151; and Krishna K. Tummala, *Public Administration in India* (Singapore: Times Academic Press, 1994). On Malaysia, refer to Robert O.

Tilman, *Bureaucratic Transition in Malaya* (Durham, NC: Duke University Press, 1964); David S. Gibbons and Zakaria Haji Ahmad, "Politics and Selection for the Higher Civil Service in New States: The Malaysian Example," *Journal of Comparative Administration* 3, No. 3 (1971): 330–348; Gordon P. Means, "Malaysia," in Kearney, ed., *Politics and Modernization in South and Southeast Asia,* pp. 153–214; Karl van Vorys, *Democracy Without Consensus: Communalism and Political Stability in Malaysia* (Princeton, NJ: Princeton University Press, 1975); R. S. Milne and Diane K. Mauzy, *Politics and Government in Malaysia* (Vancouver: University of British Columbia Press, 1978); Lloyd D. Musolf and J. Frederick Springer, *Malaysia's Parliamentary System: Representative Politics and Policymaking in a Divided Society* (Boulder, CO: Westview Press, 1979); Zainah Anwar, "Government and Governance in Multi-Racial Malaysia," in John W. Langford and K. Lorne Brownsey, eds., *The Changing Shape of Government in the Asia-Pacific Region* (Halifax: The Institute for Research on Public Policy, 1988), pp. 101–124; K. S. Nathan, "Malaysia in 1988: The Politics of Survival," *Asian Survey* 29 (February 1989): 129–139; William Case, "Semi-Democracy in Malaysia: Withstanding the Pressures for Regime Change," *Pacific Affairs* 66, No. 2 (Summer 1993); 183–206; and "Malaysia in 1993: Accelerating Trends and Mild Resistance," *Asian Survey* 34, No. 2 (February 1994): 119–126; Hari Singh, "The 1995 Malaysian General Election: Reaffirmation of Barisan Nasional Dominance," *Round Table* (July 1997): 389–409; G. Pascal Zachary, "The Malaysian Equation: Economic Crisis = Less Democracy," *In These Times* 22 (November 15, 1998): 10–11; and Murray Hiebert and S. Jayasankaran, "Wake-up Call," *Far Eastern Economic Review* 162, No. 11 (March 18, 1999): 8–11.

58. Kochanek, "The Indian Political System," p. 45.
59. Means, "Malaysia," p. 163.
60. Kochanek, "The Indian Political System," p. 69.
61. The prevalent view until recently has been that this is likely to occur, even though the party may be incapable of imposing a coherent strategy for national development. However, Pradeep Chhibber, in his 1999 book *Democracy Without Associations*, asserts that religious and caste-based parties such as the Bharatiya Janata have achieved domination, whereas "catchall" parties such as the Congress have declined.
62. Means, "Malaysia," p. 181.
63. Tummala, "Higher Civil Service in India," pp. 105-106.
64. Maheshwari, "India," p. 55.
65. Paul H. Appleby, quoted in Palmer, *The Indian Political System,* p. 132.
66. Kochanek, "The Indian Political System," p. 137.
67. Maheshwari, "India," p. 61.
68. Tummala, "Higher Civil Service in India," p. 111.
69. Jain, "Political Executive and the Bureaucracy in India," pp. 135, 143.
70. Milne and Mauzy, *Politics and Government in Malaysia,* p. 267.
71. Tilman, *Bureaucratic Transition in Malaya,* p. 137.
72. Esman, *Administration and Development in Malaysia,* p. 8. Esman's book is basically an account of a major effort at administrative reform designed to remedy such deficiencies.
73. For a view differing from mine (and from others as well) as to political-administrative

relationships in India, see Kishan Khanna, "Contemporary Models of Public Administration: An Assessment of their Utility and Exposition of Inherent Fallacies," *Philippine Journal of Public Administration* 18, No. 2 (April 1974): 103–126.

74. See Dwivedi and Jain, *India's Administrative State*, Chap. 4, p. 90, where the authors conclude that the nexus between politicians and administrators resulting from political interference has caused "a loss of morale and a state of inaction and non-performance" in the bureaucracy, and that the breaking of this nexus presents "one of the most perplexing problems of India's administrative state." Bhambhri, *Politics in India*, pp. 104–110, gives examples of what he considers improper linkages between politicians and bureaucrats. Maheshwari, "India," p. 56, concurs that there is "growing political interference in administration and, as often as not, both the civil servant and the politician have learned to accommodate each other in a wide variety of matters."

75. Esman, *Administration and Development in Malaysia*, p. 6.

76. *Ibid.*, p. v.

77. Selected sources on Egypt: Morroe Berger, *Bureaucracy and Society in Modern Egypt* (Princeton, NJ: Princeton University Press, 1957) and *Military Elite and Social Change: Egypt Since Napoleon* (Princeton, NJ: Center for International Studies, Princeton University, 1960); Grassmuck, *Polity, Bureaucracy and Interest Groups in the Near East and North Africa*; Walter R. Sharp, "Bureaucracy and Politics—Egyptian Model," in Siffin, ed., *Toward the Comparative Study of Public Administration*, pp. 145–181; Amos Perlmutter, *Egypt: Praetorian State* (New York: E. P. Dutton, 1973); Claude E. Welch, Jr. and Arthur K. Smith, "Egypt: Radical Modernization and the Dilemmas of Leadership," in *Military Role and Rule* (North Scituate, MA: Duxbury Press, 1974), Chap. 7, pp. 178–204; Shahrough Akhavi, "Egypt: Neo-Patrimonial Elite," in Tachau, ed., *Political Elites and Political Development in the Middle East*, pp. 69–113; Hamied Ansari, *Egypt: The Stalled Society* (Albany: State University of New York Press, 1986); Guilain Denoeux, "State and Society in Egypt," *Comparative Politics* 20 (April 1988): 359–373; Arthur Goldschmidt, Jr., *Modern Egypt: The Formation of a Nation-State* (Boulder, CO: Westview Press, 1988); Monte Palmer, Ali Leila, and El Sayed Yassin, *The Egyptian Bureaucracy* (Syracuse, NY: Syracuse University Press, 1988); Anthony McDermott, *Egypt from Nasser to Mubarak: A Flawed Revolution* (London: Croom Helm, 1988); Thomas W. Lippman, *Egypt after Nasser* (New York: Paragon House, 1989); Robert Springborg, *Mabarak's Egypt* (Boulder, CO: Westview Press, 1989); Nazih N. Ayubi, "Bureaucracy and Development in Egypt Today," *Journal of Asian and African Studies* 24 (January/April 1989): 62–78; Mona Makram-Ebeid, "Political Opposition in Egypt: Democratic Myth or Reality?" *Middle East Journal* 43 (Summer 1989): 423–436; E. H. Valsan, "Egypt," in Subramaniam, ed., *Public Administration in the Third World*, Chap. 6; James B. Mayfield, "Decentralization in Egypt: Its Impact on Development at the Local Level," prepared for the Annual Conference of the American Society for Public Administration, March 1991, 76 pp. mimeo.; Stanley Reed, "The Battle for Egypt," *Foreign Affairs* 72, No. 4 (September/October 1993): 94–107; Caryle Murphy, "Egypt: An Uneasy Portrait of Change," *Current History* 93 (February 1994): 78–82; Mona Makram-Ebeid, "Egypt's 1995 Elections: One Step Forward, Two Steps Back?," *Middle East Policy*

4 (March 1996): 119–136; Andrew Hammond, "A New Political Culture Emerges in Egypt," *Middle East* (April 1996): 5–7; and Eberhard Kienle, "More Than a Response to Islamism: The Political Deliberalization of Egypt in the 1990s," *Middle East Journal* 52, No. 2 (Spring 1998): 219–235.

78. R. Hrair Dekmejian, *Egypt under Nasir: A Study in Political Dynamics* (Albany: State University of New York Press, 1971), p. 284. Quoted in Welch and Smith, *Military Role and Rule*, p. 199.

79. Akhavi notes that "having purposefully chosen a rationalist, elitist model of rule and modernization from above, the military has been unable to achieve meaningful participation. In consequence, political integration in society has been weak and political mobilization artificial." "Egypt: Neo-Patrimonial Elite," p. 102. At the village level, basic transformations have not been affected. "Party membership in the rural areas tends . . . to ensure that a former traditional leader will be able to maintain his position of power and authority in the village or rural community." James B. Mayfield, *Rural Politics in Nasser's Egypt: A Quest for Legitimacy* (Austin: University of Texas Press, 1971), p. 284.

80. This 1987 statement is quoted by Makram-Ebeid, "Political Opposition in Egypt," p. 423.

81. *Ibid.*, pp. 424, 432.

82. Refer to Akhavi, "Egypt: Neo-Patrimonial Elite," pp. 87–95.

83. Welch and Smith, *Military Role and Rule*, p. 202.

84. Barbara N. McLennan, *Comparative Political Systems: Political Processes in Developed and Developing States* (North Scituate, MA: Duxbury Press, 1975), pp. 259–260.

85. Ayubi, "Bureaucracy and Development in Egypt Today," pp. 63.

86. Sharp, "Bureaucracy and Politics—Egyptian Model," pp. 158–160.

87. Akhavi, "Egypt: Neo-Patrimonial Elite," p. 103.

88. McLennan, *Comparative Political Systems*, pp. 260–261.

89. Akhavi, "Egypt: Neo-Patrimonial Elite," p. 103.

90. McLennan, *Comparative Political Systems*, pp. 260–261.

91. Palmer, Leila, and Yassin, *The Egyptian Bureaucracy*, p. ix.

92. *Ibid.*, p. 151.

93. For available sources on the Tanzanian political and administrative systems, refer to Henry Bienen, *Tanzania: Party Transformation and Economic Development*, expanded ed. (Princeton, NJ: Princeton University Press, 1970); Raymond F. Hopkins, *Political Roles in a New State* (New Haven, CT: Yale University Press, 1971); Andrew J. Perry, "Politics in Tanzania," in Gabriel A. Almond, gen. ed., *Comparative Politics Today: A World View* (Boston: Little, Brown and Company, 1974), Chap. 13; Rwekaza Mukandala, "Trends in Civil Service Size and Income in Tanzania, 1967–1982," *Canadian Journal of African Studies* 17, No. 2 (1983): 253–263; Joel D. Barkan, ed., *Politics and Public Policy in Kenya and Tanzania*, 2nd ed. (New York: Praeger, 1984), especially Goran Hyden, "Administration and Public Policy," pp. 103–124; Margaret A. Novicki, "Interview with President Ali Hassan Mwinyi," *Africa Report* 33 (January/February 1988): 27–29; Philip Smith, "Politics After Dodoma," *Africa Report* 33 (January/February 1988): 30–32; Rodger Yeager, *Tanzania: An African Experiment*, 2nd ed., rev. and updated (Boulder, CO:

Westview Press, 1989); Alfred John Kitula, "Decentralization Experience in Tanzania and Its Role in the Economic Reform Programmes in the Country: (A Review of Recent Experience)," prepared for the annual meeting of the American Society for Public Administration, March 1991, 16 pp. mimeo.; Horace Campbell and Howard Stein, *Tanzania and the IMF: The Dynamics of Liberalization* (Boulder, CO: Westview Press, 1992); Tabasim Hussain, "End of Tanzania's One-party Rule," *Africa Report* 37 (July/August 1992): 22–23; and Robert Pinkney, *Democracy and Dictatorship in Ghana and Tanzania* (New York: St. Martin's, 1997).

94. Novicki, "Interview with President Mwinyi," p. 27.
95. Perry, "Politics in Tanzania," p. 439.
96. Hyden, "Administration and Public Policy, " pp. 107–112.
97. For details, see Mukandala, "Trends in Civil Service Size."
98. For a detailed analysis, see Ali A. Mazrui, "Anti-Militarism and Political Militancy in Tanzania," in Jacques Van Doorn, ed., *Military Profession and Military Regimes* (The Hague: Mouton, 1969), pp. 219–240.
99. Perry, "Politics in Tanzania," pp. 426–427.
100. Edward A. Shils, *Political Development in the New States* (The Hague: Mouton & Co., 1962), p. 75.
101. Recent source materials on North Korean political and administrative arrangements, which are extremely limited, include Bruce Cumings, "The Corporate State in North Korea," in Hagen Koo, ed., *State and Society in Contemporary Korea* (Ithaca, NY: Cornell University Press, 1993), Chap. 6, pp. 197–230; John Merrill, "North Korea in 1993: In the Eye of the Storm," *Asian Survey* 34, No. 1 (January 1994): 10–19; Sung Chui Yang, *The North and South Korean Political Systems: A Comparative Analysis* (Boulder, CO: Westview Press, 1994), especially Part III, "The North Korean Political System: A Totalitarian Political Order," pp. 219–386; Adrian Buzo and Jae Hoon Shim, "From Dictator to Deity," *Far Eastern Economic Review* 157, No. 29 (July 1994): 18–20; Pan S. Kim, "A Comparative Analysis of Reform in Northeast Asian Socialist and Post-Socialist Countries: North Korea and Mongolia," prepared for the national conference of the American Society for Public Administration, July 1994, 34 pp. mimeo.; Kawashima Yutaka, "Can Kim's Son Rule—and Last?," *World Press Review* 41, No. 9 (September 1994): 16–21; Byung-joon Ahn, "The Man Who Would Be Kim," *Foreign Affairs* 73, No. 6 (November/December 1994): 94–109; Sung Chull Kim, ed., and others, *North Korea in Crisis: An Assessment of Regime Stability* (Seoul: Korea Institute for National Unification, 1997); Hakjoon Kim, "North Korea Falling Apart?," *Korea Observer* 29 (Summer 1998): 259–285; Yong-sup Han, "The Kim Dae-jung Government's Unification Policy: Will the Sunshine Effect Change in North Korea?," *Korea and World Affairs* 22, No. 3 (Fall 1998): 325–340; and Jinwook Choi, "North Korean Local Politics Under the New Constitution," *Korea and World Affairs* 22, No. 4 (Winter 1998): 569–591.
102. Cumings, "The Corporate State in North Korea," p. 209.
103. *Ibid.*, pp. 218–219.
104. Sung Chul Yang, "The North Korean Political System," p. 753.
105. Cumings, "The Corporate State in North Korea," pp. 208–210.
106. Sources on the Cuban political and administrative systems include Richard Fagan,

The Transformation of Political Culture in Cuba (Stanford, CA: Stanford University Press, 1969); James F. Petras, "Cuba: Fourteen Years of Revolutionary Government," in Thurber and Graham, eds., *Development Administration in Latin America*, pp. 281–293; Jorge I. Dominguez, "The Civic Soldier in Cuba," in Catherine McArdle Kelleher, ed., *Political-Military Systems: Comparative Perspectives* (Beverly Hills, CA: Sage Publications, 1974), pp. 209–238; Carmelo Mesa-Lago, *Cuba in the 1970s: Pragmatism and Institutionalization*, rev. ed. (Albuquerque: University of New Mexico Press, 1978), and *The Economy of Socialist Cuba: A Two-Decade Appraisal* (Albuquerque: University of New Mexico Press, 1981); George Volsky, "Cuba Twenty Years Later," *Current History* 76, No. 444 (February 1979): 54–57, 83–84; Jorge I. Dominguez, "Cuba in the 1980's," *Problems of Communism* 30, No. 2 (March-April 1981): 48–59; Brian Latell, "Cuba after the Third Party Congress," *Current History* 85, No. 515 (December 1986): 425–428, 437–438; Jorge I. Dominguez, "Leadership Changes and Factionalism in the Cuban Communist Party," prepared for the 1987 Annual Meeting of the American Political Science Association, 22 pp. mimeo.; Andrew Zimbalist, ed., *Cuban Political Economy* (Boulder, CO: Westview Press, 1988); John Griffiths, "The Cuban Communist Party," in Randall, ed., *Political Parties in the Third World*, Chap. 8; Sergio G. Roca, ed., *Socialist Cuba: Past Interpretations and Future Challenges* (Boulder, CO: Westview Press, 1988); Michael J. Mazarr, "Prospects for Revolution in Post-Castro Cuba," *Journal of Interamerican Studies and World Affairs* 31, No. 3 (Winter 1989): 61–90; Carlos Alberto Montaner, *Fidel Castro and the Cuban Revolution* (New Brunswick, NJ: Transaction, 1989); Irving Louis Horowitz, ed., *Cuban Communism*, 7th ed. (New Brunswick, NJ: Transaction Publishers, 1989); Sheryl L. Lutjens, "State Administration in Socialist Cuba: Power and Performance," in Farazmand, ed., *Handbook of Comparative and Development Public Administration*, Chap. 24, pp. 325–338; Susan Kaufman Purcell, "Collapsing Cuba," *Foreign Affairs* 71, No. 1 (Winter 1992): 130–145; Andrew Zimbalist, "Teetering on the Brink: Cuba's Current Economic and Political Crisis," *Journal of Latin American Studies* 24 (May 1992): 407–418; Eliana A. Cardoso, *Cuba After Communism* (Cambridge, MA: MIT Press, 1992); Jorge I. Dominguez, "The Secrets of Castro's Staying Power," *Foreign Affairs* 72, No. 2 (Spring 1993): 97–107; Enrique A. Baloyra, *Conflict and Change in Cuba* (Albuquerque, NM: University of New Mexico Press, 1993); Carmelo Mesa-Lago, ed., *Cuba After the Cold War* (Pittsburgh, PA: University of Pittsburgh Press, 1993); Susan Eckstein, *Back From the Future: Cuba Under Castro* (Princeton, NJ: Princeton University Press, 1994); Juan M. Del Aguila, *Cuba: Dilemmas of a Revolution*, 3rd ed. (Boulder, CO: Westview Press, 1994); Donald E. Schulz, ed., *Cuba and the Future* (Westport, CT: Greenwood Press, 1994); "Cuba," *Caribbean Quarterly* 42 (March 1996): 1–83; Alan Shipman, "Polishing the Long Spoon," *World Today* 54 (August/September 1998): 233–235; and Wilfredo Lozano, ed., *Cambio Politico en el Caribe: Escenarios de la Posguerra Fria: Cuba, Haiti y Republica Dominicana* (Caracas: Nueva Sociedad, 1998).

107. Mesa-Lago, *Cuba in the 1970s*, pp. 67–68.
108. Jorge I. Dominguez, "The Civic Soldier in Cuba," in Catherine McArdle Kelleher, ed., *Political-Military Systems: Comparative Perspectives*, Sage Research Progress Series on War, Revolution, and Peacekeeping, Volume IV, (Beverly Hills, CA: Sage

Publications, 1974), p. 210. Reprinted by permission of the Publisher, Sage Publications, Inc.

109. *Ibid.*, p. 236.
110. Juan M. del Aguila, *Cuba*, p. 179.
111. *Ibid.*, pp. 179–180. See also Mesa-Lago, *Cuba in the 1970s*, pp. 76–79.
112. *Cuba in the 1970s*, p. 115.
113. Petras, "Cuba," pp. 289–290.
114. See, for example, Antonio Jorge, "Ideology, Planning, Efficiency, and Growth: Change without Development," in Horowitz, ed., *Cuban Communism*, Chap. 16; and Lutjens, "State Administration in Socialist Cuba."
115. Dominguez, "Cuba in the 1980's," p. 48.
116. Volsky, "Cuba Twenty Years Later," p. 54.
117. Mazarr, "Prospects for Revolution in Post-Castro Cuba," p. 61.
118. Dominguez, "Castro's Staying Power," p. 106. He says that this possibility exists because Cuban leaders have learned these lessons from the undermining of other Communist regimes: (1) "undertake as few political reforms as possible," (2) "get rid of deadwood in the party early on, before you are forced to do so," (3) "deal harshly with potential or evident disloyalty," and (4) "do not allow a formal opposition to organize," p. 99.
119. Purcell, "Collapsing Cuba," p. 130.

10

Overview of Bureaucracies and Political Systems

Now that we have surveyed the public bureaucracies in a wide variety of existing political systems, what can be said in summary about similarities and diversities among them, and about the relationship between the type of political system and the role of administration in the system as shown by bureaucratic traits and behavior? Let us start by considering basic expectations generally held concerning the proper character and conduct of bureaucracies, and move from that to more particularized treatment of variations associated with different kinds of political systems.

POLITICAL ENDS AND ADMINISTRATIVE MEANS

With few exceptions, there is common agreement transcending differences in political ideology, culture, and style, that bureaucracy should be basically instrumental in its operation—that it should serve as agent and not as master. It is almost universally expected that the bureaucracy be so designed and shaped as to respond willingly and effectively to policy leadership from outside its own ranks. The idea that bureaucratic officialdom, either civil or military, or both together, should for any extended period of time constitute the ruling class in a political system is generally rejected. The political elite may include members of the civil or military bureaucracies, but should not consist exclusively or even primarily of bureaucratic officials. Even in regimes in which a bureaucratic elite is clearly in a position of political dominance, it will rarely claim that this is the way things should be; instead, it will usually insist that such a situation can be justified only temporarily under unusual circumstances.

Of course, this is not the same as asserting that the bureaucracy can or should play strictly a passive role, uninvolved in policy-making and uncontaminated by exposure to the political process. Rather, it is an affirmation of the primacy of political control over the administrative system, whatever the character of the political leadership. This is a fundamental tenet of the doctrine held by advocates of widely variant political alternatives, including supporters of traditional monarchy, aristocratic oligarchy, representative democracy, mass-mobilization party rule, and totalitarianism of different varieties. All agree that the state bureaucracy should be responsible to the political leadership, however intimately it may be brought into the process of decision-making by the will of the political elite.

A consensus on the way things ought to be does not necessarily ensure that they will actually be that way. Of more importance to us than an idealized concept of what the role of bureaucracy should be is an accurate assessment of what it has been and is in practice.

A perennial concern relating to bureaucratic officials is that they may stray from their proper instrumental role to one that is usurpative, converting these bureaucrats themselves into the primary power-wielders in the political system. The political role of the bureaucracy has been a matter of continuing interest in the more developed nations, and has emerged as one of the principal issues in discussions about the political future of developing countries. The tendency during much of the last half century for bureaucratic elite regimes to become more prevalent has certainly enhanced the relevancy of this issue.

The classic literature on bureaucracy does not ignore the problem but gives it relatively incidental attention. Weber himself has been criticized as not being sensitive enough to bureaucratic power considerations. Diamant considers this an unfounded view, and cites passages from Weber's writings to refute it.[1] He shows that Weber described the power position of a fully developed bureaucracy as "always overtowering," called for greater emphasis on political leadership, advised politicians to "resist any effort on the part of the bureaucrats to gain control," and warned that a nation "which believes that the conduct of state affairs is a matter of 'administration' and that 'politics' is nothing but the part-time occupation of amateurs or a secondary task of bureaucrats might as well forget about playing a role in world affairs." Weber recognized a dichotomy between policy and administration and wanted to draw a sharp distinction between the roles of the politician and the bureaucrat, but he also noted that "every problem, no matter how technical it might seem, can assume political significance and its solution can be decisively influenced by political considerations." Diamant's interpretation is that ambiguities in Weber's treatment of this matter reflect a dualism in his thinking, the severe rationality of his ideal-type constructs leading him to consider bureaucracy as a neutral tool, and his own political experiences teaching him that the power interests of the bureaucracy may threaten the mastery of political leadership.

In recent literature dealing with the role of bureaucracies, particularly in polities considered to be developed, this ambiguity in assessment of bureaucratic activity continues to be evident.

As already noted in Chapter 4, Henry Jacoby has restated and amplified Weber's concern about the "overtowering" power of fully developed bureaucracy. In his book, *The Bureaucratization of the World*,[2] Jacoby concludes that bureaucracy is necessary but dangerous, with a strong potential for usurpation. This issue received special attention in 1980 at the International Congress of Administrative Sciences held in Madrid, where one of the principal subjects considered was "problems of political control of government departments and other public agencies." R. E. Wraith, who wrote a detailed and informative report on these discussions, which included participants from a wide array of political regimes, summarized that there was "agreement that the growing impact of government and governmental agencies on everyday life has brought a more than corresponding increase in public administration which, both by its ubiquity and its sheer size, appears to 'feed on itself' and which could grow to a point when it became virtually beyond political control." There was, as well, "affirmation that in the 1980s, in the realm of political control of the executive, bureaucracy itself is in danger of being uncontrolled; that whatever may be its virtues it is not necessarily an efficient instrument of control; and that we may well be approaching a bureaucratic crisis."[3]

At the end of the decade, however, there were indications of a more reassuring conclusion. Donald C. Rowat, in a well informed analysis made late in the 1980s of the impact that recent trends had made on the role of appointed officials in the making of policy, suggested that this was the case. Primarily concerned with public administration in developed democracies, he identified several developments that supported this finding. They included political decentralization, efforts to assert greater political control over agencies outside the regular departmental framework, measures to improve bureaucratic responsiveness generally, reforms in the procedures of regulatory agencies for greater protection of individual rights, and increasing attention to and participation in policy-making by both political executives and legislators. The net effect of these changes, especially in democracies with parliamentary systems, he believed, would be a decline in the policy-making role of the bureaucracy, because "the influence of senior officials will more nearly represent the interests of society," there will be closer supervision and control over the bureaucracy, and the increased political input into policy-making will bring about a corresponding reduction in bureaucratic input.[4] Recent political events in the former Soviet Union and in the countries of Eastern Europe lend support to these views, implying that there may be an equivalent or even greater reduction occurring in the role of the state bureaucratic apparatus in developed or semi-developed countries that have not been democratic in the past.

During the 1990s, the most significant shift on a global basis, particularly in the more developed countries, has been from emphasis primarily on the roles of official governmental agencies to the sharing of responsibilities by these units with quasi-governmental or private entities in public sector policy implementation. This is increasingly referred to as a broadening of focus from "governing" to "governance." The "new public management" movement discussed in Chapter 1 has been foremost in analyzing and advocating this trend.[5] Donald F. Kettl is currently a leading spokesman for this "transformation of governance" emphasis. In *The Global Public Management Revolution: A Report on the Transformation of Governance*,[6] he describes this reform movement since the 1980s as sharing six core characteristics: productivity; marketization; service orientation; decentralization; policy separation between government's role as purchaser of services from its role in providing them; and accountability for results focusing on outputs and outcomes rather than processes and structures. Kettl chaired a priorities task force set up by the National Academy of Public Administration, which asserts in its report that "this transformation focuses on the linkages between governmental institutions and non-governmental organizations who share in doing government's work. It focuses on the relationships among institutions, more than on the structures, processes, and behavior within institutions. It focuses more on government's leadership role—charting a course for achieving public purpose—than on government's direct role in producing public services."[7] This stress on the centrality of achieving public purpose, no matter what the instrumentality used, seems to me crucial in maintaining a proper balance in the study of public management or public administration, whichever term is preferred.

Taking a longer range perspective, B. Guy Peters offers what in my view is a realistic overall medial assessment, asserting that the role of public bureaucracy is

> a distinguishing feature of contemporary government. The massive increases in the number and complexity of government functions since the end of World War II, or even the mid-1960s, have generated demands for governance that could be met most readily through an increased capacity in the public bureaucracy . . . In the contemporary welfare state, the public bureaucracy has achieved an importance that few of the major theoreticians of public administration, or of democratic government, could have imagined or condoned. . . . Despite the political pressure to minimize the policy-making role of the bureaucracy and maximize the role of true believers, the public bureaucracy remains in a powerful policy-making position. That power may simply be a prerequisite of effective government in contemporary society.[8]

RELATING BUREAUCRATIC AND POLITICAL DEVELOPMENT

With regard to the developing countries, there is little controversy as to the recent and current power role of the bureaucracy in the political system. In many instances, it has been and is admittedly too high. Views differ, however, as to the relationship between bureaucratic and political development. These sharply divergent opinions have stimulated a prolonged and vigorous debate concerning the nature of this relationship, leading in turn to contrasting suggestions as to appropriate strategy for facilitating the attainment of political development.[9]

The importance of a competent bureaucracy in a developed political system is not in dispute. All commentators would agree with Almond and Powell as to the central role of bureaucracy in the process of political development, and concur with their statement that a political system "cannot develop a high level of internal regulation, distribution, or extraction without a 'modern' governmental bureaucracy in one form or another."[10] Also, there is general agreement that in many developing nations the bureaucracy has gained ascendancy over other political institutions, and that the number of such cases has increased, at least until recently, with a resulting current imbalance in bureaucratic and political development. At issue is the question of whether the presence of a bureaucracy that is relatively developed enhances or inhibits prospects for overall political development in the long run.

Stated simply, one argument is that the existence of a strong "modern" bureaucracy in a polity with political institutions that are generally weak presents in itself a major obstacle to political development. The main counterargument is that a high level of bureaucratic development can be expected to enhance rather than hinder prospects for future overall political development.

The best known spokesman for the first point of view is Fred W. Riggs. Others sharing similar judgments include Henry F. Goodnow, Lucian W. Pye, S. N. Eisenstadt, and Joseph LaPalombara, although they cannot all be lumped together because of differences in emphasis among them and, in some instances, what seems to be a shift in attitude over time.

Riggs has presented his analysis in several versions but with the same basic theme. One of the earliest, and still one of the best, expositions of this diagnosis is his "paradoxical view," reflecting a conviction based on the implications of his "prismatic-sala" model and his case study of Thailand, that transitional societies frequently lack balance between "political policy-making institutions and bureaucratic policy-implementing structures," the consequence being that "the political function tends to be appropriated, in considerable measure, by bureaucrats."[11] He surveys the power position of the transitional bureaucracies vis-a-vis other political institutions which exercise controls over bureaucracies in Western countries—such as chief executives, legislatures, courts, political parties, and interest groups—and finds the other institutions weak in contrast to the "burgeoning growth" of bureaucracies. In such circumstances, political direction tends to become more and more a bureaucratic monopoly, and as this occurs, the bureaucrats themselves are increasingly tempted to give preference to their own group interests. As the imbalance continues and increases, the prospect for attainment of a desirable mutual interdependence among competing power centers becomes more remote.

In a later formulation, Riggs has referred to regimes with these characteristics as "bureaucratic polities," or unbalanced polities dominated by their bureaucracies.[12] His underlying distinction between balanced and unbalanced polities rests on whether or not there is an approximate balance between the bureaucracy and extra-bureaucratic institutions which he chooses to call the "constitutive system."[13] This term encompasses as subcomponents "an elected assembly, an electoral system, and a party system."[14] A polity is balanced if it maintains a reasonably stable equilibrium between the bureaucracy and the constitutive system, unbalanced if either dominates the other. The form of government found in nations generally regarded as modern is balanced, whereas many developing nations have unbalanced polities. Usually the latter have "bureaucratic polities," with the attendant tendency to inhibit political development, which Riggs has consistently argued results from "premature or rapid expansion of the bureaucracy when the political system lags behind."[15] Not only will a dominant bureaucracy have this adverse effect on the future of the political system, according to Riggs, but it also will be unlikely to meet its more immediate obligations, because it "will necessarily sacrifice administrative to political considerations, thereby impairing administrative performance."[16]

LaPalombara also called attention early to the difficulty of restricting bureaucracy to an instrumental role.[17] The risk, which is not sufficiently recognized in even the more advanced countries, is accentuated in developing nations, "where the bureaucracy may be the most coherent power center and where, in addition, the major decisions regarding national development are likely to involve authoritative rule making and rule application by governmental structures."[18] The result is the emergence in many places of "overpowering bureaucracies," with the growth in bureaucratic power inhibiting, and perhaps precluding, the development of democratic polities. In instances in which the military rather than the civil bureaucracy has the upper hand, the prospect is even more dismal. If democratic development is to be encouraged, a separation of political and administrative roles is required; and this calls for deliberate steps to limit the power of the bureaucracies in many of the newer states. He makes some specific suggestions, including a de-emphasis on goals of economic development, a shift in demands on the political system from economic to social and political realms, and a massive program of education, all designed in part to reduce the responsibility of the bureaucracy for goal-setting and goal implementation.

Henry Goodnow, generalizing about the power position of the bureaucratic elite in new states from his study of the civil service in Pakistan, reached the conclusion that the occupants of the higher civil service posts do indeed exert such predominant influence as to make the climate unfavorable for the development of democratic institutions.[19] He attributes this to the fact that they inherited power vacated by the colonial administrators, and were able easily to convert governmental institutions created to permit rule by a foreign bureaucratic elite to the service of a native bureaucratic elite, usually without facing any countervailing forces. He does not say that this trend was started by a lust for power on the part of bureaucratic officials. He concedes that they have usually taken over after some reluctance, have often been sincere in blaming the shortcomings of politicians for making this necessary, and have regarded themselves as guardians of democracy as an ultimate goal; but he feels that the urge to hold and consolidate power is deceptively strong. He is therefore skeptical about the prospects of a gradual transition from bureaucratic elite rule to democratic government, and foresees as more likely a power struggle between an increasingly rigid governing bureaucracy and an increasingly revolutionary opposition, which will destroy prospects for evolutionary changes.

Lucian Pye has taken much the same stance in discussing the political context of national development.[20] He argues that the greatest problem in nation-building is how to relate "the administrative and authoritative structures of government to political forces within the transitional societies" in the face of the usual imbalance between "recognized administrative tradition and a still inchoate political process."[21] Both external and internal factors are responsible for the situation. The nation-building efforts of the West have been almost exclusively devoted to upgrading administrative capabilities, with the creation of political capabilities left to chance. Even where nationalist movements have gained popular acceptance, they have "settled on the easy alternative of preserving their power by crowding in on the administrative structure rather than striving to build up permanent and autonomous bases of power." To Pye, such tactics indicate weakness rather than strength, and do not offer grounds for encouragement even in countries with dominant national parties. His pessimistic conclusion is that there has been an unmistakable decline in both political party vitality and administrative effectiveness in most of the new states. He apparently does not agree with those who cite the countries with dominant mass parties as showing a capacity to control the bureaucracy without hamstringing it. Pye agrees closely with Riggs in saying that "public administration cannot be greatly improved without a parallel strengthening of the representative political processes."[22] Pye also has explored the psychology of institutionalization in relation to the building of bureaucracies in new states, leading him to disagree with those who consider new states fortunate if they inherit colonial administrative structures intact. During the institutionalization of colonial authority, indigenous civil servants became imbued with "the spirit of the clerk," trained to give infinite attention to details, stress legalism in the extreme, and function with minimal discretion or imagination. Independence and nationhood meant that the old pattern of institutionalized behavior was no longer adequate. Power relationships replaced ritualized relationships, and technical skills became insufficient. In this environment of politicized tension, bureaucrats consider that their status has been threatened, and therefore turn to participation in power conflicts, calling for traits such as competitiveness, creativity, and political skills.[23]

S. N. Eisenstadt likewise has reviewed the extensive involvement of bureaucracies in the political process of new states, and has noted that they tend to fulfill functions that would more normally be carried out by legislatures, executives, and political parties, thereby impeding the development of more differentiated political institutions.[24] He appears to share the view that bureaucracies which become dominant retard the potential growth of other sectors needed to bring more balance to the political system.

These appraisals are representative of the prevalent negative judgment regarding the implications of what is taken to be the most typical bureaucratic role in developing polities. Other equally informed commentators have expressed considerably more sanguine views. Usually they do not deny the tendency for the bureaucracy to occupy what seems to be an inordinately strong position relative to other political organs, but they are inclined to regard this as inevitable, perhaps desirable, and at any rate not easily susceptible to external manipulation. Ralph Braibanti has supported this position most extensively. Others with similar views include Milton J. Esman, Bernard E. Brown, Fritz Morstein Marx, Leonard Binder, Lee Sigelman, Edward W. Weidner, and myself; LaPalombara in later writing also seems to share these views to some extent.

Braibanti, like Riggs, has addressed this problem on various occasions since the early 1960s. Given the high priority assigned to economic development in the new nations, he has pointed out that during the early stages of nation-building

> what virtue there is seems to reside in the bureaucracy. Economic development must be achieved in the matrix of constructing an equilibrium of bureaucratic power and political control. This must be done even though development requirements are inherently antagonistic to the political results of the very equilibrium which will eventuate. The achievement in disequilibrium of a condition of development which the logic of popular sovereignty demands be achieved in an unattainable equilibrium is the crucial problem in political development.[25]

During the interim period when there is no possibility of vigorous political activity in general in the society, an elitist bureaucracy with a guardianship orientation must be the principal initiator of change. The educative role it can play should be reassessed, and the problem of how such a bureaucracy "can with good grace relinquish its power and transform its function when a mature, viable political system begins to operate as the source of polity," should be studied. Under some circumstances, the military bureaucracy may be more effective than the civil bureaucracy, since it sometimes "embodies nationalist and revolutionary ideals and manifests a zeal, sense of sacrifice, and devotion to duty greater than any other element of society." Braibanti also has held out the theoretical possibility that either civil or military bureaucracy may develop representativeness and responsiveness to the public comparable to that provided by a popularly elected legislature, so that "a bureaucracy in which democratic patterns have been extended and fortified may not be the worst fate which might befall a developing nation."[26]

Braibanti has consistently maintained that a primary requisite for development is a competent bureaucratic system, and has assumed that "the strengthening of administration must proceed irrespective of the rate of maturation of the political process."[27] He argues that administrative reform does not occur autonomously, but "has a permeative effect on other institutions and structures and . . . may serve as a generant in the growth of these sectors." What is desirable is "the strategic strengthening of as many institutions, sectors, and structures as possible."[28] Pursuit of this strategy does not preclude "the further strengthening of already strong bureaucratic institutions, for the existence of a viable bureaucracy is held to be a paramount need of developing states."[29]

Esman and Brown also belong among those who acknowledge the centrality of administration in developing systems but advocate that it be strengthened further rather than downgraded. Although Esman stresses the central and growing role of administrative institutions in carrying out action programs, he does not think that bureaucrats as a group can afford to be political risk-takers, or that they are likely to contest for political leadership. He acknowledges that the efforts of political elites "must often be invested in gaining and maintaining control and direction over administrative agencies, civil and military, counteracting their tendency to achieve autonomy and independent power positions or to enhance their group interests." Nevertheless, he believes that bureaucrats, when under pressure, "usually opt for safety in order to protect their careers. When challenged by powerful opponents who themselves dispose of political power and influence, bureaucrats without strong political protection feel helpless."[30]

Brown mentions tendencies for political power to shift to the executive sector of government, and within the executive, from political officials to professional civil servants; he recognizes that this raises a serious question concerning the future of democratic government, but nevertheless feels that the pressing need is to strengthen the executive branch. The dangers of a bureaucracy that is not adequately controlled are real. They cannot be eliminated but may be reduced by trying to make the bureaucracy more representative of the society, to provide built-in checks and balances.[31]

Fritz Morstein Marx credits the merit bureaucracies which emerged in the modern nation-states of the West with having contributed to the viability of constitutional government by accommodating demands made upon the body politic, participating in giving certain demands priority over others, discharging government responsibilities expeditiously, and in general, working toward stability and continuity. He mentions the possibility, although not the assurance, of similar contributions from the higher civil service in the new nations, with the observable growth of a nucleus of trained administrators, "usually relatively young, responsive to modern ways, and simultaneously aroused partisans of the new order" who "contribute a professional outlook to the everyday conduct of governmental activities," and who "are leaving a visible imprint." Since he believes civilian career officials to be primarily motivated by "prudential neutrality" rather than by an urge to take over direct political power, he is not much concerned about the prospect of bureaucratic elite rule, and he sees the civil servants in developing countries as heavily dependent on support from political leadership in various kinds of "strongman" governments, rather than sitting in the driver's seat themselves.[32]

Various other writers can be identified with the general proposition that the risk of jeopardizing a more balanced political equilibrium in the future does not justify a deliberate policy of stifling further bureaucratic development whenever current imbalance exists favoring the bureaucracy. Lee Sigelman has argued that evidence is substantial that "the presence of a relatively modern national administrative system is a necessary precondition of, not a hindrance to, societal modernization, including political development,"[33] Hence he would favor efforts to build up such administrative capabilities where they do not currently exist. I have subscribed elsewhere to the basic view that "bureaucratic upgrading is apt to be beneficial rather than disadvantageous."[34] Weidner, in evaluating technical assistance programs in public administration, has acknowledged the desirability of maintaining a competitive balance between the political and administrative elements in the political system, but at the same time he asserts that "those responsible for technical assistance programs cannot wait for political systems, of whatever form, to mature before extending help."[35] Unwilling to concede that a strengthening of the bureaucracy will necessarily deter parallel growth elsewhere, he says that another possibility may be that an enlightened and capable bureaucracy may be willing and able to take leadership in bringing along the lagging sectors in order to meet developmental objectives. His inclination, therefore, is not to advise abandonment of bureaucratic improvement as a legitimate objective in external aid programs. LaPalombara, who earlier had voiced considerable skepticism about the wisdom of attempting to help bureaucracies already tending toward dominance, subsequently moved toward a more discriminating approach in discussing alternative strategies for developing administrative capacities in emerging countries. Given the overwhelming demands of crisis management which commonly burden developing nations, he later took the position that whatever bureaucratic apparatus a developing country may have inherited should generally be strengthened rather than weakened.[36]

As might be expected, the ongoing debate just summarized has been closely paralleled by a related divergence of opinion as to strategy for achieving balanced political development, particularly focusing on the role of external sources that may intervene in the process.

Those alarmed about bureaucratic imbalance understandably urge that aid should be forthcoming from outside only if it is realistically designed to bring about better balance in the political system. Riggs has presented the most extensive arguments for such an aid-giving strategy, under which decisions to extend or withhold aid would be dependent primarily on anticipated consequences in movement toward a more balanced polity in the recipient country. On the assumption that the imposition of control over a bureaucracy by the constitutive system is a difficult task in any event and will become more difficult as the bureaucracy becomes relatively more powerful, he recommends that deliberate measures be taken to curtail bureaucratic expansion and to strengthen potential control agencies. This would call, among other things, for a drastic reevaluation of the objectives of technical assistance programs which have tended, he believes, to assist bureaucratic proliferation and to neglect the growth of strictly political institutions. The outcome in most but not all instances is that he advocates a reduction in efforts to provide aid to bureaucracies and a corresponding augmentation of externally supplied programs to strengthen elements of the constitutive system, such as legislatures, political parties, and devices for interest-group representation.[37]

Riggs discounts the efficacy of external efforts at bureaucratic improvement except in the relatively few instances among developing countries in which a balance already exists between the bureaucracy and the constitutive system. In the case of imbalance favoring the bureaucracy, which is by far the more likely situation, Riggs says that external aid to the bureaucracy would have the dual adverse results of adding to the degree of imbalance by further building up bureaucratic power while simultaneously detracting from the quality of administrative performance. Even in polities in which the imbalance is due to bureaucratic weakness, Riggs' position seems to be that external aid may indeed be able to enhance the political power stance of the bureaucracy but at the price of a lowered operational record, since he maintains that in unbalanced polities, no matter what the form of imbalance, efforts by Western polities to strengthen the bureaucracy are likely to undermine administrative performance even more. His conclusion seems to restrict very narrowly the beneficial prospects of external inducement of bureaucratic improvement.

In bureaucratic polities in which the imbalance is due to weaknesses in the constitutive system, on the other hand, Riggs apparently is optimistic about the possibilities for successful intervention to build up the strength of these elements in the political system. He makes a number of suggestions about courses of action which might strengthen nonbureaucratic institutions, but does not indicate how these steps might feasibly be taken in the absence of a request from the political leadership of the country concerned. The need for launching "soundly conceived programs for political development"[38] is mentioned, without any practical indication as to how this is to be done. The closest he seems to come is in the suggestion that "attention be given to intensive study of the political ecology of administration as a necessary prerequisite to the formulation of effective technical assistance and a realistic foreign policy concerned with developmental goals."[39]

In addition to his basic position that assistance to bureaucracies in unbalanced polities should be withheld, Riggs also argues that as a matter of American foreign policy such aid should be declined in balanced political systems which are not democratic. In other words, one form of balance may be found in a polity in which the constitutive system is dominated by a single party rather than offering opportunities for competition among two or more parties. According to his general analysis, "our administrative doctrines are relevant to the needs of these governments, as well as to those which are democratic. However, if one goal of American foreign policy is to encourage democratic regimes, then it may well be desirable to withhold assistance to undemocratic governments, even those which could use such assistance."[40] Riggs invokes Woodrow Wilson in support of his view, arguing that Wilson weighted democratic values more highly than administrative efficiency, and therefore would be shocked to find Americans exporting administrative doctrines and practices that might be of aid to authoritarian governments.[41]

The Riggsian strategy for external inducement of balanced development thus calls for the deliberate withholding of administrative technology transfer except in the relatively few instances in which developing countries have balanced polities that are also democratic in the sense of having competitive party systems, while simultaneously adopting an aggressive posture of promoting various aid programs intended to strengthen the constitutive system, especially in its competitiveness, except in the rare instances in which imbalance exists because of dominance by the constitutive system. This policy stance is linked to the firm belief consistently expressed by Riggs that even "the most well-intentioned and supposedly 'non-political' programs of bilateral and international assistance often have the unintended effect of strengthening and expanding bureaucratic power in Third World countries," and that the bureaucratic polities being helped have surprising capabilities to maintain themselves, are unlikely to evolve into more balanced political systems, and will be curbed in the long run only if they are overthrown by Marxist or neo-traditionalist revolutionary movements.[42]

Ralph Braibanti and I, among others, have vigorously questioned key features of this strategy for inducing balanced political development from external sources. The issue is not the desirability, from the point of view of a country such as the United States, of contributing as much as possible to realization of whatever prospects may exist for movement toward a more balanced political system with democratic characteristics. Rather, the question is how this can be best accomplished, within the options actually available to aid-giving countries. One major consideration, of course, is the position taken on the point as to whether or not, in bureaucratic polities, further strengthening of already strong bureaucracies will reduce future prospects for movement toward greater balance. Riggs views such an outcome as almost axiomatic. Braibanti, on the other hand, as we have seen, believes that bureaucratic reform has a permeative effect on other institutions and structures, and that external aid for this purpose should never be withheld solely on the basis that a desirable political balance from the perspective of the donor country must be achieved first. I concur with this view.

Of course, this attitude toward providing external assistance for upgrading the bureaucracy does not preclude a similar willingness to assist in efforts to improve the capabilities of other elements in the political system. Instead, Braibanti's assumption, as already noted, is that "the strategic strengthening of as many institutions, sectors, and structures as possible is desirable."[43] However, foreign assistance to institutions in the constitutive system can be made available only subject to serious practical limitations.

Braibanti examines several aspects of this problem, including external aid programs to strengthen political parties, legislatures, community development institutions, and citizen consultative or advisory bodies.[44] For example, with regard to proposals made by Samuel Huntington and others that the United States try to strengthen political parties as part of its foreign assistance effort, Braibanti points out difficulties for both the donor and recipient countries. If the support goes only to a single dominant mass party, this would surely seem to run counter to the foreign policy goal of fostering political competitiveness. Where a two-party system is functioning, support for both parties might be possible, but on the other hand the fact of two-party competition would appear to lessen the policy motivation for intervention. Braibanti goes on to point out that "in new states in which there are more than two parties or in which there are two parties very unevenly balanced in power, active support of party organizations by the United States seems especially dangerous." He details the reasons, whether all parties are supported equally, or certain parties are "certified" and selected for assistance.[45]

As far as the country on the receiving end of political party support is concerned, reasons for resistance also exist. In some instances, a clear legal prohibition against the support of political parties by foreign sources may be in effect. In the background, whether or not such a law has been enacted, is the pervasive feeling that deliberate foreign support of parties, whether all of them or a few that are "certified," would require "probing in the most delicate tissues of the social system. Such probing is not and cannot be consistent with post-colonial sensitivities regarding sovereignty."[46]

Strengthening of legislative bodies is another frequently mentioned way of controlling bureaucratic power and improving political balance. This presents somewhat similar but fewer problems, particularly if attention is concentrated on improvement of the legislative infrastructure by providing staff services in areas such as research and bill-drafting. Transfer of parliamentary technology of this type has been successfully undertaken more frequently in recent years than in the past.

Braibanti proposes, then, what he describes as a "somewhat eclectic" general strategy for the external inducement of political development, which concentrates on the strengthening of as many institutions as possible, including bureaucratic institutions that may already be strong. Acceptability on the part of the political leadership of the recipient nation is a necessary condition for success in external aid programs, no matter what the target may be. Arguing that "it is beyond the capability of an aid-giving nation to directly and deliberately accelerate politicization," he points out that "manipulation of the larger social order . . . is no longer politically feasible and is becoming less feasible. . . . The stimulation of the political process or the deliberate strengthening of counter elites implies internal interference with domestic politics" which is unacceptable to the leaders of newly independent states.[47]

I have likewise tried to stress the utmost importance of providing an opportunity for the political leaders of new nations to choose among options as to external aid programs. More specifically, these options might include requesting assistance only for purposes of strengthening the bureaucracy and improving the level of administrative performance, combining this with external help in building up nonbureaucratic institutions, or concentrating exclusively on the latter. My view, as expressed elsewhere, is that

> for countries we are generally willing to aid, as a matter of national policy, we should not discontinue technical assistance efforts in administration because of a judgment that the political system does not at the moment conform to our specifications for a working political democracy, or even because of concern that this kind of assistance may lessen the prospect for achieving such a political system in the future.[48]

Certainly leaders in today's developing nation-states can legitimately claim that they should be able to pick and choose among possibilities for foreign assistance in whatever combination suits their own political predilections. Given this understandable attitude, prospects for success are poor for a policy of extending aid only under circumstances judged by the donor country to contribute positively to desirable political development. A combined package deal under which assistance for administrative improvement efforts will be made available only when accompanied by programs to strengthen political instrumentalities deemed to have the potential for exerting suitable controls over the bureaucracy is likely to be rejected. It almost certainly will be by an entrenched bureaucratic elite regime of the type for which the strategy is presumably most directly designed.

In short, an aid-giving country is not in a favorable position to insist on such conditions for providing help, as a method for successful stimulation of balanced political development. No blueprint for external guidance of the course of political development in emerging countries is likely to be drafted by donor country planners.

> As a matter of common sense, why should this be expected? Is there anything concerning which the sensitive leaders of new states should be expected to show more touchiness than to have foreigners tell them what they must do to achieve political development adjudged suitable by someone else's standards? . . . A crucial point to bear in mind, whatever the judgment as to balanced versus unbalanced social growth strategies, is the relative impotency of external as compared to internal political decision-makers.[49]

LaPalombara also believes that "the evidence is strongly persuasive that very little can occur by way of increasing or improving administrative capacity unless those in favor of such changes secure the overt, continuous, and single-minded support of central political leadership."[50]

TESTING THE IMBALANCE THESIS

The debate about the relationship between bureaucratic and political development and about related strategies for achieving balance in development was conducted for a considerable time with very little reference to available cross-national data which might shed light on the matter. Lee Sigelman then tried to remedy this deficiency by undertaking two separate tests of the so-called imbalance thesis.[51] Later, Richard Mabbutt made still a third test as a follow-up to the Sigelman studies.[52]

According to the imbalance thesis, as already noted, the presence of a bureaucracy that is highly developed reduces the likelihood of attaining political development. As stated by Sigelman,

> the chief components of the argument that bureaucratic development hinders the prospects of political development are the propositions that: (1) the relatively high level of bureaucratic development in new nations fosters overparticipation by the bureaucracy in the performance of

governmental and political functions; and (2) such bureaucratic over-participation stunts the growth of viable representative institutions.[53]

On the basis that data were lacking for testing the second proposition, but were available for testing the more central first proposition, Sigelman set out to do this. He started by stating more precisely the hypothesis to be investigated, as follows: "In the politically underdeveloped nations, there is a positive correlation between (1) level of bureaucratic development and (2) extent of bureaucratic over-participation in governmental and political functions."[54] Confirmation of this hypothesis would support the imbalance thesis; rejection would cast doubt upon it.

To operationalize the key concepts of bureaucratic development and bureaucratic overparticipation in terms of available data, Sigelman turned to two different sources. From Banks and Textor,[55] he made use of the variable "Character of Bureaucracy" which separates national bureaucracies into four categories, three of them relevant to developing countries. In his analysis, Sigelman equated the category "semi-modern" with a higher degree of bureaucratic development, and the categories "post-colonial transitional" and "traditional" with a lower level of bureaucratic development, producing an approximately equal division among the nations considered by using this dichotomy. From Almond and Coleman,[56] he relied on the judgments expressed by the area experts involved, in terms of the model proposed by Coleman in the concluding chapter of the volume, in classifying nations as to whether their bureaucracies are "overparticipant" or "not overparticipant" in the performance of "political" functions and of "governmental" functions, considered separately.

According to Sigelman's criteria as to what nations should be considered politically underdeveloped, fifty-seven such nations in Latin America, Asia, and Africa were common to the Almond-Coleman and Banks-Textor analyses. Using this pool of politically underdeveloped nations, Sigelman's conclusion was that the comparison shows an inverse rather than a positive relationship between bureaucratic development and overparticipation.

> The bulk of the relatively developed bureaucracies do *not* overparticip-ate: only six of the thirty developed bureaucracies overparticipate in political functions, only ten of thirty overparticipate in governmental functions. On the other hand, the vast majority of the underdeveloped bureaucracies *do* overparticipate: nineteen of the twenty-seven under-developed bureaucracies overparticipate in political functions, and fully twenty-two of twenty-seven in governmental functions.[57]

Claiming that this study effectively undercut the argument that modern bureaucracies inhibit political development on overparticipation grounds, but recognizing that such findings ran counter to commonly held views, Sigelman later replicated his first study, utilizing alternative data for re-examining the relationship between bureaucratic development and bureaucratic dominance. In retesting the imbalance theory, he substituted for the Banks-Textor classification scheme to measure bureaucratic development a variable labeled "Degree of Administrative Efficiency," used by a pair of economists to separate national bureaucracies into three categories.[58] This measure of bureaucratic development groups countries as to those with systems of public administration characterized by: (1) reasonably efficient bureaucracies without widespread corruption or instability of policy at higher administrative levels; (2) considerable bureaucratic inefficiency with corruption common and moderate policy instability; or (3) extreme bureaucratic inefficiency probably combined with widespread corruption or policy instability or both. Sigelman considered this variable an improvement on the Banks-Textor measure because it is explicitly ordinal and less ambiguous as to the criteria used for grouping nations.

For measuring bureaucratic dominance, he used in the retest the classification scheme employed by me in the original version of this study for highlighting the political role of bureaucracy in a variety of developing nations. Of the six categories in that classification plan, he grouped the traditional-autocratic and the bureaucratic elite political regimes together and scored the nations in these two groups as having "high dominant" bureaucracies, on the basis that these bureaucracies "are squarely at center stage in the play of political power." Nations in the remaining four categories, where the regimes have polyarchal competitive or dominant-party systems which keep the bureaucracy's power position relatively restricted, were scored as having "low dominant" bureaucracies. Again, Sigelman believed that he had found for the retest a better means of measuring bureaucratic dominance than the "overparticipation" ratings used in his first study, since such ratings are "an imperfect indicator of dominance, in that politicized bureaucracies do not necessarily dominate their political systems," whereas the political regime type of approach measures bureaucratic dominance "directly in terms of political-bureaucratic power arrangements."[59]

The retest sample was composed of thirty-eight developing nations common to the Adelman-Morris and Heady analyses. Cross-tabulation of the two variables revealed, as in the previous study, that the cases were arrayed in precisely the opposite pattern from that predicted by the imbalance thesis.

> Bureaucracies which are highly developed do *not* dominate less developed polities. Of all the bureaucracies which have attained a "high" level of development, . . . not a single one is politically dominant. It is rather bureaucracies at a "low" and, to a lesser extent, "medium" developmental level which dominate their political systems—the former by a whopping margin (11-2), the latter by a bare majority (9-8). The findings . . . thus present new and striking evidence that the hypothesis

of positive relationship between bureaucratic development and dominance cannot withstand empirical test.[60]

Sigelman's assertion as to the significance of his findings seems to be
justified, and to date nobody has challenged his claim that these two studies
warrant an attitude of "extreme skepticism toward the hypothesis that modern
bureaucracies dominate less developed polities."[61]

Richard Mabbutt did criticize Sigelman for conceptual and methodological
deficiencies in his research on the imbalance thesis, and undertook still another
empirical test in which he attempted to remedy these alleged defects. His
concerns were that both military and civil bureaucracies should be clearly
included in the analysis, and that the concept of "bureaucratic development"
should be revised to emphasize "weight of bureaucratic power" as the key
element presumed to produce a tendency toward high bureaucratic dominance.
His retest showed that the relationship between this revised variable measuring
weight of bureaucratic power and the variable of bureaucratic dominance was not
significant, leading once again to rejection of the imbalance thesis, and to a
conclusion by Mabbutt that "it seems clear that the imbalance thesis in its several
versions is not supported by empirical tests."[62] Mabbutt's advice is to maintain a
healthy skepticism about either a presumed positive or negative impact on the
political system as a consequence of bureaucratic development.

The analyses by Sigelman and Mabbutt have increased doubt as to the
validity of the imbalance thesis, without halting the debate about the relationship
between bureaucratic and political development. I welcomed the findings of these
studies, because they lent support to my own previously expressed views, but
account needs to be taken of considerations that might raise questions about the
conclusions reached. One is that during the passage of time since Sigelman's
second study, political regime shifts in countries in his sample may have changed
the relationships reported. It is true that at least six of the nations classified as
"low dominant" based on 1966 data later had their competitive or dominant-party
regimes replaced by bureaucratic elite regimes of some kind (Argentina, Brazil,
Chile, Ghana, the Philippines, and Turkey). However, all of these countries have
currently again moved away from bureaucratic elitism, at least for the time being.
Most of these countries fell within the group considered "medium" as to level of
bureaucratic development, so that a redistribution would produce little change in
the number of cases in which bureaucracies at a "medium" level of development
are "high dominant." The huge margin by which bureaucracies at a "low"
developmental level dominate their political systems would be undisturbed.
Similarly, there would be only a slight shift in the low incidence of cases in
which bureaucracies at a "high" developmental level are also "high dominant"
politically. It is these latter two sets of relationships, of course, that are most
important as evidence of an inverse rather than a positive correlation between

bureaucratic development and bureaucratic overparticipation or dominance in the political system.

Another contention is that experience in particular countries seems to run counter to the Braibanti argument that elitist bureaucracies may take the lead in economic and political development, and that bureaucracies should be strengthened irrespective of the rate of political maturation. Claude S. Phillips cites the Nigerian experience as a case in point,[63] contending that the public bureaucracy, with thirteen years of opportunity between 1966 and 1979, in which it was untrammeled by political control and favored with oil bonanza resources, failed to achieve either economic or political development, thus supporting the position that political institutions must be strengthened at the same time that bureaucratic institutions are being strengthened. Without disputing this interpretation of the Nigerian record,[64] I think that it is important to point out that Braibanti did not say that bureaucracies could be depended on to perform such a role, and that Sigelman's conclusions had to do with overall tendencies, not necessary outcomes in specific instances. In discounting the imbalance thesis, Sigelman emphasized that he was not denying the adverse effect of dominant bureaucracies on the emergence of vigorous political institutions. Granting that political development is likely to be hampered by bureaucratic dominance, his findings indicate that political development may be facilitated rather than thwarted by bureaucratic development, because "cross-sectionally, the higher the level of bureaucratic development, the lower the level of bureaucratic dominance. . . . Far from inhibiting the growth of political institutions, then, bureaucratic development is quite consistent with, and may well play a significant role in the promotion of, political development."[65]

Because the evidence as to general tendencies is tentative, and because of the importance of particular cases that may be exceptional, the debate about the relationship between bureaucratic and political development is sure to continue.

THE SIGNIFICANCE OF POLITICAL SYSTEM VARIATION

Certain questions were posed in Chapter 2 (see pages 78 and 79) concerning higher public bureaucracies in various kinds of polities. The comparative study of public administration has not yet advanced far enough to provide satisfactory answers to these questions in the full range of existing political systems. The problem is due in part to a lack of consensus regarding what and how to compare, but it is both more basic and more elementary than concern over conceptualization and methodology. The absence or inadequacy of reliable information on bureaucratic structures and behavior in a large majority of the nation-states of the modern world continues to be a major handicap. Despite the gradual accumulation of relevant studies, the rate of progress has been disappointing, access to much valuable work is difficult, and too little systematically organized cross-national research has been carried through to completion.

What has become more and more obvious is the extreme importance of variation among political regimes as a major explanatory factor for variation among public bureaucracies, making it crucial that efforts be intensified to remedy the existing gaps in reliable information. Meanwhile, the general state of affairs is that we are better informed about the more developed nations than the less developed, and among them, know more about the United States, Great Britain, France, and Germany than about Japan, Russia, or China. Similarly, within the ranks of the less developed nations, our knowledge, skimpy enough at best, is relatively greater in quantity and superior in quality for countries with long colonial histories prior to independence, such as India or the Philippines, or for countries that gained independence early or maintained national identity without interruption, such as the Latin American countries or Thailand, than it is for newly created Middle Eastern or African states with arbitrary boundaries marked on the map or for countries that turned to and often later rejected communism during recent decades.

Our ability to answer such questions also varies from one question to another. We are least ready to compare the internal operating characteristics of national bureaucracies. A few Western civil service systems have been studied in depth, and reassessments of their operations continue to appear. Similar research has been done in only a scattering of non-Western systems, despite an encouraging spread in recent years of scholarly activity by nationals of these countries. In many instances, reports on the workings of these systems are either not available at all, or we have only impressionistic and incidental comments to go on. We know little about internal behavioral patterns in individual bureaucracies, or about degrees of consistency or variation among them. This is an area that still urgently calls for more systematic attention.

To the second question, concerning the extent to which the bureaucracy is multifunctional, we have a somewhat sounder basis for response. At a minimum we can say that there is a relationship between political modernity and bureaucratic specificity of function. The bureaucracies in more developed countries resemble the diffracted model, with its more restricted functional activity for the bureaucracy; the bureaucracies in the less developed countries are more likely to be multifunctional, participating actively in policy- or rule-making and even in interest articulation and aggregation. Still lacking are detailed case studies on the range of bureaucratic activity in most of the less developed and some of the more developed countries. More information on a country by country basis of the extent to which reliance is being placed on quasi-governmental or private entities for public policy implementation, for example, is urgently needed.

We are best prepared to respond to the third question, on the means for exerting external controls over the bureaucracy and the effectiveness of these controls. These matters have long been of concern in developed polities, and they have more recently been explored in treatments of developing political regimes.

The principal issue here is not whether political development is unbalanced to date in numerous emerging nations when judged by standards of balance in a modernized polity that is not totalitarian. This is acknowledged, and the explanation is not hard to find. It is a combination of two basic factors: the colonial heritage of bureaucratic rule which has been carried over into the fledgling nation after independence, and the unavoidable requirement of a minimal level of administrative competence for sheer political survival. It would be political suicide for a struggling nation with inchoate nonbureaucratic political institutions to insist for the sake of balance that the bureaucracy deliberately be brought down to the same level of inadequacy.

Rather, the issue, as discussed above, is whether a bureaucratic bid for power is so predictable, and bureaucratic rule so inevitable, unless resisted, that this outcome must be countered whenever possible by constraints on bureaucratic development and by continuous and systematic upgrading of nonbureaucratic potential sources of political power. A secondary but important issue is the feasibility of such a strategy on the part of external forces which may be trying to shape the future course of a developing polity.

Admittedly, the data for a definitive response to this question are not at hand, but what we do know points toward caution rather than assurance in the use of any analytical scheme to fit developing bureaucracies into a single mold. As Fritz Morstein Marx has pointed out, "the higher civil service, viewed as an action group exerting influence upon a country's political development, usually leaves quite indistinct tracks. Its role is neither easily assessed nor predictable. Aside from institutional variables, we must allow for differences not only between countries but also between stages in each country's evolution."[66] The alternatives open to the bureaucracy range from unquestioning defense of the status quo to ardent advocacy of basic reform, with one of the possibilities being simply quiescent noninvolvement in matters of political policy. Weidner has suggested that the role of the bureaucracy, as compared with the roles of other parts of government or society, "ranges widely from country to country in regard to the original formulation and later modification and refinement of developmental values. Variations in its role in securing these values are equally great."[67]

Joseph LaPalombara has suggested that political and bureaucratic evolution be viewed "within a context of challenge-and-response, or as a process over time whereby political systems respond to changes in the kinds of demands they encounter." No particular pattern of adaptation is considered optimal for development. Recurring kinds of challenge or crisis can be identified, but they vary from one political system to another in the sequence in which they occur, their frequency, the ease or difficulty of resolution, and so forth. Transitional political systems commonly face the dilemma that they "must telescope into years the

crisis management which was accomplished over generations in older nations."
This makes it especially important that the tasks to be performed are identified
and that priorities are established among them. "It is only after one has understood
the relative priority assigned to the goals of the system that discussions about
what kinds of administrators and administrative organization are best attuned to
reaching them in a given situation make much sense." Despite their shared burden
of crisis demands, the developing countries "present a wide variety of crises
configurations and of administrative resources that might be made to deal
with them."[68]

These reminders warn of the pitfalls in grouping together all bureaucracies,
or even all bureaucracies in developing countries, and point toward the necessity
of considering the role of the bureaucracy in relation to the political system and
its goals. Such considerations have led to efforts to classify bureaucracies into
types that take into account basic orientations and operational characteristics.
Among the best-known general classifications are those of Fritz Morstein Marx
and Merle Fainsod. Morstein Marx proposed a fourfold classification of historical
and current systems into guardian, caste, patronage, and merit bureaucracies.[69]
Fainsod's classification, reviewed in Chapter 7, is most pertinent here. Based on
the criterion of the relationship of bureaucracies to the flow of political authority,
this scheme distinguishes five forms of bureaucracy: representative, party-state,
ruler-dominated, military-dominated, and ruling. In only the first two of these
categories are officials clearly responsible to, and generally responsive to, political forces outside the state officialdom. Ruler-dominated bureaucracies present
a more ambivalent situation, with the bureaucracy being the subservient personal
instrument of the ruler, but with individual bureaucrats likely to be influential if
they enjoy the confidence of the ruler, and with the regime highly dependent on
adequate bureaucratic performance. In the remaining two categories, the political
regimes are controlled by ruling elements dominated by officials of military
background in one case and civilian in the other. If military men have seized
power, they soon face nonmilitary problems that cause them to turn to civilian
administrators for advice. If the civil bureaucracy is itself the ruling element, it
must find legitimization from some other source, such as a colonial power or a
figurehead monarchy, and the loyalty of the armed forces is usually essential.

Both Fainsod's categories and the groupings used in this book are based on
a recognition that there is a significant relationship between political system
characteristics and bureaucratic system characteristics in all polities, including
those that share the designation "developing" but are far from identical either in
their political regimes or their bureaucracies. The categories chosen, however,
coincide only in part. Fainsod's party-state category is subdivided into three
groupings, and his two types of official-dominated regimes are grouped and
analyzed from a somewhat different perspective. Moreover, pendulum systems,
singled out for special attention here, are not considered directly by Fainsod.

Put in terms of the classification system we have used here, the following tentative statements summarize briefly what now seems to be known about the efficacy of external controls over the bureaucracy and the risks of bureaucratic power dominance in different types of political regimes.

1. In the more developed nations, even though political regime character-istics vary in other respects, sufficient devices for political control exist to give significant direction to the bureaucracy and to minimize the likelihood of bureau-cratic dominance while permitting substantial participation in political decision-making. The long-term trend, even in Japan where bureaucratic centrality has been most prominent, does not indicate a threat of transition to a bureaucratic elite regime, unless this tendency should appear in some of the successor states to the USSR or some of the more developed countries of Eastern Europe as their political systems continue to emerge from single-party dominance.

2. Among the less developed countries, the variation is greater. Traditional elite regimes produce what Fainsod has called "ruler-dominated" bureaucracies. The usual expectation is that these regimes are vulnerable and likely to undergo transformation. One possibility is to continue as a traditional elite regime, but with a shift from an ortho-traditional to a neo-traditional orientation, as has already occurred in Iran. More likely is a transition to a bureaucratic elite regime, as occurred some time ago in Thailand and more recently in Ethiopia, and may happen in Morocco, Jordan, or Saudi Arabia. Other alternatives for transition, of course, are also present but less probable.

3. Controls over the bureaucracy are weakest and the risks of indefinite bureaucratic power dominance are greatest in personalist and collegial bureau-cratic elite systems. Because the number of these regimes was definitely on the rise during the 1960s and 1970s, they received special attention from scholars, providing much of the basis for generalized models of developing polities, as is made evident by a comparison of the prismatic model of Riggs and his case study of Thailand, or the general views of Goodnow and his case study of Pakistan. In these systems, the military bureaucracy normally will occupy a position of primacy and the civil bureaucracy will play a secondary role. Although the civil bureaucracy is less likely than the military to initiate a takeover of power, its cooperation is vital to the continued success of most bureaucratic elite regimes. The staying capacity of these regimes is debatable. Janowitz and others who investigated the political record of the military concluded that such regimes are often transitory, and this judgment is being substantiated by recent events. Although many such regimes have been able to maintain themselves in power for considerable periods, beginning in the 1980s more polities have moved out of than into the bureaucratic elite categories. Usually the transition has been toward greater political competition, even though the prospects for maintaining it may be uncertain, especially in several African and Latin American countries. In other

cases, such as Egypt and Tanzania, the growth of a mobilizing mass party has reduced the earlier direct influence of a military or civil bureaucratic elite.

4. Numerous countries—representing various geographic regions, cultural traditions, religious preferences, and colonial backgrounds—have experienced since independence a series of movements back and forth between regimes with bureaucratic elite leadership and regimes with political leadership emerging from some form of popular selection. These pendulum systems share a record of impermanence, with fairly brief histories and uncertain futures. Because of this lack of regime longevity, the regime impact on bureaucratic characteristics is apt to be mixed, muted or blurred. Generally the result will be recurring opportunities for bureaucrats to assert themselves politically, so that these are best viewed as bureaucratic-prominent political regimes.

5. In polyarchal competitive systems that are more firmly established, the trend is toward less rather than more bureaucratic involvement in the exercise of political power, toward a better balance between the bureaucracy and other political institutions in regimes that resemble those of developed democratic polities. Even so, these are volatile systems, and their number has varied both up and down in recent decades, with the current trend being upward.

6. Among the dominant-party political systems, the prospect that a preponderance of political power will be transferred to the hands of officials in the state bureaucracy, civil or military, is generally low. This eventuality becomes increasingly remote as we move across the spectrum from dominant-party semi-competitive to dominant-party mobilization to Communist party totalitarian regimes. In terms of Western democratic standards, the imbalance that can be expected in these systems is not one that overweighs but one that underweighs the bureaucratic element in the political equation. A prediction frequently made earlier as to trends in political evolution among developing countries was that the movement would be toward a higher proportion of dominant-party regimes of some kind, but this has not materialized. Instead, except for Communist party regimes established in some Southeast Asian countries, the actual trend has been away from dominant-party systems, most often toward military regimes.

Considerations such as these point toward a multiple rather than a uniform appraisal of the present status and future prospects of the role of administration in the political regimes of the developing countries. The actual role will depend on the type of political regime, and beyond that on the specialized circumstances in the particular country. In the commendable effort to identify central tendencies, we should avoid relying too greatly on experience in a few countries and on too easy an assumption that there is any clear-cut tendency at all that has shown up so far.

This survey of bureaucratic behavior in different types of developing political systems indicates that a categorical response to the issue of whether bureaucracy is usurpative or instrumental in developing countries is inappropriate and risky, particularly if it leads to prescriptive recommendations regarding the propriety of efforts toward bureaucratic upgrading which are to be applied generally. A more realistic approach is to relate the issue of the risk of bureaucratic domination to political system subtypes. When this is done, the threat of bureaucratic monopolization of political power becomes much less menacing, despite the frequency of imbalance between bureaucratic and nonbureaucratic political institutions among developing nations.

A CONCLUDING COMMENT

The subject of comparative public administration has many ramifications. It can be studied from a number of different, although not necessarily mutually exclusive, perspectives. Some of these options have been advocated since the early days of the comparative administration movement, as discussed in the opening chapter on evolution of the field. Others are quite recent, with some of them appearing suddenly without many advance indicators, such as the opportunity now presented to analyze the process of bureaucratic retrenchment and reorganization in the former USSR and Eastern Europe. Still more can be anticipated in the future. There is general agreement that more methodological sophistication is needed in comparative administration studies. This is usually coupled with recognition of the inherent problems involved. Aberbach and Rockman have discussed some of these problems perceptively in explaining their acknowledgement that "the comparative analysis of administrative systems is a difficult undertaking."[70] In another recent assessment of the field, Robert C. Fried has also reviewed some of the reasons for "the failure to produce a science of comparative public administration," despite decades of effort dating back to the work of the Comparative Administration Group and even before.[71]

As I have stated above, my preference in trying to cope with these stubborn complexities is to encourage a multiplicity of approaches, rather than to foster orthodoxy that might stifle experimentation. Having said this, I do agree with the prevalent tendency to focus on public bureaucracies for comparative purposes, and I feel that there is great value in trying to identify factors affecting bureaucratic characteristics over as wide as possible a range of contemporary nation-states, because of the urgency of aiming toward global coverage. Without claiming priority of importance for it across the board, I have emphasized the variable of political regime type as a factor always present and likely to be significant, although its relationship to other factors may vary. Some of these prevalent factors were mentioned earlier, and have been investigated extensively. Others have been advanced more recently, and merit much more attention. One example is the degree of "stateness" in a polity and its impact on the bureaucracy, as advanced by Metin Heper and his associates.[72] Another is the suggestion by V. Subramaniam that the "derivative middle class" phenomenon in developing countries offers a basis for global comparisons.[73] Still a third, with special promise for simultaneous exploration of the relative importance of numerous factors, is the stress placed by Robert C. Fried on "the value of one kind of comparative study, the multivariate cross-national study based on a large number of cases."[74] All of these have potential and should be pursued by those who proposed them or others.

A choice of focus for a comprehensive comparative survey of public administration is unavoidable. Any choice carries with it advantages and disadvantages. We have selected the public bureaucracy of the modern nation-state as the primary focus. Further, we have concentrated on the higher bureaucracy rather than the whole bureaucratic apparatus, and on its external working relationships with other parts of the political system rather than on its internal operating characteristics. We have, however, deliberately elected to include a wide variety of existing nation-states in order to explore the role of bureaucracy in diverse settings that show marked contrasts in political system characteristics. We have found that the modern nation-state is sure to have as one of its political institutions a public service that meets the minimal structural requirements for bureaucracy as a form of organization, but that there is no standard pattern of relationships between public bureaucracy and the political system as a whole. Factors of crucial importance that affect these relationships include the stage of political development of the nation-state, its political regime characteristics, and the nature of the program goals it has chosen for accomplishment through administrative instrumentalities. Recognition of the existence of such diversity is the first step toward a fuller understanding of particular national systems of administration and more meaningful comparisons among them.

NOTES

1. Alfred Diamant, "The Bureaucratic Model: Max Weber Rejected, Rediscovered, Reformed," in Ferrel Heady and Sybil L. Stokes, eds., *Papers in Comparative Public Administration* (Ann Arbor, MI: Institute of Public Administration, The University of Michigan, 1962), pp. 79–81, 84–86.
2. Henry Jacoby, *The Bureaucratization of the World* (Berkeley, CA: University of California Press, 1973).
3. R. E. Wraith, *Proceedings, XVIIIth International Congress of Administrative Sciences, Madrid 1980* (Brussels, Belgium: International Institute of Administrative Sciences, 1982), at pp. 139, 142.
4. Rowat, "Comparisons and Trends," in Donald C. Rowat, ed., *Public Administration in Developed Democracies* (New York: Marcel Dekker, Inc., 1988), Chap. 25, at pp. 450–458.
5. A recent comprehensive overview is Lawrence R. Jones and Fred Thompson, eds., *Public Management: Institutional Renewal for the Twenty-First Century*, Research in Public Policy Analysis and Management, Volume 10 (Stamford, CT: JAI Press Inc.,

1999). See also Anthony B. L. Cheung, "Understanding Public-Sector Reforms: Global Trends and Diverse Agendas," *International Review of Administrative Sciences* 63 (1997):435–457; and Stuart S. Nagel, ed., *Critical Issues in Cross-National Public Administration: Privatization, Democratization, Decentralization* (Westport, CT: Quorum Books, 2000).

6. (Washington, DC: The Brookings Institution, 2000).

7. *Report of the Priority Issues Task Force* (Washington, DC: National Academy of Public Administration, January 10, 2000), 11 pp. mimeo., at p. 8.

8. Peters, "Public Policy and Public Bureaucracy," in Douglas E. Ashford, ed., *History and Context in Comparative Public Policy* (Pittsburgh, PA: University of Pittsburgh Press, 1992), Part III, Chap. 13, pp. 283–316, at pp. 308–309.

9. The most comprehensive source is Ralph Braibanti, ed., *Political and Administrative Development* (Durham, NC: Duke University Press, 1969). Copyright 1969 by Duke University Press. For summaries of different points of view, refer to Warren F. Ilchman, "Rising Expectations and the Revolution in Development Administration," *Public Administration Review* 25, No. 4 (1965): 314–328; and Ferrel Heady, "Bureaucracies in Developing Countries," in Fred W. Riggs, ed., *Frontiers of Development Administration* (Durham, NC: Duke University Press, 1970), pp. 459–485.

10. Gabriel A. Almond and G. Bingham Powell, Jr., *Comparative Politics: A Developmental Approach* (Boston: Little, Brown and Company, 1966), pp. 158, 253.

11. Fred W. Riggs, "Bureaucrats and Political Development: A Paradoxical View," in Joseph LaPalombara, ed., *Bureaucracy and Political Development* (Princeton, NJ: Princeton University Press, 1963), pp. 120–167.

12. Fred W. Riggs, "Bureaucratic Politics in Comparative Perspective," in Riggs, ed., *Frontiers of Development Administration*, pp. 375–414.

13. This concept and the related term "head of state," with derivative classification systems, are discussed in great detail by Riggs in "The Structures of Government and Administrative Reform," in Braibanti, ed., *Political and Administrative Development*, pp. 220–324.

14. Riggs, "Bureaucratic Politics in Comparative Perspective," p. 389.

15. Riggs, "Bureaucrats and Political Development," p. 126.

16. Fred W. Riggs, *Administrative Reform and Political Responsiveness: A Theory of Dynamic Balancing*, Sage Professional Papers in Comparative Politics, Volume 1, Series No. 01-010 (Beverly Hills, CA: Sage Publications, 1971), p. 579.

17. Joseph LaPalombara, "An Overview of Political Development," pp. 3–33, and "Bureaucracy and Political Development: Notes, Queries, and Dilemmas," pp. 34–61, in LaPalombara, ed., *Bureaucracy and Political Development*.

18. LaPalombara, "An Overview of Political Development," p. 15.

19. Henry Goodnow, "Bureaucracy and Political Power in the New States," in *The Civil Service of Pakistan* (New Haven, CT: Yale University Press, 1964), Chap. 1, pp. 3–22.

20. Lucian Pye, "The Political Context of National Development," in Irving Swerdlow, ed., *Development Administration: Concepts and Problems* (Syracuse, NY: Syracuse University Press, 1963), pp. 25–43.

21. *Ibid.*, p. 31. He makes the same point in *Aspects of Political Development* (Boston: Little, Brown and Company, 1966), p. 19.

22. "In fact," he continues, "excessive concentration on strengthening the administrative services may be self-defeating because it may lead only to a greater imbalance between the administrative and the political and hence to a greater need of the leaders to exploit politically the administrative services." Pye, "The Political Context of National Development," pp. 32–33.

23. Pye, "Bureaucratic Development and the Psychology of Institutionalization," in Braibanti, ed., *Political and Administrative Development*, pp. 400–426, particularly pp. 408–422.

24. S. N. Eisenstadt, "Problems of Emerging Bureaucracies in Developing Areas and New States," in Bert F. Hoselitz and Wilbert E. Moore, eds., *Industrialization and Society* (The Hague: Mouton, 1963), pp. 159–175.

25. Ralph Braibanti, "The Relevance of Political Science to the Study of Underdeveloped Areas," in Ralph Braibanti and Joseph J. Spengler, eds., *Tradition, Values, and Socio-Economic Development* (Durham, NC: Duke University Press, 1961), p. 143.

26. *Ibid.*, pp. 173–176.

27. Ralph Braibanti, "External Inducement of Political-Administrative Development: An Institutional Strategy," in Braibanti, ed., *Political and Administrative Development*, pp. 3–106, at p. 3.

28. *Ibid.*, p. 79.

29. *Ibid.*, p. 105.

30. Milton J. Esman, "The Politics of Development Administration," in John D. Montgomery and William J. Siffin, eds., *Approaches to Development: Politics, Administration and Change* (New York: McGraw-Hill, 1966), pp. 59–112, at pp. 81–82.

31. Bernard E. Brown, *New Directions in Comparative Politics* (New York: Asia Publishing House, 1962), pp. 49–51.

32. Fritz Morstein Marx, "The Higher Civil Service as an Action Group in Western Political Development," in LaPalombara, ed., *Bureaucracy and Political Development*, pp. 65, 92–95. See also his "Control and Responsibility in Administration: Comparative Aspects," in Heady and Stokes, eds., *Papers*, pp. 145–171.

33. Lee Sigelman, "Do Modern Bureaucracies Dominate Underdeveloped Polities? A Test of the Imbalance Thesis," *American Political Science Review* 66, No. 2 (1972): 528. See also his *Modernization and the Political System: A Critique and Preliminary Empirical Analysis*, Sage Professional Papers in Comparative Politics, Volume 2, Series 01-016 (Beverly Hills, CA: Sage Publications, 1972).

34. Ferrel Heady, "Bureaucracies in Developing Countries," in Riggs, ed., *Frontiers of Development Administration*, p. 483.

35. Edward W. Weidner, *Technical Assistance in Public Administration Overseas: The Case for Development Administration* (Chicago: Public Administration Service, 1964), p. 166.

36. Joseph LaPalombara, "Alternative Strategies for Developing Administrative Capabilities in Emerging Nations," in Riggs, ed., *Frontiers of Development Administration*, pp. 171–226, at p. 206.

37. See Fred W. Riggs, "The Context of Development Administration," in Riggs, ed., *Frontiers of Development Administration*, pp. 72–108, especially pp. 81–82.

38. Riggs, "Bureaucrats and Political Development," p. 166.

39. Riggs, "Relearning an Old Lesson: The Political Context of Development Adminis-tration," *Public Administration Review* 25, No. 1 (1965): 70–79, at p. 79.
40. Riggs, "The Context of Development Administration," pp. 82–83.
41. Riggs, "Relearning an Old Lesson," pp. 70–72.
42. Riggs, "The Ecology and Context of Public Administration: A Comparative Perspec-tive," *Public Administration Review* 40, No. 2 (March/April 1980): 107–115, at p. 114.
43. Braibanti, "External Inducement of Political-Administrative Development," p. 79.
44. *Ibid.*, pp. 79–103.
45. *Ibid.*, p. 80.
46. *Ibid.*, p. 81.
47. Braibanti, "Administrative Reform in the Context of Political Growth," in Riggs, ed., *Frontiers of Development Administration*, pp. 227–246, at pp. 229, 232.
48. Heady, "Bureaucracies in Developing Countries," p. 476.
49. *Ibid.*, pp. 478, 480.
50. LaPalombara, "Strategies for Developing Administrative Capabilities," p. 192.
51. Lee Sigelman, "Do Modern Bureaucracies Dominate Underdeveloped Polities? A Test of the Imbalance Thesis," *American Political Science Review* 66, No. 2 (1972): 525–528; and "Bureaucratic Development and Dominance: A New Test of the Imbalance Thesis," *Western Political Quarterly* 27, No. 2 (1974): 308–313.
52. Richard Mabbutt, "Bureaucratic Development and Political Dominance: An Analysis and Alternative Test of the Imbalance Thesis," 1979, 33 pp. mimeographed.
53. Sigelman, "Do Modern Bureaucracies Dominate?" p. 525.
54. *Ibid.*, italics in original removed.
55. Arthur S. Banks and Robert B. Textor, *A Cross-Polity Survey* (Cambridge, MA: M.I.T. Press, 1963), pp. 112–113.
56. Gabriel Almond and James S. Coleman, eds., *The Politics of the Developing Areas* (Princeton, NJ: Princeton University Press, 1960).
57. Sigelman, "Do Modern Bureaucracies Dominate?" p. 528.
58. Irma Adelman and Cynthia Taft Morris, *Society, Politics, and Economic Devel-opment: A Quantitative Approach* (Baltimore, MD: Johns Hopkins Press, 1967), pp. 77–78.
59. Sigelman, "Bureaucratic Development and Dominance," pp. 310–311.
60. *Ibid.*, p. 312.
61. *Ibid.*, p. 313.
62. Mabbutt, "Bureaucratic Development and Political Dominance," p. 29.
63. Claude S. Phillips, "Political versus Administration Development: What the Nigerian Experience Contributes," *Administration and Society* 20, No. 4 (February 1989): 423–445.
64. Others view the Nigerian situation differently. For example, Lapido Adamolekun, himself Nigerian, thinks that both administrative and political institutions in the country are fundamentally weak, and that the prescription that "the development of administrative institutions in new states like Nigeria should be slowed down while efforts should be concentrated on developing the political institutions . . . would be catastrophic. The most useful prescription for Nigeria should be the development of strong administrative institutions, whose functioning is reconciled with the instru-

mental conception of administration either in the tradition of European western liberal democracies or in that of states committed to Marxist democratic theory." *Politics and Administration in Nigeria* (Ibadan: Spectrum Books, 1986, in association with Hutchinson of London), p. 169.

65. Sigelman, "Bureaucratic Development and Dominance," pp. 312–313.

66. Fritz Morstein Marx, "The Higher Civil Service as an Action Group in Western Political Development," in LaPalombara, ed., *Bureaucracy and Political Development*, pp. 62–95, at p. 75.

67. Edward W. Weidner, "Development Administration: A New Focus for Research," in Heady and Stokes, eds., *Papers*, pp. 97–115, at p. 99.

68. Joseph LaPalombara, "Public Administration and Political Development: A Theoretical Overview," in Charles Press and Alan Adrian, eds., *Empathy and Ideology: Aspects of Administrative Innovation* (Chicago: Rand McNally & Co., 1966), pp. 72–107, at pp. 98–103.

69. Fritz Morstein Marx, *The Administrative State* (Chicago: University of Chicago Press, 1957), Chap. 4, pp. 54–72.

70. Joel D. Aberbach and Bert A. Rockman, "Problems of Cross-National Comparison," in Rowat, ed., *Public Administration in Developed Democracies*, Chap. 24, at p. 436.

71. Robert C. Fried, "Comparative Public Administration: The Search for Theories," in Naomi B. Lynn and Aaron Wildavsky, eds., *Public Administration: The State of the Discipline* (Chatham, NJ: Chatham House Publishers, 1990), Chap. 14.

72. Metin Heper, ed., *The State and Public Bureaucracies: A Comparative Perspective* (Westport, CT: Greenwood Press, 1987).

73. V. Subramaniam, "Appendix: The Derivative Middle Class," in V. Subramaniam, ed., *Public Administration in the Third World: An International Handbook* (Westport, CT: Greenwood Press, 1990), pp. 403–411.

74. Fried, "Comparative Public Administration," at p. 338.

Author Index

Subject Index